Greg Riley

[illegible]

Black Gold to Bluegrass

Also by Fred B. McKinley

CHINQUA WHERE?
The Spirit of Rural America, 1947–1955

Also by Greg Riley

The Ultimate Guide to 'Vairs with Air

Black Gold to Bluegrass

by

Fred B. McKinley

Greg Riley

EAKIN PRESS Austin, Texas

To

Frank Yount

FIRST EDITION

Published in the United States of America
By Eakin Press
A Division of Sunbelt Media, Inc.
P.O. Drawer 90159 Austin, Texas 78709-0159
email: sales@eakinpress.com
website: www.eakinpress.com

1 2 3 4 5 6 7 8 9
ISBN 978-1-57168-887-3
ISBN 1-57168-887-0
Library of Congress Control Number 2005923535

Contents

Preface

Fred B. McKinley and Greg Riley's *Black Gold to Bluegrass* is a first-told, meticulously researched, beautifully written and illustrated comprehensive history of the Yount-Lee Oil Company of Beaumont, Texas, and its contributions to the world of oil through bringing in the great Second Spindletop Oil Field. It also chronicles the social ramifications of the company's wealth and sale, but the book, however, goes far beyond the mere study of petroleum. Without bias, the authors meet the long-standing controversies head-on by discussing the lives of the participants, leaving the reader with a clear understanding about individual personalities, and what made them tick. In great detail, McKinley and Riley lay out the various interests of those involved, whether in horses, valuable violins, or priceless classic automobiles as we know them today.

This work, too, is the story of the man, who was most responsible for the success of the company, and his wife: Miles Frank Yount and Pansy Merritt Yount. In fact, the pair and the company were so indelibly connected that it is impossible to think of one without the other.

Much has been written on the original Beaumont Spindletop Oil Field that blew in on the morning of January 10, 1901, with the deafening roar of the Lucas Gusher, the first geyser of oil that Americans had seen. Overnight, the discovery became the genesis of a life-style—the discovery that ushered in the age of oil as fuel for the world. By the early 1920s, however, old Spindletop was barely producing—petered out, as most oilmen said. That is when the Yount-Lee company came in with innovative ideas that brought Spindletop back, this time producing more oil than the field yielded the first time. In the process, the company brought untold wealth to its stockholders.

Although a quiet man in temperament, Yount, an Arkansan by birth, was farsighted when it came to his adopted Beaumont. As a modern-day hero, to a large degree, he was instrumental in the building boom that the city experienced during the second half of the 1920s. When the Great Depression fell upon the nation, Yount and his company helped Beaumont from being affected to the extent that most of the country was. When the city could not make its payroll, Yount saw to it that municipal workers got their pay. In fact, Yount did so many benevolent things for the city that Beaumonters still look upon him as a saint and a martyr, and most people willingly admit that Beaumont would be a vastly different place had Yount lived past his untimely death at a relatively young age in 1933.

Two years later, the sale of the company for the third largest cash transaction that had taken place at that time in the United States, left his wife, Pansy, and his daughter, Mildred, immensely wealthy. Afterward, the media widely circulated every conceivable story that could be written on the Yount family, and Mildred was dubbed in headlines as one of the richest heiresses in the country.

The ramifications of such affluence enabled the interesting, sometimes contentious, rather reclusive, and enigmatic Pansy, with the help of Cape Grant, her horse trainer whom Frank originally hired and brought to Beaumont, to accomplish things that placed her years ahead of her time. Frank had developed an avid interest in fine saddlebred horses, but with his death, Mrs. Yount moved the horses from Beaumont to Kentucky, established the fabled Spindletop Farm in Lexington, and made the complex one of the most forward-thinking saddlebred breeding programs in the world—producing numerous world champions.

The book also tracks the Younts to their summer home in Manitou Springs, Colorado, and their contributions to that community, which were major ones indeed.

Prefaces must end lest the writer give the book away, but *Black Gold to Bluegrass* is a celebration in the sense that it captures a legend in history, the Yount-Lee Oil Company and what it meant on the local and national scene. The book is also a celebration in that it captures Frank and Pansy Yount—both, in their own ways, legends in their time who remain legends in ours.

HOWARD PERKINS
Director of Student Publications
Lamar University

Foreword

According to the national census of 2000, the population figure of Beaumont, Texas is 113,866, placing it as the twentieth largest city in the state. It is rich in both American and Texas history, and though many historical events occurred here, two in particular stand out above the rest. On January 10, 1901, when the Lucas Gusher blew in at Spindletop from a depth of a little over a thousand feet, it immediately produced more oil from that one well than flowed from every combined field in the entire world. Think about that for a minute and how it impacted not only the infant oil industry, but the little more than nine thousand residents, who were thrust headlong into the turbulence of an almost overnight explosion to near six times the previous number.

For a while at least, Spindletop boomed, and how so! In fact, it had more of an effect on the world economic scene than did the fabled gold and silver discoveries of the great American West, and in doing so, lay the foundations for modern day oil giants such as Gulf (Chevron), Mobil, Sun, Shell, and Texaco. But as quickly as it came in, the field tapered off and then began a marked steady decline until it finally played out. Yet before it succumbed to a slow and agonizing death, oil seekers, promoters, operators, schemers, and swindlers had long since packed their bags and gone on to new horizons, hoping to stumble across something that might parallel the spectacular proportions of the 1901 bonanza. For those who were left, however, most had given up all hope that Spindletop would ever again play an important part in the design of things; but two men, Marrs McLean and Frank Yount, refused to sign on to this notion. They believed in destiny. And as dreamers often do, they kept alive the spirit that one day, Spindletop would not only produce for a second time, it would completely eclipse its old rival, the Lucas Gusher and its siblings spawned in frenzy immediately after the initial strike. On many occasions, Frank Yount, with a seemingly contrarian business approach to that held by his contemporary counterparts, reportedly said, "Don't ever count the cost of mistakes." More than any other, this quote captures the spirit of his character and demonstrates an unwavering pursuit of finding oil in East Texas.[1]

When Yount and his team brought in "Second Spindletop" in November 1925 against all odds, they revitalized not only the old field itself, they returned pride to a city caught up in a business slump and put swagger back into the steps of those who called Beaumont and the adjoining areas home. Sure, the likes of Frank Yount, Pansy Yount, Tal Rothwell, Harry Phelan, and the incalculable others associated with the "Financial Gibraltar of Beaumont" were motivated by profit, but they also gave back to the community by unselfishly contributing time and money to worthwhile causes and charities. On two separate occasions, the Yount-Lee Oil Company single-handedly rescued the City of Beaumont, when mired in the clutches of the Great Depression, it could not meet its payroll in August and December 1932. Without question, this example revealed the true moral fiber of the corporate leadership.

After Yount's untimely death in 1933, the sale of the company followed in less than two years, but it took place amidst honor and dignity, with a financial transaction that represented the third largest in United States history to that time. Immediately thereafter, the founder's widow, Pansy, picked up stakes and moved to Lexington, Kentucky, and there, she used her massive wealth to build one of the finest horse breeding facilities and training farms found anywhere. Pansy Yount's influence on the field of "Saddlebreds" is the stuff of legend.

But today, regardless of accomplishments and recognitions within a bygone era, an unnerving irony still persists. When one travels to Beaumont now, there are visual markers that pay tribute to the Lucas Gusher. The Spindletop-Gladys City Boomtown Museum, near the Lamar University campus and under the fine direction of curator Christy Johnson, has done an extraordinary job in promoting this phase of the oil industry to the public.

What about Yount-Lee? When searching for traces of its executive officers and officials, one doesn't have to look far to find the imposing figure of Harry Phelan's magnificent estate located at the corner of Calder Avenue and Eleventh Street. Tal Rothwell's house, Vir-Beth Hall, still stands at 124 East Caldwood Drive and remains a testament of the affluence generated by the company, then perhaps the largest independent oil producer in North America—and maybe the world. Due to the diligence of others, including Ryan Smith, Director of the Texas Energy Museum located in downtown Beaumont, the office furniture that belonged to the corporation's first president is on prominent and permanent display. But as far as the individual, who put Beaumont back on the map in the middle 1920s, there are no memorials, there are no statutes, just one minor street that bears his name. Long ago, his eccentric widow ordered their house, previously located at 1376 Calder Avenue, completely demolished, as well as the family mausoleum in Magnolia Cemetery that made such headlines in Beaumont when it took shape.

Notwithstanding Fred B. McKinley's 1987 Master's thesis, "The Yount-Lee Oil Company," at Lamar University and the brief accounts by James A. Clark and Michel T. Halbouty's *Spindletop* originally published in 1952, along with Jack Donahue's biography of Michel Halbouty titled *Wildcatter: The Story of Michel T. Halbouty and the Search for Oil* published in 1979, very little information in print can be found, with the exception of limited corporate filings, microfilmed newspaper and magazine records, brief internet source material, a few pictures, fading memories, and some history books with no more than a few pages or paragraphs devoted to the subject. All of this compares in stark contrast to the day of Frank Yount's funeral, when thousands of mourners lined Calder Avenue, and grown men of a starched collar era wept openly and unashamedly.

Within the following narrative, we seek to remedy this long put-aside scenario, and by providing much needed details about all those involved in the phenomena known as Second Spindletop and beyond, we hope to accord Frank, Pansy, and the others their rightful place in history.

THE AUTHORS

Acknowledgments

During Fred B. McKinley's initial thesis research at Lamar during 1986–87, he had the distinct privilege of interviewing the grand old gentleman, Marvin Wise McClendon, former assistant secretary-treasurer and the last surviving officer of the Yount-Lee Oil Company, who personally knew and worked for Frank Yount in the corporate office. And too, he spent hours with Virginia Rothwell Birdwell, the granddaughter of T. P. Lee and daughter of Tal Rothwell, who gave of her time and added a touch of humanism to the corporate figures. Marjorie Gibson Giles, former receptionist-secretary for the company, filled in material about Frank Yount's character, and L. W. "Billy" King also provided information about the Yount mausoleum at Magnolia Cemetery. G. Frank Myers, whose report titled the "Weekly Oil Review" that appeared in the *Beaumont Enterprise*, spelled out facts and figures about Yount-Lee production records from November 1925 through July 1935. Without Mr. Myers' columns, this valuable statistical data would have been lost forever.

Even though all of these individuals named above are now gone, we are forever in their debt. But we have also heard that for every door of opportunity that closes, a new one opens. Such is the case in the second wave of research. For now, Frank and Pansy Yount's grandchildren, Kathryn Manion Haider, Mildred Yount Manion, and Ed Manion, Jr., have not only stepped forward, they have opened the family archives and without reservation, shared previously unknown source material, including primary documents and photographs never before published, not to mention the spectacular forty-odd reels of home movies, some taken prior to Frank Yount's death, that were graciously donated to the archives of Lamar University. And without Mildred Yount Manion's generous gift, *Black Gold to Bluegrass* might otherwise have gone unpublished.

Bruce Yount, Marguerite Behar, and Peggy Carter, great-nephew, niece, and great-niece of Frank Yount, respectively, filled in details about the oilman's early years both in Monticello, Arkansas and Sour Lake, Texas. Erin Barry Teare, niece of Harry and Johannah Phelan, along with the couple's grandchildren, Mary Reed Williams and Anthony McDade "Mickey" Phelan, provided keen insight into the characters of their relatives. Likewise, Hans Wright Bohlmann, the grandson of Wright Morrow, lent his valuable support, and in doing so provided a wealth of documentation relating to the Houston lawyer who became one of the giants in Texas politics during the 1940s and 1950s. Janet McClendon, daughter of Marvin McClendon, also supplied immense information about her father, Max Schlicher, and others. Joe Max Guillory, grandson of

Max Schlicher and his namesake, sketched out details about his grandfather. T. P. Lee's granddaughter, Randa Kerr Davis, assisted with the project, as well as Thomas Peter Lee, III, grandson of Bill Lee, who carries the proud name of his great-uncle T. P. Lee. Robert R. Woodward, Emerson F. Woodward's grandson, gave specifics about the oilman's involvement with Yount-Lee and details about his personality. Barbara Moor supplied descriptions of her illustrious grandfather and grandmother, Judge Beeman and Nancy Strong; and Ann Moorhouse Goolsbee expressed her recollections of Mildred Frank Yount when the two were childhood friends and playmates.

We extend our heartfelt appreciation to Howard Perkins, Director of Student Press at Lamar, who provided the Preface, editorial comments, and photographs, as well as valuable assistance with interviews, research material, and suggestions about the path this work should follow. Howard's contributions to the preservation of Beaumont's history are endless. Also, we commend—and personally thank Dr. James M. Simmons, President of Lamar University, who as a staunch and loyal supporter of Beaumont history, approved the donation, transfer, and restoration of the Yount-Manion film donated by family members; to Maxine Johnston, retired former director of the Mary and John Gray Library at Lamar University, whose funds financed the film project; and to Ramona G. Hutchinson, Lamar University Archivist, who together with Howard Perkins and Raj Kapadia, computer analyst with the College of Arts and Sciences at Lamar, so painstakingly guided the process to completion. This material will prove a priceless asset and research tool for generations to follow. Furthermore, we extend a special note of appreciation to Darwin Morris, research assistant, and Penny Clark, curator of the Tyrrell Historical Library for their time researching and verifying source material.

Deborah Harrison, Historic Manitou Springs, Inc. of Manitou Springs, Colorado, spent hours poring through county records to provide us with information relative to the Yount-Manion families' acquisition and disposal of various properties in that state, along with several photographs of homes and businesses conducted there. Most certainly without the aid of Tolley Graves, director, and Kim Skipton, curator/librarian of the American Saddlebred Museum of Lexington, Kentucky, the actual story of Pansy's contribution to the Saddlebred industry could not be told properly. Both Tolley, Kim, and their respective staffs aided in the editing process, as well as supplying research material along with numerous photographs. And to Randy McKinley, Fred B. McKinley's son, we extend our thanks for his assistance in creating the maps and other drawings.

But as with any undertaking such as this one, numerous others deserve our appreciation, because in his or her way, each of the following individuals and entities provided support, information, photographs, and leads. However, no matter how careful, it seems that someone is usually left out inadvertently, and we are most certain the same occurred here. For that, we truly apologize.

In alphabetical order by first names:

Adra Miller, Jefferson County District Clerk's Office, Beaumont, Texas
Alex Szafir, Beaumont, Texas
Alford Branch, Mt. Zion Presbyterian Church, Monticello, Arkansas
Alura Hundley, Sour Lake, Texas
Amber L. Buckley, University of Texas Health Science Center, Houston, Texas
Amelie Cobb, Beaumont, Texas

Amy Spence, Hockaday School, Dallas, Texas
Andrew Hempe, Houston Metropolitan Research Center, Houston Public Library, Houston, Texas
Andy Coughlan, Assistant to the University Press Director, Lamar University, Beaumont, Texas
Anne Dunn, Baton Rouge, Louisiana
Barbara Price, Beaumont Public Library, Beaumont, Texas
Barbie Scott, Inheritance Tax Section, Revenue Accounting Division, Austin, Texas
Becky Hill, Alma M. Carpenter Public Library and the Bertha Cornwell Museum, Sour Lake, Texas
Ben Dobson, Lewisville, Texas
Ben Rodriquez, Center for American History, University of Texas, Austin, Texas
Ben Woodhead, Beaumont, Texas
Betty Ann Long, Silsbee, Texas
Beverly Pecotte, Texas State Data Center, Austin, Texas
Bill Dreggors, Jr., West Volusia Historical Society, DeLand, Florida
Blackhawk Collection, Danville, California
Bradley C. Brooks, Indianapolis Museum of Art, Indianapolis, Indiana
Bruce Yount, Lynn Haven, Florida
Carol Tompkins, pastor of Westminster Presbyterian Church, Beaumont, Texas
Charles Goodson, Lafayette, Louisiana
Charles Hawkins, Lamar University, Beaumont, Texas
Charlotte Holliman, Mary and John Gray Library, Lamar University, Beaumont, Texas
Christine Moor Sanders, Woodville, Texas
Christy Johnson, Spindletop-Gladys City Boomtown Museum, Beaumont, Texas
City of Beaumont, Office of City Clerk, Beaumont, Texas
Connie Dollinger, Magnolia Cemetery, Beaumont, Texas
Crystal and Warren Ford, Hull, Texas.
Damon Kennedy, The Petroleum Museum, Midland, Texas
Daniel Clark, Bureau of Vital Statistics, Texas Department of Health, Austin, Texas
Darlene Mott, Sam Houston Regional Library and Research Center, Liberty, Texas
Dave Cline, Kalamazoo, Michigan
Dave Renko, Smith Barney, Charlotte, North Carolina
David Moerbe, Office of Secretary of State, Austin, Texas
Dawn Boettcher, Medina County Clerk's Office, Hondo, Texas
Deena and Bob Stuart, Rockledge Country Inn, Manitou Springs, Colorado
Dolores Arnold, Antlers Hilton, Colorado Springs, Colorado
Donaly E. Brice, Texas State Library and Archives Commission, Austin, Texas
Dolly Rush, Jefferson Country District Clerk's Office, Beaumont, Texas
Donovan Landreneau, National Weather Service Forecast Office, Lake Charles, Louisiana
Ed Edson, III, Beaumont, Texas
Eleanor Straub, Lafayette, Louisiana
Ellen Walker Rienstra, Beaumont, Texas
Evelyn King, Beaumont, Texas
Frances E. Dressman, Harris County Psychiatric Center, Houston, Texas

Fred and Dorothy Wachs, Jr., Lexington, Kentucky.
Gary Christopher, photographer, Beaumont, Texas
Gayle Strickroot, American Saddlebred Museum, Lexington, Kentucky
Geneovise Buentello, Center for American History, University of Texas, Austin, Texas
George Hosko, University of St. Thomas, Houston, Texas
Gerald H. Marvel, Spindletop Hall, Inc., Lexington, Kentucky
Hardin County Clerk's Office, Kountze, Texas
Harris County Clerk's Office, Houston, Texas
Helen Locke, Beaumont, Texas
Hill County Clerk's Office, Hillsboro, Texas
Ia Wood, Texas State Law Library, Austin, Texas
Jack Whitmeyer, Heritage Village Museum, Woodville, Texas
James Broussard, Broussard's Mortuaries, Beaumont, Texas
Jane Vidrine, University of Louisiana at Lafayette, Lafayette, Louisiana
Jannett Pieper, Kerr County Clerk, Kerrville, Texas
Jason dePreaux, Center for American History, University of Texas, Austin, Texas
Jean Garrity, Manitou Springs, Colorado
Jean Kiesel, University of Louisiana at Lafayette, Lafayette, Louisiana
Jean Wallace, Beaumont Public Library, Beaumont, Texas
Jeanette Greer, Beaumont, Texas
Jeffrey Thompson, *Saddle & Bridle*, St. Louis, Missouri
Jefferson County Clerk's Office, Beaumont, Texas
Jen Liggitt, Hockaday School, Dallas, Texas
Jennifer Canup, University of Texas Health Science Center, Houston, Texas
Jim Kelley, current owner of *Sunnyside*, Sour Lake, Texas
JoAnn and Lynn McKinley, Beaumont, Texas
Jo Ann Stiles, Beaumont, Texas
John Anderson, Texas State Library & Archives Commission, Austin, Texas
John Troesser, TexasEscapes.com, Fayetteville, Texas
Joseph Dobbs, University of Texas Libraries, Austin, Texas
Judith Walker Linsley, Beaumont, Texas
Julie Moffett Suberbielle, Houston, Texas
Katherine S. Wood, Office of the Attorney General, Austin, Texas
Kathleen L. Skinner, University of Texas, Austin, Texas
Kathy Burns, *Saddle & Bridle*, St. Louis, Missouri
Kyle Hayes, City Manager, Beaumont, Texas
Lacey Liggitt, Hockaday School, Dallas, Texas
Larry R. Faulkner, University of Texas, Austin, Texas
Laurent Brocard, Past to Present Vintage Photo Gallery, Montreal, Quebec, Canada
Leslie Lewis, Chamber of Commerce, Manitou Springs, Colorado
Linda Barth, *Houston House and Home Magazine*, Houston, Texas
Lisa Grossberg, Buckingham Hotel, New York, New York
Lolita Ramos, Jefferson County District Clerk, Beaumont, Texas
Lois Harrington, The Petroleum Museum, Midland, Texas
Lu-Ann Farrar, *Lexington Herald-Leader*, Lexington, Kentucky
Lynn Edmundson, *Historic Houston*, Houston, Texas

Manitou Springs Historical Society, Manitou Springs, Colorado
Marcie Nelson, Texas Department of Public Safety, Austin, Texas
Marionette Mitchell, University of St. Thomas, Houston, Texas
Mark Holman, Tarlton Law Library, University of Texas, Austin, Texas
Mark Show, Student Editor, University Press, Lamar University, Beaumont, Texas
Marla M. Patterson, PennWell Books, Tulsa, Oklahoma
Martha Peterson, Houston, Texas
Maryjean Wall, *Lexington Herald-Leader*, Lexington, Kentucky
Mary Clark Look, Rockport, Texas
Mary Poole, Beaumont, Texas
Mary Speer, Beaumont, Texas
Mary Stewart, Secretary to Michel Halbouty, Houston, Texas
Mary Woodward, Kerrville, Texas
Michele M. Carvell, Pikes Peak Country Attractions Association, Manitou Springs, Colorado
Michel Halbouty, Houston, Texas
Micky Bertrand, Fire Chief, Emergency Management Coordinator, Beaumont, Texas
Mike Widener, Tarlton Law Library, University of Texas, Austin, Texas
Mildred Hall, Beaumont, Texas
Miro Dvorscak, photographer, Houston, Texas
Naaman J. Woodland, Jr., Beaumont, Texas
Nancy and Hartman Smith, former innkeepers of "Rockledge," Colorado Springs, Colorado
Neal Crausbay, Sweetwater, Texas
Nicole Tanner, Hill County Clerk's Office, Hillsboro, Texas
Osler McCarthy, Staff Attorney for Public Information, Supreme Court of Texas, Austin, Texas
Paul E. Petosky, Munsing, Michigan
Paul Ridenour, Garland, Texas
Pete Hausmann, Austin, Texas
Phillip Margolis, Cozio Publishing, Rapperswil, Switzerland
Ralph A. Wooster, Lamar University, Beaumont, Texas
Ramona Davis, Greater Houston Preservation Alliance, Houston, Texas
Randy Ema, Orange, California
Randy Morgan, Kelley-Watkins Funeral Home, Beaumont, Texas
Reagan and Debbie Newton, Katy, Texas
Rhonda Volrie, Beaumont Public Library, Beaumont, Texas
Rick Barrilleaux, Chamber of Commerce, Beaumont, Texas
Robert Schaadt, Sam Houston Regional Library and Research Center, Liberty, Texas
Robert Stone, Millbrae, California
Rosa Crutchfield, Beaumont, Texas
Rose Ann Jones, City Clerk, Beaumont, Texas
Rosine McFaddin Wilson, Beaumont, Texas
Ryan Smith, Texas Energy Museum, Beaumont, Texas
Sandra Soliz, University of St. Thomas, Houston, Texas

Sherry Williams, Alma M. Carpenter Public Library and the Bertha Cornwell Museum, Sour Lake, Texas
Stephen Fox, Rice University, Houston, Texas
Stephen K. Rinard, National Weather Service Forecast Office, Lake Charles, Louisiana
Steve Reed, Bureau of Labor Statistics, Department of Labor, Washington, D.C.
Sue Boyt, Beaumont, Texas
Susan Lanning, Fire Museum of Texas, Beaumont, Texas
Susan Ramsey, Atlanta, Georgia
The Beaumont City Clerk's Office, Beaumont, Texas
The Beaumont Enterprise, Beaumont, Texas
Tim Beeson, *Houston House and Home Magazine*, Houston, Texas
Tina Broussard, City Clerk's Office, Beaumont, Texas
Tom Eblen, *Lexington Herald-Leader*, Lexington, Kentucky
Victor Farinelli, Bureau of Vital Statistics, Austin, Texas
W. T. Block, Nederland, Texas
Wayne and Polly Wright, Beaumont, Texas
William Cape Grant, Jr., The Woodlands, Texas
William Seale, Jasper, Texas
And lastly, we wish to thank George Arnold, editor, and Pat Molenaar, book designer and typesetter, of Eakin Press, because without their assistance, none of this would have been possible.

THE AUTHORS

Authors' Notes

When I first heard of Miles Frank Yount, I was a young boy of twelve. But even at that tender age, it seemed improbable to me that everything I was being told could be true. Oil wells, fabulous wealth, show stopping horses, the Chicago World's Fair, custom-bodied automobiles, Stradivarius violins, and incredible generosity—all associated with or in Beaumont, Texas? I clearly remember thinking that the old gentleman who told me the story must really be laying it on thick. At this particular time, Beaumont in the mid–1970s suffered the worst effects of inflation and had only just begun to rebound with higher oil prices.

Of course I had heard of the Mildred Building and had gone to the Spindletop Charity Horse Show, but the first is just some old apartment house, and the other is nothing but prancing horses—right? With adolescence and high school looming, I soon forgot all about Frank Yount. Many years later when I became interested in local history, I read the Clark-Halbouty book *Spindletop*. Afterward, I was amazed to learn that the Yount story was apparently true after all, but as I drove among the gas stations, laundromats, and car washes, it seemed almost impossible that Calder Avenue was once millionaire's row. However, even now if you look closely enough, you can still see remnants of the Calder that once was.

After reading *Spindletop*, I really wanted to know more about Frank Yount, but there didn't seem to be anything else out there. Unbeknownst to me at almost the same moment, Fred B. McKinley was preparing his Master's thesis on Frank's Yount-Lee Oil Company. The Texas Energy Museum didn't yet exist (at least not in Beaumont), and I had never heard of McKinley. Once again, I almost forgot about Frank Yount. In 1998 an article appeared in the *Classic Auto Register* about a lady named Pansy Yount who had a custom bodied Duesenberg automobile destroyed during a World War II scrap drive in Lexington, Kentucky. I had never heard of Pansy and certainly didn't know that she had anything to do with the Frank Yount of Beaumont. I've always been fascinated with classic cars and was well aware that today, Duesenbergs sometimes sell for over a million dollars each. Well, I wrote the editor of that esteemed publication for additional information, but I never heard anything. Another inquiry to a renowned classic car expert came back with the curt response, "If this is true, it would be like putting a Rembrandt down a wood chipper."

Looking back, that article became for me the genesis of this book. If either the editor or the car expert had satisfied my curiosity, I might never have pursued anything further. My friend Christy Johnson of the Spindletop-Gladys City Boomtown Museum in Beaumont began to connect the dots for me. "Haven't you ever heard of Spindletop Farms in Lexington," she asked, "or the Saddlebred horse awards? Certainly you've heard some of the wild speculations?" No, no, and no. I hadn't heard any of it but certainly wanted to know more.

Why hadn't anyone tried to tell a factual account of this fascinating story? I became determined, so I intended to carry it through. Soon afterward, I contacted Fred McKinley who told me that it had always been his intention to expand his thesis into a book, and it soon became apparent that we should combine our efforts with each of us using our respective talents to illustrate the aspects of the story that fascinated us the most. As we continued forward, it became equally apparent that many others were also interested. These people had just been waiting for someone to ask, "What do you know about Frank and Pansy Yount or the Yount-Lee Oil Company?" The insights and information shared by these people have been invaluable.

It is often said that truth is stranger than fiction. If we had tried to write a novel with the twists and turns of this tale, a reasonable editor might possibly have rejected it as too implausible. But this is a true story. Everything you are about to read is historical fact, regardless of how implausible it may seem.

Enjoy!

GREG RILEY
Cleveland, Texas

As is Greg, I am also a native of Beaumont. But during my growing up period, I neither remember hearing the names of Frank Yount, nor that of the Yount-Lee Oil Company, and that includes my undergraduate stay at Lamar University in the early 1960s. After graduating and then on to a business career, I returned to Lamar in the fall of 1986 to pursue a Master's degree in history. With class-room work completed by the summer of the following year, I found myself scrambling to find a thesis topic. My first choice involved something on the American Civil War, but my mentor, Dr. Ralph A. Wooster, was busily engaged in other matters, so he referred me to Dr. Paul Isaac who said that another Beaumont historian, Ellen Rienstra, had suggested that someone do a study of the Yount-Lee Oil Company. When I responded that I had never heard of it, Dr. Isaac intimated that I should go the university library and check out some articles on the subject. Two days later, an excited student banged on Dr. Isaac's door and begged him to direct the project. Thankfully, he did, and in November 1987 I completed the thesis with the assistance of Drs. Adrian N. Anderson and Ronald H. Fritze, who also served on my committee.

From that point forward, I had always kept in the back of my mind the idea that one day, I would use this material as a basis for a book, and that thought has strengthened over the years as I concluded, sadly, that most folks, even in Beaumont today, much less those across America, have either rarely or most probably never heard the name of this historically significant oil company and its colorful cast of characters. So when Greg contacted me about some information and announced that he planned to do a book as well, I was more than delighted to respond.

FRED B. MCKINLEY
North Myrtle Beach, South Carolina

Chapter One

The Early Years

"I have learned this at least by my experiment: that if one advances confidently in the direction of his dreams, and endeavors to live the life which he has imagined, he will meet with a success unexpected in common hours."

—Henry David Thoreau

The names of Second Spindletop and the Yount-Lee Oil Company are inextricably linked, but in order to study either of them properly, not to mention associated family members, partners, employees, or events, one must begin first with Miles Franklin Yount. The reasons are twofold: he not only embodied the heart, soul, and spirit of the privately-owned corporation, but also, as its president and major stockholder, he acted as the driving force on which the economic development of his contemporary Beaumont, Texas, and surrounding areas came to depend upon so greatly.

Although famous in later years as the Godfather of Beaumont, Frank Yount's early life is shrouded in mystery. But a few scant details disclose that he was born January 31, 1880 near the Drew County community of Monticello, Arkansas, where his parents, Joseph Nathaniel, a Confederate veteran, and Hattie Minerva, both natives of North Carolina, had settled soon after the American Civil War ended. During the year of Frank's birth, Rutherford B. Hayes neared the end of his first and only term as Republican president of the United States; and Queen Victoria had completed almost forty-three years on the throne of England. By the time Frank reached the age of nine, the family worked to accumulate a farm of sizeable acreage, and things were going well. But from out of nowhere, disaster soon struck and shattered the young man's childhood. For during that year, his father died at age fifty; and Frank, as the third youngest of eight surviving children, had no other choice but to take on the mantle of additional responsibilities in order to keep the family together. Even though the elder Yount's death cut short Frank's formal education in the public schools of Monticello, he continued to learn on his own, and by the age of fifteen, he demonstrated the necessary aptitude to master the fundamentals of mechanical engineering, which served him well throughout life. Whether he realized the value and necessity of contributing to his family's support and livelihood at the time, he did so eventually. In later years, he joked about how the majority of his premature, harsh, and self-administered education had been received at what he often referred to as the "University of Hard Labor." While he seldom talked to the press, he once shed some insight on the subject, albeit all too brief, when he openly discussed his most noticeable personality feature—the work ethic. "I've never been afraid of toil since I left the farm," he said. "I was raised right next to hard work; grew up to know what it was; and consequently I have never run away from it since."[1]

Miles Franklin "Frank" Yount in youth.
—Courtesy Kathryn Manion Haider.

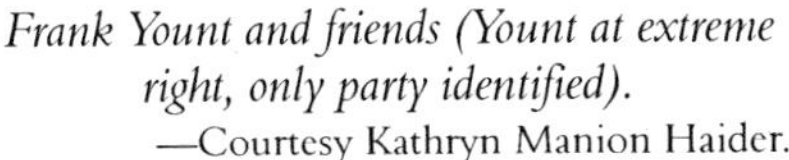

Frank Yount and friends (Yount at extreme right, only party identified).
—Courtesy Kathryn Manion Haider.

In 1897 he and a younger brother Sullie, who thought that "Frank hung the moon," moved to Winnie, Texas, and joined an irrigation crew working in the rice fields near Beaumont. During their limited leisure times, Frank and Sullie teamed up with Milton H. "Doc" Dunshie, Johnnie Webb, Jimmie Dunshie, and Will Baldwin as "they rode broncos, hunted wild ducks on the prairie ponds, fished in the gullies, [and] chased alligators." Other times the small band of close friends attended square dances, barbeques, and church socials—all part of the business of living life to the fullest. Of the six young men, Frank even then appeared to be blessed with a "certain strange wisdom that seemed to motivate his every action." But while struggling to find his true passion,

Early rotary rig at Spindletop.
—Courtesy Spindletop–Gladys City Boomtown Museum, Beaumont, Texas.

Frank Yount in youth.
—Courtesy Kathryn Manion Haider.

he made several detours along the way. After tiring of "ditch digging," as he called it, he first began his own business in 1901, contracting labor for the harvesting of rice crops in the area, and later he operated a water-well drilling service, so essential for successful rice irrigation purposes. Most other drillers had recently neglected this field, because they now concerned themselves with the far more lucrative product of oil, euphemistically known as "Black Gold." Basically, Yount had little competition and a lot of business, and in order to gain increased efficiency, he first adopted and then made quite a few design changes to the relatively new rotary process originally used in the Corsicana oil field in 1897 "capable of drilling a bore hole with a bit attached to a rotating column of steel pipe." This is the first example of several such innovations that Yount embraced long before the majority of his peers along the Gulf Coast. Even though some oilmen had previously used the system at Spindletop and Sour Lake, most still relied upon the older tried and true cable tool method based "on the percussion principle of repeatedly smashing a weighted bit into a well to gouge its way down, then hauling it back up to repeat the process."[2]

Although only twenty-four years old, a strong willed and determined Yount yearned to get into the oil business, and so he did. From 1904 until his death, with two exceptions, he associated himself with this industry in almost every phase of operation. But things got off to a shaky start in 1905 when he and Sullie invested every penny they had in a lease on Spindletop which included an old abandoned well. When they revived and converted it to the pump, however, the original lease owners swooped in, reclaimed the property, and resold it to other investors. For the moment, Lady Luck sidestepped the young dreamers, so woefully inexperienced and legally naïve. Broke and disappointed, Frank Yount turned from wildcatting and returned to the safer confines of rice threshing.[3]

After a short period, he traveled to Sour Lake, Texas, a nearby community known originally for its resort hotels. But now with the discovery of oil there, the quiet, quaint town of "less than fifteen old shacks and but one or two creditable houses and nothing to justify her making respectable pretension except her famous medicinal waters," changed almost overnight in much the same vein as Beaumont did with the bringing in of the Lucas Gusher. By November 1903 Sour Lake had grown to now include: "798 houses, 1,257 tents, 9 lumber yards, 4 livery stables, 131 stores, 7 machine shops, 7 blacksmith shops, 4 wheelwright shops, 6 hardware and implement stores, 9 markets, 1 newspaper and printer, 49 stables and corrals, 50 restaurants, 7 barber shops, 2 bakeries, 1 bank, 246 oil wells, 147 pumping rigs, 91 drilling rigs, 30 water wells, 229 boilers, 30

Rice threshing near Beaumont in the 1920s.
—Courtesy Howard Perkins Collection, Beaumont, Texas.

power and pumping plants, 29 large iron storage tanks, 143 galvanized tanks, 176 wooden storage tanks, 48 earthen storage tanks, 4 pipe lines and pumping plants to Beaumont, 9 factories, 4 sawmills, 5 dairies, 2 electric light plants, 1 waterworks, 1 opera house, 31 hotels, 54 boarding houses, 1 hospital, 122 offices, 2 cold storage plants, 1 bowling alley, 1 theater, 1 post office, 900,000 barrels of oil in storage, 8 miles of Southern Pacific Railroad tracks, 15 miles of Southern Pacific sidings, 2 depots, 2 telegraph offices, 20 miles of Beaumont and Sour Lake Electric Railroad, 2 schools, 1 church and—FIFTY-SIX SALOONS."[4]

The early boom days at Sour Lake presented a vivid picture to all those who came:

> There was everywhere in town as much mud as there was oil, for in addition to rain, the slush pits of the wells overflowed into the streets. Very quickly, the unwanted concomitant aspects of every boom town—crime, vice, drunkenness, race riots, gambling, robberies and murders—were present all over town ... Scores of law abiding but unemployed families as well as every sleazy character in search of a "fast buck" arrived, some in search of roustabout pay at $3 a day and others for profit in whatever form they could find.[5]

Such was the condition of Sour Lake when Frank Yount first arrived on the scene, hoping, praying, as a multitude of others to strike it rich. At one of the various remaining 54 boarding houses, 50 restaurants, or 56 saloons, Frank became acquainted with Peter Cannon, an established driller in that vicinity, and through Cannon, he met John Henry "Harry" Phelan, a grocery salesman from Beaumont whose route included Sour Lake, about fifteen miles away with nothing in between but a dirt road choked by dust in the dry months and turned near impassable when the frequent rains came. During regular visits to Sour Lake by his only means of transportation, a horse and buggy, Phelan took every opportunity to meet with both Cannon and Yount in order to discuss

Peter Cannon.
—Courtesy Bertha Cornwell Museum, Yount-Lee Collection, Sour Lake, Texas.

future plans. At some stage in one of these get-togethers, the three decided to form a corporation. After choosing Cannon as president, Yount as vice president, and Phelan as secretary-treasurer, the fledgling triumvirate completed the necessary paperwork on February 13, 1909, and submitted it for approval. Three days later, the Texas Secretary of State granted Charter Number 19809 to the first Yount Oil Company with a capitalization of $6,000. Of the sixty shares valued at $100 each, Cannon owned twenty-five; Yount, fifteen; Lee Wilkinson, ten; Phelan, five; and A. L. Williams held the remainder. All of the original stockholders, with the exception of Wilkinson, listed Beaumont as their principal place of residence. Though Peter Cannon claimed the title of president, Frank actually headed up the company and actively sought out leases where he proposed to drill.[6]

Yount's chosen profession would not prove an easy one. With days filled by backbreaking labor from sunup till dark and no letup in sight, Frank worked alongside his men, dirty, sweaty, and most times drenched to the skin from either the high humidity or continuous showers, performing whatever task needing doing. Charlie Jeffries, one of the many roughnecks and roustabouts at the Sour Lake field, described just a part of what Yount experienced.

> Whenever anything heavy was needed to be brought in, it was hauled by wagon as close to the road as possible; then a gang of men would take it and carry it to its destination ... The packers often had to lay down more [walking] planks; they had to twist like snakes around the obstacles. Sometimes they had to lay the load down on a friendly derrick floor, skit [skid] it across to the other side then take it up again.
>
> One hard day's work I can remember was helping pack a lot of eight-inch pipe. There was a good-sized crew of us and we would line up on each side of a joint and

> lift it up with a hand stick. Then the cautious creeping commenced. All day we went thus, back and forth, back and forth, taking plenty of time, but the work was hard and glad we were whenever quitting time came.[7]

Even in youth, Yount exhibited traits of unbridled ambition. While he worked, he dreamed about making a significant mark on the oil industry, but he could not generate the same type enthusiasm among his new business associates. When he learned that a lease on a small tract in Sour Lake went up for sale, he hastily attempted to persuade his reluctant partners that they should take advantage of the opportunity. But after hearing that the Texas Company (Texaco) had been unsuccessful in the area, no one, including Phelan, supported his recommendation. Undaunted, he tried again, and this time, the company vice president gained approval to lease an acre on the old Spindletop dome, where he drilled two wells. One produced for a while, but the other failed wretchedly. These events eventually led to the liquidation of the corporation sometime in 1911, although the actual date is vague. On paper anyway, the company was still doing business as late as January 24, because at that time, the stockholders filed an affidavit with the Texas Secretary of State, which disclosed the names of those who served on the board of directors. The only change from the original listing reflected that John Davis of Loeb in Hardin County, Texas, replaced A. L. Williams after his death.[8]

Faced with his second setback, Yount looked to the brighter side. At least now, he was rid of uncooperative partners who stalled at every turn. Thinking that a change of scenery might bring better luck, he traveled to the Texas Panhandle where he attempted to find oil there. When this effort proved unproductive, however, Yount gave up on the oil business in disgust. He returned to Beaumont in 1912, and for the next two years, he and John S. Chase operated a general repair business at 635 Main Street, which also served as the local distributorship for Cartercars and Moon automobiles. Though still dissatisfied with his individual progress, Yount tried his hand at other things, including real estate, but unfortunately his calm, reserved manner did not include a good sales technique, so both of those attempts met with dismal failure.[9]

But try as he might, Yount could not resist the lure of the oil field, so he thought hard about going back into the business. This idea intrigued him even more when he learned that oil had been found on the acreage that slipped through his fingers because of his former partners' no-confidence vote. The founders of the Poor Boy Oil Company had recently purchased that well for $15,000, and Yount never forgot about either the missed opportunity of finding oil where he thought it would be or the cash lost in the transaction. In 1913 he

Frank Yount in youth.
—Courtesy Kathryn Manion Haider.

visited Phelan, who by then had founded the Phelan-Josey Company, a wholesale grocery firm, during that same year. Yount invited his friend to form a new partnership with him, but the latter declined because at the time, his credit standing wouldn't allow any secondary business activities, much less taking a risky gamble on anything remotely akin to the oil business.[10]

Fate seemed to guide Yount back to Phelan time and again, because within two months after his initial refusal, Frank returned to his friend and asked him to use his influence to obtain a particular lease that looked promising. Phelan agreed to be the front man, so he sought the assistance of another acquaintance, Joe Hebert. With the lease successfully negotiated in 1913, Yount presented Hebert with a chance to purchase a percentage of his new company, but he refused the offer.[11]

However, when Yount extended another to M. E. "Ras" Pevito for an equal partnership, the two formed the Yount-Pevito Oil Company in early 1914 with capital stock amounting to $4,500. Yount further illustrated the fact that he held a special admiration for Harry Phelan, because without his knowledge, he reserved for him a sixth interest in the new enterprise whose shares were also held by Ambrose Merchant, T. S. Crosbie, and Ray Hankamer.[12]

Unfortunately, things did not go well for Yount-Pevito from the beginning. When drilling operations forced the company to seek additional capital to continue, Yount went to Phelan yet again. This time, he explained both good news and bad. He had found oil on the Hebert-associated lease, but in order to complete the project, he desperately needed $750, which he considered payment for Phelan's stock, the sixth interest set aside unbeknownst to him. Phelan must have been completely taken aback by the revelation, but regardless, he responded that due to the strain on his own personal finances, the funds were not readily available. Later on, however, when Phelan changed his mind and decided to help out after all, he visited his banker, and even in the face of considerable difficulty, he negotiated a loan in the amount of $750 and gave it to Yount.[13]

As with his previous experiences, Yount found it extremely difficult to maintain an agreeable, working relationship with his major partners. Once more, he wanted to purchase leases in Sour Lake, and as earlier, he failed to garner the support he needed. But in this instance, Phelan switched alliances and supported his friend to the hilt. Perhaps he was stung by the memory of his last lost prospect in Sour Lake and equally by the realization that Yount possessed an almost uncanny ability to find oil deposits there, not to mention the supposed loyalty generated by the sixth-interest episode. Obviously Phelan felt more confidence in his partner than ever before, and furthermore, he had come to conclude that no one should ever bet against Frank Yount. In spite of Phelan's vote, however, the majority sided against the most recent proposition.[14]

The latest setback only reinforced an already resolute Yount to follow through, so he sought out other more receptive prospective associates. This time he called on William Ellsworth "Bill" Lee and asked for his assistance. But Lee, who served with the production division of the Texas Company in Sour Lake, had problems of his own. His younger brother, T. P. Lee of Houston, once himself with the same company, had earlier resigned his position at Sour Lake and followed Joseph S. Cullinan under protest when the corporate offices were relocated to New York. After Cullinan founded the Farmers Oil Company, the forerunner of the American Republics Corporation, T. P. Lee and another associate, Emerson F. Woodward, joined the new venture. When Bill Lee failed in his bid to get the job as the head of the Sour Lake production division, he surmised that the bigwigs held his brother's actions against him. To Bill Lee, his future with the Texas Company looked dim. Perhaps, he thought, a possible association with Yount might provide an avenue for his departure that would eventually allow him to go into the banking business. With that as a backdrop, he called T. P. and asked for his opinion.[15]

After he considered his brother's request, T. P. Lee brought Woodward along, and the two met with Yount and discussed his proposal. Because Lee liked what he saw and heard, he instantly invested $25,000 in return for half of Yount's interest. The new venture, formed on December 22, 1914, assumed the leases of both Yount and Talbot Rothwell, T. P. Lee's son-in-law, while they operated briefly as partners. Immediately, though, a problem arose with the first choice of company title, the Yount-Rothwell Oil Company and the identical one used earlier. Texas law made it impossible to incorporate under the same name as an operating partnership without experiencing abnormal delays, so for purpose of expediency, everyone settled on the new name of Yount-Lee. They established principal offices in Sour Lake and tapped Yount as president and general manager; Rothwell as vice president and superintendent of production; and Phelan as secretary-treasurer. The new company's stock capitalization, set at $50,000, distributed 500 shares valued at $100 each. A portion of T. P. Lee's original investment went for the buyout of the old Yount-Pevito partners, excluding Phelan, and the rest went toward lease purchases and drilling operations. Although Woodward desperately wanted a piece of the new company, he told T. P. Lee that he simply didn't have the funds. After hearing that, Lee sold one-half of his interest to him and agreed to hold a block of Woodward's Texas Company stock as collateral. When the company was officially incorporated effective January 21, 1915, the owners, who were also the board of directors, controlled the following shares: Yount, 167; T. P. Lee, 120; Woodward, 125; Phelan, 83; and Rothwell, 5.[16]

Pansy Bernadette Merritt Daley Yount, seated, and standing is believed to be her sister, Belle Blanchette.
—Courtesy Kathryn Manion Haider.

Another important event in Frank Yount's life occurred in 1915, when he married Pansy Bernadette Merritt Daley, the daughter of Hosea Holly and

Sarah Frances Sherman Merritt, in Beaumont on September 15. Central Presbyterian minister E. P. Kennedy performed the ceremony. The account in the next day's *Beaumont Daily Journal* said that "the bride wore her going-away gown, a smart model in navy blue, with a "Bluebird" hat and accessories in harmony. Mr. and Mrs. Yount left on the 6 P.M. Frisco for the West where they will visit points of interest in Colorado, Washington, Oregon, and California." The article continued, "they will be away until Christmas, after which they will make their home with Mr. and Mrs. H. S. Blanchette, 1408 Bibb Avenue, while they plan together the handsome new residence which Mr. Yount will have built for his bride." Although this was the first wedding for Yount, Pansy had made the trip to the altar once before on July 20, 1905, with oil driller Charles Albert Daley of Humble, Texas, when they were married by Father William J. Lee at St. Louis Catholic Church in Beaumont located at the corner of Bowie and Orleans. This particular union, however, ended with Pansy's filing for divorce on April 10, 1915, finalized on May 24 during the same year. Throughout these proceedings, both plaintiff and defendant attested that they had been residents of Beaumont in Jefferson County, Texas, for the preceding twelve months.[17]

The actual set of circumstances that brought Frank and Pansy together are unknown, although one anecdotal version is that they met while she worked as a waitress in one of the many Sour Lake or Batson boarding houses that catered to oil field roughnecks. Batson, like most boom towns, experienced similar growing pains when drillers found oil there, and the ensuing population wave swamped the existing infrastructure. Killings at every turn, all sorts of crime, wide-open saloons, gambling, and hard drinking made the place extremely hazardous for all citizens, and besides the usual, "some 200 prostitutes crowded into Batson alone at the peak of the boom, many of them working in bawdy houses on the town's main street." With profitable operating branches at other oil fields, one such bordello, "Ann's Place," moved into Batson and set up shop. George Stoker, a local resident, recalled that the madam "had not time to get beds for her girls, but they did not let such little inconveniences deprive them of business." Although it had been years since the original growth surge, many of the same conditions that contributed to the area's notoriety still existed. Therefore, some of Frank's relatives, from a stance of protectionism filled with good intentions, did not relish the thought of his involvement with a divorced woman who lived around this type of setting, so they balked. Hence from the start, Pansy felt ostracized by her new in-laws. A longstanding feud developed between them, and most assuredly, Frank's younger

"Before Success," Frank and Pansy Yount.
—Courtesy Kathryn Manion Haider.

sister, Ida Belle, and her assertion that Pansy was never good enough for her brother, not only added fuel to the fire, but fanned the flames to fever pitch.[18]

When he returned to Sour Lake after his wedding trip, Frank found oil on the leases that he had fought so hard to purchase, and as a result, the company's financial picture as of December 8, 1916, reflected the recent prosperity. The assets now included the $25,000, the amount paid toward the stock capitalization at the time the original charter was filed in December 1914, and

> one acre of land, title owned in fee and a lease on one acre of land, eight producing oil wells, fully equipped with standard rigs, one boiler station and five boilers, treating plant, storage tanks, etc., all land and equipment above mentioned are located in the Sour Lake fields in Hardin County, Texas, the acre in fee know as Yount Lee acre #5 and the leased acre known as Jackson & Merchant acre #15. All of which being valued at twenty-five thousand dollars ...[19]

In 1917 Yount-Lee reached a milestone when it drilled the first deep well in the Sour Lake area. The Lynn No. 1 represented the beginning in a string of successes that allowed Yount and Rothwell to hire many of the locals such as William Warren Ford, who as a mechanic earned $2,467.94 in 1918, although his income for the next year slipped to $1,419.12. Nevertheless, Yount-Lee was on a roll that prompted the company's board to declare a 900 percent stock dividend on December 22, 1920. Basing the decision on the strength of the financial statement, the board also voted to increase the capital stock from $50,000 to $500,000, and to move its headquarters to a small L-shaped building on North Merchant Street for which it paid the owner a lease of $1.00 per year.[20]

A review of the net assets figure indicated clearly why the board voted the enormous increase in dividends, even though, erroneously, the balance sheet never considered the $50,000 in capital stock as a liability. At any rate, the surplus still remained at a healthy $464,866.92, satisfactory by any evaluation, but particularly stunning for a company virtually unknown only five years earlier.

Yount-Lee Oil Company
Financial Statement as of December 15, 1920

Assets	
Cash on Hand	**$ 38,520.73**
Accounts Receivable	**15,931.77**
Merchandise and Supplies	**10,461.71**
Machinery, Tools and Equipment	**149,609.47**
Buildings	**6,329.02**
Real Estate and Leases	**300,000.00**
Gross Assets	**$ 520,852.70**
Liabilities	
Accounts Payable	**$ 5,985.78**
Total Liabilities	**$ 5,985.78**
Net Assets	**$ 514,866.92**

Source: Texas Secretary of State, Charter Records, no. 28005, December 23, 1920, Office of Secretary of State, Austin, Texas.

With real cash in his pocket for the first time in his life, Frank had earlier begun construction on a Sour Lake home aptly named *Sunnyside*. He contracted with his brother-in-law, Walter Fletcher Parrish, who together with his partner, a Mr. Coleman, sometime during 1916 completed the home that still stands today on Texas Highway 105 West. One signature, most probably left behind by one of the many workmen on the project, was found later during a renovation. On a board salvaged from one of the demolished walls, the brief inscription reads: "C. B. Pearcy of Gainesville, Texas, January 20, 1916."[21]

A short while after Parrish and Coleman completed the home, an article that appeared in a local newspaper commented on its overall appearance:

> Experienced architects, decorators and landscape gardeners have given much thought to the matter, but, although they were allowed all freedom in planning the home, it is undeniably stamped with the individuality of the owner, and one is impressed with the simplicity and wholesomeness of the entire scheme from the broad sweep of the lawn to the splendid example of "preparedness" found in the kitchen.
>
> Mr. Yount himself made the plans and the architect worked out the details. And throughout the house a "homey" touch has been added by the beautiful hand decorated linens made by Mrs. Yount, who is an artist at needlework.
>
> In [the] dining room, drawing room and library the walls are finished in tan, and the furniture is of San Domingo mahogany in a light finish. The hangings are of blue and the rugs have a ground work of blue relieved with dull gold, deep orange and a suggestion of red. In the drawing room there is a magnificent leopard skin, pliant as a lady's glove.
>
> Then there is the breakfast room, all Dresden shades and roses ... The plate rail in the dining room is to be decorated by Miss Minnie Jones of Beaumont.
>
> Upstairs the bedchambers are furnished in Mexican mahogany of Queen Anne and Colonial design. There is a room of faint pink, a blue room and a rose room, each hung with harmonizing shades. The rugs are imported from Austria.
>
> If one is a good friend of the household one is admitted to the pretty green sewing room with its white wicker furniture, upholstered in black and white, and its win-

Sunnyside *under construction. Frank Yount, in suit (standing fourth from right), and Walter Parrish (standing fifth from right).*

—Courtesy Marguerite Behar and Jim Kelley.

Yount-Lee roustabout crew, Rufus Pugh and C. L. Lewis, foremen, Daisetta, Texas. Photograph by L. L. Allen.
—Courtesy Sam Houston Regional Library and Research Center, Liberty, Texas.

dows overlooking the rose beds on the lawn, dotted with palms and flanked on one side by an orchard of orange and fig trees.[22]

The Hull field provided the greatest discovery for Yount-Lee to date when on April 13, 1922, it brought in a flank well on the Stengler lease; and thereafter, overall production increased tremendously as a result of several 5,000-barrel a day achievements. On December 15, the board voted yet another dividend, the latest representing a 300 percent increase. And too, the capital stock soared to $2 million. An interesting point emerges that centers on total liabilities of less than $344 at the time, in that it is clear that Yount-Lee sustained its enormous growth pattern without incurring any real debt in the process. By today's standards of multi-billion dollar corporations, Yount-Lee's accomplishments to date do not sound terribly impressive. When one considers, however, that in January 1914 Henry Ford shocked the world by effectively doubling the working man's salary with an offer of $5 for an eight-hour day, all is placed into proper perspective.[23]

The company had been very generous to its short-term stockholders. Frank Yount and Tal Rothwell were now at the helm of a $2 million concern, and Harry Phelan's $750 investment yielded him in excess of $330,000 plus dividends, which must be considered one of the most lucrative outlays in Texas history. Woodward reclaimed his Texas Company stock from T. P. Lee with his first dividend check received in 1920, and although T. P. Lee had been reimbursed many times over for his original buy-in, over the previous years, he had given away many of his shares to his brother, Bill, and some to his daughter and her husband, Mabel and Tal Rothwell. All three parties profited heavily from the stock that T. P. Lee presented as gifts, but one of the most interesting sidelights of Yount-Lee's phenomenal return on investment up to that point is the fact that Emerson Woodward never invested one penny of his own money in the company that made him a fortune.[24]

Yount-Lee filed a financial statement on December 29, 1922, with the Texas Secretary of State's office . Once again, the net assets picture is overstated, but even with

Yount-Lee Oil Company
Financial Statement as of December 15, 1922

Assets	
Cash on Hand	$ 198,785.00
Accounts Receivable	50,357.13
Merchandise and Supplies	34,411.94
Machinery, Tools and Equipment	222,790.83
Buildings	7,354.26
Real Estate and Leases	2,000,000.00
Gross Assets	$2,513,699.16
Liabilities	
Accounts Payable	$ 343.96
Total Liabilities	$ 343.96
Net Assets	$2,513,355.20

Source: Texas Secretary of State, Charter Records, no. 28005, December 29, 1922, Office of Secretary of State, Austin, Texas.

San Jacinto Life Building.
—Courtesy Howard Perkins Collection, Beaumont, Texas.

the $500,000 in capital stock considered as a liability, the surplus remained at $2,013,355.20. In approximately two short years, the company had increased its surplus by an impressive $1,548,488.28, quite a meteoric rise, and by today's value in excess of $17 million.[25]

But even in the face of fantastic growth and virtually no debt, Frank Yount had far reaching plans for his company, and for him that meant relocation to a larger city more capable of meeting future goals. After the stockholders approved his motion on March 14, Yount-Lee moved its corporate headquarters from Sour Lake to Beaumont in 1923 and occupied a portion of the twelfth floor of the San Jacinto Life Building, located at the corner of Orleans and Fannin Streets. By 1925 employees and officers had taken additional space that now included suite numbers 1206 through 1209.[26]

However, when Yount-Lee arrived in Beaumont in 1923, the company executives found a Spindletop, described as "a little knob of land rising out of a swampy prairie," much different than it appeared twenty-two years before. At the beginning of that first day of 1901, Queen Victoria would have only twenty-two days left of her long life that would end a remarkable reign of near sixty-four years on the English throne. And most had no inkling that another sovereign was about to take charge in the United States some ten days later, with the inauguration and amazing run of the great American phenomenon, "The Black Golconda," that produced the majority of the world's petroleum reserves. The original discovery well, better known as the Lucas Gusher, struck at Beaumont at about 10:30 A.M. on January 10, 1901; and from a depth of 1,160 feet, according to Captain Lucas' log, it came in with such fury that oil shot more than a hundred feet above the derrick. The crew estimated the flow to be between 80,000 and 100,000 barrels a day, but no one really knows for sure, because an official reading was never taken at the initial, maximum force. Since the monster ran completely out of control for a ten-day period, rumors spread that the owners offered a reward of $10,000 to

The famous Lucas Gusher, 1901. Photograph by Halvor I. Ostebee, Beaumont, Texas.
—Courtesy Tyrrell Historical Library, Beaumont, Texas.

anyone who successfully capped its flow. Finally, though, the Hamill brothers, the original drillers at the site, brought the big brute into submission, but not until a million barrels of crude saturated the surrounding area of at least fifty acres.[27]

In order to understand the oil field, it is necessary to describe it in rudimentary terms. Geologically speaking, Spindletop proper is a salt dome, and it

> ... is a low surface hill of Lissie and Beaumont sands, and the salt mass is found at a depth of about 1,200 ft. It is a mile or so in diameter, steep-sided and cylindrical; and the principal oil reservoir is the cavernous limestone rock above the gypsum layer overlying the salt. There is much native sulphur in the cap rock, which does not completely cover the salt.[28]

During the early days at the field, operators discovered that the cap rock measured between twenty and thirty feet in thickness, and once they drilled through it into the salt formation below, nothing but dry holes resulted. Virtually all of them, therefore, assumed that the oil confined itself to the porous limestone stratum, so they limited the depth of the majority of the wells to less than 1,100 feet, partly due to the extreme difficulties posed by the gummy soil while drilling deeper. For those of the time, the oil's source remained a complete unknown, but during those boom days, it really didn't matter to most in Beaumont, because they considered Spindletop as king of the hill, and oil his mistress, however unfaithful she might be. Almost overnight, the small lumber and

A sea of derricks.
—Courtesy Spindletop–Gladys City Boomtown Museum, Beaumont, Texas.

rice-producing town, with a population of a little more than nine thousand, became a crowded, congested city of near six times the previous number.[29]

In glowing terms, Isaac Marcosson described the Spindletop of 1901:

> The Klondike of petroleum has witnessed the greatest rush since that eventful day when Drake drilled the first well on Oil Creek. It put the oil stock on the popular map to the acute distress of many. The Lucas gusher, the discovery well . . ., was the wonder of the day.[30]

Indeed the rush was on as five hundred derricks sprang up on about 140 acres, and the complexion of the world's infant oil industry changed immediately after the discovery. Spindletop could now outproduce the combined effort of every oil field in the entire world, but above all else, one thing became abundantly clear. The Rockefeller companies would no longer monopolize either the American petroleum business, or that of the entire world. A new kid had arrived on the block, and the big bully would take notice.[31]

The boom that resulted was like nothing the world had ever seen. In the days that followed, Spindletop not only provided excitement, it also caused a major societal upheaval when various classes of individuals, many of them undesirable, traveled to Beaumont for varied reasons. Investors and prospectors made their way there to find oil fortunes; "parasites" came to make quick money off the public by any means, whether hook or crook; some to merely study the oil experience and apply its lessons elsewhere; while others were simply curiosity seekers who wanted to see what the action was all about. Excursion trains arrived from New York, St. Louis, Philadelphia, New Orleans, and Galveston. Promotion companies brought in ready investors who wanted nothing more than to cash in on the bonanza, and many of these get rich quick seekers were treated to artificial gushers turned on purposely to excite immediate investment. These

"Open One for the Suckers." Photograph by Frank J. Trost of Port Arthur, Texas.
—Courtesy Tyrrell Historical Library, Beaumont, Texas.

unfortunate displays wasted crude by the millions of barrels, but again, most did not concern themselves with the smallest degree of conservation, because they foolishly believed that Spindletop's oil production would continue indefinitely.[32]

Regardless of the reasons, however, people congregated by the thousands, and with their influx, businesses of all types flourished. But as far as the customers were concerned, things were not as rosy as pictured beforehand. With hotels and rooming houses filled beyond their limits, many were forced to sleep on the streets, on billiard tables, or

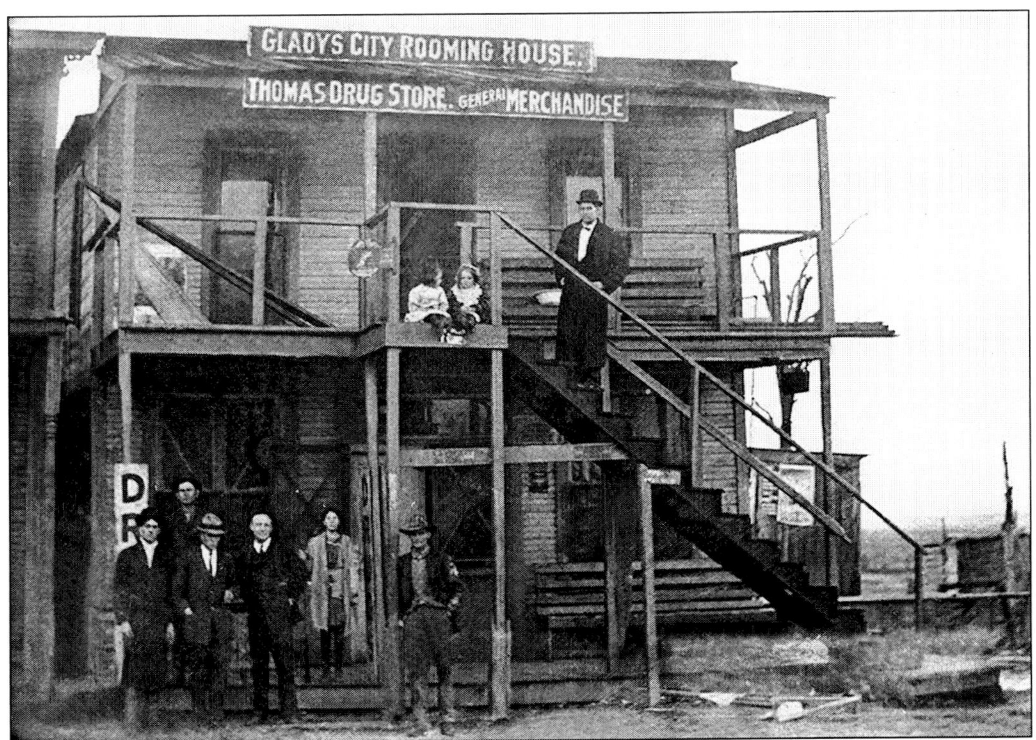

Gladys City Rooming House, Thomas Drug Store, and General Merchandise.
—Courtesy Spindletop–Gladys City Boomtown Museum, Beaumont, Texas.

wherever they could, at overblown prices, while other enterprising landlords rented out scarce rooms by the hour or in shifts to accommodate the masses. The same principle held true as long lines formed at restaurants and eating establishments that eagerly sought to get in on the action. Local farmers also got into the play by peddling coffee and food products to the hungry crowds who willingly paid whatever the market would bear. Livery stables and those who catered to the transportation trade received enormous returns as well. Likewise, land prices skyrocketed to levels previously unheard of, and those who happened to own land in the close proximity of the discovery well became extremely wealthy in a short span of time. A sixty-fourth of an acre commanded up to $7,500; but again, money meant little amid the speculative schemes and the lure of fantastic profit potential. Reportedly in the ninety days immediately following January 10, 1901, at least $50 million passed from one hand to the other on the streets of Beaumont.[33]

Thus, it is not surprising that Spindletop became widely known as "Swindletop," where vice and corruption ran rampant amidst the area as if leading the way for the Four Horseman of the Apocalypse. Many saloons, as plentiful as derricks themselves, were built on the oil field, often with rig timbers being incorporated into their very structure. Alcohol flowed freely and its plentifulness received much of the blame for fights that broke out continuously, producing both fatalities and property destruction. Ironically, the boom not only created an overabundance of crude oil, it turned Beaumont into a rough, disorderly, dangerous place for all inhabitants, law abiding or otherwise.[34]

For a short while, though, it appeared that the few skeptics who preached the doom of Spindletop might be way off their mark. True, production was nothing short of spectacular in the early stages, but the end result proved that too much of a good thing not only harmed the oil field in the long run, it also led to a dramatic decrease in the price

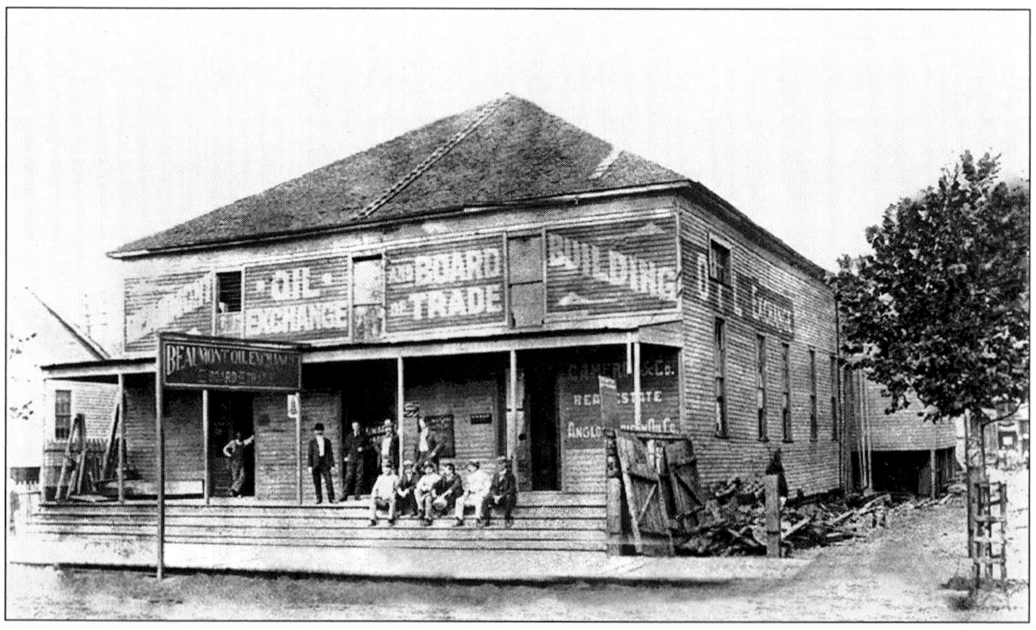

Beaumont Oil Exchange and Board of Trade Building.

—Courtesy Spindletop–Gladys City Boomtown Museum, Beaumont, Texas.

The infamous Log Cabin Saloon at Spindletop Settlement.
—Courtesy Spindletop–Gladys City Boomtown Museum, Beaumont, Texas.

Earthen oil storage pits.
—Courtesy Spindletop–Gladys City Boomtown Museum, Beaumont, Texas.

Fire on the hill.

Courtesy Spindletop–Gladys City
Boomtown Museum, Beaumont, Texas.

of oil itself. The average price per barrel produced in Texas fell to a low of 18 cents in 1901, and it took nineteen years for it to get back to $2.74. At Beaumont, however, the price fell even further during 1901–1902 to 3 cents a barrel. Since the field had come in so suddenly and with a force only dreamed of, no one had time to plan properly for so great a volume, consequently when storage facilities proved pitifully inadequate, operators managed the best they could and used earthen pits to accommodate their bounty. Regrettably, this decision led to sustained fire hazards that resulted in untold injuries and deaths along the way.[35]

By end of year 1922, when Spindletop's production dropped to a mere 295,015 barrels—the lowest point since the original discovery—it became apparent that the rush had taken its toll on a field that had operated for more than two decades without the slightest hint of restriction. So when Yount-Lee moved its headquarters to Beaumont in the spring of 1923, the company officers must have witnessed the same gloomy picture as did Isaac F. Marcosson when he toured the site in January 1924:

> Today Spindletop is practically petered out. I went there to see the aftermath of what had been a scene of frenzied output. The 140 acres where 500 derricks had creaked in the golden age of the field were almost as still as a graveyard. From a few wells a trivial amount of oil was being pumped. Decay and desolation were the dominant notes.

Marcosson continued:

A Comparison of Crude Production at Spindletop for the Years 1901 through 1936

Year	Barrels	Year	Barrels	Year	Barrels
1901	3,593,113	1913	716,374	1925	420,823
1902	17,420,949	1914	580,130	1926	14,838,281
1903	8,600,905	1915	388,266	1927	21,255,935
1904	3,433,842	1916	340,441	1928	14,332,357
1905	1,652,780	1917	380,039	1929	10,183,684
1906	1,077,492	1918	557,128	1930	5,997,913
1907	1,699,943	1919	432,660	1931	3,209,994
1908	1,747,537	1920	323,995	1932	1,442,560
1909	1,388,107	1921	321,080	1933	1,168,432
1910	1,182,436	1922	295,015	1934	1,152,010
1911	965,939	1923	309,315	1935	969,634
1912	822,916	1924	351,385	1936	844,684

Source: C. A. Warner, *Texas Oil and Gas since 1543* (Houston: Gulf, 1939), 375-376.

> A spot which once hummed with activity and held the eye, interest, and some of the bankroll of the nation, was a forlorn and well-nigh desolate stretch, cluttered up with the wreckage of other days. Only the strong smell of petroleum remained unimpaired.[36]

Even with what he observed, Frank Yount exuded confidence in all things, whether business or personally related. Soon after moving to Beaumont, he cemented the relationship with his adopted home city by purchasing a residence, along with lots 4 through 9 in the thirty-eighth block of the Calder addition. This magnificent house, located at 1376 Calder Avenue, originally belonged to Valentine and Laura Wiess (pronounced Wise), prominent members of early Beaumont society who contracted premier architect Henry Conrad Mauer for the design, and general contractors, James Wellman for the carpentry and finish work, and Matthew A. McKnight for the brick and stone. J. T. Booth installed the roof unit and "the metal cresting around the large skylight ... that emitted light to the finished attic and in turn through a large ceiling window into the third floor." As the project approached completion in 1908, the following newspaper article described the house with painstaking details.

Valentine Wiess.
—Courtesy Tyrrell Historical Library, Beaumont, Texas.

> The new home of Mr. V. Wiess, senior member of the V. Wiess Insurance Company, which is now being erected on Calder avenue and Oakland street, is des-

tined to be one of the most stately and substantial residences of its kind in this part of the country.

Mr. Wiess and his architect, H.C. Mauer, a well known citizen and architect of this city, have been at the plans of this house for some time and now state that they are nearing completion.

The residence lot is of 150 foot frontage and extends back for 300 feet towards North street. The construction of the house is to be of St. Louis pressed brick and trimmed with Carthage and Bedford stone and Texas and Georgia marble. There will be three galleries and one porticochere [sic] on the west side. There will be on each side of the residence six large columns of Bedford stone adorned with carved base and caps of the same material, and on each side of the main entrance there will be two tall polished red Texas granite columns. The house is to be roofed with asbestos cement slate, a product of the Keasby Matterson Company of Ambler, Pennsylvania, and all metal work will be of sixteen ounce copper. The floor of the front porch will be of

Henry Conrad Mauer.
—Courtesy Howard Perkins Collection, Beaumont, Texas.

Henry Conrad Mauer's Studio.
—Courtesy Howard Perkins Collection, Beaumont, Texas.

> marble tile and the doors opening on it, and the porticochere [sic] will be beveled plate glass in copper bars. It is to be of colonial style and strictly modern in all of its accessories. A drive-way and stable will be added to the work later in the year.
>
> Mr. Wiess' home will be finished throughout in hardwood, the bathroom will be finished with a marble wainscot and a tile floor. There will be six rooms on the first floor not including the butler's apartment, pantry and reception hall. The parlor will be finished in white and gold, the dining room, smoking room and library are of quartered sawed oak of the best description; the sitting room of cherry and the remainder of the lower floor to be finished in red birch.
>
> The second floor will contain six rooms also, exclusive of the bath rooms, closets and halls. All the other living apartments on the second floor shall be of white enamel except the sewing room, which will be of birds-eye maple, and the front hall, which will be finished in quartered sawed oak.
>
> The third floor will be finished and contain, if the builder does not change present arrangements, a billiard room, trunk room, bath room, store room and servants' hall.
>
> There will be thirteen fire-places in the house, and in addition, it will be heated with hot water. A freight elevator will be one of the costly features and conveniences of this modern home, and will extend from the basement to the third floor. The boiler-room will be in the basement and will be strictly fire-proof in every respect.

After the death of her husband, Mrs. Wiess decided to dispose of the property, now too expansive for her purposes, so she sold it to Yount on February 10, 1923, for $90,000 ($1,013,000 in today's evaluation). The contract, which included furniture, called for an immediate cash payment of $45,000 and the remainder at 6 percent interest, secured by a promissory note due February 10, 1924. Frank and Pansy packed their personal belongings, left their home Sunnyside in Sour Lake with all its furnishings to Frank's sister and brother-in-law, Ida Belle and Walter Parrish, and moved to Beaumont.[37]

When the Younts took possession of the Wiess house, they named it "El Ocaso"

1376 Calder Avenue. Architect's original photograph, 1908.
—Courtesy Howard Perkins Collection, Beaumont, Texas.

(The Sunset), and on the porch, they had that title etched in tile for all to see as they entered the front door. Unfortunately the home no longer stands, but at its zenith, the granite-columned eighteen-room structure rested on a foundation approximately seven feet thick. Relative to its outward façade, the granite columns, banisters, and trim work appeared as tan, with tan colored brick lending some contrast. Actually, the exterior contained very little wood whatsoever; even where it would be normally used for trim, the architect used stone in its stead. Each room reportedly had a ceiling fan, as writer Don Streater put it, "certainly a mark of luxury in 1923." El Ocaso also held a basement; four bathrooms; and three additional lavatories, with the attic used primarily for storage purposes. The entertainment floor—the specialty on the third level—contained a billiard room, a ballroom large enough to accommodate sixty couples while dancing, and a stage. Frank and Pansy Yount were never satisfied to rest on their laurels, so they immediately set about to improve the property at every level, and when they were finished, the extensive renovation included the installation of marble fireplaces by Italian artists brought over from Europe. Valuable oriental rugs and tapestries, art treasures of all sorts, rare violins, beautiful furnishings, including between 6,000 and 7,000 books, many of them first editions, all accented the living area. Outside, live oaks bought from Griffing Nursery located north of Beaumont on Old Voth Road enhanced the landscaping already dotted by giant palm trees which the same firm planted for Valentine and Laura Wiess. Later, Pansy had the ballroom converted into a large dining space where family, friends, and Frank's business associates enjoyed such treats as caviar brought in for special occasions. With Louise Ogden's able assistance, the lady of the house also entertained royally when she had to, throwing extravagant parties, especially when the guest

El Ocaso, "The Sunset."

—Courtesy Tyrrell Historical Library, Beaumont, Texas.

list included the higher-ups at Yount-Lee and Preston B. Doty, the president of First National Bank. At the conclusion of each of these get-togethers, El Ocaso's hostess passed out lavish gifts to everyone as they left her residence.[38]

In 1923 as Frank Yount renovated and decorated his new home to suit his and Pansy's individual tastes, the majority of people who lived in Hackberry, Louisiana, and in Sour Lake and Hull, Texas, recognized him as the millionaire president of a well respected and successful oil drilling firm. But in Beaumont, however, very few outside the small circle of oil acquaintances ever heard of him, much less the Lee brothers, Woodward, and Rothwell. Nevertheless, this circumstance would soon change dramatically, because in less than three years, the nation's eyes would again focus on Spindletop. But this time and for the foreseeable future, the names of Frank Yount, his partners, and associates would temporarily push aside those of Captain Anthony F. Lucas, Pattillo Higgins, John Galey, and James Guffey, the principals who had gained earlier fame on the same hill back in 1901.[39]

Alignment with Destiny

"Destiny is not a matter of chance, it is a matter of choice; it is not a thing to be waited for, it is a thing to be achieved."

WILLIAM JENNINGS BRYAN

At times, it seems that the road to fame, fortune, and riches is controlled by the dual hands of fate and destiny, and along the way, many who traverse it find the path strewn with previous failures and broken dreams too hazardous to overcome and simply reverse course. Yet regardless of these same obstacles, a select few persist and even in the face of overwhelming odds, they never give up—and they never give in. They don't understand what the word "quit" means. If the relationship, therefore, between Frank Yount and Harry Phelan can be characterized as fate, then that between Yount and Marrs McLean is described as destiny.

McLean was born at Sherman, Texas, on June 20, 1883. His parents, Edward Curd and Zerena "Rena" Hervey Marrs McLean, sent their son to the Sherman public schools and then on to Austin College, also located in the same city. After completing one year there, Marrs enrolled at the University of Texas in 1902, where he studied law. His father, a well-known Sherman attorney, wanted his son to follow him into the legal profession, but Marrs never shared that desire. So when he received a degree in 1904, he chose not to take the bar examination. Instead, he went to St. Louis, Missouri, and landed a job as an elevator operator at the Brown Shoe Factory, before deciding to become a policeman. He served on the St. Louis police force for about seven months, after which he resigned and traveled to Beaumont, where his family had moved previously in 1901. But he didn't stay there long either. Soon he was off to Noble, Louisiana, where he went to work for the Kansas City Southern Railroad. During this stint, McLean worked as a section hand and then on the railroad's experimental farm. This agricultural experience led him to the Bolivar Peninsula and High Island, Texas, where he and a brother, Jack, truck farmed for approximately three years and shipped their produce to Eastern markets. At the time, it is highly doubtful that either realized that rich deposits of undiscovered oil lay beneath the land on which they raised melons and cabbages.[1]

As a seeker of fortune, it is only natural to conclude that Marrs McLean began looking for his big break from the very moment that he arrived at High Island. When his

Marrs McLean, "Second Prophet of Spindletop."
—Courtesy Tyrrell Historical Library, Beaumont, Texas.

brother died, however, he tired of the agricultural business and went into partnership with B. E. Quinn, and together, the two built and then operated a local hotel. Later, he bought out Quinn's share of the business and moved back to Beaumont, which promised even greater opportunities. Beginning with 1907, McLean became a promoter and advertiser in the theatrical field, and his agency conducted business in Houston, Galveston, and Port Arthur, as well as Beaumont. He headed up a group of investors that purchased the Peoples Theater, which no longer exists, on Liberty Street in Beaumont, and he managed this establishment for approximately two years, until he finally succumbed to oil fever. From 1911 McLean dissociated himself from all other business activities and devoted his full attention to his new fascination with the petroleum industry.[2]

At every opportunity, he bought interests in wells at Spindletop and Vinton, Louisiana, but each provided only enough revenue for an investment in an Eagle Pass location with the Higgins Oil and Fuel Company that promptly hit a dry hole. While this latest failure proved to be a most valuable training ground, the young entrepreneur, though disappointed, received at the least a practical education concerning the pitfalls of his new vocation.[3]

Although McLean never received any formal training as a geologist, he carefully analyzed each of the salt domes that he encountered and, with well thought out observations, he soon formed a theory that portrayed him for the visionary he turned out to be.

> I pictured the vast salt plug shoving itself up through the various strata over the centuries and ages and eons. I saw the sands and shales being thrust upward by the giant plug, being pulled away from the caprock that had formerly connected them, and in the process forming perfect traps for the accumulation of migrating into lenses of varying sizes and shapes, including some that could be perfectly perpendicular, but containing oil.

This rationale asserted simply that undiscovered oil lay at the flanks of salt domes, and not just near—or at their center. Although various others had long accepted and preached this identical concept, McLean carried it much further. He believed fervently that in order to be successful, a driller needed to punch enough holes and along the way, have a little luck in the process. Undeterred in the short term, he never compromised on this idea that guided him throughout an illustrious career.[4]

In 1913 he returned to Vinton and began testing his new hypothesis. However, before finding any substantial oil deposits in that area, he sold his holdings, but this time, he retained an overriding royalty, a novel inspiration up to that point, not only from the aspect of payments but in how title to oil property is held. Widespread lease-buying became Marrs McLean's trademark, and it is highly likely that he invented the business terminology of "overriding royalty interest," which means that when a seller holds one of these, he retains a percentage of the mineral rights to a particular piece of property. In such a transaction, the buyer pays all the taxes, and if the new owner discovers oil, even in a lease obligation, royalties are paid to the seller or whoever holds an interest. Matters become further complicated when several parties are involved in a sublease situation, with each being entitled to percentage payments. However complex, McLean became a master in the art, which even today represents a significant or potential income producer among lease holders.[5]

Firmly convinced that oil would be discovered on the flanks of salt domes, McLean leased everything that became available at High Island during the period from 1915 through 1919. Then he returned to Beaumont in 1920 and began buying recently expired leases in and around the old Spindletop field, those previously held by the Gulf Production Company and located primarily on property owned by two entities: the Gladys City Oil, Gas, and Manufacturing Corporation and the McFaddin, Wiess, and Kyle Land Company. At this stage of his career, McLean turned from being an oil producer to promoter, and from this point forward, he withdrew from direct involvement in drilling, except in instances when it fulfilled a contractual requirement. His first option always: lease or purchase property, retain a royalty interest and then either sublease or sell it to another who would be ultimately responsible for production costs. He operated under the supposition that if he owned enough royalty interests, and if operators were successful enough, he would become a wealthy man by sheer volume. In the years that followed, his assumption proved most valid.[6]

As stated previously, the idea of deep flank production was nothing new, and as a matter of fact, several such attempts had already been made at Spindletop, some as early as 1917 when the Spindletop Deep Well Company drilled to 3,832 feet without finding sufficient quantities necessary to justify commercial production. Likewise, a Texas Company effort, northeast of the old dome, resulted in a total loss. Meanwhile, the Gulf Production Company tried at least seven times, once as deep as 4,718 feet, to locate the elusive pay sands, but it too walked away from a sizeable investment. These miserable failures prompted Gulf to give up many of their leases on Gladys City and McFaddin, Wiess, and Kyle acreage, an action the company would later regret. It is hard to imagine how the histories of Beaumont and especially the owners and employees of Yount-Lee might have been altered had any one of these earlier efforts been successful. Regardless, that is when Marrs McLean stepped in. After acquiring some Gulf leases in the outlying areas, he staked a site on Gladys City Square No. 12, but unfortunately for him, materials for the derrick's construction were mistakenly unloaded 300 feet away. Even when McLean discovered the error, he chose to accept the incorrect location, rather than ordering a move that would have resulted in further costly delays. Drilling at the erroneous site proceeded to a depth of 3,700 feet, and it might have gone even farther, had it not been for the derrick's destruction by hurricane force winds. The result ended in a dry hole; but destiny would later confirm that if he had held fast and retained the original location, oil would have flowed at about 3,000 feet. Interestingly enough, McLean learned the hard way that a difference of just a few feet one way or the other in a well's location determined whether it proved a success or a complete fiasco.[7]

After accepting his latest defeat, McLean tried to market his idea of deep flank production to the major oil companies, but he found that road rough going also as one by one, each turned him down without exhibiting any interest whatsoever. Flat broke, and as a last resort, he turned to the officials of the Amerada Petroleum Corporation and presented his proposal. To McLean's delight, Amerada, which later operated as the Rycade Oil Company, signed on to the project, purchased the leases on the Gladys City and McFaddin, Wiess, and Kyle acreage, and agreed to drill three test wells. In 1922 drilling began on McFaddin property, but when the first try produced a paltry fifteen to twenty barrels of crude a day, hardly enough to consider it a true well, Amerada redirected its crew. They abandoned a second attempt at 5,400 feet, and the third, on a Gladys City tract, also went bust at 3,962 feet. By 1925 with nothing to show for its labors except enormous expenses, Amerada pulled out altogether and left the matter of deep exploration at Spindletop to others. Once again, providence proved most kind to the future prospects of Yount-Lee.[8]

True to his character, McLean reassumed Amerada's leases and continued the search for any major oil company that would drill on his holdings. He approached Marland, but like the rest, it also rejected the idea. At this point, most large concerns had come to realize that deep wells had been drilled around the outlying areas of Spindletop for years without success, and from all indications, they believed that the old dome was finished as a producer of any consequence. Attitudes such as this put McLean at a standstill, and for the first time in his career, completely frustrated to the point of disgust, he ignored the obvious. It never occurred to him to look beyond the key producers and consider that just maybe someone like Frank Yount and his Yount-Lee Oil Company might be interested in his proposal.[9]

1925

Astonishingly, both Yount and McLean, along with his wife Verna and only child, Ruth, had lived for at least two years on Calder Avenue, with only one house owned by Percy H. and Bertie Wiess separating them. As acquaintances, each man knew that the other made his living in the oil business; yet, neither discussed their similar viewpoints concerning deep flank production. Since 1917 Yount had drilled deep wells at Texas locations in Sour Lake and Hull and in neighboring Hackberry, Louisiana, and in reality, deep drilling was his cup of tea. His close neighbor, McLean, had sought in vain for a number of years to find a willing producer to prove his theory, but for some reason, it took these two individuals until mid-April 1925 to realize that each shared a common goal. A chance meeting, during a walk home for lunch in which McLean openly discussed his disappointment about not being able to find anyone to drill on his Spindletop leases, began the process by which both men prospered, most probably, beyond their wildest dreams.[10]

Although his own previous experiences on the hill were less than sensational, Yount also refused to accept the premise, shared by most self-proclaimed authorities, that

Spindletop's glory days were a thing of the past. Over the years, he too witnessed the numerous botched attempts by various companies who punched holes along the rim of the old salt dome, and like McLean, Yount believed with all his being that Spindletop would not only be rediscovered, it would outproduce what it did during its heyday. But first, he had to get his hands on those leases. The more Yount thought about the possibility, the more excited he got. That very afternoon, he visited McLean at his office in the Gilbert Building and asked if he would consider doing business with him. After a short discussion, McLean and Yount struck a deal and sealed the bargain with a handshake.[11]

Within a day or two, McLean put Yount in contact with George Cave O'Brien, president of the Gladys City Oil, Gas, and Manufacturing Company, and on April 23 the two signed an agreement on five tracts totaling 408.4 acres, all in the John A. Veatch survey. Yount paid an immediate $4,000 cash bonus for the lease that called for mandatory drilling within six months of the following May 16. If, however, the oilman failed to "spud in"—begin drilling—his first well within that timeframe, he agreed to pay another $4,000 in penalties, and the process would continue, until thirty-six months elapsed, at which time Gladys City would consider the lease forfeited. But in the event that Yount's crews found oil on tract A of about fifty acres, he would be entitled to it only at the 1,500 foot level and below. Oddly enough, Gulf still retained the rights to the reserves produced from 1,500 feet and above. For its part in the overall lease, Gladys City retained a one-eighth royalty interest.[12]

George Cave O'Brien.
—Courtesy Tyrrell Historical Library, Beaumont, Texas.

On May 11 Yount concluded similar negotiations with William Perry Herring McFaddin, Wesley W. Kyle, and Percy H. Wiess, owners of two other tracts, eight-two acres located in the Spindletop Heights addition in the John A. Veatch League, and another 377 acres of the Pelham Humphreys survey. Again, Frank signed a stiff multi-claused document that called for mandatory drilling requirements by the lessors who retained the usual one-eighth royalty interest. Furthermore, Yount stipulated that he would begin his first well on that particular property no later than September 15, but if oil was not discovered there, he had to try again within sixty days. This process would continue for three consecutive six-month periods, at which time he was expected to fork over $2,500 due on a rental clause to kick in only if his efforts proved unsuccessful.[13]

Relative to agreements between McLean and Yount on May 28, the two oilmen completed their uncomplicated negotiations on a small tract in the John A. Veatch survey. As long as Yount honored his two separate pacts with Gladys City and McFaddin, Wiess, and Kyle, McLean refused to impose any mandatory requirements on his neighbor, already weighted down in legal commitments. Over the next several weeks, McLean pitched in and helped Yount obtain numerous leases from different title hold-

William Perry Herring McFaddin.
—Courtesy Tyrrell Historical Library, Beaumont, Texas.

Wesley W. Kyle.
—Courtesy Tyrrell Historical Library, Beaumont, Texas.

ers, and when all was said and done, Frank controlled about 1,200 acres of McFaddin, Wiess, and Kyle; and Gladys City leases, with McLean holding royalty interests on a great deal of that. The promoter, however, offered the driller a bit of friendly advice. Yount should make an initial attempt south of where Gulf had failed previously, just inside the dome's southeast perimeter on McFaddin property. If a dry hole resulted there, McLean more or less guaranteed Yount that if he moved out another two to three hundred feet, the second effort would definitely strike pay sands.[14]

Finally Frank Yount had the combination he always needed: the wherewithal to drill where and when he wanted, within contractual limits of course, and now, at least according to his and McLean's way of thinking, he owned some of the most favorable leases on the planet. But make no mistake, he had painted himself into a corner by obligating himself to two of the most powerful land interests in Southeast Texas, and in doing so, put the Yount-Lee Oil Company in harm's way. Thus came "make or break" time!

Yount took his neighbor's advice and commenced his latest Spindletop operations where McLean directed. Regrettably, things did not go well at the outset. Drilling on the Yount-Lee McFaddin No. 1 began by the contract date, September 15, but it produced nothing but dust. However, one lone piece of encouraging news emerged. Because the bit first encountered the salt strata some 700 feet lower than at the previous unsuccessful Gulf location, Yount took this as a positive sign; and afterward, he promptly assured his partners that he would definitely hit the next time out. Stay the course, he counseled.[15]

As expected, Yount extended the field's boundary and moved another three hundred feet from McFaddin No. 1 to the same spot where, in the late 1890s, he helped dig an irrigation ditch. And too, the location of his first failure on the hill in 1905 rested only a short distance away. Regardless, Yount remained confident, and on October 20 he started drilling on the McFaddin No. 2, just beyond the edge of the known-producing

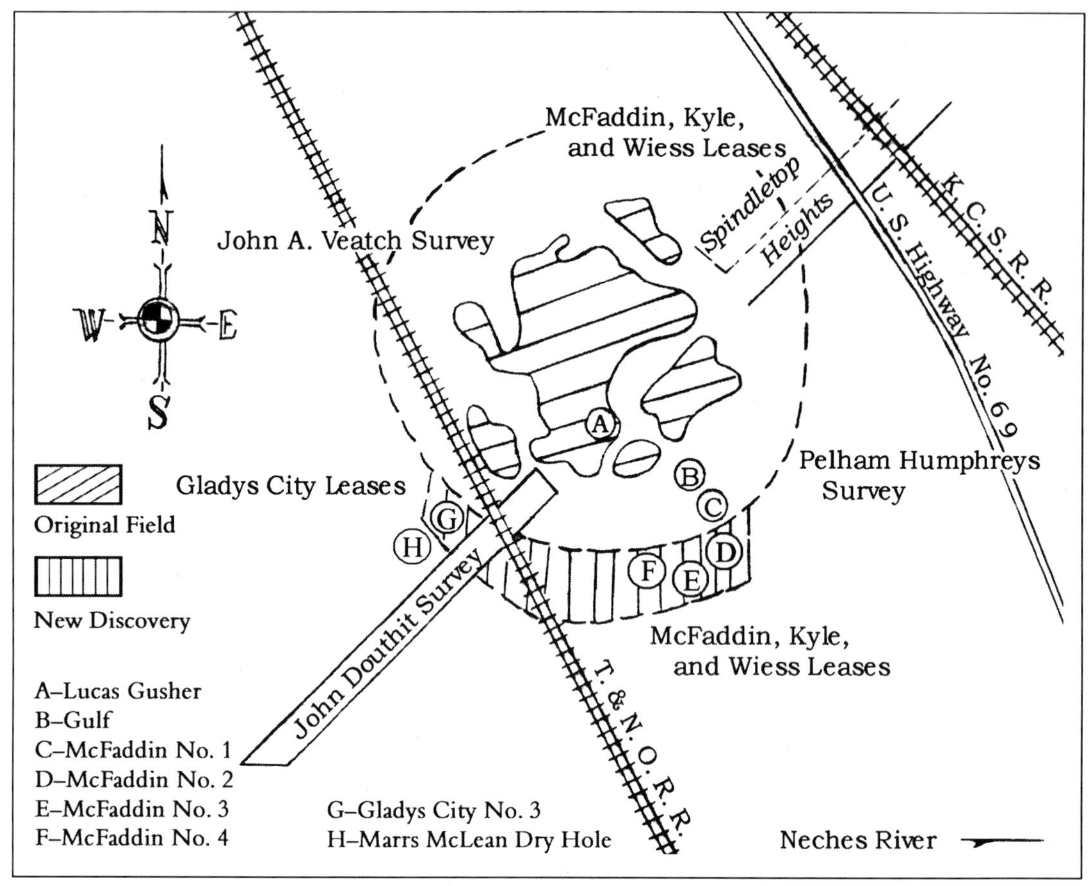

Spindletop Production Areas, January 10, 1901 to April 11, 1926.[16]

area and approximately one-half mile southeast of the Lucas Gusher. John E. "Johnny" Hatcher directed field operations at the new site, and H. H. "Dad" Kellam served as the foreman. Even though these two crusty veterans with competent and experienced hands required little supervision, the methodical company president would leave nothing to chance, not on this occasion. With so much at stake, including personal pride and business reputation, he intended to see that everything proceeded according to plan. Saturday, November 14, found him on the grounds as always, blending in among driller, roughneck, and roustabout with their grimy faces and smudged, oily work clothes. In the excitement of leaving for the field earlier that morning, he simply forgot to bring along a coat for protection against the winter weather. About noon when the men noticed and then offered him one of theirs, Frank refused to take the garment, because he thought others needed it more than he did. Finally, though, he could stand no more and ordered one to be sent from home. With the deafening roar in the background caused by the massive engine that drove the drawworks and the kelly joint, Frank continued working on the derrick floor whose wide and rough planks shook everyone who stood upon them. Occasionally, he stopped just long enough to glance at the many core samples that held promise. As the crew heaved and connected thirty-foot pieces of pipe onto another, and the crown block sent the drillstring back into the depths, everyone on the

John E. "Johnny" Hatcher, circa 1926.
—Courtesy Tyrrell Historical Library, Beaumont, Texas.

H. H. "Dad" Kellam, circa 1926.
—Courtesy Tyrrell Historical Library, Beaumont, Texas.

platform shared the same opinion. Just like Johnny, Dad, and all the rest, Yount believed that oil would be soon discovered, but the main question remained, how much?[17]

While Frank and his men strained under the difficulties posed by the biting, cold wind, and even higher anxiety, over 25,000 spectators crowded through the gates of the South Texas State Fair to partake of the annual festivities. In spite of the showers that had moved through the area earlier that morning which brought a front that lowered temperatures, nothing dampened the spirits of the huge crowd on that fourteenth of November. But even in their wildest imaginations, none could possibly predict the extraordinary event that soon followed. As darkness fell at about twenty past five that afternoon, the Yount-Lee Oil Company accomplished what others had only dreamed of for the last twenty years; it brought in a sizeable well at Spindletop. McFaddin No. 2 came in under perfect control from a depth of slightly below 2,500 feet. The well, under its own pressure and contained by a half-inch choker valve, produced at the rate of almost 1,500 barrels a day, and speculation held that if unleashed, it would have flowed between twelve to twenty thousand barrels. An ecstatic Yount left the scene temporarily and telephoned a brief message to his wife, "I've got a well, and a big one." Newspaper reports reflect that she contacted Percy Wiess and his family, who lived next door at 1316 Calder Avenue, and they immediately drove Mrs. Yount to the field for a firsthand inspection. The recent rains had left the entire area surrounding the site virtually inaccessible by automobile, and because the nearest road lay some 1,400 feet away, Pansy and her party exited and waded through the mud to the location, where she received congratulatory remarks under lantern light from the many visitors who had already arrived.[18]

Before the night was over, several hundred people, including Marrs McLean, vari-

Percy and Bertie Wiess House.

—Courtesy Sue Boyt and Susan Ramsey.

ous Yount-Lee employees (consisting of officers, clerical staff, and others who worked at different locations), along with newspaper reporters, including Ben Woodhead, a cub reporter for the *Beaumont Enterprise*, friends, and an occasional oil scout, came to witness the event and marvel at its historical significance. Woodhead later wrote:

> The main thing I recall about the actual scene at Spindletop that bleak November night is that the mud was ankle deep. Among the fifty-odd spectators on hand when I arrived, by far the most excited was Mrs. Pansy Yount, wife of the man responsible for it all.

As he turned toward his old friend Harry Phelan who had stood with him from the beginning, Frank Yount prophetically remarked, "Harry, these flanks will produce another 60,000,000 barrels of oil."[19]

In a spirit of cooperation, the Unity Oil Company lent its tanks for temporary storage, and had earlier allowed Yount-Lee to lay a pipeline and get its water for drilling from a reservoir in the vicinity. When the well came in, oil was pumped in reverse back into both the drained basin and Unity tanks, and when done, very little crude, if any, was lost during the process. Ben Woodhead further observed, "This is probably one of the few times in history that a pipe line enjoyed two-way traffic." With that said, Frank Yount achieved a feat far different from those at the Lucas Gusher, where millions of barrels were wasted before the well could be effectively brought under control and proper storage facilities erected.[20]

News of the discovery circulated quickly to the fairgrounds about half an hour after McFaddin No. 2 blew in. Later that same evening at about eight o'clock, John W. Newton, the first announcer for the Magnolia Petroleum Company's new radio station, followed with a communiqué that stunned those who heard it: "Spindletop has come back. The Yount-Lee Oil Company's No. 2 McFaddin on the south flank of the dome came in not more than an hour ago flowing an estimated 5,000 barrels of oil a day through a small choke." The new discovery became the topic of conversation there, as well as on the streets downtown, and already, rumors flew fast and furious, for within less than two hours, no one quite agreed on the well's production flow, or the time Frank's crew capped it. Whether 1,500 barrels, 5,000 or more, or whether it hit at a little past five or seven mattered little; the thought that Spindletop had come back was something to be excited about. People remembered the prosperity that the first great boom generated, and Beaumont, mired in a business slump, needed another push. The next morning, the headlines of the *Beaumont Enterprise* read "Spindle Top Yields New Oil Gusher," and written in most colorful language, the accompanying story contained the buoyant speculation that the McFaddin No. 2 would spark a new era.[21]

On Sunday, November 15, Yount received the gut-wrenching news that the new well stopped flowing altogether. It began again, however, early on Monday morning, and for the next few days, with intermittent pauses, its production varied considerably. By Wednesday the new offering brought forth only between 500 to 800 barrels a day, and it appeared that all the buildup in the community was for naught. But the ever-optimistic Yount met the challenge, put on his best marketing face, and tried to calm the voice of the skeptics who claimed that McFaddin No. 2 had come upon a small and isolated pocket that would be depleted shortly:

McFaddin No. 2, "The Discovery Well of New Spindletop."
—Courtesy Tyrrell Historical Library, Beaumont, Texas.

Crude Production at Spindletop
The First Discovery versus
Second During Peak Years

Year	Barrels	Year	Barrels
1901	3,593,113	1925	420,823
1902	17,420,949	1926	14,838,281
1903	8,600,905	1927	21,255,935
1904	3,433,842	1928	14,332,357
1905	1,652,780	1929	10,183,684
1906	1,077,492	1930	5,997,913
1907	1,699,943	1931	3,209,994
1908	1,747,537	1932	1,442,560
1909	1,388,107	1933	1,168,432
1910	1,182,436	1934	1,152,010
1911	965,939	1935	969,634
1912	822,916	1936	844,684
Totals	43,585,959		75,816,307

Source: C. A. Warner, *Texas Oil and Gas since 1543* (Houston: Gulf, 1939), 375-376.

> I expect the new well, drilled in Saturday night, to be one of the best pumpers in the entire southwest oil field, and it does prove the deep oil theory that there is a substantial pool beneath that which made Spindle Top famous in years gone by.

Marrs McLean added that he too "would not be at all surprised if there proved to be 50,000,000 barrels of oil there." Ben Woodhead put it into perspective:

> From the standpoint of profound significance, the biggest story I covered in 1925 was the bringing in of the "second" Spindletop oil field. The first producing well was McFaddin No. 2. I was shamefully ignorant of drilling terminology then (as now) and had a terrible time batting out a piece that would be acceptable to our numerous oil-oriented readers. There wasn't anything visually spectacular about McFaddin No. 2. It was a fine producer . . . a flowing well, not a gusher . . ."[22]

Regardless of its size, however, magic had been recreated. People must have believed the two oilmen, Marrs McLean, the prophet, and Frank Yount, the pioneer, because by the thousands, they visited the "Discovery Well of New Spindletop," as McFaddin No. 2 came to be called. Surely, a revival era was underway, they thought, and the juggernaut had been put in motion. In the beginning, even the local newspapers fueled the perception that Second Spindletop would be much like the first, but within a matter of days, something finally clicked when these same publications recognized that because Yount-Lee owned the choice leases on the hill, things might not be quite as advertised in their recent columns. In his usual quiet manner, Frank Yount said that the company would continue drilling on the leases of about 1,200 acres, but he added a caveat: he intended to put down wells at a steady, controlled pace, a philosophy that flew in the face of all popular opinion. Most disappointed observers failed to understand from the get-go that a revitalization of the old field would take place—and it would be one of spectacular proportions when compared to the years between 1901 and 1924, but Frank Yount and his company would do it in orderly fashion. There would be no repetition of the wild and speculative boom days associated with the Lucas Gusher, but it would take the public quite a while to come to terms with this new mind-set.[23]

In order to fulfill further lease obligations, Yount-Lee soon began another well on the north side of Spindletop, this one on a Gladys City tract. The new location, known as Gladys City No. 1, held promise as it reached a depth of 700 feet on November 18. Six days later it doubled that, but solid salt forced its abandonment. The well's eventual failure served to only strengthen the notion held by many die-hards who believed that the company wasted both its time and money in pursuing a depleted Spindletop.[24]

For a time, it appeared that these same skeptics just might be correct in their assumptions, especially when Yount-Lee seemed to abandon exploration of the old field entirely, while continuing its operations at Black Lake and Hackberry, Louisiana. And too, they were putting down new wells at Sour Lake and Hull, but for the Beaumont vicinity, activities languished. Sure the McFaddin No. 2 was alive, barely, pumping between 150 to 200 barrels each day, but otherwise, Spindletop remained curiously quiet. Things, however, were about to change. On December 14 drilling began on the McFaddin No. 3, and word spread rapidly by January 2 that the well, located about 300 feet south of its previous namesake, lay at a depth of 2,540 feet. Newspaper reports eagerly claimed that oil was expected at any time.[25]

1926

The McFaddin No. 3 came in on the night of January 13 at about 8 o'clock. This time, completely opposite of the first, the crew was caught flatfooted, and they had no time to remove the drill stem. Before everything got totally out of hand, though, the men recovered, brought matters under control, and the hectic scene that followed bore a strong resemblance to the events that occurred only 300 feet away on the previous November 14. Yount, who worked on the rig as before, excused himself briefly, long enough to once more call his wife. By now and although it went against all character traits, Frank Yount delved into the art of public relations and telephoned the two Beaumont newspapers. Shortly afterward, crowds again flocked to the hill, where they confronted the elements as before and waded through the mud for a close inspection of the latest miracle.[26]

By the next day, Yount-Lee officials heaved a sigh of collective relief. The new well held its own with a flow of 5,000 barrels, and it seemed that existing facilities—three storage tanks had been erected for McFaddin No. 2 to replace those lent temporarily by Unity—would be sufficient to hold the contents of the recent discovery. One trouble spot popped up, but it was quickly corrected. The lines that connected the Yount-Lee tanks to a nearby Gulf pipeline proved inadequate to move the volume, so crews laid down additional pipe.[27]

Yount-Lee's drilling activities continued to produce at other locations, and the number of successes far outnumbered the failures. When its Merchant No. 12 at Hull hit dry dirt, the Gilbert No. 2 at Sour Lake responded on January 18 with a modest 2,000-barrel a day showing. Crews at Welsh, Louisiana, also experienced good luck during the previous two years, and they accounted for no fewer than eleven producers.[28]

While Yount-Lee proved the deep flank theory at other fields, Spindletop seemed to be getting most of the attention. A few competitors tried desperately to get into the action there, although at this point, their efforts were not considered to be a mad scramble. But because of Yount-Lee's achievement, prices did begin to escalate. For example, the Gulf Production Company paid $72,000 for a 197-acre tract, located immediately southwest of McFaddin No. 3, to F. M. Hebert, who retained a one-eighth royalty interest. This transaction must have embarrassed Gulf, because just a few years earlier, it controlled most of the oil leases in the vicinity.[29]

From January 13 to February 5, McFaddin No. 3 produced about 120,000 barrels of grade A crude, but a particular condition continued to pose problems for company officials in their quest for maximum return on investment. In the early stages, Gulf Coast petroleum never commanded the price of that produced in other regions due to its salt water content. By seeking out an answer to the dilemma, Yount-Lee soon came up with a cutting edge technological innovation when it ushered in a process to correct the problem in the field. Company technicians designed special equipment, consisting of two steel tanks that measured ten by twelve feet, and fitted them with electric plates. They proved that by forcing the crude through the barrels and into contact with the plates, salt water separated from the oil, and in the end, the product became much more marketable.[30]

On February 5 Yount-Lee brought in the first producer since 1913, at the edge of Black Lake close to Hackberry Island, Louisiana, and the company stepped up its activities at Sour Lake. Yet on March 5 it discontinued the second attempt on Gladys City property. With this decision, Yount-Lee confined its operations at Spindletop to McFaddin No. 4, located just 300 feet from both the No. 2 and No. 3. Once more, cynics saw the Gladys City dry hole as proof positive that the wells on McFaddin property had struck an isolated pool. This upstart, Yount-Lee and the wildcatter in charge, Frank Yount, would prove, they ridiculed, to be just another flash in the pan.[31]

McFaddin No. 4 reached 3,500 feet by April 7, and two days later, it hit. Savvy industry watchers not only hailed the new discovery for the obvious, but pointed up an important piece of information that hinted of good things to come. Although located only 300 feet apart, the gravity weight of McFaddin No. 4's crude calculated at 29, compared to No. 3's 24. Considering that oil weight is defined as its measurement at a given temperature, and since the two wells produced a markedly different product, speculation arose that each drew from separate sources. A few now concluded that Frank might be on to something, and perhaps—he had discovered a new stratum of oil after all.[32]

Yount could not agree more. Aimed squarely at the Doubting Thomases, he commented on what he believed to be the bright future of Spindletop, when he said, "As much oil remains there as was ever taken out." Constantly on the offensive, he backed up his claim by making a third effort on a Gladys City tract, and on April 11 at 7 o'clock in the evening, the persistence paid off when the Gladys City No. 3, located about a half mile southwest of the old Lucas Gusher, blew in with a stream estimated to be approximately 6,000 barrels a day. As a result of this strike, one might assume that two things would happen immediately. The first is that Yount-Lee would throw every drilling rig that it could muster into all areas of the field under its control, and the second is that the new finding would set off a frenzy of competition among the other companies for the small acreage still available. Strangely enough—neither happened. Yount-Lee officials calmly announced that they planned to maintain two drilling rigs as before. One would operate on the Gladys City property and the other on McFaddin's. Frank Yount and Tal Rothwell were conservatives in that respect, and since their company dominated the hill, no real advantage to hurried production could be had. This soundly-laid strategy, although suspect at the moment, proved its worth as time progressed. In the interim, however, most operators shrugged off the latest news. Even though oil had now been discovered on both sides of the Douthit survey, the majority still believed that Yount-Lee would fail ultimately in its bid to revive Spindletop, and they waited for further developments before making any real moves to the contrary.[33]

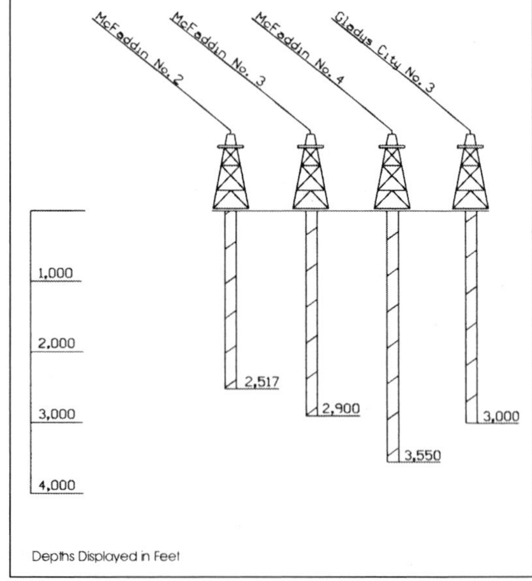

Yount-Lee Drilling Operations at Spindletop, November 14, 1925 to April 11, 1926 (indicating actual depths in feet).[34]

Partners and Balance Wheels

"Great discoveries and improvements invariably involve the cooperation of many minds. I may be given credit for having blazed the trail, but when I look at the subsequent developments I feel the credit is due to others rather than to myself."

ALEXANDER GRAHAM BELL

Although only a handful have written about the Yount-Lee Oil Company, many of those who did fell into the trap of discussing both the business entity and Frank Yount in interchangeable fashion. Admittedly, distinguishing between the two is rather difficult, especially when analyzing contributions to a grateful city that the man, Frank Yount, called home. But as in most successful corporations, whatever the size or financial structure, no one individual at the helm probably runs the entire operation without able assistance. As a company, Yount-Lee proved no exception. Never content to be just a major petroleum producer, Frank Yount's direction took many paths, from becoming deeply immersed in real-estate investments, philanthropic activities, collecting rare automobiles, violins, books, and oriental rugs, building Spindletop Stables in Beaumont to showcase his "Saddlebred" horses, developing an experimental farm for his registered Jersey cattle herd, not to mention fending off several major lawsuits initiated over questioned ownership of Spindletop acreage, any one of which might have had disastrous effects if successful.

Correctly so, Frank Yount considered himself, first and foremost, an oilman, and he proved that claim over and again to the delight of investors and the chagrin of competitors, both large and small. But due to the organization's phenomenal growth, micromanagement turned out to be a virtual impossibility, so he transitioned into an effective administrator who relied heavily upon other key officials such as Tal Rothwell and Harry Phelan, who attended daily business activities in their respective areas of expertise. Even then, the company required a vast array of talented specialists in the fields of law, accounting, engineering, and geology.

Frank Yount was, of course, the president and the largest stockholder with almost 33 percent ownership, but he had several partners and a board of directors to which he

Frank Yount, circa 1926.
—Courtesy Texas Energy Museum, Beaumont, Texas.

ultimately answered. Without question, though, none of these associates ever placed serious constraints upon his management style, and there was never any doubt in anyone's mind who was boss. While Yount exercised that function freely, still he wisely placed his trust in those who were more knowledgeable in certain areas than he.[1]

Three major partners, Thomas Peter Lee, William Ellsworth "Bill" Lee, and Emerson Francis Woodward, were content to sit on the sidelines and let Frank Yount and his Beaumont team run the show.

Thomas Peter Lee

Of these three, T. P. Lee wielded the most influence, given that he invested the capital necessary for the creation of the company in the first place, and in doing so, put spunk back into a young Sour Lake wildcatter who seemed to be continually at odds with uncooperative partners who refused him free rein and full authority. Lee provided what Frank Yount needed most: an opportunity to prove himself worthy as an oil driller.

Born on March 19, 1871, in Petroleum, West Virginia to Alexander and Martha Jane Mount Lee, T. P. left school at the age of sixteen and went to work in the oil fields, first in his native state and then in Ohio. In 1903 he moved to Saratoga, Texas, where he gained employment with the newly formed Texas Company, and when he left that organization ten years later, he had attained the rank of general superintendent of production. While there, however, he became friends with J. S. Cullinan, and the two, along with Emerson F. Woodward, Will C. Hogg, and James L. Autry, joined in 1914 to form the Farmers Petroleum Company, of which Lee became president. In 1916 he, along with Cullinan, Woodward, and other associates, organized the American Republics Corporation that later controlled twenty-one subsidiaries involved in all facets of the oil industry: prospecting, production, refining, and transportation, as well as manufacturing ships, tank cars, and oil tools. While serving on the board of directors, Lee also held the position of vice president in charge of production. But things would eventually sour between Lee and Cullinan, and several years later, they headed opposing forces bitterly engaged in a stock war for control of the corporation. Cullinan not only defeated Lee in the struggle, but he put his own son Craig into Lee's position as vice president. More than he could bear, Lee resigned and began a lucrative career in the investment field.[2]

He also became active in agriculture and cattle breeding on his ranch in Uvalde County. An avid Republican, Lee attended several national conventions as a delegate, and in 1924 he refused the party's nomination for governor of Texas. He twice married, the first to Elizabeth Mann on July 14, 1892. Before she died on June 21, 1895, however, the union produced one child, Mabel Martha, who later became the wife of Tal Rothwell. Lee's second marriage occurred on April 24, 1900, to Essie Mable Horton of Savannah, Georgia, and together, the couple had five daughters: Maude, Ethel, Maxine, Thelma, and Marjorie. Contrary to many published accounts, T. P. Lee had no sons.[3]

Thomas Peter Lee.
—Courtesy Tyrrell Historical Library, Beaumont, Texas.

The Lee home, located at 3812 Montrose (corner of Montrose and West Alabama) in Houston, yet remains as an outstanding example of the glory days of Texas oil production. But long before T. P. Lee acquired it, the mansion already had a colorful past. In 1910 John Wiley Link, a wealthy lumberman, financier, lawyer, and former mayor of Orange, Texas, saw a great opportunity in Houston, so he moved there and formed the Houston Land Corporation. Then he bought several tracts of land consisting of 250 acres on the outskirts of the city and immediately set

The Link Mansion, circa 1913.
—Courtesy Houston Metropolitan Research Center, Houston Public Library.

about improving the property, building a main street, now Montrose Boulevard, through the center of it. At this point, he began to divide the property into tracts and sold them as part of a strategy to develop the first upscale residential subdivision in the Houston area, which during the early 1900s had only a total of about twenty-six miles of decent roads. After Montrose and West Alabama were paved in 1911, Link announced that he would soon begin construction of his own home within the confines of the entire block number 41 in the Montrose addition that he purchased from his own corporation. He hired the architectural firm of Sanguinent, Staats, and Barnes to design the structure that the Young Contracting Company completed in 1912 at a cost of $60,000.[4]

The Links lived there until December 9, 1916, when T. P. Lee purchased it for $90,000, reported to be the most ever paid for a single family dwelling in the Houston area at that particular time. Expressed in today's currency values, the home would price near $1.5 million.[5]

William Ellsworth Lee

William E. "Bill" Lee, the brother of T. P. Lee, was born in Petroleum, West Virginia, on January 31, 1867. At a very early age, he began working in the oil fields and spent six years with the U. S. Oil Company in West Virginia, before moving to Ohio and then following his brother to Saratoga in 1904. He married Margaret McGuigan, a native of Parkersburg, on September 8, 1907, and the couple had six children: William Howard, Irene May, Thomas Peter, Faustine Ellen, and the twins, Donald and Ronald.[6]

William Ellsworth "Bill" Lee.
—Courtesy Tyrrell Historical Library, Beaumont, Texas.

After working for ten years with the Producers Oil Company, Bill Lee resigned and joined the Texas Company, which assigned him to the Sour Lake production division. When T. P. Lee left the Texas Company and vacated the position of general superintendent of production, Bill thought that he might be promoted to that spot, but another got the job. Though thoroughly sickened when things did not work out as planned, he stayed with the company only at the insistence of his brother. Meanwhile, he still sought another area of employment, until finally, he got his wish. With the formation of the Yount-Lee Oil Company, T. P. Lee gave him a block of stock in the new venture, and this afforded him the opportunity to break away from the oil business. Subsequently, he organized and became president of the Citizens National Bank of

Sour Lake, which became one of the most prominent financial institutions in Hardin County.[7]

Bill Lee's grandson, T. P. "Tommy" Lee, III, described his grandfather as a large man weighing about three hundred pounds and with a height of about five feet, eleven inches. He was very affectionate toward all family members, but he was closer to T. P. Lee than all the rest. Portrayed as a "man of extreme wealth with country ways," Bill Lee maintained a vegetable garden, kept various farm animals at his stately home on Montrose Boulevard, and enjoyed spoiling all of his children and grandchildren.[8]

Emerson Francis Woodward

E. F. Woodward was born on February 23, 1879 at Podunk (about 70 miles southwest of Syracuse), New York to William W. and Ida May LaGrange Woodward. Because his father made his living in the oil business in its earliest days at Titusville, Pennsylvania, Emerson wanted to follow in his footsteps. After receiving an early education in the Goodwill Hill public schools in Pennsylvania, Woodward, at the age of eleven, went to work in the oil fields, and before the end of his career, he would be affiliated with the industry in various states, including Oklahoma, Pennsylvania, Ohio, Arkansas, Louisiana, and Texas. He married Bessie McGarry in 1901 at Woodsfield, Ohio, and the couple had only one child, a son, Harley E. Woodward.[9]

The Producers Oil Company employed Emerson Woodward for eleven years, and during this stretch, he met his lifelong associate, T. P. Lee, who worked for the same firm. Woodward advanced quickly within the organization and received a promotion to assistant superintendent of its southern division, which encompassed the area from New Orleans to El Paso. Later, he helped organize the Farmers Petroleum Company, held the position of superintendent, and in 1921 became president of the Republic Production Company, one of the American Republics Corporation's subsidiaries.[10]

Emerson F. Woodward.
—Courtesy Tyrrell Historical Library, Beaumont, Texas.

Emerson and Bessie Woodward virtually raised their only grandchild, Robert R. "Bob" Woodward, from the age of eight when his father Harley died tragically in an airplane crash. Bob stated that his grandfather had a rather deep voice, stood about five feet, eleven inches, and weighed approximately 180 pounds—a strong physique built by years of hard work in the oil fields. He said that his grandfather enjoyed telling one particular story above the rest about his association with Yount-Lee. Emerson maintained an office on the twentieth floor of the Commerce Building in downtown Houston, and during its construction, he had it planned intentionally so that unannounced visitors with endless oil schemes and proposals could not enter his office directly from the hallway. The first screening occurred at the desk of R. B. Miller. Then if they made it past there, they would be sent on to the second office belonging to W. B. Barnhill, Emerson's assistant, who in some rare occasions, if he felt the deal offered any real promise, would allow them into Woodward's office. One day, such a visitor arrived and presented specifics to Miller who thought they held merit, so he sent the prospector into Barnhill's office. W. B. talked with the man a few minutes, while sizing him up, and then he asked if he knew of Yount-Lee? Without hesitation, the man replied, "Yes, I know him very well." Barnhill, who had no patience with anyone who failed to do proper research, sent the man packing. He pointed toward the exit and responded, "See that door? Go out the way you came in!"[11]

While the Lee brothers and Woodward remained engaged in their respective business affairs in Houston and Sour Lake, Frank Yount relied on two other active partners, Tal Rothwell and Harry Phelan, to help manage the Yount-Lee Oil Company's day to day activities.

Talbot Frederick Rothwell

When it came to matters of production, Yount depended most on Talbot Rothwell. Another West Virginian, Rothwell was born on February 27, 1887, to T. J. and Mary Jane Cross Rothwell. Educated in the public schools of both his native state and Ohio, he began his career in the oil fields and eventually moved to Saratoga, Texas, where he found work with the production division of the Sun Oil Company. On August 13, 1913, he married Mabel Martha Lee, the daughter of T. P. Lee, and to this union, three daughters were born: Mary Elizabeth, Essie Lee, and Virginia Mae. In 1914 he and Frank Yount formed a partnership, which later became the Yount-Lee Oil Company, of which he became vice president and superintendent of production—and eventually its president.[12]

Talbot Frederick "Tal" Rothwell.
—Courtesy Tyrrell Historical Library, Beaumont, Texas.

Rothwell felt more at ease in the field than behind his desk in the corporate office, and many acknowledged him as the consummate oilman, an expert at exploration and drilling. Tal knew virtually every phase of production. His daughter, Virginia, recalled the numerous occasions that Max Schlicher, a drilling superintendent with the firm, brought core samples

The Rothwell family home, Sour Lake, Texas.
—Photograph by Fred B. McKinley.

to the family home late in the evening, and how after her father and Schlicher smelled and tasted the samples, they decided whether to drill further, and if so, how far. As the evidence clearly shows, they usually made the correct choice. Virginia Rothwell Birdwell stated that she heard Frank Yount graciously say more than once that "Tal Rothwell is the real oilman in the company," and the fact that in 1931, the chief executive put him in charge of developing Yount-Lee's enormous holdings in the East Texas oil field clearly illustrates the supreme confidence that Yount had in his vice president. Each of these men held a deep admiration for the other, based on mutual respect. Rothwell's daughter further stated that she saw her father cry only twice; one occurred on the night that he received word that his partner and good friend, Frank Yount, had died. Other evidence of the deep friendship that existed between the two is also reflected in a statement made by R. E. Masterson, Yount's personal attorney, when he said, "the given name of his [Yount's] closest oil pal is Tal."[13]

The early success of Yount-Lee's operations allowed Rothwell to build a modest house in Sour Lake where it can be viewed today at 330 Cora Lee Street. When the company relocated to Beaumont, however, he purchased a home, which no longer stands at 888 Calder Avenue—its site now a parking lot on the east side of the former Y.M.C.A. building, now known as the Senior Citizens Y House. The family lived there until a majestic home, named Vir-Beth Hall in honor of the two surviving Rothwell daughters, Virginia and Elizabeth, could be built at 124 East Caldwood at an estimated cost of between $250,000 and $500,000 in 1929. Oddly enough, the family never employed the services of an architect, but left those details up to the staff of George R. Brown of Houston, whose firm completed the actual construction. Virginia Rothwell Birdwell later told an interviewer that "it was not well thought out," and "none of them, including her parents, ever liked the house [that] did not function well." Regardless of the

Original entrance gate at Vir-Beth Hall.
—Courtesy Sue Boyt and Susan Ramsey.

outcome, though, one thing is for certain. George Rufus Brown, the man whose name is associated with the Houston Convention Center, and the same one who co-founded Brown and Root, the world's largest construction and engineering firm, built for Rothwell, what turned out to be the lone residential dwelling he ever contracted to do in Beaumont, Texas. But this was not the only Rothwell home; similar to the Yount family, they also bought, around September 17, 1935, a summer place, simply known at "The Cottage," located on the side of Cheyenne Mountain under the Will Rogers Shrine at Broadmoor, Colorado. Each year, Mabel and "Papa Tal," the stocky oilman with a height of a little less than six feet and a weight of just under two hundred pounds, loaded up the girls and most everyone else in the Beaumont household, including chauffeur James Winchester and his wife Hazel; Suzie Davis, the cook, and headed west.[14]

"Papa Tal" Rothwell at Vir-Beth Hall.
—Courtesy Sue Boyt and Susan Ramsey.

Tal Rothwell had numerous business ties and held directorships on the boards of the Citizens National Bank of Sour Lake, the

First National Bank of Beaumont, the Lake Tool Company, and the Rex Supply Company of Sour Lake. A devoutly religious man with a gentle voice and calm demeanor, he rose as one of the leaders of the First Methodist Church of Beaumont, where he was steward and chairman of the finance committee, and the music committee. Once during the Depression, when the church needed $39,000 to complete an addition to the Sunday School building, the Rothwells contributed $30,000 to the cause. They also donated the Aeolian-Skinner organ, and a new parsonage to First Methodist. As a civic leader, Tal served on the Texas Y.M.C.A. board as a member-at-large; was vice president of the Community Chest board, and president of the board of directors of the Beaumont General Hospital, which later became St. Therese. As a devoted family man and humanitarian, he recognized the fact that some oil field roughnecks tended to drink away their paychecks immediately after receiving them. Due to a genuine concern that his employees' families were not being adequately fed and clothed, at times he summoned the wives to Spindletop and gave their husbands' pay to them directly to ensure that they would at least have the opportunity to see the money first. This type of spirit prevailed within the Yount-Lee organization, and Rothwell, like the other company officers, contributed some of his personal income to other worthy causes, which included aid to the area's needy families.[15]

John Henry Phelan

John Henry "Harry" Phelan, the secretary-treasurer of Yount-Lee, and later named as vice president and treasurer, is by far the most remembered of all Yount-Lee's people. He had been associated with Frank Yount from the early days when Yount struggled at Sour Lake, and he a traveling salesman with the Heisig-Norvell Company. Born on December 11, 1877, at Charlotte, North Carolina, Harry was one of Patrick Henry and Adele Myers Phelan's eleven children. He received an early education in the parochial schools at Charlotte, but soon after completing the ninth grade, he followed his father into the wholesale grocery business. The younger Phelan held jobs as office boy and shipping clerk in several organizations, including the Wittkowsky Wholesale Dry Goods and the Wolfe Company, and at the age of nineteen, he went to work as a traveling salesman for the J. A. Durham Company. He remained there until January 1902, when he moved to Beaumont.[16]

John Henry "Harry" Phelan.
—Courtesy Tyrrell Historical Library, Beaumont, Texas.

Heisig-Norvell offered him a similar job at a salary of $150 per month. Phelan accepted the position and remained with this

Harry and Johannah Phelan.
—Courtesy Yount-Manion Film Collection, Lamar University, Beaumont, Texas.

concern until 1913, at which time he formed his own business, the Phelan-Josey Grocery Company. For a while, though, he successfully divided his time between duties at Yount-Lee and his own firm, but in January 1927 the demands generated by the oil company's success at Spindletop forced him to choose between the two. Yount-Lee won out. Phelan, however, continued as president of Phelan-Josey, but his brother, Frank, already a vice president there, assumed the title of general manager and ran the business while Harry devoted his full attention to Yount-Lee affairs.[17]

On June 15, 1905, he married Johannah Maria Cunningham at Chicago, and three children were born to this union: John Henry, Jr., Anthony, and Margaret. The elder Phelan, an active member of the Catholic Church, became legendary for his philanthropic activities. In October 1931 he donated $35,000 to the St. Vincent de Paul Society in Austin, Texas, and he contributed considerable funds to the Home of the Holy Infancy (now Marywood), located also in Austin, that provides maternity, adoption, and foster care services. He and Johannah gave extensively to St. Anne Church and St. Anne School in Beaumont, along with numerous "organs, statues, and ..., making gifts of some 225 altars to churches throughout the country," including the one donated in 1915 to St.

Caed Mile Failte. *The Phelan Mansion shortly after completion.*
—Courtesy Tyrrell Historical Library, Beaumont, Texas.

Anthony Cathedral in Beaumont. As a recompense for his many contributions, Pope Pius XI made Harry a Knight of St. Gregory in January 1933, an honor received previously by only one other Texan and only about fifty men in the entire country. And later that same year, the Pope also granted the Phelans a private audience, a first for Beaumonters. The Catholic Church bestowed upon him numerous other awards, such as Knight of Malta and Knight in the Order of the Holy Sepulchre.[18]

In 1928 Phelan began construction of a palatial home named *Caed Mile Failte*, a Gaelic term meaning "one hundred thousand welcomes," on a 15.4-acre estate, located at the corner of Eleventh Street and Calder Avenue in Beaumont. The original estimate of the house, set at $125,000, escalated, and when completed, it ranged near $500,000 after adding in the costs of the acreage, furnishings, and other amenities, such as guest houses, art studios, a miniature golf course, stables, a swimming pool, and a $25,000 pipe organ. Architect Owen James Trainor Southwell, a long-time friend of the family who grew up with the Phelan children, designed the overall project.[19]

Dining room of Phelan Mansion.
—Courtesy University of Louisiana at Lafayette, Edith Garland Dupre Library, University Archives and Acadiana Manuscripts Collection, Owen J. Southwell Papers.

Phelan, like Yount and Rothwell, also became involved in numerous real-estate ventures, as evidenced

Ballroom of Phelan Mansion.
—Courtesy University of Louisiana at Lafayette, Edith Garland Dupre Library, University Archives and Acadiana Manuscripts Collection, Owen J. Southwell Papers.

Courtesy of The Texas Gulf Historical and Biographical Record *and with full permission of the author, Bradley C. Brooks, the current Director of Lilly House Programs and Operations, Indianapolis Museum of Art, the following represents excerpts taken from a November 1999 article titled, "Owen J. T. Southwell, Architect, and the John Henry Phelan House."*

The house that Southwell designed for his clients was a product of the American country house movement that flourished from the late nineteenth century until the time of the Second World War, with the period of greatest vitality ending as the Great Depression began. As American wealth increased and became concentrated in the hands of successful capitalists and entrepreneurs during this period, many of them sought to build expansive rural or semi-rural residences, usually in one of a number of European historical styles and often with highly developed ornamental and agricultural landscapes. The Phelan house, called *Caed Mile Failte* (Gaelic for "one hundred thousand welcomes"), was based on eighteenth-century English Palladian models, and was very much in the mainstream of contemporary American country house design in its architecture, interiors, and landscape.

Surrounding the house were extensive gardens and grounds designed by Dallas landscape architect Homer Fry. As was common for such estates, the Phelan property combined formal and informal landscape features. An aerial view ... showed that the house, which faced Calder Avenue to the south, was anchored in the landscape by formal gardens immediately to its east and west, and by an allee formed by rows of trees on either side of paired drives that extended from the Calder edge of the property to the ends of an oval drive immediately before the house's front portico. The strict orthogonal geometry of the axial gardens and the allee was balanced by less formal features such as a gently meandering diagonal drive that originated at the main entrance gate near the corner of Calder and Eleventh and approached the house from the southwest, and a similarly undulating drive that encircled the property's perimeter. At greater distances from the house were other informal features, including the swimming pool near the southwest corner of the property. Also in this area were a rustic arched bridge and a gazebo, two of a group of items on the property constructed of reinforced concrete and finished to resemble wood. This *trabajo rustico*, or rustic work, was probably the creation of Dionisio Rodriguez, a Mexican native who came to San Antonio in about 1926 and eventually worked in several states.

Even though Beaumont's urban grid would eventually encroach on all sides, at the time it was built (completed in 1930) the Phelan house dominated the landscape. Southwell designed the nine-bay, two-story house to be built in brick and limestone with a gabled tile roof of relatively low pitch. Centered on the main (south) elevation was a two-story portico, its limestone pediment supported by limestone columns described as "Greek-Corinthian" in style. Inside the portico, the exterior wall was faced with limestone, its contrast with the flanking brick walls giving strong emphasis to the verticality of the composition's central element. The front door stood within a small loggia; above it, at the center of the second floor, another loggia provided a view onto the allee. The remainder of the central block featured limestone cornices, belt courses, and keystones, louvered shutters, and brick quoins.

Southwell designed the house on a U-shaped plan, with a central block of two rooms' depth, the arms of the U enclosing the east and west sides of a spacious porch and courtyard. Circulation through the first floor was by way of a T-shaped central hall joined to twin staircases, dictating that the two rooms at the rear of the block be offset somewhat to the east and west. Softening the angles created by the offsets,

Southwell placed at these junctures small two-story porches, open on the first floor and enclosed for use as sleeping porches on the second. Five primary public rooms accounted for the majority of the first floor. Just inside the entrance door, a drawing room and music room opened off the black and white marble hall to the left (west) and right (east), respectively. Behind these were the dining room and library. Behind the library and oriented perpendicularly to it was the ballroom, which formed the eastern arm of the U shape. A breakfast room, kitchen, and pantries, also on the first floor, constituted the western arm of the U shape. Later alterations to the first floor included the enclosure of the courtyard beneath a spreading glass ceiling decorated with neoclassical tracery, the expansion of the small first floor porches into sun porches, and the removal of the original sleeping porches immediately above them.

Upstairs, the front of the central block was given over to two suites, each comprising a sitting room, bedroom, bathroom, sleeping porch, and closets. Between them, in the very center of the second floor, was a chapel. Other second floor rooms included four bedrooms, a sitting room, and a sleeping porch, along with additional bathrooms and closets.

Shortly after the house was completed, the interiors were said to be in a state of "perfection," the result of Johanna[h] Phelan's years of work and thought and study. Whatever Mrs. Phelan's contributions to the interior decorative scheme, she was substantially assisted by Southwell, who claimed overall supervision of the house's decorations as one of his contributions. He made numerous buying trips to New Orleans, choosing furniture, upholstery, decorations, and fixtures for the house, confirming that he was involved in decorating decisions at the level of individual object selection.

The most elaborate of the house's interiors were the music room, the library, and the ballroom, all located on the east side of the first floor. Perhaps best known of all, the music room was noted for its wall and ceiling coverings, twenty panels of silk satin embroidered with rococo motifs reminiscent of eighteenth-century French decorative painting.

Adjacent to and behind the music room was the library. Fully paneled in walnut, the room included Doric pilasters and entablature that provided a strong sense of architectural structure and rhythm. Finely bookmatched veneers and recessed bookcases completed the room's architectural scheme. Comfortable seating furniture and a number of conveniently placed tables and lamps made the room ideal for its intended purpose. The room was home to Phelan's collection of Texana, which he at one time hoped would become the largest such private collection in the state.

North of the library was the ballroom, at 21 by 41 feet in dimension, the largest in the house. The room was notable for its elaborate Adamesque plaster wall ornament that incorporated architectural elements, angels, and a variety of delicate floral and foliate motifs. Even more unusual was the treatment of the ceiling, which featured a large central rectangular panel of shirred silk with two large crystal chandeliers. Surrounding the fabric panel on all sides was a glass ceiling approximately four and one-half feet in width enriched with delicate tracery that echoed the Adam theme of the room.

The interiors of the second floor rooms were far less elaborate than those of the first, as was typical for private spaces such as bedrooms. The one exception was the chapel, located at the center of the floor with access from the main upstairs hallway and from the sitting rooms on either side. The chapel was partially enclosed with iron grillwork, which continued the theme of the twin staircase balustrade. Inside, the chapel featured a frieze decorated with the stations of the cross, an altar of white marble, prayer desks and chairs procured by Southwell, niches for statuary, and a second pipe organ. Deeply devoted to the Catholic church, the Phelans had secured "special permission" to construct the chapel, said to be the only one of its kind in Texas at the time.

by the following examples. He purchased several lots in downtown Beaumont, and in October 1929 paid approximately $70,000 for the large two-story frame house and three lots previously owned by the late John L. Keith and his wife Ida. Phelan's plans for the property, located at the corner of Magnolia Street and Calder Avenue, called for the construction of an apartment house with shopping facilities on the first floor. Cost estimates of the project were set at between $50,000 and $90,000. Phelan, however, built something entirely different there, choosing instead an art deco shopping center. In December 1930 he purchased a tract that measured 300 feet by 160 feet, located where Calder Avenue and Willow Street converge. The property contained buildings that housed the Gasow-Howard Motor Company (802-812 Calder Avenue) and the McNairy Lubrication Company (825 McFaddin). After paying approximately $250,000 for the site, he stated that he intended it for investment purposes only. Later, he bought 2,533 acres near Tyrrell Park for which he paid $62,544 in February 1934. The four tracts, formerly owned by W. C. Tyrrell and situated about three and one-half miles southwest of Beaumont, had been used previously for agricultural purposes.[20]

On the personal side, however, during interviews with Harry's grandchildren, Mary Reed Williams, and Anthony McDade "Mickey" Phelan; and his niece, Erin Barry Teare, each disclosed fond memories of their grandparents and uncle, respectively, and their home, due to its massive size, in which one could actually become lost. Mary recounted the occasions when her jovial grandfather would have his grandchildren line up—he had twenty-two in all—and laughingly tell them to "come here and give me a kiss; nothing makes me sick!" Other times, he would have his breakfast while sitting on the morning paper, because he did not want anyone to mix up the pages before he got around to reading it. Mickey explained how he always wore long handle underwear, and that as an extremely modest person, he would go into the large walk-in closet in his bedroom and get dressed. All described how he loved honeydew melons, and for breakfast, he always ate some with eggs, sunny-side up, on toast with bacon on the side.[21]

As a devoutly religious couple, Harry and Johannah required all their children and grandchildren to say the rosary in the home chapel, and many a time, according to Mickey, when attending plays and movies, both exited as soon as they heard the first curse word. Erin recounted the early years when her uncle and aunt had little money, and she agreed with Mickey who disputed the claim made by some that Johannah provided the $750 to Frank Yount back in 1914 from her saved household funds. "Back in those days," Mickey said, "$750 was a lot of money."[22]

With broad smiles, the two grandchildren and niece recalled the various servants such as Nettie Giersi, the housekeeper; Enoch Barnes, the chauffeur; and the butler-valet "Will Green from New Orleans." It seems that Will loved to gamble, and when he left one day and never came back, each speculated that he may have met his end when he ran afoul of those to whom he owed money.[23]

Business wise, as one of the dominant forces at Yount-Lee, Harry Phelan blended well with Yount and Rothwell, because each respected the other's knowledge and expertise. Theirs is a combination that almost every company seeks, but few have the good fortune to experience. An extremely lucky Yount-Lee thrived from it. In order, however, for Harry or any other employee of Yount-Lee, whether upper echelon or roustabout, to be successful and remain that way, they had to place their trust in another vital position in the front office, that of chief legal counsel.

Beeman Ewell Strong

Beeman Strong assumed that critical responsibility and dealt with the many lawsuits and claims against Yount-Lee's rights to oil producing lands at Spindletop and other locations. The former judge, whose handling of the company's legal affairs has frequently been described as nothing short of brilliant, experienced a colorful career. Born on September 22, 1875 near Mount Enterprise, Texas, he was the son of Creed Jentry and Mary Adelaide Crow Strong. His father, a native of Alabama, had settled in this Rusk County community sometime in 1873. During the primary grades, Beeman attended Rusk public schools, and later, he enrolled at the Summerhill Select School in Omen, Texas, where he studied under Professor A. W. Orr. At the age of sixteen, he obtained a certification to teach school, moved to Sulphur Springs, where he taught for a while before accepting a similar assignment at Lufkin. There, he became interested in law, left the teaching profession, and while at Henderson in 1897, gained admission to the bar.[24]

Judge Beeman Ewell Strong.
—Courtesy Tyrrell Historical Library, Beaumont, Texas.

In 1902 and again in 1904 the voters of Nacogdoches County elected him as County Attorney, and in 1906 he ran successfully for the post of District Attorney of the Second Judicial District that included Angelina, Cherokee, Nacogdoches, Sabine, San Augustine, and Shelby Counties. He held this position until 1907. He then resigned and went into private practice as a partner with George S. King, which lasted until his January 1909 association with S. W. Blount. This partnership, however, terminated in August 1918, when Governor Hobby appointed Strong as a member of the Commission of Appeals to the Texas Supreme Court. He moved to Austin in September of that same year and continued his duties there until January 1, 1920, when he resigned to assume the position of legal counsel for the Fidelity Trust Company and the Galena Signal Oil Company, both in Houston and interests of T. P. Lee and J. S. Cullinan. While in Houston, he served on the board of directors of the Northside Belt Railway Company, chartered on March 23, 1925. About two months before McFaddin No. 2 struck, Frank Yount lured him to Beaumont, and he became the general counsel for Yount-Lee, a position he held until July 31, 1935.[25]

Judge Strong, as most called him, married Nancy Rae Faulkner on April 19, 1904, at Concord in Rusk County. The couple had two children: Beeman Ewell Strong, Jr., born February 6, 1905, and Charlotte Rae on February 6, 1911. As a staunch member of the Democratic Party, he served as a delegate to the 1916 national convention held in St. Louis. He was a member of the American Bar Association, the Texas Bar Association, the Jefferson County Bar Association, and the Lamar Junior College [now Lamar University] Board of Regents.[26]

Beeman stood about five feet, ten inches, weighed around 210 pounds, but he carried his weight well. In the courtroom during his days as a prosecutor, he rarely raised his voice. A. D. Moore, his longtime associate at Yount-Lee, said of him, "On all occasions, when he spoke, he talked briefly, forcefully and to the point."[27]

Besides Strong, two other members of the Yount-Lee organization owned a small block of non-voting stock: Frank E. Thomas, the secretary and assistant-treasurer, and Max T. Schlicher, field superintendent.

Frank E. Thomas

Frank Thomas, the corporate figure whom the men in the field most trusted besides Frank Yount, is credited with being one of the major reasons why Yount-Lee's oil field workers delayed unionizing for so long. With pay scales comparable to the upside of most other producers, they never had the desire, because the team on the fifteenth floor of the San Jacinto Building gave them what they wanted. Purported to be Yount's alter ego, Frank Thomas led the way in human relations and made sure that he extended an open door to anyone with a problem that needed discussing, regardless of the employee's time on the job.[28]

Born on October 4, 1883, Frank was the son of George W. and Fidelia Crummer Thomas of Hartley, Iowa. In his younger years, he worked for two banks, the first at Ocheyedan in his native state, and then at Fulton, South Dakota, where he served as assistant cashier. After playing baseball for a few years, he went to work for the Chicago and Great Western Railroad at Waterloo, Iowa, and later for the New Orleans, Texas, and Mexico Railway (the Missouri Pacific). He eventually landed in Sour Lake, Texas, where he met Frank Yount, who in 1917 put him to work in a clerical capacity. Within the organization, he advanced through the ranks as office manager, assistant secretary, and then in 1933 he attained the rank as corporate secretary. He married Jo Keating at Eads, Colorado, on September 10, 1910, but she passed away in San Antonio in 1930. Sometime after that he married his second wife, Julia.[29]

Frank E. Thomas.
—Courtesy Tyrrell Historical Library, Beaumont, Texas.

Standing about five feet, ten inches in height, Thomas is reported to have been a soft-spoken man with a slender build, and as an energetic, athletic type, could do handstands when he was over forty. He became a father figure, not only to employees in the field, but equally to many in the corporate office, including Marvin McClendon who learned right away that his mentor wanted everything to be meticulously documented.[30]

Maximilian Theodore Schlicher

Maximilian Theodore "Max" Schlicher.
—Courtesy Janet McClendon.

Max Schlicher served at several locations as field superintendent. Born in 1890 he settled in Sour Lake, Texas, and like many of his associates at Yount-Lee, Max went to work in the oil fields at an early age.

While in Sour Lake, he met and befriended Frank Yount who put him on the payroll. Over the years, Yount trusted Schlicher, above most others, as his man on the ground, and wherever problems arose, Max went and took care of business. In youth, Schlicher, the tough but lovable German, stood about five feet, ten inches that packed a solid 215 pounds. He loved cigars, choosing often to chew on them rather than light up, and one rarely ever saw him without his favorite stogie or a felt hat. Characterized by his grandson, Joe Max Guillory, as a snappy dresser, Max was a devoutly religious man who attended Roberts Avenue Methodist Church in the South Park district of Beaumont. When various functions at Yount-Lee called for cooking, Schlicher stepped in and took charge of preparing the barbeque.[31]

Marvin Wise McClendon

Marvin Wise McClendon was born near Lafayette, Alabama, on April 9, 1896, the second of the three sons of Robert Pierce and Edna Earle Brooks McClendon. Edna died in 1898, and in 1907 shortly after his remarriage that same year to Alice Barnes, the elder McClendon, who had heard about the limitless opportunities in Texas, moved his new wife and his three sons, Homer, Marvin, and Earl, to Roscoe about eight miles from Sweetwater in the western part of the state. When he arrived, though, he soon found the land that he had purchased extremely rocky and most difficult to farm, but he held steadfast for about four years. Finally in 1911, he again moved his family, which by then included another son, Bill, to the small town of Ben Arnold, where he cotton farmed in the area for years. Another son, named Barnes, was born to Robert and Alice McClendon in 1913.[32]

After attending public schools in both Roscoe and Ben Arnold, Marvin McClendon

Marvin Wise McClendon, circa 1953.
—Courtesy Janet McClendon.

entered Southwestern University at Georgetown, Texas, in 1913. And by the summer of 1918, he had taught various grades in schools near Taylor and served as an English and history instructor in a private secondary institution at Weatherford.[33]

He entered the army on June 20, 1918, but he had not seen any action when word came of the Armistice that ended World War I. After receiving a discharge from service on February 18 of the following year, McClendon entered The University of Texas, and in 1920 he graduated with a degree in economics. Following that, he held several accounting jobs, until finally landing at Mattison and Block of Houston. As McClendon settled into his chosen profession, Frank Yount determined in 1924 that he required the services of a contract accountant to help manage the business of his growing oil company, so he directed Samuel G. Parks, his personal secretary, to make some inquiries. Eventually Frank's request made its way from Mattison and Block's New York office to its Houston facility. McClendon won the coveted position over a field of at least five other candidates.[34]

Samuel G. Parks.
—Courtesy Tyrrell Historical Library, Beaumont, Texas.

From December 1, 1924 until December 31, 1927, McClendon worked in Yount-Lee's office in Beaumont as a direct employee of Mattison and Block, which later dissolved, and then Mattison and Davey, its successor. On January 1 of the next year, Frank offered him a full-time job as auditor. "If you're going to have a good company," Yount remarked, "you have to put good men into it." McClendon gladly accepted the post.[35]

Frank Yount put a lot of trust into this young man from Alabama as indicated in 1929 when he sent him to New York City to negotiate with a brokerage firm, Blythe and Company, in an attempt to list the Yount-Lee Oil Company on the New York Stock Exchange. After two weeks, however, both parties scrapped the project, and McClendon returned to Beaumont.[36]

When Frank and Pansy Yount completed the construction of the Mildred Apartments in 1930, they ran into problems with insurance coverage, part of which had to do with a requirement relating to tenancy numbers. Apparently, the apartments were not being rented as quickly as planned, and in order to boost occupancy rates, Frank offered Marvin free rent if he would move into one of the vacant units. McClendon also accepted this offer, and he lived there for about three years until he and his wife, the former Marie Young, moved out in the early summer of 1936. The couple, who had married on December 16, 1933, had one child, a daughter named Mary Janet, born August 18, 1941.[37]

Marvin Wise McClendon at the Mildred Building, circa 1930–1931.
—Courtesy Janet McClendon.

Even though he never owned a single share of stock in Yount-Lee, Marvin McClendon played a pivotal role in the company's financial business dealings, and finally on January 3, 1934, the board of directors rewarded his stellar performance by elevating him to the dual position of assistant secretary and assistant treasurer. Above all others, Marvin enjoyed his association with Frank Yount, Talbot Rothwell, Harry Phelan, Frank Thomas (his mentor), Max Schlicher, and A. D. Moore. He also valued his long-standing friendship with Pattillo Higgins of First Spindletop fame. During McClendon's frequent business trips to San Antonio, he visited the old man as often as possible until Higgins' death in 1955.[38]

It is rare that any individual, especially

Frank Yount on an oil rig. Frank Yount extreme left; next to him, Harley Woodward; rest unidentified).
—Courtesy Bob and Mary Woodward.

one with Frank Yount's limited educational background, possessed the skills and insight to assemble such a cohesive team. Armed, however, with the talented and impressive lineup at Yount-Lee, it is as though the company could never be anything other than a success. And even though the reins of general power, for the most part, lay in the hands of the big three: Frank Yount, Tal Rothwell, and Harry Phelan, with Rothwell concentrating on production and Phelan on finance, the general public perceived each man, in spite of his vast wealth, power, and plush office environment, as a down to earth individual who never placed himself above the working class. That also went for the men in the field, who considered both Yount and Rothwell as just two more hands on a rig. Long after they were both millionaires, there were a number of occasions when each rolled up his sleeves and took his place alongside roughnecks to bring in several wells. Frank also applied good will to the men in the corporate office when, during the summer of 1930, he rewarded A. D. Moore and Marvin McClendon with a pleasure cruise that originated in Beaumont, destined for Cuba, Jamaica, the Panama Canal, and Mexico.[39]

Kingston, Jamaica, June 1930. Left to right: Marvin McClendon, a Mr. Chandler, Ewell Strong, and A. D. Moore.
—Courtesy Janet McClendon.

Although most certainly a strong character who reportedly operated the business as if it belonged to him personally, Frank Yount never understated the valuable input by others. He knew all that and then some would be required down the home stretch to maintain the company on the projected course of competing head-to-head with the major oil producers of the day.

Competition with the Majors

"Capitalism needs to function like a game of tug-of-war. Two opposing sides need to continually struggle for dominance, but at no time can either side be permitted to walk away with the rope."

PETE HOLIDAY

No stranger to being ranked close to the top in Texas oil production, Yount-Lee claimed third place in that category as early as 1920. But almost five years later when the McFaddin No. 2 hit, clear evidence revealed that the Beaumont-based independent had begun to arouse not only the operators' interests in Spindletop but also others who owned property in and around the area. The Beaumont City Commission got into the oil play after it leased a tract, located in the Spindletop Heights subdivision and part of the John A. Veatch and John A. Bullock surveys, to Yount-Lee on April 27, 1926.[1]

1926 (continued)

Sustaining its operations at Sour Lake, Yount-Lee brought in the Gilbert No. 3 on April 29 with a daily production of 2,000 barrels; but just as before, Spindletop stole the thunder. On May 11 the Yount-Lee McFaddin No. 5 produced twice that and more the first day alone. The drilling of the well that began as a race between the crews on McFaddin and Gladys City leases took only thirteen days to complete, and it turned out to be the shallowest of the four producers brought in thus far on the McFaddin tract. The reality that these wells flowed oil with different gravity weights from various depths at nearby locations completely baffled most oilmen. Similar to the previous 1901 Spindletop boom, one question went unanswered, the one on which many pondered continuously: where was the source?[2]

History had shown that Marrs McLean and Frank Yount shared viewpoints on the subject. To concisely describe his position, Yount pointed to the glass top of his huge conference desk, and afterward, commented:

> If I should hit that glass with a hammer hard enough to crack it all over, you would have my idea of what a dome's flank is like. The center, of course, would be the salt plug, and the cracks radiating out in all directions would represent the flank area. The strata of the surrounding area has been shattered by the rising of the salt. Anywhere, in any direction, oil might be located. The irregularity of the breakage accounts for oil being found in certain places and being drained off under a tract a few feet away.[3]

By May 13 those who wanted to lease or buy available Spindletop acreage remained in a quandary, because landowners had smartened up. They now banded together, without question, and it became clear that they were willing to hold out for profitable lease arrangements that included healthy bonus payments. Even at this late stage of the game, operators were not quite ready to meet these stiff requirements, at least not until they received more positive data. But when Yount-Lee brought in its Gladys City No. 4 on May 16, their attitudes soon changed. Ironically, the well staked on Gladys City Square No. 12 corresponded to the identical spot where Marrs McLean intended to drill years before, but an unfortunate mistake led him to change locations. From a practical stance, the Gladys City No. 4 represented the turning point at New Spindletop, and figures for the week ending May 22 indicated that the field had reassumed the limelight. It rebounded into second place in Gulf Coast daily production with 12,100 barrels, but Hull still commanded the lead with 22,000, while Orange with 11,300, ranked third. Yount-Lee, with its six producers, accounted for most of Spindletop's volume, and the company's future prospects looked even brighter.[4]

Yount-Lee's achievement sparked a new fervor at the old field. New locations, it seemed, were being put down everywhere, and derrick construction by at least six different companies continued nonstop. Not wanting to be left out in the cold, County Commissioner J. E. Turner recommended on May 31 that Jefferson County officials approve an innovative plan, whereby the county could take advantage of its rights of way and two roadways through Spindletop. Under his proposal, the county would not only lease the acreage to prospective oil drillers, it would borrow an idea from Marrs McLean's playbook, retain royalty interests in the property and of course, share in the profits. Then suddenly, County Attorney C. T. Groce blindsided the commissioners and declared the measure illegal. The controversy died down for a while, but it resurfaced in August. Doggedly, County Judge B. B. Johnson reaffirmed and then pressed the group's earlier decision to go ahead with the lease program, but in doing so, he now added a new strategy which he hoped would make the matter more palatable to the courts. He alleged that if county properties were not in current use, those specific land titles would revert back to the original owners, and in the long run, the county would suffer the consequences of ill timing and lost revenue potential. Johnson's measure, he claimed, would guarantee the county's cut of oil income. During a September showdown, however, Texas Attorney General Dan Moody, in a landmark decision, finally resolved the issue by ruling that county governments could not, under any circumstances, lease roadways or rights of way under their control for profit of any type.[5]

After completing the Gladys City No. 4, Yount-Lee increased the number of drilling rigs at Spindletop to three. Both Gulf and Unity Oil continued their operations, and on

June 3 the latter brought in a small well on one of the older sections. This led to yet further speculation that maybe the original areas of the old field still had some life left in them after all. At this point, at least 150 men worked on various projects at Spindletop, a substantial increase over less than three weeks prior. The latest production, as stated earlier, also brought about a renewed overall interest in leasing activities. B. E. Quinn, Marrs McLean's former partner in the High Island hotel venture, leased a small tract from Daisy Roche and her sister, Mrs. F. C. Joesting, and in the process, set about an almost unbelievable chain of events. Thirty days later, Quinn sold it to H. E. Hines and his brother of Huntington, West Virginia, for $6,000 and a royalty interest. On July 7 the new owners completed the Hines No. 1 Quinn, and Gulf, on the constant lookout for fresh opportunities, bought both the well and tract for the immense price of $200,000, consisting of $140,000 in cash and the remainder in oil. The preceding transaction points up the lengths that some of the major companies were prepared to take in order to get back into the competition at Spindletop, but none of that posturing mattered to Yount-Lee. Since it held already most of the valuable leases on the hill, it could very well afford a conservative approach to the millions of yet undiscovered barrels of crude that lay there for the taking.[6]

On June 26 the Gladys City No. 5 blew in, and the McFaddin No. 6 followed the next day. With successive strikes, Yount-Lee immediately announced plans to now maintain four drilling rigs at Spindletop, and it appeared that its own output, when added to that of the Gulf Company, would vault the field into the Gulf Coast production lead for the first time in almost twenty-five years. Nearby Port Arthur Road felt the effect of the boom as people rushed to the field to see the new "gushers." Yount-Lee's Davis No. 1, which came in on June 30, developed into the company's fourth producer in the same number of days. The Davis No. 1, the largest of the Yount-Lee wells at Spindletop to date, allowed the field to regain the Gulf Coast lead. Spindletop now produced more than 20,000 barrels a day; Yount-Lee contributed 16,000 of that number, and Gulf, the rest.[7]

This hot news prompted a near frenzy among oil operators, and for those who wanted to lease at Spindletop, they swallowed hard and learned to cope with inflated prices. Land once refused at $10 an acre, now marketed for as much as $6,000. And as before, Marrs McLean found himself in the right place at the right time, because in July, he leased a five-acre tract to the Atlantic Oil Producing Company for a profitable package that included a $10,000 bonus if it discovered oil, a 50 percent split on all profits, plus the retention of a 20 percent royalty interest. This lopsided agreement netted McLean a hefty three-fifths return on any future production. With such examples, operators soon blamed Yount-Lee for the effect of expanded land speculation and along with it, the inflated prices. But the company took everything in stride and increased its own drilling rigs to eight, leading the way as derrick construction at Spindletop took on proportions comparable to that of 1901.[8]

About the middle of July, Yount-Lee permanently stationed Johnny Hatcher, superintendent with previous dual responsibilities at Spindletop and Sour Lake, at the Beaumont field to oversee all local operations, and afterward, reassigned Max Schlicher to fill Hatcher's slot at Sour Lake. Spindletop's remarkable success prompted this decision, so said the announcement, and furthermore, the company had to position itself for future expansion by placing the veteran driller in command of its most critical site.

Shortly, traffic jams appeared in tandem with the recent discoveries, especially after the evening meals when entire families traveled to the outskirts of town to view the latest activities. The roadways through Spindletop proved to be a constant thorn in the side of county officials, not only from a traffic problem perspective, but due to their potential worth in millions of dollars in oil that could not be exploited legally.[9]

Caught off guard somewhat, Yount-Lee officials were ill prepared to handle the constantly increasing production levels. They faced storage problems, no question about that, but the output of upward to 40,000 barrels a day presented a second more pressing dilemma. The real question now: how would the volume affect prices? Clearly, no one at Yount-Lee wanted a repetition of the 1901 boom situation when prices plummeted to incomprehensible lows of three cents a barrel, so they formulated a master design that took the form of a tank farm, the likes of which the world had never seen. On the second of August Frank Yount confirmed that he had negotiated a massive $475,000 real-estate deal with Perry McFaddin and Wesley Kyle by which the company purchased some 1,800 acres, extending from the current lease holdings on McFaddin property all the way to the Neches River. When answering questions about the possibility that his company might construct a refinery there, Yount chose to remain vague, but he did stipulate that immediate plans called for the erection of one hundred steel tanks with a cumulative storage capacity of 5.5 million barrels of crude, and a pumping station, complete with dock facilities along the river just below the Magnolia Refinery. He reiterated that Kyle retained a one-eighth royalty interest in the property, but the agreement itself

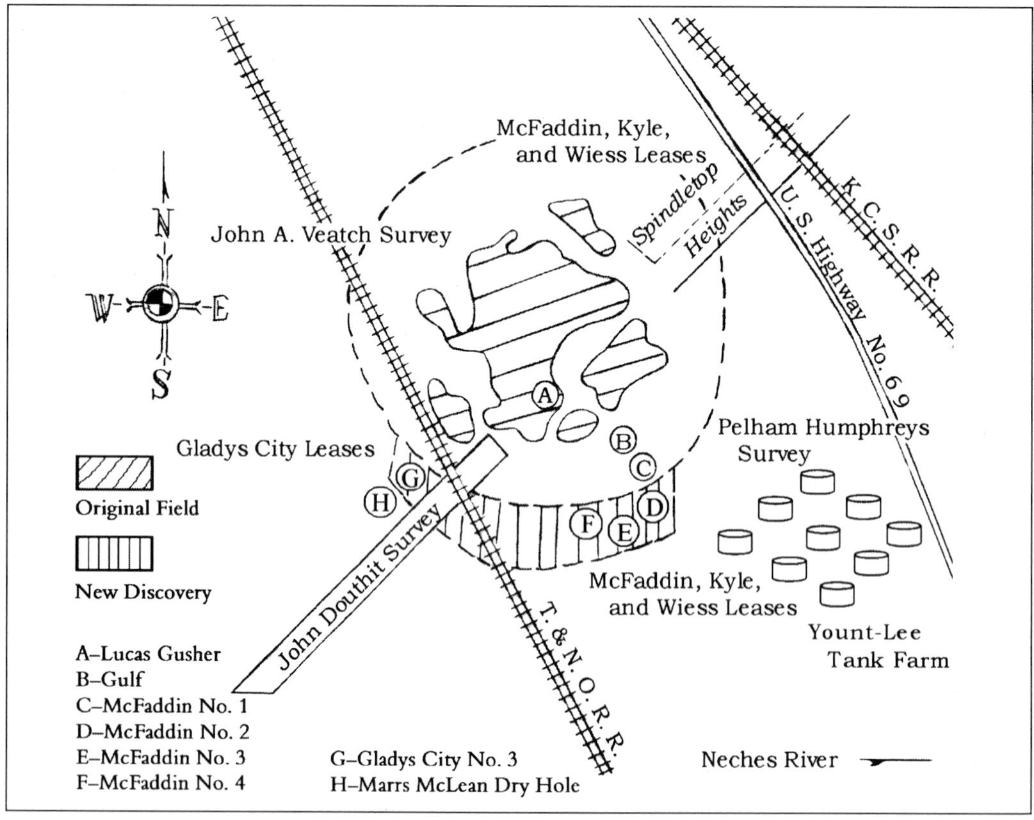

Yount-Lee Spindletop Tank Farm

did not provide for any mandatory drilling. Right away, industry watchers hailed this bold maneuver as the first major step taken by Yount-Lee to place itself among the leading producers in the oil industry. Yet, regardless of Yount-Lee's best thought out tactics, the impact of overproduction marched to the forefront on August 6 and 7, when both the Gulf Pipe Line Company and Magnolia joined in a price cutback. Grade A crude fell from $1.60 a barrel to $1.25, and that of grade B from $1.50 to $1.15. The obvious, often feared, finally came to fruition as the effect of an almost 100,000-barrel daily production at Spindletop began taking its toll on world markets.[10]

Hoping to ride out the tide until oversupplies subsided, Yount-Lee placed a $1.2 million order with the Petroleum Iron Works of Sharon, Pennsylvania, for the first of the steel storage tanks that took four train loads to transport to Beaumont. The manufacturer delivered the materials in record time, and the erection process, by Petroleum Iron Works personnel of both Sharon and Beaumont, began by the middle of August. Five weeks from the original order date, Spindletop crude began filling the first tank. For its investment in storage facilities, Yount-Lee spent nearly $3.25 million on this project, a remarkable expenditure by any measure.[11]

With Yount-Lee accomplishments on the hill and at other locations, rumors became commonplace. One report alleged that the company planned to drill on its Orange property, the George Blanch tract of about 700 acres. Officials, however, maintained silence, as they did on the newest buzz that the Pure Oil Company offered to buy all Yount-Lee holdings for about $30 million. When approached for a comment, Harry Phelan answered: "I don't want to confirm that story. Of course, we have had offers and

Yount-Lee tank farm and oil field.

—Courtesy Tyrrell Historical Library, Beaumont, Texas.

some substantial ones, but nothing has come of any of them yet." With that, he refused to say anything further and referred the reporter to Frank Yount who politely refused to discuss the matter either.[12]

Yount-Lee producers at Spindletop increased to twenty by August 22, and the next day, company officials indicated that the office staff had outgrown the existing twelfth floor offices in the San Jacinto Building. The corporate headquarters were relocated upstairs and now occupied the entire fifteenth floor.[13]

The company continued to bring in wells at a record pace, and with its Davis No. 2 on August 24 and the McFaddin No. 9 five days later, Spindletop's total production by all companies stood well above 100,000 barrels a day. With the field now leading all of Texas, Yount-Lee extended its production boundaries again, and crews spudded in a new location on Hillebrandt Road. By September 5 the firm's output represented 46,000 barrels of Spindletop's daily volume; and at an average price of $1.25 per barrel then, that would put the income at almost $2 million in today's currency.[14]

On October 29 the well that many called the "third discovery at Spindletop" blew in from a depth of 5,157 feet. The Yount-Lee Fee No. 9, estimated at 20,000 barrels a day, created a new wave of enthusiasm, which excited even the normally unflappable Frank Yount. Within the first year after its discovery at Spindletop on November 14, 1925, the company's record had been dramatic. (See table on page 21.) Yount-Lee now had thirty-three active wells and was in the process of drilling at least twelve others. Of course, there were other companies in operation at Spindletop, among them Rio Bravo, Gulf and Sun, but Yount-Lee accounted for almost half of the seventy-eight producers with a daily output of 100,840 barrels. Within that same year, more than fourteen million barrels of crude flowed from the new discovery areas whose foundation rested on Marrs McLean's prophecy and Frank Yount's gutsy, unswerving self-confidence.[15]

Throughout the years, geologists and oilmen, alike, wondered just how deep

McFaddin No. 14, J. C. Chance, driller.

—Courtesy Christine Moor Sanders.

Yount-Lee Fee No. 18, E. H. Patton, driller.
—Courtesy Texas Energy Museum, Beaumont, Texas.

Spindletop's oil stratum really went, but the technology required to drill at these enormous depths did not yet exist. On November 8 Tal Rothwell announced Yount-Lee's preparations to make just such a test. The Boykin Machine and Supply Company of Beaumont manufactured the drawworks for a new rig touted as having the capability of drilling to 10,000 feet. This "super-rotary" affair represented not only one of the largest in the world, but probably the most expensive. Rothwell said that his company had committed to spend more than $100,000 on the undertaking that would prove once and for all what lay beneath the old dome. The next day, crews under the direction of contractor D. B. McDaniels moved the mammoth rig and set it up on the location dubbed as Fee No. 17. Both Beaumont newspapers ran several articles heralding expectations that the experiment would most assuredly break the current drilling record previously set in California at over 8,000 feet. "Seventeen is going to be a lucky number for us," said Johnny Hatcher, "because we're going after the bottom of Spindle Top. Our McFaddin No. 13 is our best well but the big rig at Fee 17 should find still better." He also pointed out that if the bit hit oil at any depth before reaching the record, the well would be brought in. Unfortunately, the company abandoned the attempt at about 5,400 feet when officials received discouraging test results, and they never again revived the project.[16]

Nonetheless, Yount-Lee maintained the momentum at Spindletop, but it also drilled at other new locations. The company, therefore, constantly added to its inventory of leases and fees, the latter described as land that is owned outright. With its acquisitions team firing on all cylinders, approximately 1,600 acres in the Sophia Dean survey were obtained in northwest Jefferson County around the middle of November.[17]

The company received more good news on November 18 when its Gladys City No. 10 came in with a flow of about 15,000 barrels a day. This event prompted Frank Yount to assert, "It's a real well, not a toy, like many which have been coming in out here." The Fee No. 15 followed on December 2 with a respectable 4,800-barrel production figure.[18]

By December Yount-Lee had captivated both the citizens of Southeast Texas and Beaumont, and the local media considered everything that the organization did as news-

Yount-Lee Oil Company
Financial Statement as of December 31, 1926

Assets	
Cash on Hand	**$2,435,220.28**
Accounts Receivable	**3,115,446.45**
Material and Supplies	**538,618.81**
Equipment, Less Reserves	**1,711,071.67**
Real Estate and Leases	**1,643,928.42**
Gross Assets	**$9,444,285.63**
Liabilities	
Accounts Payable	**$1,058,511.53**
Surplus	**6,385,774.10**
Capital Stock	**2,000,000.00**
Total Liabilities	**$9,444,285.63**

Source: Texas Secretary of State, Charter Records, no. 28005, March 23, 1927, Office of Secretary of State, Austin, Texas.

worthy, however impressive or however trivial. The *Beaumont Enterprise* printed with pride the story that described the purchase of new office furniture in the amount of $16,000, and the explicit particulars reflected the luxury and beauty of the company's corporate offices, now located on the fifteenth floor of the San Jacinto Building. While Harry Phelan's office "will be furnished with a walnut suite of modern colonial style ... the office of Judge Beeman Strong ... will be a modified Louis the XIV suite in mahogany. In order that the effect of this furniture may not be lost in a single detail, the steel safe and cabinets in the room will be finished in mahogany grain that perfectly matches the other pieces." The overall expenditure, however, represented fixtures primarily for the use of Yount and Rothwell, with each company executive having "a desk, table, revolving chair, telephone stand with humidor, two side chairs, two club chairs, a waste basket and a coat pole," all in richly carved walnut manufactured by the Doten-Dunton Desk Company of Boston, Massachusetts. Alex Szafir of E. Szafir and Son Company of 373-385 Liberty Street in Beaumont handled the details of the purchase.[19]

In line with its amazing production records, the company's monetary condition grew stronger than ever, as evidenced by the Financial Statement as of December 31, 1926. Gross assets now reached over $9 million, with a surplus that amounted to 68 percent of that number, while the debt ratio remained at a low 11 percent.[20]

1927

By the end of January, figures pointed out that Yount-Lee led all Gulf Coast producers, but as is often the case, the success of a few breeds greed and contempt among others. Due to the massive amounts of money at stake, numerous parties who questioned the corporation's title to specific acreage at New Spindletop brought about a myriad of lawsuits. The most celebrated, initiated by two former stockholders and officials of the Federal Crude Oil Company, also involved B. E. Quinn, Marrs McLean's old partner. This particular litigation would play a pivotal role in Yount-Lee's future. Although Federal Crude legally incorporated on April 23, 1901, it was never highly successful at oil exploration, and had officially gone out of business on July 1, 1905 when the state revoked its charter due to failure to pay Texas franchise taxes. However, the company owned a 13.8-acre tract, lots 5 and 7 of the Douthit survey, located where Hillebrandt and West Port Arthur Roads converge, for which it paid $140,000 cash immediately after the original boom in 1901. The company drilled one well on the property, but it never produced. No further efforts were made on the tract, and eventually the owners left the area. After the court established a receivership and appointed C. L. Rudd of Beaumont to administer the title, J. F. Guilmartin, a former minority stockholder in Federal Crude, petitioned for the right and subsequent purchase of the entire acreage for only $50. Since the state held a lien of $175 on property that Rudd considered basically worthless, he received approval to sell the two lots to Guilmartin who assumed all future tax liabilities. Guilmartin then resold lot 7 for $60 to R. W. Wilson who deeded it to Quinn for $700 in 1917. During the same year, Yount purchased lot 5, the 6.9 acres, from Guilmartin for $690. Suits and counter suits were filed and appealed, until finally on October 5, 1922, L. B. Hightower, Chief Justice of the Ninth Court of Civil Appeals, affirmed Yount's legal ownership. Then on October 11, 1923, Frank transferred the deed to the property into the company name. All remained relatively quiet until Yount-Lee struck oil there, and the property value jumped approximately $12 million. With that revelation, two other previous stockholders and officials at Federal Crude saw an immediate opportunity to cash in on the bonanza.[21]

D. A. Duncan, the past president, and H. L. Fagin, the former manager, filed suit against Yount-Lee, Quinn, and Guilmartin on the basis that none of them possessed a clear title to the land, and they further proposed that the receiver had no legal right to sell it to Guilmartin in the first place. After listening to ten days of testimony, Federal Judge W. L. Estes of Beaumont handed down a decision in favor of the defendants. As expected, Duncan and Fagin continued the appeals process, until finally the U.S. Supreme Court held again for the defendants, when on June 4, 1928, it denied a *writ of certiorari* (legal instrument issued by a superior court ordering that a lower court produce its record for review) to the Fifth Circuit Court of Appeals. Immediately after the ruling, Quinn became amused when he read about how he had gained victory in the $12 million suit, when in fact, Yount-Lee had the most to lose. Quinn's property, which produced not a single well, was valued at only about $20,000, compared to that of Yount-Lee's in the millions. This litigation, however, would surface yet again.[22]

Yount-Lee put its docks on the Neches River into operation February 21, 1927. In about 3½ hours, the pumping station, equipped with two centrifugal and electrically-driven pumps, moved 16,000 barrels of oil from the storage facilities of four 55,000-barrel tanks and loaded them into the oil tanker, *Sundown Yuna*, for transportation to the Humble Oil refinery at Baytown, Texas. According to P. R. Mitchell, Yount-Lee's superintendent of the installation, plans were made to load a tanker every seventy-two hours.[23]

The company's board of directors met on March 15 and voted another increase in capital stock, this one by $100,000. The additional 1,000 shares, valued at $100 each and designated as non-voting, were awarded as a stock dividend. Of the total, Yount received 334; Phelan, 166, Tal Rothwell, 100; Mabel Rothwell, 50; Emerson Woodward, 250; and Bill Lee, 100.[24]

By the end of March, Yount-Lee's quarterly production surpassed the 3.9 million-barrel mark, a figure strong enough to place the company not only as the largest operator at Spindletop but second in Texas, ahead of Phillips, Humble, Magnolia, Texas,

Marland, Rio Bravo, Big Lake, McMan, Prairie, and Pure in that order. Gulf, however, continued to hold the overall lead.[25]

Yount-Lee maintained its sizzling pace at Spindletop through April, but on May 5 it experienced its first major accident at the field. The McFaddin No. 29 blew up while drilling at about 5,140 feet, and the well ran out of control for at least two hours. Miraculously, out of the six men who worked on the derrick at the time, only J. C. Chance and Lewis Sanders received injuries from the blast that rocked the area. Chance suffered "a fractured skull ... when a large piece of shale from the well struck him in the head," and Sanders sustained numerous cuts and abrasions when he fell a distance of some forty feet to the derrick floor. Twisted drill stem blocked the T.&N.O. train tracks, sand and gumbo covered at least ten acres, and oil sprayed automobiles more than two miles away. Field superintendent, Johnny Hatcher "estimated that rocks as large as a man's head were at one time being thrown 350 to 400 feet into the air, although the mixed column of oil, gas and mud spray, which rapidly covered the nearby field, probably did not rise more than 250 feet." Another worker, P. Bouse, described the event in his own words:

> I was eating at one of the lunch stands near the well when I heard the roaring noise and saw the derrick swaying back and forth like the mast of a ship. I saw Sanders reach for the guyline and as he did so the derrick collapsed about him. I thought sure he was falling to certain death and watched him, but did not see him when he struck the ground. Despite the danger, his fellow workmen rushed to him and carried him away from the derrick. An ambulance was called and he was sent to the hospital.

Regardless of the outcome, newspaper reports described that everyone came out ex-

McFaddin No. 28. Photograph by L. L. Allen.

—Courtesy Texas Energy Museum, Beaumont, Texas.

Wreckage of McFaddin No. 29. Photograph by L. L. Allen.

—Courtesy Texas Energy Museum, Beaumont, Texas.

tremely lucky considering the damage estimate of over $40,000. By nightfall, though, most of the wreckage had been cleared away, and new derrick construction begun. The injured workers, at first thought to be critical, recovered quickly, and a few days later, both were released from Hotel Dieu, located at 1425 Sabine Pass. Ironically, McFaddin No. 29 turned out as one of the few actual "gushers" at Second Spindletop.[26]

Over the years, Yount-Lee acquired considerable properties in downtown Beaumont, and it enhanced its real-estate program on May 7 with a transaction that involved the purchase of seven lots on Park and Forsythe Streets for $161,000 cash. It procured these lots, with an average price of $23,000 each, from Perry McFaddin, the Josey-Miller Company, A. N. Adams, N. T. Anders, and Sarah Willard. Yount-Lee officials indicated that the property was for investment purposes only, and they refused to elaborate on future plans.[27]

On July 13 Yount-Lee announced that a 150-acre tract in the Jennings oil field near Evangeline, Louisiana had been secured. Although these Houssiere-Latrielle holdings proved to be extremely valuable oil-producing territories as time passed, Marrs McLean's inroads at High Island would have a more profound influence on the immediate future of Yount-Lee. For some time, the Sun Oil Company controlled a large High Island lease, but it had been unable to find oil in any commercial quantity. Sun, therefore, offered the 800-acre Cade tract to McLean who not only took over the lease, but all equipment in the form of a drilling rig, pipelines, and casing. The two completed the agreement in July, and when asked to comment on why he wanted the previously unsuccessful property, McLean remarked:

> The general public does not understand that the early failures and dry holes around these domes are a part of the real development ... If I fail, the chances of the next man will be just that much better because he will have the benefit of my experience ...

> The hole I drilled several years ago was worth a great deal when the Yount-Lee Oil company began drilling for deep sands at Spindle Top.

With another of his farsighted approaches, McLean began the process by which he obtained almost every lease on High Island in a move that virtually ensured Yount-Lee success in that area.[28]

Considering all the recent developments, the fact remained that in order to maintain Spindletop's daily output, Yount-Lee's drilling efforts would have to be increased substantially. True, wells were being put down in record numbers, but the longevity of the older ones presented a major cause of concern. The 1901 boom tapered off very quickly when the cap rock's gas pressure deteriorated, and hints of a repeat appeared, only this time at a lower stratum. Even so, the field retained its lead in Gulf Coast production with 54,138 barrels a day, and Yount-Lee accounted for 77 percent of that.[29]

The company, however, fully recognized the effect that a potential demise of New Spindletop would have upon its balance sheet and stockholders' checkbooks, and in an effort to guarantee an inventory of future holdings for drilling purposes, officials adopted a more aggressive program of lease and fee acquisitions in Louisiana. On about September 12 it purchased an interest in property, including an overriding royalty on producing wells at the Edgerly field near Lake Charles, from the Bright Company for $225,000. Since Gulf owned the drilling rights on the tract, this transaction reflected the faith that Yount-Lee had in the area, even though it would be some time before commencing operations of its own. The proven areas of Louisiana also saw a flurry of activity during that same period, as several wells were brought in at Hackberry.[30]

With the close of 1927, figures confirmed that Spindletop's yearly output topped 21 million barrels, the largest volume that the field ever produced, surpassing even the 1902 banner year when it yielded 17 million plus. Brisk drilling during 1927 created 121 wells at Spindletop alone, and Yount-Lee owned 76 of those representing a production figure of 13,240,000 barrels. With oil selling at an average of $1.25 a barrel, the company's gross income from Spindletop, by itself, exceeded $16.5 million. Although Gulf still commanded the Texas production lead, Yount-Lee retained a second place finish with 14,720,000 barrels, ahead of

Hotel Dieu, circa 1920. From John H. Walker and Gwendolyn Wingate, Beaumont: A Pictorial History.

"Second Spindletop," Yount-Lee Oil Company. Photograph by L. L. Allen.
—Courtesy Tyrrell Historical Library, Beaumont, Texas.

Texas, Phillips, Magnolia, and Humble. The company's gross revenue on Texas wells alone, in today's currency, would be roughly $631.5 million.[31]

1928

In February and March Yount-Lee obtained more real estate by purchasing property for $300,000 on the east side of Orleans Street and on the south side of Wall Street in Beaumont from P. B. Doty, Ed Cherry, and R. E. Smith. As usual, the company never disclosed plans for the new acquisition. On March 10 it completed another transaction, this one involving the purchase of J. Cooke Wilson's Riggs Furniture Company Building and a 99-year lease on the land it occupied. On this occasion, though, neither party disclosed the purchase price. With this latest move, Yount-Lee controlled almost an entire city block, bounded by Orleans, Wall, Forsythe, and Park Streets. Charles Chaison owned the lone exclusion with a 60-foot piece of property that faced Park Street. Although it took quite some doing, the company eventually ended the hold-out and gained future control of this tract on August 7, 1930 when it concluded a 99-year lease arrangement with Mrs. Chaison.[32]

Yount-Lee also extended its holdings in Orange, and on April 10 it secured a 100-acre tract, located in the Larkin R. Thomas survey, by purchase from Jack Turner, J. D. Thomas, C. C. Thomas, Mrs. Henry Stakes, and Sam Hatton. The company paid a price of fifty dollars per acre but gave up a one-eighth royalty interest to the previous owners during the negotiation.[33]

Frank Yount, however, held other interests besides work in the oil fields, and he was especially pleased to hear that Ignacy Jan Paderewski, the former Polish premier during 1918–1919, and world-renowned classical pianist, who as part of a transcontinental tour sponsored by Steinway & Sons, piano makers extraordinaire, planned to present a concert in Beaumont on April 10. The *Beaumont Enterprise* boldly proclaimed the upcoming event nine days earlier:

McFaddin No. 39, William Stewart, driller. Photograph by L. L. Allen.
—Courtesy Texas Energy Museum
Beaumont Texas.

> When the curtain goes up at 8:30 o'clock, there will be the darkened stage, the slumbering piano with the high-backed chair before it, the docilely waiting audience. There—finally—the deity himself, frock-coated, white-necktied, aureoled, to be greeted by a standing audience.

The adoration and sacred description continued:

> An audience jamming all the available and unavailable space in the [municipal] auditorium is due the appearance here of one of the sovereign artists of our time. The Paderewski concert will be a red letter event in the city's musical history and will mark a step forward in its cultural growth.

A *Beaumont Journal* article of April 2 recounted another remarkable talent attributed to the pianist, that of a fine memory. Supposedly, he could recall names and faces after introductions years before, but in one instance, however, he admitted that he did not recognize a particular lady who came to shake his hand after a concert in a small eastern town. When questioned further, Paderewski said that he remembered the event where the woman allegedly met him, but he could not recollect her name. The lady replied, "Well ... it rained so hard that night of your concert that I could not come ... but my daughter went in my place ... and she was introduced to you after the performance ... and so I thought you might perhaps remember me." The article concluded, "Which goes to prove that even artists' memories are short sometimes and that miracles do not happen nowadays."[34]

On the morning of the scheduled concert, the *Beaumont Enterprise* printed the entire program that listed one selection composed by Paderewski himself, one by Schumann, one by Beethoven, four by Schubert-Liszt, five by Chopin, and one by Liszt. Immediately below that, Paderewski's local competition for the night appeared. The Magnolia Petroleum Company's radio station KFDM offered for its nightly broadcast from 8 to 9 P.M. the Southern Ramblers Orchestra, under the direction of Lynn Grisaffi; and from 9 to 10 P.M., its own company orchestra, directed by R. A. Dhossche, who would perform such memorable tunes as "Fascinatin' Vamp" and "I'm Going Back to the Bottomland."[35]

When Paderewski arrived by private rail car in Beaumont at 7:48 A.M. on Tuesday, April 10, he found the unseasonable weather brisk, cold, and dreary, with the temperature dropping to 42 degrees. He had traveled from New Orleans in the company of an entourage that included his wife, Madame Helena Paderewski; her secretary, Miss Helen Lubke; Eldon Joubert, transportation manager; Lawrence J. Fitzgerald, Paderewski's secretary; Joseph Stubanski, his valet-masseur; James Davis, special chef; two Pullman porters; and a waiter. Fitzgerald announced to the press that due to the inclement weather, the "master" would remain inside most of the day and take "every precaution to safeguard his health."[36]

As a connoisseur of the arts and classical music, Frank Yount not only attended that evening's concert, along with about 2,499 others, but invited the musician to extend his stay by one day, take in the sights around Beaumont and the Spindletop oil field and afterward have tea at his household. Paderewski agreed without hesitation. He had heard about the Lucas Gusher and believed such as commonplace, so he asked Yount to show him a similar well. "Frank," he remarked excitedly, "I must see one of your gushers." The surprised oilman didn't have the heart to tell the old gentleman, then about sixty-eight, that gushers had gone out of style some twenty-five years prior. After concocting a plot, later that night Frank got on the phone and ordered Johnny Hatcher to stage a gusher for Paderewski's amusement. "Johnny," he said, "we've got to have a gusher for the Maestro." Hatcher indicated that he understood, so he directed Alton Prentiss to take it from there. The next day, the driller opened a valve at the precise moment that the Yount party approached by automobile, and treated everyone to oil spewing some 200 feet above the derrick floor. After observing the field for about two hours, a grateful Paderewski said, "I have seen many oil fields in Poland and Rumania, and in many sections of the United States, but I have never seen such a field as Spindle Top. It is astounding to see so many wells producing oil in such a small area." Furthermore, he added, "Frank, I think this is the kind of music I like best." Reports point out

Ignacy Jan Paderewski in youth.
—Courtesy Buckingham Hotel, New York City.

that he was so wound up, he gave the Yount family an unexpected private concert later that afternoon in their home. After the "gusher episode," Prentiss later recounted the story to author Jim Clark during a meeting at the Houston Club. "Boy, it was a beautiful sight," Prentiss said. "It must have been making oil at the rate of 100,000 barrels a day. I soaked everybody in Spindletop in crude oil." Clark concluded, "I don't recall exactly, but I believe that was the very day we all started calling him 'Nutty,' because most of the oil workers thought Prentiss had lost his mind."[37]

Yount-Lee paid increased attention to its holdings at Hackberry in April and May 1928 when several wells were drilled in, while at Spindletop, the company launched another attempt, this one a best ever for Gulf Coast drilling depths. The Yount-Lee Quinn No. 1 reached 6,604 feet with a seven inch casing on June 12. When approached on June 16 for a comment regarding the record possibility, Johnny Hatcher remarked, "Our only object in drilling the hole is to find oil. We are not after any particular records. They are merely incidents, so far as we are concerned. The only things that will stop us on this hole are oil or heaving shale." As it turned out, the rig did encounter heaving shale at 6,755 feet, and the crew abandoned the well. In spite of Hatcher's comments, the single thing accomplished by the venture: a new Gulf Coast record that replaced another Yount-Lee mark, that of the McFaddin No. 43 when it came in at 6,700 feet.[38]

Seeking to keep its acquisition plans at intense levels, Yount-Lee negotiated a $1.5 million transaction on July 30 by purchasing 7,400 acres near Lake Charles from the Sweet Lake Oil and Land Company. The tract had been leased previously to Pure Oil which retained a seven-eighths royalty interest; Yount-Lee's purchase included the remaining one-eighth. Future prospects for the area looked good, because Pure had brought in two producers that generated a total of about 4,000 barrels a day.[39]

Also in July, Frank E. Thomas, assistant secretary-treasurer, revealed the company's plans to enlarge the storage facilities at both its tank farm and Neches River docks. Contracts were signed with the Reeves Brothers Company of Birmingham, Alabama, he disclosed, for the manufacture of four additional tanks, each with an 85,000-barrel capacity, to be erected near the current loading docks. Twenty-six others of the 55,000-barrel variety, he said, were to be installed at the tank farm. The new project, estimated to cost $900,000, became necessary because of Yount-Lee's overall increase in production and shipments from the docks to both American and European markets. Thomas further indicated that his company had recently shipped 95,000 barrels of crude to Germany and that other large orders were in the works. Three days later, he made a second announcement which included information about the size of the loading docks being doubled. Space would now be provided for two ships at one time, he stated, thereby allowing oil to be loaded at the rate of 20,000 barrels an hour, compared with the old capacity of 9,500. Thomas set the estimated cost of this additional renovation at $100,000.[40]

Eighteen lots, which bounded the Neches River and Forsythe Street, were purchased from the Keith Company for $100,000. The parties involved concluded this transaction, consisting of 8.23 acres, on August 1, and as usual, the company spokesman declined to offer any planned details for the property's future use, other than for investment purposes.[41]

During the first part of September, Yount-Lee confirmed that plans were underway to enlarge the tank farm yet again. It had placed an $800,000 order with the Reeves

Brothers of Birmingham for thirty 55,000-barrel tanks, and with the pipeline connections and other necessary equipment added in, the new project's total approached $1 million. These new tanks gave the Beaumont oil firm a cumulative storage capacity of 6,060,000 barrels. The total number of tanks found at both the storage farm and the Neches River docks now stood at 104 of the 55,000- and four of the 85,000-barrel variety. This made the company's storage facilities one of, if not the, largest in the world.[42]

Yount-Lee added more property to its inventory of assets, when on September 17 it purchased a four-acre tract, the location of the defunct Tarver Shipbuilding Company situated on the Neches River opposite the old Bowie docks, from A. H. Tarver of Shreveport, Louisiana, for $20,000.[43]

1929

By October of the previous year, Yount-Lee began to pay more attention to the Barbers Hill field and moved "Frank Yount's million dollar rig"—the one used to drill McFaddin No. 3—and set it up on the Richardson No. 1 in December. Even though Spindletop's daily output now declined considerably, the company maintained drilling operations there and even sought out new leases in and around the old field. In December of the prior year, it reached an agreement with the city of Beaumont and the W. C. Tyrrell Trust that gave the company the drilling rights on Tyrrell Park property. By retaining a combined one-eighth royalty interest, the city and the trust would share equally in possible oil earnings. A test on the tract of 6,000 acres that adjoined the park

Gladys City No. 41, L. R. Smith, driller. Photograph by L. L. Allen.

—Courtesy Texas Energy Museum, Beaumont, Texas.

became the integral part of the overall agreement, and if Yount-Lee discovered oil there, it would be required to drill on the park lease within ninety days. At the time, F. L. Bertschler, superintendent for the park, had drawn up a schematic that included an eighteen-hole golf course, zoological gardens, and playgrounds. When asked how his plans might conflict with those seeking oil, Bertschler admitted, "A slush pit makes a splendid golf hazard," but he also added that "he did not know the rule on making a hole in one with an oil well for the objective." None of this conjecture mattered, though, because Yount-Lee abandoned the test well, the Nona Mills No. 1, located on the Hillebrandt Bayou, at 6,622 feet. Unfortunately, this failure placed a damper on the city's hopes of reaping incalculable profits from the oil industry.[44]

On May 1 the *Beaumont Enterprise* printed a report that according to its Houston sources, Yount-Lee turned down a bid of $40 million the previous December by Standard Oil of New York to acquire it lock, stock, and barrel. And now, it appeared that Standard had rethought the matter and might be willing to meet the current asking price. From a marketing standpoint, Standard wanted Yount-Lee's fields for its subsidiary, Magnolia Petroleum, which valued the oil produced at the local level over that in other areas which congealed as the thermometer dropped to near and below freezing. Due to its salt water content, East Coast refiners preferred Gulf Coast petroleum as a "zero cold test lubricant . . . free running at all temperatures." And as demand increased, companies such as Magnolia, "decided that it would be more profitable to secure their own production of coastal crude which would also [guarantee] a future supply for the plants, and it was for this reason that many . . . have come to the Gulf Coast during the past several years . . ." In typical fashion, Yount-Lee never admitted its participation in these negotiations, but regardless, nothing ever came of it. Company officials responded as they always did on such issues, saying that they "knew nothing about it."[45]

Train through Second Spindletop.
—Courtesy Texas Energy Museum, Beaumont, Texas.

As the 1920s drew to a close, automobiles had taken the country by storm. With more than 23 million registrations, America's desire for the passenger car had become insatiable, and manufacturers responded willingly with a record pace in 1929 when some 5.3 million units drove off the assembly lines and onto the nation's highways.[46]

America's number one industry now produced positive effects on the country's economy as it became the single largest customer for gasoline, rubber, nickel, steel, and lead, but a developing major danger lurked just below the surface, although few yet realized it. With a buy now-pay later mentality, consumers spent too freely on this new national obsession, and for every three out of four cars purchased by 1925, a bank or finance company held an installment note. All said, with the exception of rent and insurance, consumers used almost one dollar out of every five they made on their automobiles, including the purchase, operation, and maintenance; and in the process, debts piled up as never before. One trade union official responded when asked what most men worked for: "Twenty-five percent are fighting to keep their heads above water; 10% want to own their own homes; 65% are working to pay for cars."[47]

Frank Yount and other oil producers around the country knew one thing for sure; it would take a lot of petroleum reserves to keep pace with the American dream. But on the other hand, it became equally clear that if Yount-Lee, Texas' largest independent oil company, desired to hold on to that position much longer, its officers and board of directors would have to concentrate on and develop new lease and fee holdings in other areas that promised greater potential than Spindletop.

New Horizons

"We are the first nation in the history of the world to go to the poor house in an automobile."

WILL ROGERS

While their crews continued to bring in wells at Spindletop, Frank Yount and Tal Rothwell feared that unless they discovered new production areas, the old field would eventually dry up, and history would repeat itself. Neither would permit this to happen.

1929 (continued)

Meanwhile, they concentrated drilling operations at Barbers Hill, Texas, and the Houssiere-Latrielle leases, located in the Evangeline and Jennings, Louisiana vicinity. The Yount-Lee Chambers No. 1, the company's third successful well at Barbers Hill, blew in on January 29. Another, the No. 2 Chambers, followed on March 29, and on April 5, the No. 3 made its debut. Unfortunately, the first serious setback at Barbers Hill occurred on September 20, when the Chambers No. 4 tested salt water at 6,000 feet, which forced its abandonment. While these deep-production wells indicated the presence of a new oil-bearing stratum, their counterparts at Evangeline proved at some of the deepest levels that the Gulf Coast had ever seen. The Houssiere-Latrielle No. 6 came in on June 2 from 7,410 feet, and as a result, the royalty holder on the tract, a grateful Houssiere-Laticlle Oil Company, invited the entire Yount-Lee crew to a barbecue and afterward, presented each member with a fifty dollar new suit of clothes.[1]

But just at the time when many considered Spindletop finished, the old field surrendered yet another fine producer. On April 2 Yount-Lee capped an 8,000-barrel well at the Fee No. 6 tract, located on the west side of Port Arthur Road in a section thought to be generally depleted.[2]

On other fronts, Yount-Lee maintained its real-estate acquisition program in downtown Beaumont and adjoining areas. On March 3 Harry Phelan reported that the company purchased the Union City Transfer Building at 630 Fannin Street for $10,000. Another announcement followed on March 28 with information that the company acquired lot 3 and the southwest half of lot 2 of the N. A. McMillan addition. Costing another $30,000, both properties, located at Fannin and Neches Streets, housed warehouse buildings previously owned by H. W. and C. E. Vallee. On June 5 the firm procured Block 6, consisting of six lots on Railroad Avenue and Bowie Streets, and immediately resold the parcel for $21,000 to the Wall Street Realty Company, one of Frank Yount's private business concerns. On July 12 Yount-Lee purchased an industrial site of 1,270 acres between Nederland and Port Arthur from the Harvey W. Gilbert Company for $85,000 cash, partly because two railroads, the Kansas City Southern and the interurban line of the Southern Pacific, served the tract with connections to gas and water facilities. Since Yount-Lee officials did not announce any immediate plans for the new acquisition, the question again rose about the company's possible construction of a refinery, for which this new site could be a likely candidate.[3]

Yount-Lee acquired a lease on 34.8 acres in the F. M. Gardner Survey No. 150, located seven miles west of Dayton, Texas, on August 20, 1929. The purchase price of $500,000, comprised of $300,000 in cash and the remainder in oil, went to Harvey Smith, Inc., which retained a twenty-fourth royalty interest. The seller had recently brought in a small wildcat on the property that lay on the Esperson Dome, so Yount-Lee followed up with a 7,000-foot test that unfortunately never produced. The overall lease never paid off either, and eventually on June 27, 1931, the company returned title to the original owner, Mrs. Nellie Esperson Stewart.[4]

The fantastic sums of money generated by Yount-Lee at Spindletop spawned numerous lawsuits over disputed ownership of oil-producing properties, and one of these dubious distinctions goes to the Fall Corporation of New Orleans with its August 23, 1929 filing against the company for $10 million in damages. Fall's attorneys argued that when Yount-Lee gained control of leases in the William and Pelham Humphreys survey through Perry McFaddin, he did not own clear title to the acreage. The suit, however, did not demand full restitution of profits from Yount-Lee's 113 producing wells on the tract, but it did seek 5 percent or $9 million, with an additional $1 million in interest. Trial testimony began on June 16, 1931, but the final resolution did not come until much later. On March 28 of the following year, Federal Judge Randolph Bryan ruled that McFaddin did in fact have legal title, and as such, exercised his inherent right to sell it. Yount-Lee's leases, therefore, were upheld to the relief of its board of directors—but the exuberance would not last for long.[5]

Production records dated September 7, 1929, revealed that Spindletop would soon relinquish its first-place standing on the Gulf Coast to Barbers Hill, although it still led its nearest rival 25,000 barrels a day to 23,250. A week later, Spindletop's figures diminished again, although slightly. Of the 24,977 barrels in daily volume, Yount-Lee produced 22,235; Gulf, 815; Sun, 508; Rio Bravo, 441; and the original section, 978. During that time, Yount-Lee maintained twenty rigs at Spindletop, five at Barbers Hill, two at Evangeline, and one at Johnson's Bayou. Barbers Hill finally moved into the top spot on November 27—and regretably, Spindletop never again regained the lead. Oil operators concentrated at the new field with twenty-six rigs all told, compared to just thirteen at the Beaumont location.[6]

On the national scene, disaster struck, and the focus turned away from discussing such topics as oil and the latest fashion in automobiles. On Monday, October 28 and the very next day, Black Monday and Black Tuesday, respectively, the American stock market suffered a one-two devastating knockout punch, as frantic investors unloaded shares of stock that numbered in the millions, sending the entire system into freefall. The Great Stock Market Crash of 1929 had actually begun the previous Thursday, but things would eventually worsen. In September and October, the market lost 40 percent of its value, and when November ended, investors suffered some $100 billion in losses. The spiral continued until it mercifully hit bottom in July 1932, but it would take another twenty-two years to fully recover.[7]

Businesses began to close, and by 1932 the nation's manufacturing output had fallen to less than half of that produced immediately before the crash; and in that same year of 1932, unemployment of 25 percent affected 13 to 15 million workers on whom another 30 million depended on for food. Jesse Jones, Houston financier and real-estate tycoon, later wrote:

> The national income had fallen from eighty billion dollars in 1929 to forty billion in 1932. That meant simply that the income of every individual in the United States, every farmer, businessman, industrialist, clerk, wage earner, or whatever, on the average had been cut in half. But many had no income at all because they had no work, and, in countless cases, family savings had been swept away in the collapse.

All over the country, banks that held stocks in their own investment portfolios strained under the same weight as individuals, who rushed to retrieve whatever funds were left to feed their families. Because many of these same banks did not have the necessary reserves to meet demands, they closed also, and by 1933 about 44 percent of the nation's total 25,000 financial institutions failed. In reality, the American public had lost all confidence in the economic system. For those fortunate enough to have money, most drastically reduced spending levels, and the law of supply and demand took over from there. Finally, President Franklin D. Roosevelt on March 4, 1933, declared a bank holiday, and the financial institutions were allowed to reopen only after Treasury personnel determined their soundness. This first step began the process of restoring trust, although it would take many years for it to reach the desired goal.[8]

Jesse H. Jones.
—Courtesy Tyrrell Historical Library, Beaumont, Texas.

But no description of crashing

stock prices, record-setting unemployment levels, and a collapsing monetary system can ever adequately describe the tragic misery suffered by a great many Americans. Hourly wages plummeted 60 percent, with white-collar jobs faring a little better at about 40 percent. And as if economic woes were not enough, American farmers in Kansas, Texas, Colorado, and Oklahoma contended with the unrelenting Dust Bowl that literally ruined about 100 million acres and damaged another 200 million. Suicides were commonplace with over 20,000 reported in 1931, alone. Hopelessness and hunger reached epidemic proportions. People by the throngs left their homes in the city, abandoned their farms in the rural areas, and hit the road to find work and food wherever that might lead. The nation as a whole blamed President Hoover for the debacle, and his name became synonymous with pain and suffering. With nowhere to go, displaced workers and their families set up makeshift villages and called them Hoovervilles, jackrabbits became Hoover hogs, and whether broken-down completely or simply out of fuel, automobiles pulled by horses or mules became known as Hoover wagons. Even though gas sold at an average of 18 to 19 cents a gallon, most could not afford it. For those who were forced to sleep on park benches, they covered themselves with newspapers referred to as Hoover blankets. The list goes on. The Roaring Twenties were over, and the Great Depression had set in for the long haul.[9]

While the economic death knell sounded for some, and brought others to their knees still clinging to life, Spindletop responded in tandem, in that 1929 was the last year it produced in excess of 10 million barrels of crude. Similarly, Yount-Lee's daily output at the field dropped to 30,100 barrels by January 13 of the next year (see Crude Production table on page 35 for peak years' production), and the company's ranking among Texas oil producers fell to third.[10]

"Okies" on Route 66 to California, circa 1935.
—Courtesy Franklin D. Roosevelt Library, National Archives and Records Administration, Washington, D.C.

Other matters, however, were far more serious than which field brought in the most oil. Both the glut and the quality of the oil itself became major concerns of Gulf Coast producers. The prolific discoveries in Oklahoma the previous year, along with those in Mexico, Venezuela, and West Texas, all added tremendous volume to an already flooded market. California, one of the world's greatest producers, now ranked second in the United States in 1929 with an output of 292 million barrels. Even so, Texas still held first place with 298.4 million, while Oklahoma placed third with 253.7 million. Overproduction too caused a price decline in the world oil market. Crude that had been selling for $1.21 to $1.25 per barrel now went for $.15 to $.41 less. Additionally, Gulf Coast operators had to deal with the perception of many refiners who considered this area's oil supply as inferior to the higher class product from West Texas and California. With over 14 million barrels of grade B crude laying in storage, an ultimate solution did not appear in sight. But at the least, the overproduction issue underscored the necessity for operator and driller alike to observe cost-conscious measures in daily operations. Each needed to develop more efficient programs, and only those who heeded this regimen would survive the crises.[11]

1930

An example of this new thinking and ingenuity occurred in early February, when Yount-Lee crews readied to move equipment into place at McFaddin No. 125's location at Spindletop. The field's condition, muddy from recent rains, would not permit the usual transportation by wagons, so Yount-Lee personnel converted an excavating machine to lift, carry, and place the boilers and drawworks into position. The entire procedure, which would have normally taken at least three days to complete in fair weather, took less than half a day under trying conditions.[12]

Elsewhere, Yount-Lee negotiated a large transaction on February 17 with Elizabeth Watkins of Lake Charles. The oil company purchased the Watkins Building in Lake Charles, along with 160,000 acres in fee for $1 million cash. The land, located in several parishes: Cameron, Jefferson, Davis, Rapides, Vernon, and Calcasieu, had never been tested adequately. Only one tract in the entire block produced oil, and it lay in Cameron Parish, where Shell Petroleum Corporation had but three previous discoveries.[13]

On February 20 Harry Phelan announced that the company had leased additional office space in the San Jacinto Building, and that Yount-Lee personnel would now occupy both the fourteenth and fifteenth floors. When asked to comment on the reasoning behind the move, he stated tongue-in-cheek, "It means simply that we hadn't enough office room to do business."[14]

Yount-Lee's production at Spindletop fell to new lows; even though, the McFaddin No. 125 produced on March 3 with a volume of 1,450 barrels per day. On May 20 the McFaddin No. 131 followed with a small daily output, and likewise, the No. 137 on July 28. In the meantime, the Beaumont independent continued to bring in wells at Barbers Hill. The Fisher No. 1, which had been originally capped at 6,630 feet with an output of about 600 barrels a day, created a sensation after several weeks, when for some unknown reason, its daily yield jumped to 7,600 barrels. The figures, however, dropped quickly, and by July 20 it pumped only 4,000 barrels. At first, the general consensus held that the well must have been supplied by two different sources, but since the crude's gravity weight never varied from 34.6, everyone finally agreed that the oil originated from the same strata. No one ever knew what caused the sudden surge.[15]

Proration became the topic of conversation among operators and within state agencies where the oil business played a part in their mission statements. Without question, the glut was real, and in order to keep prices from falling to the feared 1901 levels, something had to be done to curb the output. During the months that followed, the Texas Railroad Commission and its Operators Subcommittee, which held jurisdiction over the state's production, attempted to place a cap on the problem. The solution, however, proved to be most difficult. Although Yount-Lee and other similar independents objected strenuously to any form of restraint, they could afford to wait on prices to increase, because most owned their own storage facilities. Also, Yount-Lee developed markets for all the oil it could produce, and company officials felt it unreasonable to place them among other operators who required and sought out protection. As hoped, the Railroad Commission granted Gulf Coast producers a temporary reprieve in the early stages, in part due to their smaller capacity, when compared to other areas in Texas, Oklahoma, and California, and in part because of another distinctive situation. Experiments proved that if coastal wells were pinched down for long periods of time, their future worth would be jeopardized because of their salt water content. Nonetheless, proration remained a hot topic and one that all Texas operators, including Yount-Lee, would have to face in due course.[16]

The overproduction issue heated up again on October 3 with the news of Columbus Marion "Dad" Joiner's discovery well on the Daisy Bradford farm, six miles northwest of Rusk. This event opened up the East Texas field, the "Black Giant," which turned out to be of the largest ever to be discovered in the United States, outside Alaska, and it covered some 140,000 acres when in full production. Later when asked to comment on his chosen vocation, and how it eventually led to success, Joiner answered, "Wildcattin'? All it takes is guts and acreage. It seems to help some, too, if you're smart and lucky ..." On the economic front, the discovery could not have come at a worse time, given that it occurred while the Depression played havoc with most every domestic institution. The existing oil surplus swelled to outlandish proportions as new wells brought about tumbling prices. During the previous October, East Texas oil marketed for $1.10 per barrel; by December, the price had fallen to $.60; and within another six months, it slumped to the $.20 range. The Great Depression and proration had become unwelcomed partners that dealt untold misery among both large and small operators alike.[17]

The remainder of 1930 remained sluggish for Yount-Lee production. By the last day of the year, the company had only nine drilling rigs in operation: three at Spindletop; three at Barbers Hill; and one each at West Dayton, Lockport, and Hackberry. Spindletop's volume declined to 13,705 barrels a day from its 324 active wells, while Barbers Hill did somewhat better at 20,210 barrels from 151. For the total year, Spindletop produced a shade less than 6 million barrels; Barbers Hill about 8 million; and Hull a little over 3 million. As far as Yount-Lee was concerned, its officials seemed resigned to sit on the company's massive storage stockpile and wait until the market and oversupply situations eased.[18]

1931

The Texas Railroad Commission imposed another order effective January 23. Designed to limit the state's overall production, the new guidelines held the Gulf Coast to 155,000 barrels per day. Yet, at a time when proration affected the entire state, Yount-Lee looked to the future and became immediately interested in the new East Texas field. W. A. "Monty" Moncrief, John Farrell, and associates, along with the Arkansas Fuel Company, had leased about 5,000 acres near Longview in Gregg County for $1 an acre. They staked a location on the F. K. Lathrop tract and began drilling a well that attained a depth of approximately 3,500 feet by January 23. When the big well hit, it yielded over 18,000 barrels a day. However, Moncrief and Farrell, strapped by the lack of funds necessary to develop the remainder of their properties, put both the well and several leases on the auction block to raise much-needed capital. Harry Sinclair of the Sinclair Oil Company turned down their proposal of $1.75 million. Yount-Lee, however, liked the prospects and agreed to purchase a half interest in the Lathrop discovery well and about 2,400 acres under lease for about $3.5 million, divided into one cash payment of $1.5 million and the remainder in oil.[19]

Yount-Lee placed Tal Rothwell in charge of its Longview holdings, and by March 16 he began moving drilling equipment into the area under the direction of field supervisor T. W. "Red" Herrin. At the same time, Robert Penn, chairman of the Texas Central Proration Committee, who reported to the Texas Railroad Commission, warned that overproduction in East Texas would ultimately lead to 10 cents a barrel if he failed to impose stiffer levels of proration immediately. For a brief period, however, it appeared that the issue might resolve itself, when on March 26 the Lathrop operators who generated one-fifth of all new production, agreed to a self-imposed limit that allowed only 15,000 barrels each for the first thirty days with one exception: within ninety days, the maximum would be stretched to 25,000.[20]

Although Yount-Lee agreed to abide by this decision, Rothwell sought to acquire additional leases in the area. So, in April he struck a deal with Shell Petroleum that added another 600 acres to its Longview property holdings. This tract, checker boarded with the original 2,400 acres purchased earlier, cost the company another $250,000. When asked to comment on immediate plans, Frank Yount disclosed, "We won't do much drilling for a while. If production isn't cut, the way the oil business is going we'll be giving oil away before long. Producers can't make money out of it at 40 cents a barrel and it looks like it may go to 25 or 30 cents." By April 17 Yount-Lee had a total of six rigs and about one hundred men in East Texas, most of which had been moved from Spindletop, Barbers Hill, and South Dayton.[21]

Meanwhile, Marrs McLean had been active back at High Island. In September 1928 he brought in the Cade No. 12, and on November 12 of the following year, the Cade No. 16. Even with one well hitting after another, McLean tired of production matters and soon turned to a familiar face. As a result, he and Frank Yount discussed another lease buy-out, and in mid-April 1931 the two completed an agreement which involved approximately $2.6 million and 1,300 acres of land. McLean received "$200,000 in cash, $400,000 payable over a period of a year, $2,000,000 in oil, and a one-eighth overriding royalty." This time, unlike their earlier arrangement with the Spindletop leases, the two business associates did not include a single drilling restriction in the verbiage. McLean acknowledged this step as unnecessary when he said, "... the Yount-Lee company's record is such that it is regarded as being the outstanding development company in the country. There is no doubt that this company will do more drilling than it would ever contract to do."[22]

During the same period that Yount-Lee became heavily involved at High Island, another oil firm decided to get out altogether. Sun Oil sold most of its leases there to Marrs McLean in July 1927; now Gulf offered him the rest. The deal, involving 600 acres of which 300 were in fee and the remainder in leases, was concluded on April 17. McLean paid $450,000: $150,000 in cash and $300,000 out of oil proceeds. Gulf retained a 6½ percent royalty on the acreage that included seven wells that produced an average of about 400 barrels per day each. Immediately after the negotiations were completed, McLean, in turn, offered the entire package to Yount-Lee which agreed to the purchase price of $525,000: $225,000 in cash and the remaining $300,000 in oil to be delivered directly to Gulf. This transaction, finalized on April 22, netted McLean an immediate cash profit of $75,000, while he retained a 6 percent overriding royalty. Yount-Lee now controlled approximately 2,200 acres at High Island, where the only competition stemmed from Sun Oil which held only 100 acres under lease.[23]

The Beaumont firm had previously drilled at the High Island peninsula, but the early efforts of some six proved to be dusters. Too, the dome had been unkind to those who attempted to discover a solution to the heaving shale issue, the main obstacle to oil production there. Added to this, no fresh water or electricity could be had, but with collective genius provided by Earl Henry, the seasoned engineer, and a gutsy young geologist, Yount-Lee solved all three problems. First, Henry constructed an irrigation system and a pipeline that connected the Trinity River to High Island, and second, Gulf States Utilities announced on May 10 that it would run electric lines to the area at a cost to them of approximately $85,000. The heaving shale concern, however, posed a more difficult challenge for two reasons: this geological formation is extremely difficult to penetrate in the best of conditions, but when water comes into contact with it, the shale expands, fills the drilling hole, and freezes the bit into position. In the past, this latter effect caused most drillers to abandon their projects in total revulsion, but that was then, and this was now. Wherever he went and whatever project he backed, Frank Yount always seemed to be blessed with the Midas touch, so why would one expect High Island to be any different?[24]

During the 1931 spring commencement exercises at College Station, Michel Thomas Halbouty was graduated from Texas A&M University with Bachelor and Master of Science degrees in the fields of geology and petroleum engineering. He tried to find a job, but during the Depression, those were hard to come by. Finally, he landed a grunt's position with Yount-Lee which assigned him to High Island and there, Halbouty began his long, illustrious career as a "chain-puller" on a surveying crew, one of the lowest paid in the oil business. After weeks of sloshing around in the mud, fighting mosquitoes and high humidity, he began to form definite opinions about salt formations and where oil might be found. He watched closely as the crew foreman logged core samples or "cuttings," examined, and then tasted them as necessary.[25]

Up until Halbouty came along, Yount-Lee had no professional geologist on the payroll, depending instead on Frank Yount to fill that particular job description with his mystifying ability to lie on the ground, taste the soil, and determine whether or not he thought oil might be found at that exact spot. And now with the hiring of Halbouty, his main job had nothing to do with what he had been trained for. But the young man never gave up. He hung around the drilling rigs at night and became acquainted with Hannibal Westlake who suggested that he talk with Henry, the chief engineer for the company, on one of his infrequent visits to the field. Maybe, Westlake advised, Halbouty could gain access to the field logs. So that's what he did, and surprisingly, Henry, a "short, stocky, gray-haired man who chain-smoked Picayune cigarettes," let him take the material back to his boarding house, the Berwick Hotel in High Island, and study the contents. After several days Halbouty determined that the formations that produced oil at Spindletop and those he thought most promising at High Island were dissimilar, with the latter's not rising "sharply where he expected them ... because the salt shaft was not where he had expected it to be!" The next evening he dropped in on the crew working feverishly at Cade No. 21. He examined the latest core sample and noted that he looked squarely at a ten-foot core of nothing but pure salt. But before he turned away, he thought that he saw a trace of something else, maybe sediment. His interest piqued! At that very moment, the veteran toolpusher, the straw boss, and the next thing to God-Almighty on the derrick floor, Dad Kellam yelled, "All right, boys. That makes sixty feet of salt we've cored. Tear the damned rig down and let's move it to the next location." Halbouty asked, "Why?"[26]

Kellam had been with Frank Yount almost from the beginning; he was with him at McFaddin No. 2 on the night of November 14, 1925 when his crew brought in the great discovery that revived Spindletop as legend; and he had been a standout and considered one of the major reasons why Yount-Lee prospered so. Of all things, Kellam did not need any college educated, young whippersnapper who was still wet behind the ears telling him how to do his job. Why, he had forgotten more about oil (or so he thought), than Halbouty would ever learn in a lifetime. He turned to the novice and screamed above the deafening roar in the background, "I've got orders from Miles Frank Yount to drill into the salt until I can see that it's solid, then skid the rig. If you want to argue about it, argue with Mr. Yount." Halbouty reacted unexpectedly. He took a section from the bottom of the core, placed it into a discarded ice cream carton he found nearby, jumped in his old car, and started for Beaumont which lay about fifty miles away.[27]

Michel Thomas Halbouty.
—Courtesy Gittings Studio, Houston, Texas.

When Halbouty arrived at Yount's posh 1376 Calder estate long after dark, he had a difficult time gaining entry,

Street scene in front of El Ocaso showing trolley car.
—Courtesy Yount-Manion Film Collection, Lamar University, Beaumont, Texas.

and only after convincing security guards that he really was a company employee and not a crazy man, did they escort him into the house. Yount was throwing a party, and had no time to waste on a shabbily dressed chain puller from his High Island operation whom he had never met. Halbouty's persistence, however, paid off, because he convinced Frank to not only take a look at the sample but then had him agree to call the field office. Dad Kellam, he promised, would make another test tomorrow. When Halbouty returned to the site, Kellam met him with a predictable response. He snarled, "Welcome back, genius. You've cost the company a lot of time and money, and you've made Miles Yount act like a damned fool." The rest is history. Kellam did the core sample and found gray shale—and as Halbouty predicted, oil flowed. Thus began the long success story of the High Island field.[28]

But Cade No. 21 held one important advantage in that the bit never encountered the full weight of heaving shale. Others, however, had already, and that would continue not only at High Island, but at Barbers Hill and other fields in Louisiana. By now, Frank Yount had taken quite a liking to his new geologist, so he raised the young man's pay from $80 a month to an unheard of $150 and assigned him the responsibility of dealing with the overall shale problem. Halbouty responded vigorously. Working almost nonstop, he invented a formula, with the basic chemical ingredient hexametahphosphate, that proved over and again to be the long-sought-after answer. Finally, someone came up with a working mud that repelled water in the hole, and since water could no longer make contact with the shale, a well could be drilled at much deeper levels in order to locate new strata. Unfortunately, when Yount asked Halbouty about the possibility of obtaining a patent on his new product, the geologist resisted. Even when questioned repeatedly by company attorneys and counseled to reconsider, Halbouty argued against such a move. He wanted to continue as before. But others eventually stole the recipe, and soon a whole new industry developed around it. Manufacturers later sold fifty-gallon drums of drilling mud for $60, the same fifty-gallon drum that cost Yount-Lee thirty cents to make. To his credit, though, Halbouty agreed with an attorney's later statement, "You kissed off a fortune."[29]

With the heaving shale issue now in check, Yount set his sights on constructing a fifty-mile pipeline that would connect his storage facilities at High Island to those in Beaumont, so he turned again to Michel Halbouty, who admittedly knew nothing about such matters, to get things done. Harry K. Smith, the project inspector, remarked,

> It started raining the day we started the pipeline. It doesn't seem possible, but I don't believe it ever stopped raining. We built that pipeline under water. The rain brought out the snakes and it seemed as if someone was bitten every day. And we were using electric welding machines, and someone was always getting shocked. It was a mean job, from start to finish, and if Halbouty didn't know anything about pipelining before, he sure learned.

While the backbreaking project dragged on, Frank Yount recognized the burden placed on Nick Saigh, the San Antonio contractor, who agreed to take the job at a fixed price. Afterward when Frank found out that Saigh faced bankruptcy, because he overshot the bid by some several hundred thousand dollars, the oilman surprised him with two separate checks: one for the contract, and the other for the expenses incurred over that, and then some. As he handed the second check to the contractor, Frank said, "Nick, this ... covers the amount of money you overspent, plus a ten percent profit on the job."[30]

Yount-Lee, Gulf, Texas, Sun, Atlantic, and Pure Oil, the companies with the majority of the storage capacity on the Gulf Coast, began to take advantage of the East Texas production, which proved not only plentiful but cheap. Oil that sold for 7½ to 10¢ in East Texas commanded 80¢ at Beaumont; therefore, it made good economic sense to transport the crude and store it in local tanks. But how? In a classic move that stunned the competition, J. Edgar Pew, vice president of the Sun Pipe Line Company, announced plans on May 11, 1931, for the $2.5 million cooperative venture between his company and Yount-Lee, by which a 190 to 200-mile pipeline would be constructed. They purchased materials for the project from Jones and Laughlin of Pittsburgh and signed Schmidt Construction Company of Beaumont as the general contractor. When completed, the pipeline extended from Yount-Lee's loading docks on the Neches River and the Sun Docks at Smith's Bluff on the Neches ship channel to Sour Lake and then northward to Rusk and Gregg Counties. Feeder lines branched off to various parts of the East Texas field's productive areas, while two pumping stations, one in each of the East Texas counties, pushed crude at an estimated 30,000 barrels a day toward its final destination in Beaumont.[31]

As a result of this joint venture with Sun, corporate Yount-Lee formed the Yount-Lee Pipe Line Company to manage its part of the business. On June 24, 1931, the Texas Secretary of State issued Charter Number 59740 to the new enterprise, capitalized at $1 million with 10,000 shares, each having a par value of $100. The company's board of directors, which owned the entire stock portfolio, included Yount, Rothwell, and Phelan. Yount held 3,400 shares; Rothwell and Phelan each owned 3,300.[32]

Yount-Lee realized astounding success with its East Texas leases, and by December it capped a run of seventy-six producing wells without a single failure. This remarkable record of achievement seemed even more amazing when considering the fact that during this same span, about 250 men brought in a well every four or five days without one serious accident being reported. Proration, however, held down the production figures of these same wells. The seventy-six, if unleashed, could yield between 7,000 to 20,000 barrels a day per, but restrictions limited them to 100 each. Proration also hurt Yount-Lee deeply at High Island, where it kept twenty-five wells online These were able to produce a total of 25,000 barrels a day; however, state controls held them to a mere 6,800.[33]

Wanting to give their daughter the best of everything, Frank and Pansy saw to it that Mildred, from about the age of eight, received harp and violin lessons. They employed the best instructor that Beaumont had to offer, and Mrs. Lena Milam, who taught music at Beaumont High School, had guided Mildred's progress for about two years on American-made instruments. On one particular Friday night in 1930, Yount requested that Mrs. Milam come to his house and inspect three different violins sent the week before for his inspection, and from those, he would choose one for Mildred. Mrs. Milam's opinion, he explained, would go a long way in determining which one he bought. When Milam arrived, she expressed surprise at what she saw: a "Grancino, an Amati and a Guarnerius, all worth many thousands and all products of the age of the master violin makers, from 1695 to 1750." Afterward, she determined that the Grancino had the most beautiful tone, but Mildred, however, respectfully disagreed. It seemed that she personally favored the Guarnerius. Then ten-year-old Mildred excused herself, walked hurriedly from the room, and when she returned, she carried "the Grancino in a beautiful alligator leather case and a whipcord waterproof cover, trimmed with leather and equipped with triple locks." Smiling widely, "she presented the masterpiece to her astonished teacher as a token of regard." Some token of regard, because at the time, the Grancino fetched between $40,000 and $50,000 on the open market. Mildred chose to keep the Guarnerius, Frank returned the Amati, and everything ended on a happy note, maybe excepting the broker who wished to sell all three.[34]

Mildred Frank Yount.
—Courtesy Mildred Yount Manion.

From that point forward, Frank Yount maintained an acute interest in those particular instruments, not only from the analytical angle of how they were made by the masters, but his natural curiosity "prompted him to investigate the cause and reasoning which placed fine violins among the highly valued objects of art." But Yount never went into any field of endeavor without thoroughly researching it first, and he should never be considered as just another poor boy that struck at rich who blindly collected to present to others that he had finally attained a certain level of success required for entry into the social scene. Far removed from such notions, he sought out the advice of J. Moody Dawson of Houston, well known in the area for assisting others to secure rare violins and bows. With Dawson's guidance, Yount purchased for his daughter some of the most prized violins in the world, and by March 1931 newspaper sources reported that Mildred owned a million dollar collection, including: the Joseph Guarnerius, "Del Jesu," made in 1741; Antonio Stradivari, "Spanish," 1689; Stradivari, "Swan," 1737; Antonio Stradivari, "Wilhelmj," 1725; Joseph Guarnerius, "Del Jesu Chrysler," 1737; Antonio Stradivari, "Reynier," 1681; Antonio Stradivari, "Piatti," 1717; Dominicus Montagnana, 1735; J. B. Guadagnini, 1782; Andre Guarnerius, 1688; and Joseph Guarnerius/Felius Andre, 1715—some eleven in all. Put simply, Frank Yount wanted Mildred to become an artist, and he did not mind spending whatever money it took to supply her with the best tools of the trade. The newspaper article below painted the picture:

> The priceless fiddles, some of which have probably delighted kings and which have moved human feelings thruout [sic] hundreds of years, such as only a violin maker's masterpiece in the hands of a master player can, repose each in its beautiful case for her [Mildred] to play at will.[35]

Lena Milam.
Courtesy Tyrrell Historical Library, Beaumont, Texas.

Antonio Stradivari, "Piatti," 1717.
—Courtesy Cozio.com.

Yount Buys His Daughter Million Dollar Collection of World's Finest Violins

Mildred Yount, the 11-year-old daughter of Mr. and Mrs. M. F. Yount of Beaumont, Tex., and Manitou, has become the owner of the foremost collection of old violins in America. Her father has bought them for her, it is reported at a cost of at least $1,000,000. The little girl is herself studying the violin and has shown remarkable talent. In the collection are listed the following violins, given in the order of maker, name and date:

Joseph Guarneurius, "Del Jesu," 1741; Antonio Stradivari, "Spanish" 1689; Stradivari, "Swan," 1737; Stradivari, "Wilhelmj," 1725; Guarnerius, "Del Jesu Chrysler," 1737; Stradivari, "Reynier," 1681; Stradivari, "Piatti," 1717; Dominicus Montagnana, 1735; J. B. Guardagnini, 1782; Andre Guarnerius, 1688; and Joseph Guarnerius and Felius Andre, 1715.

On March 7 the Texas oil magnate and Mrs. Yount and their daughter, Mildred, presented Paul Kochanski, the famous virtuoso, in a recital at their Beaumont home and he played the numbers of the program, each on a different violin. It was violin history.

There are few great artists in the world who have as good violins, it is said, as any one of these famous violins that this 11-year-old girl owns. And they are not to her only a collection of relics. A student of the violin, their marvelous tones, which no modern hands, however cunning, can duplicate, are hers to command. The priceless fiddles, some of which have probably delighted kings and which have moved human feelings thruout hundreds of years, such as only a violin maker's masterpiece in the hands of a master player can, repose each in its beautiful case for her to play at will.

Mr. Yount is said to have a passion for music and it is reported to be Mrs. Yount's ambition to see their daughter become an artist. The child is well known in Manitou where the Yount family passes the summers at Rockledge and is a friend, as is her mother, of Mrs. D. Hampton, 1915 Wood avenue.

Two of Mildred Yount's little friends, Elizabeth and Virginia Mae Rothwell, also are known here. Mr. Rothwell is a business associate of Mr. Yount's and Elizabeth, like Mildred, is both a student of the violin and the possessor of famous violins. One she has is said to be a Guarnerius that was played by Leopold Auer, who recently died in Europe. He never himself hoped to own the superb instrument, but it was bought by another for him to use on one of his concert tours and after his death again went onto the market.

Mr. Rothwell purchased it for his daughter and it has been played at Mrs. Hampton's home and played and examined by local musicians. Just to touch this instrument has been held a privilege by violinists. It is not known what was paid for it, but probably the sum was not greatly below $80,000. The Rothwell girl has another famous violin reported to be of half the value of this one and a $10,000 instrument for everyday use. She is one of the high school stdents coming to Colorado Springs to play in the large high school orchestra that is to be a feature of the Southwestern Music Supervisors' conference at the municipal auditorium next Friday night. The two girls and their mother will be the guests of Mrs. Hampton this week. The other girl, who is younger, plays the harp. Both have shown rare talent and are said to practice assiduously, as does Mildred Yount. They have a wealth of violins probably never equaled by any child or adult violinist in the world, the nobility and royalty of Europe not excepted.

Mr. and Mrs. Yount's daughter is not to be here for this week's musical occasion, but the family is expected to pass the summer at their Manitou home, and Mrs. Yount writes Mrs. Hampton that she is counting the time until they can come.

It is estimated that 25,000,000 persons live in the 133,700 square miles of the Punjab region of India.

From Beaumont Journal, *circa 1931.*

—Courtesy Kathryn Manion Haider.

On Saturday, March 7 at 8 P.M., the Yount home played host to another recital by a world-famous musician, this time by violin virtuoso Paul Kochanski, who together with accompanist, Pierre Luboshutz, performed the entire program using Mildred's eleven different instruments. Kochanski, composer and arranger, was born on September 14, 1887, in Orel, Russia. He began studying the violin at the age of seven at Odessa, and in 1897 he immigrated to Warsaw, after which he held highly prized posts at the Warsaw Conservatory and the Imperial Conservatory at St. Petersburg. He taught at the Kiev Conservatory, and in 1921 he moved to the United States where he taught at the prestigious Juilliard School beginning in 1924.[36]

At the conclusion of the concert, Kochanski presented an autographed photograph to a thrilled Mildred; the inscription read: "To my dear friend Mildred Frank Yount with my best wishes." Why was this concert so significant, especially when such

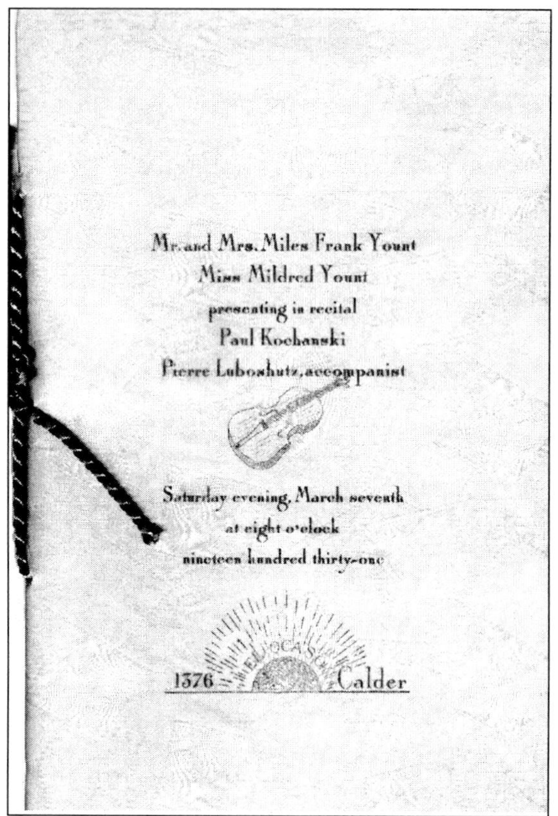

Mr. and Mrs. Miles Frank Yount
Miss Mildred Yount
presenting in recital
Paul Kochanski
Pierre Luboshutz, accompanist

Saturday evening, March seventh
at eight o'clock
nineteen hundred thirty-one

1376 Calder

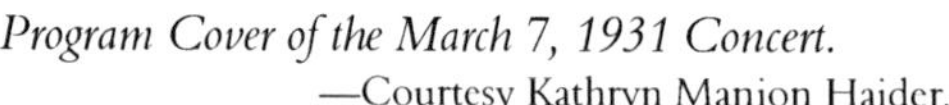

Program Cover of the March 7, 1931 Concert.
—Courtesy Kathryn Manion Haider.

Paul Kochanski, 1887–1934. Photograph by Underwood & Underwood, New York.
—Courtesy Mildred Yount Manion.

affairs were rather commonplace during the nineteenth century and well through the first part of the twentieth? Writing from Rapperswil, Switzerland, Philip Margolis of Cozio Publishing, one of the foremost and acknowledged experts of priceless violins in the world today, considers the Yount concert as "unparalleled," given that "it was certainly an uncommon event for so many rare instruments to be exhibited and played during a single performance."[37]

Ernest N. Doring of Chicago, author and expert in his own right, who had been in Beaumont to attend not only the Kochanski concert but another presented five days earlier at the city auditorium by Madame Schumann-Heinke and S. L. Rothafel, visited Yount on March 8. "I will long remember my introduction into his palatial home," Doring reported. "The cordial reception accorded me by his charming wife, who was a most gracious and genial hostess, and their daughter, will long remain a pleasant memory."[38]

But relative to Frank's expertise when discussing violins, however, Doring entered the interview with skepticism, but soon, he changed his mind. "I found him conversant with many of the fine points by which the work of the great masters is identified," he admitted. "His reading had been thorough, and he knew just what and where to look for the minute details. Although without prior experience in handling such fine specimens, ... his conversation on the subject was that of the experienced connoisseur."

When the two completed their meeting, Frank presented him an autographed photo that read, "To my friend Ernest N. Doring, 3/8/1931."[39]

But before he left, Doring, as with Ignace Paderewski before him, asked to see Spindletop up close and personal, so Frank proudly obliged. An impressed Chicagoan continued:

> Mr. Yount personally conducted a party, of which I was one, and words fail to express the amazing spectacle of the forest of miniature Eiffel Towers, the hundreds of pumps, the battalion of immense storage tanks, the miles of pipe-lines, conveying the oil directly into the holds of tank steamers lieing alongside private loading docks on the neighboring Bayou. Truly, an impressive and interesting experience, never to be forgotten.

Ernest N. Doring became a fan of Frank Yount's for life.[40]

1932–1933

Because of events that occurred at the Summer Olympics held in Los Angeles between July 30 and August 14, 1932, Beaumonters had another reason to feel proud. Mildred Ella "Babe" Didrikson Zaharias, a Port Arthur native who now lived in Beaumont, became one of the standouts when she captured gold medals in the javelin and eighty-meter hurdles competition, and a silver in the high jump. Even though she cleared the same height as the winner in the latter event, Babe received second place, because she used the unorthodox method of going over the bar head first. At the time, the rules committee considered this a foul.[41]

Ross Shaw Sterling.
Courtesy Texas State Library & Archives Commission, Austin, Texas.

On the oil front, however, the ability of the East Texas field to produce enormous volumes continued to create excruciating headaches for the Texas Railroad Commission. The field, almost from the point of discovery, suffered from proration as operators labored under constantly changing daily controls. On several occasions Ross Sterling, the Texas governor, ordered the field shut down completely to give the nation time to absorb some of the glut, but each time it reopened, though, he usually called upon national guardsmen to enforce martial law.[42]

Though often criticized for his high-handedness in dealing with the proration issue, Ross Sterling had been around the oil business most of his life, dating back to his 1903 opening of a feed store in Sour Lake during its great boom. Later, he drilled in the area and brought in two wells himself. From this modest first stage, the future governor teamed up with Harry C. Wiess, and together they co-founded Humble Oil and Refining Company, which eventually grew into Exxon. In 1930 he became chairman of the Texas Highway Commission, and in that capacity, he spearheaded the development of paved roadways throughout the state in the 1930s, along with implementing the all important 100-foot right-of-way necessary for future expansion. Additionally, these construction projects could not have come at a better time, because thousands of unemployed workers who suffered from hard times brought on by the Depression went back on the payroll.[43]

With its storage tanks filled to the limit, Yount-Lee could not help being concerned about the safety of its huge investment. The Beaumont tank farm spanned some 640 acres, and the presence of high grass and weeds created a fire hazard. In order to resolve the predicament, P. R. Mitchell, the tank farm superintendent, took it on himself to bring in some sheep, and in a relatively short period, the herd increased to about 1,301 head. During one of his inspection tours, a good-humored Yount reminded Mitchell that the corporate charter called for oil exploration, not the raising of sheep. Frank also noted that most of the ewes were expecting; in fact another 600 lambs would soon be added to the census rolls. Mitchell replied to his boss in a joking manner, "Well, in the first place, they're working for us, and in regard to the lambs, I can't help what they [the adults] do after ... hours." The industrious Mitchell also mentioned that over 4,700

Charles J. Chaison.
—Courtesy Tyrrell Historical Library, Beaumont, Texas.

William D. Gordon.
—Courtesy Tyrrell Historical Library, Beaumont, Texas.

pounds of wool had been sold at 9½ cents a pound and that sheep manure brought another $30 a ton in the marketplace. Each month, the unlikely venture provided between 15 to 30 tons of manure whose sale contributed to bottom line profits of the corporation.[44]

Litigation, which again involved the Federal Crude Oil Company, roared back at center stage, but this time with a new twist. When the U. S. Supreme Court ruled in Yount-Lee's favor on June 4, 1928, Federal Crude was a defunct corporation. The next day, Charles J. Chaison, the firm's former vice president, and others instigated a different approach to get their hands on approximately $15 million of Yount-Lee profits generated so far from lot 5 of the Douthit survey at Spindletop. This peculiar scheme involved buying the company's old stock, paying its delinquent franchise taxes, penalties and costs of $10,500, reviving the charter, and instructing their attorneys, headed up by William D. Gordon, to proceed with legal action. As expected, Yount-Lee filed an objection to the tactics and served notice that it would rigorously defend its position. Beeman Strong, the company's general counsel, determined right away that he needed help, since both he and first assistant, A. D. Moore, were busy with other legal matters. So Strong called for the services of experienced Will E. Orgain, who at the time represented the most sought after legal mind in the oil profession. After agreeing to come on board, Orgain beefed up his team by signing on R. L. Batts of Austin and F. A. Williams of Galveston, both former Texas Supreme Court justices. Not to be outdone, Gordon countered and brought to his side Nelson Phillips of Dallas, another former Texas Supreme Court judge, E. E. Easterling of Beaumont, and M. S. Duffie, also of Beaumont. After both groups concluded protracted arguments and legal posturing, the Texas Supreme Court ruled on June 20, 1932, that the suit should be tried, because Federal Crude, as an existing and legal corporation, should be entitled to its day in court.

A. D. Moore.
—Courtesy Tyrrell Historical Library, Beaumont, Texas.

Will E. Orgain.
—Courtesy Tyrrell Historical Library, Beaumont, Texas.

The case dragged on incessantly through various stages, until finally in June 1934 the Ninth Court of Civil Appeals in Beaumont ruled in favor of Yount-Lee. Federal Crude appealed again to the Texas Supreme Court. This time, however, in a turn about face, the judges refused to hear the case, claiming a lack of jurisdiction. Undeterred by his latest defeat, Gordon tenaciously pursued his clients' interests all the way to the United States Supreme Court.[45]

As 1933 drew to a close, Yount-Lee not only maintained its local market position, but also made every effort to become one of the industry giants and was well on its way to becoming a truly integrated oil company. Already, it weathered the worst of the Depression and decline in oil prices, and through it all, retained a virtual monopoly at Spindletop, such as it was. And it controlled High Island and owned other valuable holdings in East Texas, Barbers Hill, and various fields in Texas and Louisiana. Oil assets, such as one-half interest in the East Texas pipeline and a full interest in the one that connected High Island and the Beaumont tank farm, placed Yount-Lee in a most enviable position, but above all else, the Beaumont corporation had proved to most skeptics that it could compete toe to toe with the major producers in the Gulf Coast region.

Chapter Six

Godfather of Beaumont

"I am of the opinion that my life belongs to the community, and as long as I live it is my privilege to do for it whatever I can."

George Bernard Shaw

The Beaumont region had been extremely kind to Frank Yount, Tal Rothwell, Harry Phelan, and the rest of the Yount-Lee Oil Company officials and stockholders. Although the firm was worth over $2.5 million when it relocated there in 1923, Spindletop became the catalyst for a rapid increase in the company's assets, and by the end of 1926, Yount-Lee's value stood at approximately $9.5 million. As the company grew and flourished, it contributed to the overall economic progress of Beaumont and the surrounding communities along the Texas Gulf coast.[1]

The population of Beaumont proper varied greatly over the years. There were 3,296 inhabitants in 1890, but ten years later, the number increased almost threefold. The onslaught of 50,000 created by the great 1901 boom dissipated proportionately as Spindletop's production volume decreased, and the 1910 census reflected that the population settled at 20,640. As Beaumont's economy diversified, however, the next decade saw an almost 100 percent increase, and by 1920 the citizen count stood at 40,422.[2]

With Yount-Lee's discovery in November 1925 and the subsequent development of Second Spindletop, property values, as well as the tax rolls of both Jefferson County and the city of Beaumont, rose considerably. The entire area felt the boom's effect as hundreds of men went to work in the oil field. There had been approximately 150 men at work at Spindletop in June 1926, but within a three-week period, the number increased by 700. At that time, Spindletop's weekly payroll amounted to over $35,000. The Yount-Lee employee base grew also, from 20 employees the previous year to 500 by November 24, 1926, and the company's daily payroll closed in on $2,500. The total number employed by petroleum-related industries expanded by 20 percent that same year, and merchants as a whole prospered as oil provided the impetus for more jobs and greater income.[3]

Frank Yount, "Godfather of Beaumont."
—Courtesy Yount-Manion Film Collection, Lamar University, Beaumont, Texas.

Compared with the earlier boom, Second Spindletop was more orderly and businesslike, and there were certainly no "gushers," unless one of the wells accidentally blew up as had McFaddin No. 29. Things had sure changed. There were no excursion trains that brought hoards of "get rich quick" seekers, and there were none of the rowdy, rough, and tumble dealings associated with the 1901 event. Without knowing it, Marrs McLean was most responsible for this new order. When he offered his extensive lease holdings at Spindletop to Frank Yount, the Beaumont independent held a virtual monopoly on the choice property; there was simply no basis for widespread speculation. In addition, the oil industry had grown into big business, and Beaumont itself had matured. Local surveys, which were conducted at the beginning of 1926, placed the city's population at 54,469, and within a year another estimate put it at 57,963. With the growth, came the realization of a new phenomenon. Population was not only increasing, it included a new type of citizenry. A solid, more dependable working class, the kind that futures are built upon, moved into the area, as opposed to the undesirable transients of yesteryear.[4]

The Beaumont Real Estate Board sought to recognize Marrs McLean, Frank Yount, Tal Rothwell, Harry Phelan, Beeman Strong, Johnny Hatcher, and "Dad" Kellam for their positive economic impact on the city. When he announced plans for an appreciation banquet, John O. Banks, the board president, said, "The citizens of Beaumont appreciate the enthusiasm and commercial expansion that has resulted from the revival of old Spindle Top and desire to honor the men who are largely responsible for it." The program cover continued:

> The achievements of Mr. Marrs McLean and The Yount-Lee Oil Company have resulted in a wonderful prosperity to Beaumont and community. For twenty-five years, it has been the fondest hopes of our entire citizenship that some one be found who would risk fortune and reputation in developing a new strata of oil which all felt existed at old Spindle Top. Mr. Marrs McLean and The officials of the Yount-Lee Oil Company fullfilled this long felt want, and the Beaumont Real Estate Board is proud to sponsor a banquet in their honor to show some slight mark of appreciation on the part of the community.[5]

Hotel Beaumont.

—Courtesy JoAnn McKinley.

The dinner, originally set for November 30, 1926, at Hotel Beaumont never happened on that date due to a scheduling conflict that caused its postponement until December 7. With over 2,000 invitations mailed, the respondents filled the hotel's dining room and stretched its capacity to the limit, as Beaumont officials, dignitaries, and top businessmen paid $2.50 (about $26.71 in today's currency) a plate and were treated with shrimp cocktail; hearts of celery; olives; radishes; cream of tomatoes, *au croutons*; half of a milk fed chicken, grilled, *au buerre noir*; *chateau* potatoes; sifted sweet peas, *en caisse*, *au buerre*; frozen fruit salad, whipped cream, *en forme*; topped off with Neapolitan ice cream with assorted cakes; and of course, coffee. Magnolia Petroleum Company's radio station KFDM was there to broadcast the event live. J. S. Edwards served as toastmaster; Reverend T. M. Hunter gave the invocation; Steve M. King delivered a toast to the officials of the Yount-Lee Oil Company to which Beeman Strong responded; Stuart R. Smith gave the toast to Marrs McLean to which W. D. Gordon responded; and Ben Sykes Woodhead toasted the ladies of the honorees. Mrs. Harvey W. Gilbert sang a solo, and she was accompanied by Mrs. Frank T. Higgins on piano and R. A. Dhossche on flute. Mrs. Jack G. Holtzclaw concluded the evening's festivities with forecasts and the reading of a story titled, "The Famous Spindle Top Oil Field," by Marvin L. Brown that heralded the economic success stories that McLean and Yount-Lee had already brought to the community. This appreciation dinner, however, represented only the beginning of a great many to follow. Throughout the years, many individuals associated with the company received various other awards for their business and civic contributions, and eventually Frank Yount captured the highest title that an admiring public could bestow, when he became known as the "Godfather of Beaumont."[6]

BANQUET

GIVEN BY

APPRECIATIVE CITIZENS OF BEAUMONT, TEXAS,

TO

OFFICIALS OF THE YOUNT-LEE

OIL COMPANY

AND

MR. MARRS McLEAN

HOTEL BEAUMONT

EVENING OF DECEMBER SEVENTH

NINETEEN TWENTY-SIX

SEVEN-THIRTY P. M.

SPONSORED BY THE BEAUMONT REAL ESTATE BOARD

THE Achievements of Mr. Marrs McLean and The Yount-Lee Oil Company, have resulted in a wonderful prosperity to Beaumont and community. For twenty-five years, it has been the fondest hopes of our entire citizenship that some one be found who would risk fortune and reputation in developing a new strata of oil which all felt existed at old Spindle Top. Mr. Marrs McLean and The officials of the Yount-Lee Oil Company, fullfilled this long felt want, and the Beaumont Real Estate Board is proud to sponsor a banquet in their honor to show some slight mark of appreciation on the part of the community.

Program Cover.

—Courtesy Tyrrell Historical Library, Beaumont, Texas.

As a result of Second Spindletop, Beaumont's banking—the five local banks reported a \$4.5 million increase in 1927 deposits over those of the previous year—and building activities soared between 1926 and 1936. \$2.5 million in construction permits set a record in 1926, and the figure for 1927 doubled that. Announcements were made concerning large-scale projects, such as the Jefferson Theater, the Goodhue Building, the American National Bank Building, the new city hall and auditorium, the Jefferson County Courthouse, the St. Therese Hospital, the Edson Hotel, the La Salle Hotel, the Y.M.C.A. (Young Men's Christian Association) building, a combination post office and federal building, and a new Beaumont High School building, along with numerous improvements at other schools. Churches and apartment houses sprang up all over town, and at least 2,500 residences were completed during those ten years. The city also built a new central fire station, a new jail, a police station, and spent thousands on street and park improvements. Jack Hott, the general secretary for the Beaumont Chamber of Commerce, revealed in January 1928 that the previous year's building activity had been the largest in the city's history. Approximately \$20 million in new construction was in progress, and all facets of commercial, industrial, and residential development were affected. The building boom continued into 1929 when at least eighteen apartment projects and sixteen commercial buildings were begun. When the Depression hit, however, even the strong oil economy failed to sustain the fantastic growth that Beaumont had enjoyed. Even so, new construction kept pace with the population of 57,732 by producing approximately \$1 million in permits during 1931, but by the end of 1933, that figure fell to \$725,000.[7]

"Evidence of the New Prosperity"

Beaumont skyline, circa 1932. From City of Beaumont letterhead.
—Courtesy Kathryn Manion Haider.

Goodhue Building.
—Courtesy Howard Perkins Collection, Beaumont, Texas.

American National Bank.
—Courtesy Howard Perkins Collection, Beaumont, Texas.

Edson Hotel.
—Courtesy Howard Perkins Collection, Beaumont, Texas.

New City Hall and Auditorium.
—Courtesy Howard Perkins Collection, Beaumont, Texas.

Jefferson County Courthouse.
—Courtesy Howard Perkins Collection, Beaumont, Texas.

Post Office and Federal Building.
—Courtesy JoAnn McKinley.

La Salle Hotel.
—Courtesy Howard Perkins Collection, Beaumont, Texas.

Beaumont High School Building.
—Courtesy Howard Perkins Collection, Beaumont, Texas.

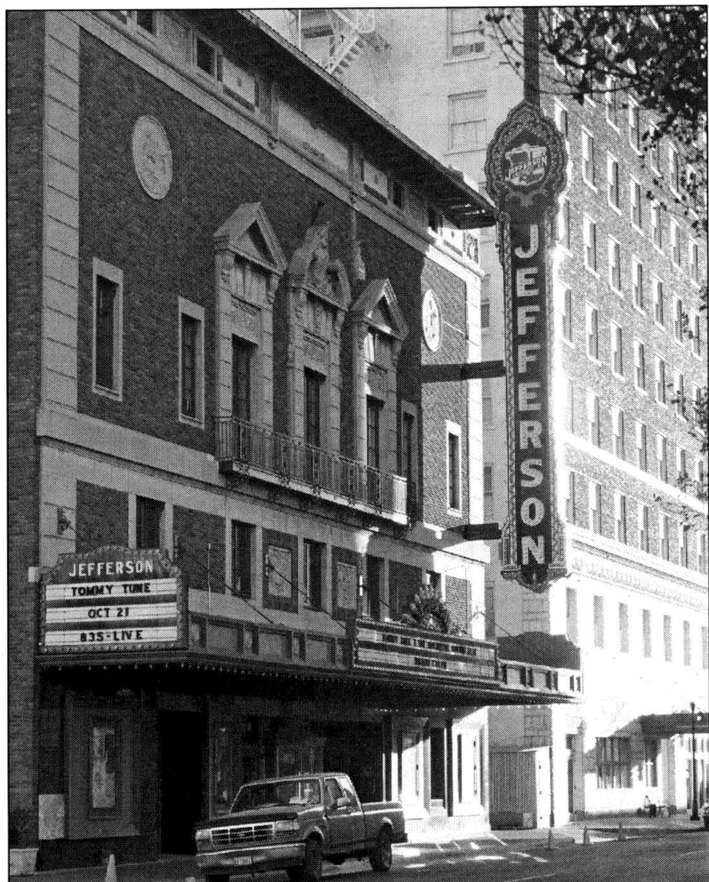

Jefferson Theater.
—Courtesy Howard Perkins Collection, Beaumont, Texas.

The Municipal Plunge (Magnolia Park Swimming Pool).
—Courtesy Howard Perkins Collection, Beaumont, Texas.

Y.M.C.A. Building.
—Courtesy Howard Perkins Collection, Beaumont, Texas.

Other cities, however, besides Beaumont honored Yount-Lee for its achievements. Galveston County had also been the recipient of strengthened tax rolls as the company successfully developed the High Island oil field, and the Galveston County Chamber of Commerce contemplated an appreciation banquet of its own. A. L. Burge, chamber representative, secured Frank Yount's approval for a recognition dinner, scheduled for May 13, 1932, at Galveston's Buccaneer Hotel. Yount, Phelan, Rothwell, Earl Henry, Marvin McClendon, Lester Burleigh and C. E. Cooper of the accounting department, and E. L. Sandel and W. C. Patton of the land department, all attended. During the function several speakers came forward and declared that the county would continue lending strong support to the Beaumont firm, and one in particular, perhaps carried away by the moment, even recommended that High Island's name be changed to Yount-Lee, Texas. By the next day, though, the proposal had been completely forgotten.[8]

Most assuredly, Yount-Lee assisted Beaumont and the surrounding vicinity indirectly by the development of major oil fields. But there were other instances, however, when both the company and its officers gave direct aid to several worthwhile causes and charities. Unfortunately, many of these deeds were never made public, but the few that were, gave valuable insight into the organization's moral character. In 1928 Beaumont Masons initiated a fund raising drive for the purpose of building a new temple at a projected cost of $350,000. When the project's contributions came up short and seemed in jeopardy, the Yount-Lee Oil Company gave $25,000 to the effort on June 20, even though Frank Yount was never a member of that particular fraternity. Similarly, the Y.M.C.A.'s efforts to raise money for the construction of its new building hit a snag, in that all contributions thus far "were made on the condition that a minimum of $300,000 was subscribed." Dr. Hastings Harrison, who served as General Secretary on the Y's board at the time, wrote later: "Mr. Yount's additional $10,000 gift to the liberal subscription that he had already made enabled us to reach the $300,000 minimum objective and caused all subscriptions that had been made to become effective." And too, several gifts were made to the Beaumont Community Chest. In November 1931 Yount-Lee and its three principal officers, Frank Yount, Tal Rothwell, and Harry Phelan, helped this organization by contributing $10,000, $4,000, $1,500, and $2,000, respectively, a total of $17,500.[9]

Without question, though, the most celebrated demonstration of Yount-Lee community involvement occurred when the city of Beaumont, hard-hit by the Depression

Emmett A. Fletcher.
—Courtesy Tyrrell Historical Library, Beaumont, Texas.

and loss of tax revenues, could not meet its payroll on approximately two hundred employees of the General Department, consisting of city officials, clerks, policemen, and firemen, who had already taken a 30 percent salary cut over the past several months. And even when they were paid, the checks came on an irregular basis, because the city attempted to maintain a repayment schedule at the local banks on previously borrowed funds. Beaumont mayor, Emmett A. Fletcher, tried to scrounge more capital, as was the usual practice, but this time, bank managers advised him that the city had lost its credit worthiness, due to over $900,000 in delinquent taxes that had accumulated over a fifteen-year period. Fletcher had been mayor from 1906 to 1918, and in 1930 city leaders drafted him out of retirement, so to speak, to lead them through troubled economic times. But even the experienced professional could not sway the bankers, who told him flatly that the national crisis made it impossible for anyone to forecast the percentage of current revenue collections that would be available for repayment of outstanding loans. They encouraged—actually patronized is a better description—Fletcher and Paul H. Millard, Beaumont city manager, to go after the required funds from the delinquent tax base instead of trying to borrow more money from them. Faced with a no-win situation in his view, a desperate Fletcher went to see Frank Yount. After hearing the mayor's case on August 6, 1932, the oilman agreed for his company to loan the city $60,000. The simple arrangement called for settlement when the city received tax revenues for the current year; Yount-Lee would earn 6 percent interest, the same as the banks' lending rate; and the city would furnish deficiency warrants as the only collateral. On August 9 the Beaumont City Commission, represented by Mayor Fletcher and Commissioners Sam Z. Powell and George A. Wells, passed the ordinance required for the issuance of the warrants. That same day, the City Council voiced its approval and finalized the Yount-Lee loan.[10]

These proceeds, however, did not last long. When the city issued paychecks for distribution on October 13, 1932, the fund was depleted once more; and from November 14 to December 15 the General Department employees went without pay entirely. On December 21 Frank Yount heard about the situation and became saddened by the news. So he made an unsolicited call to city officials and inquired about how much money they needed to pay the workers for another full month. The figure came in at $22,000.

Yount had a check drawn in that amount, and he personally delivered it to Fletcher and Millard. They struck the same type agreement as before, relative to restitution, interest earned, and deficiency warrants; but this time, Yount added a personal stipulation—the paychecks had to be dispersed before Christmas. When the City Commission met in special session on December 21, as did the City Council, both approved the issuing of $22,000 in deficiency warrants, the city obtained the supplemental loan, and its employees received their pay the very next day—and before December 25, just as Yount directed. Fire Chief Steve D. O'Conor, in a letter to Frank dated December 22, summed up the feelings of his grateful employees:

Paul Millard.
—Courtesy Tyrrell Historical Library, Beaumont, Texas.

> I wish to express to you by letter the sincere thanks of this department and myself for your kindness and thoughtful action which today has made these men exceedingly happy.
>
> It was indeed going to be a very sad Christmas for them until you came to our rescue and I want you to know that we do appreciate what you have done for us. While we may not be able to show this in a material way, we want you to feel that you have their sincere friendship and respect, and should we be able to reciprocate in any way we certainly hope and trust that you may call upon us first.

Beaumont was now indebted to Yount-Lee in the amount of $82,000 plus 6 percent interest. When the city received tax revenues of an estimated $250,000 during a two-day period of January 30–31, it repaid to Yount-Lee the full amount, which included $1,508.16 in interest, on February 1, 1933, the day after Frank Yount turned fifty-three. The extra windfall also allowed the city to wipe out its outstanding obligations to area banks, but officials sadly admitted that "they could not estimate when the next pay day for city employes would be set, all depending on whether or not the banks will lend the municipality operating funds, and the amount of the loan."[11]

But this had not been the first time that the city turned to Frank Yount for help. On May 4, 1929, local voters passed a bond issue for over $5 million that included $100,000 "for the purpose of acquiring a site for an airport for … Beaumont and providing the necessary improvements and equipment therefor." Early on, though, the city experi-

Beaumont Central Fire Station, Built in 1927.[12]
—Courtesy Howard Perkins Collection, Beaumont, Texas.

enced problems with the offering, and by the middle of June that same year, the future of the project appeared gloomy. Investors were just not buying the bonds. At that point, W. M. Crook, president of the Beaumont Aero Club, approached Frank Yount and persuaded him to advance $31,675 from Yount-Lee funds and take a note as collateral at 6 percent interest. This would at least allow the city to close the deal on the airport site. Mayor Gross gladly accepted the gesture and agreed to discuss the matter with the entire council. On June 27 the motion passed, which authorized the city manager

> ... to complete negotiations and purchase of 275.44 acres of land from the Ziegler Estate at $115.00 an acre, totaling $31,675.00 ..., same being located in the A. Savery League and bound on the East by the Neches Fresh Water Canal, on the West by Willow Marsh Drainage Ditch, on the South by the Texas and New Orleans Rail Road, and on the North by the Missouri Pacific Rail Road.

The lender received the first payment of $950.27, representing six months of accumulated interest, on December 31, 1929, and the remainder at a later date.[13]

Yount-Lee also exhibited other acts of generosity. The company donated $1,000 on May 7, 1934, to an interdenominational church building in High Island. Also, most oil firms had long since tired of the bookkeeping nightmare created by the distribution of royalty checks on fractionally owned oil-producing properties. Some of these checks were in the 30 to 40 cent range; however, laws dictated that each had to be processed monthly. Therefore, many companies, in order to reduce accounting costs, discontinued altogether the practice of purchasing small royalty leases and fee tracts. Frank Yount disclosed on May 10, 1927, that his organization would proceed as before; subsequently, all parties, regardless of their holding's size, retained the ability to participate and cash in on oil profits. In fact, A. D. Moore, one of Yount-Lee's lawyers, once recounted about how Frank insisted "that royalty to East Texas landowners be paid on a basis of 25 cents a barrel minimum even when that same oil was bringing 5 and 10 cents a barrel. He was a master in the field of human relations because his heart was as great as his mind."[14]

During a particular trial, Frank Yount's kindheartedness almost cost him, and the company, dearly. In another case over questioned ownership of productive Spindletop acreage, this one styled *Ivy Wilkinson Counce et al. v. Yount-Lee Oil Company*, Frank almost lost when he insisted on paying his witnesses over and beyond the $12.50 daily jury fee. Since these men were taking time off work—most without pay—Yount could not bear the thought. So to make up for their trouble and inconvenience, he gave them an additional $250 to $1,000 each, depending on where they lived, and how long they had to stay in town for the trial. Beaumont attorney Oliver J. Todd, who represented the plaintiffs during the final appeal, brought up the issue of Yount's payments to his own witnesses and labeled the practice, however well-intentioned, as a form of intimidation. Their testimony, he argued, should be disqualified. Although Todd's motion ultimately failed, Frank's actions could have cost Yount-Lee $20 million, the amount of damages requested by the litigants in the original motion.[15]

In another instance, Yount displayed his determination to protect the environment from the plunder of his own oil rigs. Michel Halbouty, the company geologist, had picked out a spot on which to drill at High Island when Yount took him to task. "We don't want to drill here son. We would damage those trees." He pointing to a stand of oaks and continued, "There are not many trees on this peninsula, anyway, and we ought to save all we can." Later, another conversation between the same two centered on the East Texas field. In a prophetic tone, Frank said, "Someday we'll regret every drop [of oil] we waste. See to our interests, see that we do well, but remember that the earth is our home and don't do a thing to desecrate it."[16]

High Island also benefited greatly by Yount-Lee's point of view on conservation. During operations there, crews discovered an inordinate amount of natural gas, enough in fact, to operate drilling rigs, separation units, and the pipeline pump station that pushed oil from storage tanks all the way to Beaumont. Company employees also used some of the excess for cooking purposes and to heat their homes, but even after that, much remained. At that particular time, some operators considered natural gas a byproduct nuisance, and dealt with it by simply burning it. To Yount-Lee, however, this seemed a complete waste of resources, so it gave free, whatever it could not recycle, to the citizens of High Island. In order to get the supplies, though, recipients had to provide the necessary connections to their homes. More than half took advantage of the program.[17]

Yount-Lee and its officials not only helped the general public, they adopted the same type mind-set toward their own employees and all those around them. But as a manager of the old school and in accordance with the tradition of that day and age, Frank Yount believed that a woman's place lay in the home with her children, not in some office environment, where she could be a distraction. Harry Phelan, spurred on by his wife Johannah's staunch position on the issue, also agreed. Yount-Lee, for that reason, remained basically an all-male enterprise, and it was not until August 1926 that the company hired its first female employee, Belle Marks, who operated the switchboard located on the fifteenth floor of the San Jacinto Building. Four years later, Marjorie Gibson came to the firm from Norvell-Wilder, a company in which Frank Yount owned considerable stock. Miss Gibson, not only the second but the last woman to be employed by Yount-Lee, functioned as a receptionist, typist, and also stenographer at her station on the fourteenth floor. Yet regardless of Yount's personal ideas relative to female service, he and the company took care of their people, especially during the Christmas season. In 1926 Yount-Lee dispersed $20,000 among the workers; the single requirement for participation: one had to have at least thirty days' service. In addition, field personnel received a pair of eighteen-inch Witch Elk brand work boots which would have cost them about $18 at the dry goods store. Yount wanted these particular situations to have special significance, so he made it clear that they should be considered as Christmas presents, not bonuses. That same year, Yount-Lee purchased coal in half ton quantities and gave it to several needy Beaumont families. Approximately 900 Yount-Lee employees shared $60,000 in Christmas bonuses given away in 1928, the maximum award $100 and the smallest $5. Also each married man received a box of groceries, and over 600 individuals fit within that category. That particular year, over 700 employees reciprocated, pitched in, and collected money that went toward a Christmas fund earmarked for Yount, Rothwell, and Phelan. The company distributed some $90,000 among 915 workers during the 1929 Christmas season; and in 1934, even with the Depression in full swing, about 1,135 employees received a total of $79,000. Over time, Frank Yount earned quite a reputation not only with his employees but others, as he gave away cigars, candy, and various presents to elevator operators, shoeshine boys, newsboys, and sometimes perfect strangers, along with workers of various companies that conducted business with his company. On another occasion, he sent three barrels of Texas pecans to be shared by all the children of Manitou Springs, Colorado, at Yule time.[18]

Frank also took care of his mother in Monticello, Arkansas, and his family in Sour Lake. Not only had he earlier given Sunnyside to his sister, Ida Belle, and her husband, Walter Parrish, who served as the Sour Lake Yount-Lee superintendent for years, there were other occasions when he gave them cars for Christmas. Another sister, Harriet "Hettie" Ann, and her husband Frank Hazard, received the same type gifts, but on a somewhat lower scale. Hazard, as a Yount-Lee employee in Sour Lake, had once participated in a strike against his brother-in-law bosses Walter, and the main man, Frank Yount, who kept him on the payroll regardless. Although Yount continued to give Hettie and her husband new cars also, "they weren't as nice as Ida Belle and Walter's." Marguerite Behar, Frank's niece who still resides in Sour Lake, recalls that when she was a child, her uncle came up and brought her back to Beaumont to spend time with Mildred during the summers. Reminiscing about these instances, Marguerite said, "Uncle Frank would drive us to Sunday School at Westminster Presbyterian, and a lot of times, he'd join us on the sleeping porch at night when it got too hot to stay in the house. There were three small beds out there." She continued, "Mildred slept in one, me in another, and Uncle Frank in the last. He was a very kind and generous man." Marguerite admitted that while she was growing up during the Depression, she had no idea of its crippling effect. "My dad made $500 per month in his position," she said, "and that was good money for the time." During Frank's last visit with his mother at Ida Belle's home in 1933, the oilman asked Hattie why she had failed to cash the checks that he had sent as Christmas presents. She muttered some unsatisfactory excuse, at which point, Frank had her search inside her purse, retrieve the checks, and return them. Frank mentioned that he would have to void these particular ones, because they were outdated. "I'll have new ones issued," he promised, "and send them to you."[19]

When the two Beaumont newspapers began printing stories about Mildred's lavish parties thrown on birthdays and other special occasions, Frank and Pansy felt guilty that many area children did not have similar opportunities. So they remedied the situation by giving numerous parties at local parks where all of the kids in the neighborhood were invited to attend and enjoy the same type of refreshments, ice cream, and cake that Mildred had at her recent get-togethers.[20]

Frank Yount.
—Courtesy of Kathryn Manion Haider.

Bruce Yount explained another charitable act by his great-uncle. During the fall of 1917, Bruce's grandparents, Joseph Reul and Lula Belle Yount, were killed in an automobile-train collision at a grade crossing near China, Texas, ten miles west of Beaumont on U. S. Highway 90. Their son, Harrell, a passenger in the car, survived but received serious burns that required hospitalization for about six months. Bruce said that Frank paid his dad's bills, took over as guardian, and watched after him until he reached adulthood.[21]

There were examples, still, when Frank Yount's kindness gained the attention of some who sought to prey on his good nature. Ben Woodhead commented on just one such occasion:

> As Frank Yount's fortunes rose, ... he could not escape a certain amount of notoriety. By nature he was a very self-effacing man. He lived across the street from us ... One Christmas morning Dad prevailed on him to come over for eggnog. His conversation, though guarded, was intriguing. He confided that he was continually beset on all sides by requests for financial help to this charity and that. Not only organizations but individuals too, ... Two days before, he recalled, he had received a letter from some man in North Carolina whose wooden leg had been hopelessly splintered in an accident. Mr. Yount had never heard of this character, but anyhow the latter thought it would be real nice if the oil tycoon shipped him a new leg. This sort of thing seemed to be commonplace.

As Frank talked to one reporter about the hundreds of letters received each week from various parties wanting help in one way or the other, he stated, "It makes it hard for me to hear, as I know some of these cases are really deserving, but most are frauds and are nearly always evident by the time the missive [letter] is concluded."[22]

Like Yount, the rest of the company's officers and supervisors also possessed and then exhibited a special feeling for their employees, not just because each contributed to the efficiently run organization, but because they were mostly family men. One report revealed that Yount-Lee built a house on two lots for Max Schlicher, when in June 1927, the company assigned him to supervise the company's activities at Welsh, Louisiana. Throughout the Great Depression, while scores of unemployed looked for work of any kind, Yount-Lee never reduced its work force, even while grappling with the proration issue. Although experiencing some cuts in the number of working hours, men could say one thing at least: they had a job. Because of Yount-Lee loyalty to its employees, most returned the same and refused for the longest time to become entranced by the siren song of labor unions. And similar to their superiors, many participated and donated to worthy organizations such as the Community Chest.[23]

In May 1934 roughly 1,000 employees received another company benefit, when Tal Rothwell announced that the company granted a 9 percent pay increase to every member of the production unit. Although the new pay scale, set at 83 cents per hour, did not include the office staff, Rothwell pointed out that their pay was comparable to those in like positions at other oil companies.[24]

For several years, widespread speculation held that Yount-Lee might build a petroleum building in downtown Beaumont, especially when the public learned that the company purchased large parcels of real estate there. While the Depression changed those plans, another project, unveiled on April 24, 1929, came much closer to reality. T. P. Lee, Tal Rothwell, and E. A. Hester, real-estate manager of the Guaranty Trust Company of Houston, a Cullinan and Lee interest, divulged plans for the construction of a combination theater and fifteen-story medical arts building. By the time the group appeared at a press conference, contracts were already in hand, signed by several physicians who planned to occupy the offices within the new structure. As announced, the facility would be located, most probably on Yount-Lee property, outside the downtown vicinity. Unfortunately, this undertaking suffered the same fate as the earlier proposed petroleum building, not only because of the Depression, but due to certain critical events that occurred within the Yount-Lee organization itself.[25]

The Financial Gibraltar

"It is a mistake to try to look too far ahead. The chain of destiny can only be grasped one link at a time."

SIR WINSTON CHURCHILL

Frank Yount celebrated his fifty-third birthday on January 31, 1933. During that time, he had risen from humble beginnings to president and major stockholder of a multimillion dollar oil empire and now approached the zenith of his career. It is ironic, however, that this same man, who possessed an almost timid personality, could not sell Cartercars, Moon automobiles, much less real estate during the years 1912–1914, and it is no small wonder that he progressed at all. Yet, he now headed up a company that provided a large portion of the crude necessary to fuel America's ever-expanding economic might and seemingly limitless love affair with the automobile; and in the long run, amass, both personally and through his company, one of the largest property holdings in the entire South.

Due to the corporation's privately-owned status, Yount-Lee's exact worth was then, as now, a complete mystery, although Yount reportedly once said that he wouldn't take a $100 million for it. But regardless of speculated value, Frank openly admitted that he would not sell at any price. "I have been trying to get into the oil business for 20 years," he said, "and I am not going to give up a start like this." The select few in the know held all financial details close to the vest, and they rarely publicly commented on anything and that only after the president issued his personal stamp of approval. Likewise, Yount attempted with some degree of success, to maintain a confidential private life, but Beaumont, the city that profited most by his good fortune, considered everything he did as newsworthy and portrayed him as larger than life. For his fifty-third birthday, Pansy threw a stag party and invited all of husband's close friends and, as usual, some of his business associates. Mayor Fletcher attended, along with R. W. Pack of the Sun Oil Company who presented the celebrant with "an old pipe with a line run through it with Beaumont on one end and Longview on the other," symbolizing the joint venture of Yount-Lee and Sun Oil's East Texas pipeline project. Other gifts included a miniature oil storage tank affixed with the number 1880, indicating the year of Yount's birth. Actress Norma Schearer sent a photograph with the inscription, "I have not forgotten you," while Greta Garbo mailed a toy spinning top with a note that said, "I am tired of Hollywood—I want to sit with you on Spindletop!" Of all the presents, whether serious or gag related, Frank's personal attorney, R. E. Masterson, presented him with the most historically important: a copy of a whimsical manuscript titled "The Low Down on a High Up Man," which fortunately survives to this day. Of all that is written, it is the only known document in existence that details so much about the private side of the enigmatic oilman. The text contains photographs of a youthful Frank Yount, in his twenties and before, along with a description of his personal features, his likes, dislikes, superstitions, beliefs, and much, much more.[1]

Masterson's observations, as read by Preston Doty, included:

> Frank's greatest fun in life is his work. He has been aptly called a steam engine in trousers. He remembers everything he reads and is a wizard on facts and events, recalling at an instant's notice the most minute details of instances long past. In fact, he is a walking encyclopedia. He parts his hair on the left side. In his bare feet he stands 10-1/2 inches over five feet. He tips the scales at 170 pounds ... A definite neatness marks his wardrobe. He is sort [of] a dresser. For visible clothing, he goes in for brown and dark gray. He wears a number seven hat and a number nine shoe. He puts on his left shoe last.
>
> In matters culinary, he begins breaking the fast every day with a cup of coffee, the juice of a Texas orange or grape fruit, toasted bread, strips of bacon and Post Toasties. He is very fond of vegetables of all kind, but pins the blue ribbon on collard greens. He dislikes alligator pears, bird's nest pudding and garlic. He only eats sweet potatoes semi-annually and hasn't drunk a glass of milk in ten years. He is attracted to flowers. He is an admirer of Will Rogers. He believes ... Jack Dempsey the greatest fighter that ever lived. He neither chews nor smokes. He has many prohibition friends ... sleeps in night shirts ... gets a shave every day and Sunday too. He drives his own car – a Pierce Arrow, and does his own parking in the down town garage.
>
> Jazz gives him a pain in the solar plexus. He never carries an umbrella. A hobby of his is mountain climbing, and although he has seen a century plant pass middle age, he can walk down a Globetrotter. He supported the man for President who said, "Prohibition is a noble experiment" and as a campaign slogan, held out the prospect of two chickens in every pot and two cars in every garage.
>
> When not interested, he becomes "Miles the Silent". Emotion or enthusiasm never rumples his fine gray plume, clouds his clear brown eyes or disturbs his Napoleon-like features. ... some of his epigrams: "Oil your brains occasionally with a good brand of construction thought" [and] "He profits most who serves best."
>
> His cook is Will Irwin; [and] his butler Johnnie Sam. He can't play the saxophone. He believes in reciprocity, returning coin of like kind given. Oil is his hand-maiden. He knows her anatomy from A to Z. Southern expressions still cling to him. He still says, "you all" and "H o o v a h". One of his superstitions: "That if hogs are killed while the moon is decreasing the bacon will shrink."
>
> In his first half century, he has pyramided quite a bit of mazuma [slang for money]. He rarely ever takes a dose of medicine. Insofar as possible, he stays clear of political buzzers and is well guarded by a faithful secretary. He is not a member of the Anti-Saloon League. He is Beaumont's first citizen, all wool and a yard wide, a straight and upright man, a good Presbyterian and a doer for his fellowman ...

But Masterson's one statement that "biographers cannot approach him in the flesh or in the spirit," reveals the true personality of Frank Yount and is the most telling of all his traits.[2]

A few days after Frank's birthday, the humorous "Susie Spindletop" column, written by Florence Stratton, appeared in the *Beaumont Enterprise*. The tongue-in-cheek reporting of the party also carried a gentle skewer of Dr. T. M. Hunter, Yount's pastor at Westminster Presbyterian Church.

> Now believe it or not, Doctor Hunter crashed the gate and ate just as hearty as though he had been sent a written invitation. Far be it from me to reflect in any manner on Doctor Hunter, but when a child I noticed that preachers, ministers of the gospel, always put just a little more "heart and soul" into "We thank Thee for these blessings" than most any other part of their ministerial duties.

The article concluded, "And a good time was had by all." Once again, the public at large could not hear enough about their beloved hero, the Godfather of Beaumont, his family members, close friends, and associates.[3]

Will Irwin.
—Courtesy Yount-Manion Film Collection, Lamar University, Beaumont, Texas.

Frank's culinary preferences also included cake. His favorite came in the form of a four-layer blackberry jam variety complete with cream fillings and crushed pecans in between, and whole pecans on the top. Marguerite Behar claimed that her uncle would never accept Christmas gifts from anyone in the family, but he made an exception with his sister Ida Belle when she prepared her specialty for him every year.[4]

Yount, his wife, Pansy, and daughter, Mildred, born on May 2, 1920, and adopted by the couple while they lived at Sour Lake, were the subject of numerous newspaper articles through the years. In spite of the publicity, however, most attempts to gain an accurate insight into the oilman's personality seemed to always fall short of the mark, that is, from the reporter's perspective. Maybe, the press anticipated too much from this self-made man who disliked talking to any of its corps. And as an extremely private man, he always held back, and even with his close neighbors, the Woodhead family, he guarded his conversation. But in July 1928 N. Dean Tevis, who wrote for the *Beaumont Enterprise*, sat down with Yount during a rare interview that lasted for more than hour, and afterward, he walked away with one of the most intimate discussions that anyone outside family or friends ever recorded. Beginning with November 14, 1925, when Yount brought in the McFaddin No. 2, a host of reporters had hounded him for an interview. Tevis, who eventually won the honor, prefaced his article as follows:

> For more than two years writers have sought the story of Frank Yount from his own "lips." It remains well within the realm of fact that his personality—the real man behind the desk— has been bathed in more than a little foolish mystery. They wanted to know the real Frank Yount. They wanted to take him apart. With entirely human failing they had not seen a story ... [of] Frank Yount working in a blacksmithy, driv-

> ing a team of sweating mules, working with begrimed face and hands on a balky gasoline engine or perched under a broiling sun on a rice threshing machine. Nor did they see romance in Frank Yount in the role of a "roughneck" in an outlying oil field. No one noticed ... [him] when he was carefully, thinkingly laying the foundations for the success which was to be his when his star should rise.

Mildred Frank Yount. Photograph by Van Dyke Studios, Beaumont, Texas.

—Courtesy Mildred Yount Manion.

When he entered the oilman's office, Tevis noted that his subject had a plain "trace of sentiment in his thin rather finely cut face, set with penetrating hazel eyes beneath hair that is beginning to gray." The reporter further described how the interviewee reacted:

> Frank Yount rises to greet the visitor. He smiles, not the broad smile of your politician nor the chuckle of a humorist—for he always has about him a certain dignified reserve—but a very welcoming smile from a pair of eyes that always look very directly at you. The man behind the desk is clothed in a cool summer suit. He is adept at toying, though he does this in no nervous fashion, with a pencil, ... He takes little notes and comprehensive sketches having to do with what he is talking about as he proceeds.

"There is nothing of the fairy tale about my life," Yount interjected. "It is, rather, the story of work lasting from 12 to 20 hours a day and attending to my business. . . . It has not been luck. We placed derricks and rigs, and sent down holes where the oil lay."[5]

In June 1933 Yount exposed a few more of his innermost thoughts to another correspondent; these centered, most appropriately, also on work ethics:

> The majority of people today have not found happiness. They lack initiative, enterprise. Our forefathers worked and found happiness in that manner. A lot of folks could take a lesson from them. Too many people today follow the line of least resistance, expect to gain their objectives through the medium of least effort. Too many folks [are] getting by—not giving everything they have to life.[6]

Indeed, Frank Yount followed his own advice. He worked hard and fully expected everyone around him, especially those in his company, to do the same. Not averse to getting his hands dirty, he pulled some duty on a derrick floor long after he became a

Frank and Mildred Frank Yount at El Ocaso.
—Courtesy Yount-Manion Film Collection, Lamar University, Beaumont, Texas.

millionaire, but the ultimate risk taker in the oil field knew where to draw the line when it came time to lay out capital for other investments. He never dabbled in the stock market, although he did own considerable shares in companies where he knew the principals. Aside from those of the Texas Corporation (later Texaco), based in New York, and those of his own company, Yount purchased stock in local operations only, including six in Sour Lake: Schlicher Oil, the Citizens National Bank, Sour Lake Investment Company, Rex Supply Company (owned by his brother Lee), Lake Tool Company, Lake Chevrolet; sixteen in Beaumont: the First National Bank, Beaumont Cotton Compress, Hotel Beaumont, the Edson Hotel, Phelan-Josey Grocery Company, Phelan Grocery Company, Beaumont Iron Works, Wall Street Property Company, Norvell-Wilder Hardware; Norvell-Wilder Supply, Beaumont Implement Company, Beaumont Brick Company, Savoy's, Inc., Plumbing and Heating Company, Thames Drug Company, Beaumont Cement Company; and one in Port Arthur, Standard Brass. And too, Frank Yount believed firmly in the future of the real estate business.[7]

Long before the discovery at Second Spindletop, he helped charter the Wall Street Property Company on September 5, 1922, which began with a capitalization of $76,000 (760 shares of stock valued at $100 each). The original directors included Preston B. Doty, T. S. Reed, C. C. Lewis, Ed C. Cherry, Harry Phelan, Walter J. Crawford, and James Donohoe. John Cashen, Frank Yount, Stuart R. Smith, R. E. Smith, Jesse W. Stuart, and W. T. Williams rounded out the list of investors. During a meeting held on March 14, 1928, the entire group voted to increase the capitalization from $76,000 to $380,000, and afterward allowed the purchase of the additional $304,000 in shares by Frank Yount, Talbot Rothwell, Harry Phelan, Ed C. Cherry, Beeman Strong, Max Schlicher, Johnny Hatcher, Frank Thomas, J. C. Jones, Marvin McClendon, E. L. Sandel, and Sam Parks. From all appearances, Frank Yount brought many of his company associates in on a good thing. Yount was the largest stockholder, from its inception, in the organization formed first as strictly a profit venture and then later used during the Depression as an instrument to prop up property values in Beaumont. He and his fellow stockholders could have well taken advantage of the many who had to—or wished to—sell, even at distressed prices, but Frank never for a minute considered this shortsighted approach. As an astute businessman, he knew that a strong Beaumont economy served everyone's best interests.[8]

Labeled somewhat as a paradox, Frank Yount enjoyed his hard-earned money and never minded spending it. He appreciated the finer things in life and went after them with all the zeal he used in searching for oil. On August 22, 1927, he purchased Rockledge, a summer home at Manitou, near Colorado Springs, from Edward H. and wife, Ray Wilson Heath, for the sum of $50,000. Architect William W. Stickney of Pueblo, Colorado, drew the original plans for this magnificent example of Craftsman style elegance in January 1913. Nestled on a mountain side in a 27-acre estate, Rockledge contained twelve rooms, including three master bedrooms, each equipped with a private bath and sleeping porch. On Sunday, March 18, 1928, the *Beaumont Enterprise* ran an article with photographs that described both the home itself and the surroundings.

> The site, originally a steep hillside of unpromising aspect, has been splendidly developed from a landscape aspect, at the same time capitalizing the use of native pines and cedars found on it, care being taken to retain virtually all of them. Every variety of Colorado wild flower is to be found within the grounds.
>
> The house is gained by a driveway spiraling through the hills and forming loops between which are the lawns and forests of indigenous plants and trees.
>
> On the hill back of the house vegetable gardens and orchards have been made possible by terracing. Here wild cherry and plum abound. On the west side of the house where the mountain outlook is particularly fine, a rustic courtyard has been developed, the chief of which is a pergola of native cedar.
>
> The house of Colorado stone, ivy covered

Rockledge.
—Courtesy Kathryn Manion Haider.

Rockledge.
—Courtesy Kathryn Manion Haider.

Living room at Rockledge.
—Courtesy Deena and Bob Stuart.

Library at Rockledge.
—Courtesy Kathryn Manion Haider.

and typically English, seems to grow out of its setting, so well adapted is this type of architecture to the location. The front of the house commands a view of Pike's Peak glimpsed through the intervening mountains. To the rear a view of the Garden of the Gods, and on the east side a landscape of natural terraces leading to the valley below leave nothing of beauty to be desired in a landscape of almost incomparable beauty.

Scarcely less lovely is the interior of the house with its paneled oak walls and beamed ceilings, its spacious rooms bespeaking hospitality. ... The library of great proportions is distinguished by a huge fireplace, extending almost across the length of one wall and made of rock quarried from the estate. Quarters are provided for a retinue of servants.

The house, now in the hands of the decorators, will consistently develop the idea of an English interior.

To paraphrase Rupert Brooke: There is some corner of a foreign field that is forever Texas, for Mrs. Yount floats a Texas flag about her estate.

Summers at Rockledge provided the Yount family with a welcomed respite from the heat, high humidity, and mosquitoes that entered their pre-air-conditioned home in Beaumont. Likewise, other lucky friends and visitors on occasion, like Bill Grant, the son of a Yount employee, said that many who suffered with asthma such as he did, traveled west for the summer to "take the airs." While there, Mildred enjoyed trying her hand at fishing in one of the many ponds in the immediate area stocked with "so many trout that you were assured of catching all you wanted."[9]

Mildred, Pansy, and Frank Yount at Rockledge.
—Courtesy Mildred Yount Manion.

Yount's other businesses included

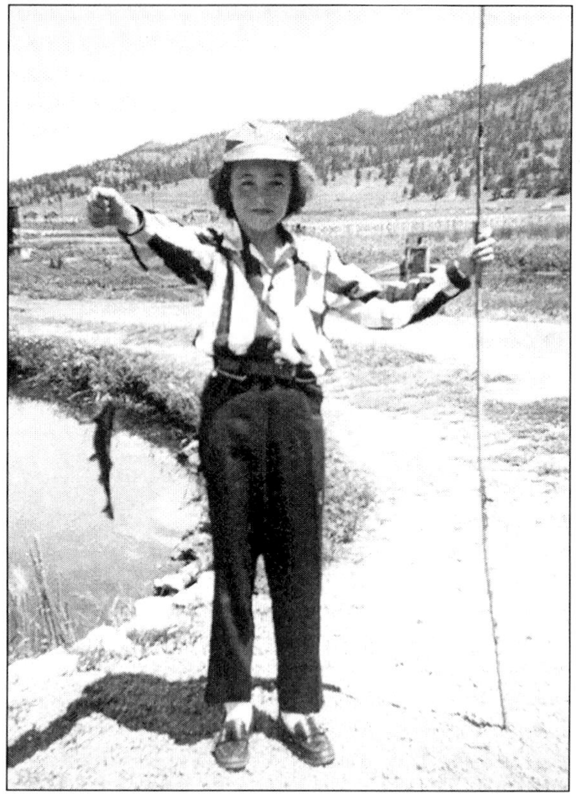

Mildred Frank Yount at Manitou Springs, Colorado, circa 1930.

—Courtesy Kathryn Manion Haider.

a quarry, also close to Manitou Springs, bought from Robert D. and Alice Maude Sandford Weir on September 9, 1929. The Beaumont oilman invested over $35,000 in this venture which sat on seventy-five acres, located at Rainbow Falls near Pike's Peak, where workers mined a product known as Manitou Greenstone. Named for its brownish-green color and advertised as durable as granite, the quarry marketed it mainly to commercial contractors who used it in the construction of churches and schools. Samples of the greenstone can be found today at the base of the Jefferson County Courthouse, and within the walls of the post office building and the Temple to the Brave in Pipkin Park, all in Beaumont. During November 1930, N. L. Ross, in charge of Yount's Colorado quarry, visited Beaumont and explained "that stone for the new Jefferson county courthouse, to be used as trimming, is

Manitou Springs, Colorado, quarry with headframe in distance.[10]

—Courtesy Deborah Harrison.

being quarried at this time and ... 10 carloads or more will be required for the structure. It will be fabricated at the Vermont Marble company's works at Houston." The Yount quarry also supplied the greenstone used in the post office at Manitou Springs, Colorado.[11]

Temple to the Brave.
—Courtesy Tyrrell Historical Library, Beaumont, Texas.

There were numerous other instances of Yount's personal involvement in real estate. In March 1928 he, together with Phelan and Rothwell, purchased a vacant lot, located at Alamo and Laurel Streets, for $22,500 from R. L. Autrey of Houston; and on a Calder site, diagonally across the street from their Beaumont home, the Younts bought from Daniel Bowie Clark and his wife Zoe Alice three lots, which had been the site of the famous upscale Oaks Hotel that burned in 1908, and another three from J. H. and Laura Broocks. The Broocks' residence was torn down, but Clark, who served the city of Beaumont for forty-two years as health inspector and fire marshal, had his relocated where it still stands, though altered somewhat, at 1895 McFaddin. Mary Clark Look, daughter of Daniel and Zoe Alice, says that her mother commented, "The move was quite a big deal in Beaumont, and folks came from miles around to see it. By dusk, the workers could go no further, so we spent the night in the house right there in

U. S. Post Office, Manitou Springs, Colorado.
—Courtesy Paul E. Petosky and Deborah Harrison.

the middle of the street where Mariposa [now Martin Luther King] intersects McFaddin."[12]

With everything cleared away, Frank and Pansy had a complex built on the property and named it for their daughter Mildred. This eclectic structure, with a Mediterranean motif and a mission tile roof, includes a three-story apartment building with eighteen units, entry doors made of bronze, a roof garden, bronze gutters, and "some windows are either leaded or art glass." The contractor imported stone from the Yount's Manitou Springs, Colorado, quarry and used it in the entrance hall. Furthermore, the compound has nine business spaces designated for shopping, and a separate garage built to accommodate twenty-five cars. The Austin Company of Texas began the apartments first, followed by the commercial space, commonly referred to as the "arcade," and when totally completed by October 1, 1930, the project cost about $1 million, including the property. A *Beaumont Enterprise* article of July 3, 1929 added:

> The building will be a substantial addition to the commercial section which is developing within a radius of a block of it. Directly opposite the arcade is a Gulf filling station; diagonally, the Thames Calder drug store and the Calder market, while on the other block are a Magnolia filling station, Perkins Drug Store; a Piggly Wiggly store and the Log Cabin refreshment stand. On Broadway and Mariposa, a block away ... [is the] recently opened Munro drycleaning plant.[13]

Frank Yount first conceived the idea of the Mildred Building when during his travels to California, he came to admire the terra cotta design of structures found there. While touring the manufacturing plant of the Gladding-McBean Company in Los Angeles, makers of terra cotta blocks, Frank mentioned to the manager that he would someday use this same material in a Beaumont project, because its composition would lend itself well to the humid conditions and damp climate of the Texas Gulf Coast. He studied the feasibility of building his project for about two years before finally engaging architect P. E. Robinson of Cleveland, Ohio, "who designed the building, ... [including] an apartment house of the Mediterranean type with a stucco exterior." But at this point, however, the original plans deviated somewhat. Since the inclusion of the terra cotta blocks necessitated a more formal look, Yount and Robinson eventually developed a style reminiscent of the Spanish renaissance of the sixteenth and seventeenth centuries. They took cues directly from Spanish noblemen's palaces: "lintels and ornamental window heads from the Palacio de Monteroy at Salamanca, an ornate cresting and bronze gates from the Plaza de la Plateria at Santiago, several shields and heraldic designs from

Mildred Apartments, 1415 Calder Avenue (left), and "The Arcade" (beginning right), as they appear today.
—Courtesy Howard Perkins Collection, Beaumont, Texas.

sculptural panels in the palace of Don Alonso de Fonsica at Salamanca and lesser details from similar buildings in Seville, Toledo and Leon. Wood details mimic the cloister of Lupiana."[14]

A June 8, 1930, article in the *Beaumont Enterprise* printed photographs of both the exterior and interior of the Mildred Apartments and described the units with painstaking particulars through the eyes of a first time visitor. When opened in July,

> the entrance to the building is one of the imposing features of the structure. Through heavy bronze doors, the visitor enters a small vestibule which is separated from the lobby by doors of bronze grill work. By means of telephone he communicates with the resident whom he wishes to see, and if this person desires to receive the visitor, he will push a button which will unlock the doors.
>
> Mounting a few steps, the visitor finds himself in a lobby which is flanked on one side by a stone mantel over a gas fireplace and on the other by an elaborate console table. Hangings of Spanish design, softly colored windows and tiled floors add to the attractiveness. Exposed beams are of a composition which cannot be distinguished from ancient, carved wood. Elevated slightly above the entrance lobby and framed by a textured arch [hangs a portrait of 10 year old Mildred Yount, painted by William Edmundson of Cleveland, Ohio,] a monument to his [Yount's] adoration of his only child ... whose name the building bears.
>
> Then up another short flight of steps to the corridor where flooring is of rubber tile, alternate light and dark squares. A handsome Spanish chest and a damask hanging are ornamental features here. The stairway, extending upward at the right is of tile bordered by bronze grills. An electric automatic elevator also is available to tenants and visitors.[15]

Each of the eighteen individual apartment units (eleven two- and seven one-bedroom) were completely furnished by pieces manufactured by the Shaw Company of Cambridge, Massachusetts which reproduced them in sixteenth and seventeenth century Spanish and Italian designs made from solid walnut. "Desks are of Italian tooled leather. Painted ladderback chairs, walnut tables and carved high-backed dressers are used in dining rooms. Living room furniture includes comfortable divans, several chairs, tables of different designs and desks. A stone mantle tops each gas fireplace."[16]

Stained glass window in apartment building. Photograph by Fred B. McKinley.

Frank and Pansy stamped their approval on every detail, and when completed, all apartments contained most every modern convenience that could be had in 1930s America: draperies, paintings, ceiling fans, metal kitchen cabinets, Frigidaires (popular name brand refrigerator), carpeted floors, except in solariums, kitchens, and bathrooms, choice of gas or electric ranges, exhaust fans and vent hoods, porcelain sinks and laundry trays, drain boards made with nickel and silver, gas fireplaces, steam heat (electric in the bathrooms), central vacuum units, garbage chutes, indoor parking for automobiles, and even something called, "the radio-victory system," an aerial (antennae) and a special outlet provided for every tenant, that eliminated irritating static when listening to one's favorite programs. In a harsh and humid climate, tenants enjoyed "central refrigeration, meaning electric refrigerators had their 'cool' piped in to each individual unit from the basement." Each unit also contained "a Murphy Bed, carefully hidden in a working wall."[17]

Relative to the arcade, the precursor to the modern shopping center, the Younts had the interior of its fourteen units finished far less elaborately. The original tenants included: the Zoghev Oriental Shop, the Thames Drug Company in the two corner spaces facing Calder Avenue and Mariposa Street, J. S. Blain Grocery and Market, which faced Mariposa, M. E. Strange Barber and Beauty Shops, Cave Interior Decoration Company, Cox and Blackburn Refrigeration Sales, and an unnamed florist located immediately adjacent to the apartments "in order that the more commercial businesses may not intrude too closely upon the residents." Only one of these fell outside the Spanish influence in design, that being the Zoghev with its oriental atmosphere.[18]

The arcade locations rented very quickly, but apparently the apartments did not follow the same path, partly because Frank "is unwilling to lease the [latter] until tenants may be assured of the minimum annoyance. Construction on the arcade building must be completed or practically so, in order that residents of the apartment house will not be disturbed by the noise of construction." The article continued, "Although nearly all the space in the arcade building has been leased, and none of the apartments is yet rented, Mr. Yount shows no perturbance."[19]

But during the early stages of construction, however, things did not go quite as smoothly as the general contractor and subcontractors hoped. Even with the simple act of excavation, Frank continued to be involved. While glaring at a growing mound of dirt dredged out for the foundation, he took a handful, ran it through his fingers, and said, "We'll have to go deeper. We haven't reached the solid earth yet." He got his wish, and eventually, concrete pilings that supported the structure extended eighteen feet deep, all the way to solid bedrock. When Frank Yount built something, he not only wanted the best—he wanted it to last.[20]

Furthermore, to the complete surprise of every member of the construction crew, Pansy also exerted her influence. As a teenager and young man, Ed Rollins, a Beaumont native and graduate of South Park High School, worked for the Gulf Manufacturing and Lumber Company in Beaumont which had the contract with the Austin Company to provide much of "the custom millwork ordered by the architect" for the Mildred complex. Because Rollins got along so well with the older clientele, his bosses assigned him the responsibility of soothing problem issues that cropped up from time to time, and in this position, Rollins came to know the foreman on the Yount job, George M. Hunting of Dallas, who described with great tribulation his dealings with Mrs. Yount. Howard Perkins, who rented from Rollins for about nine years, heard the following account by him over and again, and he always repeated it the same way. Relayed through Perkins, Rollins' words paint a portrait of Pansy as a strong-willed business person—a woman ahead of her time—who looked after the family's best interests:

> The foreman became extremely upset and paranoid with Mrs. Yount. She watched them constantly, was standing on the sidewalk waiting for them by 6:30 every morning, and stayed with them most of the day watching—sometimes trying to supervise what they were doing. If the men went up a ladder where she could not see what they were doing, she went up the ladder, too. The men, in 1929, were certainly not used to a woman being around, let alone taking that kind of active interest in what they were doing—and seemingly policing them at the same time.
>
> When they were ready to put the millwork in the building, she and the foreman really began to clash. She objected to practically everything and ordered up changes, which was also unnerving to them at Gulf. Everyone received mixed signals. She loved traditional 18th-century interiors, Adams, Chippendale, Sheraton, etc., and wanted those inside the building rather than the Mediterranean interiors planned to coincide with the style of the exterior, except everyone at that time in Beaumont referred to the style as Spanish.
>
> The foreman would come into Gulf and express his frustrations with her. It was the beginning of the Depression, and all the men were afraid for their jobs and really afraid of Pansy. When she went home (across the intersection), she reported when she would return.
>
> Either the foreman or one of his superiors called Mr. Yount, asking that he call her off. He replied, "Why do you think she is over there? I have to work and can't be there. She and I discuss that building every night over supper." Mr. Yount did seem to find it amusing that they were afraid of her and told him that when she wanted something changed, explain to her why she could not have that and she would understand.
>
> Without telling my bosses, I lent her a book for a weekend that explained sizing interior millwork for the rooms and the importance of keeping everything in proportion to the size of the rooms. I asked that she get it back to me early Monday morning, and she did. Evidently she had devoured it, because after that, the foreman would come in not saying anything about Mrs. Yount.
>
> One day I asked the foreman, "How are you and Mrs. Yount getting along?" He replied that he did not realize how much she knew about interiors. He stated that she had decided to go with the architect's plans—that she really knew the sizing of mill work in relation to the size of rooms, and was always asking if he was sure that the molding was not a little large for the space or if it was undersized. Everything toward the end seemed to work very smoothly although it had not started out that way. I never told the foreman, or my bosses, about lending her the millwork reference book which had been written for architects and millwork makers.[21]

On February 25, 1930, a purchase negotiated with Earl Hankamer of Sour Lake brought 730 acres, situated on the Beaumont-Sour Lake Road west of Elizabeth, to Yount's array of assets, and the land, which had been used for rice planting, carried all mineral rights. Yount indicated that he bought it for investment purposes only. In May 1933 he purchased a 650-acre tract that adjoined Beaumont's Calder Terrace addition, near his farm. W. M. Crook and A. M. Kaufman sold the acreage to Yount for a reported $80,000 in cash. And in Manitou Springs, Colorado, on October 31, 1930, he paid an undisclosed sum to Lafayette M. Hughes for a private street, including some existing buildings, all valued at about $100,000. Pike Street, 60 feet wide and 200 feet long, would eventually be the site of an arcade and other improvements. At the end of November 1930 Yount revealed that he contracted Douglas Steinman, an architect based in Beaumont, to draw the plans. "A large amount of Manitou greenstone, from Mr. Yount's Colorado quarries will be used," the *Beaumont Enterprise* wrote, "and the wood will be left in its natural state and stained. Large columns of the greenstone will be used along either side of the street." Also in this same article, N. L. Ross, Yount's head of quarry operations, said, "the stone ... which will be used in the Colorado arcade, will not be [polished], but left more in the rough state, which many believe to be more attractive than the completed product." With the development almost finished by early summer 1931, the *Colorado Springs Gazette and Telegraph* further described it on June 21:

> What Mr. Yount has done is to take the street, a private thorofare [sic] a block long, and set down into it this unique structure, built on heavy foundations, of beautiful Manitou greenstone and a wealth of concrete, timber and glass. A vast crowd can find shelter underneath its broad roof when it rains and shade when the sun shines bright. There are under the roof four octagonal store buildings, glass on all sides. With fountains, benches and other conveniences for rest and recreation, the arcade can be visualized as the pivot for the milling throng of pleasure seekers in Manitou this summer.

Prior to the Yount family purchasing there, the area had gained national attention with its natural "soda" springs. The *Gazette and Telegraph* continued, "This water is drunk either in Manitou or at home from bottles, by a large slice of the population of the country. It never loses its vogue. It becomes constantly more popular. It is drunk for its flavor and for the medicinal value that people find in it."[22]

In Colorado, Yount decided to turn his drilling expertise toward searching for a somewhat unfamiliar prize. Long before, many of the locals extolled the perception that hot water lay directly beneath Manitou Springs, and if found, it would prove a great

Arcade entrance, Manitou Springs, Colorado.
—Courtesy Manitou Springs Historical Society.

"Hot Water Drilling Crew and the Oil Baron." From left to right: C. H. Caldwell, H. H. Roxbury, Harry Watson, O. W. McLeod, and Frank Yount. From Gazette and Telegraph *(Colorado Springs), September 14, 1930.*

benefit to the area as an additional draw for tourists who sought out the water for mineral bath purposes. So Frank selected a spot near a fault line at Rainbow Falls in the area of Ute Pass, where he began drilling to prove once and for all if it were really true. But right away, things went badly, as the crew struggled to drill through solid rock. An optimistic, yet realistic, Yount commented, "I would like to go about 2,000 feet deep, but it would be almost out of the question to drill so deep in hard stone." When it became apparent, however, that granite posed a more formidable obstacle than that of salt, cap rock, and heaving shale found on the Texas Gulf coast, he eventually abandoned the project.[23]

Although Frank Yount shunned the limelight and refused to serve in any type of public office during his earlier years, Beaumont leaders persuaded him in 1930 to take a more active part in the guidance of his adopted city. On May 27 Mayor Emmett Fletcher appointed him as a member of the Beaumont Port Commission, and on January 6 of the following year, Governor Ross Sterling named him as a University of Texas regent. During that same month, the 15-member panel assigned the responsibility of studying and making necessary adjustments in the salary structure of Jefferson County officials, elected him chairman. He also served as vice president of the Beaumont General Hospital board, and as a member of another panel, he helped regulate the activities of the South Texas State Fair.[24]

Frank's enthusiasm and relentless approach to finding oil spilled over into his personal life, where he engaged several hobbies. But even here, he was never content to settle on a lackadaisical style, settle for second best, and he, therefore, usually excelled in everything. The poor boy who started out from Monticello, Arkansas, in spite of his current wealth, needed to prove to everyone that he had what it took, but most of all, he had to exceed the demands of his principal critic—Frank Yount. But there was more to the mix. From an almost unbelievable viewpoint, he developed into a caring and totally unselfish individual, and as such, he held a genuine desire to help his fellowman. Yount wanted to put Beaumont on the map with one of the finest horse training facilities in the country, and he set about to do just that. He hired William Capers "Cape" Grant, a dashing saddle horse trainer of known reputation, to guide the newly-constructed Spindletop Stables, located on his Calder Road property on the west side of Beaumont. Yount first met Grant in April 1933 at the Dallas Polo Club, where the latter had taken a job as stables manager after attempting various times, unsuccessfully, to establish his own stable and breeding facilities. Even then, however, Cape had estab-

William Capers "Cape" Grant.
—Courtesy American Saddlebred Museum, Lexington, Kentucky.

Cape Grant (right) and Captain Paul at Spindletop Stables, Beaumont.[25]
—Courtesy Kathryn Manion Haider.

lished quite a professional reputation. One writer observed:

> He [Cape] had developed into one of the greatest catch riders in history and was in great demand at all large shows as an extra rider when stables had more than one stake horse. They all realized that Cape Grant was one man that could mount a strange horse and had the uncanny ability to get along with it and get the best out of it. The experience he obtained in riding so many strange horses for the various owners was of untold value and proved to be a priceless asset …

Frank and Cape hit it off immediately. In Frank, Cape saw an opportunity to prove himself to the world of Saddlebreds, and Frank was equally impressed by the younger man's brash personality—and yes, his flamboyance—his can do attitude, and previous accomplishments that included being judged "The Best Boy Rider" in 1911, 1912, and 1913 at the Texas State Fair held annually in Dallas. Later Cape competed on a horse named The Virginian and rode "to victory in eleven straight shows before he was defeated at Des Moines by the invincible Roxie Highland." Then, he rode The Title, and "showed him in seventeen shows, the horse losing but two gelding classes and never being farther back than fourth in the championships."[26]

Grant explained his revolutionary ideas on training and breeding American Saddlebreds to Yount who immediately ended the search for his own stables manager, after concluding that Cape was the right man for the job. So Frank immediately purchased six horses from his new trainer, put him under contract, and gave him a new car. Cape also got $200 per month regular salary, drawing privileges against future income, an expense account that covered just about everything, including riding clothing, and half of the profits generated by the enterprise. Soon, Frank moved Cape along with his wife, Nola, and his two young sons, Silas and Cape, Jr. "Bill," and put them up free of charge in his Mildred Apartments. Bill vividly recalls the arrival in Beaumont and likens their lavish second-story unit to a fairy palace that contrasted sharply with the family's dreary living accommodations just days before when he, his father, mother, and Silas shared a small, cramped two-room house outside Dallas with his aunt Kathryn Hunt and her family, and at least part of the time with Cape's brother Jack. As a youngster thrown into unaccustomed luxury, much less the tight security measures, Bill said that the self-locking front door and intercom system at the new digs gave him fits, and that he constantly found himself stranded on the outside with no way to gain admission except by buzzing the family apartment.[27]

Bill "Kid" Grant and Dorothy "Dot" Hilliard.
—Courtesy Kathryn Manion Haider.

On May 13 Frank gave Cape what amounted to a blank check and directed him to hit the road and assemble the best horses that money could buy. Frank told Grant, "You find 'em, and the barn will be ready when you get back." On many other such occasions, Dr. John Yost, a local Beaumont veterinarian, accompanied both Grant and Yount in search of the best horse flesh in the country.[28]

Cape Grant (left) shaking hands with Mildred Frank Yount; Dot Hilliard (right).
—Courtesy Yount-Manion Film Collection, Lamar University, Beaumont, Texas.

Besides Paris Grand and Beau Peavine, sired by Jean Val Jean and out of Fair Acres Vanity Fair; the Spindletop Stables early on consisted of Chief of Spindletop, bought from George B. Lane of

Frank Heathman.[29]
—Courtesy American Saddlebred Museum, Lexington, Kentucky.

Raymore, Missouri, Night Alarm (Mildred's horse), Tradewind, My Mary, Blue Bonnet McDonald, Dan, Alice, Sally Foot, Texas Ranger, and a few others. Gladiola Pruitt, a reporter with the *Beaumont Enterprise*, described the three-year-old Tradewind as "most different ... distinguished with a white stripe down the nose as well as two white ankles." And according to the same report, "any account of the ... stables, without some mention of 'My Mary' would be disastrous to the one telling the story. For this horse is the particular pet of Mrs. Yount, the one that she ordinarily rides." Speaking fondly of My Mary, Cape said that the mare "is the only one of her kind in the country, an ideal companion, a horse with a splendid disposition, perfect manners, gaited, but one riding her ... could carry a glass of water without spilling it." Before long, however, Cape realized that he needed assistance, so he hired first Frank Heathman, who was on the Yount payroll as early as July 4, 1933, and later "Careful Carl" Pedigo, as his second in command, decisions that proved to be very sound as time wore on.[30]

Never one to do things by half, Frank Yount had constructed his stables with the most modern specifications. The Saturday, June 10, 1933, *Beaumont Enterprise* reported:

> The site is a most natural and beautiful one. All around the barns are tall trees, shading it. In front of the barn is a ring, two rings in fact, a large one and a smaller one. The barn itself is almost entirely fireproof, and the most comfortable one for the horses that could be imagined. It is built on a foundation, and rat proofed. Down the center is a wide hall, 16 feet across. On either side are the stalls, large and roomy. Doors are at both ends, one leading to the stables hall and the other outside. Nearly 150 feet in length, there is sufficient space for a score or more of horses. In addition to this, there is a saddle and harness room. In this connection, a word about the saddles would likely not be amiss, for they are the latest in design, some being of English importation from the Barnsby company. There is perfect ventilation through the building.[31]

The description continued:

> To one side of the barn is a large grove, in which there are oaks, magnolias and many other kinds of trees. It will be from this point, over toward the Voth road, that the bridle paths will be built, approximately four miles in length. It is possible that a loop path will be established. The property acquired by Yount recently, on which the en-

> tire layout is being established, lays between the Calder road and the Treadaway place... It contains some of the most attractive wooded land in that section.... Various other improvements are also planned, including a lodge to which Mrs. Yount will give her special attention. A feature of the lodge will be the large living room on the first floor, in which will be constructed an immense fireplace, with Manitou greenstone brought for it from the Yount quarries in Colorado.

Bill Grant recalled the location about five miles out of downtown Beaumont going west on Calder Road. "The stables were on the right," he said, "and the dairy farm on the left." Grant remarked also that a bayou ran further west just beyond the stables, about three-quarters of a mile. "It [Hillebrandt Bayou] isn't like now, the water was clear and beautiful, and the fish practically jumped on the hook." He continued, "I really liked to fish." His most vivid memory, however, is that of the enormous fence surrounding the track, constructed of interlocking boards, painted gleaming white; and the stable which sat about fifty yards from the track with its several stalls to each side, the large feed and tack rooms. He laughed and said, "Sometimes when I'd be in the barn, I'd go into the feed room, grab a big handful of oats and eat them on the spot." Another source, Ed Edson, III, indicates that he spent years living in a home located at 5615 Clinton Street which sits on the property that originally contained Spindletop Stables.[32]

Reportedly, Frank spent over $150,000 on the project that shortly included a small herd of about fifteen horses, among them one that would soon become the stables' pride and linchpin, the beautiful chestnut stallion, Beau Peavine, for which Cape paid about $20,000, an almost unheard of price for what could be basically described as an unproven four-year-old that had only been shown sparingly. In fact, Beau Peavine is the only horse among Cape's early selections with any real experience, however limited. When asked what he looked for in a horse, Grant replied, "It is type, soundness and something undefinable that is almost felt but not seen. The color ... is immaterial." On June 8 Cape returned with his string to Beaumont where Frank had fullfilled his promise to have everything ready. Initially, the so-called professionals criticized Grant for his choices, including Beau Peavine, but eventually, time would erase such mistaken beliefs. None of this conjecture, however, mattered the least bit to Frank who always gave a person a reasonable time to prove himself. On June 27 an excited Mildred got her first look at the new stables. Her diary entry for that date read: "We went out to the stables this morning and saw our new horses & Mr. Grant the new horse trainer." She followed with another passage on July 13 marked "Extra. My first horseback lesson by Mr. Grant and [I was] the first to ride Whirlwind ..."[33]

One particularly interesting story involves the purchase of Frank Yount's favorite, Paris Grand, from Forrest Fugitt of Hamilton, Missouri. After Yount and Grant struck the bargain with Fugitt, the sentimental seller requested to spend the last night in the stable with his horse before he was taken to Beaumont. All agreed, and the following morning, Fugitt reluctantly turned him over, just like he said he would. Later, Frank personally rode Paris Grand at the Beaumont Horse Show in the Plantation Gait category, and even though the animal "misbehaved a little, the judges declared he was such a fine specimen that he must be given the first prize." During the same show, Mildred also won second prize on Dan.[34]

Although most observers probably envisioned the dreams of the two, boss and trainer, as rather grandiose, Frank and Cape made plans to show the horses at the upcoming World's Fair—and they intended not only to compete but to bring home some ribbons and trophies. Others scoffed, stating that, even with years of experience, much less a stable not yet seven months old filled with unseasoned contestants, no one could realistically accomplish such a feat. When Grant fielded questions on how he thought Beau Peavine would perform at Chicago, he answered, "I have high hopes . . . and knowing him, many Beaumonters will not be at all surprised if he comes back to this city with the much coveted silver cup for the junior class, and places Beaumont for all time, in the horse world." The trainer's remarks must have seemed somewhat foolish to insiders who knew the stiff competition that he would face in Chicago: entries like Chief of Longview from the W. P. Roth stables in Redwood, California; and others sent by Mary Gwyn Fiers of Oklahoma City, the Longview Farms of Kansas City; and various establishments based in Kentucky.[35]

When Frank, Pansy, and Mildred, who brought along her best friend "Dot" Hilliard, arrived in Chicago a few days early to see the sights at the World's Fair before the upcoming events at the horse show, they found the weather still fairly warm, but a cold front moved through unexpectedly, catching everyone completely off guard. Frank concluded that both Mildred and Dot required extra clothing, so he personally took them to a department store and bought identical fur coats for the young ladies. If the Texans, however, were unprepared for Chicago, nothing can be remotely said of the horses that represented Spindletop Stables.[36]

To the shock and amazement of the Saddlebred establishment, several Yount entries, including Chief of Spindletop, Beau Peavine, and Night Alarm, the first black horse owned by Spindletop Stables, either became champions at the October 1933 Horse Show, or placed high on the competition scale, and in doing so, gave credence to the upstart facility in Beaumont, Texas. Right before Cape entered the ring atop a small brown horse, Frank asked "what that little fellow was going to do?" Grant remarked that the horse's name was Chief of Spindletop. "Well," Frank laughed and replied, "he'd better win with that name." In this, his debut, the Chief took top honors in the Three-Year-Old Stake, along with a trophy that bore the inscription, "Given in loving memory of A. Montgomery Ward—for his great love of horses and fine sportsmanship—by his daughter Marjorie Montgomery Ward Baker." On top of that, the Chief placed second in the Model Class. Night Alarm, the other novice, placed second in the Combination Class, and though Beau Peavine managed but a second place finish in the $500 Five-Gaited Junior Stake and third in Fine Harness, he did well in the eyes of Frank, Pansy, and Cape. Before the Chicago show finished, however, Cape introduced Frank to Carl Pedigo, considered in his own right as one of the best trainers in the country who handled the great champion Belle Le Rose. Pedigo brought three horses with him to the fair hoping that their performances might enhance their value and prompt others to purchase them. One of his entries, Lady Virginia, a beautiful black mare that took three out of four classes, so impressed Cape that he urged Frank to buy her for Spindletop Stables. So again, Frank complied, and before the week ended, Lady Virginia, with Cape up, placed fifth in the Championship Stake won by Roxie Highland.[37]

Both Beaumont newspapers reported each and every event in the greatest of details, in much the same manner as contemporary publications proclaim a local sport team's most recent triumph. Although most certainly a proud moment for area admirers, Frank, precisely as with Second Spindletop before, would never be satisfied with just a

Carl Pedigo.
—Courtesy American Saddlebred Museum, Lexington, Kentucky.

few wins. There would be other victories, he predicted, so many in fact that the dynasty he and Cape would build together would set the standard for future Saddlebred championships. Unfortunately, this successful outing at Chicago would prove to be Yount's one single opportunity to see his shining new stables compete on the national level, but in the interim, his critics stood in awe, wondering what had just happened.

Many other Beaumonters attended the Chicago World's Fair in 1933, including Zoe Alice Clark and daughter Mary, who once lived diagonally across the street from the Younts. Mary vaguely remembers going to the horse shows, but when they arrived back home, she vividly recalls the thrill of a lifetime waiting for her in the backyard, where during her absence, Frank Yount had paid for someone to build an eight by ten feet playhouse for her, just because he thought it would be a nice thing to do.[38]

Another Yount pastime included an eighty-five-acre Jersey cattle farm, also located on West Calder Road, under the direction of F. J. Helmke, manager. Like his counterpart at the stables, Helmke set about to create one of the best in the area with the full support of his boss who armed him with an open checkbook. As a base, he purchased much of the original stock from the Henderson Breeding Farm at Ruston, Louisiana, which produced previous world champions, and even though he began with a quality herd, selective breeding, and pasture land experimentation improved it considerably. Jefferson County agricultural extension agent, J. F. Combs, pitched in and lent his expertise in recommending the planting of specific clovers and grasses. Helmke also stocked the farm with numerous Duroc hogs, chickens, ducks, turkeys, and peacocks. One newspaper article stated that many of the hogs born in March 1933 now weighed about 350 pounds, and in a pampered environment, they "eat cafeteria fashion, when and what they want, picking out their food." When the 1933 South Texas Fair Livestock Show rolled around, both owner and manager decided to use the event to exhibit their stock, so they chose the best they had to offer: two young Jersey calves, Wonder Girl and Fair Lady, and two adults, a female named Theatre Cup Louise, and Yount's most prized bull, Golden King's Jerry. One article, appearing in the *Beaumont Enterprise*, led with "Yount's Jersey Cows Wear Khaki Kimonos And Have Hooves Manicured For Fair." The piece went on to elaborate how the khaki blankets were used to protect the bovine hopefuls from insects, and that their hooves were manicured for the best possible appearance. True to his billing, Jerry walked away with grand champion honors, and everyone on the farm payroll, including Yount, beamed with pride.[39]

Frank loved automobiles too, so much in fact that he amassed quite a collection. He began with a handbuilt 1918 model Locomobile limousine, and followed up with a leg-

1927 Pierce-Arrow.

—Courtesy Kathryn Manion Haider.

endary Pierce-Arrow. But during one of his trips to New York, he found three more that suited his fancy. According to Mickey Phelan, his grandfather Harry often told him the account about how Frank nonchalantly walked up to a salesman and expressed the desire to purchase two of the latest models and have them shipped back to Beaumont. A somewhat surprised dealer responded that he would have to contact Frank's bank to determine whether his check would clear before he made good on any promises, considering that the custom-bodied Duesenberg priced over $10,000, and a Cord L-29, the world's first production front-wheel-drive auto, added another $3,100, putting the total transaction at a then astronomical $13,000, plus the shipping costs to Southeast Texas. At the time, Frank, if he had wanted, could have bought a Ford sedan for a mere $600, so in reality, for the same amount he planned spending on the Duesenberg and the Cord, he could have had twenty-two new Fords. Speculation aside, however, the salesman put in a call to Preston B. Doty, president of the First National of Beaumont. When Doty advised the astonished New Yorker that "if the check is less than $10 million, we'll honor it," Frank got his automobiles, both 1929 models, consisting of a Duesenberg "Willoughby" sedan, and a five-passenger Cord sedan, both delivered to him about the same time the National Auto Show opened in January 1929.[40]

Preston B. Doty.

—Courtesy Tyrrell Historical Library, Beaumont, Texas.

Frank with his 1929 Duesenberg "Willoughby" sedan, black exterior color (background), and 1929 Cord, five-passenger sedan, dark maroon exterior color (foreground). From the Walker Collection.
—Courtesy Tyrrell Historical Library, Beaumont, Texas.

The Duesenberg sedan came equipped with a straight eight-cylinder engine "of 265 horsepower, capable of a speed of 90 miles an hour in second gear and 135 an hour in high." Both the sedan and the Cord, with front wheel drive, were "upholstered in the finest of grey imported broadcloth, [and] on the dashboard of the Duesenberg are signals showing when the battery water is low, how the grease is working, etc."[41]

Apparently Frank was so impressed with the Duesenberg sedan that he ordered another model from the same manufacturer, this one a 1929 Judkins coupe, delivered a short while later. Since many surmised that Frank had wheels in his head, and furthermore, since he never went into anything with blinders on, it is highly likely that he researched the automobiles at great length. As such, he would have been well aware of the Duesenberg brothers' celebrated racing accomplishments at the Indianapolis 500 and the French Grand-Prix. Other wealthy and famous owners of these cars included the likes of Greta Garbo, Clark Gable, Jimmy Cagney, and Gary Cooper. P. K. Wrigley of chewing gum fame, along with various kings and potentates, who also possessed the car termed as "Duesies." Even today most people who use the common phrase, "Isn't it a Doozie?" are completely oblivious to the fact that it originally described a car. Eventually, Frank owned three of the custom-built Duesenbergs, and this status elevated him to a lofty level, attained by few anywhere.[42]

1929 Duesenberg coupe (believed to be Frank Yount's).
—Courtesy Randy Ema, Inc.

These fabulous automobiles created quite a sensation in Beaumont with their appearance: the rakish Cord standing only sixty-one inches tall, and the 265 horse-power Duesenbergs with their mind-boggling power when compared to the 40 horse-power Ford sedans of the day. Beaumonters widely reported that Frank's front-wheel-drive Cord could "turn a square street corner at fifty miles an hour."[43]

In 1931 as did many Duesenberg owners, Frank purchased another special automobile, this one an Austin Coupe presented to his eleven-year-old daughter as a gift. This diminutive little car, which appears much like a shrunken Duesie, counted among its owners the likes of Al Johlson, Buster Keaton, Marion Davies, and Laurel and Hardy. Basically, most used these unbelievably small vehicles as play things, as demonstrated by film from the Yount-Manion family archives that shows Mildred happily circling the driveway at El Ocaso in her motorized toy.[44]

Mildred Frank Yount's 1931 Austin Coupe.
—Courtesy Yount-Manion Film Collection, Lamar University, Beaumont, Texas.

Frank rounded out his collection with the purchase of a 1933 Dodge.

As stated previously even from youth, Yount liked to invent things, and this talent carried over into improvements that he saw could be made with oil field drilling equipment. On September 15, 1920, he filed an application with the United States Patent Office in which he claimed his invention will "provide in a pump piston, a piston body, the packing receiving groove of which is tapered from the following end of the piston forwardly, thereby permitting the use of unit packing." On March 22, 1921, he received Patent Number 1,372,262. He followed up on August 13, 1923, with a second application stating "this invention relates to new and useful improvements in a tong, and has particular relation to a novel type of latch, by means of which the tong jaws may be secured around the pipe or tool joint, or other round object to be turned." The government issued patent number 1,499,435 on July 1, 1924. Yount requested a third patent on June 11, 1925, this time for "a line guide for draw works designed to guide the cable, or line on to the cable operating drum of the draw works in such manner that the cable will be uniformly wound, or

1933 Dodge.
—Courtesy Kathryn Manion Haider.

Yount
Wire Line Guide
or Spooling Attachment

A Dreadnaught Product

Yount Wire Line Guide
(Patented)

YOUNT WIRE LINE GUIDE
or Spooling Attachment

Conceived and designed by practical Oil Men to prolong the life of wire line by controlling its spooling and preventing its abuse in service.

1.— SPOOLS THE LINE PERFECTLY.— On or off the drum, fast or slow, the casing line weaves smooth and even, never piles up or crowds. So simple in action the line itself governs its operation.

2.— LINE ALWAYS IN CONTROL— Close but almost frictionless contact with the line prevents the abusive whip and gaps in the line which with constantly changing load strains cause undue vibration and often results in stranding of lines in heavy duty.

3.— ADJUSTABLE to the exact direction of the line so that the strain is never imposed on the sheaves of the guide.
Proportioned to spool hoisting drums up to 42 inches in width.
Easily attached to the head-board of any rotary draw works.

4.— CONSTRUCTION, Dreadnaught.

The Casing Line automatically and positively spooled permits speed with safety. The Yount Guide pays dividends by protecting your wire line investment.

Yount Cat Line Spool
and Cat Line Protector
(Patent Applied For)

Serving the Cat Line in a similar capacity, the Cat Line Spool and Protector are necessities for safe and efficient operation from the Cat Head. They fit any draw works.

1.— The SPOOL or upper pulley smooths out operation for the several hoisting purposes on which a line to the cat-head is used and eliminates cutting the head-board timbers.

2.— The PROTECTOR or side spool provides protection for No. 1 draw works post and saves the cat-line when making-up or breaking-out pipe from the cat-head.

PRICES

YOUNT WIRE LINE GUIDE
or Spooling Attachment

Complete, Ready to install ....380 lbs. $100.00
(Prices slightly higher West of Rocky Mountains)

PARTS

Part Number	Name	Weight	Price
Y-10	Mounting Brackets	Each 72	$20.00
Y-11	Sheaves	Each 48	15.00
Y-24	Shaft	Each 41	8.50
Y-21	Adj. Screws with Nuts	Each 2½	3.50

YOUNT CAT LINE SPOOL
and CAT LINE PROTECTOR

Cat Line Spool Complete (For Head-Board) ....86 lbs. $30.00

PARTS

Part Number	Name	Weight	Price
Y-6	Sheave (Pulley)	Each 46	$14.00
Y-20	Shaft only	Each 6	1.50
Y-8	Head Bracket	Each 18	8.50
Y-9	Clevis Bracket	Each 10	6.50

Cat Line Protector Complete (For Post) ....72 lbs. $30.00

PARTS

Part Number	Name	Weight	Price
Y-13	Roller Pulley	Each 40	$15.00
Y-12	Brackets, Upper and Lower,	Each 10	5.50
Y-19	Shaft only	Each 12	4.00

MANUFACTURED BY
Beaumont Iron Works Co.
BEAUMONT TEXAS, U. S. A.

DISTRIBUTED BY
Frick-Reid Supply Co.
GENERAL OFFICES: TULSA, OKLA.
West of the Missippi—Stores Everywhere

This Seal Appears on All Genuine Dreadnaught Equipment, and is a Guarantee of Quality.

Yount Wire Line Guide Sales Brochure.
—Courtesy Mildred Yount Manion.

spooled, onto the drum, without its turns becoming crossed and thereby injured." Even before January 19, 1926 when he received Patent Number 1,570,116, Beaumont Iron Works Company manufactured this particular invention for Yount under the trade name of *Dreadnaught*, distributed by Frick-Reid Supply Company of Tulsa, Oklahoma.[45]

He submitted another application on November 18, 1926, for a counterweight whose purpose "is to counterbalance the weight of the rods of the well …, but must likewise be capable of being secured firmly in position over the center of balance of the walking beam, so that it will not unbalance the walking beam, and render the operation of disconnecting and re-connecting the rods extremely difficult." Patent number 1,616,100 was issued on February 1, 1927. On June 14 of the following year, Yount submitted another specific request relating to a flame arrester "which is so constructed that it will not fail either in its flame arresting function or in its venting function, due to action thereon of heat, the elements or the fumes of the stored oil." He received patent number 1,755,624 on April 22, 1930. Yount filed a fifth application on May 16, 1929 indicating that it related to the previous patent number 1,570,116. The current invention, he said, "is to provide in a sheave type line guide means for effectively lubricating the line passing through the guide and at the same time lubricating the bars upon which the sheaves are slidably and rotatably mounted." He received patent number 1,809,921 on June 16, 1931. And finally on November 3, 1932, he submitted a request for another "to avoid the expense and trouble caused by the use of fluid cooled brake flanges, by the provision of a fluid cooled brake band." That patent, number 2,008,633, was issued on July 16, 1935. As of November 13, 1933, however, only two of these were actually producing income, these being numbers 1,570,116 and 1,616,100 that brought in a combined total of $449.56.[46]

At the age of fifty-three, Yount personally received one of the highest honors that his city could bestow. On June 14, 1933, the Rotary Club named him as "Distinguished Citizen" of Beaumont during a luncheon at Hotel Beaumont. J. S. Edwards, past president of the club, presided during the ceremony, attended by Pansy, Mildred, Preston P. Butler, C. A. Easley, and others, including special guests, Dr. and Mrs. T. M. Hunter, Mayor E. A. Fletcher, Dr. and Mrs. John Yost, R. E. Masterson, Mrs. Jack "Stannie" Stansbury, Mrs. P. B. Doty, Mrs. C. A. Easley, Mrs. J. S. Edwards, Mr. and Mrs. Will E. Orgain, Mrs. Beeman Strong, and Miss Charlotte Strong. In a lengthy oration, Edwards called Yount a "citizen and neighbor to the people of Beaumont," and he also added:

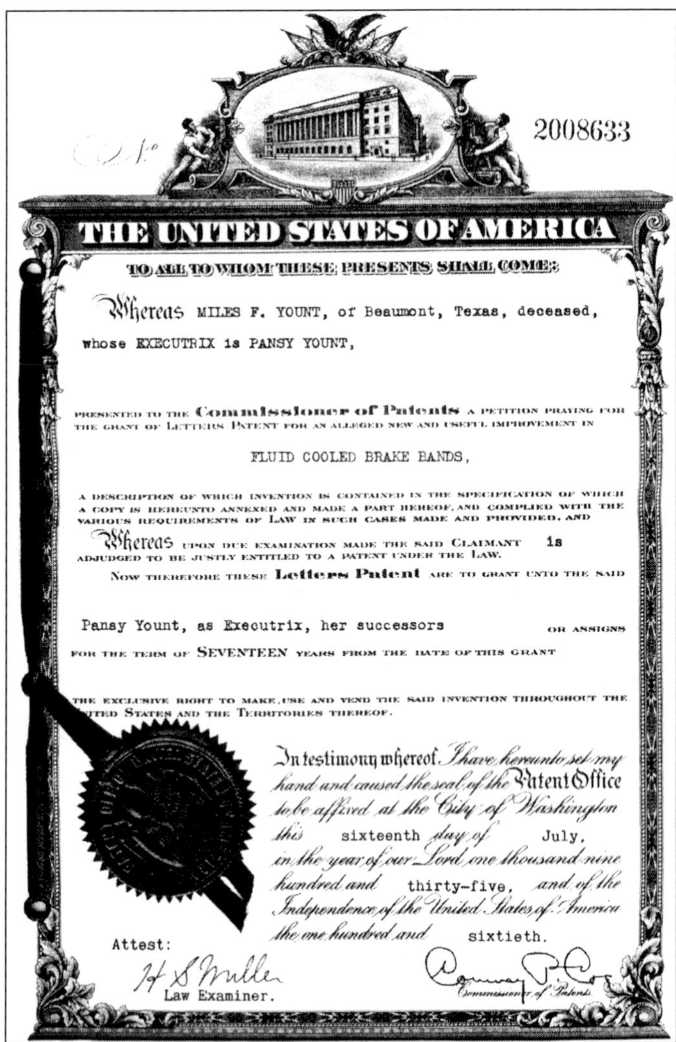
No. 2008633

THE UNITED STATES OF AMERICA

TO ALL TO WHOM THESE PRESENTS SHALL COME:

Whereas MILES F. YOUNT, of Beaumont, Texas, deceased, whose EXECUTRIX is PANSY YOUNT,

PRESENTED TO THE **Commissioner of Patents** A PETITION PRAYING FOR THE GRANT OF LETTERS PATENT FOR AN ALLEGED NEW AND USEFUL IMPROVEMENT IN

FLUID COOLED BRAKE BANDS,

A DESCRIPTION OF WHICH INVENTION IS CONTAINED IN THE SPECIFICATION OF WHICH A COPY IS HEREUNTO ANNEXED AND MADE A PART HEREOF, AND COMPLIED WITH THE VARIOUS REQUIREMENTS OF LAW IN SUCH CASES MADE AND PROVIDED, AND

Whereas UPON DUE EXAMINATION MADE THE SAID CLAIMANT is ADJUDGED TO BE JUSTLY ENTITLED TO A PATENT UNDER THE LAW.

NOW THEREFORE THESE **Letters Patent** ARE TO GRANT UNTO THE SAID

Pansy Yount, as Executrix, her successors OR ASSIGNS

FOR THE TERM OF SEVENTEEN YEARS FROM THE DATE OF THIS GRANT

THE EXCLUSIVE RIGHT TO MAKE, USE AND VEND THE SAID INVENTION THROUGHOUT THE UNITED STATES AND THE TERRITORIES THEREOF.

In testimony whereof *I have hereunto set my hand and caused the seal of the* Patent Office *to be affixed at the City of Washington this* sixteenth *day of* July, *in the year of our Lord one thousand nine hundred and* thirty-five, *and of the Independence of the United States of America the one hundred and* sixtieth.

Attest:

Law Examiner.

Commissioner of Patents.

Patent number 2,008,633.

—Courtesy Kathryn Manion Haider.

The serious economic situation that has for four years prevailed in this section, and still continues, has placed many of his neighbors and friends, and right here let me say that he considers all the citizens of this community his neighbors and friends, in a position of being seriously affected and in some instances without even the means of livelihood, and this good man, this citizen, has, without hope or desire of reward, created business where business had disappeared. I speak of our honored guest, Mr. Frank Yount.

Yet, regardless of his wealth, estimated in the low range of $16 million ($238 million in

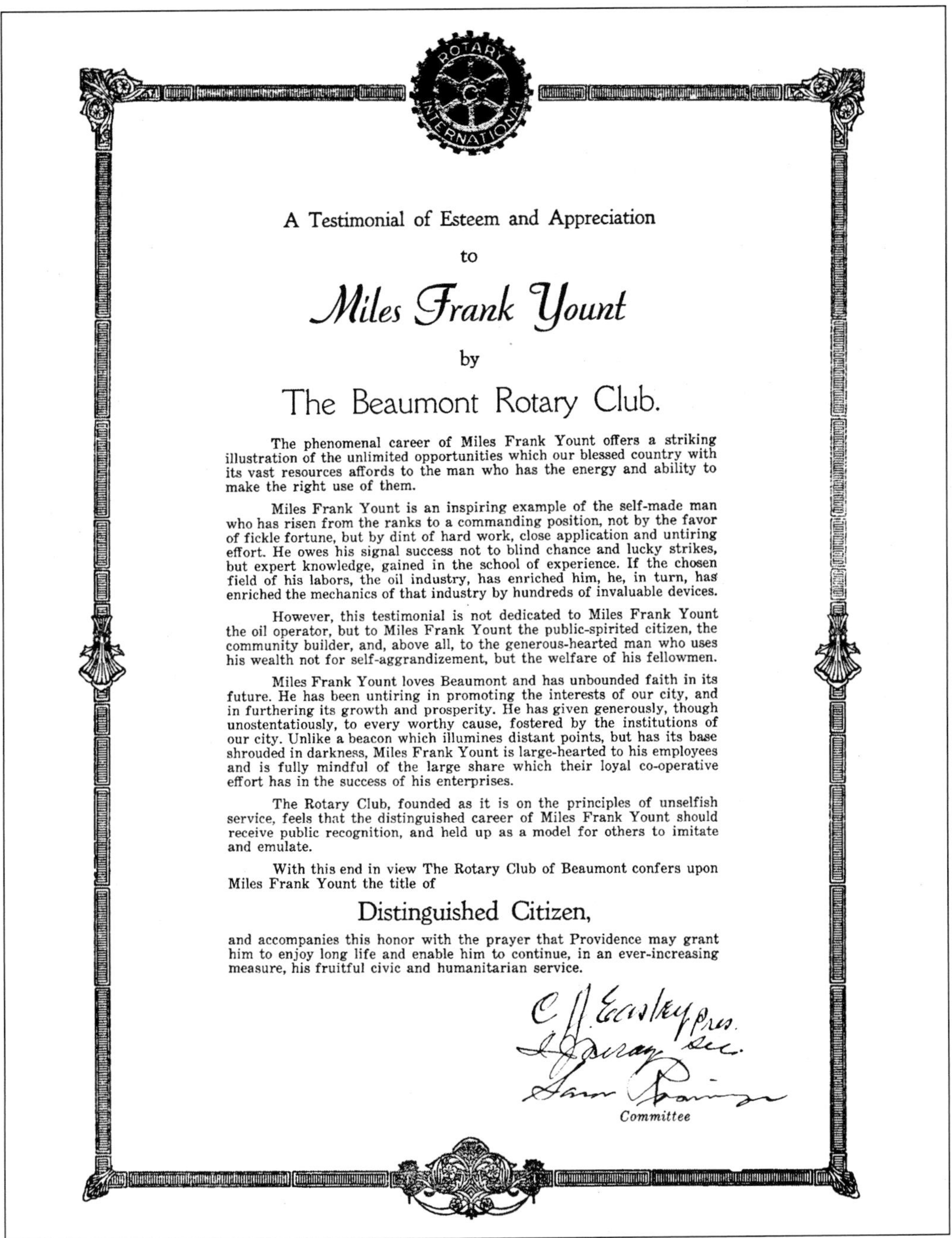

ROTARY INTERNATIONAL

A Testimonial of Esteem and Appreciation

to

Miles Frank Yount

by

The Beaumont Rotary Club.

The phenomenal career of Miles Frank Yount offers a striking illustration of the unlimited opportunities which our blessed country with its vast resources affords to the man who has the energy and ability to make the right use of them.

Miles Frank Yount is an inspiring example of the self-made man who has risen from the ranks to a commanding position, not by the favor of fickle fortune, but by dint of hard work, close application and untiring effort. He owes his signal success not to blind chance and lucky strikes, but expert knowledge, gained in the school of experience. If the chosen field of his labors, the oil industry, has enriched him, he, in turn, has enriched the mechanics of that industry by hundreds of invaluable devices.

However, this testimonial is not dedicated to Miles Frank Yount the oil operator, but to Miles Frank Yount the public-spirited citizen, the community builder, and, above all, to the generous-hearted man who uses his wealth not for self-aggrandizement, but the welfare of his fellowmen.

Miles Frank Yount loves Beaumont and has unbounded faith in its future. He has been untiring in promoting the interests of our city, and in furthering its growth and prosperity. He has given generously, though unostentatiously, to every worthy cause, fostered by the institutions of our city. Unlike a beacon which illumines distant points, but has its base shrouded in darkness, Miles Frank Yount is large-hearted to his employees and is fully mindful of the large share which their loyal co-operative effort has in the success of his enterprises.

The Rotary Club, founded as it is on the principles of unselfish service, feels that the distinguished career of Miles Frank Yount should receive public recognition, and held up as a model for others to imitate and emulate.

With this end in view The Rotary Club of Beaumont confers upon Miles Frank Yount the title of

Distinguished Citizen,

and accompanies this honor with the prayer that Providence may grant him to enjoy long life and enable him to continue, in an ever-increasing measure, his fruitful civic and humanitarian service.

C. J. Easley Pres.

Sec.

Committee

Frank Yount's Distinguished Citizen Award.

—Courtesy Mildred Yount Manion.

Miles Franklin Yount.

—Courtesy Mildred Yount Manion.

today's currency), and the vast personal recognition that he attained through the years, the oilman remained modest—and steady as a rock. The term applied to his company, "the Financial Gibraltar of Beaumont," fitted most appropriately, and due in large order to Yount's personal generosity, the city eventually overcame its economic crisis.[47]

Frank Yount died of a heart attack on November 13, 1933. Although newspaper reports indicated that he seemed in perfect health up to that time, an associate, Marvin McClendon, said that he witnessed Yount taking his pulse on several occasions and asserted that he probably knew that he suffered from heart problems. Furthermore, Ben Woodhead, who lived across the street from the Yount family, wrote years later:

> His death was regarded as "sudden." And yet our family physician, Dr. Guy Reed, told Dad a few days later that he had examined Mr. Yount for a life insurance policy about a year before, and had felt duty bound to turn down the application. Heart condition, as I recall.

Most others, however, had no clue, like long-time acquaintance, W. M. Crook, who said, "Only two or three days before his passing, I encountered him on the street in front of the San Jacinto Building, shook hands with him, enjoyed the friendly interest kindled in his eye and realized the sincerity of his greeting."[48]

Over the course of the next several days, a few details emerged about the millionaire's last hours. Frank had gotten up that Monday morning as usual, dressed, and ate the breakfast that his personal cook, Will Irwin, prepared for him. He was excited about the day ahead, to a great extent, because his new five-passenger black and gold Duesenberg J-472 (Judkins-bodied Berline) sedan, which he bought while attending the Chicago World's Fair the month before, had just arrived by rail the previous Saturday. He owned two Duesenbergs already, one a coupe, his "Sunday car," and the other a sedan, both 1929 models, but to Frank this one—the cosmetic queen, Elizabeth Arden, owned its identical twin—had more pizzazz. At first glance during the auto show, he not only became infatuated with the motor, he fell in love with the accessories. One newspaper report stated that the Judkins Berline contained "special compartments ... built in the back portion of the front seat" and even included as standard equipment, "a moving picture camera." Frank and Everett Randall (Mildred's bodyguard and Frank's part-time chauffeur) picked up the long, sleek beauty, and drove it home where it would remain parked until someone purchased license plates.[49]

That Monday morning, early, Frank took his "work car," the Pierce-Arrow, and drove himself to the office, where he spent a rather uneventful day. The only thing considered out of the ordinary occurred that afternoon when the plates were bought for the new Duesenberg. Frank got home at the usual hour, and around dark he sat at a desk in his home office located on the first floor, right off the hallway leading to the west side entrance of the house. Mary Powell, whom Frank and Pansy employed to home school Mildred, had just completed her daily duties and walked down the same hall to go outside and be picked up by her husband, Joe, who had just got off work. Mary passed by the doorway to Frank's office, saw him busily poring over some papers, ducked her head in, and bid him with the customary farewell. Yount smiled and responded simply, "Goodnight, Mrs. Powell."[50]

That evening Frank and Pansy entertained a few friends, including her brother,

1933 Duesenberg "Judkins Berline" sedan, black and gold exterior color.

—Courtesy Kathryn Manion Haider.

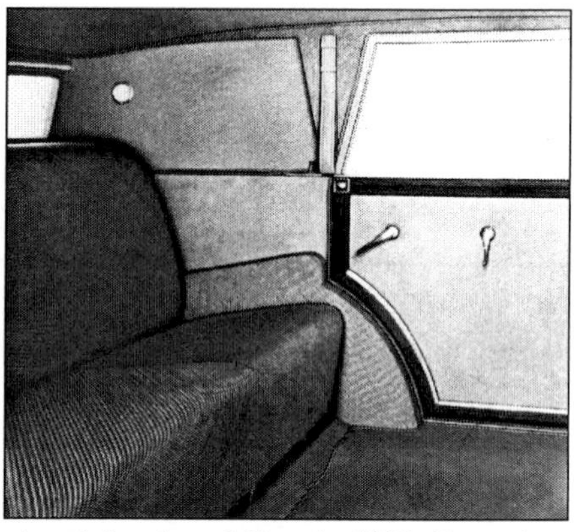

Actual interior of Yount's 1933 Duesenberg "Judkins Berline" sedan.

—Courtesy Randy Ema, Inc.

265 H.P. Duesenberg Straight 8 Engine.

—Courtesy Blackhawk Collection, Danville, California.

Emmett Merritt, and R. E. Masterson, long-time friend, confidant, and family legal advisor. The small group joked and talked about planning a Christmas party. And too, Frank was excited for another reason. His beloved horses, led by Night Alarm, Chief of Spindletop, and the incomparable Beau Peavine were already at Kansas City for an upcoming event. He planned to take Pansy and Mildred up there within the next couple of days and join Cape Grant who promised to blow away the competition. During the small get-together that evening, all had a good time, and each attendee said later that Frank seemed in good spirits, and that he appeared to have never felt better. After his guests left, Frank retired for the night to his second floor bedroom at about 10:30, but a few minutes later, Mildred heard a noise and ran to investigate. There, she found her father slumped in a chair, at first unresponsive, and then she saw him fall lifelessly to the floor. Panic stricken, Mildred summoned Pansy who put in an immediate call to the family physician, Dr. Hugh E. Alexander, but when he arrived, he soon abandoned all efforts to revive the one whom many considered invincible. At this point, Alexander could do nothing but hang his head and express sympathy. He performed a clinical diagnosis on the spot, and ordered no autopsy. In his professional opinion, there was no need. With the outcome, a massive heart attack, so clearly obvious, Alexander determined that Frank suffered a coronary occlusion as a probable result of a thrombus. He put the oilman's death at 11:30 P.M.[51]

From here, however, things began to take on a very bizarre overtone. Instead of directing that Frank's body be removed to a local mortuary, Pansy had it placed back into his bed where he had been just a few minutes before. Furthermore, the widow made the quick decision that no one, with the exception of some members of the immediate family, close friends, and business associates would be allowed to view her husband's

The following represents a photocopy of Frank Yount's death certificate located at the Jefferson County Courthouse in Beaumont, Texas.

CERTIFICATION OF VITAL RECORD

City of Beaumont, Texas

TEXAS STATE DEPARTMENT OF HEALTH
BUREAU OF VITAL STATISTICS
STANDARD CERTIFICATE OF DEATH

1 PLACE OF DEATH STATE OF TEXAS
COUNTY OF Jefferson — Registrar's No. 537
CITY OR PRECINCT NO. Beaumont No. 1376 Street Calder
If in an Institution, give name of Institution instead of Street and No.
Length of residence in city where death occurred 36 yrs. ... mos. ... days ... ? How long in U. S. if foreign born? ... yrs. ... mos. ... days ...

2 FULL NAME OF DECEASED Miles Frank Yount
Residence: No. 1376 Street Calder — If non-residence give city, or town and state

PERSONAL AND STATISTICAL PARTICULARS

3. SEX: Male
4. COLOR OR RACE: White
5. Single Married Widowed Divorced (Write the word): Married
5a. If married, widowed, or divorced HUSBAND of (or) WIFE of: Pansy Merritt Yount
6. DATE OF BIRTH (month, day, and year): January 31st, 1880
7. AGE: 53 Years 9 Months 12 Days. If LESS than 1 day, ... hrs. or ... min.
8. Trade, profession, or particular kind of work done, as spinner, sawyer, bookkeeper, etc.: Oil Producer
9. Industry or business in which work was done, as silk mill, saw mill, bank, etc.:
10. Date deceased last worked at this occupation (month and year): November 13th, 1933
11. Total time (years) spent in this occupation: 18
12. BIRTHPLACE (city or town) (State or country): Monticello, Arkansas
13. NAME (Father): Joseph Nathaniel Yount
14. BIRTHPLACE (city or town) (State or country): Virginia
15. MAIDEN NAME (Mother): Hattie Minerva Yount
16. BIRTHPLACE (City or town) (State or county): Virginia
17. INFORMANT: Mrs. Frank Yount
(Address) Beaumont, Texas
18. BURIAL, CREMATION, OR REMOVAL Place: Magnolia Date Nov. 16, 19 33
19. UNDERTAKER: Pipkin & Brulin Company
(Address) Beaumont, Texas
20. FILE DATE AND SIGNATURE OF REGISTRAR: Nov. 17th 19 33 L. O. Bernhagen

MEDICAL CERTIFICATE OF DEATH

21. DATE OF DEATH (month, day, and year): November 13th, 19 33
22. I HEREBY CERTIFY, That I attended deceased from November 13th, 19 33, to November 13th, 19 33
I last saw him ~~alive~~ dead on November 13, 19 33, death is said to have occurred on the date stated above, at 11:30 P.m.
The principal cause of death and related causes of importance were as follows: Coronary occlusion probably a thrombus — Date of onset: 11/13/33
Other contributory causes of importance:
Name of operation ... date of ...
What test confirmed diagnosis? Clinical Was there an autopsy? No
23. If death was due to external causes (violence) fill in also the following:
Accident, suicide, or homicide? ...
Date of injury ..., 19...
Where did injury occur? ... (Specify city or town, county, and State)
Specify whether injury occurred in industry, in home, or in public place.
Manner of injury ...
Nature of injury ...
24. Was disease or injury in any way related to occupation of deceased? ...
If so, specify ...
(Signed) Hugh E. Alexander M. D.
(Address) Beaumont, Texas

HF121979

This is to certify that this is a true and correct reproduction of the original record as recorded in this office. Issued under authority of Sec. 191.051, Health and Safety Code.

Issued: March 26, 2004

Marcia Gauthier
Local Registrar

CITY OF BEAUMONT TEXAS

DEPARTMENT OF PUBLIC HEALTH VITAL STATISTICS CITY OF BEAUMONT

WARNING: It is illegal to duplicate this copy.

American Bank Note Company

ANY ALTERATION OR ERASURE VOIDS THIS CERTIFICATE

remains. Frank always shunned the limelight during life, she explained, and now she would honor his wishes after death. All that seemed perfectly logical coming from a grieving widow who had just seen her world turned upside down, but her next decision raised eyebrows. Frank's body, she ordered, would be kept at 1376 Calder Avenue until the burial.[52]

At 11:30 P.M. on Monday, November 13, 1933, Frank Yount's amazing winning streak had unfortunately run its course and so abruptly met its end. On the morning that followed, Joe and Mary Powell awoke to a fair day, and before the day was out, the temperature would reach 76 degrees. The sun had risen at 6:40 A.M., and everything seemed normal enough, that is until they read the headlines of the *Enterprise*. Only then, in total disbelief, did Mary realize that she was one of the last few people who saw Frank Yount alive.[53]

The death sent shock waves through the financial structure of Beaumont, and citizens, both influential and ordinary, wept and mourned his passing as if they had lost a member of their immediate family. For them, Frank Yount had actually become much more than that. He had become their savior, their salvation, their hero, their role model, and the spirit of the American dream, all wrapped into one. His celebrated rags to riches story and his aspirations represented a glorious future, most thought, and as long as Frank Yount remained alive, Beaumont felt safe and secure. Why, Frank had even personally staved off, temporarily at least, the Great Depression! When many employers throughout the country were laying off workers in record numbers, Yount-Lee kept men on the payroll. Sure, some had to contend with a few less hours each week, but more importantly, they still had jobs. In fact, others even received salary raises. William Gray Ford, a company employee who lived in Beaumont, had seen his annual income rise steadily from $1,504.83 in 1929 to $2,257.38 in 1933. Imagine that, a 50 percent increase, and in the heart of the Depression, making today's equivalent of $32,332.63. Just ask anyone on the street; everyone knew who made those kinds of things happen. Who else, but Frank Yount? And during the darkest days of Beaumont history, he had seen that city workers—not once but twice— received paychecks back in 1932 when local banks turned a deaf ear to the pleas of Mayor Fletcher for additional funds. No one, including Fire Chief Steve O'Conor, cared that Yount-Lee actually loaned the city the money and got 6 percent interest. None of that really mattered except the knowledge that Frank Yount came through in the clutches. And back in June 1929, when Yount-Lee advanced $31,675 in company funds to help the city purchase land on which to build an airport, everyone knew that Frank made that call as well.[54]

For those and countless other crusades in which he assumed command, Frank Yount demonstrated that he knew best, and that was good enough for the city fathers who sincerely believed, as did others, that the man whose office graced the fifteenth floor of the San Jacinto Building would lead the way in building a Beaumont to be reckoned with. And when he was done, the city would rival, if not totally surpass, the giant metropolitan Houston just ninety miles down the road as the kingpin of the economic bully pulpit of Texas, not to mention the cultural aspect with all its impact. Frank Yount, if he'd only lived, they said, would have been to Beaumont what Jesse Jones was to Houston. Yes, Frank Yount had become more than a mere mortal. By now, he had become legendary, a knight in shining armor, and along the way, this quiet, conservative, unassuming individual evolved into an icon.[55]

Hastings Harrison summed it up best. "In this day of insecurity, uncertainty and unprecedented need," he said, "the world can ill afford to lose such a citizen and benefactor."[56]

Pansy wanted her husband's funeral to be a small service, with just a few friends and family in attendance—the way Frank would have liked it. But in complete contrast, his passing took on an air and ceremony, a certain pomp and circumstance of royalty and pageantry that resembled in many ways the procession and burial of an American president. After the city council's regular session on Wednesday, November 15, Mayor Fletcher proclaimed that city offices would close at noon the next day in remembrance of their patron. Banks announced similar decisions as well, and Judge P. D. "Pete" Renfro, acting in place of County Judge B. B. Johnson, issued a special proclamation that all departments would lock their doors from 2:00 until 4:00 P.M. on the sixteenth. Administrators at Mildred's former school, Dick Dowling Junior High, called for dismissing classes at 2:00 P.M., and directed the flag to be flown at half mast. Harry Phelan ordered all branches of his wholesale grocery firm located in Beaumont, Port Arthur, and DeQuincy, Louisiana, closed at noon. Numerous other offices and businesses followed suit. By Thursday noon, several hundred visitors, included an estimated half of all Yount-Lee employees, had made their way to the family home to pay brief visits, and out of frustration, Pansy abandoned trying to keep track of them.[57]

Immediately after Frank's death, flower arrangements of all descriptions began arriving at El Ocaso, and within an hour of the funeral, two hundred and seventy-eight wreaths, sprays, easels, baskets, and pot plants were delivered, so many in fact that they filled, then completely overflowed the first story front rooms of the mansion, the entrance porch, and veranda, and the excess used to line both sides of the walkway leading from the street to the house. Just about every blooming flower was represented, ranging from the most popular mums and pom-poms to a few carnations. The McFaddin family sent a large easel of red roses and orchids, doubtless the most expensive of the lot; but common folks, many who probably had no money to spare, dug deep and reciprocated as well. Eighty Western Union telegrams and fourteen postal telegraphs originated from points all over the nation, including Texas, California, Colorado, Arkansas, Mississippi, Illinois, New York, Oklahoma, Ohio, Louisiana, Missouri, and Pennsylvania. Some came from far away as Paris, France. Seventy-four letters of various lengths, some hand-written, some typed, some pre-printed cards, were mailed to Pansy and Mildred from people all across the country who stated that they had seen the shocking news about Frank's death in their hometown newspapers that carried the Associated Press story. One of the most poignant letters, however, arrived from Laura E. Wiess, the original owner of El Ocaso, who now lived in San Antonio.

> Dear Mrs. Yount,
>
> It was with great sorrow that I learned of the passing of Mr. Yount. I feel that no one can sympathize with you more than I, as my great sorrow was also in that home. It brought back to me so vividly the passing away of Mr. Wiess. I wish you to know that I would have tendered my sympathy sooner, but I can no longer see to read nor write, and had no one to write for me. I feel that Beaumont has lost one of its best and most influential men with the passing of Mr. Yount. He always commanded my greatest esteem. I pray that the Lord will comfort you in your hour of sorrow.

Rank strangers like Mickey Levito, a little girl, eleven years old, who resided at 1005 Avenue D in Beaumont, felt compelled to write as well, and in heartrending fashion, she explained that during the Depression her family had lost everything they owned except their house. She did not complain for herself personally, however, but concluded, "... you [Mrs. Yount] lost most of all, the great man of Beaumont." Resolutions of sorrow streamed in by the droves, including those from the Beaumont Council of the Boy Scouts of America, the Beaumont Rotary Club, the Port Commission of the City of Beaumont, the College Street Branch of the Young Men's Christian Association, and the regents of the University of Texas, just to name a few. Ernest N. Doring, who had earlier interviewed Frank about his interests in violins, sent his condolences from Chicago, while G. A. Bryant, Jr. of the Austin Company of Cleveland, Ohio, which built the Mildred Building and Apartments, also expressed his deepest regrets.[58]

Mr. and Mrs. Ed Humphries of High Island conveyed "appreciation of one of the last acts of kindness of the late Mr. Yount for donating the gas line and gas into the building we are using for a school cafeteria. It is a wonderful help to us, also the children, enabling them to eat their meals in a warm room on the coldest day. And while speaking of the children, let me say a word in their behalf. Had you have looked this whole world over, you could not have found a more prouder group of children, and at the same time, a more sorrowful group of children as when they gathered their nickels & dimes together to buy "Uncle Frank," as they lovingly called Mr. Yount, a wreath."[59]

Courtesy Tyrrell Historical Library, Beaumont, Texas, the following represents a portion of the minutes taken at the regular semi-annual meeting of First National Bank of Beaumont's Board of Directors held on December 30, 1933. Read aloud by director T. S. Reed, the part paying honor to Frank Yount, himself a former director, appears on page 980.

On November thirteenth, nineteen hundred and thirty-three, the Death Angel called into eternal life Miles Frank Yount. It can be truthfully said that no one will be more missed, no memory more cherished, for ineffaceably stamped upon Southeast Texas and the neighboring section of Louisiana will be the imprint of his genius for organization and development; his loyal, sincere affection for friends; his supreme devotion to home life; his deep interest in the finer things of life.

The story of Miles Frank Yount is a story of achievement, and where that story is fully told, the man stands revealed as one who possessed remarkable vision and insight. Few who have not had intimate knowledge of his business connections have any accurate idea of the far reaching consequences of Mr. Yount's contribution to the industrial life of Southeast Texas. He possessed a faith backed by courage, integrity and ability, striking qualities of leadership, qualities that made it possible for him to amass a large personal fortune, and at the same time increase the prosperity and happiness of his neighbors.

While today all Beaumont mourns the passing of Miles Frank Yount, he has left to friends, acquaintances, and associates an immortal legacy—the remembrance of a "mighty oak," a man among men, whose influences of honor and responsibility toward his fellow men will continue to bless those of generations to come.

The following board members were listed:

W. P. H. McFaddin, Jr.	H. W. Gardner	P. B. Doty
Ben D. Jackson	E. E. Plumly	T. S. Reed
Tom Andrus	C. H. Chambers	H. A. Dodd
C. E. Broussard	Stuart R. Smith	L. P. Tullos
W. P. H. McFaddin	Robert Corley	J. S. Gordon

Aurelia (Mrs. Benjamin Rush) Norvell offered her personal condolences to "My dear Mrs. Yount and Mildred" and ended "with a deep feeling of friendship & the hope that God will give you strength to "carry on." Other prominent Beaumonters such as Nena Wiess (Mrs. W. A.) Priddie, Signora Wiess (Mrs. Alex) Marshall wrote, as did Lizzie Edwards, whose husband James penned a short poem titled "Tribute to Mr. M. F. Yount."[60]

The news of Frank's death quickly made its way to Monticello, Arkansas, where his mother, Hattie, had one of her grandsons, Harrell Yount, immediately drive her to Texas. The couple left about 1:00 P.M. on Tuesday and arrived in Sour Lake some ten hours later after traveling approximately 393 miles, a harrowing trip given the condition of the roads in between and Hattie's advanced age of eighty-four. Since she had last visited the area as recently as June, each of her relatives in Arkansas and Sour Lake expressed grave concern for her welfare considering the fact that she too suffered with heart problems.[61]

When Cape Grant got the news in Missouri, he asked Pansy what to do. Should he scrap the plans, come back to Beaumont, or what? She told him that Frank would have wanted everything to proceed as usual, so she issued absolute instructions to "ride Chief of Spindletop, Beau Peavine and your other horses in Kansas City, and ride them to win." At about 10:30 Thursday morning, the family gathered in Frank's bedroom where his body still remained in bed. Pansy allowed entrance to a select few: Mildred; brother Emmett; a small city delegation; Dr. T. M. Hunter, pastor of Westminster Presbyterian where Frank and Mildred attended; and other close friends, including R. E. Masterson, corporate officers at the Beaumont location, and those who resided in Houston: T. P. Lee, Bill Lee, and Emerson Woodward. But on one of the saddest notes of all, Pansy denied Frank's

Hattie Minerva Yount Uptegrove.

—Courtesy Marguerite Behar.

own elderly mother, Hattie, and his family members from Sour Lake, along with their respective spouses and children, admission to the house in order to pay their final respects. She did, however, put up the Yount family at various apartments at the Mildred Building across Calder Avenue, and from there, they were expected to get to the cemetery on their own.[62]

Shortly before noon, Keith Hotchkiss of Pipkin and Brulin Funeral Home directed his fellow employees to place Frank's body inside the massive bronze cast casket, weighing more than 1,300 pounds, just the night before expressed in from Chicago. With that done, Masterson tearfully walked forward and deposited a tube, also made of bronze, at the side of his departed friend. The small container held a brief life history of the Texas oilman. Written on parchment, it read:

> THE HISTORY OF A LIFE
> Name: Miles Frank Yount
> Address: 1376 Calder Avenue, Beaumont, Texas
> Born: January 31, 1880
> Died: November 13, 1933
> Birthplace: Near Monticello, Ark.
> Father's Name: Joseph Nathaniel Yount
> Mother's Name: Hattie Minerva Yount
> Family: Pansy Merritt Yount, wife. Mildred Frank Yount, daughter
> Religious affiliation: Presbyterian
>
> ADDENDA
>
> Miles Frank Yount was a pioneer in the discovery and development of salt dome oil fields in the gulf coast section of the United States of America.
>
> He was a mechanical genius and his inventions aided and assisted in the development of the petroleum industry of his time.
>
> The Yount-Lee Oil company of which he was president, drilled to a new depth of 9,863 feet.
>
> He was indeed born to be a builder and a developer. He dreamed of a great and glorious city of Beaumont.
>
> His life exemplified the virtue expressed in the passage of scripture which says: but the greatest of these is charity. He was a godfather to his host of employes.
>
> He was devoted to his wife and daughter and his home life was a miniature heaven on earth.
>
> Miles Frank Yount is gone, but his spirit still lives.

When Masterson stepped back, everyone left the room except Pansy and Mildred who viewed the body for the last time. After a few minutes, about when the clock struck twelve noon, Hotchkiss ordered the casket sealed, and then he summoned a stout group of twelve pallbearers to take it downstairs to the first floor front room in the southwest corner of the house and place it underneath a large French mirror. From then until 3:00 P.M., multitudes filed by and paid homage. Ranging from those of affluence and political stature on the high end to the lowest roustabout in the field, people from all stations in life, for a while at least, walked on the same level and shared a common bond.[63]

The day of the funeral, Thursday, November 16, most all business activity in High Island ceased for at least an hour. Some 3,000 people gathered outside the Yount home; cars lined Calder Avenue and Oakland Street for blocks. All Yount-Lee operations stopped, and over 800 employees came to pay respects to their fallen leader. Flags at the city hall and the Jefferson County Courthouse, among others, flew at half staff. No further visitors were allowed to enter the house after 2:45; there was no further space. Inside, Ross Sterling, the former Texas governor and his family stood silent, as well as current and former University of Texas regents: Beauford H. Jester, chairman of the board from Corsicana; John T. Scott of Houston; Willmot M. Odell of Fort Worth; Robert L. Holliday of El Paso; Louis J. Sulak of LaGrange; Charles I. Francis of Wichita Falls; Edward Randall of Galveston; Leslie C. Waggener, Jr. of Dallas; Kenneth H. Aynesworth of Waco; Edward E. Crane of Dallas; and H. J. Lutcher Stark of Orange. Ras Pevito, Frank's old partner at Sour Lake back in 1914, put aside his past differences and attended the service. The twelve pallbearers had been there since Wednesday. All were employees of the Yount-Lee Oil Company, and they included: S. A. Hatcher, drilling rig superintendent at High Island; Max Schlicher, general superintendent for all Louisiana operations; A. L. Barrow, production superintendent; G. L. Young, drilling rig superintendent stationed at Edgerly, Louisiana; C. R. Trahan, Hackberry, Louisiana, superintendent, T. W. "Red" Herrin, superintendent of the East Texas Division; H. H. "Dad" Kellam, High Island superintendent, J. C. Chance, Hull field drilling superintendent; M. Camp, foreman of the Spindletop tank farm, W. Gilbert Prince, Texas district supervisor; G. W. Davis, Louisiana production superintendent; and E. B. Maske, Barber's Hill superintendent. Various oil companies, some allies, such as Sun Oil represented by R. W. Pack; and others, direct and fierce competitors of Yount-Lee, also came, among them Gulf, the Texas Company, and Magnolia. The small service that Pansy originally planned had become a large scale event, orchestrated by a grateful community as a whole.[64]

At about 3:00 P.M, Dr. Hunter escorted the family from the second floor, and a silence fell about the place as Pansy and Mildred walked into the room. Too, some could not believe their eyes, because on this most solemn of all occasions, Pansy slammed the door on another tradition in a manner that flew in the face of all accepted social mores of the time. Instead of wearing the customary black funeral attire, she chose a red dress in its stead, because Frank had not only bought it for her recently, he personally made the selection. If it was good enough for Frank, she determined, it was certainly good enough for his funeral ceremony. After all, she remained in charge of these proceedings, and she really didn't care what anyone thought! Hunter sensed the crowd's reaction, so he directed the service to begin immediately, and a KFDM Radio crew of two, Roy Wise and a Mr. Cierson, broadcast it live

Dr. Thomas Marshall Hunter, Minister, Westminster Presbyterian Church.
—Courtesy Westminster Presbyterian and Tyrrell Historical Library, Beaumont, Texas.

over the airways and by public address system to those who waited outside. Three of Yount's own violins, the Piatti-Stradivari, the Reynier-Stradivari and the Dominicus Montagnana, were prominently used in the service by Charlotte Strong (Mildred's friend), J. Moody Dawson of Houston who had helped Frank put together the fantastic collection, and Lena Milam, Mildred's violin instructor, to play the oilman's favorite song, *Ave Maria* by Shubert, with accompaniment by Josef Evans. Stirred by the music and the occasion, Will Irwin and other African-American servants stood in the background, lowered their heads and cried. Both inside and out, a guard of detectives made sure that everything remained under control; Captain L. B. Maddox, Glen Gallier, J. H. Mulligan, Henry Thomas, Hugh Bayne, Demmie Hayes, Doyle Wingate, John McCain, and J. H. Allen acted on behalf of both local law enforcement agencies.[65]

In part, Dr. Hunter's address is as follows:

> Frank Yount told me he thanked God that he could disperse so many shadows. Judged according to this judgment, this friend our ours has brought hope to many a discouraged man, removed hunger and want from many a despairing home, and lifted the shadow that enveloped many a soul in darkness. And he told me that every day he thanked God that he was able to do these things.
>
> You called Frank Yount a rich man. He brought nothing into the world and he carries nothing out. But there are some investments that cannot be taken away—an orphan fed, a boy educated for a useful life, a girl trained for womanhood. These investments he cannot lose and in years to come they will be paying dividends, some 60, some a hundred fold. We should not estimate a man's worth … by his accumulations of worldly goods, but by what he has done with these things.
>
> The only riches that he [Frank] has taken with him are the kindnesses that he has done; the friends he has won—the love of mankind. And I believe that could he speak to you today, when he sees things so clearly, that Frank Yount would say, "Do not praise me, but give all the glory to God, Who in His own way, put these things into my heart.[66]

Steve D. O'Conor.
—Courtesy Fire Museum of Texas, Beaumont, Texas.

After Dr. Hunter concluded his remarks, the pallbearers lifted the heavy casket with the assistance of others and carried it to the hearse parked at the curb. Police Chief Carl Kennedy and Fire Chief Steve D. O'Conor supervised that part of the ceremony as several motorcycle officers, including Captain J. T. Swanzy, George Stafford, J. B. Como, Ray Yaw and L. E. Davis, took up their assigned places both in front, to the side and in back of the procession. All down Calder, then onto Magnolia and finally to Pine Street, massive crowds lined the streets and watched the slow-moving cortege on its way to Magnolia Cemetery. The pallbearers rode in the first two cars, and the family followed the hearse in between. When the large motorcade drove through the cemetery's main gates, a Spindletop Stables' employee leading Frank's own riding horse, a brown gelding, stepped in front and escorted it toward the hillside grave, protected overhead by an enormous tent. Pansy sat motionless, grief stricken—but unable to shed a tear. After a brief and solemn service, "Paris Grand ... seemed to bow his head as they led him from the graveside." Walter Gunn and his Boy Scout troop spread about and urged the onlookers who gathered next to the protective fence to stay put, while two hand-picked policemen, George Stafford and J. B. Como, remained throughout the night and for the next several, guarding the area. A newspaper reporter wrote, "The services were over ... just as El Ocaso—the Sunset—fell across the petroleum domain which Miles Frank Yount, more than any other man, created and through which he became the benefactor of the city of Beaumont and its people." Afterward, Pansy and Mildred returned to their home—El Ocaso—to face an uncertain future.[67]

Frank Yount's body would stay at the burial site until his widow made a decision about a combination mausoleum and chapel to be constructed of Manitou Greenstone, which cost an estimated $100,000 to $150,000. Obviously, plans were already in the making, because on November 17, 1933, W. M. Schultz, a Yount-Lee corporate employee, wrote to Pansy: "If I can be of any service to you in the building of the Mausoleum ... I will be only too glad to do so." Two days later, a tearful, yet composed, Pansy told a reporter that she would attempt to implement her late husband's numerous plans for Beaumont, though she admitted that some were still unknown even to her. She voiced unwavering support for Spindletop Stables, vowed to see to it that all activities there continued, "and be built up as she was able." "You must remember," she continued, "that the estate must pay the inheritance tax." Pansy intimated that for the next eighteen months, all activities would be hamstrung due to an extremely heavy tax burden. But before the interview concluded, however, Frank Yount's widow dropped a bombshell in what was then a very segregated area by describing her concept for Frank's mausoleum. "The building," she said, "will be interdenominational. I have been asked today to erect it for certain denominations. This I do not care to do, for the reason that I want it to be a place of worship for everyone, white and black, who knew Frank Yount, and those who, though they never saw him, loved him. I want it to be his perpetual resting place and his memorial. It is about all that I can do for him."[68]

On November 20, 1933, Homer J. Tucker, executive secretary of the College Street Branch of the Young Men's Christian Association—the particular location designated for African-Americans—responded to Pansy's recent comments:

> The kindness of your husband and the fine unselfish expressions you made in the *Sunday Enterprise* regarding the interdenominational chapel ... have created a keen desire on the part of many colored people to express their appreciation to you. My work with Mr. A. D. Moore and Judge Beeman Strong ... has taught me something about the unique life of Mr. Yount.[69]

And along the same lines, Aaron Jefferson, editor-manager of the *Beaumont Informer*, an African-American weekly newspaper based in Beaumont at 2068 Irving Avenue, wrote to Pansy on November 23:

> You will find enclosed several clippings from *The Beaumont Informer* issue of

> November 18th. We were indirectly informed that you desired a few clippings of that particular issue.
>
> We may say that this is a very feeble way of expressing the esteem in which Mr. Yount was held by Negroes who knew him and those who only knew of him, they knew he was a friend to man.
>
> While quiet and unassuming there are many Negroes who spoke of him in the very highest terms as being kind, generous and appreciative. The untimely passing of your devoted husband ... is an ... [irreparable] ... [loss] to humanity and the ... *Informer* and the Negroes of Beaumont took this method to let you and the world know that they respected him in life and honor him in death for he was an exceptional character.
>
> According to a news story appearing in the *Enterprise* Sunday Nov. 19th, the *Informer* wish[es] to express its appreciation for the courageous Christ like position you took in this matter and the undaunted courage to herald it to the world, while Miles Frank Yount has passed on, to not be forgotten, his many acts and deeds of kindness shall live after him, in his good wife humanity has a benefactor.
>
> I am enclosing under separate covers a marked copy of *The Beaumont Informer* which is an expression of our faith and devotion.

One of the articles that Mr. Jefferson referred to mentioned that [Frank Yount] respected all people and that "his Negro employes received the utmost consideration in the way of fair and impartial working conditions and wages," and that during his funeral service, Pansy provided "adequate space ... for the Negro employes in the home and procession."[70]

Although it would take quite a while for Pansy's controversial comments about the "interdenominational" issue to die down, it took even longer for the intended mausoleum to take shape. But finally, some twenty-nine months later, on April 19, 1936, the *Beaumont Enterprise* reported that Pansy had approved the plans drawn and submitted to her by Colorado architect, Charles E. Thomas; and she put N. L. Ross, head of the family's quarry operations in Manitou, Colorado, in charge of its construction. The memorial would eventually sit on an 80 by 120 foot plot, and the building itself measured 62 by 18 feet overall. Other important details included the following:

> Space surrounding the mausoleum will be landscaped and planted with flowers and shrubs which were Mr. Yount's favorites.
>
> Back of an arched entrance will be a room, 15 by 22 feet, in which six crypts will be located. Mr. Yount's body will occupy one crypt and the remainder will be for members of his family. A flower room, measuring 10 by 10 feet, will adjoin the main entrance.
>
> Carefully selected stone from the Manitou, Colo. quarries, marble stained glass for the tall arched windows and a quantity of sedately wrought bronze decorative fixtures will go into the building of the memorial.

Ross and his workers completed the edifice by April 30, 1937, and—afterward Frank's body was placed there for all time, at least according to plan.[71]

With Frank's death, numerous newspaper articles described Mildred as heir to a tremendous oil fortune. Although some often inflated the correct amount by large sums, the effect, nonetheless, remained the same. When Masterson filed the inventory

The Yount family mausoleum (only known photograph of Frank Yount's second resting place).

—Courtesy Magnolia Cemetery, Tyrrell Historical Library, and *Texas Gulf Historical and Biographical Record*, Beaumont, Texas.

for the Yount estate, the story that Mildred's share would be a little over $4 million made the front page of the *Beaumont Enterprise* on April 12, 1934. Teenager Betty Johnson of Palisade, Colorado, saw an identical article in the *Rocky Mountain News* and felt obligated to write Mildred on May 23: "Dear Little Girl: I read... that you couldn't have any fun or go to school with your playmates because you have four million dollars. You have my sympathy, and I would like to help you if possible." Miss Johnson went on to explain that she came from a good home, as her father was a doctor. She also supplied further references such as Mr. Tilton, the banker, Mr. Bancroft, the grocer, or any of the area preachers. If Mildred would only come and visit her, she emphasized, no one would know her true identity, and while there, the two could spend their time hiking, skating, and swimming. Betty concluded, "Please investigate and come. Will you?" But not all the letters received were natured so, and as a matter of course, the publicity generated all types of marriage proposals and crackpot responses. Pansy feared for Mildred's safety, as well as her own. Ever since the infamous Charles A. Lindbergh, Jr. kidnapping on the night of March 1, 1932 from his family's home in Hopewell, New Jersey, Frank, first, and now Pansy, more than ever, voiced concern about potential threats to her thirteen-year-old.[72]

Film frame shows Mildred Frank Yount receiving an etching of the USS Frigate Constitution, *"Old Ironsides," from its Commander Louis J. Gulliver. The ship docked at the Port of Beaumont on March 11, 1932.*

—Courtesy Yount-Manion Film Collection, Lamar University, Beaumont, Texas.

Even before then, however, Frank and Pansy had legitimate reasons to worry about their young daughter's wellbeing. Mildred first met Dorothy Hilliard during the second grade while both were students at Millard Elementary, and albeit Dot came from a family whose economic status compared nowhere near that of the Younts, Mildred cared less, so the two, "Dot" and "Millie," became fast friends. Afterward, Dot visited the Yount household frequently, and Mrs. Hilliard, Marguerite Katherine, frequently took the two youngsters on shopping excursions to downtown Beaumont. But dire events would soon mold and strengthen the new camaraderie that lasted a lifetime when unexpectedly, one day a man showed up at the school and announced that he was there to take Mildred to her music lessons. During these unsophisticated and more trusting times, no one really thought this out of the ordinary, and even Mildred, herself, failed to question the man's identity. Luckily, though, Dot intervened. Anxiously, she told her teacher that she had never seen this man before, and certainly he was no member of the Yount staff. Finally, Dot's pressing the issue raised an alarm, and when school officials began to question the stranger, he ran away. Pansy and Frank never forgot this episode, and from that day forward for the rest of their years, they saw to it that Dot Hilliard was taken care of. In fact, Pansy assumed the role as Dot's surrogate mother, choosing to refer to herself as "Mother Fox," the protector. Frank and Pansy also hired a bodyguard for Mildred, and everywhere she went, Everett M. Randall was close by, even at Sunday School, where "Randy," remained in the hall, watching diligently.[73]

So with the current publicity barrage about Mildred's massive wealth filling newspaper columns, Pansy took extra precautions. For additional protection, she turned to the current Beaumont Police Chief, Carl Kennedy, lured him away from a secure post that he had held since 1925, and installed him as manager of the Yount estate with offices in the Mildred Building, effective June 1, 1934. Beginning his colorful career in law enforcement at age twenty, Kennedy previously worked as a deputy sheriff in Hardin County for five years during the Batson, Sour Lake, and Saratoga oil boom, before joining the Jefferson County Sheriff's Office as chief deputy under Tom Garner. On the Beaumont scene, Kennedy made quite a name for himself, chasing moonshiners and bootleggers during the Prohibition era.[74]

While security for some is a necessity, others consider it as interference. After seeing the Yount home, whether routinely or for the first time, most observers of the day could not help expressing awe at its grandeur, and comment, "What a way to live!" But now as many of these same folk caught a fleeting glimpse of armed guards moving about inside the protective fencing, the remark, "What a way to live!" took on an entirely different context.[75]

Carl Kennedy, Beaumont Police Chief and a confiscated moonshine still during Prohibition, circa 1925.

—Courtesy Tyrrell Historical Library, Beaumont, Texas.

Beaumont Police Station during the 1920s.

—Courtesy Howard Perkins Collection, Beaumont, Texas.

Passing the Mantle

"Courage and perseverance have a magical talisman, before which difficulties disappear and obstacles vanish into air."

John Quincy Adams

In the interim, however, Pansy Yount had to deal with other important issues besides the mausoleum—and the possibility of Mildred's abduction, so she now turned attention to her late husband's estate. At first glance, Frank's will, dated June 25, 1932, is a straightforward instrument, calculated to meet all contingencies and in accordance with Texas common law statutes. By law, one-half of the assets or about $4 million went automatically to his widow, and as Frank further stipulated, his daughter inherited the remainder. The will itself, first filed in Probate Court on December 5, 1933, and reviewed before Christmas Eve, led to Pansy's appointment as executrix of the estate and guardian of her daughter's financial affairs. Overnight, Mildred became one of the country's wealthiest heiresses, and newspapers placed her on a shortlist of the elite, "ranked along with the "dollar princess" daughters of the Morgans, du Ponts, Dohertys, McCormicks, and Fields as one of the possible successors to Miss Doris Duke ..." Even though Yount-Lee stock represented the bulk of Mildred's fortune at almost 86 percent, the amount is considerable nonetheless, and in today's currency values would exceed $57 million. But in spite of everything at stake, with only mother and minor child involved, no one perceived that any person might possibly contest the provisos that Frank and his attorney R. E. Masterson planned so carefully and wrapped in a concise package that took only one typewritten page.[1]

On May 24, 1934, the same day that graves were being dug in West Dallas, Texas, for the notorious bank robber and killer duo, Clyde Barrow and Bonnie Parker, Masterson filed a state inheritance tax return for Mildred's portion of the estate valued at $4,000,072.76 (see Appendix 1). Working jointly with the Internal Revenue Service, the state comptroller's office immediately moved to protect its interests by filing a lien against the entire estate until all inheritance and federal estate taxes, both amounting to a total of $778,979.91, were paid in full. But the millionaire heiress and Pansy, as

Mildred Yount Listed Among Possible Successors to 'Wealthiest Girl in U. S.'

MISS MILDRED YOUNT of Beaumont, 14-year-old daughter of Mrs. M. F. Yount, is ranked along with the "dollar princess" daughters of the Morgans, du Ponts, Dohertys, McCormicks, and Fields as one of the possible successors to Miss Doris Duke as the wealthiest girl in the nation.

Recognition as one of the richest girls in the country is accorded Miss Yount in an Associated Press feature story published Sunday on the front page of the Kansas City Star.

Miss Duke left the position of America's wealthiest girl open when she was married recently.

Story in the Star

Following is the story:

A new bloom of "dollar princesses" peeped forth today in the garden of golden flowers from which, only this week, matrimony plucked the wealthy Doris Duke.

Miss Duke, now honeymooning with James Cromwell, was the best known of America's— of the world's —eligible heiress. The Duke fortune, estimated as high as 50 million dollars, grew from tobacco.

The distinction, and often the grief, of being an heiress to fabulous fortunes formerly was shared with Miss Duke by Barbara Hutton, now the wife of Prince Mdivani. The fortune she inherited was built by her grandfather, F. W. Woolworth, from nickles and dimes in the "five and ten."

A New Crop Coming On

But with these two gone, the air still - full of heiresses to fortunes of oil, brick, banking, merchandising, steel timber and all the things that go for great wealth.

Names that are synonyms for money—Morgan, du Pont, Doherty, McCormick, Field,—fill the list.

Louise C. Morgan, granddaughter of J. P. Morgan, is 18 and a debutante of the current New York season. She is one of the attractive and eligible heiresses.

Some persons believe Ethel du Pont, "princess of Delaware" and daughter of Eugene du Pont, is the wealthiest unmarried American heiress. Her name has been mentioned often in connection with that of Franklin D. Roosevelt, Jr., a student at Harvard.

Miss Mildred Yount, of Beaumont, Texas, is at the age of 14 one of the country's wealthiest heiresses—a fortune estimated at 20 million dollars of Yount-Lee Oil company wealth.

Talented Violinist

Music rather than money, however, is Miss Yount's joy. Possessing several rare violins, she plays with skill that hass been applauded. She loves to ride the blooded horses of her mother's famous Spindle Top stables at Beaumont.

Miss Mildred Yount

The young woman now attends the Hockaday school at Dallas and was awarded recently the Hockaday medal for highest grades among freshmen.

Matrimony has taken in late years three Chicago heiress—Florence Crane, born to plumbing millions, Betty Offield, whose grandfather was William Wrigley, Jr., of chewing gum fame and Rosemary Baur—but there remain the beautiful Narcissa Swift of the family that made a mint from meat, and Katrina McCormick, whose father was the late Senator Medill McCormick.

The west coast has lost within the year one of its—and America's —wealthiest daughters through the marriage of Dorothy Spreckles, sugar heiress to a French newspaper publisher.

Income of $3000 a Day

One of the most charming and talented of American beauties-of-gold is Hazel Forbes the 24-year-old heiress to a 30-million dentifrice fortune. With an income of $3000 a day from her fortune, Miss Forbes is concentrating upon a career in the movies. All the money she earns before the camera is devoted to charitable works. She has said she is in the movies for the sheer joy of working in that profession. She has denied repeatedly all rumors of romance.

Dorothy Fell, daughter of Mrs. Ogden Mills, is one of the nation's wealthy unmarried young women, whose engagement has been predicted frequently in recent months but still is—so far as announcement has gone—unattached. It was whispered last year that she might marry Woolworth Donahue, himself an heir to Woolworth wealth, but nothing came of it.

Daughter by Adoption

Henry L. Doherty's daughter-by-adoption, Helen Lee Doherty, is regarded as unusually attractive. Two years ago she entered the diplomatic service.

There are, too, Lucille, Evelyn, and Marie Dupont who, like Ethel can look forward to the prospect of unusual wealth.

There is Priscilla St. George, whose grandfather was George F. Baker, a man of many millions.

The huge Frick fortune casts its golden shadow on Adelaide and Francis Frick. Barbara Field, daughter of the Marshall Fields, will some day control big chunks of a fortune founded on the merchandising genius of the first Marshall Field.

Barbara Phipps, daughter of Henry Carnegie Phipps, can look ahead to the day when she may have more money than she knows what to do with.

From Beaumont Enterprise, *February 21, 1935.*

—Courtesy Kathryn Manion Haider.

R. E. Masterson.
—Courtesy Tyrrell Historical Library, Beaumont, Texas.

The following represents a transcription of Frank Yount's last will and testament located at the Jefferson County Courthouse in Beaumont, Texas. For historical presentation purposes, the authors have made every effort possible to retain the integrity, terminology, grammar, and abbreviations of the original, including misspellings and omissions.

LAST WILL AND TESTAMENT
OF
M. F. YOUNT.

THE STATE OF TEXAS,)
COUNTY OF JEFFERSON) IN THE NAME OF GOD, AMEN:

I, M. F. YOUNT, a resident of Beaumont, in Jefferson County, Texas, being of sound mind and memory, and desiring to dispose of the property with which God has been pleased to bless me, do make and publish this my Last Will and Testament, hereby revoking any and all wills by me heretofore made.

FIRST:

It is my will that my body be buried in a Christianlike manner.

SECOND:

All of the property which I own is community property of myself and my wife, Pansy Yount, and in making this will I am devising and bequeathing my one-half interest in all of said community property.

THIRD:

I hereby GIVE, DEVISE and BEQUEATH to my beloved daughter, Mildred Yount, all of the property, real, personal or mixed, of which I may die seized and possessed, or am interested in at the time of my death, to own and hold in fee simple title.

FOURTH:

I hereby constitute and appoint my beloved wife, Pansy Yount, Executrix of this my Last Will and Testament, and direct that no bond or other security be required of her as such Executrix.

FIFTH:

It is my will that no other action shall be had in the County Court in the administration of my estate than to prove and record this will, and to return an inventory and appraisement of my estate and list of claims.

IN TESTIMONY WHEREOF, I have hereunto set my hand, at Beaumont, Texas, this, the 25th, day of June, A. D. 1932, in the presence of the undersigned witnesses, who attest the same at my request.

executrix, experienced cash-flow problems, because as of November 13, 1933, less than $300,000 remained on deposit at the First National Bank of Beaumont and the Exchange National Bank of Colorado Springs. Even with bonds and notes considered, they represented an additional pool of slightly above $32,000, not much help given the gravity of the situation. With the initial payment of inheritance taxes on August 21, 1934, the financial position deteriorated even further. The estate still owed another $557,725.55, and none of this took into account that Pansy's separate obligations only made matters worse. After reviewing Frank's drawings for a spectacular home and an "American Saddlebred" horse facility, originally planned for Beaumont, she now seriously considered relocating everything to Lexington, Kentucky, but before moving forward, however, she needed an immediate cash infusion. Therefore, Pansy's scrambling for liquidity certainly contributed greatly to the process that led to the eventual sale of the Yount-Lee Oil Company. And too, the overwhelming sum levied by state and federal taxation units against the estate heaped on top of Pansy's list of mounting problems; and to her, the more than three-quarters of a million dollars—reported to be the largest in Texas to that point—represented nothing other than blatant abuse of authority. Thus began her bitter and extensive hatred toward the Internal Revenue Service and the programs that grew out of FDR's "New Deal" policy.[2]

With pressure appearing at almost every turn, Pansy faced another brief scare on Thursday, February 28, 1935, the latest from totally unexpected sources, when her late husband's aged mother, Hattie Minerva Yount Uptegrove, and some other family relations filed a suit that challenged the legality of the oilman's will. The reason: Frank's generosity extended toward them throughout the years, they believed, seemed at odds with his final bequest. Represented by R. W. Wilson, an attorney with offices in Pine Bluff, Arkansas, Frank's relatives, including brother, Nolan Alfred Yount of Wilmot, Arkansas; sister, Mary Ellen Yount McKeown and her husband, James Walter McKeown of Drew County, Arkansas; and another sister, Alice Virginia Yount and her husband (a distant cousin), Sullie Yount, also of Drew County, joined Hattie in alleging that the document filed in probate back in December 1933 "was not the last will and testament of the late Mr. Yount." Furthermore, the complaint contained mention "that the late Mr. Yount died without having any natural children surviving." Arguments were set for 9:00 the morning of April 4, but when the contestants failed to show any evidence to the contrary, Jefferson County Judge B. B. Johnson upheld the original probate ruling. Pansy further substantiated her case by presenting papers which proved that Mildred had been legally adopted in Hardin County on December 28, 1920. Even though no one ever again officially challenged either Frank's will or Mildred's adoption, part of the family's unsuccessful attempt of getting at the estate's assets evolved into a bitter pill too hard for Pansy to swallow and further widened the schism already created long ago between the two camps. And until recently, few probably realized the extent of the damage to Mildred personally, because she had taken the clipping of the March 4, 1935, article in the *Arkansas Democrat* titled "Monticello Woman Sues to Break Will of Millionaire Son, Deceased Oil Magnate," and placed it within her diary, no doubt reflecting hard about the "no natural children" remark. Another quirk of fate exists also. Just fourteen days prior to the suit being filed, Pansy still possessed sympathetic feelings for Frank's mother, because she admonished Mildred, "I received a letter from Grandma ... If you have time to breathe do write her a line." She continued, "I am going to write to her and we will do our best to cheer her up."[3]

When Pansy's brother-in-law Walter Fletcher Parrish died at age fifty-two in September 1930, Ida Belle was left alone to raise a family and keep up the house in Sour Lake, but as long as Frank lived, he helped out. When he died, however, Pansy discontinued all assistance, and to make matters worse, Frank's brother, Lee attempted to wrest ownership of Sunnyside. Ida Belle won the latter battle, but in order to make ends meet, she took in oil field workers and pipeliners who paid one dollar a day for room and board. From then on, relationships soured even further, with Ida Belle talking scornfully about Pansy in "that big old house on Calder Avenue with all that oil money." Even so, Frank's favorite sister never used her personal opinions of Pansy as a jumping off point to join with Arkansas family members who filed suit against the Yount estate over the questioned will. And for that matter, neither did Lee Yount, nor his other sister Hettie and her husband Frank Hazard, all of whom lived in Sour Lake.[4]

With Yount's death, the company's stockholders, who held the whole of the 21,000 shares of stock, of which 20,000 carried voting rights, had met on the previous January 3rd at 2:00 P.M. and elected Pansy, Emerson Woodward, Harry Phelan, Tal Rothwell, and T. P. Lee as directors. At 2:30 P.M., the board meeting followed, and as a result of a motion by Woodward, seconded by T. P. Lee, and approved by the five members, Tal Rothwell ascended to the presidency. Understandably, this accomplishment created one of the proudest, yet bittersweet memories of the Rothwell family. Phelan became vice president, while retaining the treasurer title; Frank Thomas elevated to secretary; Marvin McClendon assumed the dual responsibilities as the assistant secretary and assistant treasurer; and Beeman Strong remained as the general counsel. The minutes of the meeting also reflected that Rothwell's salary was now placed at $3,000 per month, and that of Harry Phelan fixed at $2,500, both effective January 1, 1934. None of the other officers received an increase. Before they adjourned, however, Pansy made a motion, seconded by T. P. Lee, and adopted unanimously, in which the board members "resolved that a ten per cent (10 percent) cash dividend be paid by the Company to its stockholders each sixty (60) days during the year 1934." Pansy had established her foothold among the male-dominated boardroom, and even though the minutes never included it, the group discussed the idea of taking Yount-Lee to the next level: refining and getting into the retail gas business. Woodward stalled and counseled everyone "to

Talbot F. Rothwell.
—Courtesy Sue Boyt and Susan Ramsey.

stay with what we know, and that's finding oil." No one offered any real resistance, so after putting that possibility to rest, there is little doubt how the majority now felt. Yount-Lee would be put on the auction block at the earliest opportunity, but before that happened, those in control would see to it that reserves of some $4 million in cash and negotiable notes would be drawn down and placed into the hands of the stockholders.[5]

While the company reins were still in familiar hands—and its financial footing remained in an enviable position, bolstered by both a massive cash position and another $1.7 million in accounts receivable, most employees felt uneasy, fearing change in the wind. After all, rumors had floated for sometime that some oil giant would come along sooner or later and make a bid that no one could possibly turn down. But Frank was around no longer to make sure that did not happen. McClendon said that he too sensed the inevitable, but he had no concrete evidence on which to base his opinion. "Just one of those feelings," he said, "nothing you could put your hands on." Yet, reports coming from Rothwell, the new chief executive, as late as February 6, 1935, claimed that the firm's plans for the coming year were similar to those of the past, and that nothing occurred at the February 5 annual stockholders' meeting that would be of any real public interest.[6]

Everyone tried to carry on normal operations in the field after Frank Yount's death; however, there were no real developments, with a few exceptions. On May 21 of the previous year, an announcement indicated that two tracts of oil-producing land had been acquired, for which $50,000 was paid. One, located in Harris County, consisted of 982 acres in the new Hockley field; the other of 628 acres was situated in Jefferson County at Big Hill. After Johnny Hatcher, the general drilling superintendent for Texas operations, died, W. Gilbert Prince, a superintendent who had been with the company for ten years, replaced him.[7]

Sometime in the latter part of 1934, the steamroller momentum generated by Frank slowed to a crawl, and T. P. Lee, backed by Emerson Woodward, soundly concluded that Yount-Lee would never be the same without its founder. Others had suspected or known that already but refused to bring it up for reasons of pride. Total production had slipped to about 20,000 barrels a day, and it seemed as if the combined effects of proration and Frank's death had cast a pall on the once dynamic operation that perhaps would never recover. Frank Yount, the integral cog in the wheel, the glue that held everything together, and the center square, could never be replaced by Tal Rothwell—no matter how hard he tried—Harry Phelan, or any of the rest. T. P. Lee and his right-hand man, Emerson Woodward, might do better, but neither had the time to devote to the Beaumont firm; they had other duties in Houston. Also, there had been another earlier sign that revealed a chink in the armor of the once mighty oil company. Frank Yount often prided himself on running an operation free and clear of encumbrances from labor unions. After all, he kept his men happy, and above that, he took care of their families. But the Great Depression and Frank's death had changed attitudes. Workers, who once turned deaf ears to such

John E. "Johnny" Hatcher, circa 1929.
—Courtesy Tyrrell Historical Library, Beaumont, Texas.

outlandish notions, now listened to statements from labor union representatives who told them that President Roosevelt encouraged memberships in such organizations. Perhaps, they thought, unionization might not be such a bad thing. All of this came to a head on April 18, 1934 when Harold LeClaire Ickes, interior secretary and oil administrator for the Roosevelt administration, "approved today a decision of the petroleum labor policy board that the Yount-Lee Oil company of Beaumont had interfered with the right of employes to organize and bargain collectively with the company." Rothwell's terse response followed immediately. He disputed the allegation and said candidly, "We never fired a man for joining a union and won't . . ."[8]

Since Frank's death, Woodward made no secret that he wished to sell the company, take his money, and go on to other things that interested him more, such as horse racing and competitive trap shooting. And now with the recent developments, T. P. Lee shared his partner's opinion. Woodward put in a call to Wright Francis Morrow, a Houston attorney, whom T. P. knew through Fidelity Trust Company, where Morrow served as general counsel and Lee on the board of directors. Woodward asked Morrow to come by. He and T. P. wanted to discuss the possibility of the company's sale, and if Morrow could find a buyer, he would profit handsomely from a tremendous brokerage fee.[9]

At the time, few people outside the lawyer circle in Houston knew this Wright Francis Morrow, but most everyone associated with Texas jurisprudence recognized the name of his distinguished father, Wright Chalfant Morrow. The elder Morrow first began practicing law in Hillsboro, Texas, in 1887, taught law at the University of Texas, held a district judgeship in Hill County, served in the Texas senate from 1912 to 1916 at which time he was elected to the Texas Court of Criminal Appeals at age fifty-eight. In 1921 his peers appointed him as the presiding judge, and the following year, he waged a spirited successful campaign for reelection to the Court of Criminal Appeals against Judge A. J. Harper of El Paso whom the Ku Klux Klan supported. Morrow held his position as presiding judge until he retired some eighteen years later. So when Wright Francis Morrow, the son at age forty-two, discussed the sale of Yount-Lee with T. P. Lee and Emerson Woodward, he spoke with authority, armed with the background and close family advice to pull off one of the most impressive business deals in the history of oil.[10]

Wright Francis Morrow.
—Courtesy Tyrrell Historical Library, Beaumont, Texas.

After his and Woodward's discussion with Wright Morrow, Lee, in turn, talked individually with each of the stockholders who controlled the total block of 21,000 shares. He made a convincing argument, and each one agreed to sell at the right price. When this information became public knowledge as early as February 27, 1935, most Beaumont residents reacted in total disbelief and openly criticized Yount-Lee's owners for their action. *How dare they sell?* One must consider, however, that these stockholders were businessmen and women who were looking after their self interests, and if they were going to sell, now would be the right time, while the stock retained a reasonably high value. Timing now meant everything.[11]

With the owners in complete agreement, Morrow visited banker, Melvin A. Traylor, president of the First National of Chicago, who substantiated a report that Standard Oil of Indiana and its subsidiary, the Stanolind Oil and Gas Company, were definitely interested in purchasing oil-producing properties and reserves. However, Traylor made it crystal clear that neither company would pursue an outright purchase of Yount-Lee, nor its capital stock. While that news shattered Morrow's grand visions of brokering the sale and reaping a huge windfall, he still held out hope. He then asked Harry Weeks, a lawyer from Fort Worth, and H. I. Wilhelm, an accountant who specialized in tax matters, to guide him during this process, and these two sought out specifics from the Internal Revenue Service. According to Guy T. Helvering and Robert H. Jackson, tax commissioner and general counsel for the IRS, respectively, an individual, speculative purchase by Morrow, as opposed to a bulk agreement, would prove beneficial, because each owner would be entitled to a legal 25 percent capital gain on all stock held for over twenty years. Equipped with that advice, Morrow approached T. P. Lee and Woodward with a daring, innovative plan. If he purchased Yount-Lee and liquidated the assets, he surmised, he would be free to offer Stanolind whatever properties they wanted, and afterward, sell off the rest for, perhaps, an amazing return on his investment. And too, Morrow argued, this type of individual agreement would most certainly save the stockholders a bundle of cash when it came time to pay income taxes on capital gains. But in order to continue the negotiations with Stanolind, all stockholders had to be in complete accord. Almost *ad nauseam*, Morrow hammered this one point over and again: if any one pulled out, for whatever reason, the entire deal would be called off. And too, Morrow reiterated that he could neither represent Yount-Lee stockholders nor Stanolind directly; otherwise, he would violate IRS restrictions.[12]

Lee carefully measured all options. Though he approved of the idea personally, there were others to consider. So he agreed to talk once more with each individual stockholder, and when he did, everyone decided to let Morrow follow through and see how everything played out. After he received more encouraging comments from Stanolind officials, Morrow took the progression one step further. From each Yount-Lee stockholder, he obtained separate options, which stated that they would sell directly to him if he could arrange an acceptable deal with Stanolind. The Houston attorney, likewise, received a similar option from Stanolind, and as part of the overall interim accord, the Standard subsidiary sent a battery of lawyers, accountants, and D'Arcy Cashin, a nationally-known outside field appraiser, to Beaumont to begin the arduous process of evaluating Yount-Lee assets included in the proposed purchase.[13]

Morrow's option with Stanolind remained in effect until April 23, 1935. But as of March 29, the company had yet to complete its evaluation, and it appeared highly likely that the agreement would expire beforehand. There were other obstacles to overcome as well. Yount-Lee's long-standing nemesis, Federal Crude, vaulted back into the picture, when its attorneys filed for an injunction in the Fifty-Eighth District Court in Beaumont to forestall the sale, at least until they settled the $15 million property suit against Yount-Lee. Tenaciously, Federal Crude lawyers argued for time. They had petitioned the U. S. Supreme Court to take jurisdiction in the matter, plus if Stanolind completed the sale with Morrow before the Court reached a possible final favorable verdict to Federal Crude, all assets would be so intermingled, it would be extremely difficult to determine whose properties would be subject to levy.[14]

Even Edward G. Seubert, president of Standard Oil, expressed doubts on April 11 that the necessary appraisal could be completed by the cut-off date. In retrospect, it is entirely possible that he and his company employed delaying tactics in order to see what the Federal Crude outcome would be. Five days later Yount-Lee's fortunes seemed to take a turn for the worse. On April 16 Judge George Cave O'Brien of the district court heard one and a half hours of testimony by opposing sides, and the following day, he reached a decision. While it fell short of an outright injunction, O'Brien did order that $15 million from the proceeds of the sale—if it went through—be held in trust until the Supreme Court weighed in. Yount-Lee immediately appealed the ruling to the Ninth Court, and on April 22 that body, represented by Chief Justice Daniel Walker, Associate Justices J. M. Combs and W. B. O'Quinn, sided with the plaintiff and reversed the lower court's ruling. Meanwhile, Stanolind officials, including the company president himself, Frank O. Prior, had set up shop at the Yount-Lee headquarters on April 16. The office atmosphere changed overnight from a relatively normal calm to a scene of hectic comings and goings as T. P. Lee, Woodward, Morrow, and his associates, along with Stanolind employees and other officials, made their way among Yount-Lee staffers of about twenty-five who were used to a highly efficient and regimented work schedule.[15]

As expected, Morrow's option did expire at midnight on April 23, but the negotiations continued anyway. With its appraisal finally finished days later, Stanolind told the Houston attorney that it would pay to Morrow slightly less than $42 million for the desired properties, which did not include "some $4,000,000 in cash and negotiable notes, valuable Beaumont and Lake Charles properties, certain oil and bank stocks, some business enterprises and other Yount holdings including undeveloped oil properties . . ., and $1.7 million in accounts receivable."[16]

While Stanolind officials met with their counterparts and Wright Morrow at Yount-Lee's Beaumont boardroom, tempers flared. Privately, Bill Lee had asked Michel Halbouty to conduct a separate appraisal of Yount-Lee's oil-related properties, and he estimated those near the $135 million mark, almost $93 million more than Cashin's. When Cashin spoke out, Lee suggested that perhaps he should explain how he arrived at his total. After all, Bill said, his guy came up with a much higher number. Hearing this proposition, Prior became enraged. He pointed directly at Halbouty and exclaimed to Lee, "He's your geologist. If we had used our geologist, he might have come up with a figure of twenty-four million. But we've used an impartial geologist, as we agreed to do, and he's come up with his figure."[17]

Bill Lee then turned to Halbouty and asked his opinion. Michel argued loudly that Cashin's appraisal fell way short, and before long, everyone in the room got into a shouting match. Prior demanded that Halbouty leave the meeting, and reluctantly, Bill Lee so directed. Inside, the heated negotiations continued, but the Stanolind president never caved in. However, Pansy Yount, T. P. and Bill Lee, Woodward, Rothwell, Phelan, and the others blinked, and after a short conference, all voted to accept Cashin's appraisal and along with it, Stanolind's final bid. Clearly, everyone wanted out; besides who would come along in the near term and offer that type of money?[18]

Two major obstructions, however, remained in the way of the final transaction. Litigation before the U.S. Supreme Court threatened to derail everything, but on April 29 all parties received the long awaited announcement that the Court ruled on the merit of the Federal Crude complaint. It refused to take jurisdiction in the matter. Thus, Yount-Lee gained a final victory in its claim to 6.9 acres of some of the most productive oil land at Spindletop, over which the wranglings and legal maneuvers had lasted for eight long years.[19]

During the sale negotiations with Morrow so far, Yount-Lee attorneys had uncharacteristically overlooked a major point of contention. Even though Pansy administered her late husband's estate, she did not have legal permission to dispose of any asset, much less the stock. Furthermore, if she failed to obtain court approval to do so, the Yount-Lee sale would have to be postponed, maybe indefinitely. Tensions ran high.[20]

On May 24 R. E. Masterson presented her case to the Sixtieth District Court and argued that his client should be allowed to sell the entire block of shares. Why? Because she desperately needed the money to satisfy more than $691,000 in expenses, which included state and federal estate fees, unpaid federal income taxes for 1932, and those estimated for 1933, let alone additional state and county property obligations. The list seemed endless. The estate at that time, Masterson said, had only $50,000 in cash to apply toward all outstanding debts. Actually, Pansy needed much, much more. The attorney never mentioned the estate's other debts of $368,038.91 that included Frank's outstanding personal note due Yount-Lee in the amount of $300,000, which as of November 13, 1933, had accumulated $3,739.73 in interest. Added to that, he purposely omitted the real reason, because near this very time, Pansy toured the most successful horse farms around the nation, gathering ideas on how they operated. In fact, she already decided to move both her residence and Spindletop Stables from Beaumont to Kentucky; and relative to her planned house of gigantic proportions, she took delivery of these preliminary blueprints on the previous January 2. For these projects to get off the ground, however, she needed cash, and a lot of it.[21]

On July 3 Judge R. L. Murry of the Sixtieth District Court announced his decision. He approved Pansy's request for the sale of the Yount-Lee stock, valued at $6,866,666.66 according to the inventory and appraisal of Frank Yount's estate as of April 11, 1934. Now, for the time being, everything seemed back on track. Sale negotiations could proceed, but as before, it ran headlong into another major barrier. With the Yount-Lee stockholders' asking price for each of the 21,000 shares set at $2,200, the total package amounted to an incredible $46,200,000 (almost $637.7 million in today's valuation). Stanolind agreed to pay Morrow an exact figure of $41,803,030.48, so if he held out any hope of completing what he had begun, the Houston attorney had to come up with the difference—an amount that would scare off most normal men—otherwise his personal expenditures thus far, estimated at over $40,000, would be for naught. The sum, certainly staggering, at first appeared insurmountable given that the nation continued to struggle in the throes of the Great Depression. Everywhere, programs initiated by the federal government to create new business in bad economic times put a strangle hold on loans involving the oil business, and one major source, the Reconstruction Finance Corporation headed up by Jesse H. Jones, a powerful

Houston banker and real-estate developer, had cut off such government loans completely.[22]

Back on December 7, 1931, President Herbert Hoover recommended the establishment an emergency Reconstruction Corporation, but it did not become a reality until he signed the act creating it on January 22 of the following year. In his address, Hoover declared the new agency's purpose as:

> ... to stop deflation in agriculture and industry and thus to increase employment by the restoration of men to their normal jobs. It is not created for the aid of big industries or big banks. Such institutions are amply able to take care of themselves. It is created for the support of the smaller banks and financial institutions, and through rendering their resources liquid to give renewed support to business, industry, and agriculture. It should give opportunity to mobilize the gigantic strength of our country for recovery.

Ironically, Jones and Morrow were friends, but that didn't matter. The new board's policy did not include lending money to oil interests, period, and Jones stated the reasons why:

> First, the oil business was profitable; it was able to command money when other kinds of business could not; secondly, if we loaned a man money to drill an oil well and another man owning the adjoining property sought a loan for the same purpose, we would be honor-bound to accommodate him. So, as a policy, we simply decided against lending to the oil industry, though we had ample opportunities, from Texas and probably from another state or two.

For Morrow, millions teetered in the balance, and he would not give up so easily. He had fight left in him yet.[23]

As Jones battled to steer Texas' dependence on agriculture and oil into chemicals and steel, Morrow sought the help of another friend. He went to see his banker, William A. Kirkland of the First National Bank of Houston. When presenting his loan request, though, Morrow played down the bank's overall risk factor. Since he could liquidate some $4 million in assets immediately after the proposed sale, he stated, the bank's exposure would be lessened tremendously. In fact, Morrow added that First National would benefit for years to come, not only from the positive publicity created by the bank's participation in such a large-scale affair, but with additional monies that might remain on deposit there for quite a while. Although Morrow made his case, Kirkland, nonetheless, had to honor his own bank's loan limit. He simply could not extend the amount required by Morrow, despite speculation about safety in collateral and no matter how good the plan or its outcome. In fact, Kirkland could lend no more than $300,000, but as an innovator, he did not shut the door completely. Instead, he offered promise. If he could similarly convince his correspondent bank, the National City Bank of New York, to go along with the deal, perhaps operating together, the two might come up with something positive. Morrow, Kirkland said, would just have to sit tight for a few days. Kirkland went to work on the deal and after discussing it with his counterpart at National City, the two banks joined in a loan, secured by Yount-Lee assets, among them the $4 million in cash and negotiable bonds that would be immediately applied to the outstanding loan balance. When said and done, the two banks had only one thing to worry about: could Wright Morrow deliver on the difference of $396,969.52? Relieved at this point to be clear of one stumbling block, at least, Morrow continued his negotiations with Stanolind, but much work remained before he could rest easy.[24]

T. P. Lee and Harry Phelan had long since divided some of their company shares among associates and family members; Strong, Thomas, and Schlicher had acquired some non-voting issues along the way; but otherwise, the proportion of stock owned by the other majority holders remained basically the same as when they established the company some twenty years before. Expectedly, public curiosity about the sale intensified when details began to leak out to the press, and as early as February 27, 1935, Stanolind felt pressure to admit that negotiations were actually underway. But with Yount-Lee officials, they were, as usual, tight lipped. When a reporter contacted Harry Phelan for a comment on July 28, he replied, "The deal really is in *status quo* but we ought to have something ... in the next day or two." In reality, things were going according to schedule. Mildred's personal diary entry for the same date reflects: "Last night Mother [and] Aunt Floy left for Houston on business," and the next day, she added, "Wrote to Mom in Houston. They are going to sell the Yount-Lee Oil Company, Daddy's company." Then on the August 1, she wrote, "They say ... [it] is going to be sold for $14 million. Money isn't everything."[25]

While Yount-Lee stockholders and their attorneys traveled to Houston, Standard Oil's board of directors met on July 29 and agreed to loan Stanolind $41,803,030.48 with which to conclude the purchase. Company accountants deposited that amount into a new account at the First National Bank of Houston on July 31, the very day that the Houston bank played host to the parties who completed the third largest financial transaction in the United States to that time, and the greatest relative to the oil industry.[26]

Early on, Wright Morrow made it his business to find out about potential liabilities that posed an overall threat to his future financial position. The accounts receivable represented $1.7 million, a hefty sum considering Depression times, but he could deal with that. The most troubling issue, however, took the form of pending litigation that created uncertainties. Wright Morrow hated uncertainties. What if Yount-Lee lost some or all of the outstanding lawsuits against it over ownership of oil producing leases and fee properties, not only at Spindletop, but other locations? How might these adverse rulings affect the overall stock price of Yount-Lee shares—and Morrow's ability to sell off other assets? As an attorney, Morrow used his skills and came up with another masterful plan that called for indemnities that would protect him from such unfavorable possibilities; consequently, he negotiated as part of the agreement what must be considered as a coup d'état. All Yount-Lee stockholders, all fifteen of them (sixteen if Pansy and Mildred are counted separately and not as one in the estate), agreed to pony up millions and have the sum allocated to three separate escrow accounts based on each owner's percentage of stock relative to the total number of shares outstanding. And in the process, they demonstrated the extent of just how badly they wanted out, and how far they were willing to go to make it happen.[27]

The first account that protected Morrow from unfavorable litigations' effect on falling stock prices amounted to right at $1.6 million; the second, $4.5 million, sheltered him from judgments in causes of action now pending or instituted within two years of the sale closing date; and the third, another $2 million, related to adverse judgments arising out of suits brought about prior to December 1, 1934. Altogether, these three separate escrows insulated Wright Morrow from negative rulings that might arise out of fifteen separate lawsuits, involving properties extending from the East Texas field all the way to Spindletop.[28]

The actual sale closing, a carefully orchestrated affair, began at 9:00 in the morning at First National Bank in Houston. A. W. Peake, Standard and Stanolind chairman of the board, presided over the proceedings, divided into three distinct stages to maximize income tax savings. First National provided one of its vice presidents to act as a "stakeholder," who during the first step, watched closely as Morrow presented checks to each seller. Then each endorsed their respective instruments and relayed them to the stakeholder, who also received the properly assigned stock certificates and leases from the sellers themselves. During the second phase, Morrow accepted the resignation of all Yount-Lee directors and officers, since he now conditionally owned 100 percent of the company stock. Quickly, he held a meeting in which a new board and officers were elected, after which he declared the company in a state of liquidation. All documents associated with this stage were also placed in the stakeholder's possession. The third step resulted in Stanolind's delivery of a check, earmarked for the purchase of specified properties, in the amount of $41,803,030.48, to Morrow who endorsed and passed it on. Then Peake asked if there were any objections. Since he received none, he directed the stakeholder to distribute all checks, stock certificates, and property titles to each of the appropriate parties.[29]

Shortly after 3:00 that same afternoon, Morrow made the announcement to the press. In the rush to meet its printing schedules, the respected *Houston Chronicle* led with the headline, "Stanolind Pays $48,000,000 For Yount-Lee," and the associated article carried details of the sale that even today perpetuate the myth of who actually bought Yount-Lee, and how much they actually paid.[30]

William Kirkland, the First National banker who observed the entire proceedings, said:

> By nightfall the funds in the new accounts of Stanolind and of Morrow, which had more than doubled the Bank's deposits for the day, had been paid out, but most of the money remained on the Bank's books in the names of the individuals who had

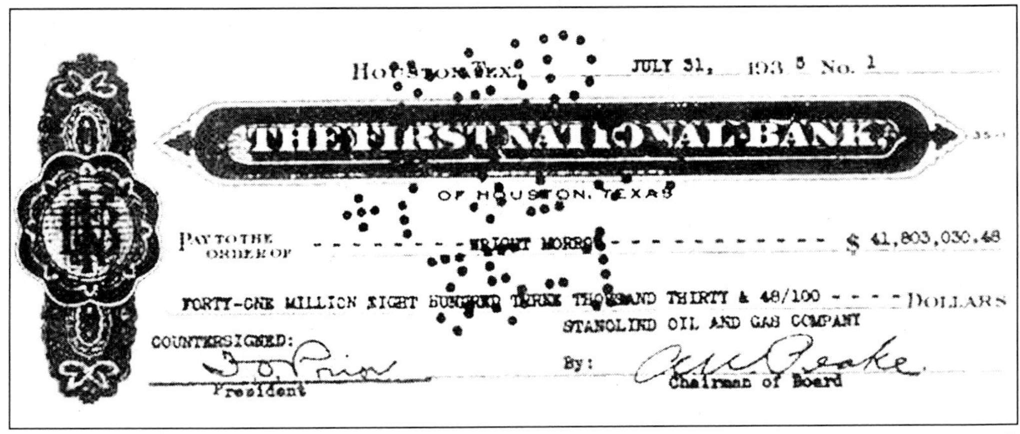

JULY 31, 1935 No. 1

THE FIRST NATIONAL BANK OF HOUSTON, TEXAS

PAY TO THE ORDER OF WRIGHT MORROW $ 41,803,030.48

FORTY-ONE MILLION EIGHT HUNDRED THREE THOUSAND THIRTY & 48/100 DOLLARS

STANOLIND OIL AND GAS COMPANY

COUNTERSIGNED: President

By: Chairman of Board

—Courtesy *Texas Gulf Historical and Biographical Record*, Beaumont, Texas and First City Bancorporation of Texas.

> sold their Yount-Lee stock or in Beaumont banks for their accounts. Deposits at the close of July 31 were $83 million and a day later were still $71 million. Though the proceeds of the sale were gradually transferred or invested, a healthy amount stayed on deposit for a long time, and after that red letter occasion, the "New Bank" grew steadily in volume of business and profits.[31]

In effect, Morrow's prophesy came true. The First National Bank of Houston owed much of its future success to three parties: the Stanolind Oil Company, Yount-Lee stockholders, but most of all to the tenacity and the don't-give-up attitude of Wright Morrow, perhaps the first corporate raider of modern times.

With the transaction concluded, Stanolind had acquired Yount-Lee assets which included approximately 680 wells that produced a net of between 18,942 to 20,000 barrels daily, the Spindletop tank farm, the Neches River dock and storage facilities, over 5 million barrels of oil in storage, the Yount-Lee interest in the East Texas pipeline, and full interest in the pipeline that connected Beaumont and High Island. Yount-Lee also turned over leases and fee land that involved 283,000 acres of which about 280,000 were undeveloped, almost 99 percent of the total. This acquisition immediately increased Stanolind's production by 9 percent, and its new total daily production of 72,000 barrels placed the company as fourth among producers on the Gulf Coast. Wright Morrow received all other Yount-Lee assets, which included real-estate holdings; the Beaumont properties alone were valued at over $900,000. For their part in the sale, Yount-Lee stockholders received $46,200,000, distributed as follows: the Yount estate, $15,106,666.74; Emerson Woodward, $11,330,000; Tal and Mabel Rothwell, $4,532,000; Harry Phelan and family, $7,553,333.48; Bill Lee, $3,399,000; and the gentleman who put up the original $25,000 that made it all possible, T. P. Lee, $3,399,000. The three who owned non-voting stock, Strong, Thomas, and Schlicher, received $293,333.26 each. Additionally, Strong had subdivided some of his stock and put it in his wife Nancy's name, so a portion of his funds went to her.[32]

Mabel Martha Lee Rothwell.
—Courtesy Sue Boyt and Susan Ramsey.

The proceeds to each shareholder mentioned above, however, represented a gross amount, at least for the time being, and in no way represents what they walked away with on July 31, 1935. An $8,076,737 deduction, taken immediately off the top, has to be taken into account.

The Phelan family, November 25, 1955. From left to right: A. M. "Mickey," Margaret Phelan Reed, Johannah, Harry, and John Henry, Jr.

—Courtesy Mary Reed Williams.

Beeman Ewell and Nancy "Nannie" Rae Strong, circa 1953. Photograph by Gittings Studio, Houston, Texas.

—Courtesy Barbara S. Moor.

Summary of Escrow Accounts[33]

Stockholder Name	Escrow 1	Escrow 2	Escrow 3	Total Escrow Fund
Yount, Pansy M., individually and as executrix of Frank Yount's estate	515,567.97	1,471,428.57	653,968.25	2,640,964.79
Woodward, Emerson F.	386,675.97	1,103,571.43	490,476.19	1,980,723.59
Phelan, Harry	106,367.18	303,571.43	134,920.64	544,859.25
Phelan, Johannah	106,367.18	303,571.43	134,920.64	544,859.25
Phelan, J. H., Jr.	15,016.54	42,857.14	19,047.62	76,921.30
Phelan, Anthony M.	15,016.54	42,857.14	19,047.62	76,921.30
Reed, Margaret	15,016.54	42,857.14	19,047.62	76,921.30
Rothwell, Talbot	116,002.80	331,071.43	147,142.86	594,217.09
Rothwell, Mabel	38,667.59	110,357.14	49,047.62	198,072.35
Lee, Thomas P.	116,002.80	331,071.43	147,142.86	594,217.09
Lee, Bill	116,002.80	331,071.43	147,142.86	594,217.09
Strong, Beeman	5,130.65	14,642.85	6,507.93	26,281.43
Strong, Nancy	4,880.38	13,928.58	6,190.47	24,999.43
Thomas, Frank E.	10,011.03	28,571.43	12,698.41	51,280.87
Schlicher, Max T.	10,011.03	28,571.43	12,698.41	51,280.87
TOTALS	**1,576,737.00**	**4,500,000.00**	**2,000,000.00**	**8,076,737.00**

With the total escrows affixed to individual shareholders, the following table expresses the net amount each actually received as of July 31, 1935.

Net Proceeds of Sale Summary[34]

Stockholder Name	Gross Sale Proceeds	Total Escrow Fund	Net Sale Proceeds
Yount, Pansy M., individually and as executrix of Frank Yount's estate	15,106,666.74	2,640,964.79	12,465,701.95
Woodward, Emerson F.	11,330,000.00	1,980,723.59	9,349,276.41
Phelan, Harry	3,116,666.74	544,859.25	2,571,807.49
Phelan, Johannah	3,116,666.74	544,859.25	2,571,807.49
Phelan, J. H., Jr.	440,000.00	76,921.30	363,078.70
Phelan, Anthony M.	440,000.00	76,921.30	363,078.70
Reed, Margaret	440,000.00	76,921.30	363,078.70
Rothwell, Talbot	3,399,000.00	594,217.09	2,804,782.91
Rothwell, Mabel	1,133,000.00	198,072.35	934,927.65
Lee, Thomas P	3,399,000.00	594,217.09	2,804,782.91
Lee, Bill	3,399,000.00	594,217.09	2,804,782.91
Strong, Beeman	150,333.26	26,281.43	124,051.83
Strong, Nancy	143,000.00	24,999.43	118,000.57
Thomas, Frank E.	293,333.26	51,280.87	242,052.39
Schlicher, Max T.	293,333.26	51,280.87	242,052.39
TOTALS	**46,200,000.00**	**8,076,737.00**	**38,123,263.00**

The only written evidence offered by any Yount-Lee stockholder after the sale on how they felt about it came from Mildred and later, Bill Lee. Pansy and her daughter must have exchanged words of anger, because soon after, Mildred made the following notations in her diary: "I feel so much like crying. It is so silly, but I do care ... I wish we could make up truly.... Things won't be like they were." By these reflective statements, Mildred could have proved the lone holdout, the one who might have nixed the whole affair, but Pansy, as the executrix who controlled the purse strings, set the rules. Years later, Bill Lee openly and strongly criticized the deal, especially when he learned that even Michel Halbouty's estimate was nowhere near what it should have been. But none of that mattered, really, because Halbouty's figure was never taken seriously by Standard or Stanolind, and all of Yount-Lee's stockholders—over the objections of a minor made to her mother—signed the agreement with their eyes wide open. "It was the greatest giveaway in history," Bill Lee said. "We gave away billions!"[35]

Stanolind took over Yount-Lee's field operations effective August 1, 1935. Immediately, the public raised questions that concerned several key issues, among them the future of all Yount-Lee employees and the community's relationship with the new owners and the local office, if there was one. Acting quickly and decisively, Stanolind speculated that once prospective employees passed a physical examination, approximately 80 percent of Yount-Lee field personnel would be switched from one company payroll to the other. However, the prospects of the corporate office employees were not as good, because on August 1, they were greeted by two memorandums posted outside the main office entrance. One signed by Frank O. Prior, the Stanolind president, read in part:

> The Stanolind Oil and Gas company hereby gives notice that it is not employing any of the former Yount-Lee employes except such employes that it specifically notifies as hereinafter provided.

The other from Roger Guthrie, one of the new Yount-Lee officers and Morrow's brother-in-law, said:

> Because of this [the sale] it is necessary to terminate the employment of all employes of the Yount-Lee Oil company and or Wright Morrow except those whose services are required in handling the remaining affairs of the Yount-Lee Oil company ... Any employe whose services are desired further by the ... company will receive separate and individual notice to that effect.

This must have been a very sobering experience for the office employees who had remained loyal all those years, but over the next few days, the reality sank in. Things, however, settled down quite a bit when on August 2, the company named W. Gilbert Prince, a former Yount-Lee supervisor, as Stanolind's superintendent for its new Beaumont district office. When he took over, some of the Yount-Lee office personnel transferred to his workplace; some moved to Stanolind's Tulsa location, while others like Marjorie Gibson Giles decided to leave altogether.[36]

Michel Halbouty also faced a career choice. After all, he made $750 a month at Yount-Lee, and even for oil company geologists, that was extremely good money during the Depression. But as he put it, Halbouty did not want "to become just another name in a large, integrated company," so he passed on Stanolind's offer to keep him on board, albeit at a reduced salary. Halbouty also turned down bids by other oil companies. At Yount-Lee, he was used to free wheeling, and he did not want any big organization cramping his style. At Bill Lee's suggestion, Glenn McCarthy, the former Beaumont boy turned wildcatter, wanted to hire Halbouty, but he could only pay the geologist about forty percent of his current salary. That is when Lee (McCarthy's father-in-law) stepped in with a possible solution and offered to make up the difference. However, Halbouty thought it over and turned down the proposal. "If Glenn ever found out about it," he responded, "he'd break my damn neck!"[37]

In early August, Mildred traveled to Rockledge, and apparently by then, the tiff with her mother had run its course, because she had begun asking for a new car days before. On the thirteenth, Judge Masterson arrived with the joyful news; Mildred could now have the Ford roadster that she wanted. The two drove to Denver, where they picked up the automobile and ate at the Cosmopolitan Hotel, before returning to Manitou Springs. On September 1 Mildred received more good news; Masterson advised her that she could have a new car every summer.[38]

Mildred's 1934 Ford roadster.
—Courtesy Kathryn Manion Haider.

Wright Morrow wasted no time and began immediately to dismantle what was left of the Yount-Lee infrastructure. On September 2, 1935, he changed the company's place of business from Beaumont to Houston, and on December 24 of the following year, he decreased the capital stock to $420,000 or 4,200 shares at $100 each. Again on July 22, 1937, he reduced the capital stock even further, this time to a mere $1,000. Finally, the officers and the board of directors, consisting of Wright Morrow, president; Roger Guthrie, vice president; George P. Murrin, secretary; Harry C. Weeks, director; and H. I. Wilhelm, director, filed a corporate dissolution request with the Texas Secretary of State's office on November 4, 1943, and when the state complied on December 6, the liquidation was complete.[39]

With Stanolind's purchase of specific assets, namely oil and oil-producing and related properties, Yount-Lee as a viable company ceased to exist on July 31, 1935, but it folded into the pages of history with dignity. Within its twenty-year life span, the corporation's economic and civic contributions to Beaumont and the entire Gulf Coast reached unprecedented proportions, and in fact, will most likely never be duplicated. The entire Gulf Coast beamed with pride, because it had been home to one of the largest independent oil operators in the country, and by most indicators, probably the most successful anywhere during its heyday. Afterward, former stockholders, officers, and many of its employees continued to generate strong leadership within their respective cities, towns, and communities, but for Pansy Yount, however, it came time to look past all these glorious accomplishments. Now she would concentrate on matters in Lexington, Kentucky.

Black Gold to Bluegrass

"Do what you feel in your heart to be right—for you'll be criticized anyway. You'll be damned if you do, and damned if you don't."

ELEANOR ROOSEVELT

If the public at large viewed Frank Yount as an enigma, then his widow represented a more challenging subject, even for those who thought they knew her best. After all, Frank's position as president and chief executive of the Yount-Lee Oil Company put him at the forefront, and whether he liked it or not, he had no alternative but to accept leadership roles, make sporadic public appearances, and grant an occasional interview to satisfy the demands of the press and appreciative fans. On the other hand, no credible evidence exists that Pansy ever talked to one single newspaper reporter prior to Frank's death. A few days afterward, however, she finally broke the silence by disclosing future plans for continuing Spindletop Stables and building an "interdenominational" chapel at Magnolia Cemetery which would serve as Frank's great monument and final resting place. This latter revelation stirred up quite a controversy that lingered for years, and as one so succinctly put it, "settled with Beaumonters [in 1933] like the explosion of Vesuvius with the people of Pompeii . . ."[1]

Because Frank Yount contributed at one time or another to most every worthwhile cause and charity event in Beaumont, he came by a well deserved title. But what may come as a surprise to some, is that Pansy continued his efforts. During the late 1933 Community Chest drive, the Advanced Gifts Division announced a record-setting total so far of $52,036, and of that amount, Pansy donated an $8,000 personal check, which when added with those of the other Yount-Lee officers, amounted to $16,000. Preston Doty, who headed up the campaign, commented:

> the close associates Mr. Yount left behind him are carrying on is something Beaumont may be proud of and thankful for. It shows their fine spirit, their broad vision which the death of their leader is not dimming. The community should be full of gratitude ... Theirs is the same brand of vision as Miles Frank Yount possessed.[2]

Pansy Merritt Yount.
—Courtesy American Saddlebred Museum, Lexington, Kentucky.

But few people in Beaumont really knew anything about Pansy, her likes and dislikes, her religion, her values, nor anything of her past. Until the interview held on November 18, 1933, only five days after her beloved husband's death, most identified her simply as the oilman's loyal and devoted wife, the lady who kept to herself in the family mansion at 1376 Calder, and the mother of Frank's daughter, Mildred Frank, whose life, so far, could be followed within the society pages of the *Beaumont Enterprise* and the *Beaumont Journal*. Up to now, Pansy chose to remain in the shadows where she felt most comfortable.[3]

Pansy Bernadette Merritt was born in Orange, Texas, on February 21, 1887 to the union of Hosea Holly and Sarah Frances Sherman Merritt. Unfortunately though, before Pansy reached the age of ten months her mother died, leaving behind a father and the other children to raise her the best way they knew how, and within the Catholic faith. Altogether, she had seven siblings, all older: brothers Emmett, Byron, Travis, Huil; and three sisters: Belle, who married Iva Tevis first, and then Hardy S. Blanchette; Raphael, who married Sid McClure; and Floy Augusta, who married Grayson B. Watkins.[4]

Pansy's father died in May 1894, so kinfolk brought the seven-year-old from Orange to Beaumont, and at age eighteen, she married oil driller Charles Albert Daley. But when that stormy relationship of about ten years ended in divorce on May 24, 1915, she found herself alone, and in order to survive, she landed in Batson, Texas. Most accounts agree that she worked as a waitress in a boarding house where she met Frank. A little less than four months after her divorce from Daley, Pansy and Frank married on September 15, 1915. Although copies of Mildred's formal adoption papers have not been located as of late, Anthony McDade "Mickey" Phelan tells the story that he heard from his grandfather. Harry Phelan felt sorry for the couple because they could not have children, so upon his recommendation, Frank traveled to a New Orleans orphanage and brought home to his wife a little red-haired girl. Records show Mildred's date of birth as May 2, 1920, and Pansy proved to the court's satisfaction back in April 1935 that her daughter had been legally adopted while she and Frank lived in Hardin County. But contrary to her religion's accepted beliefs at the time, Pansy allowed her husband to rear Mildred as a Protestant within the congregation at Westminster Presbyterian Church, where in March 1932, she received baptismal rites as an adult member.[5]

Pansy Merritt Yount became a product of her early environment; forged in a man's world and in the rough and tumble oil fields of Sour Lake, Saratoga, and Batson, filled with roustabouts, roughnecks, wildcatters, drillers, contractors, and hellions of all sorts who worked hard and played even harder. Such men swore openly and often, drank to excess routinely, and could hold their own with the devil himself. As a natural consequence, she learned to curse and mimic some ways of crassness. Yet, after Pansy and Frank married and while they still resided in Sour Lake, one reporter labeled her "an artist at needlework," and credited her for giving Sunnyside a "homey" touch with abundant hand-decorated linens. On May 2, 1929, Pansy presented a Shoninger brand piano to Millard School in honor of Mildred's ninth birthday. The piano, she said, would be used in the school's newly completed auditorium that seated about 300. Pansy "told the children that music means love and the presentation of the instrument was the way in which she and Mildred had decided to show their love for the pupils, teacher and principal of that school." One of the students, Emma Dru McMicken, made the acceptance speech, and Miss Effie Piland, the principal, voiced her appreciation as well. After a group performed the song, "We Love you Mrs. Yount, Yes, We Do," the program concluded. These are but a few examples of Pansy's sensitive disposition, and another occurred during Ernest Doring's interview of Frank on March 8, 1931, when he referred to her as "a most gracious and genial hostess."[6]

But Pansy had another side. She literally hated any involvement in the social scene whatsoever, unless it was a time and place of her choosing. Furthermore, because she detested those whom she described as "putting on airs," a few of her contemporaries portrayed her as not being able to fit in, to adjust to culture, in fact, in some instances, downright rude and never rising to the level expected of "The Godfather of Beaumont's" wife. One such case in point attested to by several sources, who wish to remain anonymous, claimed that she also had quite a temper. After the Younts moved to Beaumont in 1923, Mrs. Aurelia Norvell, the influential wife of Benjamin Rush Norvell, Beaumont bank president and civic leader, dropped by their home on several occasions for the purpose of inviting Pansy to various teas. Each time, though, Pansy refused and made endless excuses, hoping that Mrs. Norvell would give up and leave her alone. But Mrs. Novell persisted and came by once too often. When the maid answered the doorbell and realized the caller's identity, she walked upstairs and announced to her mistress that Mrs. Norvell waited inside the front door. Pansy snapped, "Go back and tell that woman that I'll never be home to her!" When the nervous maid complied exactly as directed, an embarrassed and visibly shaken Mrs. Norvell backed up, fell off the front porch and into the flower bed, before regaining her footing and making a hasty retreat to her automobile.[7]

Pansy Bernadette Merritt.
—Courtesy Kathryn Manion Haider.

As demonstrated by this alleged event, Pansy confirmed that by and large, she cared less what others thought of her actions. Furthermore, she could have built Frank's mausoleum and kept quiet about that "interdenominational thing." She could have built up Spindletop Stables with the amazing start already realized; and with the huge inheritance that

Frank left behind, she certainly had the means to fulfill her husband's dreams of constructing a magnificent home on the Calder Road property that already contained the stables and the Jersey farm.[8]

Yet again, Pansy seemed to be a lightning rod for controversy. She began to soon develop sternness in attitude, a commanding presence perceived by some as kindness with an undertone of steel. In an era where strong-minded females, who regularly displayed a take-charge attitude, were considered aberrant, some just called her "uppity." But beneath the façade that a few referred to as "a woman with country ways," she found the footing necessary to survive in big business. After shunning the elite of Beaumont society for years, she now further angered many of the general population by speaking openly of allowing Frank's mausoleum and the chapel inside to be used by folks of all races, white and black, and of all denominations, including those of the Jewish faith. And within two years, she would find herself embroiled in other heated decisions; one involved her participation in selling Beaumont's most recognizable and loved business institution—the Yount-Lee Oil Company. Put plainly, most did not understand, and they asked the logical question. "Why would she do that?" During the first meeting after Frank's death, the Yount-Lee Board voted Pansy to succeed her husband as director. In that role with an almost 33 percent ownership of the company, she could have insisted that Yount-Lee continue as before, and with the combined strength of Harry Phelan's and the Rothwells' voting shares, the Lee brothers and Woodward would have had no choice but to either sell their part and get out, or toe the line. In spite of statements to the contrary, there was no real necessity to sell her Yount-Lee stock to raise funds for paying inheritance taxes, regardless of what her attorney Masterson argued before the courts. At the snap of a finger, Pansy could have easily borrowed the required capital locally and repaid the loan on an installment basis of her preference. But underlying all the legal theatrics, and unbeknown to the general public, Pansy had other plans in the making that would tarnish her local reputation even more.[9]

Her interest in Saddlebred horses remained intense since the death of her husband, and she was now more determined than ever to keep alive Frank's dream by building one of the most fantastic facilities ever conceived. As with Frank, she had fallen in love with the breed that traced it roots from the Galloway and Hobbie horses of the British Isles that gained popularity in North America in the 1600s. Selective breeding with the Narragansett Pacer of Rhode Island and the Thoroughbred produced offspring that found their way all across the region, and by the time of the American Revolution, Colonial cavalry used them extensively. Later, breeders mixed their bloodlines with Morgans and Standardbreds, and eventually the Saddlebred as known today made its mark at horse shows held in Virginia and at the 1856 St. Louis Fair. Before long, Kentucky claimed the breed as its own, and the term *Kentucky Saddlers* came to be used commonly. By 1861 the Saddlebred had become the most popular riding horse in North America, and during the War Between the States, both sides engaged in this terrible and bloody conflict depended upon the strain "born with the walk, trot and canter, plus the inherent ability to learn the slow gait and rack." Robert E. Lee's own Traveller was such an example that "demonstrated incredible endurance and dependability on long marches and under fire."[10]

Relative to characteristics, the American Saddle Horse Association offers the following description:

Yount-Lee Stockholders' Share Ownership
Expressed in terms of total ownership, ownership percentage, and total voting shares
(As of January 3, 1934)

Stockholder Name	Total Shares	Owner Percentage	Voting Shares
Yount, Pansy M., individually and as executrix of Frank Yount's estate	6,866 ⅔	32.6983	6,666 ⅔
Woodward, Emerson F.	5,150	24.5238	5,000
Phelan, John Henry "Harry"	1,416 ⅔	6.7460	3,333 ⅓
Phelan, Johannah (wife of Harry)	1,416 ⅔	6.7460	
Phelan, John Henry, Jr. (son of Harry)	200	.9524	
Phelan, Anthony M. (son of Harry)	200	.9524	
Reed, Margaret Phelan Reed (daughter of Harry)	200	.9524	
Rothwell, Talbot	1,545	7.3571	1,500
Rothwell, Mabel (wife of Talbot)	515	2.4524	500
Lee, Thomas P.	1,545	7.3571	1,500
Lee, William E. "Bill"	1,545	7.3571	1,500
Strong, Beeman	68 ⅓	.3254	
Strong, Nancy Rae "Nannie" (wife of Beeman)	65	.3096	
Thomas, Frank E.	133 ⅓	.6350	
Schlicher, Max T.	133 ⅓	.6350	
TOTALS	**21,000**	**100.0000**	**20,000**

Sources: Stock Purchase Agreement, dated July 29, 1935, between all Yount-Lee stockholders of record and Wright Morrow of Houston. This previously unpublished document is in the private collection of Kathryn Manion Haider; Minutes of Stockholders' and Directors' Meeting, Yount-Lee Oil Company, January 3, 1934. This previously unpublished document is in the private collection of Mildred Yount Manion. Even though he divided his stock among his wife and three children, Harry Phelan held the proxy on all 3,333 1/3 voting shares. Pansy Yount, Phelan, and Rothwell, all serving on the board of directors effective January 3, 1934, still represented the "Big Three," that controlled 12,000 of the 20,000 voting shares or 60 percent.

American Saddlebreds range in size from 15 to 17 hands [high] and average about 15.3. According to *Modern Breeds of Livestock*, "The American Saddlebred horse has a refined head with small ears and long neck with considerable arch. The withers [highest part of the back] should be well above the height of the hips. The Saddlebred is of good proportion, presenting a beautiful overall picture. Its conformation enables the breed to perform well in all equine events especially dressage, jumping, carriage and endurance. A distinguishable trait is high intelligence. Alert and curious, Saddlebreds possess personality, making them people oriented." Saddlebreds come in all colors, as there have never been color restrictions.[11]

1934

Just as Cape Grant predicted, Frank's horses blew away the competition at the American Royal in Kansas City during late 1933 when both Beau Peavine and Chief of Spindletop placed high on the money list. Beau won the Five-Gaited Stallion Stake, and

Lady Virginia, Cape Grant up.
—Courtesy American Saddlebred Museum, Lexington, Kentucky.

Lady Virginia, the newcomer to Spindletop Stables, took the Under-15.2 Stake, but lost the championship to Roxie Highland, the acknowledged walk-trot queen of saddle horses owned and ridden by Mary Gwyn Fiers of Oklahoma City. Veteran horsemen were hard put to remember a time when Roxie tasted defeat. She had taken scores of titles in Kentucky, Missouri, and in the Mississippi Valley classics, but for some reason, Fiers had never shown her at the National Horse Show held annually in New York's Madison Square Garden. Pansy took the loss to Roxie at Kansas City unusually hard, so immediately after the show that particular night, she found her trainer in the tack room. She promptly commanded, "Buy her Cape." Grant responded, "She's not for sale, Mrs. Yount." Then Pansy directed once more, "Buy her Cape." By now the message rang loud and clear. Cape was expected to purchase the famous mare, whatever the cost, and bring her to Beaumont. Sometime in March, he contacted Fiers and made an offer. Eventually, the two completed the deal at the annual Southwestern Exposition and Fat Stock Show in Fort Worth with Pansy paying $20,000 for the ten-year-old, three-gaited world's champion that she presented to Mildred as a gift. Mildred still grieved for her father, and Pansy hoped that the present would help alleviate some of the sadness. Critics, on the other hand, mocked Roxie's acquisition, claiming that Mrs. Miles Frank Yount's brash trainer had neither the capability nor finesse to show Roxie in top form, and that her winning ways would end on a sour note. Before the dust settled, however, and the last chapter was written, Grant would remind these same critics repeatedly that he came by the nickname "Capable Cape" honestly.[12]

The current season began in earnest on February 21 with the Miami Biltmore Horse Show, but before departing Beaumont on the Southern Pacific, Grant commented, "No horses have ever been in finer condition than this string." When asked about the animals' quarters, he replied, "The express car accommodations are among the best I have ever seen and the horses are comfortable." Pansy and Viola Ransom went also, and when they arrived in Miami, they stayed at the Biltmore Hotel. Cape and his assistant, Frank Heathman, took seven horses—Texas Ranger, Tradewind, Sea Breeze, Guida Knight, Beau Peavine, Lois Harrison, and Chief of Spindletop—along with their four groomsmen to the event, and they concluded the session five days later with an impressive sweep, winning four of the five stakes. Combined with earlier successes at the

1933 World's Fair in Chicago and the American Royal at Kansas City—a few days after Frank Yount's death—Spindletop Stables by its unequaled meteoric rise now attracted much of the attention of the nation's Saddlebred circuit. In September, Roxie, now wearing the blue and red colors of Spindletop Stables, won the Over-15.2 Three-Gaited Championship Stake at the Kentucky State Fair in Louisville; but Beau Peavine, however, managed but a fourth place finish in the Five-Gaited Championship. Chief of Spindletop, with Carl Pedigo up, generated quite a bit of controversy when he concluded competition with a paltry fifth place tie in the Five-Gaited Gelding Stake; but in the Junior Five-Gaited Stake with Christian Barham judging, he bounced back and took reserve champion honors behind Dixiana Farm's All American. At the St. Louis National Horse Show, Roxie, with Cape Grant up, faced a field of fourteen others, and for the third time at this event, she won the championship in her class and along with it a prize of $1,000. One reporter wrote of Roxie, "She worked smoothly and regally in all the required gaits, and the balconies, filled with the largest crowd of the week, showered applause down upon her as she pranced daintily around the ring, a statuesque animal with coppery glints in her chestnut hide and a thin white blaze in her forehead." No one, including the harshest of critics, now doubted that Cape could ride Roxie successfully. At the American Royal in October, Beau Peavine returned to top form, kept up the pace, and walked away with double victories in both the Five-Gaited Stallion and Fine Harness Stakes, with Roxie taking the Three-Gaited Championship.[13]

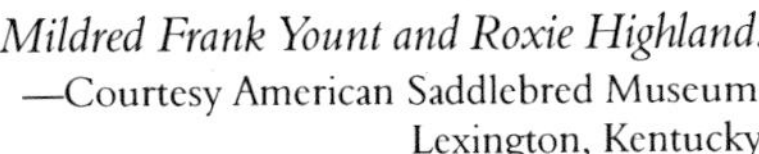

Mildred Frank Yount and Roxie Highland.
—Courtesy American Saddlebred Museum, Lexington, Kentucky.

Tradewind at Miami, Cape Grant up.
—Courtesy American Saddlebred Museum, Lexington, Kentucky.

The winning ways continued in November at the National Horse Show in New York City's Madison Square Garden, where Roxie's first ever appearance there made headlines. When the competition ended on the thirteenth, Spindletop Stables owned a total of thirteen ribbons and three grand

LEFT:
Chief of Spindletop at Miami, Cape Grant up.
—Courtesy American Saddlebred Museum, Lexington, Kentucky.

BELOW:
Roxie Highland, Cape Grant up.
—Courtesy American Saddlebred Museum, Lexington, Kentucky.

championships, the best record of any stable represented. As highly anticipated, Roxie won honors in both her classes, Beau Peavine in all three of his, and Tradewind continued his streak by taking the Combination Harness and Saddle Class, for which he received the Mountain Echo Challenge Trophy. But if any lingering doubts persisted whether the so-called "infant stable in Beaumont" could really compete with the big boys, they were wholly erased at the Chicago Livestock Exposition Horse Show during the first part of December. Though the new International Building, just completed a few days before, could not hold the overflow crowd of spectators, the results were spectacular nonetheless. Roxie won both of her three-gaited classes; Chief of Spindletop took the $500 Junior Stake (for four-year-olds and under) and the open $1,000 Five-Gaited Stake; and Beau Peavine won the Five-Gaited Saddle Horse Stallion Class and placed reserve in the Fine Harness Open. Tradewind, who placed second in the Combination Harness and Saddle Horse Stake, also won the Three-Gaited 14.2 and Over Class. After the concluding ceremonies, Pansy received numerous congratulatory telegrams and floral tributes from admiring supporters all over the country, including Mayor Pete Renfro of Beaumont, and when Cape and the horses arrived back in Southeast Texas a few days later, all were hailed as conquering heroes with their collection of forty-seven trophies won at five of the most prestigious shows in America. For the time being, however, Pansy announced plans to stay over in the windy city for several more weeks, no doubt savoring the latest victories that placed her in a most envious position amongst the lofty scale of blue bloods. Moreover, Cape relished the fact that some were beginning to refer to him "as one of the greatest of the saddle horse men of all time."[14]

Beau Peavine
—Courtesy American Saddlebred Museum, Lexington, Kentucky.

1935

On Christmas day 1934, during the holiday break, Mildred visited New York, where she got a teenager's thrill by meeting songster Rudy Vallee at one of his shows. A few days later, on January 11 she returned to Hockaday. Pansy called from Beaumont and told her that she had received a letter from the idol, and on January 18, Pansy brought the letter to her daughter in Dallas. Mildred answered the correspondence, but in her diary, she admitted frankly that she expected no answer. But much to the youngster's surprise and elation, Mildred got of all things in the mail, an autographed photo of her hero received on the twenty-eighth. She wrote, "I phoned Mother & broke the news."[15]

In May with Yount-Lee sale negotiations proceeding, Pansy used her business savvy learned from Frank who always put a lot of study into every field of endeavor he entered. While one of Tradewind's silver trophies and pictures of the other Yount horses were proudly and prominently displayed in the window of the Thames Drugstore at the Mildred Building, Pansy, in the company of constant companion, Edith Stansbury, whom everyone called Stannie, and her trainer, Cape Grant, toured several successful horse breeding farms in Texas, Oklahoma, Kansas, Missouri, and Kentucky for the purpose of obtaining a clearer understanding of how they operated. But this is where the oilman's widow deviated from her late husband's plans for Beaumont. She sought out the opportunity to rid herself of bad memories in Southeast Texas, believing that a fresh start in Kentucky might provide the answer. Whispers, rumors, and insinuations from some circles in Beaumont hurt the normally thick-skinned Pansy deeply. Cape Grant often encouraged a change, and recommended to Pansy that Spindletop Stables would not only flourish, but meet its true potential at the heart of Bluegrass Country, none other than Lexington itself. Here, he said, both of them could begin anew, and leave behind the sordid attempts, not only to link the two romantically, but the narrow-minded speculation that together, they might have actually participated in some dastardly plot to kill her famous husband.[16]

With conspiracy theories flowing like oil from East Texas fields, finally, Pansy had enough! With her mind made up and half of the almost $12.5 million in immediate funds derived from the sale of her Yount-Lee stock, she contacted Mary C. Tipton, a real-estate agent of considerable reputation in Lexington and expressed an interest in purchasing a good-sized farm. Tipton soon found the perfect place, the 836-acre Shoshone Stud Farm, owned by W. R. Coe, located "at the corner of the Ironworks and Newtown Pikes for a price reported to be about $400,000." While Pansy, Stannie, Mildred, and Cape waited in Lexington, discussions took more than three weeks before the Yount and Coe interests finally reached an understanding. Both Hugh Fontaine, who served as manager of Shoshone Farm, and the law firm of Stoll, Muir, Townsend, and Park represented the seller during the negotiations of the sale completed on Saturday, September 7, 1935. Cape could not contain his excitement; he put in a telephone call that same night to his assistant trainer, Carl Pedigo, in Beaumont and told him to start preparing. Coe immediately announced his retirement from the racing business and said that his string of about eighty horses would be sold at auction. Conversely, Pansy and Cape stated that Beau Peavine and the other Beaumont horses, including Frank's favorite, Paris Grand, would be moved at once to their new home, even before Pansy took official title to the property, effective the first day of December. And as soon as possible, she said, "Pansies would be planted in the fields, to give everything a touch of color."[17]

Pansy shocked the horseworld when she announced the retirement of Roxie Highland from the show circuit and that she would be used as a broodmare. On Saturday, November 9, right after an exhibition at the Madison Square Garden Horse Show, the bugle sounded, Cape Grant entered the ring astride Roxie, and the two were met with a thunderous applause. Mat S. Cohen, the master of ceremonies, broadcast the event over the loudspeakers; the following represents only a portion of the message:

> Ladies and gentlemen, before you is the grand champion, three-gaited saddle horse of America. ... In her show career extending over a period of eight years, [she] has shown 260 times, winning 258 firsts, including championships, grand championships and two reserve championships. Her cash winnings ... were in excess of $65,000, besides numerous cups and trophies. She is the only horse that has ever won the H. F. McElroy $1,000 Challenge Cup at the American Royal, Kansas City, Mo., six times, in six consecutive years. In fact, it is said that Roxie Highland has been exhibited at more shows, shipped more miles, shown before more different judges, won more championships, grand championships and money, than any three-gaited horse that ever lived.
>
> ... In conclusion, it is only right and proper to state that Roxie Highland is the only three-gaited saddle horse ever exhibited at the principal horse shows ... from Seattle, Wash., to New York; she has thrilled the hearts and received the plaudits of a greater number of people than any other three-gaited horse the breed ever produced, and while she is yet in her prime, Mrs. Yount should receive the commendation of the horse loving public in retiring this great grand champion from active tanbark contests, in order that she may be given an opportunity to produce a son or a daughter nearer the class and quality of its famous dam than any horse yet produced, and yet, to many, her retirement will be regretted in that no one of this generation has ever seen, or will see, the equal of America's three-gaited sweetheart, the invincible, the

incomparable, Roxie Highland!

With escort in arm, Pansy walked to the center of the ring where she received "two beautiful trophies and a host of flowers, after which the band played 'My Old Kentucky Home,' while Cape Grant led the flower-bedecked mare slowly from the arena amid such applause as was never heard in historic Madison Square Garden!"[18]

Roxie Highland's retirement ceremony at Madison Square Garden.
—Courtesy American Saddlebred Museum, Lexington, Kentucky.

Soon afterward, Pansy publicized the purchase of "the immortal road horse Senator Crawford from George Brandeis, Omaha, Neb., through B. B. Tucker, for an astonishing $30,000." Imagine how the masses, affected by the calamity of the Great Depression, felt when they read that by-line. Nonetheless, Cape and his horses continued into the 1935 season with more remarkable wins—and purchases. At the Milky Way dispersal, Cape bought Calumet Armistice for $7,000, and like Senator Crawford, Calumet remained under contract to noted roadster trainer R. C. "Doc" Flanery of Illinois, who soon drove him to victory in several championships classes. At the New York Horse Show, Chief of Spindletop won the Five-Gaited Gelding Class and the $1,000 Stake; and at Chicago, he took top honors in the open Five-Gaited Division and along with it, the reserve championship.[19]

Calumet Armistice and Doc Flanery.
—Courtesy American Saddlebred Museum, Lexington, Kentucky.

From the beginning, Pansy encouraged all of the children she met to "read a good book" and get a good education; and the same approach applied to her daughter. In her early years, Mildred attended Millard Elementary, and then she enrolled briefly at Dick Dowling Junior High, located immediately behind El Ocaso. One afternoon while Mildred walked home, this time alone for some

Left to Right: Everett "Randy" Randall, Pansy Yount, Stannie Stansbury, Mildred Frank Yount, Mose Rawlins and wife, Beulah "Boo" Rawlins, Johnnie Sam; Mildred Building under construction in background, circa 1929.
—Courtesy Mildred Yount Manion.

reason, two men tried to grab her, but she pulled away and ran. After that, Frank and Pansy kept their daughter at home, and from that point forward, tutors were brought in.[20]

No doubt, Mildred did not care the least bit for being taken out of the public school system, because she commented, "It doesn't seem as though I'm like other little girls. I can't even play without being watched, and now I can't even go to school with my playmates." With these words spoken in April 1934, Mildred actually, without quite understanding why, described her life, past, present, and future. Moreover, she had never been like most other little girls. Ever since the day Frank and Pansy brought her into their home, she could never be anything but different. Constant press coverage, kidnapping threats, at least two attempted abductions, private tutors, the death of a famous father, an inheritance of over $4 million, all combined to set her apart from most normal folk. In that respect, Mildred became a victim of circumstances, first cut off from her doting father when she was only thirteen, and less than

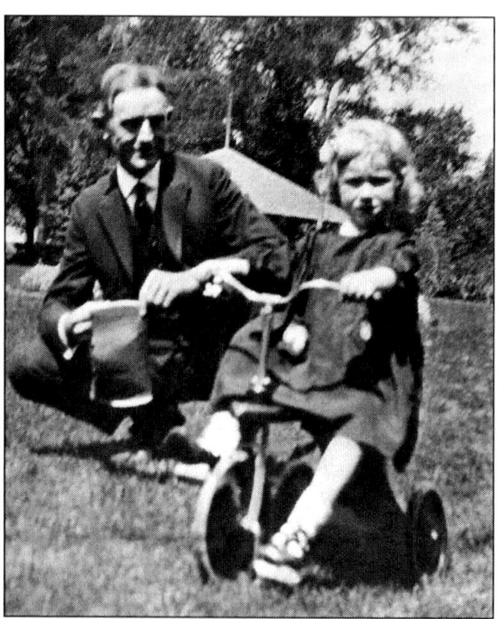

Frank Yount and daughter Mildred Frank Yount.
—Courtesy Mildred Yount Manion.

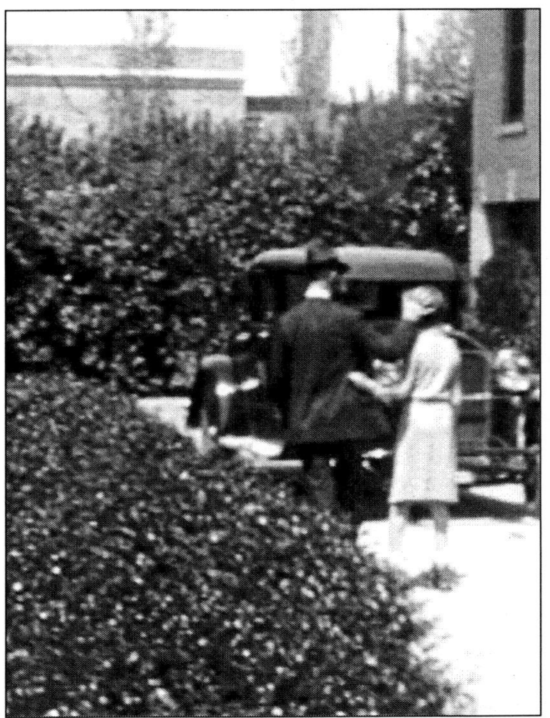

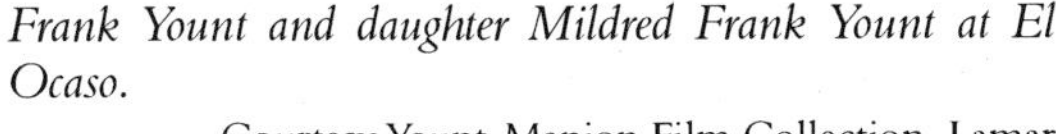

Frank Yount and daughter Mildred Frank Yount at El Ocaso.

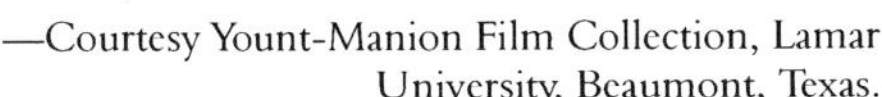

—Courtesy Yount-Manion Film Collection, Lamar University, Beaumont, Texas.

Ela Hockaday.

—Courtesy Hockaday School, Dallas, Texas.

one year later, detached from her mother when she was sent to continue her studies in Dallas. Dot Hilliard, whose expenses were paid completely by "Mother Fox," also went along to keep her daughter company at Hockaday. This institution for the select few, founded by Ela (pronounced Eela) Hockaday in 1913, was more or less a "finishing school" for young ladies who took "basic courses of a liberal arts education, as well as music and other skills calculated to the achievement of excellence in academics, athletics, and fine character."[21]

In actuality, Mildred felt abandoned at Hockaday, cast out on her own for the first time in her life, and had it not been for Dot Hilliard, no one could have bridged the gap between familiar surroundings in Beaumont and the strange new ones found in North Texas. While the two were students there, Dot, whom Bill Grant fondly recalled as an individual "seemed touched by angels," provided at least part of Mildred's lost self-assurance. According to Reagan Newton, the quiet and reserved "Millie" came alive when his mother walked into a room. "Mom seemed to animate her," Reagan said, "and she quickly became almost a different person." Reagan added that Dot "was the only person in Millie's circle who moved freely from the real world to that of the Yount's, and as such, provided the millionnairess with a ground." After the two lifelong friends were graduated, and both returned to Beaumont, Mildred always started her day by calling Dot, who married Trent Newton, promptly at 7:00 A.M., and this ritual continued throughout adulthood. However, despite her best friend's influence, Mildred, for the rest of her life, constantly labored with the loss of security that she so much required, and yearned for, in order to maintain balance in her ever-changing world.[22]

1936

Relative to their interests in Beaumont, Pansy and Mildred's year began with a windfall. The two, who still jointly owned an 85-acre tract that connected to the family's dairy farm in Beaumont, signed over a three-year lease to the Texas Company on March 20 "for $100,000 cash and $63,750 payable in oil produced, plus a one-seventh royalty." According to the *Beaumont Enterprise* report, this particular transaction "proves another instance of the vision of the man who made the Yount-Lee Oil company one of the country's greatest independent organizations." Also on the twentieth, other events—more important to the national scene—occurred. Frank Scofield, Internal Revenue collector for the Southern District of Texas, issued statements that in effect signaled a remarkable improvement on the American economic front. In a report to his Washington superiors, he said that the surprise up tick of 149 percent over the same quarter for the previous year "swelled the total collections so far to their unbelievable totals." In Trenton, New Jersey, Mark O. Kimberling, warden of the prison that held Bruno Richard Hauptmann, announced that invitations were mailed out to those who would witness the execution of the tried and convicted abductor and murderer of the Lindberg baby. Unless Governor Harold G. Hoffman intervenes, Kimberling said, the execution will occur "shortly after 8 o'cock on the night of March 31." Meanwhile in Germany, Adolf Hitler continued his saber rattling and tirades against the terms of the Versailles Treaty, solidifying a fanatical view that he would "accept nothing which infringes on German honor." But in Kentucky, however, Pansy and her trainer concentrated on matters at hand.[23]

There is no doubt that Spindletop Stables owed most of its success to Cape Grant, the proven professional who always seemed to get the best out of any horse entrusted in his care. Maxine Carter, who worked for *Saddle & Bridle* magazine, remarked, "To me, Cape Grant was the most magnificent rider I've ever seen. He was class from the word go and his presence added more ... to the show ring than the rest of them put together." The formal look, including a silk top hat, the white shirt and tie, the long riding attire, and boots, all added to the mystique that mesmerized and delighted crowds wherever he went. When Grant climbed into the saddle, he turned into a fierce competitor who gave no quarter, and one writer, in particular, recalled the lengths that he sometimes undertook to capture a crown.

> He [Cape] liked to tell the story of how he was once showing Chief of Spindletop early in his career, and he felt the judge was not giving them an adequate look.
>
> When the horses were reversed, he stopped on the rail, undid the strap on his jodphur britches, and hiked up his pants, baring his leg.
>
> It was on the rail side, away from the judge, but the crowd could see his bare leg and went wild. The judge was hoodwinked into thinking they were cheering for the horse, and Cape and Chief left the ring with blue.[24]

But Cape Grant, the epitome of confidence on a Saddlebred, had weaknesses for the

William Capers Grant.
—Courtesy American Saddlebred Museum, Lexington, Kentucky.

fairer sex and fast automobiles, especially the latest model of Ford. William Capers Grant, Jr. was born on January 5, 1899 to parents William, Sr. and Mary Alice Reynolds Grant, and one wonders perhaps if his parents ever considered that one definition of the derivative Caper is "to prance." Reportedly, Cape's father first put his son onto a horse at age two, but "thoughtlessly led the mare under a low clothes line, thereby giving Cape his first ride and his first fall." The youngster grew up around horses, and his proud father promoted the love that grew into an obsession. From many accounts, Cape, Jr. also had a quick temper, and given the right scenario, he demonstrated a high degree of proficiency in the art of profanity. Bill Grant recalled as a child in rural Beaumont driving along with his dad in a new Ford that came equipped with a radio, which in those days represented a rarity among a vehicle's standard accessories. "When Dad hit a pot hole in the road," he said, "the radio would frequently go out and have to be repaired. This happened often and would set ... [him] to cussing a blue streak."[25]

Circumstances, aggravated by prolonged absences from his wife Nola who still lived in Beaumont with her sons, caused an irreparable rift, and in fact, Cape officially walked out of the relationship in September 1934, about seventeen days before his youngest son, Miles Frank, was born. For a while, though, Nola held out hope for reconciliation. But when she finally gave up and filed for divorce on February 21, 1936, some suggest that Pansy paid $50,000 to Nola for seeking the settlement when she did. At this point, however, such an allegation can never be proved, but if Pansy did give money to Nola Grant, it may have well been out of the kindness of heart, a trait that she demonstrated repeatedly throughout her life. But aside from that, Pansy also wanted to rid her talented trainer of worries and outside distractions brought on by the marital split, but reasons, whatever the source, mattered little. When court action finalized the decree about two months later, Cape and Nola's seventeen-year marriage, which began on March 5, 1919, ended.[26]

In direct opposite of his brilliant accomplishments of late in show rings throughout the country, Cape's personal problems seemed to increase. On Thursday evening, May 7, it appeared that ironic tragedy might once again strike at the heart of a Yount enterprise and take out two of its most talented members. He and assistant Owen Hailey, who took the place of recently departed Carl Pedigo, had been to downtown Lexington, and they were returning to the farm by way of the Newtown Pike. When they neared Fasig Tipton curve, Cape's new car blew a tire, left the road, and both he and passenger were ejected. Passersby found them unconscious lying on the roadway, and shortly, they were transported to St. Joseph's Hospital in Lexington for treatment of critical injuries. Cape sustained "numerous broken bones about the neck and shoulder, [and] there were fractures of certain ribs and vertebra." Apart from receiving several blood transfusions, Grant suffered a concussion, and in the short term, some thought that he might not sur-

Owen Hailey.[27]
—Courtesy American Saddlebred Museum, Lexington, Kentucky.

vive. When she heard about the accident, Pansy summoned Dr. William T. White from Dallas, and when he arrived at the trainers' bedsides, the physician declared "that Cape is over the hill, so to speak, and ... he will undoubtedly experience a satisfactory recovery barring unforeseen eventualities." As for Hailey's condition, Dr. White announced that most of his wounds were limited to facial cuts and bruises. Although these would prove painful, he said, "Owen will be up and at 'em very shortly."[28]

Several well-wishers came by to see the two patients, and while visiting with Owen, an individual remarked that in one respect, he lucked out; since he worked for Pansy Yount, there would be no need to worry about financial obligations. Some even suggested, openly, that Owen ought to consider suing his employer, the results of which, they rationalized, would put him on easy street. These remarks, whether intended as a joke or serious advice, spelled disaster. When the report made its way back to Pansy that her assistant trainer planned on taking her to court, she fired him on the spot. Not only that, she balked when asked to pay Hailey's medical expenses, giving validity to the prospect that the recent outing with Cape had nothing to do with business whatsoever, but everything to do with tomfoolery. Owen always claimed that he got the raw end of the deal for it was he who prepared Spindletop's horses for the next competition, and deservedly so, he was scheduled to ride them to victory. Several skin grafts and operations later, Hailey recovered health wise, but for the rest of his life, he carried the effects of facial scarring—and as the story goes, unpaid medical bills. His supervisor, Cape, not only survived the ordeal, but by the time of the Kentucky State Fair's Fall opening, he was well enough to ride. His previous experiences as a catch rider paid off big time.[29]

The Chief, with Cape up, strutted his stuff at the event held in Louisville, where he walked away with the Gelding Division and the $10,000 Stake, along with the World's Grand Champion Five-Gaited Saddle Horse Crown. Pansy could not be present due to illness, and unfortunately, she missed one of the most spectacular victories ever achieved by her stables. One observer wrote:

> The largest crowd ever to witness a Kentucky show was standing, led by A. B. Chandler, Governor of the Commonwealth, singing My Old Kentucky Home. As the final note faded, the following hush was shattered by the sharp, clear call of the starter's bugle. The in-gate was opened wide and Chief of Spindletop, with Cape Grant in the saddle, burst into the ring. The crowd roared its approval, Cape smiled his and the Chief expressed his in the execution of an animated slow-gait down the center of the arena. Something clicked, everyone was satisfied. It was an omen. A new Champion would rule the Bluegrass and the Show Horse World![30]

What the crowd did not know is that a few nights before, just after 12:00 P.M., Cape took the Chief to the arena for a practice ride. Recently, the horse had pulled up lame, and the trainer wanted to determine beforehand if he could manage the routine. Pansy and a few other Spindletop employees came along to see the secret workout, and afterward much to their delight, Cape expressed confidence enough to keep the gelding in the lineup. The next passage points up the extent and the tenacity of the competition among handlers, and like grandmasters on a chessboard, Cape and his arch-rival, manager and trainer Charles C. Dunn of Dixiana, demonstrated why they were the best.

1936 Five-Gaited World Grand Champion. Chief of Spindletop, Cape Grant up.

—Courtesy American Saddlebred Museum, Lexington Kentucky.

> The night of the Stake, Cape Grant made it a point to be first to enter the ring. He figured that if the crowd saw the Chief first, no other horse could distract their attention; and again he was right. Mr. Grant knew that Night Flower was the horse to beat and that his gelding was faster at the rack than the mare. Consequently he placed his horse directly behind Night Flower during the slow-gait work-out and when the call came to "let 'em go!" Chief of Spindletop passed the Dixiana mare and moved away. When the horses were stripped for judging, Cape moved the gelding to a position beside the mare so that the judges could get a definite comparison. While the second division horses were working, Charlie Dunn, being one of the smartest ring generals in the country, took Night Flower to the east end of the arena and put her into her fine slow-gait. But when he turned around there was the smiling Cape with Chief of Spindletop slow-gaiting for all he was worth.

As many times previously, not only did Cape best Charlie Dunn this round, he rubbed salt in the open wound by winning the Dixiana Perpetual Trophy and collecting a private bet satisfied with the traditional state fair's "jug band" playing at the Chief's stall. Author M. F. Bayliss issued a glowing compliment to the Chief when he said, "Mrs. M. F. Yount of Spindletop Stables, Lexington, Ky., is the owner of this distinguished parader and Cape Grant, a no foolin' real horseman, the one who takes him to the wars." But lost somewhat in the fanfare of the Chief's splendid showing and subsequent win, Beau Peavine, with Cape up, also claimed victory in the $10,000 Stallion Division, beating out another of Dunn's best, Dixiana's Pirate Gold, as well as King Cane owned by the Minton Hickory Farm, and Proctor's Red Light out of the Pinehurst Stable of Orange, Texas, in that order. During the contest, Cape trounced his former assistant,

Carl Pedigo, who had left Spindletop's employ to go to work for Mr. and Mrs. Edgar Brown, Jr., who owned fourth-place finisher, Proctor's Red Light.[31]

After years of struggling to make the big time, Cape Grant had finally reached the top of his profession, and when it seemed that things could not get any better, the following appeared in the November classified section of a top trade magazine under a bold-faced, underlined special notice:

> In the Special Christmas Volume of the National Horseman, there will be an added inducement—the third installment of undoubtedly the most authoritative group of saddle horse articles ever published (FAMOUS SADDLE HORSE TRAINERS AND THEIR METHODS, by PETE MONROE), will be run on the life and unpublished methods of CAPE GRANT (WILLIAM CAPERS GRANT), one of the greatest and most famous saddle horse showmen of all time![32]

Immediately after acquiring Shoshone, which Pansy renamed as Spindletop Farm, she set about to increase the scale of her new acquisition. She purchased several adjacent tracts, paying anywhere from $175 an acre to $250, and sometimes more, until the total expanse involved some 1,066 acres, making it a little larger than rival Dixiana Farm nearby. With everything done, "Spindletop had 11 barns with 108 stalls, 75 separate paddocks, 18 miles of white board fence, and ten miles of hard road. Two lakes were built, Lake Mildred, which covered twelve to fifteen acres; and Lake Roxie, which contained a horseshoe-shaped island." Pansy brought in Percheron horses, Hampshire hogs, Suffolk sheep, foul of every description—Egyptian geese, Chinese geese, snow geese, wood ducks, and the Sebastopol, a native of Russia—and on top of it all, she constructed a new home.[33]

For that, Pansy relied upon Louisville architect E. T. Hutchings, who along with N. L. Ross, a longtime Colorado associate of the Yount family, completed Spindletop

Spindletop Hall under construction, June 1937.

—Courtesy Kathryn Manion Haider.

Hall in 1937 at a cost of over $1 million, not including the property and contents. At that time and era, this massive residence of forty rooms and a total of more than 45,000 square feet represented grandeur almost beyond comparison. Many called it "a masterpiece which has no parallel in Kentucky." The architect and builders made use of the latest technology at every turn, and in many ways, much of it is considered modern even by today's standards. A brief description follows, but for a more detailed version, refer to Appendix 2.

> There are three kitchens, each equipped with automatic photoelectric doors to prevent accidents. With 600,000 cubic feet in the structure, each room has its own thermostat.
>
> The music room on the first floor contained a custom-built organ, which took the entire summer to build and install. It cost $55,000 and could be played manually or with paper rolls like a player piano, controlled from any of six stations throughout the house. There were 7,000 volumes in the library, which also had an oriental rug valued at $40,000. The roofs of the mansion and some of the adjacent buildings are copper. The guttering, downspouts, and plumbing are also copper. The front doors made of bronze cast cost $14,000.
>
> A 30-by-60-foot seamless carpet in the living room was woven in Scotland, and the dining room rug from Czechoslovakia was designed to match the ceiling.
>
> Living quarters, including servant's rooms, are upstairs. There are seven bedrooms and two four-room suites. The bathrooms are decorated with custom-made, hand-painted tile.
>
> Twin winding staircases connect the three floors of the mansion. The Saddle Horse Lounge, where many a story was told and many a deal was made, is on the

South Terrace of Spindletop Hall.

—Courtesy Kathryn Manion Haider.

Grand entrance hall. Photograph by Lafayette Studios, Lexington, Kentucky.
—Courtesy Kathryn Manion Haider.

Elizabethan living room. Photograph by Lafayette Studios, Lexington, Kentucky.
—Courtesy Kathryn Manion Haider.

French powder room. Photograph by Lafayette Studios, Lexington, Kentucky.
—Courtesy Kathryn Manion Haider.

Gothic library. Photograph by Lafayette Studios, Lexington, Kentucky.
—Courtesy Kathryn Manion Haider.

William and Mary music room. Photograph by Lafayette Studios, Lexington, Kentucky.
—Courtesy Kathryn Manion Haider.

Terraced rose garden. Photograph by Lafayette Studios, Lexington, Kentucky.
—Courtesy Kathryn Manion Haider.

Aviary at Spindletop Farm.
—Courtesy Kathryn Manion Haider.

> lower level. It is decorated in Spindletop red and blue. Valet and barbershops are adjacent as is a billiard and game room.
>
> The ballroom, also on the lower level, has a floor of hardwood parquet constructed to have some give so as not to tire the dancers. The kennel is next to the ballroom.

Pansy with "Lucky."
—Courtesy Mildred Yount Manion.

The architectural firm of Lord and Burnham of Cleveland, Ohio, designed the aviary, consisting of separate houses for the pigeons and parrots. Pansy also owned many types of dogs and loved them everyone, especially a toy Pomeranian that followed her about every step. After an interview with Pansy, author Elizabeth Simpson commented that "Lucky ... takes his business of bodyguard with absurd seriousness."[34]

With Spindletop Hall finished in 1937 and after Pansy moved in, she threw several parties planned to unveil the masterpiece to the horse world. Christian Barham attended one of the first, and allegedly, when the famous Saddlebred show judge walked into the enormous Oak Room, he looked around in amazement, and with wide eyes, exclaimed, "What a great place to show colts!"[35]

During the construction phase of her Lexington mansion, as well as after, Pansy traveled considerably, choosing to divide her time between Lexington, and her homes in Beaumont and Manitou Springs, with Rockledge serving as a summer retreat from

Onaledge.
—Courtesy Jean Garrity.

The Antlers Hotel.
—Courtesy Antlers Hilton, Colorado Springs, Colorado.

about the first of June through the middle of September. By early 1936, many improvements had been made to the original property in Colorado: the guest house Onaledge had been purchased from Roland Bautwell, owner of the nearby Craftwood Inn; newly-completed double tennis courts "partly surrounded by a stone wall and climbing red blossing [sic] vines;" a lake for boating; and a massive swimming pool. Every possible amenity served the pleasure of a lucky few who could also choose from other forms of entertainment such as theater parties, dancing, croquet, hiking, horseback riding, and driving out to eat at the Antlers Hotel in Colorado Springs. One newspaper article that described Rockledge recites like a travelogue: "Cedar trees in their natural setting, red cliffs, stone steps, winding greenstone flag walks, rustic chairs and benches, formal

Mildred Frank Yount and Stannie Stansbury.
—Courtesy Yount-Manion Film Collection, Lamar University, Beaumont, Texas.

chairs and tables and smooth terraces make a beautiful setting about which dozens of pet dogs romp . . ."[36]

Because rather large groups stayed on for a month at a time, Louise Ogden, Pansy's faithful companion and the person in charge, prescribed measures to keep the decorum. Gentle reminders posted on framed cards found throughout Onaledge read, "For the benefit of our guests. Breakfast, 7:30 to 8 o'clock. Coffee in the solarium or courts at 10. Luncheon at 12:30. Cocktails on the island at 6 o'clock. Dinner, 7 o'clock." Besides Mrs. Ogden, the first gathering in July 1936 included another regular, Stannie Stansbury. Also the likes of Martha Jane Starr of Hutchinson, Kansas; Guy Merritt, Dan Masterson, George Holland, Jane Plummer, and Martin Johnson of Beaumont; two of Cape's sons, Bill "Kid" Grant and Silas; and Harriet White of Kansas City joined Mildred and her closest friend, Dot Hilliard, as they casually lounged at the home and grounds that covered 150 acres, where "within protective high wire fences and locked gates for the young people gathered there . . ., the days glide by like life in a fairy tale." Bill Grant recalled the height of the fence at about eighteen or nineteen feet, and that it extended around the entire property, which seemed, to him, in many ways like a compound. Pansy, he concluded, had some special penchant for cyclone-type metal fencing, but even so, the added fortification did little to keep wild varmints from steering too close for comfort. Bill mentioned one such occasion when Pansy and Stannie spotted a mountain lion on the premises. Stannie, expectedly nervous, resorted to a rather ridiculous tactic and ordered Pansy to "stay put, while I get help." Later on, within the security afforded by the rock home's interior, everyone thought the remark hysterically funny. When the summer's festivities ended in mid-September, Mildred returned to her studies at the exclusive Hockaday School in Dallas, where she had enrolled on September 24, 1934; and Pansy returned to Kentucky.[37]

Mildred Frank Yount and Dot Hilliard.

—Courtesy Yount-Manion Film Collection, Lamar University, Beaumont, Texas.

Spindletop Farm

"We sell the best and show the rest."
Spindletop Farm's Motto

When considering the many accomplishments of the stables thus far, it is hard to believe that it had been in operation for just over three years, but in this time span, however brief, Spindletop had won virtually all that could be won. With Lady Virginia's limited showings, Roxie Highland's full retirement to brood in late 1935; and Beau Peavine to stud the following year, at first glimpse, it seemed to some that at the height of success most only dreamed of, Pansy was simply going to walk away and allow her competitors a free pass to reclaim their previous prominence within the Saddlebred industry. In reality, though, Spindletop was undergoing a clever transition by way of unchartered territory. Pansy now decided to let Cape spend whatever resources were required to turn Spindletop from one the best show horse training facilities around to the best Saddle Horse breeding farm in the country. By this decision, Spindletop would be the first to seek out and purchase some of the most titled broodmares and studs, and instead of merely showing them on the tanbark, would allow these horses to build pedigrees that many champions of this day link to their own. This is Pansy Yount's true legacy.

The actual turning point can be traced to the Chief of Spindletop's surprising feat at Louisville in 1936 when he captured the World Championship Five-Gaited Crown. Even before, however, Cape had already taken steps in the new direction by placing the first advertisement in the May 1936 issue of the *American Horseman*.

> Dealers in and Breeders of Registered American Saddle Horses. A liberal supply of prospective champions including yearlings, two-year-olds, three-year-olds and aged horses constantly on hand, together with high class pleasure horses most suitable for small shows, as well as proven champions of both divisions of the Saddle Breed. Visitors welcome ... inspection invited ... correspondence promptly answered ... satisfaction guaranteed. W. Cape Grant, General Manager—Lexington, KY. Box 161 Phone 4760.[1]

Lady Virginia's retirement ceremony. Photograph by Lester Rounds.
—Courtesy American Saddlebred Museum, Lexington, Kentucky.

1937

After Louisville in 1936, Spindletop stepped up its breeding operations, and cast Senator Crawford, based out of "Doc" Flanery's Chicago area stable, as the mainstay on the show circuit. Cape had already begun adding such show ring notables as Belle Le Rose, Clara Bow, Ardella King, Dancing Daffodil, Sue Rex A, Virginia Highland, Belle Rita, Elizabeth Greis II, and Sweet Kitty Belairs as broodmares, and now to bolster the base at stud, he bought the renowned sire American Ace from Mrs. L. L. Rowland of Pennypack Valley Farm for $15,000, reported to be a record price paid for a stallion.[2]

Aside from being a show ring champion, Belle Le Rose's background is extremely colorful. Ed Ballard, a wealthy hotel owner from French Lick, Indiana, purchased the mare during the 1933 Chicago World's Fair Horse Show, along with Flashing American, for which he paid about $40,000 for the pair. He then sent both horses to Bettydot Stables in Dayton, Ohio for training under Earl Teater. But before Earl could show either horse, he was badly

American Ace.
—Courtesy American Saddlebred Museum, Lexington, Kentucky.

hurt in an accident. Having recovered by the St. Louis show in 1934, he trotted Belle Le Rose to her most impressive win so far by beating out Beau Peavine, Golden Dawn, and Night Flower. After that, however, Belle's career stalled, that is, until Carl Pedigo took her on. At this point, Belle Le Rose became Pedigo's first World Grand Champion. When Carl went to work for Cape Grant in Beaumont, Ballard sent his horses to Charles Cook of Louisville, but without proper guidance, Belle languished on the circuit. However, everything came to a head in November 1936. While in Hot Springs, Arkansas, Ed Ballard was killed in a gangland slaying, and early the following year, all of his horses were dispersed. When Cape Grant got wind that Belle Le Rose was up for sale, he bought her immediately. Pansy's trainer remembered well his previous loss to Ballard's mare, and now with the mission of Spindletop Stables changing from showing to breeding, Belle Le Rose fit right into the program of concentrating "those good genes and they will carry on."[3]

Pansy Yount.
—Courtesy Kathryn Manion Haider.

While Pansy oversaw the finishing touches on Spindletop Hall, Mildred continued her studies at Hockaday in Dallas. But regardless of distance, mother and daughter remained extremely close, communicating as often as possible. At every opportunity and especially during breaks from school, Mildred visited her mother either at Manitou Springs or Lexington, and on one of these occasions, Pansy surprised her daughter with a very special present: another automobile, none other than a new, stylish 1937 La Salle convertible sedan.

With Spindletop going full tilt with its new program, Beau Peavine and Sweet Kitty Belairs produced Burma Sapphire, the first and only foal registered by the farm in 1936. And when 1937 rolled around, everyone awaited the highly anticipated arrival of the foal of Roxie Highland and Beau, but sadly the stud colt named The New King died of pneumonia a few months later. But the team of Beau Peavine and Dahlia Dare did produce a healthy filly, Viola Ransom, who would later take many titles to her credit. Other members of the 1937 crop included Jean Lafitte and Star of Spindletop.[4]

Walt Disney Studios released its film *Snow White and the Seven Dwarfs* during Christmas 1937, and it immediately became a smash hit. Considered the first commercial success of its type, the movie spawned an extensive industry of all types of collectibles, in much the same vein as the "Beanie Baby" phenomena of recent times. Pansy took the idea and had built on the grounds of Spindletop Hall cottages for each of the seven dwarfs and afterward invited many of Lexington's children, as well as those of her own employees, to enjoy this unique playground. While no evidence of what happened

Mildred and her La Salle, June 1937.
—Courtesy Kathryn Manion Haider.

Roxie Highland and The New King. Photograph by Lester Rounds.
—Courtesy American Saddlebred Museum, Lexington, Kentucky.

Burma Sapphire. Photograph by Lester Rounds.
—Courtesy *Saddle & Bridle* magazine, St. Louis, Missouri.

to this pint-sized village exists, one newspaper reporter wrote affectionately about one of the best attractions "that Lexington never had was the Seven Dwarfs park with the live, miniature horses prancing around the little cottages where the dwarfs lived."[5]

1938

On January 23 Pansy received and entertained a group of distinguished visitors at Spindletop Hall. Under the auspices of the Lexington Board of Commerce committee, a delegation of United States Senators and other officials were there to not only tour Spindletop but other horse farms as well. The group had been in Louisville the previous night, where they attended a banquet held in honor of Alben W. Barkley of Kentucky who had recently announced his reelection bid to the U. S. Senate. Proudly, Cape Grant introduced everyone, including Senator Barkley and his manager

Shackelford Miller, Jr.; Marvin H. McIntyre, one of President Roosevelt's secretaries; the future president and then Senator Harry S. Truman of Missouri; Senators Joseph F. Guffey of Pennsylvania; Matthew M. Neely of West Virginia; Lewis Schwellenbach of Washington state; and Sherman Minton of Indiana to Chief of Spindletop and the rest of the stable's pride. From there, the group toured the dairy, cattle barns, and smokehouse. Afterward, Pansy hosted a reception where the dignitaries enjoyed coffee and cake before departing for Washington, D.C. that afternoon.[6]

Mildred and a group of students from Hockaday School visited with Vice President John Nance "Cactus Jack" Garner in the senate office building on April 5. And while they were there, they had their photo taken with the colorful character from Uvalde, Texas, who by 1937 had become "the second most powerful man in Washington," and next to Roosevelt, "the single most important man in the New Deal." Given Pansy's extreme distrust of FDR and his welfare policies, it is ironic that Pansy's daughter, with only Dot Hilliard separating them, stood with the man whom the president depended on to get his controversial legislation pushed through congress. And it is equally ironic that Garner, "as an old-line Democrat," later broke with his boss over the same issue when "the New Deal drifted toward welfare-state concepts."[7]

For years the Thoroughbred industry practiced the concept of marketing livestock by selling yearlings. Spindletop Stables soon adopted this same methodology, and on April 20 it conducted its first sale with the likes of Queen of Spindletop, Bet a Million, Viola Ransom, and Rajah of Spindletop. After Pansy and Cape treated everyone to a barbecue, auctioneers Johnston and McClure of Missouri kicked off the sale at 1:30 P.M. While few touted the initial offering as a true success, it did demonstrate the farm's commitment to innovation; its horses were sold at the actual last bid and without reserve. It seems inconceivable that Spindletop sold the best stock in this manner, but re-

Vice President John N. Garner and Hockaday students, April 5, 1938. To right of Garner, Dot Hilliard, wearing hat and holding coat; and then Mildred Yount.

—Courtesy Kathryn Manion Haider.

The first Spindletop sale. Photograph from National Horseman, *May 1938.*

—Courtesy American Saddlebred Museum, Lexington, Kentucky.

gardless, would-be bidders most probably thought it too good to be true, feeling there certainly had to be a catch. So on this day, many onlookers passed up several bargains, because they did not yet understand the rules. However, another more far reaching implication involved the stable's promise to never again "compete in the show ring against any horse they had sold." For all intents and purposes, this one single informal guarantee effectively ended Spindletop's show career.[8]

Mildred celebrated her eighteenth birthday on May 2, and soon after, she graduated from Hockaday. During the previous summer, though, while at Manitou Springs, Cape Grant introduced Mildred to Edward Daniel Manion, a young law student from Tulsa whose father, John Raymond Manion, worked as an executive with Sinclair Refining Company. On Monday morning at 11:20 o'clock, June 27, the two were married in what was described as a "simple ceremony," officiated by four priests at St. Paul's Catholic Church in Lexington. Long-time family friend and attorney R. E. Masterson of Beaumont gave away the bride, Dot Hilliard served as maid of honor; and Ed's brother, Ray L. Manion, stood by as best man.[9]

After the ritual, Pansy held a breakfast reception at Spindletop Hall between 1:30 and 3:00 in the afternoon. When reviewing the list of attendees, one might logically assume the number to be rather small, in that most consisted of the Yount's friends from Beaumont and Colorado, along with the Manions' relatives and guests. Besides these few, the only Lexington names reported included Rev. Joseph E. McKenna, who read the wedding service, Mr. and Mrs. Roy F. Williams (Mrs. Williams was Spindletop's business manager), Miss Frances Williams, Cape Grant, and Rev. George O'Bryan. Much ado has been made in some circles of the allegation that "several prominent members of Lexington society, who had been invited, were conspicuous with their absence." The fact remains, nonetheless, that Pansy, for reasons of security, and Mildred, in complete agreement with her mother, planned the marriage from the start to be kept as secret as possible, and neither the ceremony, nor the reception that followed were ever intended to be large-scale social events. Furthermore, when the *Beaumont Enterprise* hit the streets and newsstands early June 27, the article about the wedding contained the statement: "A simple ceremony is planned for this morning with only members of the immediate families of the principals and close friends in attendance." Regardless of size, however, Pansy had Spindletop Hall decorated to the hilt. White satin runners, which lined the winding staircases, beautiful table settings, and elaborate floral arrangements, all accentuated the occasion befitting the marriage of a fairy prince and princess.[10]

At four o'clock that afternoon, the new Mr. and Mrs. Ed Manion left for New York

Edward Daniel Manion, 1938.
—Courtesy Kathryn Manion Haider.

Mildred Frank Yount at Hockaday.
—Courtesy Hockaday School, Dallas, Texas.

Yount-Manion wedding party.
—Courtesy Kathryn Manion Haider.

Mildred Frank Yount and Ed Manion wedding reception.
—Courtesy Kathryn Manion Haider.

Pansy Yount and Cape Grant, seated left; Carl Kennedy, standing.
—Courtesy Kathryn Manion Haider.

Pansy Yount and Cape Grant.
—Courtesy Kathryn Manion Haider.

and Canada before taking a wedding trip to Europe, followed by a stopover at Rockledge, and then back to Beaumont where they took up residence at El Ocaso about October 1. Even before the couple returned, however, Ed received some good news. Obviously, Pansy made a call that put her new son-in-law on the prestigious board of directors at the First National Bank of Beaumont, but for regular employment, Ed had a job waiting for him in R. E. Masterson's law practice. Mildred's diary entry for October 29 reads in part: "Ed got his first salary check today." Before the marriage, Pansy still worried about Mildred's security. Reams of reports held in the private collection of Kathryn Manion Haider point up that this particular issue seemed to reach new levels in 1938 when Pansy received one report after the other from private detectives who reported back on the activities of her only child. Pansy could now rest easy, somewhat, and quit worrying so much about her daughter's safety.[11]

Cape hired K. K. "Eddie" Gutridge to work for the stable on a part-time basis, and when it came time for the show at Louisville, Gutridge successfully argued for entering Lady Virginia and her filly foal by American Ace in the competition. Everyone else, including Grant, believed the effort futile, though, assuming that the two would never place more than second in the Mare and Foal Class. Belle Le Rose and her filly, Belle of Spindletop by Beau Peavine, they said, would certainly win the blue ribbon. However, Gutridge had other ideas. The part-time trainer claimed to know "that Lady Virginia would crane her neck an extra foot if you put up your hand like there was food in it." So, that's what he did, and to Cape's surprise, Lady Virginia and Lady Augusta won their outing. Eddie remarked that "Mrs. Yount was so pleased, she put a color picture of Lady Virginia and her foal on the Christmas cover of Saddle & Bridle." Much later, when asked by an interviewer to make a comment about his employer, Gutridge said, "Mrs. Yount was an enthusiastic, kind lady, as nice as she could be."[12]

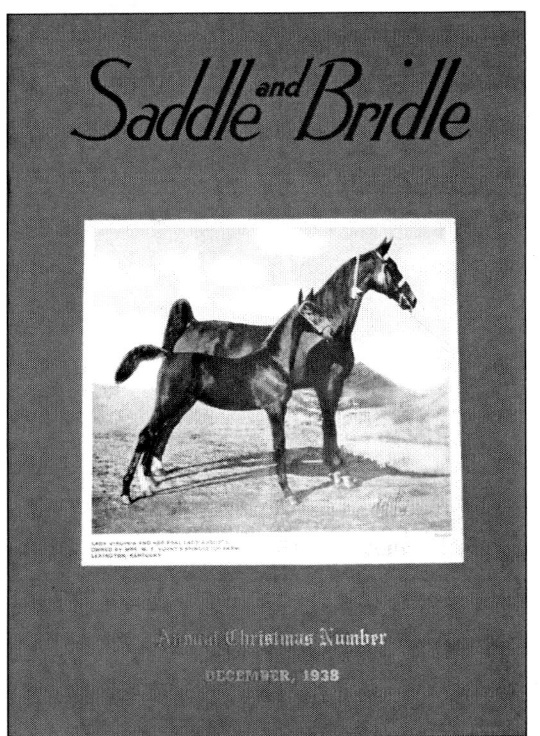

Lady Virginia and her foal, Lady Augusta.
—Courtesy *Saddle & Bridle* magazine, St. Louis, Missouri.

1939

The sting of losing Roxie Highland's stud colt had subsided somewhat, especially when the mare's second breeding to Beau Peavine produced Roxie Highland of Spindletop—but seven weeks after the chestnut filly foal arrived, the unthinkable happened. Roxie developed acute indigestion (colic) on February 20, and even though three first-rate veterinarians worked nonstop to try to save her, she passed away within hours. Right after Roxie had fallen ill, farm personnel contacted Henry Graddy of Versailles, Kentucky, and had him bring

Roxie Highland with foal, Roxie Highland of Spindletop. Photograph by Lester Rounds.
—Courtesy American Saddlebred Museum, Lexington, Kentucky.

in his famous foster mare Mary Graddy to serve as a wet nurse for the young filly. Pansy and Cape were both out of town at the time, but when she heard about the death of Mildred's priceless beauty, Pansy issued immediate instructions to have the horse buried with appropriate ceremonies in the beautiful little parkway just south of Spindletop Hall, on the drive leading to the training stables. There she was interred in her show blanket, hood, halter and bandages. Her grave was covered with a blanket of lilies and other floral designs arranged by a local florist.

Roxie's statue.
—Courtesy American Saddlebred Museum, Lexington, Kentucky.

"Roxie was good to everybody," a remorseful Cape Grant remarked. "She was pleasant to be around and to work with, and was the most sensible horse I ever rode. She knew what she was expected to do in the show ring and always did it." The bronze statue in her memory, which Pansy had placed at Spindletop, was removed later, and it is now located at the south end of the building that currently houses the American Saddlebred Museum.[13]

Tom Murphy joined Cape's staff as assistant trainer this year, and the future champion and world's grand champion Edith Fable, sired by American Ace and out of Bugle Anne, made her first wobbly appearance. With high hopes, Spindletop conducted its second annual

Roxie Highland's funeral.
—Courtesy American Saddlebred Museum, Lexington, Kentucky.

yearling sale on April 26. This time, twenty head sold for a total of $12,300—much better than the first one—but the average price of $426 for the top horses did little to lessen the frustration. But again, as before, Cape could blame no one but himself—and Pansy, because they insisted on selling notables Dancing Daffodil, Belle of Spindletop, Rockledge, Mighty Midget, and others, without reserve. However, no amount of disappointment after the sale could ever compare to Roxie's recent death, an event that would continue to cast a long shadow for some time to come.[14]

As the 1930s drew to a close and the Great Depression took its last few gasping breaths before heaving the death rattle, the ever-growing menace of war loomed on the European front. Locally, however, Lexington hospitals were undergoing a particular problem of their own. Many babies, born prematurely, "needed supplementary nourishment to survive." According to Mrs. J. Ed Parker, who relayed this story to a *Lexington Herald* reporter, when Pansy learned of the crisis, she remembered the old adage about a goat's milk being far more digestible than that of a cow's. With that, she sent her farm manager to bring in some of the best Nubians of the milking variety that he could find. Soon, Ed "Fitz" Fitzpatrick returned with about twenty head, and they took up residence in "the first goat barn in the area constructed, based on plans sent from the University of New Hampshire." The Nubians thrived in their new environment, and after drinking the milk donated by Pansy's dairy, so did the premature babies. Due to their seemingly overnight improvement, many of the tykes were released to their parents' home care prior to Christmas.[15]

1940

Although she was ill and could not attend, Pansy had Senator Crawford retired at the final performance of the January National Western Stock Show in Denver, where for the sixth straight year he took the blue in the $1,000 Roadster Stake. For the ceremonies, the band played the Colorado state song as the great champion entered the ring wearing a blanket of some three dozen orchids and 150 gardenias. Those who were present, as well as those who tuned in on the Mutual Radio Network's live broadcast from coast to coast by its affiliate KFEL of Denver, heard of the great champion's whole host of accomplishments. Senator Crawford, the announcer said, held the distinction of never being defeated in a trotting contest. During his

Senator Crawford's retirement ceremonies at Denver, Colorado. Third from right: "Doc" Flanery, in glasses; Mrs. R. C. Flanery, his wife, fourth from right.

—Courtesy American Saddlebred Horse Association, Lexington, Kentucky.

Cosmopolitan Hotel, Denver, Colorado.
—Courtesy http://homepages.rootsweb.com/~rocky/PostcardHTML/cosmopolitan.html.

eight-year career begun in 1932, he won 159 blue ribbons and 57 grand championship events, performed in 11 states and Canada, and logged more than 50,000 miles in his travels. The Lexington Board of Commerce president Gilmore Nunn; and Russell Nuzum, a board of commerce member, and president of the Lexington Rotary Club, presented Spindletop Farm with a trophy; and C. R. Jones, manager of the National Western Horse Show, did likewise. When the horse departed from the ring, the band played "My Old Kentucky Home." On the previous day, however, some 150 folks gathered at the Cosmopolitan Hotel in Senator Crawford's honor, and some even seriously suggested that the horse himself participate in the festivities. But the program's chairman, R. C. "Doc" Flanery, knew full well that the Senator's spirited temper would never condone such a thing, so he put the matter to rest. A spokesman said, "We just couldn't do it. Why? Well, you know, there's a lot of glassware and the Senator might have become excited." After the retirement ceremony, Senator Crawford was brought to Kentucky where he was supposed to spend the rest of his days; however, he became depressed—actually downright mean—and reportedly yearned for his trainer, Doc Flanery. Soon afterward, Pansy sent the horse, along with his hot temper, back to the Chicago area, where she continued to pay for his full upkeep just as she had all along.[16]

Elsewhere, on February 6, 1940, the M. F. Yount estate with N. L. Ross acting as agent, signed a three-year lease with Florence E. and A. O. Maltby for the famous Navajo Indian Store in spaces designated as No. 1 Arcade and No. 264 Manitou Avenue in Manitou Springs. The lease total set at $2,400, escalated from the first payment of $125 to the last of $250 in September 1942. Also in 1940, Sister Belle was foaled at Lexington, followed the next year by Beau Le Rose Peavine, but for some reason, Cape gave up on the breeding stallion American Ace, sold at an undisclosed price to J. Truman Ward,owner of Maryland Farm, of Brentwood, Tennessee .[17]

The War Years

In our current day and amidst the justified fears of terrorism brought on by the tragedy of September 11, 2001, it is often forgotten that previous generations of Americans also experienced the same angst. During World War II, the possibility that Japan might invade from the West was taken very seriously. And too, the constant sightings of German U-Boats off the Eastern seaboard and elsewhere led some to believe that an imminent attack by Hitler's Luftwaffe would reduce to ruin the Texas Gulf coast oil fields, its refineries, and much of the nation's petroleum reserves, not to mention the loss of thousands of lives. Mildred and Ed Manion thought their children might be safer, for a while, in Lexington. So they sent them to visit Spindletop Hall to experience "the run of a 40-room mansion, pony cart rides over a 1,000 acre farm, a real live menagerie of farm animals to feed and pet, sumptious [sic] parties at Christmas and on birthdays." Kathryn Manion Haider, who shares the middle name of Bernadette with Pansy, reminisced fondly about her famous grandmother. "She was a character," Kathryn said. "She loved the good life and never did anything halfway. If she had a horse, it had to be the best horse. A cow had to be the best cow. She was not well educated … but I remember her as a lecturer. She used to tell me I should get the best education I could." During a recent interview, Kathyrn further discussed her stays at Lexington, where she got to know Cape Grant, sometimes called "Uncle Catty-Corner." "I remember him as a Clark Gable type." She continued, "He let us get our hands dirty and ride horses all by ourselves. I always thought of him as a kind person …"[18]

Kathryn Manion and Cape Grant, riding at Spindletop Hall, circa 1945.

—Courtesy Kathyrn Manion Haider.

During the war, the government sold bonds to help finance combat operations, and women by the thousands went to work in the factories and munition plants to replace men folks who left to fight the Japanese, Germans, and Italians in faraway places, such as Guadalcanal, Anzio, Sicily, the Ardennes, and Buna beach. Moreover, on the domestic front, Americans from almost every walk of life were forced to get by on much less and dealt with stringent rationing on food products and gasoline. To help ease one of these situations, Agricultural Secretary Claude R. Wickard, in late December 1941,

Mildred Yount Manion riding at Spindletop Farm; Cape Grant at right, circa 1945.

—Courtesy Kathyrn Manion Haider.

Southern California Work Projects Administration poster.
—Courtesy Library of Congress, Washington, D.C.

Philadelphia Salvage Committee poster encouraging scrap drives to aid the war effort.
—Courtesy Library of Congress, Washington, D.C.

suggested that ordinary citizens should get involved by planting Victory Gardens, and "with that, millions of … [those] who had never known a hoe from a trowel began planting lettuce, tomatoes, beets, carrots, peas and radishes in such unlikely sites as their own backyards, the Portland (Oregon) Zoo, Chicago's Arlington Racetrack and the yard of the Cook County Jail." Another program, designed partly out of necessity and partly as a morale booster for supporting troops in the field, called for recycling numerous items, including steel, iron, tin, rubber, and paper. Scrap drives were common throughout the country, but at times, public zeal went overboard when discarding objects intended for conversion into war materiel. Though these examples seemed perfectly logical at the time, after the war ended, many who contributed wished they had not acted so hastily in donating memorabilia like irreplaceable cannon from previous wars, various park statues, and other treasured keepsakes and heirlooms.[19]

Pansy Yount, it seemed, had about everything a person could ever want: a loving and educated daughter, a successful son-in-law, grandchildren, fine homes, a magnificent farm, championship caliber Saddlebreds, amenities by the score—and she also had a patriotic streak. As such, she wanted to do her part, and although some might find her actions unjustified from today's perspective, she personally "drove her huge Judkins-Berline Model J. Duesenberg onto the scales on the Fayette County courthouse lawn and announced she was donating it to the scrap drive." Imagine the shock of the volunteers and nearby spectators on that particular Saturday in October 1942, when Pansy put the very car, which Frank Yount took delivery of two days before he died on November 13, 1933, on the chopping block. The attendants at the weigh station tried desperately

Frank's tireless Duesenberg weighs in.

—Courtesy Randy Ema, Inc.

to talk her out of it, contending that the car was worth much more intact than at salvage prices. But Pansy refused to budge. With her mind made up, she ordered, "No, make it into a tank." When she left, however, no one had the heart to do as she directed, so local army personnel devised a plan. Quietly, they moved it to the Bluegrass Ordnance Depot, and repainted it "olive drab and festooned with white-stenciled stars and ID numbers." But the secret did not stay hidden for long. When the depot commander used it conspicuously as a parade vehicle, Pansy soon learned about the subterfuge. She quickly had the car confiscated and brought back to Spindletop Farm, where she personally watched as her workman dismantled the classic, closely akin, as one concluded, to "putting a Rembrandt down a wood chipper." When her employees were done literally cutting the car into pieces, she accompanied them to the municipal scrap heap and watched as they unloaded the remnants of the once beautiful, black and gold, special ordered Duesenberg. Coincidentally, there were only two like it in the entire world. Frank and Pansy owned one of course, and cosmetic queen Elizabeth Arden of nearby Maine Chance Farm in Lexington, which sent Jet Pilot to win the 1947 Kentucky Derby, once owned the other.[20]

Nineteen hundred and forty-three proved a banner year for Spindletop's program, continuing with the birth of three of its most famous mares: Carolina Caroline, Rita Le Rose, and Marie Bosace. And with the arrival of 1944, several more soon to be legendary foals followed, among them Abie's Genius and Beau Yount, sired by Beau Peavine and out of Belle Le Rose. This extraordinary colt, Beau Yount, would eventually be chosen to replace his sire as the stables' top producing stallion.[21]

Cape, however, yearned still for the excitement of show ring competition, so he spent a lot of his time judging, and in the process, received some pretty good reviews. On the farm, Beau Peavine, now aged fifteen, had been Spindletop's top stud, but breedings had fallen off some as of late, given that the stables had all but deserted the show ring circuit. To renew potential customers' interest in the horse, Cape brought the

Broodmares and foals at Spindletop Farm. Broodmares, left background, Belle Le Rose; foreground left to right, Sweet Kitty Bellairs (white face), Lady Virginia, and Iowana.
—Courtesy American Saddlebred Museum, Lexington, Kentucky.

great champion out of retirement for a special exhibition at the 1944 Lexington Junior League Horse Show just before the Three-Gaited Grand Championship Stake to show everyone in attendance that his horse remained in top form, regardless of his age. Afterward Beau Peavine "was presented with a lovely basket of flowers at the close of the performance," and later on, most probably, additional inquiries regarding his stud fees, advertised in the low range of $75 to a high of $150.[22]

In Colorado on July 24, 1944, Pansy transferred ownership of Rockledge and the Arcade property to Mildred; and on the seventeenth of the previous month, she sold Onaledge to Ruth Roeser and Mary Jane Biehn. The Roeser family also operated the nearby Craftwood Inn as a restaurant.[23]

Post-War Years

With the surrender of the Japanese and the war over in 1945, Spindletop roared on with the births of stallions Abie's Royal Irishman and Lexington Leader; and the foaling of two nice fillies: Susie Key and Mona Kai. Pansy transferred the last of the Colorado properties out of her name on October 10, 1946, when she sold the quarry to Robert C. Whiteley of Denver for an undisclosed sum. But early in 1947, controversy again cropped up in Beaumont. During one of Pansy's numerous visits to Frank's mausoleum, she discovered loose sand on the floor, and became quite alarmed. Even though it would be years later before the term "Quality Assurance" assimilated into mainstream America's vocabulary, Pansy knew well what it meant—and what she expected. Much to everyone's dismay, she had intended the elaborate memorial to last indefinitely; thus, she immediately hired a team of experts, a structural engineer and a geologist, to make a thorough inspection and get back to her quickly. Confidently, the two never imagined her reaction when they boasted that "the structure would last at least six hundred years." Not long after that, an angry Pansy Yount drove to the cemetery office and approached the manager, Willis Clyde King. In no uncertain terms, she promptly ordered, "I don't want anything around here that will fall down after I'm gone with the Yount name on it. Tear the damn thing down." But before King could act in response, however, further details had to be gotten out of the way. Pansy called Carl Kennedy, her Beaumont estate manager, and set the plans in motion. In her quest for the best, she approved the purchase of a $40,000 "ledger and grave vault," consisting of 5,000 pounds of bronze crafted by the Meierjohan-Wengler Company in Cincinnati. Then, sometime within thirty days after March 28, King's crew, assisted by local mortuary personnel, moved Frank's body, placed it in temporary facilities until the mausoleum could be torn down, and for the final time, the oilman was interred at the original site of the dismantled edifice during a private ceremony attended only by Pansy and members of the immediate family.[24]

In Lexington, Abie's Baby was foaled in 1947, and during the following year, Spindletop registered Miss Dixie Rebel, a spectacular filly foal sired by Beau Peavine and out of Abie's Irish Rose. Later on at the farm's auction, Cape sold the mother and daughter pair for about $8,500 to Mr. and Mrs. John Oman, III, owners of Oman Stables in Franklin, Tennessee, and within the next two seasons, the youngster won the "weanling, yearling and two-year-old futurities at the World Championship Horse Show at the Kentucky State Fair.[25]

On Tuesday, September 27, 1949, at ten o'clock in the morning, Pansy married Cape Grant at Spindletop Hall in a small private ceremony attended by a few friends, including Carl Kennedy and Stannie Stansbury who came up from Beaumont. Some folks back in Southeast Texas, as expected, expressed shock at the occasion, while others really did not care one way or the other. From the latter's point of view, Pansy and Cape had traveled together for so long on the Saddlebred circuit, it seemed that they had been a couple for years anyway.[26]

Cape Grant and Pansy Yount at wedding.
—Courtesy Kathryn Manion Haider.

Bill Grant said that he always believed that Pansy used his dad as a security officer, more or less to ensure the family's protection from undesirables, and Cape testified later that his responsibilities did, in fact, include that very proviso. Others like David Howard Corcoran, concluded, probably more nearer to the actual truth, that the security issue cut another way. No doubt, Cape Grant ranked as a superstar among a short list of trainers that most stables would have loved to have had on their payroll; and similar to highly sought after championship athletes of contemporary times, if Cape had been a free agent, he could have found suitable employment at any given moment. Even though all compensation records of Spindletop Farm have long since been destroyed, rest assured, Cape Grant received top pay—$500 per month and all expenses during Depression times according to his statement—and most likely, no outside offer would have come close to matching what he made there. Plus, Cape liked to wear the best clothes and drive the newest and fastest car; and Pansy saw that he remained happy, evidenced by her presenting him with a new Packard in 1934 and a Ford in July of the following year. By this marriage of convenience on both their behalves, perhaps in reality, Pansy did ensure Cape's staying around, but relative to long-term loyalty to her farm and stables, that became a matter of future contention.[27]

A separate report, however—though possibly another of the endless rumors—circulated that the couple had actually been married more than ten years earlier. Lynn Weatherman relayed the following account that purportedly took place in 1938 as told by Arthur Van Ronzelen, the founder and first publisher of *Saddle & Bridle* magazine.

> Cape and Mrs. Yount had come to St. Louis and called him from the downtown Jefferson Hotel where they always stayed. The Saddle & Bridle offices were located in midtown, several miles west at the Chase Hotel. Cape Grant invited Van Ronzelen and the late Virginia Powell, a well-known employee and then Associate Editor, to join them for dinner. They responded, but when Mrs. Yount learned of Van's forthcoming marriage, she was disturbed that the bride-to-be had not joined them and insisted on hosting another party for Van and Jayne the next evening at the Chase.
>
> The Van Ronzelens vividly remember that as the party progressed and the cocktails flowed freely, Mrs. Yount and Cape Grant confided to them, that they had recently been secretly married aboard an ocean liner, by the captain, on the high seas.

But regardless of why, when, or where they were first married, Cape and Pansy left soon after the official wedding breakfast and headed straight for Beaumont by automobile.[28]

Chief of Texas, sired by Beau Yount and out of Abie's Irish Rose, foaled that same year at Spindletop, but for Cape, no accomplishment on the horse breeding front could ever replace the thrill of showing horses in the ring to a thunderous applause. He had been in the doldrums for some time now, so when his friend William J. "Bill" McIlvain told him that the owners of the Dufferin Stock Farm in Toronto, where Bill worked as

Coach and Four, consisting of Waltz Time, Dinner Dance, Curtain Call, and Stage Hand. Atop front: Cape Grant on whip; Bill McIlvain. Atop back: Stannie Stansbury, forefront; Mrs. Lou Winges. Photograph by John R. Horst.

—Courtesy American Saddlebred Museum, Lexington, Kentucky.

trainer at the time, had put a four-in-hand team of Hackney horses on the market, Cape bought the lot and began exhibiting them as a special attraction all across the country.[29]

1950–1952

At a time when Cape's vigor renewed somewhat, Pansy's interests in Saddlebreds seemed to wane considerably. But when Bill McIlvain came to Spindletop, most everyone on the sidelines took this as proof positive that perhaps the stables would return in a serious way to show business. McIlvain began immediately to train a new string that included Juanita Watkins, Mildred Manion, Chief of Texas, and Abie's Royal Irishman, the latter sired by Beau Peavine and out of Abie's Irish Rose. In his description of the latter, J. H. Ransom, noted Saddlebred author, wrote:

Abie's Royal Irishman. Photograph by John R. Horst. From American Horseman/Sportologue *(July 1952).*

—Courtesy American Saddlebred Museum, Lexington, Kentucky.

> This beautiful horse is one of the sort that horsemen dream of and seldom see as he is a magnificent specimen. He is a gorgeous chestnut with one of the longest necks seen on any saddle horse, exquisite quality and finish and a big full tail that drags the ground. He has the speed of an express train, goes high in front and a popping pair of hocks that move like pistons with terrific drive and action.

While Cape added Spindletop Bourbon to the farm's impressive list of champions, competitor Doss Stanton took Miss Dixie Rebel to the 1951 Kentucky State Fair. But just before she made her appearance in the Three-Year-Old Fine Harness Stake, Pansy and Cape repurchased the mare for about $20,000, and she entered the ring under her new colors of blue and red, handily defeating Treasured Token and Star Final to take the title. Also during the same show, Cape made his last appearance with the famed Coach and Four. Later, Cape bought some fine show ponies in 1952 at the Carolanne Farm dispersal in Norfolk, Virginia; and he continued to work with Abie's Royal Irishman—but nothing really seemed to reignite the flame that once burned within.[30]

Miss Dixie Rebel; Cape Grant on whip. Photograph by John R. Horst.

—Courtesy American Saddlebred Museum, Lexington, Kentucky.

Return to the Lone Star State

"All that we are is the result of what we have thought. Believe in your own thoughts, be confident and self-reliant."

PANSY M. YOUNT[1]

From her Beaumont office at the Mildred Building, on July 8, 1957, a normally confident and self-reliant Pansy wrote to her daughter Mildred, who toured Europe in the company of her husband's long-time secretary Sallie Blain. In her own hand, the seventy-year-old admitted that she had recently gone through some rough spots, as she put it, a "bad spell of sicking." Continuing, Pansy said, "I think I am going to sell my farm. Pray that I do if it is the Lord, is willing for me to do it." It is apparent that still, she did not feel well; the scrawl, misuse, and misplacement of words identified that. But one message rang loud: with these simple statements, the die was cast.[2]

On the previous twenty-ninth of August, Father Joseph E. McKenna of St. Paul Church in Lexington wrote to Mildred. He mentioned that he had spent a week in Beaumont recently, and during that time, he "had a heart to heart talk with your good mother." McKenna continued, "I told her of her serious illness, [and] I explained how she could be reconciled to God and the Church." Although the distinction between physical and spiritual illness is rather blurred, it is clear from McKenna's letter, nonetheless, that Pansy had reached a crossroad, in that her marriage to a divorced man put her in direct opposition to the teachings of her faith. In order to receive absolution, Holy Communion, anointment at the time of her death, and have the funeral services conducted inside a Catholic Church, McKenna advised her "to give up Mr. Grant by a 'Will Act,' … [which] would not affect his property rights or her [temporal] relations with him …" In closing, the priest informed Mildred that he had left with Pansy his "Relic of St. Ann." "If anything would happen to her, I know you would send it to me. She may live for years, or go in a hurry. Who knows? The good sisters consider her condition serious." McKenna also referred to several relics in Pansy's possession, such as St. Vincent de Paul; St. Joachim; and St. James, the Apostle, and that he planned to send

Pansy Yount Grant at Spindletop Hall.
—Courtesy Mildred Yount Manion.

Mildred a "First Class" Relic of St. Andrew, the Apostle, the brother of St. Peter, all to be used while praying for her mother.[3]

There were, however, other underlying issues that caused Pansy to conclude that now just might be the best time to sell the Kentucky property. In an article contained within the July 1981 issue of *Saddle & Bridle*, writer Lynn Weatherman described an alleged incident that occurred in 1952 when several members of the Lexington Junior League visited Spindletop Hall for the purpose of soliciting a contribution for the upcoming horse show, which Pansy helped found and liberally supported. Supposedly, Pansy invited the ladies out to the sprawling mansion, and when they were seated, she left the room. While returning, she inadvertently overheard one of them say, "Isn't it a shame that someone like her owns a place like this." Weatherman went on to explain how this remark "was the straw which broke the camel's back."[4]

Whether this episode has at its base fact or fiction, it is true that in Lexington, as with Beaumont, Pansy never cared about mixing with high society. Frankly, she always felt more at ease around those whom she counted as true friends, such as Fred B. Wachs, Sr., the respected general manager and publisher of the *Lexington Herald-Leader*; the revered John Gray, former banker and president of Lamar University in Beaumont, and his wife Mary; long-time attorney R. E. Masterson; Louise Ogden, who for years served as her quasi-social chairman; Viola Ransom; Stannie Stansbury; Ed "Fitz" Fitzpatrick, her farm manager; and numerous others in whose presence, she could just be herself—and without pretension of "putting on airs," the very thing she found the most despicable. Perhaps this business with the Junior League ladies represented nothing more than just another rumor in the mill, but if Pansy actually did hear such a coldhearted remark, there is no doubt that she would have sent every one of them scurrying, followed by a more than ample dose of expletives as they ran toward the door. And after chalking the

John and Mary Gray.
—Courtesy Mildred Yount Manion.

whole thing up to thoughtless tongue-wagging by a bunch of societal inconsiderates unable to contain their envy, she would have promptly brushed the matter aside. After all, she had heard worse things. Why should this be handled any differently?

In truth, though, Pansy tired of the personal—and financial—demands placed upon her by Spindletop itself. Besides lingering illnesses, injury contributing to the diminished health of the once energetic millionaire, who traveled continuously with her magnificent horses as they performed on the tanbark at shows all over the country. And during the breathers in between, she split whatever time was left at homes in Manitou Springs, Beaumont, and DeLand, Florida.

In Colorado, Pansy titillated the residents of Manitou Springs about the possibility of building a branch of Spindletop Stables there, and in Florida, she bought a small Chris-Craft pleasure yacht and named it what else but "Spindletop." She had Father John P. Cotter of the Church of the Holy Rosary "christen the vessel and invoke the blessings of God on her and persons who sail on her." While visiting her home, which she called "The Woodlands," in DeLand, located at 500 East New York Avenue, Pansy often fished on the nearby St. Johns River. According to Bill Dreggors, Jr., current resident and head of the local historical society, he once worked for Pansy as a maintenance man, and he also heard from his father many accounts about her fishing escapades. One involved a favorite guide, Dick Flowers, who said that during one such outing, Pansy lost her tackle to a big bass just before a storm hit, forcing the two reluctant fishermen to leave the river. But as soon as the weather permitted, Pansy got back in the boat and insisted that they return "to the same spot where she not only caught the one that got away, but also recovered her tackle."[5]

Pansy's Florida property consisted of the main residence, a large garage with servants' quarters above, and another brick house used alternately for guests and a caretaker. Bill Dreggors, Jr. said that Pansy was very particular about everything. Sometimes she walked outside, and usually without uttering a sound, stood and watched the workers, including him, as they manicured the lawn and continually removed moss from the surrounding trees, and vines from the azaleas. But when she did speak, Dreggors added that she never used a demanding or critical tone. And as for her personal appearance, Pansy dressed so casually, one could have easily mistaken her for a house maid.

"The Woodlands."
—Courtesy Kathryn Manion Haider.

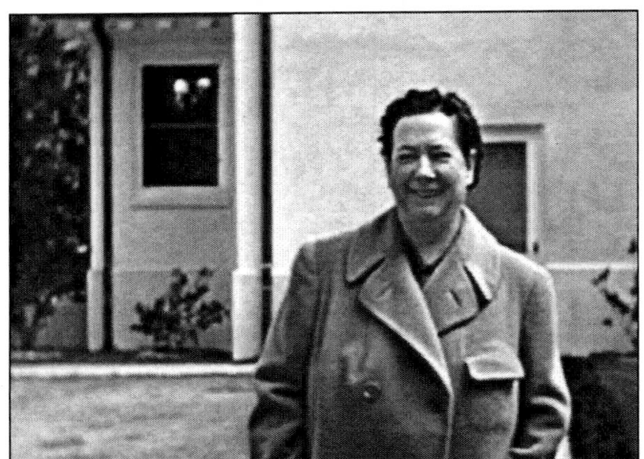

Pansy Yount at "The Woodlands."
—Courtesy Yount-Manion Film Collection, Lamar University, Beaumont, Texas.

Photograph taken at "The Woodlands." From left to right: Judge R. E. Masterson, Stannie Stansbury, Pansy Yount, and Mildred Frank Yount.

—Courtesy Mildred Yount Manion.

Although she made no attempt to join local society, everyone knew about her extreme wealth, and because her only apparent interest seemed to be fishing, they found this quite odd. While in the area, she relied on locals mostly, employing Tony Visconti as chauffeur and Carl Murz as caretaker. Cape Grant, he said, rarely accompanied Pansy to DeLand, but when he did, she introduced him simply as "her farm manager." After the marriage, however, Pansy seemed to lose interest in the place altogether and promptly sold the property to Max Acree, the local Ford dealer.[6]

During one of their trips to Texas, specifically on April 22, 1950, Cape and Pansy were involved in a serious automobile accident at Liberty, just west of Beaumont, when another car driven by Willie L. Mitchell turned in front of them. All were taken to Mercy Hospital nearby and treated. In addition to internal injuries, Pansy's included a crushed pelvis, but Cape lucked out, escaping with minor wounds to the head and leg, while Mitchell received "a broken right arm and possible rib fractures." Whereas the outcome certainly could have been worse for all involved, the effects of Pansy's pelvic injury nagged on—and now, arteriosclerosis began to take its toll.[7]

For whatever reason, though, whether by combined hurtful remarks and gossip from some circles of local society, constant travel, sickness, injury, the demands of maintaining Spindletop Hall and the adjoining 1,066 acres, or whether she felt cut off from her only child who now lived in Beaumont, Pansy made her decision, first to sell her beloved horses, and then, leave Lexington for good. At her direction, Cape contracted Tattersalls, the premier auction house in the area, and had them plan a dispersal sale on Spindletop Farm grounds. The weather turned out well with a lot of buyers on hand, and on the afternoon of July 9, 1952, auctioneer George Swinebroad began the event with the announcement, "Here she comes." Everyone crowded in close to catch a glimpse of Miss Dixie Rebel who "trotted, in her elegant form, up through the center of the track." Active bidding began at $1,000 but quickly climbed to a final of $10,000 by Robert Baskowitz of St. Louis, Missouri. S. J. Campbell of Argyle Stables in Mt. Caroll, Illinois, paid $8,000 for the Coach and Four, represented by Waltz Time, Dinner Dance, Curtain Call, and Stage Hand, all made famous by Cape in exhibitions at horse shows nationwide. In addition, twenty-eight other Spindletop horses were sold (see Appendix 5). Although some hailed the event at Spindletop Farm as a complete dispersal, it was not. Pansy could not bear the thought of selling her pride and joy, so Beau Peavine, along with a few select older mares, would not be listed among those for sale. But when the sun set over Spindletop late that Wednesday afternoon, most of the others were gone at unbelievable low prices, generating a total of only $52,400, averaging just $1,747 each. For Cape and Pansy, the results were undoubtedly disappointing. Plus, the sale proved a sobering experience, not only to them but to most other horsemen, including fierce competitors of yesteryear, when it finally sunk in that the flame of Spindletop had been extinguished forever, and that the stables' colors of blue and red would reign supreme no longer in the Bluegrass. The farm's epitaph, however, had been written years before, but it would live on within the offspring of the foals produced there and through blood lines that continue well in today. (See Appendices 3 and 4).[8]

From the date of the dispersal, Spindletop remained virtually idle, and the distinction of being the last horse registered as bred by the farm goes to the March 1954 foal Spindletop Denmark, sired by Beau Yount and out of Roxie Highland of Spindletop. Cape and Pansy were in Beaumont, when on August 27, 1957, they got the distressing news that Beau Peavine—the winner at one time or another in all leading shows he entered and whose name graced Spindletop Farm's letterhead—died in Kentucky at age twenty-eight. Cape commented that "the animal had been in apparent good health up to the moment of his death. He had been brought in from pasture Tuesday night, fed and watered, and was found dead in his stable Wednesday morning." He concluded, "Beau Peavine will be buried on Spindletop Farm and a tombstone will mark his achievements as one of the world's great show horses." During his lifetime, the great stallion sired 104 offsprings: 47 stallions and 57 mares. And while there is no record of Pansy's remarks when she learned of Beau's passing, the following quote by Stephanie M. Thorn most probably summarized her true feelings, especially when remembering that Frank counted him among the first in his new Beaumont stables back in 1933:

> Nothing is more sacred as the bond between horse and rider ... no other creature can ever become so emotionally close to a human as a horse. When a horse dies, the memory lives on because an enormous part of his owner's heart, soul, very existence dies also ... but that can never be laid to rest, it is not meant to be ...[9]

Finally on February 21, 1959, the inevitable hit the newspapers, "Show-Place Spindletop Farm Bought for $850,000 for U. of K.," followed three days later with another detailing the sale completion. For the many who read the associated articles and took in their true scope, Pansy had done the unimaginable; she had actually sold Spindletop Hall and the 1,066 acres that went with it for only $850,000, considering that the home alone took over $1 million to build, Shoshone Farm cost about $400,000 by itself, plus another $165,000 or so for the additional 230 acres to bring it to its current size. However, none of this took into account all the various improvements: a two-story brick home for the maintenance supervisor, Randall Reed, and one for Jack Grant, the current farm manager, sixteen tenant houses, numerous barns, a 6,500 square-foot greenhouse, a swimming pool, bath houses, the aviary, and other ancillaries built since 1937. "Seven miles of chain-link fence eight feet high" and other interior fencing contributed another $137,000, and when all added up, the original investment could well be in the $2.5 million range. The appraisal value on the house was put at about $500,000, and that of the surrounding acreage at near $1.8 million. And now the selling price—$850,000! Had Pansy lost her mind? Why, it almost seemed like a gift.[10]

In fact, that is just about what the transaction represented—sort of. For the reasoning process to become clearer, however, one must turn backward and presume that Pansy might be accused of a lot of things, rightfully so, but losing her mind was never one of them. Long before, she had taken the pseudonym of "Mother Fox" in her protective approach with Dot Hilliard, Mildred Frank's close friend, and now she relied on the same characteristics and slyness of this particular animal when it came to the Internal Revenue Service, which she hated with a passion. She vividly recalled the tremendous outlay of $778,979.91 that she paid in estate and inheritance taxes after Frank died, and now wisely, Pansy sought to lessen the tax burden on capital gains when she sold her Kentucky property. Along with her personal attorneys and those of the buyer, she crafted a novel gift-purchase contract that maximized savings. When Pansy transferred the deed on February 24, 1959, she elected to receive a down payment of

$150,000 from the state sometime immediately after July 1, and agreed thereafter to accept from the Kentucky Research Foundation a ten-year payout with nine equal installments of $75,000 and the last at $25,000, all at an annual finance rate set at 3 percent.[11]

In his statement to the press, University of Kentucky vice president Leo M. Chamberlain, who also served as the president of the foundation, explained:

> As has been indicated in newspaper reports, the transaction represents a sizable "gift" to the foundation and ultimately to the university. The university considers itself extremely fortunate to be the beneficiary of such an investment as this one made possible through the Kentucky Research Foundation and the Commonwealth of Kentucky.

At an earlier luncheon held on January 30, Governor A. B. "Happy" Chandler told a Lexington Optimist Club audience that "the property was offered to the university and the university only by Mrs. Pansy Grant . . ." There is no doubt that Pansy knew exactly what she was doing. She did not want to see her Kentucky properties fall into the hands of a competitor farm, and if guarantees could be had to ensure that at least part of her legacy be preserved, the current approach seemed the best.[12]

When Pansy packed up and left Fayette County, Kentucky, for good, she brought with her Viola Ransom, "Fitz" Fitzpatrick, and individual property that reportedly filled nine moving trucks and trailers. When the vehicles arrived in Beaumont, she sorted through everything, and "then returned a vanload of the furniture, a gift . . . valued at more than $61,000." Once again, The University of Kentucky and its research foundation, with the earlier contribution of her amazing collection of carriages and other tapestries with their enormous appraisals, benefited greatly by Pansy's generosity.[13]

One somewhat amusing piece of information immediately came to light, however, when the new owners discovered that the home with over forty rooms, costing about $1 million to build, had no filter for the swimming pool that measured forty by seventy feet. When asked how Pansy's workers performed maintenance on the 120,000 gallons of water held therein, a spokesman for the university stoically replied, "Whenever Mrs. Yount wanted to change the water, she just pulled the plug."[14]

Actually, some four years earlier, Pansy and Cape moved back into El Ocaso, empty of Mildred and her family, who had vacated it after buying their home at 650 Thomas Road from C. Fletcher Graham, Jr., vice president of the White House Dry Goods Company, at the time one of Beaumont's most elite department stores. But with Pansy's return to Beaumont, nothing in her lifestyle changed dramatically. As before, she remained a virtual recluse, excepting visits to her daughter's house and an occasional shopping trip downtown to buy clothing at the White House. Cape set up an office in the Mildred Building and advertised himself as an investor and dealer in livestock. Employees at the nearby offices of the KFDM Radio Station frequently rushed to the window to watch the much-talked about horse trainer who struck a fine pose with his fancy outerwear and high riding boots as he walked across Calder Avenue on his way to work. Mickey Phelan also said that several times he went with his father for lunch to Moncla's Restaurant, close by the Mildred Building, and often he saw Cape sitting at his regular table in the back enjoying a big juicy steak.[15]

But living in Frank's house never quite suited Cape, and for Pansy, as with Laura

Wiess before her, it contained too many memories of her late husband. The couple began looking around for suitable alternatives, and they settled on Vir-Beth Hall. Mabel Rothwell had died in November 1953, and her great home had passed to her daughter, Virginia Mae Birdwell, who offered it for sale. When Pansy bought it in early 1956, she began to renovate immediately. In character, she had a chain-link fence, which survives to this day, built around the entire perimeter, and soon she began moving all of the shrubbery and plants, along with the furniture from El Ocaso to her new estate. In short order, the fantastic home built by Valentine Wiess in 1908 and bought by Frank Yount in 1923, appeared forlorn and stripped of aesthetic appeal, both inside and out.[16]

On May 2, 1958, the announcement came: "Landmark Being Demolished Here." El Ocaso, a showplace by all standards would go by way of so many other spectacular homes on Calder Avenue, once called "Millionaires' Row." It would be taken down by late summer, so said Cape Grant, "for sentimental reasons and to save on taxes."

The Manion home at 650 Thomas Road.

—Courtesy Mildred Yount Manion.

Vir-Beth Hall, circa 1956. Original photo gift of the Beaumont Enterprise, *circa 1977.*

—Courtesy Howard Perkins Collection, Beaumont, Texas.

El Ocaso, 1955. Original photo gift of the Beaumont Enterprise, *circa 1977.*

—Courtesy Howard Perkins Collection, Beaumont, Texas.

Though the words were spoken by Grant, they were most assuredly scripted by Pansy, because of their similarity to those she used when she directed Frank's mausoleum to be torn down. Furthermore, Cape concluded, "When you're gone, you don't know what will happen to a place like that. I'd hate to see it used as anything but a home."[17]

Private citizens and local historical societies—some say *en masse*, while others claim a mere handful—appealed to Pansy, Cape, and Mildred, but nothing worked. One group, spearheaded by members of the Beaumont Junior League, asked that Ben Irby, a local architect, present a proposal whereby pledges of at least $90,000 would be used to save the building. Apparently, Irby talked directly to Cape, who responded, "Too much has been made of this fellow Frank Yount and his house. We don't care how much money you raise, we're going to tear it down." Finally, Kell Jones and Son Contractors of Beaumont completely stripped and gutted it of everything valuable. Certain items were snatched up by Beaumonters and some by out-ot-towners; others made their way into refuse piles. The thirteen different kinds of marble from across the world imported to decorate the home; the beautiful architecturally-designed custom-made woodwork of mahogany, quarter-sawn oak, bird's eye maple, and cherry; the elaborate main staircase winding upward to the third-floor ballroom and a separate billiard parlor; the ornate Otis brass elevator that ran from the basement all the way to the third floor; the prized marble mantles that craftsmen from Italy had originally installed; and the multiple banks of Tiffany windows, as well as the smaller ones, were virtually given away. Surprising as it may seem today, by the late 1950s, art-glass windows and doors had fallen out of demand in the design market and did not begin to make a comeback until the late 1960s. With everything of value soon gone, including the extremely ornate beveled glass doors, with cooper canes instead of lead for durability; the surrounding door columns of Texas red granite; and the dark green, glazed tiles from the huge roof—and the home itself demolished, the Jones crew turned to the final stage. When they eventually managed to gouge out the seven-foot-deep, steel-reinforced, concrete foundation, haul away the debris, and fill in the gaping hole left behind, El Ocaso, including its gigantic, two-story granite columns and capitals, its stone balustrades, its granite and marble porch floors, and its fire-proof construction, literally passed into the sunset. No wonder the locals bragged when the Younts bought the place from Laura Wiess in 1923 that after fifteen years of weathering the rain-soaked Southeast Texas climate and sitting on what people commonly referred to as Beaumont swamp gumbo mud, the house was so well-constructed that no carpenter had ever been called back to even adjust a door or a window. El Ocaso, built for the centuries, had scarcely celebrated its fiftieth birthday, when Pansy had it demolished while in perfect condition—perfect right down to the upholstered, silk damask interior wall coverings and the granite, marble, Missouri and Indiana stone, and St. Louis pressed-brick exterior with windows that at night displayed lights in a vast array of sparkles and colors to the delight of passers-by along Calder Avenue.[18]

Aside from a precious few photographs; some recently discovered film, memories; a small section of the Page brand chain-link fence and a portion of the original brick wall, both across the back of the property that spans an entire city block; along with remnants of the concrete floor of the four-car garage and servants quarters equipped with a fireplace, few traces of its physical location exist today. Some of the gigantic live oaks that surrounded the property still stand, but a car wash now occupies the spot where the house rose gigantic from the soil, with a convenience store and coin laundry covering the part of the block where Pansy installed a large outdoor swimming pool and planted scores of different varieties of camellias and azaleas, as well as every other shrub imaginable, on the meticulously manicured grounds.[19]

Beaumont historian Howard Perkins spoke to the foreman of the demolition crew who caustically mentioned that his company had radically underbid the job. The reason: regardless of the massive size, who would have guessed that any architect would have designed and overbuilt the home as he did? In essence, Jones should have submitted a bid at least three times larger, and when he approached Pansy for additional monies to cover the shortfall, she summarily told him "to go to hell."[20]

The relations between Cape and Pansy had steadily worsened, and less than a year after El Ocaso came tumbling down, so began one of the most controversial divorce actions in Beaumont history. Amid allegations of his infidelities and her ungovernable temper, Cape Grant struck first, and the money fight began. On March 3, 1959, presiding Judge Owen M. Lord of the Domestic Relations Court in Beaumont granted to Cape a temporary restraining order against his wife based on several accusations, one among them: "The defendant [Pansy] has been and is now making serious threats of bodily harm against the plaintiff [Cape], and that upon one occasion the defendant has armed herself with a .380 automatic pistol, and that upon one occasion, the plaintiff has been forced to disarm the defendant." In connection with his restraining order petition, Cape filed for divorce on the same day, claiming that he was entitled to half of the couple's joint property, valued a few months earlier at about \$4.5 million. When alerted to Cape's activities and not to be outdone, Pansy's attorney, A. D. Moore, immediately countered by filing a cross-action divorce petition on behalf of his client.[21]

From left to right: Pansy Grant, Cape Grant, Stannie Stansbury, and Louise Ogden.
—Courtesy Kathryn Manion Haider.

The heated trial commenced on October 26, 1959, and the respective combatants took to the stand. Pansy testified that Cape had taken unfair advantage of her after their marriage, in that he systematically looted the assets of Spindletop Farm. In fact, she said, between the years 1949 and 1955, the entertainment complex lost some $666,768.12. Although Cape agreed in part, he replied angrily that the stock breeding program had always made money due to his efforts—and sacrifices implemented to keep the facility afloat during the Depression, including dropping the portion of his contract that allowed a 50 percent retention of profits. Without him, Cape boasted, Spindletop's success story would have been written much differently. As expected, Pansy denied his assertion. She shouted, "That's a lie! Make him prove it!" When the long drawn out testimony about an errant husband's alleged sordid affair with Mrs. Lucille Odom, and how property might be divided fairly concluded, a jury of twelve exited the courtroom to ponder evidence in a record that filled thousands of pages. On November 17 they handed down a decision, and one month later Judge Harold R. Clayton of the 136th Judicial District Court in Beaumont published his decree, the contents of which met with rage from both parties. A shocked Cape learned that Pansy, and not he, received the divorce. Pansy's married name was restored from Grant to Yount, and she maintained the greater part of her estate. However, Cape did not walk away a total loser, because the ruling granted to him at least a part of his request for property division. He received 4,000 shares of stock in Texaco; 3,200 in General Motors; 2,000 in Norvell-Wilder Supply; along with a certain proration of dividends, and all personal property owned by him, including vehicles, jewelry, bank accounts, and safety deposit boxes in his name. (See Appendix 6 for full details). In open court, attorneys from both sides announced exceptions and their intentions to file appeals, which they did on the spot. When Clayton denied a request for a retrial on February 10 of the following year, Pansy, who wanted Cape to have nothing at all, and Cape, who thought he should be entitled to an equal share, appealed to the Ninth Supreme Judicial District of Texas, which also sat in Jefferson County. When this particular court refused also to allow a new trial, Cape and Pansy filed petitions with the Court of Civil Appeals in Waco, Texas. Grant paid $5,000 to Beaumont attorney, W. G. Walley, for his representation, and gave him an I.O.U. for another $10,000, to be deducted from funds only if his action against Pansy prevailed. When the latest Court reaffirmed the previous decision set forth in Judge Clayton's original 1959 ruling, both tried yet again. Finally on May 17, 1962, when the Court of Civil Appeals refused to reconsider earlier verdicts, the matter ended. And while there is no way to accurately determine the figure that Cape actually received, the value of his appraised property, set in August 1962 exceeded $422,000.[22]

With nothing left for him in Beaumont, Cape moved back to Dallas, where he established residence at 3544 Rosedale. Now aged sixty-three, alone, and facing health problems that worsened by the day, he often felt guilty about leaving his first wife and his three sons, so he sought to make amends. He had already rewritten his will to include all four, but now he wanted more. He visited Nola in Hillsboro sometime during the middle of May 1962. While there, however, Cape suffered a massive stroke, and he was rushed to nearby Grant-Buie Medical Center, where he remained a patient in critical condition in his own son's hospital. In a strange turn of events, on the twenty-eighth—eleven days after Cape lost his final bid to break the divorce terms with Pansy—Methodist minister Thad E. Son, reunited the marital bond between the retired horse trainer and his first wife. Ironically, though, on the day of the wedding, the man responsible for so much of the show-ring success of Spindletop Farm and Stables, and whose talent influenced such world-class horsemen as Frank Heathman, Carl Pedigo, Tommy Murphy, Owen Hailey, and Bill McIlvain, took his last breath. Two days later, he was buried at Restland Cemetery in Dallas.[23]

Cape's brief will, dated February 9, 1961, left "all cash, jewelry, automobiles (one 1958 Ford Thunderbird), trailers, and boats" to Nola, appointed her as executrix of the estate, and recommended that she give each of their sons $1,000 apiece; his sister Kathryn Hunt of Dallas, $2,000; and the prized pair of Llewellyn Setters to his friend Walter C. Davis of Reinzi, Mississippi. The larger part of his estate, however, represented the shares of Texaco stock received in the divorce settlement with Pansy. When Nola's attorney William B. Martin filed the order fixing the inheritance tax on an appraised estate value of $422,186.62, taxes were calculated at $11,560.66. On August 27, 1963, when Nola paid that amount to Robert S. Calvert, Comptroller for the State of Texas, she wrapped up the financial affairs of her late husband. (See Appendix 7).[24]

At her Caldwood home, Pansy showered affection on her three grandchildren all reared in the Catholic faith: Kathryn Bernadette born on April 6, 1939; Mildred on February 26, 1941; and Ed, Jr. on August 23, 1943. Continuing where they left off with their mother, Mildred Frank, when she was a child, the two Beaumont newspapers reported on parties, dances, trips, and educational progress. Virtually everything the Manion children did made the social news. But as the youngsters grew and matured into young adults, Pansy's health began to fail rapidly, followed by a debilitating stroke. Honoring her mother's wishes, however, Mildred Frank kept the extent of its devastating effect from her three children.[25]

Thereafter when Kathryn, Mildred, Jr. and Ed, Jr. visited their grandmother, Pansy was out of bed, fully dressed, sitting in a chair, and none of them suspected that she remained virtually paralyzed from the waist down. Sometime later, she slipped into a coma, and immediately before her death, set at 11:34 A.M. Sunday, October 14, 1962, the entire family congregated at her side. Dr. J. C. Crager, the heart specialist in attendance, asked Mildred Frank to take her children outside. When she returned to the room a short time later, she witnessed her mother slip away. The lady who felt more comfortable in print dresses, the lady whose attire often caused some to confuse her as a ser-

The Manion children, left to right: Kathryn, Mildred, and Ed.
—Courtesy Kathryn Manion Haider.

The Manion family. Ed, Sr. standing left; in front of him is Mildred, Jr., then Ed, Jr., Mildred Frank, and Kathryn.
—Courtesy Kathryn Manion Haider.

vant, the lady who seldom wore the dazzling accumulation of furs and jewelry at her disposal (see Appendix 6), the lady who built Spindletop Hall and Farm and helped establish the Spindletop Horse Show in Beaumont, the lady who caused a great deal of controversy in both Beaumont and Lexington, and the lady whose hair never grayed from its natural dark brown, died at the age of seventy-five as a result of kidney failure brought on by the onset of uremia, with a secondary diagnosis of arterioscleroses. When Mildred Frank announced the death to Kathryn, Mildred, Jr., and Ed, Jr., she remarked in front of them, "Well, now I have no one." When they tried to reassure her of their total support, she replied, "Yes, I know. But it's not the same." These remarks, however, should be interpreted in their proper context. Mildred Frank saw this as another disconnect from the security first lost when her father died, and now repeated with the loss of her mother on whom she depended so significantly.[26]

Pansy got her church service after all. At 10:00 A.M. on October 16, Monsignor E. A. Holub conducted the funeral mass at St. Anne Church in Beaumont, where Pansy held membership. Her friend from Lexington, Fred Wachs, Sr., served as pallbearer along with Joe A. Fischer of New York City, and the rest from Beaumont, M. R. Geisendorff, Ed Fitzpatrick, W. S. Young, Jr., Harry M. Heffner, Jr., Sam S. Roberts, and confidant John Gray. Afterward, she was taken to Magnolia Cemetery and laid to rest beside Miles Franklin Yount. With all said and done, this seemed a fitting end to a saga that began when the two first met in a boarding house, where Pansy worked as a waitress and Frank roomed, both hoping for some sort of break that would lead them to better things. Little did either know.[27]

Throughout her lifetime, Pansy—a true study in contradictions—had been many things to many people who offered a myriad of personal interpretations along the way: respected, loved, charitable, vengeful, uncompromising, misunderstood, overbearing, not well educated, lecturer, fun loving, recluse, friend, enemy, a great cook, a splendid entertainer, a woman who could not entertain whatsoever unless helped by others, an astute business person, and oddly, a person whom some took advantage of. In actual fact, however, at some point in her life each of these images fit; and similar to personality traits, her physical features also varied considerably, evidenced by photographs that rarely ever show comparable characteristics. Despite the somewhat melodramatic pitch, author Elizabeth Simpson described Pansy best as "instinctively kind and impulsively generous, entirely devoid of artifice and with a fine appreciation of beauty in every form. With loyalty and courage she stood shoulder to shoulder with a man whose memory is loved the length and breadth of Texas. They were friends with a deep understanding of each other—companions—dreamers ..."[28]

During the fall of 1962, Peter Wells, Beaumont attorney, filed Pansy's last will and testament, dated February 8, 1960, in Jefferson County Probate Court. The eighteen-page instrument began by stating that none of her estate would be left to her only child, Mildred Frank, because her father had already provided for her handsomely. To understand the true significance of how Pansy reached this decision, and the love that went into it, refer to Appendix 8. The proceeds were to be distributed as follows: lucrative trust accounts were set up for each of the Manion grandchildren, and two of them, Kathryn and Ed., Jr., received cash gifts in the sum of $200,000; Mildred Yount Manion got the Caldwood home (Vir-Beth Hall) and most all of its contents; faithful friend and companion Viola G. Ransom received $50,000 in cash, and Ed Fitzpatrick got $25,000 in cash also. Pansy directed that the amount obtained by selling all of her jewelry and precious stones, appraised at $148,614.92, be donated to the Masonic Home for Crippled Children in Lexington, and that her "four great tapestries and the 'Yount Silver' given to me by Mr. Yount" should go to the University of Texas. (See Appendix 8).[29]

The final appraisement report of her assets, filed on January 14, 1964, reflected a gross value of $6,097,841.15, almost $2.1 million more than what she started with in November 1933 when Frank died and left her half of his portfolio (see Appendix 9). After fulfilling all components of the will, the remainder went into the Manion grandchildren's trust accounts, tax free, with all fees paid by the estate. Pansy's probate file shows two inheritance tax payments, both to the State of Texas; $274,165.70 on May 7, 1964 and the other $201,744.86 on July 7, 1966. Peter Wells received a letter from the Internal Revenue Service dated August 15, 1969 that stated, in effect, all estate taxes had been paid, and all audits concluded.[30]

Seated background, left to right: Pansy and Mildred Frank. In foreground, left to right: Mildred, Jr., Ed, Jr., and Kathryn.

—Courtesy Kathryn Manion Haider.

In order to clear her grandmother's belongings from the house that she inherited, Mildred, Jr. contracted with the Samuel Hart Galleries of Houston to conduct an estate sale. But first, Parke-Bernet, the famous New York auction firm, sent a team of appraisers to Beaumont, and with the help of family friend Dot Hilliard Newton, they completed the staggering inventory and catalogued thousands of items from Spindletop Hall in Lexington, the "Woodlands" in DeLand, Florida, Onaledge in Manitou Springs, Colorado, as well as Vir-Beth Hall in Beaumont. But before sending eighteen van loads of furnishings and accessories of every sort to Houston, and the rest to Cropper's Antiques, owned by Bernice and Ferdinand Cropper, located at the Mildred Building, Mildred held a private sale at the home, where her father's friend Texas Governor John Connally, his wife, Nellie, and a few others purchased items "from the collection of rare art treasures and authentic period furniture."[31]

The Hart Galleries' Main Street location was not large enough to accommodate the upcoming event, so they rented a building at 5510 Greenbriar, across from Rice University stadium. "There is no question but that this is one of the most important estate auctions ever announced in the South," Samuel Hart said. "The collection is so extensive, it took four days just to inventory the linens." Hart and his wife, Charlotte, had printed over 2,500 catalogues, thinking that they would have enough for the scheduled two-week sale. However, neither foresaw the enormous turnout. Although the first gavel did not fall until Sunday, January 12, the public got its first look at the exhibit on the day before.

> They came in slacks, they came in mink coats, they came in suits, they came in cocktail dresses, but boy, they really turned out ... On Saturday, the day items were just on exhibit, some 10,000 people jammed the spot, necessitating traffic officers to control the crowds. [The catalogues] were gone in the first two hours Saturday, and he's [Samuel Hart] frantically trying to get more printed before tonight's session. There are over 4,000 items catalogued, with over 2,685 slated to go this week.[32]

On Sunday, the first day, about 1,500 interested parties showed up. With brisk sales "at the rate of 100 to 150 ... an hour, four young women kept scurrying down the aisles to record the names of purchasers, [and] seven porters hauled desks, vases, and paintings to the viewing stand." One of the more spirited bids of the first day came from N. C. Soward, who represented Dr. Silas Grant, Cape's son from Hillsboro, who badly wanted the collection of "36 English china plates, each decorated with a different horse from the Yount [Kentucky] stables." Soward lost out to a young lady named Eidman, but he gained some measure of success, however, when she sold him twenty-four for $20 each.[33]

When the sale finished, over 4,000 pieces of "antiques, art treasures, furniture, pianos, linens, silverware and silver pieces, paintings, bric-a-brac, and oriental rugs," brought a little over a half million dollars, and Samuel Hart estimated it be "the biggest sale of its type in Texas," attended by between 25,000 to 35,000 patrons. The collection of oriental rugs was so large that Hart devoted a special sale on January 17 to auction off fine examples of Kerman, Sarouk, Kashan, Bokhara, Sheraz, Derganzin, Camel Hair, Kazak, along with twenty-five Navajos and Serapis.[34]

Epilogue

From all accounts, Mildred Frank Yount, who married Ed Manion on June 27, 1938, had been always gracious and kind, demonstrated at the age of nine when she set up a makeshift soft-drink stand on the steps and lawn of her Calder Avenue home. When a reporter questioned the purpose, Mildred smiled and responded, "Everybody is doing his bit on the new church." The meager earnings, $3.50 for selling fifty bottles of pop over a two-day period, went to the building fund of Westminster Presbyterian.[1]

As evidenced in numerous diary entries extending from 1933 though 1938, Mildred, who had grown to a height of about five feet and three inches, still with reddish hair, loved to ride horses, attend movies, and contrary to some reports that she never again played a musical instrument after her father died, she did at least on one occasion. A May 12, 1937, diary entry read: "Played harp at recital for some club at tea. Scared stiff; got refreshments though."[2]

Jeanette Greer also mentioned that her mother, Mrs. Herbert Mulder, made tamales and sold them from the family home, where Mildred dropped by often to make purchases. While she waited for her order to be counted out and wrapped, she perched upon a stool and partook of some of the tasty morsels. "Mildred seemed to always bring a token of appreciation and present it to Mom," Jeanette said, "even if it was nothing more than a bottle of ketchup purchased from the neighborhood store."[3]

But regardless of their lofty financial status, the Manions had to meet the problems of the everyday world, some humorous, whereas others took sadder overtones. While Mildred and Ed lived at El Ocaso, they sought out a new cook, but the quest took them no further than across the street to their neighbor Mrs. Woodhead who employed Billy Overton, a well-educated African-American. Perhaps, they asked, Billy might work for them part of the time. After Mrs. Woodhead considered the proposal, she suggested a compromise. Since her children were all grown, she required only the morning meal prepared for her, so that left the rest of Billy's day free to work for the Manions. When he heard the suggestion for the first time, however, the stern, most times uncompromising, and always "snooty" Billy thought it outright ludicrous, but finally with some

Mildred Frank Yount Manion.
—Courtesy Mildred Yount Manion.

persuasion, he agreed, albeit with strong reservations. Settling in at the new household, surprisingly, he found that he liked the family, regardless of a few rough spots to overcome in the short-term. Apparently during the initial adjustment period, Ed would come in from the office, walk into the kitchen, and inquire, "What are we having for dinner?" The aloof and extremely formal Overton never appreciated the fact that anybody walked into "his kitchen and his domain," much less a person possessing the audacity to ask him what he had prepared for the evening meal. So after chasing Ed out with a big spoon on several occasions, his employer quit the "annoying practice," and from then on waited patiently for the meal to be served to determine what it actually represented. Evidently, though, Overton's attitude toward Pansy never changed. He stated bluntly that he never cared for her visits to 1376 Calder, because "she would order up a ham for lunch and a roast for dinner, take a slice for herself, and then feed some to her dog that sat beside her at the dining room table. She cut the dog's slice with her knife and fork, and after they were through, whatever was left went into the garbage." Overton viewed a dog's place in the home other than in the dining room, and Pansy's condoning such a practice, combined with wanton wastefulness, as the epitome of bad taste.[4]

After witnessing her mother's actions, Mildred too developed the identical habit of discarding leftovers. Overton recounted one particular situation that involved an old black man who had worked for the Younts when Mildred was young, and now he continued working for her as an adult, even though he was nearly ninety years old, feeble, and extremely weak. Mildred had always ordered Overton to throw out all unused food, but one day he had enough. He marched up to Mildred's bedroom and knocked on the door. When the lady of the house responded, he quickly stated, "Mildred, you're going to hell!" Startled, with tear-filled eyes, she immediately asked why he had made such a remark. "Well," Billy replied, "go over to the window and look at that old man sitting in the back yard. He has taken care of you all your life, even walked you to school, and watched after you as if you were his own. His wife is dead, and because he's not eating properly, he's getting weaker by the day. I can't even fix him a plate for his supper." Somewhat bewildered, Mildred questioned, "Why didn't I think of that?" She promptly ordered Billy to set the dining room table, give the old man a good meal, and by all means, she said, "Let him eat on the good china." But to Overton, even this Good Samaritan thing had limits, and as far as he was concerned, Mildred totally over-reacted. He countered by arguing emphatically that he would never allow hired help to take a meal in the formal dining room; instead, he would let him eat in the kitchen. So he did, and from that point forward, Mildred saw to it that the old man never again left the house at the end of the work day without first having a proper supper.[5]

During late February 1952, Mildred sold the Arcade property in Manitou Springs, Colorado to Floyd S. Padgett; while in Beaumont, as part of her father's estate distribution, she inherited ownership of the Wall Street Property Company founded by Frank and others back in 1922. On September 13, 1955, she and Ed, along with various current stockholders, sold the firm and its assets, consisting of five buildings in the downtown area, for $400,000 cash to Ted E. Moor of T. E. Moor and Company, and Peter W. Maida of Peter W. Maida Insurance and Realty Company.[6]

Relatively speaking, however, when comparing the press coverage devoted to Frank Yount, and Pansy during her second marriage to Frank and her third to Cape Grant, Ed and Mildred's lives after their wedding were rather incidental, with few exceptions. Ed served on fund drives for several causes, one among them as chairman of the advance memorial gifts division of the $900,000 effort in 1958 "to build a new Catholic School at the corner of Washington Avenue and 25th Street." Later on that same year, the *Beaumont Journal* printed a story about the couple's planned six weeks' vacation, accompanied by their three children, and Ed's secretary, Sallie Blain. "They leave New York City June 20 [1958] aboard the SS Ile de France bound for Europe," and before returning home on August 1, the Manions toured Paris, Madrid, Granada, Cordova, France, Ireland, and Brussels. Between the efforts of Pansy, the First National Bank of

The Manions aboard the Queen Mary. From left to right: Kathryn; Mildred Frank, seated; and Mildred, Jr.
—Courtesy Kathryn Manion Haider.

Beaumont, and Betty Gilbert, Mildred and Ed's stateroom remained filled with fresh flowers; and Pansy arranged for them to take their meals at the Captain's table. On an earlier separate trip, the family, accompanied by friend, Louise Ogden, and servant, Beulah Rawlins, cruised aboard the *Queen Mary*.[7]

Ed Manion, Jr., bought for his grandmother a show dog in the form of an AKC registered black Labrador Retriever named Monkscroft Peter, "Pete," for short, and unveiled him as a present sometime in 1959 or the following year. Pansy thought the world of Pete, and when she died, the dog passed to Mildred Frank who idolized him in more ways than one. It seemed that the Lab represented Mildred's last link to her mother, and besides, she just naturally took to him as a family pet. As the dog aged, he became ill, and Mildred did everything in her power to save him, taking him almost daily to a veterinarian in Port Arthur for shots and treatment. When his health failed to improve, Roy "Marty" Martin, chauffeur, drove Mildred, and her daughter, Mildred, Jr., along with Dot Newton and Pete, to Texas A&M University in College Station, where clinic doctors diagnosed the dog's illness as prostate cancer. When she heard that Pete could not be saved, Mildred had him put to sleep, and then afterward, at the urging of the same doctors, she also agreed to an autopsy, only with assurances that this action would help other animals in the future. Mildred brought Pete's body back to her home, and had Whitney Melancon, the head gardener bury him in the back yard and then construct a cross as a grave marker. It took Mildred a long time to get over the loss of Monkscroft Peter.[8]

Mildred's charitable contributions extended far beyond. On June 27, 1963, Sister Mary Richard, administrator of the St. Elizabeth Hospital in Beaumont, sent a letter to the Manions expressing "appreciation ... for the check that you so kindly presented me with yesterday. This of course, represents full payment of the seventy-five thousand dollar balance on the pledge of the late Mrs. Yount." In May of the following year, the Manions again made news when they donated $75,000 to a St. Elizabeth Hospital expansion project, to which the *Beaumont Enterprise* opined, "... in the case of the Manion gift, it is inspiring and encouraging to the community when those especially blessed with worldly goods are willing to share their blessings with programs that benefit the people as a whole."[9]

All through the years, Mildred looked forward to her visits to Rockledge, but when the State of Colorado took part of its property for a highway bypass project and paid her less than $100,000, she became upset. This subdivision prompted her decision to sell out completely, so she found a buyer, and by early 1969 she signed a contract by which the house and its remaining acreage would be sold for about $190,000. "Back in those days," Ed Manion, Jr. said, "the stock market was skyrocketing and real estate values were quite low and not increasing much as inflation was flat." Mildred planned on making one last trip to the home in January 1969 for the purpose of closing it down, and she wanted her namesake daughter, who lived in Houston at the time, to accompany her and Sallie Blain. Mildred could not go, but she counseled her mother, who had a known condition of high blood pressure, to make sure that she carried the necessary monitoring equipment with her on the plane trip. Ironically, whether explained by premonition or forces coincidental, it seems that before Mildred left her home in Beaumont, the rather unusual occurred; she summoned all the servants around her, hugged, and kissed them everyone, as if bidding farewell for the last time. At Rockledge on the twenty-ninth at about 5:00 P.M., Sallie Blain walked downstairs to prepare afternoon cocktails, and when she returned she found Mildred, with a reddened face, slumped backwards in a chair and completely unresponsive. Frantically, Sallie put in a call to the volunteer fire department at Manitou Springs, but when a team arrived, they could do nothing other than to administer oxygen. In the interim, Sallie had also telephoned Mildred's local decorator, Marshall Morin, and asked for assistance, but by the time he got there, Mildred was already gone. When her body arrived at Penrose Hospital in Colorado Springs, an autopsy revealed a brain aneurism as the cause of death of Mildred Frank Yount Manion, the oil heiress and mother of three, who had not yet reached her forty-ninth birthday. On the thirtieth, an air ambulance took her back to Beaumont for the final time.[10]

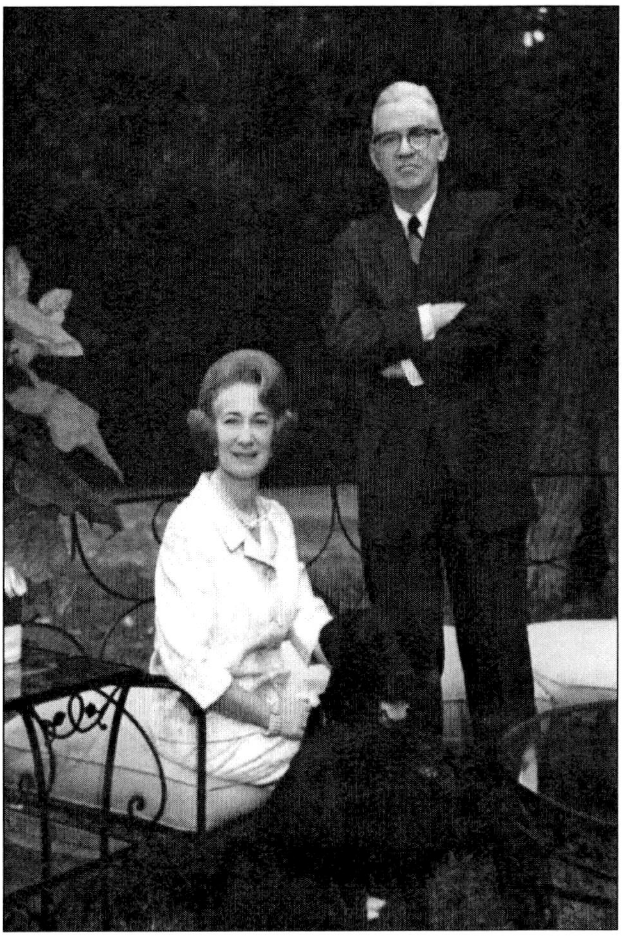

Mildred Frank and Ed Manion, Sr.
—Courtesy Kathryn Manion Haider.

Like her mother's, Mildred's funeral was held at St. Anne Church, and the Right Reverend Monsignor E. A. Holub once again found himself delivering a funeral for a member of the Yount family. Dr. Julian Fertitta, Glenn McGowan, Walter Crawford, Trent Newton, Peter Wells, John Gray, Joe Broussard, II, W. C. Gilbert, Jr., and Dr. J. C. Crager served as pallbearers, and after the service, which began at 4:00 in the afternoon, Broussard's Mortuary, in charge of all arrangements, oversaw Mildred's burial next to her mother at Magnolia Cemetery.[11]

Mildred's holdings were tremendous. When W. P. Machemehl, senior vice president and trust officer of the First Security National Bank in Beaumont, filed the inventory and appraisement of Mildred's separate property holdings on July 2, 1970, her estate totaled in excess of $12 million, with heirs listed as Ed, Sr. and their three children.[12]

After Mildred died, a devastated Dot Hilliard Newton lost much of her bubbly personality. In the early 1970s, she traveled to Denver to visit her son Reagan and his wife Debbie, and for old times' sake, they all decided to drive to Manitou Springs and see Rockledge. Without calling ahead, the three knocked at the door, and when the current owner responded, they identified themselves, explained their purpose for being there, and that Dot had been Millie Yount Manion's closest friend. When the owner remarked,

Ed Manion, Sr.
—Courtesy Kathryn Manion Haider.

"Yes, I know Millie," the visitors were immediately stunned by the statement and asked the man to explain what he meant. "Because," he said, "Millie haunts Rockledge." The episode so completely upset Dot that she refused to enter the premises. The three left immediately, and never went back.[13]

Mildred Frank's children recalled their mother as a chain smoker. Ed, Sr. smoked also, and that probably contributed to various heart attacks and strokes beginning about 1964. He finally succumbed on October 5, 1986, and was buried at Magnolia Cemetery in the family plot with Mildred Frank, Pansy, and Frank.[14]

On February 5, 1973, Kenneth Warren who represented Kenneth Warren & Son, Ltd., violin dealers and makers out of Chicago, wrote to the Trust Department of the First Security National Bank of Beaumont. The Manion heirs had requested an appraisal of the last violin owned by the family, which had been acquired by Frank Yount for his daughter, Mildred, years before. Warren's opinion follows:

> The violin, an authentic example of the work of Joseph filius Andreas Guarnerius of Cremona, Italy, made in the period of 1710-15, bearing a reproduction label of the type employed by this master, date undecipherable, has a present day value of $12,000. We regard it as a good example in a good state of repair, aside from the top.

Warren also identified the accompanying bow as made by J. Henry of Paris, circa 1850–60, and placed its value in the order of $800. Both the violin and the bow were sold the first part of March 1973 to a man who lived in Conroe, Texas. He bought it sight unseen, and went all the way to Chicago to pick up his new purchase. The selling price $12,800, the exact amount of the appraisal.[15]

The *Beaumont Enterprise* reported on November 14, 1974, that Jackie Harmon, president of Harmon Chevrolet Corporation of Orange, purchased the Mildred Buildings for $265,000 from Kathryn, Mildred, and Ed and that the First Security National Bank of Beaumont financed the transaction. This represented the last of the original houses, buildings, and entities owned by Frank and Pansy Yount, with the exception of land and personal items retained by the three grandchildren.[16]

After the Second Spindletop discoveries, Marrs McLean essentially sold his drilling and production business to concentrate on politics. After moving to San Antonio in

Yount-Manion plot, Magnolia Cemetery, Beaumont, Texas. Photograph by Fred B. McKinley.

1937, he worked tirelessly for the Republican Party in which he served as finance chairman of the Texas unit from 1938 until 1952 and as a member of the National Finance Committee in 1946. He eventually supported Ohio Senator Robert A. Taft in his failed bid for his party's nomination in 1952. Over the years, McLean and his wife, Verna, became well known for their philanthropic activities. They donated money toward Beaumont's new Y.M.C.A. building in 1929; to the same city's Little Theater building in the 1920s; and later on, to Lamar University's engineering library. Also, they lent considerable financial support that helped Baylor University of Waco construct the physical education building, the Armstrong-Browning Library, and the Marrs McLean Science Building. In 1951 Baylor honored McLean with an honorary degree. After a long and illustrious career, "The Second Prophet of Spindletop," died in San Antonio on May 18, 1953. Following the death of her husband, Mrs. McLean continued the philanthropic efforts by contributing to San Antonio's Trinity University and to the University of Texas Press. Both Marrs, who died about a month before his seventieth birthday, and Verna, who passed away in 1981, are buried in Beaumont's Magnolia Cemetery.[17]

Wright Morrow acknowledged in 1944 that he had made about $500,000 on the Yount-Lee deal. Yet oddly enough, the vast amount of press clippings held in his file at the Center for American History, University of Texas at Austin, contains not one single reference to his connection with one of the most impressive independent petroleum producers of its time, but instead lauds him as a political mover and shaker in the Texas Democratic Party until his death on December 17, 1973, at age eighty. President Truman once offered him the ambassadorship to Belgium, but Morrow refused. For many years, he served his party as national committeeman from the Lone Star State, but Wright lost the job after declining to support Adlai Stevenson during the 1952 presidential campaign. Morrow continued to hold a membership in the Democratic Party, even though he openly endorsed and campaigned for Republican candidates on many levels. Dwight D. Eisenhower nominated him as alternate delegate to the United Nations

Wright Francis Morrow.
—Courtesy Hans Wright Bohlmann.

General Assembly, but the Senate Foreign Relations Committee denied confirmation, at the alleged insistence of Lyndon B. Johnson.[18]

What about the remaining former officials, directors, stockholders, and others employed by the Yount-Lee Oil Company? At age sixty-seven, T. P. Lee died of a coronary occlusion on February 4, 1939, and he was buried at Glenwood Cemetery in Houston, two days later. But his home remained in the possession of his family until July 9 of the following year when family members, including Mrs. Essie Lee, sold the property to Saint Thomas College for $120,000. At the wishes of all heirs and executors, the college separated the payment into two parts: $6,000 in cash and the remaining $114,000 as a donation, guaranteed by a promissory note dated September 1, 1946, made payable to the William M. Rice Institute for the Advancement of Literature, Science and Arts of Houston. The home, now referred to as the Link-Lee Mansion, and its surrounding acreage, became the basis of the founding of the University of St. Thomas which still occupies the site today. In particular, the house serves as the university's administration building. It is listed on the National Register of Historic Places, and as a landmark of both the State of Texas and the City of Houston.[19]

Bill Lee moved from Sour Lake to Houston, where he devoted himself to investments. He became a distinguished financier, a member of the River Oaks Country Club, Houston Club, Yacht Club, Mount Olive Lodge No. 3, A.F. and A.M. of Parkersburg, West Virginia, and the Shrine and Knights Templar. Bill Lee lived to be sixty-nine years old, and at the time of his death on October 28, 1936, brought on by bronchial pneumonia, he made his residence at 4218 Montrose Boulevard in Houston. Like his brother, T. P. Lee, Bill is buried at Houston's Glenwood Cemetery.[20]

One of Bill's daughters, Faustine, married Glenn Herbert McCarthy, popularly known as "Diamond Glenn," a legendary wildcatter who built the world famous Shamrock Hotel in Houston. Purportedly, McCarthy, a close friend of Howard Hughes, inspired the character of Jett Rink found in Edna Ferber's best-selling novel *Giant*. Another of Bill Lee's children, William Howard, married into Hollywood royalty not once but twice: first to actress Hedy Lamarr from December 1953 until the couple

Link-Lee Mansion as it appears today.
—Courtesy Miro Dvorscak, Photographer, Houston, Texas.

divorced in 1960; and then to Gene Tierney from 1960 until she died of emphysema in Houston on November 6, 1991.[21]

Emerson Woodward in January 1924 advanced $28,000 to build the Houston Gun Club on Westheimer Road, and he actively participated in his favorite hobby of trapshooting in the company of friends such as Henry A. "Hank" Hausmann of LaGrange, Texas, and Forest McNeir, a fellow Houstonian. His expert marksmanship earned for him places in the National Trapshooting Hall of Fame, which inducted him on August 24, 1973, and in the Texas Trapshooters Association Hall of Fame, which reciprocated in 1983. One of his records "in 1933 … set a yearly ATA [American Trapshooters Association] 16-yard average record of .9950 that was not broken or tied until 1965," some thirty-two years later.[22]

Forest McNeir wrote admiringly of the fierce competitive nature demonstrated by the cigar-champing Woodward:

> E. F. was a beautiful shot. When he threw his head down on that gun stock with that big black cigar unlit in his mouth, his head became a part of the gun. He shut one eye … wore a glove on his right hand, stood correctly, and observed every rule. I never heard him complain about any targets. If they were hard he knew the other fellow was having just as much trouble as he was. His unbounded confidence in himself made him what he was—one of the world's best.

Emerson Woodward and his shooting pals. From left to right: Emerson F. Woodward, Henry A. Hausmann, J. T. Caldwell, C. L. Dupuis, and Forest McNeir.

—Courtesy Pete Hausmann.

> When some fellow was telling him how it ought to be done, E. F. would listen until he got tired and then say, "If you are so damned smart, why ain't you rich?"[23]

After the Yount-Lee sale to Wright Morrow, Woodward announced, "Well, I sold the last of my oil interests today. I've got nothing to do but fool with horses." Emerson kept his word, retired from the oil business and spent much of his time occupied with the sport of the kings. During the late 1930s and early 1940s, on his ranch, Valdina Farms, spanning 18,127 acres located in both Uvalde and Medina counties in Texas, hence the name Valdina, he raised, trained, and sent his horses such as Valdina Myth, Valdina Orphan, and Rounder to racetracks all over the country. These entries competed head to head with some of the best the racing world had to offer. Valdina Myth finished first at the 1941 running at Kentucky Oaks; Valdina Orphan, with jockey Carroll Bierman aboard, ran third at the 1942 Kentucky Derby; and Rounder "became the only horse to ever outrun 1941 Triple Crown winner and Horse of the Year Whirlaway in wire-to-wire fashion." For his contributions to the industry, the Texas Horse Racing Hall of Fame inducted him as a member in 2001.[24]

Emerson and his wife were also recognized for their philanthropic accomplishments. According to Jack Meyer, their pastor at the Heights Church of Christ in Houston, "They financed an orphanage in Hope, Arkansas . . . , built the Church of Christ at College Station, contributed heavily to the Boles Orphans home at Quinlan [Texas]. They sent many girls through the Abilene Christian college, paying all their expenses."[25]

Unfortunately, an automobile driven by Woodward collided into the side of a train at a grade crossing near D'Hanis, Texas, close to Hondo in Medina County, and the accident claimed both his life and that of his wife, the only other passenger in the vehicle. Bessie Woodward died of injuries on May 22, 1943, and Emerson followed at age sixty-four two days later while a patient at the Medina Hospital in Hondo. A double funeral was held in Houston at Heights Church of Christ, and they were entombed in a mausoleum at the city's Forest Park Cemetery.[26]

Tal Rothwell maintained an office on the fifteenth floor of the San Jacinto Building, where he looked after his family's personal investments. He died at age sixty-two on December 16, 1949. Afterward Mabel donated the Rothwell Bible Chair and Wesley Foundation to Lamar State College of Technology (now Lamar University), and the dedication was held on February 8, 1953. However, while discussing the terms of her will with Marvin McClendon and Martin Davis, certified public accountants; Harry Garnham, the Rothwell business manager for years; and Ken Linsley, another connection to the estate, she died suddenly of a heart attack in her home on November 14 of that same year. Both "Papa Tal" and Mabel are buried at Beaumont's Magnolia Cemetery.[27]

Harry Phelan—the man who smiled sheepishly and for the amusement of an interviewer, once said that he didn't "know anything about the oil business"—gave much of his time and some of his wealth to his beloved city of Beaumont. In return, the Beaumont Rotary Club named him as 1940 citizen of the year, and in 1951 he received the prestigious Laetare Medal, conferred by the University of Notre Dame to outstanding Catholic laymen. He became known far and wide for his philanthropic acts, but the greatest of these occurred in early 1957 when he and Johannah donated their home and estate to the Sisters of Charity of the Incarnate Word. The home, now vacant, and grounds are a part of the St. Elizabeth Hospital complex. Harry Phelan died at age seventy-nine in Beaumont on May 19, 1957, and is buried at the city's Magnolia Cemetery.[28]

Upon Harry's death, Johannah (Kathryn Manion Haider's Godmother) succeeded him as a director of the First Security National Bank. She continued the course set by the couple earlier, and as a result in 1959, the Catholic Church elevated her to the rank of lady commander in the Order of the Holy Sepulchre. She died on February 18, 1966 and lies beside her husband.[29]

Rothwell Bible Chair and Wesley Foundation.

—Courtesy Sue Boyt and Susan Ramsey.

Harry and Johannah Phelan.
—Courtesy Kathryn Manion Haider.

Harry and Johannah's three children, all minority stockholders, kept to their parents' example as civic, business, and religious leaders who sought to build a bigger and better Beaumont. John Henry, Jr. died at the age of fifty-five on October 30, 1961; followed by Margaret Phelan Reed on April 23, 1988; and finally A. M. "Mickey" on March 30, 1993. All are buried at Beaumont's Magnolia Cemetery.[30]

Beeman Strong organized his own law firm of Strong, Moore & Strong and established offices in the San Jacinto Building of Beaumont. His associates included his son, Ewell, and A. D. Moore, his former assistant at Yount-Lee. He continued on the political scene, and served as a delegate to the 1936 Democratic Convention in Philadelphia as an influential member of the Rules Committee, so much so that when he first arrived, the mayor presented him with keys to the city. He held several directorships, including a seat on the board of the First National Bank of Beaumont, and in later years, he also served as that particular bank's general counsel. Beeman Strong stayed personally involved in his private law practice and worked daily until about 1958 when his health began to fail. During his lifetime of eighty-four years, Strong earned and carried the respect of everyone who ever came into contact with him.[31]

After her husband's death on March 27, 1960, "Nannie" Strong sustained a long and memorable career in Beaumont promoting the arts, and for thirty-one years, she served as president of the Beaumont Music Commission that brought famous entertainers to the city such as Nelson Eddy, Jeanette MacDonald, the Trapp Family Singers, Isaac Stern, Rodgers and Hammerstein, Mary Martin, and Van Cliburn. The late Merita Mills, a music critic and a former amusements editor for the *Beaumont Enterprise*, said that Nancy Strong did everything from booking and signing the contract to "meeting the artists at the station or the airport, setting up a newspaper interview, having the concert grand tuned, the dressing room filled with flowers, the palms on the stage, the ushers assembled, the tickets printed, the billboards plastered, the hall at the right temperature, the stage hands summoned and the hotel reservations ready." Nancy Strong died on August 14, 1964, and both she and Beeman are buried at the city's Magnolia Cemetery.[32]

Max Schlicher, along with Frank Thomas and Marvin McClendon, "formed . . . the Schlicher-Thomas Company, which engaged in the acquisition of oil and gas properties

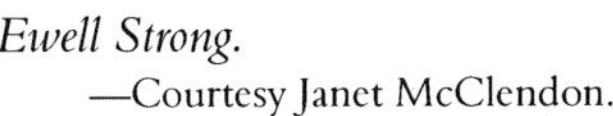

Ewell Strong.
—Courtesy Janet McClendon.

Beeman Strong.
—Courtesy Tyrrell Historical Library, Beaumont, Texas.

in Louisiana and Texas. They dissolved the company in 1942." Later in life, Max retired to a simpler life on his farm of about two acres right off Eleventh Street in Beaumont, where he spent a lot of time playing with his grandson and raising chickens, calves, and sheep. Schlicher was eight-two at the time of his death on March 31, 1972. He is buried at Beaumont's Forest Lawn Memorial Park.[33]

During an interview conducted on September 9, 1987, Marvin McClendon sat behind an enormous desk that he surprisingly identified as once belonging to Frank Yount, and while pointing to other furniture about the room, he emphatically stated, "In fact, all this belonged to Frank!" But to demonstrate how some things come full circle, McClendon had actually served in the capacity as purchasing agent who signed the order for the original 1926 transaction. Yount's huge desk and related items were eventually donated in August 1991 to the Texas Energy Museum, where they remain on permanent display. But in another ironic twist of fate, E. Szafir and Son, the local company who filled the furniture order in the first place, once located its business and occupied the same site on which the museum stands today.[34]

As the grand old gentleman of Yount-Lee, Marvin McClendon outlived the rest of his fellow corporate officers. And if one's hard work contributes to longevity, he certainly accomplished that as well, because past his ninety-fourth birthday, he maintained an active practice at the Petroleum Building, now the Century Tower, in Beaumont. Throughout his long life, Marvin retained a strong sense of humor and demonstrated a compassionate attitude toward his fellowman. In youth, he is remembered as a robust and slender individual with a height of about six feet, one inch; but as a product of poor times that permanently etched his character, he never strayed far from a conservative stance, both personally and financially. At age ninety-five, he passed away on June 26, 1991, and is buried alongside his wife, Marie, at Forest Lawn Memorial Park in Beaumont.[35]

Michel Halbouty did in fact team up with the hard drinking "Diamond Glenn" McCarthy and helped him bring in many successful wells before striking out on his own. But while they worked together, the relationship between the two is characterized by one author as "something like King Kong and Godzilla agreeing to share the same apartment." Halbouty also made his mark writing history, and along with co-author Jim Clark, the two penned *Spindletop*, the first definitive work on the oil field published in 1952. Long recognized for his tireless efforts as an oil conservator, he passed away in Houston on November 6, 2004, at the age of ninety-five.[37]

Nancy Rae Strong and Nelson Eddy.[36]
—Courtesy Tyrrell Historical Library, Beaumont, Texas

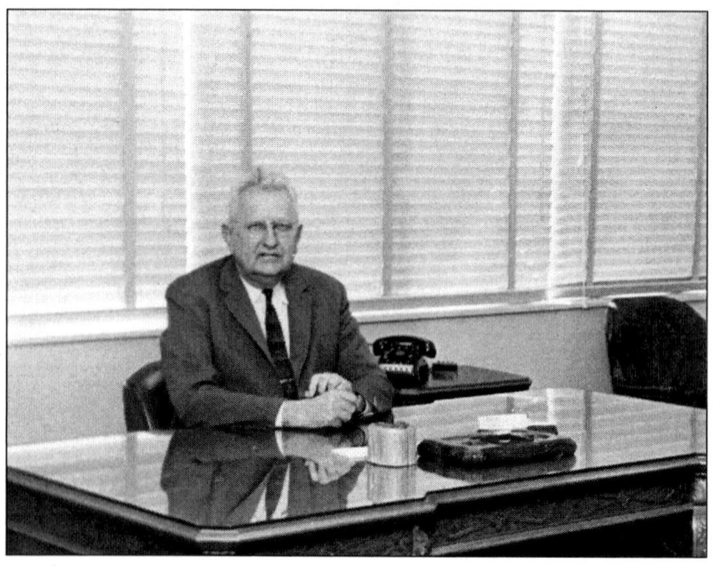

Marvin Wise McClendon seated at Frank Yount's desk in April 1961.
—Courtesy Janet McClendon.

Earlier on August 3, 1942, tragedy struck another former Yount-Lee employee. Samuel G. Parks, who first served Frank Yount as secretary and later Tal Rothwell, fell to his death from the fifteenth floor of the San Jacinto Building in Beaumont. Shortly beforehand, Parks had sent a janitor, Leo Sam, to get him a drink of water. Reportedly, Parks had not been feeling well, and on that particular morning at about 8:00, he felt faint. When Sam returned, however, Parks was gone. A short time later, someone noticed Park's body on the roof unit of the three-story San Jacinto annex. No one witnessed him plunge twelve stories below, so speculation

Sunnyside *as it appears today. Photograph by Fred B. McKinley.*

arose that he must have walked to an open window to get a breath of fresh air, and passed out. Park's body was taken to Oakwood Cemetery in Tyler, Smith County, and buried in the family plot with his mother, Nancy Cora Gibbs; father, Theodore Wilson Parks; and other kinsmen.[38]

As for Frank and Pansy's first home at Sour Lake, Sunnyside not only survives, its current owner, Jim Kelly, who lives there full time, is in the process of restoring it.

The name—Spindletop—lives on in the Bluegrass State. The University of Kentucky currently uses Spindletop Hall for its Faculty, Staff, and Alumni Club; and the American Saddlebred Museum, the major depository for information on the farm's activities, was organized in 1961 as the American Saddle Horse Museum. Governor Bert T. Combs dedicated the facility on July 12 of the following year, but since then, it has been moved from its original location in the Carriage House and now operates in a stand alone building at the Kentucky Horse Park.

Lawsuits concerning titles to land at Spindletop oil field in Beaumont, and specifically that of the McFaddin's, continue to the present day. AND—just like Frank in his time, there are those who believe still, without reservation, that "as much oil remains there as was ever taken out." Only the future will determine whether another will step forward and fill the shoes of the oilman whom Glenn H. "Diamond Jim" McCarthy classified as "the greatest optimist I have ever known." "To me," McCarthy continued, "optimism means a combination of courage, vision, industry, and faith. No man I have ever known possessed these qualities in greater measure than did Frank Yount."[39]

Main training barn at Spindletop Farm, as it appears today.
—Courtesy American Saddlebred Museum, Lexington, Kentucky.

Chief of Spindletop's grave marker at Spindletop Farm.
—Courtesy American Saddlebred Museum, Lexington, Kentucky.

Appendix 1

Note: The following represents a transcription of Frank Yount's Estate Inventory and Appraisement, a probate document located at the Jefferson County Courthouse in Beaumont, Texas. For historical presentation purposes, the authors have made every effort possible to retain the integrity, terminology, grammar, and abbreviations of the original, including misspellings and omissions. Furthermore, we made no attempt to determine whether the calculations are correctly stated.

NO. 5224) IN THE COUNTY COURT OF
ESTATE OF M. F. YOUNT, DECEASED) JEFFERSON COUNTY, TEXAS.

Inventory and appraisement of the Estate of M. F. Yount, deceased, produced before the undersigned appraisers, on the 11 day of April, A. D. 1934, by Pansy Yount, executrix of the Estate of M. F. Yount, deceased.

SEPARATE PROPERTY OF SAID M. F. YOUNT, DECEASED.

1	"Piatti" Stradivarius	$ 30,000.00	
1	Solitaire diamond ring	400.00	
1	Diamond Stud	400.00	
4	Amethyst stones (Colorado)	10.00	
1	Watch	50.00	
	Personal effects	100.00	
TOTAL OF M. F. YOUNT SEPARATE PROPERTY			$30,960.00

COMMUNITY PROPERTY

REAL ESTATE:

In Jefferson County, Texas

1. Lots four to nine (4 to 9) inclusive in Block thirty-eight (38) of the Calder Addition to the City of Beaumont, Texas, home place, 1376 Calder Avenue.

Value of Ground	$15,000.00	
Value of Improvements	35,000.00	$50,000.00

2. Lots one to six (1 to 6) inclusive in Block ten (10) of the Calder Addition to the City of Beaumont, Texas, Mildred Buildings and Mildred Apartments, 1400 Block Calder Ave.		
Value of Ground	$ 30,000.00	
Value of Improvements		
Mildred Bldgs.	56,000.00	
Mildred Apts.	114,000.00	200,000.00
3. Lots eleven (11) and East half of Lot ten (10) in Block 4 of the Calder Addition to the City of Beaumont, Texas, 1000 Block Calder Ave. being a vacant lot adjoining Andrus Motor Co. Bldg.		4,000.00
4. West half of Lot two (2) and all of Lot 3 in Block 48 of the Averill Addition to the City of Beaumont, Texas, 2600 Block, Liberty Ave.		1,030.00
5. Undivided half interest in Lots 1 to 26, Block 8 of Averill Addition to City of Beaumont, Texas, on Long Avenue.		8,250.00
6. Lots East 94', 686 and 687, Block 29, City of Beaumont, Texas, 402–32 Tevis Street, Elks Bldg.		60,000.00
7. Lots Nos. 453 to 457 inclusive in Block No. 61 original town of Beaumont, Texas. (Decedent owned one-half undivided interest)		7,500.00
8. Tracts 1 and 9, Plat D–7 of the James Drake Survey, City of Beaumont, Texas, North of French School (Earl Street)		
Value of land	$ 4,800.00	
Value of improvements	2,400.00	7,200.00
9. Tract No. 1, Plat B–8, J. W. Bullock Survey City of Beaumont, Texas, South of Booker Heights, a negro subdivision.		1,800.00
10. Tract 19, Plat A–2 of the David Brown Survey of the City of Beaumont, Texas, Herring St. Extension.		3,000.00
11. 30.19 Acres of H. Williams League, known as W. F. Treadway Tract No. 1. 85.02 Acres in C. Williams League, known as W. F. Treadway Tract No. 2. On Calder Road in Jefferson County, Texas.		
30.19 acres at $500.00 per acre	$15,000.00	
85.02 acres at $150.00 per acre	12,750.00	
	$27,750.00	
Value of improvements	10,650.00	38,400.00

12. Lots Nos. 34, 35 and South half of Lot No. 36, in Block No. 9 of the Caldwood Addition to the City of Beaumont, Texas		2,600.00
13. 400.61 acres of land in A. Houston League, known as the Hugh Long Tract, near Amelia, in Jefferson County, Texas.		21,330.00
14. 400.76 acres of land in A. Houston League, in Jefferson County, Texas, bought from C. Doornboss		16,030.40
15. 9.23 acres of land in James Gerish, Sr. League 779.86 acres of land in E. Rains Survey, in Jefferson County, Texas, bought from Earl Hankamer.		19,727.25

In Hardin County, Texas

1. Two acres of land out of the Minerva Merchant 24 acres subdivision in the Stephen Jackson League at Sour Lake, Texas, bought from Ambrose Merchant, et al, on November 27, 1915, being the old homeplace of M. F. Yount.		
Value of land	$ 500.00	
Value of improvements	3,500.00	4,000.00
2. Lots 39, 41, 42, 45, 46, 51, and 52 of the Oakland Addition to the City of Sour Lake, Texas		
Value of land is $50.00 each	$ 350.00	
Value of improvements	150.00	500.00
3. T. F. Rothwell, Trustee, an undivided 1/5 interest in a certain properties at Sour Lake, Texas, known as the Citizens National Bank, business site consisting of the bank home and 3 other buildings, on November 13, 1933, the bank was paying a rent of $50.00 per month and the two other buildings were being rented for $50.00 and $25.00 per month each. One was vacant which has the rental value of $25.00 per month.		
Value of said 1/5 interest		6,000.00
4. 204.3 acres of land in the A. A. Burrell League on Village Creek, north of Kounze, being used by the Boy Scouts as a playground. This property was bought from Southwest Settlement and Development Co. on July 27, 1927.		1,021.50

In Liberty County, Texas,

1. Part of Lot 1, Block 21 of the Town of Liberty, Texas, being the old natatorium owned

jointly with M. E. Pevito.
Value of 1/2 interest — 50.00

2. A two and one-half acre interest out of a 10 acre tract of land in the West portion of the W½ of a certain 37-1/2 acre tract of land in the Jessie Devore League at Hull, Texas, purchased from H. H. Lee on August 4, 1919 as per deed recorded in Vol. 87, page 483, in the Deed Records in Liberty County, Texas. This property is non-productive. — 25.00

3. A 1/4 interest in a 74 acre tract of land in the East half of a certain 250 acre tract of land out of the T. and N.O. Section, No. 2, conveyed to M. F. Yount, et al, by F. E. Peeler on November 21, 1921 as per deed recorded in Vol. 114, page 285 of the Deed Records of Liberty County, Texas. The other owners are Nellie A. Sterling, W. J. Hart, and C. D. Smith. W. J. Hart lives on the property, his address being Nome, Texas. Value of 1/4 interest — 185.00

<u>In Tyrrell County, Texas</u>

1. An undivided 1/4 interest amounting about 205¼ acres in a 1231 acre tract of land in the Lem Barton Survey, Abstract No. 2312, Cert. No. 325 or 326, Survey 7, Lot 162 near Sanderson, Texas. — 820.00

TOTAL — $453,469.15

<u>At Manitou, in El Paso County, State of Colorado</u>

1. Rockledge Property:
Part of SW ¼ of Section 4, Tract 14, S, R67W and adjoining and adjacent land as described on the attached blue print, consisting of about 12 acres of land.

Appraised value of land	$ 7,500.00	
Improvements to the ground	7,500.00	
Main dwelling	20,927.94	
Value of caretaker's house	2,633.97	
Cow barns, chicken houses, tool houses, dog house, bird house	526.25	$ 39,088.16

2. Arcade Property:
Part of 37, Section 4, Manitou, and adjoining and adjacent property owned by the Estate of M. F. Yount, deceased, consisting of business buildings.

Value of land	$10,000.00	
Value of improvements	15,000.00	25,000.00

3. Greenstone Quarries:
South half of Southeast quarter of Section 31, Tract 13, S, R 67W, containing 75 acres of land

Value of land	$6,200.00	
Value of machinery and buildings	8,676.80	14,876.80
	TOTAL	$78,964.96

STOCK IN CORPORATIONS:

Name	Capital Stock	Certif. No.	No. Shares	Total Par Value	Market Value
1. Schlicher Oil Company Sour Lake, Texas	$ 6,000.	2	29	$ 2,900.	
	Market Value 29 Shares @ $80.00				2,320.00
2. Standard Brass and Manufacturing Co. Port Arthur, Texas	$125,000.	47	916	22,900.	
	Market Value 916 Shares @ $25.00				22,900.00
3. Beaumont Cotton Compress Company Beaumont, Texas	$ 50,000.	5	10	1,000.	
	Market Value 10 Shares @ $50.00				500.00
4. Beaumont Hotel Operating Co. Beaumont, Texas	$	55	10	100.	
	Market Value 10 Shares @ $10.00				100.00
5. The Citizens Nat'l Bank of Sour Lake Sour Lake, Texas.	$ 50,000.	35	20	2,000.	
		76	5	500.	
		84	5	500.	
		146	15	1,500.	
		160	35	3,500.	
		162	5	500.	
		165	4	400.	
			89	8,900.	
	Market Value 89 Shares @ $50.00				4,450.00
6. Sour Lake Investment Company Sour Lake, Texas	$ 32,000	1	30	3,000.	
		22	4	400.	
			34	3,400.	
	Market Value 34 Shares @ $50.00				1,700.00

Name	Capital Stock	Certif. No.	No. Shares	Total Par Value	Market Value
7. The First National Bank of Beaumont Beaumont, Texas.	$400,000.	399	13⅓	1,333.33	
		650	10	1,000.00	
		655	3	1,300.00	
		677	184	18,400.00	
			220⅓	22,033.33	
	Market Value 220⅓ Shares @ $150.00				33,050.00
8. The Edson Hotel Company Beaumont, Texas.					
(Common)	$500,000.	10	25	$2,500.	
(Preferred)	500,000.	21	25	2,500.	
			50	5,000.	NO VALUE
9. Rex Supply Company Sour Lake, Texas.	$ 45,000.	12	17½	1,750.	
		25	37½	3,750.	
		41	35	3,500.	
		55	49	4,900.	
		62	10	1,000.	
			149	14,900.	
	Market Value 149 Shares @ $125.00				18,625.00
10. Lake Tool Company Sour Lake, Texas.	$ 15,000.	1	30	3,000.	
		21	7½	750.	
			37½	3,750.	
	Market Value 37½ Shares @ $100.00				3,750.00
11. Phelan-Josey Grocery Company Beaumont, Texas	$250,000.	81	20	2,000.	
		87	20	2,000.	
		130	10	1,000.	
		163	165	16,500.	
		206	215	21,500.	
		256	26	2,600.	
Phelan Grocery Company Beaumont, Texas		276	25	2,500.	
		278	124	12,400.	
		283	31	3,100.	
		295	20	2,000.	
		296	17	1,700.	
		314	8	800.	
			681	68,100.	
	Market Value 681 Shares @ $75.00				51,075.00

Name	Capital Stock	Certif. No.	No. Shares	Total Par Value	Market Value
12. Yount-Lee Oil Company					
Beaumont, Texas	$	9	166⅔	16,666.66	
		12	1500	150,000.00	
		24	5000	500,000.00	
		107	200	20,000.00	
			6866⅔	686,666.66	
	Market Value 6866⅔ Shares @ $1,000.00				6,866,666.66
13. Beaumont Iron Works Company					
Beaumont, Texas	$ 700,000.	100	78	$ 7,800.	
	Market Value 78 Shares @ $25.00				1,950.00
14. Wall Street Property Company					
Beaumont, Texas.	$ 380,000.	12	100	10,000.	
		19	25	2,500.	
		32	18	1,800.	
		34	104	10,400.	
		45	988	98,800.	
		57	250	25,000.	
			1485	148,500.	
	Market Value 1485 Shares @ $40.00				59,400.00
15. Norvell-Wilder Hardware Company					
Beaumont, Texas	$ 500,000.	78	25	2,500.	
		82	20	2,000.	
		103	45	4,500.	
		148	48	4,800.	
		222	117	11,700.	
		247	114	11,400.	
		255	35	3,500.	
		259	315	31,500.	
		260	169	16,900.	
		269	100	10,000.	
Norvell-Wilder Supply Company		285	5	500.	
		289	10	1,000.	
		294	31	3,100.	
		297	242	24,200.	
		301	9	900.	
		308	20	2,000.	
		311	9	900.	
		313	5	500.	
		314	90	9,000.	
		315	8	800.	
			1417	141,700.	
	Market Value 1417 Shares @ $125.00				177,125.00

Name	Capital Stock	Certif. No.	No. Shares	Total Par Value	Market Value
16. Beaumont Implement Company Beaumont, Texas					
(Common)	$	188	24	2,400.	
(Preferred)		18	12	1,200.	
			36	3,600.	
		Market Value of Common Stock			NONE
		Market Value of Preferred Stock @ $25.00			300.00
17. Beaumont Brick Company Beaumont, Texas	$	29	133	$13,300.	
		30	30	3,000.	
		31	37	3,700.	
			200	20,000.	
		Market Value 200 Shares @ $25.00			$ 5,000.00
18. Savoy's Inc. Beaumont, Texas	$ 20,000.	17	50		NO VALUE
19. Plumbing and Heating Company Beaumont, Texas		5	40	4,000.	NO VALUE
20. The Texas Corporation New York, N. Y.		181451 to 181455, incl.		(COst)	
			500 (35½)	17,750.	
		181363 to 181375, incl.	1300 (35½)	46,150.	
		181546 to 181611, incl.	6600 (35½)	234,300.	
		0397122	64 (27½)		
		191398 to 191447, incl.	5000 (27½)	139,260.	
			13,464	437,460.	
	Market Value 13464 Shares @ $26.50 (Par $25.00)				356,796.00
21. Lake Chevrolet Company Sour Lake , Texas	$	22	16	800.	
		Market Value 16 Shares @ $50.00			800.00
22. Thames Drug Company Beaumont , Texas		72	50	5,000.	
		Market Value 50 Shares @ $50.00			2,500.00

Name	Capital Stock	Certif. No.	No. Shares	Total Par Value	Market Value
23. Beaumont Cement Sales Company Beaumont , Texas			10	1,000.	
	Market Value 10 Shares @ $150.00				1,500.00
				TOTAL	$7,610,507.66

MISCELLANEOUS PROPERTIES:

1. Automobiles (cars were listed in code):

1	Duesenberg Coupe, 1929 Model	$1,575.00	
1	Duesenberg Sedan, 1929 Model	1,000.00	
1	5-passenger Cord Sedan, 1929 Model	369.50	
1	Locomobile Limousine, 1918 Model	200.00	
1	Austin Coupe, 1931 Model	137.70	
1	5-passenger Dodge Sedan, 1933 Model	646.95	
1	5-passenger Duesenberg Judkins Sedan	5,000.00	
1	Chevrolet Coupe (Delivery), 1932 Model	333.00	
			$ 9,262.15

2. Household furnishings and effects:

(a)	Homestead	$44,736.50	
(b)	Mildred Apartment	15,237.00	
(c)	Rockledge, Manitou Colo.	5,343.00	
			65,316.50

3. Yount Dairy Farm, Calder Road:

1	Milking Machine	$ 50.00
1	Milk Cooling Unit	50.00
1	Barrell Churn	5.00
1	Cream Separator	30.00
1	1/8 H.P. Motor	5.00
1	1/3 H.P. Motor	7.50
1	3/4 H.P. Motor	12.00
1	Clipping Machine	7.50
1	Hot Water Heater	20.00
1	Light Farm Wagon	20.00
1	Draft team harness	20.00
1	8 inch plough	4.00
1	Scraper	2.00
1	Chevrolet Truck, 1930	40.00
1	Chevrolet Coupe Pickup, 1931	272.70
1	Electric Incubator	40.00
1	Commercial Brooder	50.00
2	3-gal. Thermos cans	5.00
4	5-gal. cans	2.00
1	Pr. Draft Horses	175.00
2	Range ponies	45.00
1	Part Shetland pony	15.00

14	Spring pigs	84.00	
1	Boar	15.00	
3	Age sows	45.00	
30	September pigs	70.00	
14	Peking Duck	7.00	
7	Toulouse Geese	7.00	
35	Pigeons	5.00	
34	Barred Rock Chickens	13.50	
78	White Leghorns	31.20	
100	Baby Chicks	5.00	
9	Turkeys	9.00	
11	Peafouls	11.00	
32	Guineas	9.00	
7	Hives of Bees	10.00	

Cattle on Place:

1	Cow	$ 100.00	
1	Cow	50.00	
	Cow Y 13	55.00	
	Bull Y 5	50.00	
	Cow Y 9	75.00	
	Cow Y 11	35.00	
	Heifer Y 14	35.00	
	Heifer Y 15	35.00	
	Heifer Y 18	25.00	
	Cow 555	60.00	
	Heifer 13 H	40.00	
	Cow 559	60.00	
	Bull H 62	50.00	
	1 Grade Cow	20.00	
	3 Heifer Calves	60.00	
3	Milk Cows from Colorado		
	1 @ $20.; 2 @ $60. each	140.00	
1	Bull	10.00	
GRAND TOTAL			$ 2,099.40

4. Show Horses and Equipment at Spindle Top Stables:

Show Horses:	Cost	Value
Beau Peavine	$ 6,000.00	$6,000.00
Night Alarm	1,250.00	1,250.00
Trade Wind	1,250.00	1,250.00
Roosevelt	1,100.00	1,100.00
Shirley Gray	1,000.00	1,000.00
Chief of Spindle Top	1,000.00	1,000.00
Lady Virginia	3,250.00	3,250.00
Belle Rita	700.00	350.00
Texas Ranger	400.00	250.00
Girl Friend	350.00	350.00
Sea Breeze (George)	400.00	250.00

	Lois Harrison	265.00	265.00	
	Paris Grand	500.00	300.00	
	My Mary	210.00	210.00	
	Sally Foot	150.00	150.00	
	Dan	270.00	150.00	
	Alice	270.00	100.00	
		18,365.00		17,225.00

<u>Equipment</u>:

1	1933 Chevrolet Sedan (Code Price)		535.80	
1	Show Buggy	$400.00		
1	Set Super Quality Brand Show Harness	200.00		
1	Race Bike	100.00		
1	Colt Cart	147.79		
4	Wal. Fin. Beds with Springs and Mattress	238.00		
4	Cots with Mattresses and Blankets	86.00		
	Blacksmith tools			
	Forge	$27.50		
	Anvel	23.75		
	Reed Vise	13.60		
	Foot Leveler	6.00		
			$ 70.85	
8	Special Tack Trunks		269.70	
1	Set Silver Trimmed Jogging Harness		48.50	
3	Special Show Saddles		294.71	
3	Special Riding Saddles		254.13	
16	Show Bridles		369.49	
24	Special Blankets with lettering		405.00	
			$2,884.17	
	Less 33-1/3 depreciation		961.39	$ 1,922.78

5. Building at Spindle Top Stables:		
Cost of stables and other improvements	$13,518.00	
Less 10% depreciation	1,351.80	12,166.20
6. Miscellaneous property at Spindle Top Stables:		100.00

Spindle Top Stables– – – TOTAL $31,949.78

7. Patents:

3–22–21	Pump Pistons	No.	1372262
7–01–24	Tongs		1499435
*1–19–26	Line Guides		1570116
*2–01–27	Counterweights		1616100
4–22–30	Flame Arrester		1755624
6–16–31	Sheaves		1809921

*These two patents are the only ones producing any revenue. The total received from these patents the last three years is as follows:

1931—	$ 269.53
1932	120.91
1933	59.02
	$ 449.56

Average per year—$ 139.85
Capitalized at 10% makes a valuation of $ 1,398.50

TOTAL $ 110,026.33

CASH, NOTES, MORTAGES AND INSURANCE:

1. a. Cash in the First National Bank of Beaumont, Texas, as of November 13, 1933. (This balance is subject to adjustment on account of a number of outstanding checks.)		$ 299,010.00
b. Cash in Exchange National Bank, Colorado Springs, Colorado		405.78
2. $1,400.00 of 6% bonds of the Beaumont Iron Works Company of Beaumont, Texas		
Value of bonds	$1,400.00	
Accrued interest to Nov. 13, 1933	16.75	1,416.75
3. $2,500.00 of 6% Beaumont Country Club bonds. These bonds are in default.		
Value of bonds (Face)	$2,500.00	
Accrued interest to Nov. 13, 1933	227.50	
Value 50% of face		1,250.00
4. One Note of Beaumont Surgical Hospital of Beaumont, dated Feb. 25, 1928 for $50,000, due three years after date, at 6% interest payable semi-annually. Secured a mortgage on Lots 1 and 2, Block 16, Calder Addition to the City of Beaumont, Texas, said property being known as the Beaumont General Hospital. This note is one of a series of notes, aggregating $106,000.00. All notes in default and no interest has been paid on same.		
Principal of note	$50,000.00	
Accrued interest, Nov. 13, 1933	14,400.00	
Value		20,000.00
5. Amount due from E. Farris, et al, for merchandise sold as per contract, dated October 20, 1932. The debtor is in default.		
Total amount due under the contract $19,419.74		
Value, 1/2		9,709.87

6. Life Insurance Policies Nos. 8175 J	$30,000.00		
" " " " 8197 J	20,000.00		
	50,000.00	This insurance is property of beneficiaries named.	
Great Southern Life Insurance Company Payable to Pansy Yount, wife, and Mildred Yount, daughter.			
Policy No. 31,460, same company, payable to Pansy Yount.	10,000.00		
	$60,000.00		
		TOTAL	$ 331,792.40

DEBTS OF DECEDENT

1. Note payable to the Yount-Lee Oil Company, dated December 8, 1930 for $300,000.00 at 5% interest to July 1. 2½% thereafter. Interest due from June 1, 1933.		
Principal of note	$300,000.00	
Accrued interest to Nov. 13, 1933	3,739.73	
		$303,739.73
2. Note payable to the Guardian Trust Company assumed in the purchase of the Elks Building Property on Nov. 13, 1931 on which there is due the sum of $13,000, with interest from Oct. 1, 1933 at the rate of 8% per annum.		
Principal of note	$ 13,000.00	
Accrued interest	125.37	
		$ 13,125.37
3. Unpaid income tax for year 1932—		$ 25,734.66
Income tax for year 1933—(Estimated)		90,000.00
Property taxes for year 1933—		18,423.34
4. Funeral expense		$ 16,500.00
5. Miscellaneous debts		$ 9,673.81
6. Administration expenses (Estimated)		$ 25,000.00
	TOTAL	$502,196.91

DEBTS OF DECEDENT

Contingent Liability (Ascertained)

Endorsement of M. F. Yount on the following notes in the First National Bank of Beaumont. The liability is certain on these notes.

Name:	Date:	Int.	Paid To:	Due:	Amount:	Collateral:
1. L. W. Beach	9.30.33	8%	12.1.33	Demand	$ 2,500.00	None
2. A. Benedict	4.30.33	8%	None	Demand	5,740.00	Deed of Trust dated 11/21/29. Lot 7, Blk. 33 Dallas, Tx. 62 Shs. Plumbing and Heating Co.
3. A. Benedict	4.30.33	8%	None	Demand	319.53	None
4. M. Burge	4.30.33	6%	7.24.33	Demand	5,398.13	200 Shs. Texas Corp. (sold)
			(Amount of note $10.620.72) The above collateral was sold by the bank resulting in a deficiency indebtedness of $5,398.13.			
5. Plumbing and Heating Co.	4.30.33	6%	12.1.33	Demand		Also endorsed by Beeman Strong and T. F. Rothwell
		(Amount of note $13,500)				
Plumbing and Heating Co.	5.13.33	6%	12.1.33	Demand		Also endorsed by Beeman Strong and T. F. Rothwell
		(Amount of note $1,825.00)				
Plumbing and Heating Co.	4.30.33	6%	12.1.33	Demand		Also endorsed by Beeman Strong and T. F. Rothwell
		(Amount of note $175.00)				
	(Total $15,500.00) 1/3				5,166.66	
	Total amount - - - - - - - - -				$19,124.32	

DEBTS OF DECEDENT

Contingent Liability (Unascertained)

Name:	Date:	Int.	Paid To:	Due:	Amount:	Collateral:
1. W. W. Prather	9.21.33	6%	12.20.33	12.20.33	$ 200.00	None
2. Harry Brown and Ida Francis Brown	9.25.33	8%	12.24.33	12.24.33	300.00	Deed of Trust, Lots 7 & 8, Blk #30, Calder Highlands, Bmt. Tex., also Lot 49 Sec. E, Forest Lawn, Bmt.

Name:	Date:	Int.	Paid To:	Due:	Amount:	Collateral:
3. C. E. Kennedy	5.1.33	8%	12.1.33	Demand	325.00	None
4. Lake Tool Co., Inc.	4.30.33	6%	12.1.33	Demand	12,000.00	Also endorsed M. L. Yount & T. F. Rothwell
5. Emmett Merritt	1.31.33	6%	12.1.33	Demand	500.00	Deed of Trust, dated 2/18/30, Lot #12, Blk. #4, Kirby Add., Bmt. Tex.
6. M. S. Murchison	4.30.33	6%	12.1.33	Demand	120.00	None
7. Rex Supply Co	4.30.33	6%	12.1.33	Demand	10,000.00	Also endorsed by M. L. Yount & T. F. Rothwell
8. Bruce Richardson	4.30.33	6%	12.1.33	Demand	25,000.00	None

DEBTS OF DECEDENT

Contingent Liability (Unascertained)

Name:	Date:	Int.	Paid To:	Due:	Amount:	Collateral:
9. E. L. Sandel	4.30.33	6%	12.1.33	Demand	4,105.00	40 Shares Wall St. Property Company
10. W. M. Schultz	9.16.33	6%	12.1.33	Demand	955.00	None
11. Thames Calder Pharmacies & M. G. Thames	4.30.33	6%	12.1.33	Demand	$15,000.00	Chattel Mortgage on furniture, fixtures & equipment, store in Mildred Bldg.

Total amount ———————— $ 68,505.00

SUMMARY OF ESTATE.

		Colorado	Texas	
Separate Property of M. F. Yount, deceased				$ 30,960.00
Community Property:		Colorado	Texas	
Real Estate		$78,964.96	$ 453,469.15	
Stocks			7,610,507.66	
Miscellaneous Property:				
Automobiles			9,262.15	
Household Furnishings		5,343.00	59,973.50	
Yount Dairy Farm			2,099.40	
Spindle Top Stables				
Horses	$17,225.00			
Equipment	2,458.58			
Buildings	12,166.20			
Miscellan.	100.00			
			31,949.78	
Patents			1,398.50	
Cash, Note, Mortgages, etc.		405.78	331,386.62	
		$ 84,713.74	$ 8,500,046.76	
Debts due by decedent:				
Notes payable	$316,865.10			
Taxes (Income)	115,734.66			
Taxes (Property)	18,423.34			
Miscellaneous	9,673.81			
Endorsements (certain)	19,124.32			
Endorsements (uncertain)	$68,505)			
		$ 479,821.23		
Total Community – – – – – – – – – – –		$ 8,020,225.53		
One-half Community				$ 4,010,112.76
				$ 4,041,072.76
Funeral Expenses	$ 16,000.00			
Administration (Est.)	25,000.00			
				41,000.00
				$ 4,000,072.76

Appendix 2

Note: Author Elizabeth Simpson, in her book titled The Enchanted Bluegrass *(Lexington: Transylvania Press, 1938), devoted one complete chapter, spanning pages 245 through 281, which details the splendor of Spindletop Hall just after its completion. The authors wish to express their appreciation to Ms. Simpson and her publisher for this spectacular description of the Yount estate.*

SPINDLETOP HALL

N. L. Ross, Colorado Springs, was engaged as the contractor, and E. T. Hutchings, Louisville architect was asked to draw plans for the house, following the clearly defined ideas of its owner. For thirty years she had planned to build a home, and every detail had been carefully thought out before she consulted an architect. She wanted a home where comfort would out-weigh every other consideration, yet it must be beautiful as any palace of a fairy princess, for it was to be the background of her only child, Mildred Frank Yount, namesake of her husband. It should have mantels and tapestries and rugs from the far corners of the earth, and it should have beds and chairs and sofas of deepest luxury.

Wide wrought-iron gates swing back to give entrance to the magnificent estate down an avenue of maples. Gnomes peer out from behind the trees, and "the little people" rest among the perennial borders that line the lawn enclosure.

Six large fluted pillars support the portico of the north entrance to the Georgian, red brick mansion, and six pilasters are against the dressed stone wall that lines the face of the veranda. The copper roof has turned a lovely green, and the deep cornice is decorated with Adam swags below the rows of dentils. Wrought iron balconies break the severity of the façade at upper windows, and large arched windows flank the double entrance doors.

The interior is gloriously beautiful. Poised and serene, its splendor of dimensions, exquisite frescoing, priceless rugs and tapestries, and sumptuous carved paneling take nothing from its atmosphere of ease and enjoyment. It is primarily a home, lived in and loved. Not one small item of comfort has been sacrificed for beauty's sake. Each chair and sofa has its table and footstool nearby, its lamp and ash tray and portfolio or magazine. Yet it is all in such quiet good taste, rich as some old feudal castle, home-like as any fireside where children romp with dogs and slippered householder smokes his favorite brier.

Halbert White, Kansas City decorator, working with Mrs. Yount, has created a masterpiece that has no parallel in Kentucky.

Its fine architectural details are evident from first glance into the great entrance hall, with its graceful flowing line of stair rising at each side of the wide doorway. The windows are hung with heaviest Italian silk velvet in a shade of rosy red and the steps are carpeted in red chenille to match the imported carpet of Georgian design, a motif that is reflected in the moulded ceiling.

"Master Fortesque," by Sir William Beechey, waves a friendly greeting from the carved trumeau of the chimney piece, and Capo di Monte urns and stein adorn the shelf of the old English Georgian mantel of statuary marble from Wonersh Park, Guilford, Surrey. Chairs and benches are in the Chippendale manner, as is the table that has a top of Egyptian marble. The stair is white, three designs alternating in the spindles, and Corinthian columns supporting the balcony, take on a shell pink glow. A handsome lantern swings from the ceiling.

Near the door of the French powder room hangs a Renaissance tapestry, "The Hunt," woven about 1600, with a wide and intricate border.

The powder room on the left of the hall might well have been a little salon of Marie Antoinette, with its walls of palest flesh pink, the designs of the carving emphasized in gold leaf. The panels are of green silk brocade. A huge French mirror fills the shallow alcove at the end of the room above the dressing table. Gray painted French chairs and sofas are covered with coral velvet and the draperies are of Louis XV hand woven silk brocade of biscuit color and polychrome, made for the room in Lyons, France. Paintings of great French courtesans adorn the walls, and light falls from a crystal prism chandelier in the center of the room. The floor is laid in marquetry.

Double doors at each side of the hall fireplace open into the Elizabethan living room and Georgian dining room, and a door on the right gives access to the William and Mary music room, the walls wainscoted to the ceiling in walnut. A tapestry hangs above the Eighteenth Century mantel of white marble with Alps green frieze and pilaster backing designed by Kent in 1735, and taken from a house designed by him on Marlborough street, London.

The draperies are a gorgeous William and Mary design woven in heavy silk damask of rich apricot. The valances are all solid wood and all of the surfaces, including the mouldings, have the damask pasted on in exact copies of authentic William and Mary work now preserved in one of the great English museums. A Royal Saronk rug covers the floor, and the crystal chandelier is a thing of unusual beauty. A little rosewood melodeon, one of the finest examples of these instruments in existence, stands near the door into the living room, and a Kimball organ at one end of the room may be turned on in twelve other places in the house.

A harp of decorated satinwood and gold, designed for the musically talented daughter of the house, stands near the grand piano, and a case built into the fireplace end of the room holds the collection of rare violins that belonged to Mr. Yount. In his fervid pursuit of knowledge in diversified fields Mr. Yount became interested in violins when his daughter first showed signs of unusual talent. He read everything available concerning artists and instruments and soon became a most discriminating collector, conversant with the many fine points by which the great masters are identified.

As the foundation of his collection he acquired two Stradivari. One is the "Reynier," 1681, and the other the "Piatti," 1717. Both are remarkably well preserved with their original varnish, rich in color. Other famous violins in the collection include examples of the work of Dominicus Montagnana, Andreas Guarnerius and his son, Joseph, Joannes Baptisa [Baptista] Guadagnini, and Jacobus Stainer. Fine bows include several by Francois Tourte, Peccatte [Pecatte] and Jean Baptiste Vuillaume.

A few steps at the left of the fireplace lead down to the library, paneled in Gothic oak, with a high, hammer-beam ceiling. The English Tudor gray stone mantel was removed from Trentham Hall, Straffordshire, one of the seats of the Duke of Sutherland. A wonderful old Brussels tapestry of early Renaissance weaving, formerly the property of Emperor Franz Josef, hangs above it, and the iron fender, its wide top covered with brown leather, forms a fireside seat. Back of the spacious green velvet sofa is a hand tooled and illuminated Spanish leather chest that holds a lamp of the Han period pottery, more than 2,000 years old.

Parchment lamp shades are copies of a Blanche of Castile tapestry in the J. P. Morgan collection and a Charles VII tapestry in the Metropolitan. Oriental rugs of almost unbelievable worth are strewn over the floor, for Mr. Yount was also an avid collector of rugs and rare editions, and became an authority on them. Books on shelves that line the walls are reached from a spiral library ladder. Windows and doors are arched in Gothic style, and hangings are of linen, hand embroidered in England with the wool crewel stitch, following traditions of the Henry VIII era. One of the treasures of the room is a Seventeenth Century Royal Venetian brocade a fragment of a Doge's robe, that is extremely rare. A similar brocade is in the St. Louis Art Museum.

The Elizabethan living room, thirty by sixty feet in dimensions, with walls of Gothic oak carved in parchment-fold panels, has a frieze of three alternating designs of Elizabethan strap work.

The ornamental plastered ceiling is reproduced from an Elizabethan room in an old English country house. The elaborately carved mantel bears the inscription, "East, West, Home's Best." A rug nearly 3,000 [obvious error; probably meant 300] years old hangs above it. A green seamless chenille rug of luxurious depth of pile covers the floor to the baseboard.

One wall space, eleven by fifteen feet, is covered by a Flemish Renaissance tapestry of the Sixteenth century, a scene from the series of the Wars of Alexander the Great, depicting his last triumphal march. It was formerly the property of the Hapsburg family and was brought to America by once-wealthy Russian refugees.

Lamp shades are copies from tapestries in European museums, and one is a Sixteenth Century Persian manuscript. Red brocatelle in bold Italian design was woven for the draperies.

Pictures in the room include a George Henry Harlow canvas, a Thomas Lawrence portrait, "Miss Briggs," a Benell portrait of Mildred Yount in her riding clothes, and one of Mr. Yount by the same artist: T. Cachaud's "Clair de lune," and California Haze," by Edgar Payne.

A chest holding Capo di Monte urns has above it a Venetian mirror with red and gold border. A massive carved and inlaid chest to hold a radio was adapted from a court cupboard of the year 1575. On its top is a world-famous Japanese family, celebrated for its ebony carving. When death took the aged father, and his two sons were killed in battle, the sets of elephants they had made became the prizes of collectors everywhere.

A stringer table holds a silver punch bowl, a duplicate of the Dixiana perpetual trophy won by Chief of Spindletop in the 1936 Louisville horse show the night he became the five-gaited world champion.

The dining room, with its walls of cool Adam green, is resplendent with five crystal chandeliers, prism sidelights and touches of gold-leaf outlining the panels. The rug, woven for the room in Czechoslovakia, is in the softest shades of pearly gray, rose, buff and blue greens, and the Georgian pattern of scrolls and flowers is repeated in the moulded ceiling. "Spindletop Hall" is woven inconspicuously into the narrow border in front of the fireplace, and the initials of Mrs. Yount and her daughter are faintly discernible in the corner scrolls.

The fine old mantel, made in 1750, was imported from the New York mansion of Otto Kahn and sold when the place was dismantled. It is fashioned of Cararra marble with twin black and gold marble columns at each side, and a convent Siena frieze inlay. It originally adorned Shapwick Hall, Somerset, England.

Set into the over-mantel is a painting, "Arabs on Horseback," one of the finest canvases of Adolph Schreyer, signed and framed by the great artist. Lime green Lalique glass jars are on the mantel shelf.

Atop a decorated linen cabinet is a Royal Copeland platter. The dining table, with its Egyptian marble top, is one of a string that can be made to seat a large number of guests. A silver closet, glass enclosed, fills the end of the room opposite the fireplace, and doors on either side opening into the butler's pantry are opened by electric "eyes."

The draperies are of superb Royal blue and gold Louis XV Chinoiserie designed by the famous Pillmonte.

Above a long serving table is a Seventeenth Century Royal Gobelin tapestry, twelve feet wide and eleven high, delineating the episode of Carol and Ubaldo at the Fountain of Laughter in the Romance of Rinaldo and Armeda, from Tasso's "Jerusalem Delivered." The tapestry formerly was in the collection of Clarke-Thornhill Esq., and hung in Rushton Hall, the beautiful Tudor castle in Northamptonshire, England.

Both the living room and dining salon open on the south side of the mansion with its broad terrace, lacy wrought iron balustrade and pillared circular portico. The porto cochere, with decorative iron gates, is approached from the library. All outside doors are of bronze with grille fretwork.

The service end of the house includes a white-titled butler's pantry, its shelves holding Wedgwood, Royal Doulton and Dresden, handwrought silver and delicate crystal. A salad pantry adjoins it, and in the large white kitchen, Will Irvine [Irwin], chef in the service of the family for twenty-five years, rules supreme. From his enthusiasm one gets a perfect picture of the master he served so devotedly, and of the mistress who holds the affection and deep loyalties of those in her employ.

The staff dining room, service chair, flower room and pantries open on the rear hall.

Mrs. Yount's suite is on the second floor, opening off the balcony opposite the entrance doors of the north terrace, and its windows look out on the sunken rose garden.

Done in the period of Louis XV, its oyster white paneling is on walls of buff, with a deep moulded frieze. The fireplace is of dove gray marble and is one of a pair taken from an ancient French chateau. Above the mantel is Nicholas Largilliere's portrait, "Lady of the Court." Draperies are of gold and silver satin damask, and the chandelier and side lights are French gilt mesh interspersed with pastel enamel flowers. French portraits, divans and chairs upholstered in rose velvet, a French cherry commode, and a pale ivory baby grand piano, artistically decorated, give the room an air of delicate charm. The floor is carpeted in French blue. Benell portraits of Mrs. Yount's parents, Hosea Holly Merritt and Sarah Frances Sherman Merritt, hang at the end of the room.

The adjoining bedroom in the mode of Louis XVI has twin French beds draped with blue and putty damask of authentic Louis XVI design, and oval miniatures of Mildred Yount as a little girl hang just above the low headboards. Rose pointe lace covers the lamp shades, and a French mirror hangs over the dressing table. Near the fireplace is a George Ford Morris sketch in oil of "Tiny," once a favorite Pomeranian member of the household.

On the shelves of a French cabinet are treasures suitable for museums. There is a lorgnette of blue enamel and diamonds that Napoleon gave to his beloved Josephine; a watch with a fine miniature in enamels that once belonged to Alexander II of Russia that was given to Mr. Yount by a Russian prince; a set of Spanish earrings, comb and necklace of cameos set in gold filagree brought out of Madrid during the revolution; and family pieces inherited by Mrs. Yount from her mother and aunt, including long amethyst ear drops and brooch, a handsome pin of a single large amethyst surrounded by diamonds and embossed with a white cameo head; barbarie silver and turquoise matrix jewels made for Indian princesses, and jewelled evening bags and strings of coral and amber, and a star sapphire ring of such size and color as to represent a king's ransom.

The dressing room adjoining the bedroom, its walls filled with hanging closets, was decorated by Dennis Prectyl, Cincinnati artist, and forms the connecting link with the bathroom that is tiled in green with mirrored wall above the dressing table and the tub in the center of the room.

Adjoining Mrs. Yount's suite is that of her daughter who was married in June to Edward Manion, Tulsa, Okla [they were married on June 27, 1938]. It is said to be the only complete Angelica Kaufmann apartment in America. Its satinwood and cane furniture was faithfully copied from pieces of late Eighteenth Century period in England and decorated in the manner of the great Kaufmann.

An original Adam mantel, designed by one of the Adam brothers, is in the sitting room, with Angelica Kaufmann's original canvas, "Mrs. Maister," hanging above it. Mirrors hang over the pair of delicate galleried commodes at each side of the fireplace. The paneled walls are of egg-shell, the carpet is turquoise, and the upholstering of chairs, chaise longue and divans is of satin damask in pale shades of blue, pink and ivory. (Summer draperies and slip covers on many pieces through the house conceal the magnificence of the damask that is an important feature of the furnishings.) The lamps are Wedgwood, and the silver and crystal chandelier shows the Adam influence. A baby Steinway grand piano stands in strong contrast to the smallest of fine and ancient melodeons. A portrait of "Mrs. Perry," by George Harlow, hangs on one wall, and nearby stands a silver trophy that was presented to Mildred Yount by the city of Beaumont the night that Roxie Highland, her national champion five-gaited mare, was retired at Madison Square Garden in 1935.

Holding a place of prominence in the room is a pleasing portrait photograph of Mr. Yount in academic robes of regent of The University of Texas.

The bedroom of the apartment, with four-post, canopied bed, has a life-size portrait of Mrs. Yount by Benell. The rug is of peach chenille, and the furniture is similar in line and coloring to that of the sitting room. The hangings are of eggshell and blue striped taffeta with cut-petal trimmings, and the permanent draperies of the bed are egg-shell taffeta. A cabinet is filled with all the little bibelots that children love. Some are exquisite miniature tea services of Georgian silver. Some are charm bracelets from ten-cent counters—all are cherished momentoes of birthday anniversary parties in which school friends from every condition of life were included.

As heiress to the largest fortune in the southwest, the idolized only child of the house, Mildred Yount Manion, not yet in her twenties, is sweetly thoughtful and considerate of others, unspoiled, and touchingly appreciative of even the smallest tokens of friendship. Utterly unaffected, eagerly devoted to outdoor life, educated at one of the smart and exclusive boarding schools of the west, she is charmingly fitted to take her place at the head of the beautiful Yount establishment, El Ocaso, in Beaumont.

The dressing room of the suite, with closets painted in pastel colors, has diaphanous draperies, and slender, high-backed chairs are covered in oyster white damask. The blue-tiled bath, with tub in the center and mirrored side wall, has glass-enclosed showers, and the light fixtures have pear-shaped prisms.

Another suite has spacious couches and lounge chairs, a Chippendale chest-on-chest, a massive desk and a desk-chair covered with natural pig-skin. A ceiling fan is above the chandelier. The draperies are hand blocked linen of Georgian design in an exceptionally beautiful fabric. A painting of a western landscape hangs over the black and white marble mantel and at one side is a painting of the meeting of Robert E. Lee and "Stonewall" Jackson.

Four guest suites are on the second floor. One is a replica of Mr. Yount's room at El Ocaso, with Spanish furniture, Oriental rug, red damask hangings, and Paul Doering water colors.

Another is paneled in cream with green carpet, lavender taffeta draperies, dainty dressing table and chaise longue.

One, in shades of pink and blue, has walls adorned with F. Kaufmann seascapes, and the adjoining bath is tiled in pink and cream.

A single Italian bedroom with bath, the apartment of Mrs. Yount's secretary-companion, is in tones of wisteria and green. And two early Kentucky bedrooms and bath are on the third floor.

Stairs descend from the great entrance hall to the saddle lounge in the basement done in worm-eaten chestnut paneling, and blue and red leather, the colors of the Spindletop stable. The massive chimney is built of greenstone and redstone quarried on the Yount property in Colorado. It has faint coloring of green and pink and is a touch of the West added as a tender bit of sentiment. A large buffalo head hangs above the opening of the fireplace. Shades on the lamps are copied from century-old Maryland hunting scenes.

On the walls are stag heads and George Ford Morris paintings of Beau Peavine and Chief of Spindletop, and crayon sketches by the same artist. Photographs of Senator Crawford, champion road horse, and Calumet Armistice, both of the blood of Peter the Great, are hung alongside the ribbons won at the Chicago Jubilee Show.

Carriage lanterns are used in the lighting fixtures, and a table is ingeniously fashioned of cart wheels and singletrees.

The men's room, opening to the left, has walls decorated with wisteria blossoms.

The Kentucky tap room is a fascinating replica of an old wayside tavern. It, too, has a fireplace of Colorado stone, and paneled walls. The bar has a brass rail, and bar-room slogans are framed around the mirrors. The high-seated chairs are the western bar-room type with spotted ponyskin and cowhide cushions. A pair of Lillywhite canvases hang on the walls. The large front window with many small panes is flanked by doors opening on a court which comprises the ballroom, the verandas of the tavern enclosing it. The dance floor is constructed with a slight give to prevent the dancer's tiring. The powder room has silver walls adorned with cherry blossoms and hung with Chinese dolls in costumes of the various dynasties.

The dog room, arranged with bath facilities and decorated in typical canine manner, is occupied by the Pomeranian house dogs and a prized Griffon, one of only two or three in America, as they are seldom able to stand the ocean voyage.

The game room, with green canvas walls and white and black inlaid floor, has a billiard table, sofas and card tables. A series of the old English prints by Richard Blome hang here.

The laundry, a cold storage room for furs and another for meats, an hors d'oeuvre kitchen and boiler room complete the basement.

The south terrace of the house looks out on the rose garden outlined with yews and approached by wide steps of stone. On either side are bewitching bronzes of children playing with frogs, Bonnie MacLeary's inimitable "Ouches."

In the center of the rectangular lily pool is a charming bronze fountain figure, "Joy of the Water," by Harriet W. Frishmuth, one of the greatest of contemporary sculptors whose work is to be found in private estates and great museums throughout America.

At the right of the garden is the large swimming pool with chute-the-chute and white terrace furniture and the brick bathhouse has a colonnade center designed for *al fresco* tea. A tennis court, built of composition and painted green, lies between the bathhouse and the stable for pleasure horses, with the kennels beyond.

Architects fairly tore their hair at the proximity of stable and kennels, but to no purpose. Mildred Yount wanted her riding horses near enough the house to go out and saddle them herself, and her wishes were law from the time she was able to prattle baby-talk. She and her father were closely companionable. They rode together almost daily, and no business was ever important enough for him to break an engagement with his daughter. So her mother carried on in the same indulgent way, and Della, Mildred's first pony, along with My Mary, her choice mount, is stabled in plain view of the pillared portico. Mr. Yount's riding horse, Paris Grand, had a stall there, too, as have several other riding horses provided for guests. A Woodward park coach recently has been added to the collection of ancient vehicles.

In the kennels are Scotties and Sealyhams, Great Danes, Llewellyn setters, Dalmatians, pointers and foxhounds, each breed with its own run. Electrified doors of kennels and dairy sizzle every fly that aspires to enter.

Spindletop Farms, however, is more than an elegant and costly whimsy with Mrs. Yount. It is conducted as a sort of experiment farm where various breeds of stock and fowls are being perfected under the best possible conditions.

Hampshire hogs, a registered Aberdeen-Angus herd, a flock of Shropshire sheep, and milk goats are carefully bred and culled. The Jersey dairy herd is headed by Kahokas Dream Not, imported from the Isle of Jersey and winner of several championships. Adams Model, international prize winner among Percheron horses and the first imported Percheron brought to Kentucky, is in the stud at Spindletop.

White Leghorn chickens, turkeys, peacocks, ducks, geese, pigeons and bantam chickens are in the various enclosures.

The service court, with garages and servants' apartments, is at the extreme left end of the mansion, and the greenhouse, within stone's throw, is filled with roses and violets, camellias and gardenias and chrysanthemums.

A grove of trees in the midst of which a barbecue pit has been built, embowers lovely Lake Mildred which covers an area of twelve acres. Black swans mingle among the snowy white ones that glide on its glassy surface, and small boats lie at anchor near the banks. Another lake five acres in size and known as Lake Roxie is on another part of the farm, an island in its center offering a sanctuary for birds.

Appendix 3

Note: From 1936–1954, Spindletop Farm bred approximately sixty-seven horses, and another thirty or so, not bred by the farm, were registered by the owners during that time frame. Courtesy of the American Saddlebred Museum in Lexington, Kentucky, the following represents a partial listing. For a description of the abbreviations used, consult the Glossary.

Abie's Baby 47302

BHF. By Beau Peavine and out of Abie's Irish Rose (BHF). Only foal of 1947 that the farm bred. Dam of eleven-time WC fine harness horse CH Colonel Boyle 637752 (sire of WC Step Lightly 73117, RWC CH Colonel Windsor 48340, and RWC CH Sherry My Sherry 85635); WC sire Broadland's Kilarney 50136 and Grassland's Specialty 61073 (second dam of CH Six Pence Event 68326) and Grassland's Irish Rose 59200 (dam of CH First Look 49952).

Abie's Genius 24057

By The Genius and out of Abie's Irish Rose (BHF). Sire of CH Betty's Gloriann 85834.

Abie's Royal Irishman 25361

By Beau Peavine and out of Abie's Irish Rose (BHF). Broodmare sire of WC CH Genius Society 47814.

Beau Le Rose Peavine 19601

By Beau Peavine and out of CH Belle Le Rose. Sire of RWC CH Dixie Aristocrat 37034 and RWC CH Rose's China Silk 60163.

Beau Yount 22139

By Beau Peavine and out of CH Belle Le Rose. Winner at Lexington Junior League Show of two-year-old five-gaited competition. Sire of RWC Fine Harness Chief of Texas 34090, WC Lovely Model 48240, and Bless My Buttons 61957 (dam of WC CH Zeberdee 70099).

Belle of Spindletop 27124

By Beau Peavine and out of CH Belle Le Rose. WC. Dam of WC sire Grand Command 43843.

Burma Sapphire 24337

By Beau Peavine and out of Sweet Kitty Bellairs. First horse registered as bred by Yount. Placed third in the Three-Gaited Junior Stake in 1939 for Cape Grant.

CH Carolina Caroline 35691

By Beau Peavine and out of Carolina Moon. WC.

Chief of Texas 34090

By Beau Yount and out of Abie's Irish Rose (BHF). WC.

CH Edith Fable 28563

By American Ace and out of Bugle Anne 23837. WC. Third dam of CH Broadway News.

Fair Virginia 36267

By Beau Peavine and out of Lady Virginia. Second dam of WC CH Lilly Merrill, and third dam of WC CH That Special Flavor.

Lexington Leader 25359

By Bourbon Genius and out of CH Belle Le Rose. He sired only nine registered foals. He is the sire of Ruth Ann Peavine 56823, the second dam of WC Spirit's Gay Miss L E and CH Nobody's Business 12374.

Marie Bosace 36064

By Beau Peavine and out of Iowana. BHF Dam of BHF Lifetime Affair 79024 [dam of WC CH Valley Venture 70403 (photo *American Saddlebred* July 1988, 21), CH Roz 99011 (photo *American Saddlebred* July 1988, 14), CH Lifetime Memory and Bold Affair 72266, the grandsire of WC The Red Ferrari], WC CH Stonewall's Crescendo 44737 (sire of WGC CH Black Irish 69078 and CH Cavalleria), Our Anne Marie 63507, WC sire Stonewall's Beau Peavine 44736, and Sweet Deception 66313 (second dam of WC CH Callaway's Regatta 104224).

Miss Dixie Rebel 45334

By Beau Peavine and out of Abie's Irish Rose (BHF). WC.

Mona Kai 40752

By Beau Peavine and out of Lady Virginia. Dam of Ruth Ann Peavine 56823 who is the second dam of CH Nobody's Business 112374 [photo *American Saddlebred* (July 1992), 12], and WC Spirit's Gay Miss LE 95656.

Rita Le Rose 35692

BHF. By Beau Peavine and out of CH Belle Le Rose. WC. Dam of Anita Le Rose (dam of WC sire Jamestown and WC CH Chantilly Rose, dam of WGC CH Man on the Town), CH Starheart's Black Magic, and WC sire Starheart Peavine.

Roxie Highland of Spindletop 28510

By Beau Peavine and out of Roxie Highland. Dam of Spindletop Bourbon (sire of the second dam of WC CH A Touch of Champagne).

Sister Belle 30360

By Beau Peavine and out of CH Belle Le Rose. Third dam of WGC CH Sky Watch.

Sophia Van Cleve 43040

By Beau Peavine and out of Miss America. Dam of RWC Plainview's Sophia Van Cleve (photo in *National Horseman* (Dec. 1958). Plainview's Sophia produced Sophia's Sweet Conclusion, dam of CH Jennifer Logan.

Spindletop Denmark 37071

By Beau Yount and out of Roxie Highland of Spindletop. Foaled in 1954. The last horse bred by Yount. Sire of Hill Haven's Beauty (second dam of WC Worthy's Temptress).

Viola Ransom 25682

By Beau Peavine and out of Dahlia Dare. 1939 WC ASHB Futurity for two-year-olds. Dam of High Finance 29127, WC ASHB Futurity for two-year-olds.

Appendix 4

Note: Courtesy of the American Saddlebred Museum in Lexington, Kentucky, the following represents a partial listing of horses owned by Spindletop Farm, Lexington, Kentucky. For a description of the abbreviations used, consult the Glossary.

Abie's Baby 47302 (Bred by Yount)

BHF. By Beau Peavine and out of Abie's Irish Rose (BHF). Only foal of 1947 that the farm bred. Dam of eleven-time WC fine harness horse CH Colonel Boyle 637752 (sire of WC Step Lightly 73117, RWC CH Colonel Windsor 48340, and RWC CH Sherry My Sherry); WC sire Broadland's Kilarney 50136, Grassland's Specialty 61073 (second dam of CH Six Pence Event 68326); Grassland's Irish Rose 59200 (dam of CH First Look 49952); and also the dam of Rudmarvel 52993 who sired The Fraline 58496, dam of Hide-A-Way's Gypsy Josie 73955.

Abie's Irish Rose 17230

BHF. By American Born and out of Kathryn Haines. Used as a broodmare, first purchased by Spindletop in 1943, sold in 1948, bought back in 1951, and died at the farm. Abie's Irish Rose, a full sister to American Ace, won the KSF 1927 Yearling Stake. Dam of:

Abie's Baby 47302 (BHF) (Bred by Yount);
Abie's Genius 24057 (Bred by Yount);
Abie's Royal Irishman 25361 (Bred by Yount);
Chief of Texas 34090 (Bred by Yount), WC;
Miss Dixie Rebel 45334 (Bred by Yount), WC;
CH Ridgefield's Genius 22806. Sire of five-time WC CH I've Decided, WC City Hall, WC Genius Co-Ed, WC Hail to Genius (action photo in *American Saddlebred*, July 1995 issue, CH section);
and Rose Genius 25426. WC 1937 ASHB Futurity Weanling, WC Weanling Breeder's Stake, and 1938 Yearling Breeder's Stake.

Abie's Royal Irishman 25361 (Bred by Yount)

By Beau Peavine and out of Abie's Irish Rose (BHF). Sire of Miss Garbo, dam of WC CH Genius Society.

Ace's Patrician Lady 44004

By American Ace and out of RWC Star of Spindletop. 1949 WC A.S.H.B Futurity for Two-Year-Old Fine Harness, and dam of WC CH Broadland's Patrician Lady 71855.

American Ace 11025

By American Born and out of Kathryn Haines. Spindletop bought American Ace for $15,000 in 1937 as an outcross stallion, and then sold him in 1941 to Maryland Farm. He sired WGC CH Edith Fable 28563 (bred by Yount). When owned by Spindletop, American Ace also sired Pennypack's Pride (BHF), Ace's Beauty, Ace's Japanette, Ace's Charm, Ace O'Goshen, WC

Ace's Linda Lee, and Emerald's Sweet Sue.

Beau Le Rose Peavine 19601 (Bred by Yount)

By Beau Peavine and out of CH Belle Le Rose. Sire of RWC Five-Gaited Amateur Stallion/Gelding CH Dixie Aristocrat 37034, and RWC Five-Gaited Ladies Mare CH Rose's China Silk (photo *American Saddlebred*, Aug. 1988, 15).

Beau Peavine 12027

By Jean Val Jean and out of Fair Acres Vanity Fair. RWC in Fine Harness Stake in 1934 and fourth in the Five-Gaited Stallion Stake in the same year. WC Five-Gaited Stallion in 1936. His dam was a daughter of Lord Highland, sire of Roxie Highland. Foaled in May 1929, Beau Peavine was owned in name of Miles Frank Yount of Beaumont, Texas until his death. During the 1944 Lexington Junior League competition, Cape Grant exhibited Beau Peavine just before the three-gaited championship and was presented with a basket of flowers at the end. Spindletop began sponsoring the Three-Gaited Junior Stake that year with a challenge trophy in Beau Peavine's name, which still exists today. Sire of (partial list):

Abie's Baby (BHF) (Bred by Yount);
Beau Le Rose Peavine (Bred by Yount);
Beau of Grandview;
Beau Yount (Bred by Yount);
Burma Sapphire (Bred by Yount);
CH Carolina Caroline (Bred by Yount);
CH Fair Virginia (Bred by Yount);
CH Gay Gallant;
Grassland's Charm;
Marie Bosace (BHF) (Bred by Yount);
Miss Dixie Rebel (WC) (Bred by Yount);
Queen of Spindletop;
and Rita Le Rose (BHF) (Bred by Yount).

Beau Yount 22139 (Bred by Yount)

By Beau Peavine and out of CH Belle Le Rose (BHF). Winner at Lexington Junior League Show of two-year-old five-gaited competition. Sire of RWC Fine Harness horse Chief of Texas 34090 (dam was BHF Abie's Irish Rose), WC Lovely Model 48240, and Bless My Buttons 61957 (dam of WC CH Zeberdee).

CH Belle Le Rose 21495

BHF. By American Born and out of Anita Auburn. Purchased as broodmare in 1936. CH Belle Le Rose, a bay, was originally named Anita Moreland by her owner, Herbert Woolf, for his friend Bob Moreland. Her name was changed in 1932 after Woolf lost his temper when Moreland's horse, Dark Rex, beat Roxie. Belle was the first WGC for Earl Teater in 1934 under owner Ed Ballard. Spindletop purchased her for approximately $7,000 when Ballard was murdered in 1937 by a Detroit gangland figure in Hot Springs, Arkansas, and all of his horses were dispersed. She did not foal in 1937, but when bred to Beau Peavine, she produced a filly in 1938 named Belle of Spindletop. CH Belle Le Rose and Belle of Spindletop won the 1938 class for broodmares and foal at the KSF (American Saddlebred Museum has the trophy in its collection). In 1934 at the St. Louis National Show, she won the five-gaited championship, and her eventual stablemate, Beau Peavine was reserve. Dam of:

Beau Yount;
Lexington Leader;
Rita Le Rose (BHF);
and Sister Belle, second dam of Aries Golden Gift, the dam of WGC CH Sky Watch.

Belle of Spindletop 27124 (Bred by Yount)

By Beau Peavine and out of CH Belle Le Rose. WC in broodmare and foal class at the KSF in 1938 with her dam, CH Belle Le Rose. Broke records for sale of two-year-olds when at the Pendleton sale in St. Louis, she went for $5,500. Dam of WC sire Grand Command 043843.

Belle Rita 20132

By Red Harrison and out of Black Daisy Dare. Dam of 1935 WC Junior Five-Gaited Mare Belle Sarita. Photo of Belle Sarita in KSF Book. Dam of Father Crowe, sired by Beau Peavine. Father Crowe's photo in *1940 Blue Book*, 113.

Belle's Jacque 30585 (Bred by Yount)

By Jean Lafitte and out of Sister Belle. Sire of Blossom Time, a reserve winner at Rock Creek in 1958. See photo in *National Horseman*, July 1958 issue, 83.

Burma Sapphire 24337 (Bred by Yount)

By Beau Peavine and out of Sweet Kitty Bellairs. First horse registered as bred by Yount. Placed third in the Three-Gaited Junior Stake at the 1939 KSF for Cape Grant.

CH Carolina Caroline 35691

Multi WC ladies/amateur five-gaited mare – no foals.

Chief of Spindletop 12934

1936 WGC and WC Five-Gaited Gelding Competition winner. *Horse World Magazine* (Jan. 1949): Lon Cox said, "Cape Grant and George Lee bought for a very nominal amount a young chestnut stallion with a flaxen mane and tail from a farrier named George Lane at Raymore, MO. Had one foal before being gelded. Later, as a gelding, he became famous as Chief of Spindletop." Photo in *KSF* book.

Chief of Texas 34090 (Bred by Yount)

By Beau Peavine and out of Abie's Irish Rose. Foaled in 1949 and first registered as Big Deal. WC Kentucky County Fair Five-Gaited in 1956. RWGC Fine Harness in 1957. Photos found in 1956 and 1957 *KSF* book.

Dahlia Dare 11299

By Rex Peavine and out of Nancy Karsner. Dam of Viola Ransom 22682, 1939 WC ASHB Two-Year-Old Futurity.

Dancing Daffodil 21631

WC Junior Five-Gaited in 1937. Photo in *KSF* book with Cape Grant up.

CH Edith Fable 28563 (Bred by Yount).

By American Ace and out of Bugle Anne. Foaled in 1939. WGC Three-Gaited 1945 and 1946. Sold as a weanling to Welch Greenwell, then to Mrs. Lib Sharp, and then to Jean McLean Davis. Dam of The Fable 53936, the second dam of CH Broadway News.

Fairy Slippers 22209

By Kalarama Rex. Purchased by Yount as a broodmare. She won the Spindletop Trophy at the KSF as a two-year-old. Sold to Maryland Farm along with American Ace. Dam of Ace's Fairy 33160, the RWC three-year-old in the Three-Gaited Futurity in 1945. Third dam of My Brigadier, the sire of WC Prize Contender.

Father Crowe 16299

By Beau Peavine and out of Belle Rita. Photo of Father Crowe in *1940 Blue Book*, 113.

Jean Lafitte 16181

By Jean Valentino and out of Lillian Monroe. First named Valrodare; RWC in the 1937 KSF Yearling Stake. Sired Lafitte's Gay Scandal, winning walk-trot-mount belonging to Judy Kaufman in 1958 and 1959 (his photo is in *National Horseman*, Dec. 1958). Also sired Belle Lafitte, shown as Sweater Girl.

Kathryn Manion 44065

By Beau Peavine and out of Briney Breezes. Dam of CH Spellcaster; photo *American Saddlebred* (July 1988), 17.

Lady Virginia 27191
By Russell Lad and out of Eva Trotwood. 1933 World's Fair and American Royal winner. Won the under two class at Kansas City the year that Frank Yount died [1933], and was second to future stablemate Roxie Highland in the stake that same year. Dam of Fair Virginia 36267 (by Beau Peavine) who was bred by Yount. Fair Virginia produced BHF Ensign's Fair Virginia 55305, dam of WC CH Lilly Merrill 63856 (registered as Lily Merrill) and Flavor Taste 59807, dam of WC CH That Special Flavor. Photo of Lady Virginia in *1933 Blue Book*, 144.

Lexington Leader 25359 (Bred by Yount)
By Bourbon Genius and out of Belle Le Rose. He sired only nine registered foals. He is the sire of Ruth Ann Peavine 56823, the second dam of WC Spirit's Gay Miss L E and CH Nobody's Business 12374.

Marie Bosace 36064 (Bred by Yount)
By Beau Peavine and out of Iowana. BHF Dam of BHF Lifetime Affair 79024 [dam of WC CH Valley Venture 70403 (photo *American Saddlebred* July 1988, 21), CH Roz 99011 (photo *American Saddlebred* July 1988, 14), CH Lifetime Memory and Bold Affair 72266, sire of Golden Hit 86089, the sire of WC The Red Ferrari], WC CH Stonewall's Crescendo 44737 (sire of WGC CH Black Irish 69078 and CH Cavalleria), Our Anne Marie 63507, WC sire Stonewall's Beau Peavine 44736, and Sweet Deception 66313 (dam of WC CH Callaway's Regatta 104224). Also dam of CH Best Expression (photo *American Saddlebred* July 1991, 3).

Mildred Manion 51021
By Beau Peavine and out of Kalarama Heiress.

Miss Dixie Rebel 45334 (Bred by Yount)
By Beau Peavine and out of BHF Abie's Irish Rose. Foaled in 1938. ASHB Futurity Two-Year-Old Fine Harness, and WC Yearling Futurity and WC ASHB National Futurity weanling. Third dam of Sultry Sultana 117846 and second dam of Sultan's Americana 72563.

Mona Kai 40752 (Bred by Yount)
By Beau Peavine and out of Lady Virginia. Dam of Ruth Ann Peavine 56823, the second dam of CH Nobody's Business 112374 (photo *American Saddlebred* July 1992, 12) and WC Spirit's Gay Miss L E 95656.

Pennypack's Pride 25760
By American Ace and out of Jean Acker. BHF. Dam of RWC Dainty Daffodil, WC Fairview's Theme Song, and Oman's Anacacho Maytime, the dam of WGC CH Yorktown and WC CH Valley Lane's Tender Mist.

Queen of Spindletop 21606
First foal by Beau Peavine and out of Sweet Kitty Bellairs. Registered as Girl Friend. She was also shown under the name Queen of Cloverdale.

Rajah of Spindletop 15339
By Proctor's Red Light and out of I No. 1937 KSF third in the five-gaited championship for Cape Grant under name of Rajah of Spindletop. Shown as Man of Destiny by H. C. Barham. 1940 WC Five-Gaited Stallion.

Rita Le Rose 035692 (Bred by Yount)
BHF. By Beau Peavine and out of CH Belle Le Rose. Junior five-gaited champion that was sold as a three-year-old for $21,500. Dam of:

Anita Le Rose 061319, dam of Jamestown 59456 (sire of three-time WC The Uptown Girl, WGC Gimcrack 79439, WC Oh Dear! 104722, WC Champagne and Caviar 107937). Anita also produced CH Chantilly Rose (dam of WGC CH Man On The Town; photo *American Saddlebred,* July 1991, 17);

Rita's Delight 072555;

Rita's Star 044186;

CH Starheart's Black Magic;
Starheart's Challenger;
and Starheart Peavine 043077.

Rose of Spindletop 33412
By Beau Peavine. Dam of Indiana Peavine 38179, sire of three-time WC CH Glenview's Warlock, WC CH Star Scene, five-time WC CH Lilly Merrill, three-time WC CH Burning Tree's Brandywine, and successful sire CH Spellcaster 56559 (who was out of Kathryn Manion 44065).

CH Roxie Highland 15855
By Lord Highland and out of Nannie McDonald. 1934 WC Three-Gaited Over Two for Spindletop.

Roxie Highland of Spindletop 28510 (Bred by Yount)
By Beau Peavine and out of Roxie Highland. Dam of Spindletop Bourbon 34589 who sired Ledgewood Mai Tai and A Touch of Bourbon, second dam of CH Touch of Champagne 74569. Photo of Spindletop Bourbon in *National Horseman* (March 1957), 62 and 77.

Senator Crawford
Standardbred. 1936 WC Roadster to Wagon with Appt. and 1938 WC Roadster to Wagon Stake.

Sophia Van Cleve 43040 (Bred by Yount)
By Beau Peavine and out of Miss America. Dam of Plainview's Sophia Van Cleve, the RWC County Fair Three-Gaited (photo in *National Horseman*, Dec. 1958). Plainview's Sophia Van Cleve produced Sophia's Sweet Conclusion, dam of CH Jennifer Logan.

Spindletop Denmark 37071 (Bred by Yount)
By Beau Yount and out of Roxie Highland of Spindletop. Foaled in 1954. The last horse bred by Yount.

Star of Spindletop 25647 (Bred by Yount)
By Beau Peavine and out of Sweet Kitty Bellairs. Dam of RWC Ace's Patrician Lady (by American Ace), and second dam of WC Broadland's Patrician Lady. Star is also the dam of Ace's Gay Reflection 34491 (see *Tattersalls* Nov. 1957, hip number 69).

WC Susie Key 40753
By Beau Peavine and out of Rousalka.

Sweet Kitty Bellairs 14093
First horse purchased by Pansy Yount at Spindletop in Lexington. Dam of Queen of Spindletop, Chief of Manitou, Burma Sapphire, and Star of Spindletop.

Tradewind
One of the first horses purchased by Frank Yount in Beaumont. First time shown in Florida, won four times in the Three-Gaited Division. See *Blue Book 1933*, 127.

Viola Ransom 25682 (Bred by Yount)
By Beau Peavine and out of Dahlia Dare. WC. Dam of WC High Finance 29127.

Appendix 5

Note: Besides Miss Dixie Rebel and the Coach and Four, represented by Waltz Time, Dinner Dance, Curtain Call, and Stage Hand, twenty-eight other horses owned by Spindletop were sold at the July 1952 dispersal.

Name of Horse	Sold For	Bought By
Abie's Baby	$ 1,000	Ike Lanier of Danville, KY
Abie's Royal Irishman	5,000	G. Koenig of Philadelphia, PA
Chief of Texas	4,500	Louis Greenspon of St. Louis, MO
Ducky West	100	H. S. Whittenburg of Louisville, KY
Floy Watkins	450	Ike Lanier of Danville, KY
Grassland's Charm	1,600	T. D. Adams of Indianapolis, IN
Inky Imp	1,600	H. M. Boock of Logan, OH
Kalarama Kathleen	1,150	W. W. Evans of Jeffersontown, KY
Kathryn Manion	1,000	T. D. Adams of Indianapolis, IN
Lady Lafitte	650	George Gwinn of Danville, KY
Lexington Leader	4,500	Robert C. Beatty of Washington, PA
Little Rose Delight	1,000	Elizabeth Kittell of Nashville, TN
Marie Bosace	800	Robert E. Boettcher of Springfield, OH
Mildred Manion	1,450	Lewis C. Tierney of Charleston, WV
Miss Monroe	1,400	Ed Malerick of Lincoln, IL
Mona Kai	300	Dr. G. V. Howard of New Richmond, OH
Nancy's Beau	2,700	Louis Greenspon of St. Louis, MO
Peggy Odom	300	J. Howard King of Lexington, KY
Rose of Spindletop	300	George Gwinn of Danville, KY
Roxie Lafitte	850	J. Howard King of Lexington, KY
Silver Masterpiece	1,400	Thomas Murphy of Danville, KY
Sissy Peavine	150	F. H. Eddy of Lexington, KY
Sophie Van Cleve	800	R. C. Tway of Louisville, KY
Spindletop Bourbon	150	James E. Krueger of Cleveland, OH
Spindletop Ike	150	R. L. Mansell of Medina, OH
Spindletop Princess	300	Lee B. Thomas of Anchorage, KY
Susie Kettman	400	George Gwinn of Danville, KY
The Virginia Princess	400	Eli Long of Delaware, OH

Appendix 6

Note: The following represents a transcription of the divorce decree of William Capers Grant v. Pansy M. Grant located at the Jefferson County Courthouse in Beaumont, Texas. For historical presentation purposes, the authors have made every effort possible to retain the integrity, terminology, grammar, and abbreviations of the original, including misspellings and omissions.

Entered Dec. 17, 1959	NO. 49117-C	
W. C. GRANT	)	IN THE DISTRICT COURT OF
VS.	)	JEFFERSON COUNTY, TEXAS
PANSY M. GRANT	)	136TH JUDICIAL DISTRICT

DECREE

On the 26 day of October 1959, came of, to be heard the above entitled and numbered cause wherein, W. C. Grant is Plaintiff and Cross-Defendant, and Pansy M. Grant is Defendant and Cross-Plaintiff; and came the said parties, W. C. Grant, Plaintiff and Cross-Defendant, and Pansy M. Grant, Defendant and Cross-Plaintiff, and announced ready for trial; and came a jury of twelve good and lawful men, who, being duly impaneled and sworn and having heard the pleading, the evidence and the argument of counsel, on their oaths and in response to the special issues, definitions and explanatory instructions submitted to them by the Court, on the 17th day of November 1959, make the following respective findings:

SPECIAL ISSUE NO. 1

Do you find from a preponderance of the evidence that the acts or conduct of the defendant, Pansy M. Grant, toward the Plaintiff, W. C. Grant, if any constituted such excesses, cruel treatment or outrages of such a nature as to render their further living together as husband and wife is supportable?

You will answer "We do" or "We do not"

Answer:"We do not."

SPECIAL ISSUE NO. 2

Do you find from a preponderance of the evidence that the acts or conduct, if any, of W. C. Grant toward Pansy M. Grant constituted such excesses, cruel treatment or outrages of such a nature as to render their further living together as husband and wife insupportable, as that term is defined in this charge?

You will answer "We do" or "We do not".

Answer, "We do."

And the Court having adopted the findings of the jury as to such Special Issue Nos. 1 and 2, it is ORDERED, ADJUDGED and DECREED by the Court that the prayer and request of the

Plaintiff, W. C. Grant, for a divorce from the Defendant, Pansy M. Grant, be and it is hereby denied; and it is further ORDERED, ADJUDGED and DECREED by the Court that the Cross-Action of the Defendant, Pansy M. Grant, for a divorce from the Cross-Defendant, W. C. Grant, be granted and that upon the prayer and request of Cross-Plaintiff, Pansy M. Grant, the bonds of matrimony heretofore existing between Cross-Defendant, W. C. Grant, and Cross-Plaintiff, Pansy M. Grant, be and they are hereby dissolved, and the Cross-Plaintiff, Pansy M. Grant, is granted a divorce from the Cross-Defendant, W. C. Grant.

And it further appearing to the Court that the Cross-Plaintiff, Pansy M. Grant has requested that her former name of "Pansy Merritt Yount" be restored; and the Court having found that such should be done!

It is therefore ORDERED, ADJUDGED and DECREED by the Court that the Cross-Plaintiff, Pansy M. Grant, be and she is hereby restored her former last name of "Yount" so that hereafter she will be legally known as and called by the name of "Pansy Merritt Yount", although in this Decree she is hereinafter referred to as "Pansy M. Grant", such being the name under which she appears of record in the pleadings herein.

And it further appearing to the Court, and the Court having found, under the undisputed evidence, that these certain properties hereinafter described, each and all, constitute and are the separate property and estate of the Defendant and Cross-Plaintiff, Pansy M. Grant, to-wit:

1. Lots 1 to 6, inclusive, Block 10, Calder Addition to the City of Beaumont, Texas, as more particularly described in Item 1 of Paragraph 11 of defendant and cross-plaintiff's first amended answer filed herein.

2. All of Block 30, Calder Addition to the City of Beaumont, according to the plat of said addition, and more particularly described in Item 2 of Paragraph 11 of defendant and cross-plaintiff's first amended answer filed herein.

3. All of that certain 400 acres of land, more or less, out of and a part of the A. Houston League in Jefferson County, Texas, and more particularly described in Item 3 of Paragraph 11 of Defendant and cross-plaintiff's first amended answer filed herein.

4. All of that certain 786 acres of land, more or less, in Jefferson County, Texas, and being a part of the E. Raines Survey, as more particularly described in Item 3 of Paragraph 11 of defendant and cross-plaintiff's first amended answer filed herein.

5. All of Lots 39, 41, 42, 51, 52 and 40 feet x 141.5 feet off the West side of Lot 46, of the Oakland Addition to the Town of Sour Lake, Texas, all part of the Ambrose Merchant 24-acre tract in the Stephen Jackson league, Hardin County, Texas, and a 2-acre tract out of the M. Merchant 24 acre tract in the Stephen Jackson League, more fully described in a deed recorded in Vol. 168, page 312 of the Deed Records of Hardin County, Texas, as more particularly described in Item 5 of Paragraph 11 of defendant and cross-plaintiff's first amended answer and Paragraph 1 of her trial amendment filed herein.

6. All of those certain cemetery lots in Magnolia Cemetery in Beaumont, Texas, registered in the name of M. F. Yount, Mrs. M. F. Yount, or Mrs. Pansy Yount, Independent Executrix of the Estate of M. F. Yount, being Lots 6 and 7, Section ?, and Lots 65, 66, 79, 80, 81, 94 and 95, Section P, according to the Map of Magnolia Cemetery, and being the same cemetery lots referred to and described in Item 8, Paragraph 11 of defendant and cross-plaintiff's first amended answer and Paragraph 2 of her trial amendment filed herein.

7. All those certain royalties on minerals reserved (a) in Deed, Pansy Yount, Independent Exec., Estate M. F. Yount, to W. B. Mabry, dated 8/30/34, recorded Vol. 194, p. 454, Deed Records, Liberty County (Exhibit D-28); and (b) in Partition Deed, Pansy Yount, Indiv. and Exec. Estate M. F. Yount, Dec'd, and Mildred Yount Manion, dated 6/6/44, recorded Vol 590, p. 69, Deed Records, Jefferson County (Exhibit D-9).

10. All those certain Annuity contracts as follows, to-wit:

(1) Kansas City Life Insurance Co., Policy 69501 October 31, 1935.
(2) Kansas City Life Insurance Co., Policy 69502 October 31, 1935.
(3) New York Life Insurance Company, Policy 305669 February 14, 1936.
(4) Travelers Insurance Company, Policy 1917700 February 14, 1936
(5) Southwestern Life Insurance Co., Policy 427502 May 21, 1940.
(6) Equitable Life Insurance Co., Policy 10708535 July 28, 1940.
(7) John Hancock Mutual Life Ins. Co., Policy 062514 June 21, 1940.

And being the Annuity Contracts set forth in Paragraph 13 of defendant and cross-plaintiff's first amended answer filed herein.

11. All of those certain ten (10) promissory vendor's lien notes of date the 24th day of February, 1959, executed by the Kentucky Research Foundation, payable to the order of Mrs. Pansy M. Grant, nine (9) of said notes, numbered 1 to 9, inclusive, each for the amount of $75,000.00, maturing serially on or before the year from date as indicated by the number of the note, bearing interest at the rate of 3% per annum from date until paid, and one note, being No. 10, in the sum of $25,000.00 with interest thereon at the rate of 3% per annum; said notes having been given in part payment for real properties (1065.897 acres) situated in Fayette County, Kentucky, conveyed by this defendant, Pansy M. Grant, joined proforma by her husband, W. C. Grant, to the Kentucky Research Foundation by deed of date February 24, 1959;

17. Eighteen Hundred and Sixty-three (1863) shares of stock in the First National Bank of Beaumont, Texas, now registered in the name of Pansy M. Grant.

20. Thirteen Thousand Two Hundred and Eighty (13,280) shares of stock in Norvell-Wilder Supply Company, now registered in the name of Pansy M. Grant.

22. Seventy-five (75) shares of stock of Standard Brands, Inc., registered in the name of Pansy M. Grant.

23. Thirty-four Thousand Three Hundred Eight & 62/100 (34,308.62) shares of stock in Texas Corporation (formerly The Texas Company) registered in the name of Pansy M. Grant.

25. Thirteen Hundred Seventy-two (1,372) shares of stock in the Tyrrell Hardware Company registered in the name of Pansy M. Grant.

27. The following jewelry, which was deposited in Lock Box 818 listed in the inventory marked P-3, and identified by the witness, J. A. Fischer, and being the following items numbered as set forty in said inventory and as described by said witness, J. A. Fischer, to-wit:

(8) Two clips each containing one emerald and numerous diamonds and being a pear-shaped emerald and diamond clip brooch combination containing 2 pear-shaped emeralds, 6 square cut diamonds, 126 baguettes diamonds, approximately 373 round diamonds.

(9) Ring with large blue stone and diamonds on either side encased in blue box marked H. S. Fischer, Inc. and being a lady's faceted sapphire ring set in platinum mounting, weight 57.50 carats, 4 fancy cut diamonds in mounting.

(10) Large solitaire diamond ring encased in blue box from Pohndorf's, Denver, Colorado, and being a lady's round diamond ring platinum mounting approximate weight 10-1/2 carats, 46 round diamonds in mounting.

(11) One large solitaire marquise shaped diamond ring in black box and being lady's marquise diamond ring, weight 11/66 carats, platinum mounting, contains 2 marquise diamonds.

(13) Large round diamond ring with baguettes on either side, in blue box from Linz, Dallas, and being round diamond ring, weight approximately 25 carats (premier).

(14) Large square shaped emerald ring with truncated diamonds on either side in blue box from W. S. Fischer, Inc. and being lady's faceted green emerald ring, weight 25.85 carats, platinum mounting contains 2 fancy cut diamonds.

(18) Dinner ring with high rounded light blue stone surrounded by diamonds from H. S. Fischer, Inc. (in rose colored box) and being lady's star sapphire ring, high dome, Approx. weight

51-1/2 carats, platinum mounting contains 12 baguette diamonds, 60 round diamonds.

(19) Ring with emerald cut diamond and emerald cut emerald side by side with baguettes on either side from H. S. Fischer, Inc. (in rose colored box) and being lady's 2-stone emerald cut diamond & green emerald ring set in platinum. Emerald cut diamond weight 9.29 carats. Green emerald weight 9.45 carats. 2 baguettes .74 carats.

(20) Marquise shaped diamond ring with small diamonds on either side in blue velvet box and being lady's black marquise diamond ring, weight 3.78, platinum mounting, contains (?) round diamonds.

(22) Pearl and diamond eardrops from Victor Bo(?) Co., Lexington, Ky. (in blue box) and being pair of diamond and pearl drop earrings containing 2 round oriental pearls, triangular diamonds, 4 square cut diamonds, 12 baguette diamonds and 52 round diamonds.

(26) Bracelet with square blue stones and diamonds encircling in box marked "?" (in handwriting) and being diamond & sapphire bracelet (?) 2 round diamonds, 4(?) (?) sapphires.

(29) Large round diamond in filigree setting in blue box from Victor (?) Co., Lexington, Ky. and being lady's round diamond ring approximate weight 4 carats, no diamonds in mounting.

(40)(?) drops, wish diamonds and light. blue sapphire in blue box from M. S. Fischer and being pair of star sapphire diamond drop earrings in platinum, 2 star sapphires, 34 baguette diamonds, 12 fancy cut diamonds, 2 half moon diamonds, 6 marquise diamonds, 36 round diamonds.

(44) Diamond bracelet, baguettes, marquise and round shaped diamonds, in blue box from H. S. Fischer, and being marquise diamond and platinum bracelet, 5 marquise diamonds through center, 22 round diamonds, 248 baguette diamonds.

(46) Single-strand pearl necklace with three diamonds in catch (clip) and being pearl necklace containing 78 oriental pearls weighing approximately 672 grams diamond clasp contains 3 large round diamonds and 2 small round diamonds.

(47) Set of 4-strand pearl necklace (one strand detached at one end) and 4-strand pearl bracelet with diamonds from J. A. Fischer, New York, in blue leather case, and being 3 strand cultured pearl necklace with diamond & cultured pearl clasp. Extra pearls from the original set and 4 strand pearl & diamond bracelet.

(48) Bracelet with dark blue stones and diamond from H. S. Fischer (blue case), and being diamond end cut sapphire bracelet in platinum, 70 cut sapphires through center, 300 round diamonds, approx.

(49) Diamond pendent on diamond chain from Black, Starr & Frost Gornham, Inc., New York, and being diamond & platinum lorgnette with diamond chain. Lorgnette contains 3 large round diamonds in center, 4 triangular diamonds, 62 baguette diamonds, 56 small round diamonds. Chain contains 83 round diamonds.

(51) Long earrings with diamonds, and blue and green round stones. In blue box from H. S. Fisher, Inc. and being pair of diamond sapphire & emerald drop earrings in platinum, 48 round diamonds, 22 baguette diamonds, 8 (?) sapphires, 8 (?) emeralds.

(56) Eardrops with green stones and diamonds and diamond brooch in rectangular shape with safety clip, both in chamois bag in white box from P. Edw. Villerinot, Lexington, and being emerald & diamond eardrop containing 2 pear shaped emeralds, 2 (?) emeralds, approx. 52 round diamonds, and diamond & platinum has brooch containing 1 marquise diamond in center, 20 baguette diamonds, approximately 214 round diamonds.

(57) Earrings with large yellow-colored stone and diamonds in black box marked Mauboussin, New York, and being pair of marquise diamond drop earrings containing in the pair 2 yellow marquise diamonds approx. 17 carats, 108 round diamonds.

(61) Diamond eardrops in white box from Pohndorf's Denver, Colo., and being pair dia-

mond & platinum drop earrings containing 114 small round diamonds.

(62) Lady's diamond wrist watch in blue box from Victor (?) Co., Lexington, and being lady's diamond & platinum mesh bracelet watch, 17 Jewel Clycine movement, 6 baguette diamonds, 217 round diamonds.

(64) Emerald and diamond bracelet in blue box from H. S. Fischer, Inc., and being faceted emerald & diamond bracelet containing 100 round diamonds, (?)5 baguette diamonds, 42 faceted emeralds, 6 fancy cut emerald.

(65) Sapphire and diamond bracelet containing 5 matched star sapphires, (?) baguette diamonds, approx. 100 round diamonds.

Also the following articles of jewelry identified by the witness, J. A. Fischer, in
The home in Caldwood, to-wit:

(a) Lady's star sapphire ring

(b) A diamond horse

(c) A star sapphire necklace

(31) All of the furniture, furnishings, fixtures, silver and personal property of every kind and character situated in the premises described as Lots 9, 10, 11, 12 and 13, Block 3, of the Caldwood Addition to the City of Beaumont, Jefferson County, Texas, described in the inventory and as marked by the witness, Mildred Manion, in the copy of said inventory received as evidence as Exhibit D-40, such items being marked by the witness with the letter "D".

(35) All furniture, fixtures, furnishings and equipment in the Mildred Apartments and Arcade listed on Lots 1, 2, 3, 4, 5 and 6, Block 10, of the Calder Addition to the City of Beaumont, Jefferson County, Texas, with the exception of the items listed and identified by the witness, Geisendorff, in Exhibit D-44.

And the jury having special issue submitted to them by the Court concerning the hereinafter described items of real and personal property, to-wit:

1. Home in Caldwood Addition, Jefferson County, Texas, being Lots 9 to 13, inclusive, Block 3, of the Caldwood Addition to the City of Beaumont, Jefferson County, Texas, and being the property purchased in Caldwood on February 7, 1956. (Special Issue No. 3)

And the jury having special issues submitted it by the Court concerning the hereinafter described items of real and personal property, to-wit:

(1) Cemetery lots purchased in September, 1957, and being lots 57, 58, 73, 82, 83 and 84, in Section 16, according to the map of Magnolia Cemetery, Jefferson County, Texas.
(Special Issue No. 7)

(2)Two Hundred (200) shares of stock in General Motors Corporation evidenced by certificates numbers H563-770 and H563-771, registered in the name of Pansy M. Grant.
(Special Issue No. 13)

(3)Thirteen Hundred (1,300) shares of stock in General Motors Corporation, evidenced by Certificates numbered H298-680 to H298-691 inclusive, and H298-700, registered in the name of Pansy M. Grant.
(Special Issue No. 15)

And it is further appearing to the Court, and the Court having found under the undisputed evidence, that certain shares of the capital stock of General Motors Corporation, hereinafter described, were by stock dividends and/or stock splits added to certain shares of stock, said shares of stock as added by stock dividends being as follows:

Four Hundred Twenty-nine (429) shares of the capital stock of General Motors Corporation issued as a stock split and based upon shares found by the Jury in answer to special Issues Nos. 13 and 15 to be community property of the Plaintiff, W. C. Grant, and Defendant, Pansy M. Grant.

And it further appearing to the Court and the Court having found from admissions in the pleadings and under the undisputed evidence that all contents of the Safety Deposit box No. 2668 in the name of W. Cape Grant, in the First National Bank of Beaumont, constitute and are the separate property and estate of the Plaintiff and Cross-Defendant, W. C. Grant.

And the Court being of the opinion that the finds of the Jury in special issue Nos. 3 though 21 be, in all things, set aside, the same are hereby set aside and are not binding upon the Court; and the Court being of the further opinion that the relief hereinafter awarded is sustained by the record and should be granted.

And, further, that the division of the estate of the parties hereinafter decreed is fair, just and equitable, with due regard to the rights of the respective parties, their respective ages, physical conditions and earning capacity, it is accordingly

ORDERED, ADJUDGED AND DECREED that the Plaintiff and Cross-Defendant, W. C. Grant, be awarded, and there is hereby set aside to him, to be hereafter owned and held by him absolutely, free and clear of all claims, rights, title or interest of the Defendant and Cross-Plaintiff, Pansy M. Grant, the following items of property comprising a part of the estate of the parties, to-wit.

(1) Four Thousand (4,000) shares of the capital stock of TEXACO, INC., a corporation, being a part of the total shares of the capital stock of said corporation evidenced by certificate issued in the name of Pansy M. Grant;

(2) Three Thousand Two Hundred (3,200) shares of the capital stock of GENERAL MOTORS CORPORATION, a corporation, being a part of the capital stock of said corporation evidenced by certificates issued in he name of Pansy M. Grant;

(3) Two Thousand (2,000) shares of the capital stock of NORVELL-WILDER SUPPLY COMPANY, a corporation, being a part of the total shares of the capital stock of said corporation evidenced by certificates issued in the name of Pansy M. Grant;

(4) A sum of money equal to one-fourth (1/4th) of the dividends received by the said Pansy M. Grant from the 29th day of June, 1959, to the date of this judgment and decree by reason of ownership of the shares of capital stock mentioned in the temporary order of this Court in this cause in regard to the division of dividends as provided in said order, less such sums as have been paid by the said Pansy M. Grant to the said W. C. Grant in accordance with said order dated the 29th day of June, 1959;

(5) All motor vehicles, trailers, boats, jewelry, personal wearing apparel, furniture, furnishings and other person property in the possession of the said W. C. Grant on this date.

(6) All bank accounts in the name of W. C. Grant, the same being a checking account in said party's name with the American National Bank of Beaumont under the name of Cape Grant, and a checking account in said party's name with the Prentiss County Home Bank of Booneville, Mississippi;

(7) All contents of Safety Deposit Box No. 2668, in the name of W. Cape Grant, in the First National Bank of Beaumont, Texas; and it is further

ORDERED, ADJUDGED AND DECREED that all other property of the parties owned, held, claimed by said parties on the date of this judgment and decree, whether real, personal or mixed, corporeal or incorporeal, and whether heretofore the same has constituted community or separate property of the parties, whether or not hereinabove listed, except the property specifically described and enumerated above as being awarded to the said W. C. Grant, be and the same is hereby awarded to the said Pansy M. Grant, in fee simple and absolutely, free and clear of any and all claims, rights, titles and interests of the said W. C. Grand in and to the same ; and it is further

ORDERED, ADJUDGED AND DECREED that, the Court having heretofore, by said order dated the 29th day of June 1959, in this cause, set aside for the use and benefit of the parties hereto, one-fourth only of a part of the community income received by said parties after the date of said order, and having provided that all other community income received by the parties should be retained and conserved for the purpose of paying community obligations (?) at the time of final judgment herein, and all costs of this proceeding, save and except that item of cost pertaining to the taking of the inventory of furniture and furnishings in the residence in Caldwood, which shall be paid fifty (50) percent by each party hereto, shall be paid out of such community funds received and retained by the said Pansy M. Grant from the date of the filing of this suit to the date hereof, and any balance remaining shall be the sole and separate funds of said party.

The parties hereto are ORDERED and directed by the Court to execute and deliver any and all instruments of transfer, assignment or releases necessary and proper to effectuate the division of the estate of the parties hereinabove ordered, adjudged and decreed to be made.

SIGNED, RENDERED, ENTERED AND FILED this 17th day of December, A. D. 1959.

HAROLD R. CLAYTON
JUDGE PRESIDING

To which action, order and ruling of the Court is making said findings and entering said judgment, as hereinabove set forth, and insofar as said action, order and rulings, findings and judgment are adverse to the claims and contentions of the Plaintiff, W. C. Grant, the (?); and to which action, order and ruling of the Court in making said findings and entering said judgment, as hereinabove set forth, and insofar as said action, order, ruling, findings and judgment are contrary to, and in conflict with the verdict of the Jury, and adverse to the claims and contentions of Defendant, Pansy M. Grant, the said Defendant, Pansy M. Grant, then and there, in open court, excepted and is allowed her exception.

SIGNED AND ENTERED this 17th day of December, A. D. 1959.

HAROLD R. CLAYTON
JUDGE PRESIDING

Appendix 7

Note: The following represents a transcription of the Will and associated probate documents of W. Cape Grant located at the Hill County Courthouse in Hillsboro, Texas. For historical presentation purposes, the authors have made every effort possible to retain the integrity, terminology, grammar, and abbreviations of the original, including misspellings and omissions.

FILED JUNE 25, 1962
GLENN MORGAN, Clerk County Court,
Hill County, Texas

WILL
Page 1
February 9, 1962
W. Cape Grant
Mildred Building
P. O. Box 2028
Beaumont, Texas

THE STATE OF TEXAS COUNTY OF JEFFERSON

Know all men by these presents that I, W. C. Grant of the County of Jefferson and State of Texas, being of sound mind and memory and desiring to so provide for the disposition of my estate that there may be no confusion concerning the same after my death, do hereby make declare and publish this my last will and testament, here by revoking all wills, codicils and or letters of authority by me theretofore made.

I will and direct that at the time of my death, I be given a Christianlike funeral of extreme modesity and at a very nominal cost, and that my just debts including funeral expenses and expenses of my last sickness be paid by my Executrix hereinafter appointed, as soon after my death as can conveniently be done without the unnecessary sacrifice of any of the properties of my estate.

After the payment of my just debts, funeral expenses, and expenses of my last sickness I will, give and bequest unto my beloved first wife, Nola E. Grant, now residing at 1302 Lorrain, Austin, Texas, all cash, jewelry, automobiles, trailers, boats, all proceeds from property settlement now in litigation save one fourth of the latter which is to be paid to W. G. Walley, my attorney in this litigation and I am not further obligated in this matter to any one including Everitt B. Lord and Jack R. King, both of whom were hired by W. G. Walley with the distinct understanding he would pay for any service rendered by these out of his one-fourth of the recovery.

There is also an I. O. U. for ten thousand dollars signed by W. G. Walley that is in my attache brief case the combination to which is 608 this was a cash loan made by me to W. G. Walley with the understanding he would repay me in cash or that it would be deducted from the amount recovered in the lawsuit Grants VS Grant. In the event of no recovery his fee of $5000.00 was piad by me at the time suit was filed. What is meant is simply this $10,000.00 is to be deducted from one fourth of the recovery or W. G. Walley owes my estate the sum of $10,000.00.

I recommend to my executrix that she give each of our three sons one thousand dollars each. And to my beloved sister Kathryn Hunt of Dallas the sum of Two thousand dollars in loving memory of her gracious care and love to our Mother in her last years.

To my wonderful and dear friend Walter C. Davis of Reinzi, Mississippi, Route 2, I will and bequeath my pair of Liewellen Setters imported from England and any and all of their direct off-spring along with the English Setter Spindletop Wing Commander after the following condition is finished that Walter C. Davis will dispose of all other Setters or pointers owned by me as quickly as possible, keeping one half the proceeds therefore for himself and paying over to my executrix Nola E. Grant, the remaining half with no other expense to my estate. This will shall give Nola E. Grant, Full authority to sign any transfer, or to register any young dogs I might have on hand being at all times guided by the instructions of my good friend (Bill) W. H. Brown, Editor of the American Field Publishing Co., 222 West Adams St., Chicago 6, Illinois.

For the record as of this date:

My 1959 Ford Station Wagon, personal effect, some jewelry and the above mentioned

I. O. U. will be found at Hilltop Kennels, W. C. Davis place Reinzi Rouge 2, Miss. Also my 56 foot Hensley High style house trailer. My 1958 Thunderbird is at Broadway Filling Station corner Broadway & Mariposa, Bmt. 2 Lyman Coats Trailers Motors and some other equipment are at Burns outboard Motors 4711 Port Arthur Rd. Beaumont, Texas.

In House trailer in attache brief case mentioned above will be found keys to American National Bk of Beaumont.

In this box will be found jewelry and other personal items also a deed to cemetery lot in Dallas where I wish to be buried. I expect to ask my beloved first wife Nola E. Grant to be buried with me on this lot and it is my considered desire that she do so, and that no other shall ever be buried on this lot.

I hereby nominate and constitute my beloved Nola E. Grant, sole executrix of this my last will and testament and direct that no bond or other form of security be required of her as such and that the courts take no further action hereon than to admit this will to probate and record, and to cause the return of an inventory, appraisement and list of claims as provided by law.

W. C. (Cape) Grant

May 28th, 1960

FILED June 14, 1962

GLENN MORGAN, Clerk County Court

Hill County, Texas

APPLICATION

THE STATE OF TEXAS) IN THE ESTATE OF

COUNTY OF HILL) NO. 7337 WILLIAM CAPERS

GRANT DECEASED

TO THE HONORABLE JUDGE OF THE COUNTY COURT OF HILL COUNTY, TEXAS.

Now comes Nola E. Grant, as applicant and shows to the court.

1.

That she resides and is domiciled in Dallas County, Texas.

2.

That William Capers Grant died at the age of 63 years on the 28th day of May 1962, at Hillsboro in the County of Hill in the State of Texas.

3.

That at the time of his death the said William Capers Grant resided and had his domicile in the County of Hill aforesaid.

4.

That at the time of the death of William Capers Grant he was seized and possessed of personal property of the probable value of in excess of $25,000.00 consisting of Jewelry and common stock in various corporations.

5.

William Capers Grant left a written will duly executed when he was 62 years of age and of sound mind and herewith filed in which your applicant was appointed executrix and which will was wholly in the handwriting of the testator.

6.

No child was adopted or born to the decedent after the making of the will.

7.

The heirs and devisees of William Capers Grant are as follows:

(1) Nola E. Grant, his surviving widow who resides in Dallas County, Texas.

(2) Silas W. Grant, married to Betty Grant, a son, of the decedent, residents of Hillsboro, Texas.

(3) Miles Frank Grant, a son of the decedent, a single man over 21 years of age, a resident of Dallas Texas, now in the armed forces.

(4) William Capers Grant III a son of the decedent, married to LaVera Grant, who resides in London, England.

(5) Kathryn Hunt, wife of Don Hunt, sister of decedent a resident of Dallas, Texas.

(6) Walter C. Davis, marital status unknown, a friend of decedent and a resident of Reinzi, Route 2, Mississippi.

8.

Your applicant the executrix named in such will is qualified and is not disqualified by law to accept letters testamentary.

9.

The decedent was first married to Nola E. Grant the applicant in the year 1918 and was divorced from Nola E. Grant in about 1936. Thereafter he married Pansy M. Grant and was divorced from her on December 17, 1959. Decedent did not remarry until May 28, 1962 at which time he remarried Nola E. Grant his first wife.

Wherefore your applicant prays that citation be issued as required by law, that said will be admitted to probate, that letters testamentary be issued to your applicant, and that such other and further orders be made as to the court may seem proper.

MARTIN & MARTIN
Attorneys for Applicant
62 West Elm
Hillsboro, Texas
By: Wm. B. Martin

ORDER

ESTATE OF) IN THE COUNTY COURT OF
WILLIAM CAPERS GRANT) NO. 7337 HILL COUNTY, TEXAS
DECEASED)

On this the 31st day of August, 1962, came on to be considered the application of Mrs. Nola E. Grant, Independent Executrix of the last will and estate of William Capers Grant, Deceased, also know as W. C. (Cape) Grant, in the above entitled and numbered cause, for an order permitting the distribution and transfer of 5510 shares of Stock in Texaco, Inc., to Mrs. Nola E. Grant, or her assigns, and the Court having found that the administration on the Estate of

William Capers Grant is an independent administration and that the Executrix has invoked the jurisdiction of the Court for the specific purpose of, securing an order authorzing the transfer and assignment of the said stock to Mrs. Nola E. Grant, and the Court having found, after hearing all of the evidence both for and against the said application, that the same should be granted and that the transfer agent for the stock of Texaco, Inc., should be authorized to transfer the same to Mrs. Nola E. Grant, who is the beneficiary of the same under the terms of the will of William Capers Grant.

IT IS THEREFORE ORDERED, ADJUDGED AND DECREED by the Court that the distribution of 5510 shares of stock in Texaco, In., shall be effected and that the same shall be transferred and assigned to Mrs. Nola E. Grant, the beneficiary of the same, or to her of said will of the Estate of said William Capers Grant.

Nola E. Grant

SWORN TO AND SUBSCRIBED by the said Nola E. Grant, before me this 25th day of June 1962, to certify which witness my hand and seal of office.

GLENN MORGAN, County Clerk
Hill County, Texas
By Esther Blanchard, Deputy

SEAL
FILED JUNE 25, 1962
GLENN MORGAN, Clerk County Court,
Hill County, Texas

ORDER FIXING INHERITANCE TAX

IN THE MATTER OF THE ESTATE OF) HILL COUNTY, STATE OF TEXAS
)
W. C. GRANT, DECEASED) TRANSFER TAX

On this 29 day of August, 1963, came on to be considered the matter of determining the cash value of said estate and the amount of inheritance tax to which the same is liable and after having heard testimony and considered the inventory and the report of appraisement, and after having heard all the parties desiring to be heard, and upon the whole record, and being fully advised.

FIND AND DETERMINE that said deceased died on the 28th day of May, 1962; and that said estate has been appraised at its actual market value as provided by law.

It is therefore ordered that the said report of appraisement, together with the recommendations for taxation and exemption by said appraisers, be and the same is hereby approved and

It is further ordered, upon said report that the cash value of the several successions, estates, annuities, gifts, transfers, appointments, interest, etc, subject to taxation or exemption by reason of the death of said decedent under the laws of this State and the tax to which the same are severally liable, be and the same are hereby assessed and fixed as follows:

Beneficiary and Relationship of Decedent	Appraised actual market value	Statutory exemption	Taxable cash value	Rate	Fixed Tax
Nola E. Grant, Wife	377,959.75	25,000.00	352,959.75	1-4%	11,368.39
Silas W. Grant, Son	44,226.87	25,000.00	19,226.87	1%	192.27

Total tax assessed: $11,560.66

Wherefore, it is ordered that the administrator (executor) be and he is hereby authorized and directed to pay and deliver forthwith to the Comptroller of Public Accounts the sum of $11,560.66, as and for inheritance tax to which said heirs, legatees or devisees are liable and charge the same to the respective shares as taxes herein.

It is further ordered that said appraisers' compensation and expense incurred be fixed at no dollars.

J. Howard English
County Judge, Hill County, Texas

Examined and approved this the 27th day of August, 1963

Robert S. Calvert
State Comptroller

STATE SEAL

No. 54357 ORIGINAL $11,560.66

Austin, Texas

RECEIVED FROM ESTATE OF W. C. GRANT, Eleven Thousand five Hundred Sixty and 66/100 Dollars in payment of inheritance tax assessed against Estate of W. C. Grant, Deceased, resident of Hill County, inherited by Nola E. Grant and Silas Grant, heirs.

Robert S. Calvert, Comptroller of Public
Accounts for the State of Texas

August 27, 1963
STATE SEAL
FILED AUGUST 29, 1963
GLENN MORGAN, Clerk County Court,
Hill County, Texas

Appendix 8

Note: The following represents a transcription of Pansy M. Yount's last will and testament located at the Jefferson County Courthouse in Beaumont, Texas. For historical presentation purposes, the authors have made every effort possible to retain the integrity, terminology, grammar, and abbreviations of the original, including misspellings and omissions, with the exceptions of Provision THIRTEEN, Sections I through X that deal with the lengthy description of establishing and administering the three separate trust accounts for the three grandchildren.

THE STATE OF TEXAS)
KNOW ALL MEN BY THESE PRESENTS:
COUNTY OF JEFFERSSON)

THAT I, Mrs. Pansy M. Yount, heretofore known as Pansy M. Grant, and prior to that as Pansy M. Yount, a resident of the County of Jefferson and State of Texas, being of sound and disposing mind and memory and above the age of twenty-one years, do make and publish this my last will and testament, hereby revoking all wills and codicils to wills by me at any time heretofore made.

I have given much thought and consideration concerning the welfare of my daughter, Mildred Yount Manion, and her children, for whom I have a great love and affection. However, since Mildred has received a large estate from her father, she is already amply provided for and for that reason I am not including her in my will.

FIRST

I desire and direct that my body be buried in a Christianlike manner, according to my circumstances in life, and I direct that all of my legal debts be paid out of my estate as soon as practicable after my death by my Executors hereinafter appointed.

SECOND

I hereby nominate, constitute and appoint my good friend, Dr. J. C. Crager, my good friend and accountant, M. R. Geisendorff, and my daughter, Mildred Manion, Joint Independent Executors of this, my Will, and Trustees of the Trust Estates provided for herein.

It is my desire and I hereby direct that in the administration of my estate neither my Executors nor my Trustees shall be required to furnish bond of any kind, and that no other action shall be had in the County Court in relation to the settlement of my estate than the probating of this, my will, and to have returned an inventory, appraisement, and list of claims of my estate as required by law.

THIRD

My said Executors shall have full power and authority to bargain, sell and convey all lands and other properties, real and personal, for cash or credit, or in discharge of a debt, for such consideration and on such terms as they shall determine to be in the best interest of my estate, with full power and authority to collect and receive all monies and proceeds of said sale or sales; they shall have full power to manage, encumber, mortgage, partition, lease, rent, distribute, exchange and otherwise dispose of said land and other properties; they shall have full power and authority to make additions, alterations or repairs to commercial buildings or other property; they shall have full power to vote, sell, assign, transfer, exchange, encumber, pledge, hypothecate, or otherwise deal with any and all corporate stocks owned by my estate for such consideration and on such terms as they shall determine; they shall have full power and authority to execute any and all leases, including oil, gas and mineral leases, and execute mineral deeds, royalty deeds and assignments, mineral pooling and unitization agreements and mineral division orders; they shall have full power to release, settle, adjust, compromise and otherwise dispose of any and all claims against or on behalf of my estate; and my said executors shall have power and authority to determine the consideration and the terms upon which any and all of the aforesaid transactions are made, and in all other respects to exercise the functions of ownership of said property as unlimitedly as I would or could if living, present and acting.

FOURTH

In the event any one of the three named in Article SECOND hereof as Independent Executors and Trustees should predecease me, or should any one of them for any reason whatsoever fail or refuse to quality as such Executor or Trustee of this my will, or in the event any one of them should die or resign during the time he or she is acting as my Executor or Trustee, then it is my will and desire that my attorney, A. D. Moore, shall act with the survivors or remaining two of the three named, and such three (including A. D. Moore as the third) shall constitute Joint Independent Executors of this my will and Trustees of the Trust Estates provided for herein, with the same powers, rights, exemptions and duties herein conferred upon the said Dr. J. C. Crager, M. R. Geisendorff and Mildred Manion.

If a second one of the three Executors and Trustees originally named, or if A. D. Moore should predecease me, or should any one of them for any reason whatsoever fail or refuse to qualify as Executor or Trustee of this my will, or in the event any one of them should die or resign during the time he or she is acting as my Executor or Trustee, then it is my will and desire that The First National Bank of Beaumont shall act with the remaining two so that such three shall constitute Joint Independent Executors and Trustees of this my will with the same powers, rights, exemptions and duties herein conferred upon the said Dr. J. C. Crager, M. R. Geisendorff and Mildred Manion.

If at any time circumstances should develop under which only one or none of the individuals above named, Dr. J. C. Crager, M. R. Geisendorff, Mildred Manion or A. D. Moore, should be in position to act as one of my Executors and Trustees, then it is my will and desire and I hereby direct that The First National Bank of Beaumont, Beaumont, Texas, shall act with the remaining one or alone, as the case may be, as Independent Executor and Trustee with the same powers, rights, exemptions and duties originally conferred upon the said Dr. J. C. Crager, Mr. M. R. Geisendorff and Mildred Manion.

FIFTH

I give, devise and bequeath to the University of Texas my four great tapestries and the "Yount Silver" given to me by Mr. Yount, provided I own same at the time of my death.

SIXTH

I give, devise and bequeath to the Masonic Home for Crippled Children (by whatever name it is known) at Lexington, Kentucky, all proceeds from the sale of my jewelry and precious stones which I may own at the time of my death. In this connection I direct that, as soon as practicable after my death, such jewelry and precious stones be sold by my Executors, at public or private sale, under the terms, upon the conditions and for the consideration my said Executors in their sole and uncontrolled discretion my determine to be satisfactory, and after deducting expenses incurred in connection with such sale or sales, including any commissions or fees paid, the net proceeds shall be delivered to said home.

SEVENTH

I give, devise and bequeath to my granddaughter, Mildred Yount Manion, my homestead in Caldwood where I am now residing, including all improvements thereon situated; and together with the furniture and furnishings, chinaware, silverware, crystal, rugs, draperies, paintings, portraits, pictures, household goods, bric-a-brac, my clothing and personal effects; but excluding any items which may be otherwise specifically disposed of by the terms of this will.

EIGHTH

I give, devise and bequeath to Mrs. Viola G. Ransom, Beaumont, Texas, a faithful friend and companion, the sum of Fifty Thousand ($50,000.00) Dollars in cash.

In the event the said Mrs. Viola G. Ransom should predecease me, then this bequest shall lapse and said sum shall become a part of the residue of my estate and disposed of as hereinafter provided.

NINTH

I give, devise and bequeath to Ed Fitzpatrick of Beaumont, who has served me faithfully through a good many years, the sum of Twenty-five Thousand ($25,000.00) Dollars in cash.

In the event the said Ed Fitzpatrick should predecease me, then this bequest shall lapse and said sum shall become a part of the residue of my estate and disposed of as hereinafter provided.

TENTH

I give, devise and bequeath to my granddaughter, Kathryn Bernadette Manion, the sum of Two Hundred Thousand ($200,000.00) Dollars in cash.

In the event my said granddaughter should predecease me, then this bequest shall lapse and said sum shall become a part of the residue of my estate and disposed of as hereinafter provided.

ELEVENTH

I give, devise and bequeath to my grandson, Edward Daniel Manion, Jr., the sum of Two Hundred Thousand ($200,000.00) Dollars in cash.

In the event my said grandson should predecease me, then this bequest shall lapse and said sum shall become a part of the residue of my estate and disposed of as hereinafter provided.

It is my judgment that it is wise for my homestead in Caldwood, including improvements, furniture and furnishings, to go to one of my grandchildren and not be partitioned among the three of them. This I have provided for in Article SEVENTH hereof. However, because of my desire not to favor one grandchild over another, I have made the foregoing special bequest to my grandson, Edward Daniel Manion, Jr., and the special bequest to my granddaughter, Kathryn Bernadette Manion, set forth in Article TENTH hereof.

TWELFTH

It is my will and desire, and I hereby direct, that the special bequests set forth above shall pass to the recipients thereof free and clear of legal debts, Estate and Inheritance taxes and expenses of administration; that all legal debts, Estate and Inheritance taxes and expenses of administration be paid out of the residue of my estate.

THIRTEENTH

It is my will and desire and I hereby direct that after the payment of legal debts, estate and inheritance taxes, expenses of administration and the special bequests mentioned above, all of which shall be paid to the legatees free and clear of taxes, all of the remaining property, whether real, personal or mixed, or whatever situated, of every nature, class, or kind, now owned or hereafter acquired by me, whether in present enjoyment or expectancy, of which I may die seized and possessed, or as to which I may have the right of disposition at the time of my death, shall pass to and vest in Dr. J. C. Creager, M. R. Geisendorff and Mildred Manion, jointly, as Trustees in each of the three (3) Trusts hereinafter set forth; said devise to said Trustees for each Trust being for the benefit of my grandchildren, Kathryn Bernadette Manion, Mildred Yount Manion, Edward Daniel Manion, Jr., and/or the issue of said grandchildren as hereinafter provided, each of said Trusts being upon the terms and conditions and for the uses, trusts and purposes hereinafter set forth, to-wit:

[*Sections I through X deal with the establishment of and the administration of three separate trust accounts for the three grandchildren, and for the purposes of this Appendix, are not detailed here.*]

FOURTEENTH

If any provision of this will violates the law against perpetuities, that portion of the Trusts subject to such provision shall be administered as herein directed for the period permitted by law, and forthwith thereafter such part of these Trust Estates so affected shall vest in the beneficiary enjoying or who may be entitled to the same at the expiration of said period.

FIFTEENTH

Should ancillary proceedings be necessary in the State of Kentucky relative to any property I may own in that State, and my Executors do not qualify in such proceedings, then and in that event I nominate, constitute and appoint Fred Wachs, of Lexington, Kentucky, as ancillary executor *cum testamento annexo*.

SIXTEENTH

I most lovingly ask my devisees and legatees, in loving harmony, in all things, to aid my Executors in carrying out my wishes as expressed in this will; and in order, if possible, to insure this, it is my will, and I do now here expressly provide, and make it a condition precedent to the taking, vesting, receiving or enjoying of any property, benefit or thing whatsoever under and by virtue of this will, that no such devisee or legatee shall in any manner contest this will or the probate thereof, or in any manner aid in any such contest. I further will and provide that, should any devisee or legatee so contest, or in any manner aid in any such contest, he shall thereupon lose and forfeit all right to any benefit and all right or title to any property or thing herein directly or indirectly devised or bequeathed to him; and as to every such right, title, property or thing, it is my will and desire and I hereby direct that same shall pass to the Trusts or Trust of such of my grandchildren as do not contest or aid in a contest of this will or its probate; and shall pass to such Trusts or Trust in equal portions; and thereafter such right, title, property or thing shall be administered and subsequently distributed in the same manner as if it had been originally devised to such Trusts or Trust.

SEVENTEENTH

At the time of the execution of this will, I am involved in a divorce suit with my husband, W. C. Grant. The case has been tried in the District Court of Jefferson County, Texas, and on December 17, 1959, on my cross-action, I was granted a divorce from my husband, and in said judgment my former name of Pansy M. Yount was restored to me. The judgment entered in that case is being appealed by both sides and if affirmed as to the divorce will be retroactive to December 17, 1959. Therefore, in executing this will I am using the name Pansy M. Yount, but specifically declare that I am the same person as Pansy M. Grant who has been married to W. C. Grant, and the same person who prior to my marriage to W. C. Grant was Pansy M. Yount, widow of M. F. Yount.

IN WITNESS WHEREOF, I have hereunto subscribed my name in the presence of John E. Gray and W. P. Machemehl, who have hereunto subscribed their names as attesting witnesses at my request, and in my presence, and in the presence of each other, to whom I have declared this to be my Last Will and Testament, this 8th day of February, 1960.

Appendix 9

Note: The following represents a transcription of Pansy M. Yount's actual probate document located at the Jefferson County Courthouse in Beaumont, Texas. For historical presentation purposes, the authors have made every effort possible to retain the integrity, terminology, grammar and abbreviations of the original, including misspellings and omissions. Furthermore, we made no attempt to determine whether the calculations are correctly stated.

NO. 21,928

THE ESTATE OF	)	IN THE COUNTY COURT OF
PANSY M. YOUNT,	)	JEFFERSON COUNTY, TEXAS
DECEASED	)	PROBATE DIVISION

INVENTORY AND APPRAISEMENT OF ESTATE

Inventory and Appraisement of the Estate of Pansy M. Yount, deceased, produced before the undersigned Appraisers on the 5th of December, A. D. 1963, by Mildred Yount Manion, M. R. Geisendorff and J. C. Crager, Independent Executors of the Estate of said Pansy M. Yount, deceased.

SEPARATE PROPERTY

A. Cash:

Item No.	Description		Value at date of Death
1	Funds on hand (not deposited)	$ 7,617.29	
2	First Security National Bank- P. M. Yount Acct.	5,072.48	
3	First Security National Bank- Special Acct.	35,050.50	
4	First Security National Bank- Separate Acct.	25,776.21	
5	First Security National Bank- M. R. Geisendorff, Agent	39,565.90	
6	American National Bank	2,024.43	
7	Office–Petty Cash Fund	245.50	
8	Cash–Safe-Deposit box	15,395.00	$ 130,747.31

B. Notes Receivable:

No.	Description	Shares	Amount	Total
1	Kentucky Research Foundation Nos. 4-10 inc. each in the amount of $75,000.00 except Note #10, which is for $25,000.00, due annually at 3%		475,000.00	
2	Promissory Notes of Joe Fischer, New York City, 2 at $6,500.00 each, no interest and due Dec. 5, 1962, and Jan. 5, 1963, Dated Oct. 4, 1962		13,000.00	$ 488,000.00

C. Stocks:

No.	Description	Shares	Amount
1	American National Bank of Beaumont, Texas – Com. @ $77.00 per share		
	Cert. #2786	73 Shares	
	Cert. #2881	24 Shares	
		97 Shares	$ 7,469.00
2	General Motors Corp. – Com. @ $54.00 per share – Cert. Nos. R684-179 through R684-191, 13 certificates for 100 shares each	1,300 Shares	70,200.00
3	First Beaumont Corporation – Com. Cert. #37 @ price paid	2,525 Shares	6,312.50
4	First Security National Bank, Beaumont, Texas – Com. @ $23.00 per share, Cert. #1514	10,712 Shares	246,376.00
5	Norvell-Wilder Supply Co., Beaumont, Texas – Com. @12.00 per share		
	Cert. #2333	13,312 Shares	
	Cert #2349	1,528 Shares	
		14,840 Shares	178,080.00
6	Standard Brands, Inc. – Com. @ $58.00 per share		
	Cert. #N 135901	100 Shares	
	Cert. #NF388489	50 Shares	
	Cert. #N144551	100 Shares	
		250 Shares	14,500.00
7	Texaco, Inc. – Com. @ $53.00 per share		
	Cert. #E 274526	100 Shares	
	#E 278601	100 Shares	
	#EO 682759	14 Shares	
	#EO 32888	26 Shares	
	#E 342690	100 Shares	

	#EA 83819 10,000 Shares		
	#EA 83820 10,000 Shares		
	#EA 83821 10,000 Shares		
	#EA 83822 10,000 Shares		
	#EA 83823 10,000 Shares		
	#EA 83824 10,000 Shares		
	#EA 83825 5,000 Shares		
	#EA 83826 <u>1,000 Shares</u>		
	66,340 Shares	3,516,020.00	
8	Tyrrell Hardware Co. of Beaumont, Texas – Com. @ $14.75 per share Cert. #373 1,372 Shares Cert. #374 <u>120 Shares</u> 1,492 Shares	22,007.00	
9	Central District Warehousing Corp., Lexington, Ky., issued to Spindletop Farm – Cert. #3930 7 Shares	7.00	4,060,971.50

D. <u>Real Estate – Jefferson County, Texas:</u>

1	Lots 1 to 12 inc., Block 38, Calder Addn. to the City of Beaumont, Tex.	175,000.00
2	Lots 1 to 6 inc., Block 10, Calder Addn. to the City of Beaumont, Tex.	280,000.00
	3-Story Terra Cotta Apartment House with 18 furnished apartments. 1-Story Terra Cotta Building, known as Arcade Building with 11 store spaces or offices. 1-Story Garage located in rear of Arcade Building	
3	Lots 9 to 13 inc., Block 3, Caldwood Addn to the City of Beaumont, Tex. 3-Story brick residence with basement & 32 rooms. 2-story brick garage with living quarters above.	75,000.00
4	400 Acres – A. Houston League subject to Pipeline Right of Way Contracts and Easements @ $400.00 per acre	160,000.00
5	720.16 Acres in J. Gerish, Sr. and E. Raines Survey less 3.159 acres conveyed to Gulf States Utilities Co. of Beaumont, Tex. In 1957, and subject to Pipeline Right of Way Contracts and Easements – @ $400.00 per acre	286,800.00

	Hardin County, Texas:		
6	Lots 39, 41, 42, 51 and 52 of Oakland Addn. to the City of Sour Lake, Tex. Unimproved	500.00	
	Harris County, Texas:		
7	S 1/2 of Lot 10; all of Lots 11, 12 & 13, Block 22, Bayside Terrace, A Subdivision out of the W. P. Harris Survey 2-Story frame residence – rooms are furnished.	40,940.00	
	Tyler County, Texas:		
8	122.20 acres, more or less, William B. McAlister Survey, Abstract No. 463	15,000.00	1,033,240.00
E. Minerals:			
1	25 % interest in 40 acres, more or less, being Lots Nos. 39 and 47 of the Theodore F. Kock Subdivision of the F. Valmore League in Chambers County, Texas	1.00	
2.	017560 R. I. in 12.06 acres, more particularly described in Unit Designation dated Feb. 3, 1943, Records in Volume 159, Page 505, Deed Records of Hardin County, Tex. Under lease to Highland Oil Co., Sour Lake, Texas	1,000.00	
3.	08333 R. I. in 400 acres, A. Houston League of Jefferson County, Texas, being produced by Texas Co.,	7,000.00	
4.	001442 R. I. in 9.23 acres, being a part of Lots 1 & 4 in outer Block #21, and all or part of various streets in the City of Liberty, Liberty Town Tract League, Abstract 395, Liberty County, Texas	1.00	
5	1/2 Minerals in Lot 45 and West 40 feet of Lot 46, Oakland Addn. to City of Sour Lake, Texas	1.00	
6	1/2 Minerals in that certain 2 acre tract out of the M. Merchant 24 Acre Tract in the Stephen Jackson League, Hardin County, Texas	1.00	8,004.00
F. Personal Property:			
1	Jewelry	140,000.00	

2	Household Furnishings	75,000.00	
3	Automobiles:		
	Chrysler Station Wagon, 1959, Three-seat wagon sold 12-15-62	1,300.00	
	1954 Chrysler Imperial 7 passenger Sedan – Sold 12-15-62	550.00	
	1953 Rolls Royce Limousine – Sold 12-15-62	3,550.00	
	1961 Ford 4-door Country Squire Wagon, three seated	1,000.00	
	1956 Ford 1/2 Ton Pick-up truck	500.00	
	1961 Ford 3/4 Ton Pick-up with steel body for transporting dogs	1,000.00	
4	1 two-horse trailer – Dutch Boy, 1961	100.00	
5	1 – 16' shop built plywood boat and two wheel shop built trailer. Sold 12-20-62	75.00	
	1 – two wheel trailer sold 12-22-62	50.00	
6	Dogs – Setters & Pointers_	100.00	223,225.00
	Total		$5,944,187.81

Authors' Note: When the final appraisal was filed on January 14, 1964, the gross amount had reached $6,097,841.15.

Endnotes

Preface

1. *Beaumont Enterprise*, Nov. 14, 1933 (quotation).

Chapter One

1. Frank Yount's Death Certificate, no. 537, Jefferson County Bureau of Vital Statistics, Jefferson County Courthouse, Beaumont, Texas; *Beaumont Enterprise*, June 15, 1933 (quotation); Joseph L. Clark, *The Texas Gulf Coast: Its History and Development*, 4 vols. (New York: Lewis Historical, 1955), III, 109; Walter P. Webb et al., *The Handbook of Texas*, 2 vols. (Austin: Texas State Historical Association, 1952), II, 949; *Who Was Who In America, 1897-1942*, vol. 1 (Chicago: Marquis, 1950), 1393; "Queen Victoria," Spartacus Educational Online, http://www.spartacus.schoolnet.co.uk/PRvictoria.htm [accessed June 22, 2004]; Mt. Zion Presbyterian Church Cemetery Records, Monticello, Arkansas; Peggy Carter telephone interview with Fred B. McKinley, July 27, 2004. Mrs. Carter indicated that Frank had three older sisters: Alice Virginia (born 1867), Mary Ellen (born 1871), Harriet Ann (born 1873); two older brothers: Martin Lee (born 1869), Nolan Alfred (born 1875); one younger brother, Sullie Woodford (born 1882) who died in 1917 of a ruptured appendix; and one younger sister, Ida Belle (born 1884). Another brother, William Baxter, born in 1877, died at the age of two. Most sources, including Mrs. Carter, show the native state of Frank Yount's parents as North Carolina. Yount's death certificate, however, erroneously reflects the state as Virginia, although two handwritten notes on it appear to have been entered at a later date than the typed original. According to Mt. Zion Presbyterian Church Cemetery Records, Joseph Nathaniel Yount died on Feb. 16, 1889.

2. *Beaumont Enterprise*, July 3, 1928; Nov. 14, 1933; *Beaumont Journal*, Nov. 14, 1933 (first and second quotations); Mary Speer telephone interview with Fred B. McKinley, Dec. 16, 2004; W. T. Block, *Sour Lake, Texas: From Mud Baths to Millionaires, 1835–1909* (Liberty, Texas: Atascosito Historical Association, 1995), 66, 72; James A. Clark and Michel T. Halbouty, *Spindletop* (New York: Random House, 1952), 217–218; Judith Walker Linsley, Ellen Walker Rienstra, and Jo Ann Stiles, *Giant Under the Hill* (Austin: Texas State Historical Association, 2002), 21, 22 (third and fourth quotations); R. E. Masterson, *The Low Down on a High Up Man Towit: Miles Frank Yount* (n.p., n.d), 5; "Yount, Miles Frank," *The Handbook of Texas Online*, http://www.tsha.utexas.edu/handbook/online/articles/view/YY/fyo16.html [accessed June 22, 2004].

3. *Beaumont Enterprise*, July 3, 1928.

4. Block, *Sour Lake,* 56 (first quotation), 57 (second quotation), 139.

5. Ibid., 57 (quotation).

6. Clark and Halbouty, *Spindletop*, 218–219; Anthony McDade "Mickey" Phelan interview with Fred B. McKinley, July 14, 2004, Beaumont, Texas; Texas Secretary of State, Charter Records, no. 19809, Feb. 16, 1909, Office of Secretary of State, Austin, Texas; "Sour Lake, TX," *The Handbook of Texas Online*, http://www.tsha.utexas.edu/handbook/online/articles/view/SS/hjs20.html [accessed Sept. 26, 2004].

7. Block, *Sour Lake*, 88 (quotation).

8. Clark and Halbouty, *Spindletop*, 219; *Beaumont Enterprise*, Nov. 14, 1933; Charter Records, no. 19809, Feb. 16, 1909.

9. Clark and Halbouty, *Spindletop*, 218–219; *Beaumont Enterprise*, July 18, 1926; *Directory of the City of Beaumont, 1912–1913* (Houston: Southern Press, 1912), 22, 275.

10. Clark and Halbouty, *Spindletop*, 220; *Beaumont Enterprise*, May 20, 1957.

11. Clark and Halbouty, *Spindletop*, 220.

12. Ibid.; *Beaumont Enterprise*, Nov. 16, 1933; Hardin County Deed Records, vol. 59, Hardin County Courthouse, Kountze, Texas; emails from David Moerbe, Corporations Section, Office of the Secretary of State, Austin, Texas (dmoerbe@sos.state.tx.us) to Fred B. McKinley, North Myrtle Beach, South Carolina, Mar. 19, 22, 2004, indicate that the Texas Secretary of State has no record of the Yount-Pevito Oil Company as either a corporation or partnership or a Pevito (Peveto) Oil Company.

13. Clark and Halbouty, *Spindletop*, 220–221; Phelan interview with McKinley, July 14, 2004; John Conway, "Celebrating the Birth of Texas Oil," *Texas Co-Op Power* (Jan. 2001), http://www.texas-ec.org/tcp/101oil.html [accessed June 24, 2004]. In his article, Conway outlines a second version of Harry Phelan's source for the $750: "The family legend recounts that Phelan's wife, Johannah, provided the funds from household savings that she'd been carefully putting away." However, Mickey Phelan disputes the claim that his grandmother, Johannah, came up with the money. He believes that his grandfather, Harry, did in fact borrow the $750 from a bank, because Johannah would not have had access to that amount, considered large during their current state of financial affairs.

14. Clark and Halbouty, *Spindletop*, 220–221.

15. Ibid., 221.

16. Ibid., 222; *Beaumont Enterprise*, July 3, 1928; *Houston Post*, Nov. 15, 1933; Charter Records, no. 28005, Jan. 21, 1915; Hardin County Deed Records, vol. 65, 208; Ellis A. Davis and Edwin H. Grobe, eds., *The New Encyclopedia of Texas*, 2 vols. (Dallas: Texas Development Bureau, n.d.), I, 1058; emails from Moerbe to McKinley, Mar. 19, 22, 2004, indicate that the Texas Secretary of State has no record of the Yount-Rothwell Oil Company as either a corporation or partnership, or the Rothwell Oil Company. When calculating the division of the 500 original shares of the Yount-Lee Oil Company, Frank Yount got half or 250, but because he reserved a sixth-interest for Phelan, the latter got 83. T. P. Lee's half interest started at 250 also, but he immediately gave five to Talbot Rothwell and then he sold 125 to Woodward, who now held 25 percent ownership of the company.

17. Jefferson County Marriage Records, file no. 11590A (Yount and Daley), vol. 12, 159, file no. 4657A (Daley and Merritt), vol. 5, 474, Jefferson County Courthouse, Beaumont, Texas; St. Anthony Cathedral, Diocese of Beaumont Records, Beaumont, Texas; Father James F. Vanderholt, Carolyn B. Martinez, and Karen A Gilman, *Diocese of Beaumont: The Catholic Story of Southeast Texas* (Beaumont: Diocese of Beaumont, 1991), 208–213; (Clark, *Texas Gulf Coast*, III, 110; *Beaumont Daily Journal*, Sept. 16, 1915 (quotations); Jefferson County Divorce Records, file no. 10979 1/2, vol. 8, 238, Jefferson County Courthouse, Beaumont, Texas; *Beaumont City Directory, 1914* (Houston: Morrison & Fourmy, 1914), 205; Merritt Family Bible, in private collection of Kathryn Manion Haider; Elizabeth Simpson, *The Enchanted Bluegrass* (Lexington: Transylvania Press, 1938), 265; Pansy Merritt Yount's Death Certificate, no. A2592, Jefferson County Courthouse, Beaumont, Texas reflects Pansy's mother as Sarah West. Both the Merritt Family Bible and author Elizabeth Simpson show Pansy's mother as Sarah Frances Sherman Merritt. Sarah Frances Merritt died Dec. 13, 1887 and Hosea Holly Merritt on May 13, 1894, according to the Merritt Family Bible, in private collection of Kathryn Manion Haider. The Sept. 16, 1915 article in the *Beaumont Daily Journal* that described Frank and Pansy Yount's wedding also contained a mention that Pansy had lived in Beaumont for more than a year with this same sister who married Hardy S. Blanchette. The 1914 *Beaumont City Directory* listed Charles A. Daley, oil well driller, as a resident at the Heisig Apartments in Beaumont. St. Louis Church was a predecessor of St. Anthony Cathedral on which the latter's construction began in 1903 and concluded in 1907. Father William J. Lee, who drew up the plans for the new building named for St. Anthony of Padua, died on July 29, 1918, and he is buried at the foot of the altar.

18. Marguerite Behar, Frank Yount's niece and daughter of Ida Belle Yount and Walter Fletcher Parrish, who later became superintendent of Yount-Lee's Sour Lake division, interview with Fred B. McKinley, July 16, 2004, Sour Lake, Texas; Carter telephone interview with McKinley, July 27, 2004; "Prostitution," *The Handbook of Texas Online*, http://www.tsha.utexas.edu/handbook/online/articles/view/PP/jbp1.html [accessed Oct. 12, 2004] (first quotation); Linsley, Rienstra, and Stiles, *Giant Under the Hill*, 176 (second quotation); Mildred Frank Yount's Baby Book. Relative to the dissention between Pansy and her sister-in-law, Ida Belle Parrish, it is ironic, however, that Frank and Pansy named Ida Belle and her husband, Walter Parrish, as Mildred's Godmother and Godfather, respectively, on Aug. 1, 1920 when Rev. E. P. Kennedy christened her in the Presbyterian Church. This same baby book reflected that Dr. W. J. Blewett served as Mildred's physician, and Fanny Wakefield as her nurse.

19. Charter Records, no. 28005, Dec. 27, 1916.

20. Ibid., Dec. 23, 1920, 2; Marguerite Behar telephone interview with Fred B. McKinley, July 28, 2004;

Crystal Ford, wife of Warren Ford, telephone interview with Fred B. McKinley, June 9, 2004; Crystal Ford (cford@academicplanet.com) email to Fred B. McKinley, North Myrtle Beach, South Carolina, Aug. 16, 2004. Warren Ford's grandfather, William Warren Ford, who lived in Sour Lake at the time, worked first as a mechanic and later in the Engineering Department of Yount-Lee for at least three years: 1918, 1919, and 1920. Also, Warren Ford's father, William Gray Ford, worked for the company, beginning most probably in 1929 and ending in 1935.

21. Behar interview with McKinley, July 16, 2004; Jim Kelley interview with Fred B. McKinley, July 16, 2004, Sour Lake, Texas (quotation). Mr. Kelley, the current owner of Sunnyside, found the board with Pearcy's inscription during the ongoing restoration project. It remains in his private collection.

22. Newspaper article, publisher unknown, undated, copy in possession of Greg Riley (quotation).

23. Clark and Halbouty, *Spindletop*, 222–223; Charter Records, no. 28005, Dec. 29, 1922; Vincent Curcio, *Chrysler: The Life and Times of an Automotive Genius* (New York: Oxford University Press, 2000), 207–208.

24. Clark and Halbouty, *Spindletop*, 222–223; *Beaumont City Directory, 1921–1922* (Houston: Morrison & Fourmy, 1921), 520. According to the latter source, Frank Yount served as vice president of the Phelan-Josey Grocery Company. Over the years, Yount owned numerous shares of stock in Harry Phelan's business.

25. Charter Records, no. 28005, Dec. 29, 1922; U. S. Department of Labor, *Bureau of Labor Statistics, Washington, D. C.*, http://data.bls.gov/servlet/SurveyOutputServlet [accessed June 24, 2004]. The $17 million figure is based on a comparison of consumer price indices of 16.9 for Dec. 1922 and 189.1 for May 2004.

26. Charter Records, Mar. 23, 1923; *Beaumont City Directory, 1925–1926* (Houston: Morrison & Fourmy, 1925), 492. A plaque located on the front of the San Jacinto Life Building, located at 595 Orleans in Beaumont, reads, "Dedicated Feb. 21, 1922." There are actually sixteen floors, but the top one is used exclusively for storage of equipment such as radio antennae and the like.

27. Clark and Halbouty, *Spindletop*, *xiii* (quotation); Christine Moor Sanders, *Spindletop: The Untold Story* (Beaumont: Spindletop-Gladys City Boomtown Museum, 2000), 107; *Beaumont Enterprise*, Jan. 29, 1928; Wallace Davis, "History Repeats Itself–Spindletop is Concrete Example," *Oil Weekly* 40 (Aug. 27, 1926), 37–42; C. A. Warner, *Texas Oil and Gas since 1543* (Houston: Gulf, 1939), 70; Thelma Johnson et al., *The Spindletop Oil Field: A History of Its Discovery and Development* (Beaumont: Neches Printing, 1927), 12; *Houston Chronicle*, Nov. 27, 1927; "The Texas Corporation," *Fortune* 1 (Apr. 1930), 50; Queen Victoria, *Spartacus Educational Online*; Conway, "Celebrating the Birth of Texas Oil"; Archie P. McDonald, "When Oil Became an Industry," *TexasEscapes.com*, http://www.texasescapes.com/DEPARTMENTS/Guest_Columnists/East_Texas_all_things_historical/OilIndustryHi story1200AMD1.htm [accessed June 21, 2004].

28. E. N. Tiratsoo, *Oilfields of the World* (Beaconsfield, England: Scientific Press, 1973), 262.

29. Everette A. Martin, "A History of Spindletop Oil Field," (M.A. thesis, University of Texas, 1934), 65; Paul Wagner, "Spindletop's History-Making Comeback Lacks Human Background of Old," *National Petroleum News* 18 (Sept. 22, 1926), 73; *Beaumont Enterprise*, July 3, 1928; *Abstract of the Twelfth Census of the United States, 1900* (Washington: GPO, 1902), 47; Davis, "History Repeats Itself," 37; Clark and Halbouty, *Spindletop*, 45–46.

30. Isaac F. Marcosson, *The Black Golconda* (New York: Harper, 1924), 149.

31. Ibid., 150; Clark and Halbouty, *Spindletop*, 78–79. Ten days before the Lucas Gusher hit, Standard Oil controlled 83 percent of petroleum production in the United States which totaled 58 million barrels. Aside from Russia, only the Dutch East Indies, Austria-Hungary, and Romania produced small quantities.

32. Davis, "History Repeats Itself," 37; Marcosson, *The Black Golconda*, 150–221; W. T. Block, "Lucas Gusher Fever Affected So Many Folks, Far and Wide," *WTBlock.com*, http://www.wtblock.com/wtblockjr/lucus_gusher.htm [accessed June 25, 2004].

33. Davis, "History Repeats Itself," 37; Marcosson, *The Black Golconda*, 150–221.

34. Davis, "History Repeats Itself," 37; Marcosson, *The Black Golconda*, 150–221.

35. Ralph Arnold and William J. Kemnitzer, *Petroleum in the United States and Possessions* (New York: Harper, 1931), 570; Wagner, "Spindletop's History-Making Comeback," 75.

36. Marcosson, *The Black Golconda*, 149–150 (first quotation), 221 (second quotation).

37. Howard Perkins (hap70119@hotmail.com) email to Fred B. McKinley, North Myrtle Beach, South Carolina, Aug. 16, 2004 (first quotation); *Beaumont Enterprise*, Feb. 5, 1908, (second quotation); Jefferson County Deed Records, vol. 224, 71, Jefferson County Courthouse, Beaumont, Texas; Florence Stratton, *The Story of Beaumont* (Houston: Hercules, n.d.), 160–162; *Beaumont Journal*, Feb. 15, 1923; *Beaumont City Directory, 1923* (Houston: Morrison & Fourmy, 1923), 520; *Beaumont City Directory, 1925–1926*, 492; Don

Streater, "Another Day," *Beaumont Enterprise*, Feb. 16, 1973; Contract of Sale Between Mrs. Laura E. Wiess and M. F. Yount, Feb. 10, 1923; Behar interview with McKinley, July 16, 2004; Kelley interview with McKinley, July 16, 2004; Consumer Price Index, All Urban Consumers, U. S. Department of Labor, *Bureau of Labor Statistics*, ftp://ftp.bls.gov/pub/special.requests/cpi/cpiai.txt [accessed June 27, 2004]. The $1,013,000 figure is obtained by comparing consumer price indices of 16.8 for Feb. 1923 and 189.1 for May 2004. According to prominent Beaumont historian, Howard Perkins, the home's architect, Henry Conrad Mauer, referred to skylights as "glass ventilators," and after selling the home to Frank and Pansy Yount, Laura Wiess moved to 888 Calder Avenue, owned by her late husband's brother, William. That home no longer exists either.

38. *Beaumont Enterprise*, Nov. 17, 1933; Feb. 16, 1973; Aug. 31, 2002; Streater, "Another Day," (quotation); Perkins email to McKinley, Aug. 16, 2004; Helen Locke interview with Howard Perkins, Nov. 15, 2004, Beaumont, Texas.

39. Clark and Halbouty, *Spindletop*, 218, 232.

Chapter Two

1. *Beaumont Enterprise*, May 10, 1933; May 19, 1953; Magnolia Cemetery Records, May 20, 1953, Beaumont Texas; Thelma Johnson et al., *The Spindletop Oil Field: A History of Its Discovery and Development* (Beaumont: Neches Printing, 1927), 52; James A. Clark, *Marrs McLean, A Biography* (Houston: Clark Book Co., 1969), 6–8; "McLean, Marrs," *The Handbook of Texas Online*, http://www.tsha.utexas.edu/handbook/online/articles/view/MM/fmcbp.html [accessed Mar. 18, 2004]; Jack Donahue, *Wildcatter: The Story of Michel T. Halbouty and the Search for Oil* (McGraw-Hill: New York, 1979), 2 . The latter source explains that "High Island was not an island at all. It was so named because its elevation of forty-seven feet made it the highest point between Point Bolivar, at the tip of the peninsula, and Sabine Pass, the peninsula's inland extremity."

2. *Beaumont Enterprise*, May 19, 1953; Johnson, *The Spindletop Oil Field*, 52; Clark, *Marrs McLean*, 12–13.

3. Clark, *Marrs McLean*, 18; *Beaumont Enterprise*, May 19, 1953.

4. Clark, *Marrs McLean*, 21–22 (quotation).

5. Ibid., 19–20; James A. Clark and Michel T. Halbouty, *Spindletop* (New York: Random House, 1952), 207; *Beaumont Enterprise*, May 19, 1953.

6. *Beaumont Enterprise*, Mar. 14, 1931; Nov. 15, 1925; Clark and Halbouty, *Spindletop*, 207–208.

7. Everette A. Martin, "A History of Spindletop Oil Field," (M.A. thesis, University of Texas, 1934), 66–67; Carl C. Rister, *Oil! Titan of the Southwest* (Norman: University of Oklahoma, 1949), 226; Johnson, *The Spindletop Oil Field*, 14–15; Clark, *Marrs McLean*, 48–49; Paul Wagner, "Spindletop's History-Making Comeback Lacks Human Background of Old," *National Petroleum News* 18 (Sept. 22, 1926), 75; C. A. Warner, *Texas Oil and Gas since 1543* (Houston: Gulf, 1939), 205; *Beaumont Enterprise*, May 17, 1926; "What's Oil Doing on the Spindletop Dome?" *Paleontological Research Institution, Ithaca, New York*, http://www.priweb.org/ed/pgws/backyard/spindletop/spindletop_oil2.html [accessed Apr. 24, 2004]. The latter source concludes that if the Lucas had been located fifty feet to the south, the drillers would not have struck oil.

8. Wagner, "Spindletop's History-Making Comeback," 75; Warner, *Texas Oil and Gas*, 205.

9. Clark, *Marrs McLean*, 50–51.

10. Ibid., 51–53; Johnson, *The Spindletop Oil Field*, 15; Jefferson County Deed Records, vol. 222, 578–579; vol. 224, 71, Jefferson County Courthouse, Beaumont, Texas; *Beaumont City Directory, 1925–1926* (Houston: Morrison & Fourmy, 1925), 492. The latter source also shows Frank Yount as president of Beaumont Brick Works, and this same directory, page 342, reflects Marrs and Verna McLean's residence as 1262 Calder Avenue. This house was torn down ca. 1948 when Tom Felton purchased the property and built a Lincoln-Mercury dealership on it. The site is now occupied by the Alamo-San Jacinto Glass Company. Percy H. Wiess was the son of Valentine and Laura Wiess.

11. Wallace Davis, "History Repeats Itself—Spindletop is Concrete Example," *Oil Weekly* 40 (Aug. 27, 1926), 36; *Beaumont City Directory, 1929* (Houston: Morrison & Fourmy, 1929), 347; *Beaumont City Directory, 1937* (Houston: Morrison & Fourmy, 1937), 277. Both the 1929 and 1937 city directories show Marrs McLean's office address as 312–315 Gilbert Building. Contrary to some published sources, Marrs McLean and Frank Yount never had offices in the same building. McLean's located his in the Gilbert Building, first at 315 and later at 312–315; and Yount located his in the San Jacinto Building. The two respective buildings are about two blocks apart.

12. Jefferson County Deed Records, vol. 252, 452–459.

13. Jefferson County Deed Records, vol. 254, 526–531. McFaddin owned a five-eighths percentage of this property; Kyle, two-eighths; and Wiess, the final one eighth.

14. Davis, "History Repeats Itself," 36; Clark, *Marrs McLean*, 53; *Beaumont Enterprise*, Nov. 15, 1925; Nov. 16, 1925; "McLean, Marrs," *The Handbook of Texas Online*. The John Douthit survey consists of 13.8 acres located between McFaddin, Wiess, and Kyle; and Gladys City properties; it was not part of the lease agreement between McLean and Yount or those between Gladys City or McFaddin, Wise, and Kyle, and Yount.

15. *Beaumont Enterprise*, Nov. 15, 1925; Clark, *Marrs McLean*, 54–55.

16. Wagner, "Spindletop's History-Making Comeback," 75.

17. *Beaumont Enterprise*, Nov. 15, 1925; Apr. 4, 1930; Fred B. McKinley, "The Yount-Lee Oil Company," (M.A. thesis, Lamar University, 1987), 32–33.

18. *Beaumont Enterprise*, Nov. 15, 1925 (quotation).

19. Ibid., Apr. 4, 1930; Ben Woodhead, *Beaumonter at Large* (n.p.: n.p, 1968), 72 (first quotation); Clark and Halbouty, *Spindletop*, 224, 225 (second quotation); "Spindletop Oilfield," *The Handbook of Texas Online*, http://www.tsha.utexas.edu/handbook/online/articles/view/SS/dos3.html [accessed June 24, 2004].

20. *Beaumont Enterprise*, Nov. 15, 1925; Apr. 4, 1930; Woodhead, *Beaumonter at Large*, 72 (quotation).

21. *Beaumont Enterprise*, Nov. 15, 1925; John H. Walker, and Gwendolyn Wingate, *Beaumont: A Pictorial History* (Virginia Beach: Donning Publishing Company, 1983), 143; Clark and Halbouty, *Spindletop*, 223, 224–225 (quotation). As pointed out by Clark and Halbouty, natural "gushers" during Second Spindletop did not normally occur, unless in the case of accidental blowouts. At this point, the oil business had matured considerably, and wells were usually brought in under total control. Newspaper reporters and many oilmen of the day, however, continued to use the term due to its colorful appeal. Magnolia's experimental radio station, which began broadcasting on October 21, 1924, later became KFDM Radio. The station's identification letters KFDM "Kall for Dependable Magnolene" were part of a commercial marketing ploy by Magnolia to advertise its own brand of gasoline.

22. *Beaumont Journal*, Nov. 16, 1925 (first quotation); *Beaumont Enterprise*, Nov. 16, 1925 (second quotation); Nov. 19, 1925; Woodhead, *Beaumonter at Large*, 72 (third quotation).

23. *Beaumont Enterprise*, Nov. 16, 1925.

24. Ibid., Nov. 19, 1925; Nov. 25, 1925; *Beaumont Journal*, Nov. 28, 1925; Jefferson County Deed Records, vol. 252, 455.

25. *Beaumont Enterprise*, Nov. 26, 1925; Jan. 3, 1926; Jan. 5, 1926.

26. *Beaumont Enterprise*, Jan. 14, 1926; *Beaumont Journal*, Jan. 14, 1926. From 2,900 feet, the McFaddin No. 3 flowed an estimated 5,000 barrels a day.

27. *Beaumont Enterprise*, Jan. 15, 1926; Jan. 17, 1926.

28. Ibid., Jan. 17, 1926; Jan. 19, 1926; Jan. 23, 1926.

29. Ibid., Jan. 22, 1926.

30. Ibid.

31. Ibid., Feb. 6, 1926; Feb. 15, 1926; Mar. 6, 1926.

32. *Beaumont Enterprise*, Apr. 8, 1926; Apr. 10, 1926.

33. *Beaumont Enterprise*, Apr. 11, 1926 (quotation); Apr. 12, 1926.

34. Ibid., Jan. 16, 1926; Apr. 10, 1926; Apr. 12, 1926; Apr. 4, 1930.

Chapter Three

1. Judith W. Linsley and Ellen W. Rienstra, *Beaumont, A Chronicle of Promise* (Woodland Hills: Windsor, 1982), 92.

2. *Houston Post*, Feb. 5, 1939; T. P. Lee's Death Certificate, no. 412, Bureau of Vital Statistics, Texas Department of Health, Austin, Texas; *Beaumont Enterprise*, Jan. 7, 1928; Joseph L. Clark, *The Texas Gulf Coast: Its History and Development*, 4 vols. (New York: Lewis Historical, 1955), IV, 441; Ellis A. Davis and Edwin H. Grobe, eds., *The New Encyclopedia of Texas*, 2 vols. (Dallas: Texas Development Bureau, n.d.), I, 306. According to the latter source, the twenty-one subsidiaries of the American Republics Corporation were: American Petroleum Company, Federal Petroleum Company, Fidelity Securities Company, Intracoastal Towing & Transportation Company, Papoose Oil Company, Pennsylvania Petroleum Company, Pennsylvania Car Company, Pennsylvania Shipyards, Inc., Pennsylvania Tank Car Company, Pennsylvania Tank Line, Penstock Construction Company, Petroleum Coal & Iron Company, Petroleum Community Store Company, Petroleum Export Association, Inc., Petroleum Iron Works Company of Ohio, Petroleum Iron Works Company of Pennsylvania, Petroleum Land Company, Petroleum Protective Association, Inc., Petroleum Supply Company, Pueblo Oil Company, and Republic Production Company.

3. *Houston Post*, Feb. 5, 1939; Clark, *Texas Gulf Coast*, IV, 441; Virginia Rothwell Birdwell, granddaughter of T. P. Lee and daughter of T. F. Rothwell, interview with Fred B. McKinley, Aug. 25, 1987, Beaumont,

Texas; Davis and Grobe, *New Encyclopedia of Texas*, I, 306; *Houston Chronicle*, Feb. 5, 1939. According to the latter source, T. P. Lee was a thirty-second degree Mason, a member of the Arabia Temple Shrine and the International Order of Odd Fellows of Parkersburg, West Virginia. He was president of the Petroleum Building Company, director of the Fidelity Trust Company of Houston and the Citizens State Bank of Sour Lake. He also served in the Spanish American War and allegedly knew Theodore Roosevelt personally. Socially, he was a member of River Oaks Country Club and the Houston Country Club.

4. Winifred A. Duffy, *John Wiley Link* (Houston: D. Armstrong Co., 1974), 31–34; Madeleine McDermott Hamm, "When Montrose Was Young," *Houston Chronicle*, Aug. 17, 1975; Rev. Sean P. Horrigan, "Links to Houston Pioneers," *UST* (University of St. Thomas) *Magazine* (Winter/Spring 2001), 10–13.

5. Harris County Deed Records, vol. 374, 129–130, Harris County Courthouse, Houston, Texas; Harris County Deed Records, vol. 1510, 22–30; Map Records of Harris County, vol. 4, 3, Harris County Courthouse, Houston, Texas; Hamm, "When Montrose Was Young,"; Horrigan, "Links to Houston Pioneers," 10–13; Consumer Price Index, All Urban Consumers, U. S. Department of Labor, *Bureau of Labor Statistics*, ftp://ftp.bls.gov/pub/special.requests/cpi/cpiai.txt [accessed June 27, 2004]. The $1.5 million figure is obtained by comparing consumer price indices of 11.6 average for Dec. 1916 and 189.1 for May 2004.

6. Davis and Grobe, *New Encyclopedia of Texas*, II, 1678; James A. Clark and Michel T. Halbouty, *Spindletop* (New York: Random House, 1952), 221–222; *Houston Chronicle*, Oct. 29, 1936; Bill Lee's Death Certificate, no. 50083, Texas Department of Health, Austin, Texas; Thomas Peter "Tommy" Lee, III telephone interview with Fred B. McKinley, Sept. 16, 2004. Mr. Lee stated that his father, T. P. Lee, II, carried the name of his uncle who had no sons of his own.

7. Davis and Grobe, *New Encyclopedia of Texas*, II, 1678; Clark and Halbouty, *Spindletop*, 221–222; *Houston Chronicle*, Oct. 29, 1936; Birdwell interview with McKinley, Aug. 25, 1987.

8. Lee telephone interview with McKinley, Sept. 16, 2004.

9. Emerson F. Woodward's Death Certificate, no. 1615, Medina County Clerk's Office, Hondo, Texas; Davis and Grobe, *New Encyclopedia of Texas*, I, 330. The Davis and Grobe entry shows Woodward's date of birth as February 23, 1879, while the death certificate has February 23, 1878.

10. Davis and Grobe, *New Encyclopedia of Texas*, I, 330.

11. Lee telephone interview with McKinley, Sept. 16, 2004 (quotation).

12. Clark, *Texas Gulf Coast*, IV, 440; Davis and Grobe, *New Encyclopedia of Texas*, I, 1058; *Beaumont Enterprise*, Dec. 17, 1949.

13. Birdwell interview with McKinley, Aug. 25, 1987 (first quotation); *Beaumont Enterprise*, Mar. 14,1931; R. E. Masterson, *The Low Down on a High Up Man Towit: Miles Frank Yount* (n.p., n.d), 14 (second quotation).

14. Birdwell interview with McKinley, Aug. 25, 1987; *Beaumont Enterprise*, Oct. 17, 1926; Dec. 30, 1928; July 20, 1930; *Beaumont City Directory, 1925–1926* (Houston: Morrison & Fourmy, 1925), 413; Howard Perkins (hap70119@hotmail.com) emails to Fred B. McKinley, North Myrtle Beach, South Carolina, July 29, 2004 (quotations), Sept. 15, 2004; Mildred Frank Yount, personal diary entry, Sept. 17, 1935; Sue Boyt telephone interview with Fred B. McKinley, Nov. 18, 2004. Marguerite Behar, long-time resident of Sour Lake and Frank Yount's niece, verified the site of the Rothwell home there. When the Rothwells relocated to Beaumont, they lived in the house at 888 Calder Avenue, where Laura Wiess moved when she sold her 1376 Calder Avenue residence to Frank Yount. The convention center in Houston today bears the name of George R. Brown.

15. Birdwell interview with McKinley, Aug. 25, 1987, Beaumont, Texas; *Beaumont Enterprise*, Oct. 16, 1929; Mar. 10, 1931; Aug. 4, 1931; Nov. 13, 1931; Jan. 11, 1933; Dec. 17, 1949; Rosa D. Crenshaw and W. W. Ward, *Cornerstones: A History of Beaumont and Methodism, 1840–1968* (First Methodist Church Historical Committee: Beaumont, 1968), 79–80; Boyt telephone interview with McKinley, Nov. 18, 2004. From Greg Riley's personal inspection, the old location of the Rex Supply Company still exists in a long narrow building on Highway 105 in Sour Lake. A dimly painted sign, although readable on one side only, states: "Rex Supply-Heavy Hardware and Oil Field Supplies." Also, the First National Bank Building in downtown Beaumont still survives as a monument to the amazing wealth centered in Southeast Texas during this era.

16. Clark, *Texas Gulf Coast*, III, 69; Thelma Johnson et al., *The Spindletop Oil Field: A History of Its Discovery and Development* (Beaumont: Neches Printing, 1927), 53; *Beaumont Enterprise*, May 20, 1957.

17. Clark, *Texas Gulf Coast*, III, 69; *Beaumont Enterprise*, Jan. 19, 1927; Clark and Halbouty, *Spindletop*, 218.

18. *Beaumont Enterprise*, June 7, 1927; Dec. 28,1927; Jan. 1, 1929; Aug. 18, 1929; May 20, 1957; Feb. 19, 1966; Bradley C. Brooks, "Owen J. T. Southwell, Architect, and the John Henry Phelan House," *The Texas*

Gulf Historical and Biographical Record, vol. 35 (Nov. 1999), 15 (quotation); Father James F. Vanderholt, Carolyn B. Martinez, and Karen A. Gilman, *Diocese of Beaumont: The Catholic Story of Southeast Texas* (Beaumont: Diocese of Beaumont, 1991), 208–213. The Feb. 19, 1966 *Beaumont Enterprise* article explains that Harry and Johannah Phelan met "in the home of Mr. and Mrs. James J. Frasher in Beaumont where he was making his home at the time and was employed with a local grocery firm."

19. *Beaumont Enterprise*, May 20, 1957; *Beaumont Journal*, Feb. 19, 1966; Brooks, "Owen J. T. Southwell," 5, 7.

20. *Beaumont Enterprise*, June 29, 1929; Oct. 5, 1929; Feb. 4, 1930; Dec. 25, 1930; Feb. 6, 1934; *Beaumont City Directory, 1931* (Houston: Morrison & Fourmy), 474; Perkins email to McKinley, Oct. 11, 2004. Talbot Rothwell, who owned this Keith homestead and adjoining property (300 feet by 160 feet lot, located where Calder Avenue and Willow Street converge) for about four months, sold it to Gasow-Howard Motor Company for $30,000 on June 28, 1929 (the date of deed filing).

21. Mary Reed Williams interview with Fred B. McKinley, July 14, 2004, Beaumont, Texas; Anthony McDade "Mickey" Phelan interview with Fred B. McKinley, July 14, 2004, Beaumont, Texas; Erin Barry Teare interview with Fred B. McKinley, July 14, 2004, Beaumont, Texas.

22. Williams interview with McKinley, July 14, 2004; Phelan interview with McKinley, July 14, 2004 (quotation); Teare interview with McKinley, July 14, 2004. Phelan also added that at the time, his grandfather and grandmother were strapped for funds, because they were donating altars to various Catholic churches.

23. Williams interview with McKinley, July 14, 2004; Phelan interview with McKinley, July 14, 2004; Teare interview with McKinley, July 14, 2004.

24. Thomas C. Richardson, *East Texas: Its History and Its Makers*, ed by Dabney White, 4 vols. (New York: Lewis Historical, 1940), IV, 23; Marcellus E. Foster and Alfred Jones, eds., *South and Southeast Texas* (n.p.: Texas Biographical Association, 1928), 134–187; Ellis A. Davis, ed., *The New Encyclopedia of Texas*, 2 vols. (Austin: Texas Historical Society, n.d.), I, 466.

25. Richardson, *East Texas: Its History and Its Makers*, IV, 23; Foster and Jones, *South and Southeast Texas*, 134–87; Davis, *New Encyclopedia of Texas*, I, 466; Strong Family Records, in private collection of Barbara Moor, Beaumont, Texas; *Beaumont Enterprise*, Mar. 28, 1960; *Beaumont Journal*, Mar. 28, 1960; "Northside Belt Railway," *The Handbook of Texas Online*, http://www.tsha.utexas.edu/handbook/online/articles/view/NN/eqn4.html [accessed Mar. 18, 2004]. After Aug. 1, 1935, Strong organized his own firm of Strong, Moore & Strong and established offices in the San Jacinto Building of Beaumont. His associates included his son, Ewell, and A. D. Moore, his former assistant at Yount-Lee.

26. *Beaumont Enterprise*, Mar. 28, 1960: *Beaumont Journal*, Mar. 28, 1960; Grobe, *New Encyclopedia of Texas*, I, 466; Strong Family Records.

27. Strong Family Records; *Beaumont Enterprise*, Mar. 28, 1960 (quotation).

28. Clark and Halbouty, *Spindletop*, 235–236.

29. Davis, *New Encyclopedia of Texas*, II, 1630. After July 31, 1935, Frank Thomas joined with Max Schlicher and Marvin W. McClendon, and the three formed the Schlicher-Thomas Oil Company of which Thomas became president.

30. Janet McClendon interview with Fred B. McKinley, July 15, 2004, Beaumont, Texas.

31. Joe Max Guillory, grandson of Max T. Schlicher, telephone interview with Fred B. McKinley, July 26, 2004.

32. McClendon interview with McKinley, July 15, 2004.

33. Ibid.; "Roscoe, TX," *The Handbook of Texas Online*, http://www.tsha.utexas.edu/handbook/online/articles/view/RR/hjr13.html [accessed Aug. 8, 2004].

34. McClendon interview with McKinley, July 15, 2004.

35. Ibid (quotation).

36. Ibid.

37. Ibid.

38. Ibid.; Minutes of Directors' Meeting – Yount-Lee Oil Company, Jan. 3, 1934, 1.

39. Clark and Halbouty, *Spindletop*, 217; Marvin W. McClendon interview with Fred B. McKinley, Sept. 9, 1987, Beaumont, Texas; Janet McClendon (mcclendonjanet@sbcglobal.net) email to Fred B. McKinley, North Myrtle Beach, South Carolina, Dec. 8, 2004; Helen Locke telephone interview with Fred B. McKinley, Dec. 31, 2004.

Chapter Four

1. *Beaumont Enterprise*, May 1, 1926; May 12, 1926; May 13, 1926.

2. Ibid., May 1, 1926; May 12, 1926; May 13, 1926. McFaddin No. 5 struck at approximately 2,500 feet.

3. James A. Clark, *Marrs McLean, A Biography* (Houston: Clark Book Co., 1969), 61 (quotation).

4. *Beaumont Enterprise*, May 14, 1926; May 17, 1926; May 23, 1926.

5. Ibid., May 30, 1926; June 2, 1926; Aug. 19, 1926; Sept. 5, 1926.

6. Ibid., June 4, 1926; Aug. 1, 1926; James A. Clark and Michel T. Halbouty, *Spindletop* (New York: Random House, 1952), 227.

7. *Beaumont Enterprise*, June 27, 1926; June 28, 1926; June 30, 1926; July 1, 1926; July 2, 1926.

8. Ibid., July 4, 1926; July 9, 1926; July 16, 1926; Clark and Halbouty, *Spindletop*, 226.

9. *Beaumont Enterprise*, July 20, 1926; July 27, 1926; July 29, 1926; Aug. 1, 1926.

10. Ibid., Aug. 3, 1926; Aug. 4, 1926; Aug. 7, 1926; Aug. 8, 1926; Nov. 14, 1933 (gives location of Yount-Lee dock facilities); Virginia Rothwell Birdwell, granddaughter of T. P. Lee and daughter of Talbot Rothwell, interview with Fred B. McKinley, Aug. 25, 1987, Beaumont, Texas. During the interview, Mrs. Birdwell indicated that when she was a child, her father took her to an undisclosed site surrounded by a tall fence, and he told her that this would be the future location of Yount-Lee's refinery. Mrs. Birdwell said that her father spoke adamantly about the plans and that he expressed no doubts that the project would come to pass.

11. *Beaumont Enterprise*, Aug. 8, 1926; Sept. 11, 1926. Petroleum Iron Works of Pennsylvania, a subsidiary of the American Republics Corporation, was one of T. P. Lee's companies.

12. *Beaumont Enterprise*, Aug. 4, 1926; Aug. 7, 1926 (quotation).

13. Ibid., Aug. 23, 1926; Aug. 24, 1926; *Beaumont City Directory, 1927–1928* (Houston: Morrison & Fourmy, 1927), 545.

14. *Beaumont Enterprise*, Aug. 25, 1926; Aug. 28, 1926; Aug. 30, 1926; Sept. 1, 1926; Sept. 6, 1926; Sept. 27, 1926; "U. S. Crude Prices Hit 21-Year High," *Associated Press Online*, http://dailynews.att.net/cgi-bin/news?e=pri&dt=040728&cat=news&st=newsd843um600&src=ap [accessed July 28, 2004]. This latter source shows that oil was selling at $42.90 a barrel on this date. That would put Yount-Lee's daily income from Spindletop alone at about $1,973,400 in today's currency.

15. *Beaumont Enterprise*, Oct. 30, 1926; Nov. 7, 1926.

16. Ibid., Nov. 9, 1926; Nov. 10, 1926 (quotation); Feb. 12, 1927; *Beaumont Journal*, Nov. 9, 1926; Nov. 14, 1933; "New Oil-Fields Under Old," *Literary Digest* 92 (Feb. 12, 1927), 23; "New Oil Fields Are Found Far Beneath Old," *Popular Mechanics* 47 (May 1927), 766; Everette A. Martin, "A History of Spindletop Oil Field," (M.A. thesis, University of Texas, 1934), 80; Christine Moor Sanders telephone interview with Greg Riley, June 4, 2004. According to the Nov. 14, 1933 *Beaumont Journal* article, Yount-Lee later drilled two more wells much deeper than the Fee No. 17. One occurred during the spring of 1933 at Double Gum Island, ten miles west of Winnie, and it went to a depth of 9,434 feet; the second, the Boyt No. 1, located about a mile away, drilled to 9,865 feet. Neither attempt, however, produced oil after heaving shale forced abandonment.

17. *Beaumont Enterprise*, Nov. 18, 1926.

18. Ibid., Nov. 19, 1926 (quotation); Dec. 3, 1926.

19. Ibid., Dec. 17, 1926 (quotations); *Beaumont City Directory, 1925–1926* (Houston: Morrison & Fourmy, 1925), 579.

20. Texas Secretary of State, Charter Records, no. 28005, Mar. 23, 1927, Office of Secretary of State, Austin, Texas.

21. *Beaumont Enterprise*, Feb. 13, 1927; Feb. 17, 1927; June 6, 1927; Jefferson County Deed Records, vol. 232, 336–337; vol. 262, 378–379, Jefferson County Courthouse, Beaumont, Texas.

22. *Beaumont Enterprise*, Feb. 13, 1927; Feb. 17, 1927; June 6, 1928; *Fagin v. Quinn*, 277 U. S. 606 (1928); *Federal Crude Oil Co. v. Yount-Lee Oil Co. et al.*, 52 S.W. 2d 56, 57–58 (1932); Clark and Halbouty, *Spindletop*, 258–259.

23. *Beaumont Enterprise*, Feb. 22, 1927; Feb. 23, 1927; Feb. 25, 1927.

24. Charter Records, no. 28005, Mar. 23, 1927.

25. *Beaumont Enterprise*, Mar. 3, 1927. Gulf held the lead with 6,672,353 barrels.

26. Ibid., Mar. 25, 1927; Mar. 31, 1927; May 6, 1927; May 10, 1927; May 15, 1927; *Beaumont Journal*, May 5, 1927; Thelma Johnson, et al., *The Spindle Top Oil Field: A History of Its Discovery and Development* (Beaumont: Neches Printing, 1927), 47 (first quotation), 48 (second and third quotations); *Beaumont City Directory, 1953* (Houston: Morrison & Fourmy, 1953), 188, 238; John H. Walker and Gwendolyn Wingate,

Beaumont: A Pictorial History (Virginia Beach: Donning Publishing Company, 1983), 121. The Port of Beaumont bought Hotel Dieu, a local Beaumont hospital, and its property overlooking the Neches River. The building no longer stands

27. *Beaumont Enterprise*, May 8, 1927.

28. Ibid., July 14, 1927; July 23, 1927 (quotation). McLean's statement referred specifically to the occasion when he staked a site on Gladys City Square No. 12 at Spindletop, but the materials for the derrick's construction were mistakenly unloaded 300 feet away. When he drilled at the location not originally intended, he hit a dry hole.

29. *Beaumont Enterprise*, Aug. 2, 1927; Aug. 5, 1927.

30. Ibid., Sept. 14, 1927; Nov. 6, 1927; Nov. 13, 1927; Mar. 31, 1928.

31. Ibid., Dec. 23, 1927; Mar. 18, 1928; C. A. Warner, *Texas Oil and Gas since 1543* (Houston: Gulf, 1939), 375–376, Marcellus E. Foster and Alfred Jones, eds., *South and Southeast Texas* (n.p.: Texas Biographical Association, 1928), 135; "U. S. Crude Prices Hit 21–Year High," *Associated Press Online*, http://dailynews.att.net/cgi-bin/news?e=pri&dt=040728&cat=news&st=newsd843um600&src=ap [accessed July 28, 2004]. This latter source shows that on this day, oil was selling at an average $42.90 a barrel. Using that figure, Yount-Lee's gross income from Texas wells alone would equate to near $631.5 million in today's currency.

32. *Beaumont Enterprise*, Feb. 28, 1928; Mar. 11, 1928; Aug. 8, 1930.

33. Ibid., Apr. 11, 1928.

34. Ibid, Apr. 1, 1928 (first and second quotations); *Beaumont Journal*, Apr. 2, 1928 (third and fourth quotations); "Ignacy Jan Paderewski," *Buckingham Hotel Online*, http://buckinghamhotel.com/Performing_Paderewski.cfm [accessed Aug. 11, 2004]. This web site provided the following quote: "The relationship between Paderewski, Steinway, and Carnegie Hall made the Buckingham Hotel the obvious choice for his visits; Steinway Hall was next door and Carnegie Hall just across the street. It offered Paderewski spacious accommodations, "peace and quiet" and delicious food, according to both his notes and those who traveled with him."

35. *Beaumont Enterprise*, Apr. 10, 1928; Oct. 20, 1932. The latter source, dealing with the dedication of the Temple to the Brave in Pipkin Park, Beaumont, states that as of that date, R. A. Dhossche served as director of the Beaumont High School Band.

36. *Beaumont Journal*, Apr. 10, 1928 (quotation); *Beaumont Enterprise*, Apr. 1, 1928; Apr. 6, 1928; Apr. 11, 1928.

37. Jim Clark, "When Paderewski Saw a Gusher," *Houston Chronicle*, Oct. 25, 1964 (first, second, fifth, and sixth quotations); *Beaumont Enterprise*, Apr. 11, 1928; Apr. 12, 1928 (third quotation); Clark and Halbouty, *Spindletop*, 234 (fourth quotation).

38. *Beaumont Enterprise*, June 17, 1928 (quotation); Apr. 29, 1928; May 2, 1928; May 6, 1928; May 22, 1928; June 13, 1928; July 24, 1928.

39. Ibid., July 31, 1928.

40. Ibid., July 11, 1928; July 14, 1928.

41. Ibid., Aug. 2, 1928.

42. Ibid., Sept. 9, 1928; Oct. 30, 1932; Nov. 14, 1933. The latter article reflects the tank farm capacity figure at 6,650,000 barrels.

43. Ibid., Sept. 18, 1928.

44. Ibid., Dec. 12, 1928; Dec. 19, 1928; Jan. 9, 1929; Jan. 26, 1929; May 25, 1929.

45. Ibid., May 1, 1929 (quotations). Throughout the years, such sale rumors were commonplace.

46. *The Fabulous Century*, 7 vols. (New York: Time-Life Books, 1969), III, 256.

47. Ibid (quotation).

Chapter Five

1. *Beaumont Enterprise*, Jan. 30, 1929; Mar. 30, 1929; Apr. 6, 1929; June 4, 1929; June 8, 1929; June 30, 1929; July 10, 1929; Sept. 21, 1929.

2. Ibid., Apr. 3, 1929.

3. Ibid., Mar. 4, 1929; Mar. 29, 1929; June 6, 1929; July 13, 1929.

4. Ibid., Aug. 21, 1929; June 28, 1931.

5. Ibid., Aug. 24, 1929; June 16, 1931; Mar. 29, 1932.

6. Ibid., Sept. 8, 1929; Sept. 12, 1929; Sept. 21, 1929; Nov. 28, 1929.

7. *The Fabulous Century*, 7 vols. (New York: Time-Life Books, 1969), III, 128; "Black Thursday 1929," *About.com*, http://mutualfunds.about.com./cs/history/a/black_thursday.htm [accessed June 25, 2004]; "Black Monday – 1929," *About.com*, http://mutualfunds.about.com/cs/1929marketcrash/a/black_monday.htm [accessed June 25, 2004]; "Black Tuesday – 1929," *About.com*, http://mutualfunds.about.com/cs/1929marketcrash/a/black_tuesday.htm [accessed June 25, 2004].

8. *The Fabulous Century*, IV, 23; "The Year in Review: 1934," *Reminisce* (July/Aug. 2004), 19; "Stock Market Crash," *PBS.org*, http://www.pbs.org/fmc/timeline/estockmktcrash.htm [accessed June 25, 2004].

9. *The Fabulous Century*, IV, 23–27; "The Year in Review: 1934," 19.

10. *Beaumont Enterprise*, Jan. 14, 1929; C. A. Warner, *Texas Oil and Gas since 1543* (Houston: Gulf, 1939), 375–376.

11. *Beaumont Enterprise*, Jan. 19, 1930; Feb. 23, 1930; James A. Clark, *Marrs McLean, A Biography* (Houston: Clark Book Co., 1969), 85–86; J. H. Russell, "Improved Drilling and Production Methods in the Gulf Coast Fields," *The American Institute of Mining and Metallurgical Engineers*, no. 1618-G (Nov. 1926), 1–4.

12. *Beaumont Enterprise*, Feb. 7, 1930.

13. Ibid., Feb. 18, 1930.

14. Ibid., Feb. 21, 1930 (quotation); *Beaumont City Directory, 1931* (Houston: Morrison & Fourmy, 1931), 453.

15. *Beaumont Enterprise*, Mar. 4, 1930; May 21, 1930; July 21, 1930; July 23, 1930; July 29, 1930.

16. Ibid., July 31, 1930; Aug. 15, 1930; Aug. 26, 1930; Aug. 27, 1930; Oct. 2, 1930.

17. Thomas C. Richardson, *East Texas: Its History and Its Makers*, ed. by Dabney White, 4 vols. (New York: Lewis Historical, 1940), I, 431–433; E. N. Tiratsoo, *Oilfields of the World* (Beaconsfield, England: Scientific Press, 1973), 259; Jack Donahue, *Wildcatter: The Story of Michel T. Halbouty and the Search for Oil* (New York: McGraw-Hill: 1979), *v* (quotation), 19.

18. *Beaumont Enterprise*, Dec. 31, 1930; Jan. 3, 1931; Feb. 3, 1931; Warner, *Texas Oil and Gas*, 375–376.

19. *Beaumont Enterprise*, Jan. 25, 1931; Mar. 1, 1931; Mar. 14, 1931; Richardson, *East Texas: Its History and Its Makers*, I, 433; James Presley, *A Saga of Wealth* (New York: G. P. Putnam's Sons, 1978), 126.

20. *Beaumont Enterprise*, Mar. 14, 1931; Mar. 17, 1931; Mar. 22, 1931; Mar. 27, 1931.

21. Ibid., Apr. 10, 1931 (quotation); Apr. 18, 1931.

22. Clark, *Marrs McLean*, 87 (first quotation); *Beaumont Enterprise*, Sept. 2, 1928; Nov. 13, 1929; Mar. 14, 1931; Apr. 19, 1931 (second quotation).

23. *Beaumont* Enterprise, Apr. 23, 1931; Clark, *Marrs McLean*, 87.

24. *Beaumont Enterprise*, May 10, 1931; Dec. 23, 1934.

25. Donahue, *Wildcatter*, 1–6.

26. Anthony McDade "Mickey" Phelan interview with Fred B. McKinley, July 14, 2004, Beaumont, Texas; Donahue, *Wildcatter*, 6, 7 (first quotation), 8 (second quotation), 9 (third quotation). The Picayune cigarette was a popular brand of that time sold in East Texas and Louisiana.

27. Donahue, *Wildcatter*, 9 (quotation), 10.

28. Ibid., 10–13, 14 (quotation), 15–19.

29. Ibid., 16, 35–39, 40 (quotation); *Beaumont Enterprise*, May 10, 1931; Dec. 23, 1934.

30. Donahue, *Wildcatter*, 44, 45 (first quotation), 46 (second quotation).

31. James A. Clark and Michel T. Halbouty, *Spindletop* (New York: Random House, 1952), 235; *Beaumont Enterprise*, May 12, 1931; May 20, 1931; Aug. 20, 1931.

32. Texas Secretary of State, Charter Records, no. 59740, June 24, 1931, Office of Secretary of State, Austin, Texas; *Beaumont Enterprise*, June 26, 1931.

33. *Beaumont Enterprise*, Apr. 22, 1931; May 16, 1931; Dec. 30, 1931; July 8, 1933; Dec. 23, 1934.

34. Ibid., undated, ca. 1930, in possession of Fred B. McKinley (quotations); Ernest N. Doring, "Collecting Violins–The Yount Collection," *Violins & Violinist* (Apr. 1938), 7–13.

35. Doring, "Collecting Violins," 9 (first quotation); *Gazette and Telegraph* (Colorado Springs), Mar. 22, 1931; *Beaumont Journal*, undated, ca. 1931, in possession of Fred B. McKinley (second quotation).

36. Program for the Paul Kochanski Concert of Mar. 7, 1931, in private collection of Kathryn Manion Haider; *Houston Chronicle*, Mar. 8, 1931; "Paul Kochanski," *Polish Music Journal*, vol. 1, no. 1 (Summer 1998), http://www.usc.edu/dept/polish_music/PMJ/issue/1.1.98/kochanski_part1.html [accessed Mar. 17, 2004]. According to the latter source, when Kochanski died of cancer in 1934, "more than 1500 mourners including nearly every prominent musician in New York attended his memorial, and 41 internationally-known personalities of the music world comprised the list of honorary pallbearers."

37. Photo of Paul Kochanski with inscription, in private collection of Mildred Yount Manion (first quotation); Philip Margolis (pmargolis@cozio.com) email to Greg Riley, Waycross, Georgia, May 23, 2004 (second quotation).

38. Doring, "Collecting Violins," 9 (quotation); *Houston Chronicle*, Mar. 8, 1931.

39. Doring, "Collecting Violins," 8 (second quotation), 9 (first quotation).

40. Ibid., 11 (quotation).

41. John H. Walker and Gwendolyn Wingate, *Beaumont: A Pictorial History* (Virginia Beach: Donning Publishing Company, 1983), 170–175; "Zaharias, Mildred Ella Didrikson [Babe]," *The Handbook of Texas Online*, http://www.tsha.utexas.edu/handbook/online/articles/view/ZZ/fza1.html [accessed Sept. 15, 2004]. Zaharias went on to become one of the greatest amateur and professional women golfers of all times, and today, her adopted city of Beaumont honors her memory at the Babe Didrikson Zaharias Museum and Visitors Center located at 1750 Interstate 10 East. Zaharias died of cancer in 1956.

42. *Beaumont Enterprise*, May 16, 1931; June 16, 1931; July 4, 1931; Aug. 17, 1931; Aug. 18, 1931; Aug. 20, 1931; Sept. 1, 1931; Sept. 5, 1931; Sept. 9, 1931; Sept. 19, 1931; Oct. 11, 1931; Nov. 6, 1931; June 16, 1932; July 19, 1932; "Sterling, Ross Shaw," *The Handbook of Texas Online*, http://www.tsha.utexas.edu/handbook/online/articles/view/SS/fst42.html [accessed Nov. 9, 2004].

43. "Ross S. Sterling," *Texas State Library & Archives Commission*, http://www.tsl.state.tx.us/governors/personality/sterling-p01.html [accessed Nov. 9, 2004]; "Sterling," *Handbook of Texas Online*. When Sterling ran for the Texas governorship the second time, Miriam A. "Ma" Ferguson defeated him. He returned to his base in Houston and made another oil fortune, serving as president of the Sterling Oil and Refining Company from 1933 to 1946. He died on Mar. 25, 1949, and is buried in Houston's Glenwood Cemetery.

44. *Beaumont Enterprise*, Aug. 9, 1931 (quotation).

45. Clark and Halbouty, *Spindletop*, 259–60; *Beaumont Enterprise*, June 21, 1932; June 8, 1934; Dec. 13, 1934; *Federal Crude Oil Co. v. Yount-Lee Oil Co. et al.*, 52 S.W. 2d 56, 57–58 (1932).

Chapter Six

1. Texas Secretary of State, Charter Records, no. 28005, Dec. 29, 1922; Mar. 23, 1927, Office of Secretary of State, Austin, Texas.

2. *Thirteenth Census of the United States, 1910* (Washington: GPO, 1913), III, 795; *Fourteenth Census of the United States, 1920* (Washington: GPO, 1921), I, 85.

3. *Beaumont Enterprise*, June 2, 1926; June 4, 1926; July 17, 1926; Nov. 25, 1926; July 19, 1930; Nov. 16, 1930.

4. Ibid., Dec. 9, 1925; Nov. 6, 1927; *Beaumont City Directory, 1925–1926* (Houston: Morrison & Fourmy, 1925), 7; Federal Writers' Project, *Beaumont: A Guide to the City and Its Environs*, American Guide Series (Houston: Anson Jones, 1939), 118.

5. *Beaumont Enterprise*, Nov. 11, 1926 (first quotation); Beaumont Real Estate Board, Banquet Program, Dec. 7, 1926 (second quotation), in private collection of Kathryn Manion Haider. According to the latter source, the Beaumont Real Estate Board of Directors was comprised of John O. Banks, president; E. Conway Broun, first vice president; C. B. Shepard, second vice president; H. C. Schwaner, treasurer; B. E. Quinn, director at large; and Mrs. F. M. Sheffield, executive secretary. R. E. Smith, H. W. Gilbert, Ross Combest, B. E. Quinn, Burt Morrison, and J. S. Edwards served on the Banquet Committee. Harvey W. Gilbert headed up the Reception Committee. All twenty-seven (27) active members of the Beaumont Real Estate Board were listed. They included Ames & Company, John O. Banks, J. V. Brock, Broun E. Conway Company, Robert Corley Company, Weyman B. Dunlap, Jr., J. S. Edwards, Sam Fertitta, W. A. Garrabrant Company, Harvey W. Gilbert and Company, Hesig and Morrison, Johnson and Fletcher, H. B. Lindsay, Marshall and Higgins, Norval M. McKee, O. H. Pennock, B. E. Quinn Realty Company, James E. Ray, Roberts Insurance Agency, Sid Stern, C. B. Shepard, T. V. Smelker and Company, R. E. Smith and Company, Southern Realty Company, Texas Realty Company, George J. Todd, and Tyrrell-Combest Realty Company.

6. *Beaumont Enterprise*, Nov. 14, 1926; *Beaumont Journal*, Dec. 8, 1926; *Houston Post*, Nov. 15, 1933; James A. Clark, *Marrs McLean, A Biography* (Houston: Clark Book Co., 1969), 67–69; Banquet Program, Dec. 7, 1926; U. S. Department of Labor, *Bureau of Labor Statistics*, ftp://bls.gov/pub/special/requests/cpi/cpiai/txt [accessed June 15, 2004]. The $2.50 to $26.71 price comparison ratio comes from the latter source.

7. *Beaumont Enterprise*, Jan. 1, 1927; Jan. 2, 1927; Feb. 6, 1927; Feb. 26, 1927; Apr. 12, 1927; Dec. 13, 1927; Jan. 13, 1928; Mar. 24, 1929; Jan. 2, 1932; Dec. 28, 1933; Federal Writers' Project, *Beaumont*, 119–134; *Fifteenth Census of the United States, 1930* (Washington: GPO, 1932), vol. 3, pt. 2, 972; *Beaumont City Directory, 1933* (Houston: Morrison & Fourmy, 1933), 11; "Official State Historical Markers of Jefferson County,

Texas," *Jefferson County, TX Online*, http://www.co.jefferson.tx.us/landmrks.htm [accessed Oct. 11, 2004]. Many of the buildings constructed during the boom generated by Second Spindletop (those that still exist) are designated as historic landmarks.

8. *Beaumont Enterprise*, Mar. 22, 1932; May 11, 1932; May 13, 1932; May 14, 1932.

9. Ibid., June 21, 1928; Nov. 13, 1931; Virginia Rothwell Birdwell, granddaughter of T. P. Lee and daughter of T. F. Rothwell, interview with Fred B. McKinley, Aug. 25, 1987, Beaumont, Texas; Dr. Hastings Harrison to Mrs. Frank Yount, Nov. 23, 1933 (quotations); "Official State Historical Markers of Jefferson County, Texas." The latter source indicates that the effort actually raised $316,000, and that "Dr. Harrison was responsible [in 1928[for securing the first Y.M.C.A. board member [B. A. Steinhagen] of the Jewish faith in the United States ... and for beginning the Garth Friendship Club for 200 underprivileged boys, Steinhagen in 1936 provided a building for Blacks." The Y.M.C.A. Building was recorded as a Texas historic landmark and in the National Register of Historic Places, both in 1979. The marker is located at 934 Calder Avenue, Beaumont, Texas.

10. *Beaumont Journal*, Aug. 6, 1932; Ben Woodhead, *Beaumonter at Large* (n.p.: n.p., 1968), 94; *Beaumont Enterprise*, Aug. 7, 1932; Minutes of City Commission and City Council, vol. 9, 557, Office of City Clerk, Beaumont, Texas; Minutes of Ordinances, vol. 6, 971, Office of City Clerk, Beaumont, Texas.

11. *Beaumont Enterprise*, Oct. 29, 1932; Nov. 14, 1932; Dec. 22, 1932; Feb. 1, 1933 (quotation); Feb. 2, 1933; *Beaumont Journal*, Dec. 21, 1932; Minutes of the City Commission and City Council, vol. 9, 612; Minutes of Ordinances, vol. 6, 1005; Frank Yount's Death Certificate, no. 537, Jefferson County Bureau of Vital Statistics, Jefferson County Courthouse, Beaumont, Texas; Steve D. O'Conor to M. F. Yount, Dec. 22, 1932; Woodhead, *Beaumonter at Large*, 94. The latter source details that although Emmett Fletcher won reelection in 1932, the 1934 silent vote of the common worker ousted him in favor of P. D. "Pete" Renfro. By then, many considered Fletcher, a man of means, as too much a part of the old Beaumont establishment, and Renfro's appeal rested on the perception that his "relatively modest personal holdings," made him "much more palatable to the rank and file."

12. Howard Perkins to Fred B. McKinley, North Myrtle Beach, South Carolina, Oct. 20, 2004. Architect Wallace B. Livesay designed this particular building. During the 1920s, the city hired Livesay and others to draw plans and replace older structures originally designed by Henry Conrad Mauer earlier in the century, because small bays would not accommodate the larger sizes of modern fire-fighting equipment. The station pictured is almost identical to the original, with the exception of larger doors and different window arrangements. Built in 1927, at a cost of $85,000 according to on-site records, the building now serves as home to the Fire Museum of Texas.

13. Minutes of Ordinances, No. 52-L, (first quotation); Minutes of Ordinances, Datebook for 1929, (second quotation); *Beaumont Journal*, May 1, 1929; May 2, 1929; May 4, 1929; June 27, 1929; June 28, 1929; W. M. Crook to Mrs. M. F. Yount, Nov. 21, 1933.

14. *Beaumont Enterprise*, May 11, 1927; May 8, 1934; James A. Clark, "Frank Yount, High Island's Overhang, and a Pipeline," *Houston Post*, Jan. 17, 1954 (quotation).

15. James A., Clark and Michel T. Halbouty, *Spindletop* (New York: Random House, 1952), 261-264.

16. Jack Donahue, *Wildcatter: The Story of Michel T. Halbouty and the Search for Oil* (McGraw-Hill: New York, 1979), 41 (second quotation), 45 (first quotation).

17. *Beaumont Enterprise*, Nov. 14, 1933.

18. Ibid., Aug. 24, 1926; Dec. 25 1926; Apr. 26, 1927; Dec. 16, 1928; Dec. 22, 1929; Dec. 22, 1934; Feb. 21, 1930; *Beaumont Journal*, Dec. 25, 1926; Marvin W. McClendon interview with Fred B. McKinley, Sept. 9, 1987, Beaumont, Texas; Marjorie Gibson Giles, former receptionist-secretary of the Yount-Lee Oil Company, telephone interview with Fred B. McKinley, Sept. 24, 1987; Anthony McDade "Mickey" Phelan interview with Fred B. McKinley, July 14, 2004, Beaumont, Texas; newspaper article, publisher unknown, undated, ca. 1930, copy in possession of Fred B. McKinley.

19. Marguerite Behar interview with Fred B. McKinley, July 16, 2004, Sour Lake, Texas (quotations).

20. Mildred Yount Manion telephone interview with Howard Perkins, Dec. 19, 2004.

21. Bruce Yount telephone interview with Fred B. McKinley, Oct. 18, 2004. According to this source, Joseph Reul Yount and his brother Lee were partners in the Rex Supply Company of Sour Lake.

22. Woodhead, *Beaumonter at Large*, 72–73 (first quotation); *Houston Chronicle*, Nov. 27, 1927 (second quotation).

23. *Beaumont Enterprise*, June 4, 1927; Dec. 22, 1929; Nov. 27, 1930; May 15, 1934; Birdwell interview with McKinley, Aug. 25, 1987; Marvin W. McClendon interview with McKinley, Sept. 9, 1987.

24. *Beaumont Enterprise*, May 15, 1934.

25. Ibid., Apr. 25, 1929; Nov. 14, 1933; *Beaumont Journal*, Apr. 24, 1929. Written the day after Frank Yount's death, the *Beaumont Enterprise* article, Nov. 14, 1933, details the widespread speculation that the oilman had plans already drawn for a great house, costing in the millions, to be built on Calder Road beyond the Caldwood Addition. According to the writer, the drawings "are laying with Yount's effects." Though not proven, these plans most probably became the basis for Spindletop Hall of Lexington, Kentucky.

Chapter Seven

1. Frank Yount's Death Certificate, no. 537, Jefferson County Bureau of Vital Statistics, Jefferson County Courthouse, Beaumont, Texas; *Beaumont Enterprise*, Nov. 14, 1933 (first quotation); "Susie Spindletop," *Beaumont Enterprise*, Feb. 5, 1933 (second, third, and fourth quotations); R. E. Masterson, *The Low Down on a High Up Man Towit: Miles Frank Yount* (n.p., n.d), 7–17.

2. Masterson, *The Low Down on a High Up Man*, 7–16, 17 (quotation). The mention of Yount's supporting the man who said, "Prohibition is a noble experiment," refers to Herbert Hoover, who in 1928 was elected in a race with Democratic rival, Alfred E. Smith, the first Catholic nominated to run for president. During the campaign, Hoover used the slogan: "A chicken in every pot and a car in every garage." Masterson's comments about two chickens and two cars reflected Yount's optimistic viewpoint of business, and if everyone worked hard enough, they would share in the American dream.

3. "Susie Spindletop," (quotations); Mary Speer telephone interview with Fred B. McKinley, Dec. 16, 2004. During this interview, Mrs. Speer remarked that her late husband, J. V. Speer, who was a member of Westminster Presbyterian Church, said that Frank Yount gave Dr. Hunter a new car every year.

4. Marguerite Behar interview with Fred B. McKinley, July 16, 2004, Sour Lake, Texas.

5. *Beaumont Enterprise*, July 3, 1928 (quotations); Ben Woodhead, *Beaumonter at Large* (n.p.: n.p.), 73; Merritt Family Bible, in private collection of Kathryn Manion Haider. This latter source shows Mildred as being born on May 2, 1920.

6. *Beaumont Enterprise*, June 15, 1933 (quotation); James A. Clark and Michel T. Halbouty, *Spindletop* (New York: Random House, 1952), 237–238; Magnolia Cemetery Records, Beaumont, Texas; Bruce Yount telephone interview with Fred B. McKinley, Oct. 18, 2004.

7. *Beaumont Enterprise,* Aug. 26, 1927; Mar. 18, 1928; Oct. 21, 1928; Jefferson County Probate Records, M. F. Yount, cause no. 5224, vol. 44, 395, Jefferson County Courthouse, Beaumont, Texas.

8. Texas Secretary of State, Charter Records, no. 3854500, Sept. 5, 1922, Office of Secretary of State, Austin, Texas; *Beaumont Enterprise*, Sept. 14, 1955. The Wall Street Property Company dissolved on Sept. 13, 1955 when Ted E. Moor of T. E. Moor and Company; and Peter W. Maida of the Peter W. Maida Insurance and Realty Company purchased it for about $400,000 in a cash transaction that included five parcels of property in downtown Beaumont.

9. Warranty Deed no. 425913, transfer of property from Edward H. and wife Ray Wilson Heath to M. F. Yount, Aug. 22, 1927, El Paso County Courthouse, Colorado Springs, Colorado; M. F. Yount, cause no. 5224, vol. 44, 395; *Beaumont Enterprise*, Aug. 26, 1927; Mar. 18, 1928; Oct. 21, 1928; W. C. "Bill" Grant interview with Greg Riley, Oct. 11, 2004, The Woodlands, Texas (quotations); *Beaumont Enterprise*, Nov. 14, 1933; *Rockledge Country Inn*, http://www.rockledgeinn.com/ [accessed May 14, 2004]; original blueprints of Rockledge, in private collection of Kathryn Manion Haider.

10. A headframe, a mining apparatus located over a mine shaft or in this situation a quarry, is used for raising and lowering materials.

11. Warranty Deed no. 459675, transfer of property from Robert D. and Alice Maude Sandford Weir to M. F. Yount, Sept. 9, 1929, El Paso County Courthouse, Colorado Springs, Colorado; *Beaumont Enterprise*, Oct. 31, 1930; Nov. 28, 1930 (quotation); Mar. 8, 1931; Jan. 17, 1932; Oct. 20, 1932; Jan. 14, 1933; Jefferson County Probate Records, M. F. Yount, cause no. 5224; Mildred Yount Manion telephone interview with Fred B. McKinley, Oct. 15, 2004; Federal Writers' Project, *Texas: A Guide to the Lone Star State*, American Guide Series (New York: Hastings House, 1940), 198–199; Paul E. Petosky (ppetosky@chartermi.net) email to Fred B. McKinley, North Myrtle Beach, South Carolina, Oct. 21, 2004. Designed by architect Wallace B. Livesay and dedicated on Oct. 19, 1932 as a project of the Colonel George Moffett Chapter of the Daughters of the American Revolution, Lelia Tatum Pipkin, regent, the "Temple to the Brave" is located on a pie-shaped lot bordered by Pennsylvania Avenue, Emmett Avenue, and the 1300 block of Sabine Pass in Beaumont. Frank Yount donated the greenstone, and that the Yount-Lee Oil Company gave the rose window [on the backside]. The building contains numerous symbolic patriotic elements: three small stained glass windows on each side reflect Texas under the rule of six flags; the circular window at the back shows the flags of the allied nations during World War I; while the large Gothic window above the door

replicates the army, navy, and the air corps, all dedicated to world peace. The particular building, which houses the Manitou Springs Post Office, located in El Paso, County, Colorado, was built in 1940. Relative to N. L. Ross' statement concerning greenstone fabrication at the Vermont Marble Company's works at Houston, the term "fabrication" had to do with polishing. Some architects, however, preferred to use the product in its natural, rough state.

12. *Beaumont Enterprise*, Mar. 11, 1928; Mary Clark Look telephone interview with Fred B. McKinley, Dec. 4, 2004 (quotation); Howard Perkins (hap70119@hotmail.com) email to Fred B. McKinley, North Myrtle Beach, South Carolina, Dec. 6, 2004. The Clarks had originally purchased their home from Dr. J. W. Garth; and even today in Beaumont, it is referred to as the "Garth house."

13. *Historic Beaumont, Texas, A Driving Tour* (Beaumont: City of Beaumont, n.d.), brochure, item no. 18 (first quotation); *Beaumont Enterprise*, Jan. 23, 1929; July 3, 1929 (second quotation); Nov. 14, 1974; Description of the Improvements: Mildred Apartment Building, Arcade Commercial Building, and Garage Building, Hall & Hall Realtors, 1974 Appraisal, in the private collection of Mildred Hall, Beaumont, Texas, puts the total square footage for the various units as: apartment building, 25,745; commercial building, 11,794; and garage, 5,814. In the Nov. 14, 1974 *Beaumont Enterprise* article, Phil Hall said that the Mildred project cost $724,227. With the property and various improvements added in, however, the $1 million dollar figure (permit amount included in the Hall & Hall appraisal) is much closer.

14. *Beaumont Enterprise*, June 8, 1930 (quotations).

15. Ibid (quotation). The article indicated that Mildred Yount's name "appears also in the glass of one of the lobby windows, and on the entrance lanterns."

16. Ibid (quotation); Mar. 26, 2001; Hall & Hall's 1974 Appraisal. According to the latter source, only the two-bedroom units had fireplaces.

17. *Beaumont Enterprise*, June 8, 1930; Mar. 17, 1972 (quotation). As an employee of the Cox and Blackburn Company, L. W. Beach installed the Frigidaires, and he later became the manager of the apartment house. According to the Mar. 17, 1972 article, the Guenther Art Galleries of Cleveland, Ohio provided the paintings.

18. Ibid (quotation); "Official State Historical Markers of Jefferson County, Texas," *Jefferson County, TX Online*, http://www.co.jefferson.tx.us/landmrks.htm [accessed Oct. 11, 2004]. Both the Mildred Apartments and the Arcade building are designated as a Texas Historic Landmark (1999) and are listed also in the National Register of Historic Places (1978).

19. *Beaumont Enterprise*, June 8, 1930 (quotations); Chilton O'Brien to Allen Grover, *Fortune Magazine*, ca. 1934. Although the first source never disclosed the leasing fees of the one and two bedroom apartment units; the second indicated that the apartments originally rented from between $175 to $325 monthly.

20. *Beaumont Enterprise*, June 8, 1930 (quotation).

21. Ibid.; Perkins email to McKinley, Sept. 10, 2004 (first quotation); Ed Rollins interview with Howard Perkins, undated, Beaumont, Texas (second quotation). Perkins detailed the contents of numerous discussions with Ed Rollins, who relayed the story to him about Pansy Yount's involvement in the Mildred Complex project. According to the *Beaumont Enterprise* article, June 8, 1930, other contractors on the job, both located in Kansas City, included: decorations by Henry Menze and "carpets and draperies by the Keith Carpet and Furniture Company ..." The furniture, though manufactured by the Shaw Company of Cambridge, Massachusetts, was purchased through Ryder's Furniture and Carpet Company, one of Beaumont's most exclusive furniture stores; the Bailey-Reynolds Company of Kansas City provided the light fixtures; and B. D. Carney did the "California stucco wall texture and plastering."

22. Warranty Deed no. 477959, transfer of property from Lafayette M. Hughes to M. F. Yount, Oct. 31, 1930, El Paso County Courthouse, Colorado Springs, Colorado; *Beaumont Enterprise*, Feb. 26, 1930; June 8, 1930; Nov. 9, 1930; Nov. 28, 1930 (first and second quotations); May 21, 1933; *Gazette and Telegraph* (Colorado Springs), June 21, 1931 (third and fourth quotations).

23. *Gazette and Telegraph* (Colorado Springs), Sept. 14, 1930 (quotation); June 21, 1931.

24. *Beaumont Enterprise*, July 7, 1927; Jan. 31, 1928; May 28, 1930; Jan. 7, 1931; Jan. 24, 1931; *Daily Texan* (Austin), Nov. 14, 1933, reported: "In his capacity as member of the Board of Regents, Mr. Yount served as chairman of the economic committee on the College of Mines and Metallurgy and on the committees in charge of the buildings and grounds, University lands, and the medical branch of the University of Galveston."

25. Captain Paul (last name unknown) sold Persian rugs, and was more or less classified as an entrepreneur who found items that Frank and Pansy Yount wanted to buy. After moving to Palm Beach years later, he apparently led a life of luxury with a wealthy widow.

26. J. H. Ransom, ed., *Who's Who and Where in Horsedom: The Directory for Horseman* (Princeton, IL: Ransom Agency, 1948), I, 101, 103 (first quotation); *Beaumont Enterprise*, June 10, 1933; Aug. 27, 1933; Sept. 24, 1933; Oct. 24, 1933; Oct. 27, 1933; Nov. 14, 1933; Mar. 4, 1934; Pete Monroe, "Famous Saddle Horse Trainers and Their Methods," *National Horseman* (Dec. 1936), 247; 248–249 (second quotations); "W. C. Grant Advertisement," *Saddle & Bridle* (Apr. 1930), 38. While Spindletop Stables operated in Beaumont, most newspaper references show it as Spindle Top Stables. The same applies to Chief of Spindle Top; his actual registration bears that out. When the stables and horse of the same name later moved to Kentucky, most references contain the single name of Spindletop. For purposes of clarity, regardless of time period, the names of both the stables and horse are indicated with the single name.

27. Monroe, "Famous Saddle Horse Trainers," 249; *W. C. Grant v. Pansy M. Grant*, no. 49117-C, vol. 23, 16, Divorce Records, Jefferson County Courthouse, Beaumont, Texas; W. C. "Bill" Grant interview with Greg Riley, Oct. 11, 2004, The Woodlands, Texas.

28. "Spindletop Hall," *American Saddlebred* (Jan./Feb. 1991), 41 (quotation); *Beaumont Enterprise*, June 10, 1933; Monroe, "Famous Saddle Horse Trainers," 249; Mildred Frank Yount, personal diary entry, May 12, 1933 indicates that she met Cape Grant for the first time on that date.

29. Ransom, *Who's Who and Where in Horsedom*, IV, 380 (photo source).

30. *Beaumont Enterprise*, June 10, 1933 (quotations); Lynn Weatherman, "The Saga of Spindletop Farm," *Saddle & Bridle* (July 1981), 28; Grant interview with Riley, Oct. 11, 2004; *Kentucky Horseman* (Sept. 1935), 46; George B. Lane to C. J. Cronan, Sept. 18, 1933; Chief of Spindletop Registration no. 12934 and transfer to M. F. Yount, Sept. 21, 1933; Mildred Frank Yount, personal diary entry, July 4, 1933; Mildred Frank Yount's Scrapbook. This latter source shows Carl Pedigo as assistant trainer to Cape Grant in the summer of 1933. Grant was so impressed with Pedigo's handling of CH Belle Le Rose when she took the 1933 World's Grand Championship in the Five-Gaited Class, he hired him. During Grant's interview, he recalled that Carl Pedigo had a daughter named Sarah Jean. When Frank Heathman left Spindletop Stables, he went to work for William P. Roth's Why Worry Stables.

31. *Beaumont Enterprise*, June 10, 1933 (quotation).

32. Ibid (first quotation); Grant interview with Riley, Oct. 11, 2004 (second, third, fourth, and fifth quotations); Ed Edson, III telephone interview with Fred B. McKinley, Nov. 2, 2004. Mr. Edson said that his mother and father, Mamie White McFaddin and Ed Edson, Jr., respectively, moved into the Kennedy house when he was nine years old; he lived there until about age fifty-two when he sold both the home and the remaining 2 ½ acres.

33. *Beaumont Enterprise*, June 10, 1933 (first quotation); Aug. 27, 1933; Sept. 24, 1933; Oct. 24, 1933; Oct. 27, 1933; Nov. 14, 1933; Mar. 4, 1934; Ransom, *Who's Who and Where in Horsedom*, I, 101; Mildred Frank Yount, personal diary entry, June 27, 1933 (second quotation); July 13, 1933 (third quotation); Monroe, "Famous Saddle Horse Trainers," 249; "Spindletop Hall," *American Saddlebred*, 41. This latter source states that Grant purchased Beau Peavine from Herbert Woolf of Kansas City, and Chief of Spindletop from George Lane of Raymore, Missouri.

34. *Beaumont Enterprise*, June 10, 1933 (quotation); Mildred Frank Yount, personal diary entry, May 13, 1933.

35. *Beaumont Enterprise*, June 10, 1933 (quotation).

36. Reagan Newton, son of Dorothy Hilliard Newton, interview with Greg Riley, Oct. 28, 2004, Katy, Texas.

37. *Beaumont Enterprise*, June 10, 1933; Aug. 27, 1933; Sept. 24, 1933; Oct. 24, 1933; Oct. 27, 1933; Nov. 14, 1933; Nov. 19, 1933 (first and second quotations); Mar. 4, 1934; Ransom, *Who's Who and Where in Horsedom*, I, 101; Monroe, "Famous Saddle Horse Trainers," 249 (third quotation), 252; "Chicago World's Fair Horse Show," *Saddle & Bridle* (Dec. 1933), 16–17; "Spindletop Time Line–1934," American Saddlebred Museum, Lexington, Kentucky, 1. The A. Montgomery Ward referred to is the one of retail fame.

38. Look telephone interview with McKinley, Dec. 4, 2004.

39. *Beaumont Enterprise*, Oct. 30, 1932; Nov. 5, 1932; Jan. 29, 1933; Nov. 4, 1933; Jan. 13, 1935; *Beaumont Journal*, 1933 South Texas State Fair Section, undated (quotations), copy in possession of Fred B. McKinley. When the Younts and Helmke purchased their Jersey stock from the Henderson Breeding Farm in Ruston, Louisiana, J. A. Blondin managed that facility. Later Pansy Yount hired Blondin and made him manager of her farm. In January 1935 the Yount enterprise received the first ever permit given to a Texas dairy that is equivalent to an actor being honored with an Oscar. The prestigious Jersey Cattle Club, with headquarters in New York City, said that the Beaumont farm could now use its national trademark in the caps of bottled milk sold on the open market. Only about one hundred of such awards had been given previously.

40. Anthony McDade "Mickey" Phelan interview with Fred B. McKinley, July 14, 2004, Beaumont, Texas (quotation); George H. Damman, *The Encyclopedia of American Cars, 1919–1929* (Glyn Ellen, IL: Crestline, 1977), 83–88, 120–129, 140–153; Jefferson County Probate Records, M. F. Yount, cause no. 5224, vol. 59, 395, Jefferson County Courthouse, Beaumont, Texas; newspaper article, publisher unknown, ca. 1929, copy in possession of Fred B. McKinley. According to the latter source, the salesman worked for the Stutz Company.

41. Newspaper article, publisher unknown, ca. 1929, copy in possession of Fred B. McKinley (quotations).

42. Damman, *Encyclopedia of American Cars*, 120–129; Randy Ema, leading Duesenberg expert, telephone interview with Greg Riley, July 20, 2004.

43. John H. Walker, and Gwendolyn Wingate, *Beaumont: A Pictorial History* (Virginia Beach: Donning Publishing Company, 1983), 145 (quotation).

44. Damman, *Encyclopedia of American Cars*, 15–22; Yount-Manion Film Collection held in Lamar University Archives, Mary and John Gray Library, Beaumont, Texas.

45. Specification of Letters Patent, no. 1,372,262 (first quotation), no. 1,499,435 (second quotation), no. 1,570,116 (third quotation), *United States Patent and Trademark Office*, http://www.uspto.gov/ [accessed Sept. 8, 2004]; *Yount Wire Line Guide or Spooling Attachment—A Dreadnaught Product*, a sales brochure. According to Patent and Trademark Office, all of the patent drawings and descriptions shown and quoted in the text fall within the "fair use guidelines," because of their extreme age, and also due to the fact that all have expired.

46. Specification of Letters Patent, no. 1,616,100 (first quotation), no. 1,755,624 (second quotation), no. 1,809,921 (third quotation), no. 2,008,633 (fourth quotation), *Patent and Trademark* Office; M. F. Yount, cause no. 5224, vol. 55, 395; Ryan Smith, Director of the Texas Energy Museum, Beaumont, Texas (rsmithtem@msn.com), email to Fred B. McKinley, North Myrtle Beach, South Carolina, Aug. 6, 2004. The last patent was issued to "MILES F. YOUNT, of Beaumont, Texas, deceased, whose EXECUTRIX is PANSY YOUNT." The original of this particular instrument is in the private collection of Kathryn Manion Haider.

47. *Beaumont Enterprise*, Mar. 8, 1931; June 15, 1933 (quotations); Nov. 14, 1933; M. F. Yount, cause no. 5224, vol. 55, 395; U. S. Department of Labor, *Bureau of Labor Statistics, Washington, D. C.*, http://data.bls.gov/servlet/SurveyOutputServlet [accessed June 24, 2004]; Stock Purchase Agreement between Yount-Lee Stockholders and Wright Morrow, July 29, 1935, in private collection of Kathryn Manion Haider. The latter document sets the value of each share of Yount-Lee stock at $2,200. Therefore, the appraisal contained within the probate records is vastly understated. When the revised value of another $8,239,992.00 (6,866.66 X $1200] is added in, Yount's net worth actually exceeded $16 million dollars. Comparing consumer price indices of 12.7 for June 1933 and 189.1 for May 2004, that equates to about $238 million in today's currency.

48. Marvin W. McClendon interview with Fred B. McKinley, Sept. 9, 1987, Beaumont, Texas; Woodhead, *Beaumonter at Large* (n.p.: n.p., 1968), 73 (first quotation); W. M. Crook to Mrs. M. F. Yount, Nov. 21, 1933 (second quotation); *Beaumont Enterprise*, Nov. 14, 1933. Frank Yount had his one-page will prepared for signature on June 25, 1932.

49. *Beaumont Journal*, Nov. 14, 1933 (quotation); *Beaumont Enterprise*, Nov. 14, 1933; Nov. 15, 1933; Nov. 16, 1933; Nov. 18, 1933; *Houston Post*, Nov. 15, 1933; Nov. 17, 1933; Bob Wilson, "I Love a Parade," *Classic Automobile Registry* (Feb. 27, 1998), 29; Ema telephone interview with Riley, July 20, 2004.

50. Mildred Frank Yount, personal diary entry, Nov. 13, 1933; *Beaumont Journal*, Nov. 14, 1933; Mildred Hall telephone interview with Fred B. McKinley, June 23, 2004 (quotation); Phelan interview with McKinley, July 14, 2004; "Charles Lindbergh, An American Aviator," *CharlesLindbergh.com*, http://www.charleslindbergh.com/kidnap/index.asp [accessed Sept. 12, 2004]. Mr. Phelan said that he was born in 1931, and soon after the infamous Charles A. Lindbergh, Jr. kidnapping on the night of Mar. 1, 1932 from his family's home in Hopewell, New Jersey, Frank Yount cautioned, many times and strongly, that Harry Phelan and Anthony McDade Phelan be especially diligent to ensure that no one carried out such actions against Mickey, Jr.

51. *Beaumont Journal*, Nov. 14, 1933.

52. Ibid., *Beaumont Enterprise*, Nov. 17, 1933.

53. Hall interview with McKinley, June 23, 2004; "Weather Report," *Beaumont Enterprise*, Nov. 14, 1933.

54. *Beaumont Journal*, Nov. 16, 1933; *Beaumont Enterprise*, Nov. 14, 1933; Nov. 15, 1933; Nov. 16, 1933; Nov. 18, 1933; *Houston Post*, Nov. 15, 1933; Nov. 17, 1933; newspaper article, publisher unknown, undated,

copy in possession of Fred B. McKinley; Minutes of City Commission and City Council, vol. 9, 763–764, Office of City Clerk, Beaumont, Texas; Crystal Ford (cford@academicplanet.com) email to Fred B. McKinley, North Myrtle Beach, South Carolina, Aug. 16, 2004; Consumer Price Index, All Urban Consumers , U. S. Department of Labor, *Bureau of Labor Statistics*, ftp://ftp.bls.gov/pub/special.requests/cpi/cpiai.txt [accessed June 27, 2004]. The consumer price indices comparison of 17.1 for 1929; 13.0 for 1933; and 186.2 for Feb. 2004 is taken from this latter source. According to the undated newspaper article listed above, members of Beaumont's "Wing Over Club" initiated a move to rename the municipal airport as Yount Field, but nothing ever came of it.

55. Rosine McFaddin Wilson telephone interview with Fred B. McKinley, Apr. 17, 2004; Glenn H. McCarthy, Speech to Beaumont Optimist Club, Nov. 8, 2004, 4.

56. Dr. Hastings Harrison to Mrs. Frank Yount, Nov. 23, 1933 (quotation).

57. *Beaumont Journal*, Nov. 16, 1933; *Beaumont Enterprise*, Nov. 14, 1933; Nov. 15, 1933; Nov. 16, 1933; Nov. 18, 1933; *Houston Post*, Nov. 15, 1933; Nov. 17, 1933; Minutes of City Commission and City Council, vol. 9, 763–764.

58. *Beaumont Journal*, Nov. 16, 1933; Mrs. Laura E. Wiess' letter to Pansy Yount, Dec. 4, 1933 (first quotation); Mickey Levito's letter dated Nov. 20, 1933 (second quotation). The statistics for the Western Union telegrams, the postal telegraphs, floral arrangements, sympathy letters, and cards are the result of a count of those actual documents found in the private collection of Mildred Yount Manion. The corporate resolutions and other sympathy letters mentioned are also in that same collection. The Austin Company had contracted earlier for the construction of the Mildred Building and Apartments.

59. Ed and Mrs. E. Humphries to Mrs. M. F. Yount, Nov. 23, 1933, (quotation); Ernest N. Doring, "Collecting Violins–The Yount Collection," *Violins & Violinist* (Apr. 1938), 7–13.

60. Aurelia Norvell to Pansy and Mildred Yount, undated (quotation); Nena Wiess Priddie to Pansy and Mildred Yount, Nov. 15, 1933; Lizzie Edwards to Pansy and Mildred Yount, undated; J. S. Edwards, "Tribute to Mr. M. F. Yount." All of these original documents are in the private collection of Mildred Yount Manion.

61. *Beaumont Journal*, Nov. 15, 1933; Rev. Dr. Alford Branch (alford_branch@hotmail.com) email to Fred B. McKinley, July 29, 2004, North Myrtle Beach, South Carolina.

62. *Beaumont Journal*, Nov. 16, 1933; *Beaumont Enterprise*, Nov. 14, 1933; Nov. 15, 1933; Nov. 16, 1933; Nov. 17, 1933; Nov. 18, 1933; *Houston Post*, Nov. 15, 1933; Nov. 17, 1933; Marguerite Behar interview with Fred B. McKinley, July 16, 2004, Sour Lake, Texas; Peggy Carter telephone interview with Fred B. McKinley, July 26, 2004.

63. *Beaumont Enterprise*, Nov. 16, 1933; Nov. 17, 1933 (first quotation); *Beaumont Journal*, Nov. 15, 1933; Nov. 16, 1933 (second quotation). The casket and vault arrived in Beaumont on the night of November 15, and it took twenty men to carry both the casket at more than 1,300 pounds and the copper vault at another 800.

64. *Beaumont Journal*, Nov. 16, 1933; Nov. 18, 1933; *Beaumont Enterprise*, Nov. 17, 1933; *Houston Post*, Nov. 15, 1933; Nov. 17, 1933; Pipkin & Brulin Company, *Registry of Visitors*, original in private collection of Mildred Yount Manion; Harry Yandell Benedict, University of Texas president, sent a Western Union telegram to Beeman Strong indicating "severe cold threatening grip made me afraid to travel today." That particular telegram is in private collection of Mildred Yount Manion.

65. *Beaumont Enterprise*, Nov. 17, 1933; *Beaumont Journal*, Nov. 16, 1933; Pipkin & Brulin Company, *Registry of Visitors*; Ernest N. Doring, "Collecting Violins," 7–13; Billy Overton interview with Howard Perkins, undated, Beaumont, Texas. During that era, widows were expected to wear the traditional garb of black during funerals, as were men and women attendees.

66. *Beaumont Enterprise*, Nov. 17, 1933 (quotation).

67. Carter telephone interview with McKinley, July 26, 2004; John H. Walker and Gwendolyn Wingate, *Beaumont: A Pictorial History* (Virginia Beach: Donning Publishing Company, 1983), 98, *Beaumont Enterprise*, Nov. 17, 1933 (quotations); Nov. 19, 1933; Sept. 10, 1937. The latter article details that Dr. T. M. Hunter, the minister of Westminster Presbyterian for the last fifteen years, died at his residence on Sept. 9, 1937. Westminster Presbyterian was formed on May 8, 1921 when the congregation of Central Presbyterian merged with that of First Presbyterian.

68. W. M. Schultz to Mrs. M. F. Yount, Nov. 17, 1933, in private collection of Mildred Yount Manion (first quotation); *Beaumont Enterprise*, Nov. 18, 1933; Nov. 19, 1933 (second, third and fourth quotations); Apr. 19, 1936.

69. Homer J. Tucker to Mrs. M. F. Yount, Nov. 20, 1933. The letterhead contains a listing of the

Committee on Negro Work, made up by Beeman Strong, chairman; Daniel Walker, vice chairman; and A. D. Moore, Secretary. Both Strong and Moore were Yount-Lee Oil Company officials.

70. Aaron Jefferson to Mrs. M. F. Yount, Nov. 23, 1933 (first quotation); *The Beaumont Informer*, Nov. 18, 1933 (second and third quotations).

71. *Beaumont Enterprise*, Apr. 19, 1936 (quotation); Magnolia Cemetery Records, Apr. 30, 1937.

72. *Beaumont Enterprise*, Apr. 12, 1934; Feb. 21, 1935; *St. Louis Daily Globe-Democrat*, Sept. 10, 1935; Hall telephone interview with McKinley, June 23, 2004; Phelan interview with McKinley, July 14, 2004; "Charles Lindbergh, An American Aviator," *CharlesLindbergh.com*; Betty Johnson to Mildred Yount, May 23, 1934 (quotations).

73. Newton interview with Riley, Oct. 28, 2004; Reagan Newton (rhnewton@sbcglobal.net) email to Fred B. McKinley, North Myrtle Beach, South Carolina, Nov. 2, 2004; Hall telephone interview with McKinley, June 23, 2004.

74. *Beaumont Enterprise*, May 19, 1934; *Beaumont Journal*, May 19, 1934. Beaumont Police Chief, Carl Kennedy, announced his resignation on May 18, 1934. L. B. Maddox replaced him.

75. Don Streater, "Another Day," *Beaumont Enterprise*, Feb. 16, 1973 (quotations).

Chapter Eight

1. Jefferson County Probate Records, M. F. Yount, cause no. 5224, vol. 54, 361; 55, 395, Jefferson County Courthouse, Beaumont, Texas; Consumer Price Index, All Urban Consumers, U. S. Department of Labor, *Bureau of Labor Statistics*, ftp://ftp.bls.gov/pub/special.requests/cpi/cpiai.txt [accessed June 27, 2004]; *Beaumont Enterprise*, Nov. 28, 1933; Apr. 13, 1934; Feb. 21, 1935 (quotation). The first *Enterprise* article refers erroneously to a policy of $30,000 written by the San Jacinto Life Insurance Company. Frank Yount's probate records clearly point out that all three insurance policies were written by Great Southern; two of these, numbers 8175J and 8197J, in the amounts of $30,000 and $20,000, respectively, listed Pansy and Mildred as co-beneficiaries. The third, policy number 31,460, listed Pansy as the sole recipient. There were 6,866 2/3 total shares of Yount-Lee stock, valued at $1,000 each, amounting to $6,866,666.66. The comparison of indices 13.2 for Dec. 1933 and 189.1 for May 2004 is taken from the Consumer Price Index above.

2. M. F. Yount, cause no. 5224, vol. 54, 361; 55, 395; W. C. "Bill" Grant interview with Greg Riley, Oct. 11, 2004, The Woodlands, Texas; *Beaumont Enterprise*, May 25, 1934; Aug. 21, 1934; newspaper article, publisher unknown, Sept. 5, 1935, copy in possession of Fred B. McKinley; Barbie Scott, Inheritance Tax Section, Revenue Accounting Division, Texas State Comptroller's Office (barbie.scott@cpa.state.tx.us), email to Fred B. McKinley, North Myrtle Beach, South Carolina, June 1, 2004, confirmed the initial payment of $221,254.36 due in inheritance taxes on Aug. 21, 1934. Frank Yount's entire estate was valued at $8,020,225.53, and as of May 24, 1935, the date that Masterson filed the inventory for Mildred's portion of the estate, only $229,010 cash remained. The inheritance tax total of almost $779,000 was the largest inheritance tax ever collected in Texas up to that point. The blueprints for Pansy's Kentucky estate are in private collection of Spindletop Hall in Lexington, Kentucky.

3. *Beaumont Enterprise*, Mar. 1, 1935 (first quotation); Mar. 20, 1935; Apr. 4, 1935; M. F. Yount, cause no. 5224, vol. 59, 255; vol. 59, 256; vol. 59, 257; vol. 59, 258; *Arkansas Democrat* (Little Rock), Mar. 4, 1935 (second quotation); Pansy Yount to Mildred Frank Yount, Feb. 14, 1935. With reference to Pansy's mention about receiving a letter from Grandma, there is no explanation as to what Hattie Minerva Uptegrove communicated. According to Mt. Zion Presbyterian Church Cemetery Records, Hattie Minerva Yount died on Nov. 16, 1936. She outlived her famous son, Frank, by three years and three days.

4. Marguerite Behar interview with Fred B. McKinley, July 16, 2004, Sour Lake, Texas (quotation); *Beaumont Enterprise*, Mar. 1, 1935.

5. Minutes of Stockholders' Meeting – Yount-Lee Oil Company, Jan. 3, 1934; Minutes of Directors' Meeting – Yount-Lee Oil Company, Jan. 3, 1934, 1 (first quotation), 2–4; Robert R. Woodward telephone interview with Fred B. McKinley, Oct. 4, 2004 (second quotation); Don Streater, "Beaumont Really Does Need Frank Yount," *Beaumont Enterprise*, Jan. 5, 1984. There were 21,000 total shares of capital stock in the Yount-Lee Oil Company of which 20,000 carried voting rights: the Yount estate held 6,666 2/3; E. F. Woodward, 5,000; Harry Phelan, 3,333 1/3; T. P. Lee, 1,500; Tal Rothwell, 1,500; Bill Lee, 1,500; and Mable Rothwell (Tal's wife), 500.

6. *Beaumont Enterprise*, Feb. 6, 1935; Marvin W. McClendon interview with Fred B. McKinley, Sept. 9, 1987, Beaumont, Texas (quotation).

7. *Beaumont Enterprise*, Nov. 3, 1933; Nov. 18, 1933; Feb. 27, 1934; May 22, 1934; Oct. 19, 1934.

8. Woodward telephone interview with McKinley, Oct. 4, 2004; James A. Clark and Michel T. Halbouty, *Spindletop* (New York: Random House, 1952), 238–245; *Beaumont Enterprise*, Apr. 19, 1934 (quotations); *Houston Chronicle*, Feb. 5, 1939; "Memorials–Wright F. Morrow," *Texas Bar Journal* (Mar. 1974), 282.

9. Woodward telephone interview with McKinley, Oct. 4, 2004; Clark and Halbouty, *Spindletop*, 238–245.

10. *Wright C. Morrow Papers, 1922–1942*, Tarlton Law Library, University of Texas at Austin; "Memorials–Wright F. Morrow," 282; Francis Wright Morrow's Death Certificate, no. 94200, Texas Department of Health, Austin, Texas; Clark and Halbouty, *Spindletop*, 238–245; "From Morrow to the Future: A New Home for the Mental Sciences Institute," *University of Texas-Houston*, http://theleader.uth.tmc.edu/archive/2002/july/morrow_house.html [accessed Apr. 01, 2004].

11. Clark and Halbouty, *Spindletop*, 238–245; Stock Purchase Agreement, dated July 29, 1935, between all Yount-Lee stockholders of record and Wright Morrow of Houston.

12. Clark and Halbouty, *Spindletop*, 238–245.

13. Ibid., 238–245; *Beaumont Journal*, June 7, 1933; *Beaumont Enterprise*, Mar. 28, 1935; Jack Donahue, *Wildcatter: The Story of Michel T. Halbouty and the Search for Oil* (McGraw-Hill: New York, 1979), 48.

14. *Beaumont Enterprise*, Mar. 30, 1935; Apr. 5, 1935.

15. Ibid., Apr. 17, 1935; Apr. 18, 1935; Apr. 22, 1935; Apr. 23, 1935; *Beaumont Journal*, Apr. 17, 1935; Marvin W. McClendon interview with Janet McClendon, Sept. 9, 1987, Beaumont, Texas, tape in private collection of Janet McClendon.

16. *Beaumont Enterprise*, Apr. 24, 1935; May 25, 1935; Clark and Halbouty, *Spindletop*, 242 (quotation).

17. Donahue, *Wildcatter*, 48, 49 (quotation).

18. Donahue, *Wildcatter*, 49–50.

19. *Beaumont Enterprise*, Apr. 30, 1935; *Federal Crude Co. v. Yount-Lee Oil Company*, 295 U. S. 741 (1935).

20. *Beaumont Enterprise*, Apr. 24, 1935; May 25, 1935; M. F. Yount, cause no. 5224.

21. *Beaumont Enterprise*, May 25, 1935; "Mrs. Yount of Spindletop Studies Methods at Outstanding Breeding Establishments," *Kentucky Horseman* (May 1935), 17; Kathryn Manion Haider interviews with Greg Riley, Nov. 20–21, 2004, Northbrook, Illinois; M. F. Yount, cause no. 5224; email from Barbie Scott, Inheritance Tax Section, Revenue Accounting Division, Texas State Comptroller's Office (barbie.scott@cpa.state.tx.us) to Fred B. McKinley, North Myrtle Beach, South Carolina, June 1, 2004, confirmed that the estate paid $557,725.55 in inheritance taxes on Aug. 30, 1935. Relative to the payment of the federal tax obligations by Pansy and Mildred Yount, Kathryn Manion Haider, granddaughter of Frank and Pansy Yount, has possession of a letter, dated July 15, 1936 from the IRS office in Austin, Texas directed to attorney R. E. Masterson in Beaumont, that reads in part: "You are advised the records of this office show that all Federal Estate Taxes assessed against the above-named estate [M. F. Yount] have been paid in full and that the case is closed." The $691,000 in expenses included $557,725.55 in state and federal estate taxes, $25,734.66 in unpaid federal income taxes for 1932, an estimated $90,000 in federal income taxes for 1933, and another $18,423.34 in state and county property taxes. To further complicate the issue, Mrs. Haider, also has possession of a sworn statement dated Feb. 1, 1939 from George H. Sheppard, Comptroller of Public Accounts for Texas, indicating that the M. F. Yount estate overpaid the $557,725.55 by $2,880.00 due to an error in evaluation "placed on the estate by the Federal Government; that the State of Texas is now due the M. F. Yount Estate the amount of $2,880.00; that this department has not issued warrant in payment of this refund for the reason there is no appropriation available for its payment." A second email from Scott to McKinley, June 24, 2004, stated that records on hand do not reflect whether the state ever issued the refund.

22. *Beaumont Enterprise*, July 4, 1935; July 12, 1935; M. F. Yount, cause no. 5224; William A. Kirkland, *Old Bank-New Bank, The First National Bank of Houston, 1866-1956* (Houston: Pacesetter, 1975), 85–86; Clark and Halbouty, *Spindletop*, 241–242; "Jones, Jesse Holman," *The Handbook of Texas Online*, http://www.tsha.utexas.edu/handbook/online/articles/view/JJ/fjo53.html [accessed June 24, 2004]; Consumer Price Index, All Urban Consumers, U. S. Department of Labor, *Bureau of Labor Statistics*, ftp://ftp.bls.gov/pub/special.requests/cpi/cpiai.txt [accessed June 27, 2004]. The consumer price indices comparisons of 13.7 for July 1935 and 189.1 for May 2004 are taken from the latter source.

23. Jesse H. Jones, *Fifty Billion Dollars: My Thirteen Years with the RFC (1932–1945)* (New York: Macmillan, 1951), ix–x (first quotation), 234–235 (second quotation).

24. Kirkland, *Old Bank-New Bank*, 85–86; Clark and Halbouty, *Spindletop*, 241–242; *Beaumont Enterprise*, July 12, 1935; "Jones, Jesse Holman," *The Handbook of Texas Online*; "First City Turns Corner on Final Days," *Houston Business Journal*, http://houston.bizjournals.com/houston/stories/2003/11/10/story2.html [ac-

cessed Oct. 9, 2004]. The First National Bank of Houston evolved into the First City Bancorporation of Texas, and as of this writing the corporation is under liquidation.

25. *Beaumont Enterprise*, July 29, 1935 (first quotation); July 30, 1935; Aug. 2, 1935; Clark and Halbouty, *Spindletop*, 242–244; Mildred Frank Yount, personal diary entries, July 28, 1935; July 29, 1935; Aug. 1, 1935 (second and third quotations). Mildred's reference to the $14 million sale amount is an obvious referral to and transposition of the actual figure in excess of $41 million.

26. Clark and Halbouty, *Spindletop*, 242–244; Standard Oil of Indiana, Board of Directors Minutes, July 29, 1935, Amoco Corporation, Chicago, Illinois, 8; Kirkland, *Old Bank-New Bank*, 85. In the latter source, Kirkland wrote, "On July 31, 1935, when the bank's total deposits were something over $41 million, a single deposit of almost $42 million was made by a new customer-for-a-day, the Stanolind Oil and Gas Company of Tulsa, Oklahoma, soon to be Pan American Petroleum Corporation, and now Amoco." Amoco has since become a part of the conglomerate British Petroleum.

27. Stock Purchase Agreement, dated July 29, 1935.

28. Ibid.; Kirkland, *Old Bank-New Bank*, 87–88. The fifteen (15) suits are: *Roy D. Calloway v. Arkansas Fuel Company*; *S. Walker Turner v. Yount-Lee Oil Company*; *Gus Davis v. F. L. Luckel*; *Velma Lee Craig v. Taylor W. Lee*; two separate cases styled *Joe McCook v. Amerada Petroleum Corporation*; *J. R. Fenton v. Minnie Jones*; *R. W. Curtis v. Yount-Lee Oil Company*; *H. F. Worley v. Yount-Lee Oil Company*; two separate cases styled *E. Cockrell v. W. O. Work*; *H. B. Fall et al. v. Yount-Lee Oil Company*; *C. H. Wilkinson v. Yount-Lee Oil Company*; *Mrs. Jeanette Mann et vir. v. Yount-Lee Oil Company*; *Federal Crude Oil Company v. Yount-Lee Oil Company*. Due to the protracted litigation, the authors made no attempt to determine the final results of any of these particular cases, or how they adversely affected each shareholder's equity in the overall escrow matter. In his book, *Old Bank-New Bank*, source referenced above with page numbers for the following quotation, Kirkland mentioned the escrow accounts specifically: "... transfers and conveyances of oil properties from Morrow to Stanolind plus checks to establish certain escrows for known and unknown contingencies were given by Morrow to the stakeholder ..." This latter statement when taken out of context and without the benefit of reviewing the Stock Purchase Agreement, dated July 29, 1935, probably led *Spindletop* authors, Clark and Halbouty, to incorrectly conclude on page 243 that "he [Morrow] had to assume all of the company's liabilities, including several important lawsuits and innumerable minor claims."

29. Kirkland, *Old Bank-New Bank*, 85–88; Fred B. McKinley, "The Yount-Lee Oil Company and the Second Spindletop Oil Field," *Texas Gulf Historical and Biographical Record* (Nov. 1988), 11–29.

30. *Houston Chronicle*, July 31, 1933.

31. Kirkland, *Old Bank-New Bank*, 85–87 (quotation).

32. *Beaumont Enterprise*, Aug. 1, 1935; *New York Times*, Aug. 1, 1935; *Wall Street Journal*, Aug. 1, 1935; Paul H. Giddens, *Standard Oil Company (Indiana), Oil Pioneer of the Middle West* (New York: Appleton-Century-Crofts, 1955), 560–561; Emmett Dedmon, *Challenge and Response, A Modern History of Standard Oil Company (Indiana)* (Chicago: Mobium, 1984), 45; Clark and Halbouty, *Spindletop*, 246–247; Stock Purchase Agreement, dated July 29, 1935.

33. Stock Purchase Agreement, dated July 29, 1935.

34. Ibid.

35. Mildred Frank Yount, personal diary entries, Aug. 2, 5, 1935 (first quotation); Donahue, *Wildcatter*, 50 (second quotation).

36. *Beaumont Enterprise*, Aug. 2, 1935 (first and second quotations); Aug. 3, 1935; Aug. 4, 1935; *Beaumont Journal*, Aug. 1, 1935; Marvin W. McClendon interview with McKinley, Sept. 9, 1987; Marjorie Gibson Giles, former receptionist-secretary of the Yount-Lee Oil Company, telephone interview with Fred B. McKinley, Sept. 24, 1987.

37. Wallace Davis, *Corduroy Road: The Story of Glenn H. McCarthy* (Houston: Anson Jones Press, 1951), 129 (first quotation), 130 (second quotation).

38. Mildred Frank Yount, personal diary entries, Aug. 13, 1935; Sept. 7, 1935.

39. Texas Secretary of State, Charter Records, no. 28005, Sept. 3, 1935; Dec. 31, 1936; July 27 1937; Dec. 6, 1943, Office of Secretary of State, Austin, Texas.

Chapter Nine

1. *Beaumont Enterprise*, Nov. 19, 1933; Howard Perkins, Director of Student Press, Lamar University (hap70119@hotmail.com), email to Fred B. McKinley, North Myrtle Beach, South Carolina, Aug. 2, 2004 (quotation).

2. Newspaper article, publisher unknown, ca. Dec. 1933, copy in possession of Fred B. McKinley.

3. *Beaumont Journal*, May 3, 1929; May 4, 1929; Emmett A. Fletcher to Mildred Yount, May 2, 1932. In this latter source, Beaumont Mayor Emmett Fletcher presented Mildred with keys to the city in honor of her twelfth birthday.

4. Pansy Merritt Yount's Death Certificate, no. A2592, Jefferson County Bureau of Vital Statistics, Jefferson County Courthouse, Beaumont, Texas; *Births*, *Marriages*, Merritt Family Bible; *Beaumont Enterprise*, Oct. 15, 1962; *Beaumont City Directory, 1916* (Houston: Morrison & Fourmy, 1916), 156; Magnolia Cemetery Records (Belle Blanchette), lot no. 35, sec. 7, Beaumont, Texas.

5. *Beaumont City Directory, 1904–1905* (Houston: Morrison & Fourmy, 1905), 62; Merritt Family Bible; Anthony McDade "Mickey" Phelan interview with Fred B. McKinley, July 14, 2004, Beaumont, Texas; *Register of Baptisms*, Westminster Presbyterian Church, Beaumont, Texas; Jefferson County Marriage Records, file no. 4657A, vol. 5, 474, Jefferson County Courthouse, Beaumont, Texas. The latter source reflects that Pansy B. Merritt and Charles A. Daley were married by Rev. William J. Lee in Beaumont on July 20, 1905; and the Merritt Family Bible adds that the ceremony occurred in a Catholic church. According to the 1904–1905 *Beaumont City Directory*, Pansy Merritt resided with her sister Belle and husband H. S. Blanchette at 763 Washington, Beaumont, Texas.

6. Newspaper article, publisher unknown, undated, in possession of Greg Riley (first quotation); *Beaumont Journal*, May 2, 1929 (second and third quotations); Ernest N. Doring, "Collecting Violins–The Yount Collection," *Violins & Violinist* (Apr. 1938), 9 (fourth quotation); "Bernard Shoninger," *The Jewish Historical Society of Greater New Haven*, http://pages.cthome.net/hirsch/bshon.htm [accessed Oct. 4, 2004].

7. By their requests, the sources that provided this material, including the quotation that described the Aurelia Norvell episode, are withheld.

8. *Beaumont Enterprise*, Nov. 19, 1933.

9. Ibid., Nov. 19, 1933; Reagan Newton interview with Greg Riley, Oct. 28, 2004, Katy, Texas; Stock Purchase Agreement between Yount-Lee Stockholders and Wright Morrow, July 29, 1935; Minutes of Stockholders' Meeting – Yount-Lee Oil Company, Jan. 3, 1934; Minutes of Directors' Meeting – Yount-Lee Oil Company, Jan. 3, 1934 .

10. "American Saddlebred," *American Saddle Horse Association,* http://www.imh.org/imh/bw/ash.html#breed [accessed Oct. 12, 2004] (quotations).

11. Ibid (quotation).

12. J. H. Ransom, ed., *Who's Who and Where in Horsedom: The Directory for Horsemen* (Princeton, IL, 1948), I, 101; *Kentucky Horseman* (Sept. 1935), 46; Pete Monroe, "Famous Saddle Horse Trainers and Their Methods," *National Horseman* (Dec. 1936), 251; Lynn Weatherman, "The Saga of Spindletop Farm," *Saddle & Bridle* (July 1981), 27; *New York Sun*, Oct. 27, 1934; "Spindletop Hall," *American Saddlebred* (Jan./Feb. 1991), 42; *Star-Telegram* (Ft. Worth, Texas), ca. 1935, in possession of Fred B. McKinley; Anne Dunn (trumpetasb1@cox.net) email to Fred B. McKinley, North Myrtle Beach, South Carolina, Nov. 27, 2004; Anne Dunn (trumpetasb1@cox.net) email to the American Saddle Horse Museum (now American Saddlebred Museum), Nov. 5, 2003. The two latter sources include an account by an African-American farrier named Oscar Clay who said that he worked for Pansy Yount at the time. Clay described various details including Lady Virginia's loss to Roxie Highland, the event that prompted Pansy Yount to buy the walk-trot queen.

13. Ransom, *Who's Who and Where in Horsedom*, I, 102 (quotation); *New York Sun*, Oct. 27, 1934; *Beaumont Enterprise*, Feb. 16, 1934 (first and second quotations); Oct. 24, 1934; newspaper article, publisher unknown, undated, copy in possession of Fred B. McKinley (third quotation); Weatherman, "Saga of Spindletop Farm," 27; "Spindletop Hall," *American Saddlebred* (Jan./Feb. 1991), 42; Mat S. Cohen, "Spindletop's Meteoric Ascent to Prominent Position," *Kentucky Horseman* (Aug. 34), 23. The term, such as "Cape Grant up," refers simply to who is riding the horse, in this case Cape Grant.

14. Ransom, *Who's Who and Where in Horsedom*, I, 102; *New York Herald Tribune*, Nov. 11, 1934; Mar. 5, 1939; *Beaumont Enterprise*, Dec. 8, 1934; Dec. 9, 1934; newspaper article, publisher unknown, undated, copy in possession of Fred B. McKinley; *Kentucky Horseman* (Jan. 1935), 11; "Yount Horses Return Home with 47 Trophies from the Five Greatest Shows in America," newspaper article, publisher unknown, undated, copy in possession of Fred B. McKinley.

15. Mildred Frank Yount, personal diary entries, Dec. 25, 1934; Jan. 11, 18, 1935; Jan. 28, 1935 (quotation).

16. *Beaumont Journal*, Feb. 16, 1935; "Mrs. Yount of Spindletop Studies Methods at Outstanding Breeding Establishments," *Kentucky Horseman* (May 1935), 17; Newton interview with Riley, Oct. 28, 2004; William Seale interview with Greg Riley, Dec. 17, 2004, Jasper, Texas. The speculations discussed herein are a matter of common knowledge.

17. *Lexington Leader*, Sept. 7, 1935 (first quotation); *Gazette and Telegraph* (Colorado Springs), Sept. 10, 1935; *New York Herald Tribune*, Mar. 5, 1939; Kathryn Manion Haider interviews with Greg Riley, Nov. 20–21, 2004, Northbrook, Illinois (second quotation).

18. Monroe, "Famous Saddle Horse Trainers,"250–251 (quotations); "Spindletop Hall," *American Saddlebred* (Jan./Feb. 1991), 42.

19. Weatherman, "Saga of Spindletop Farm," 29 (quotation); "Spindletop Time Line," American Saddlebred Museum, Lexington, Kentucky, 1; "Spindletop Hall," *American Saddlebred* (Jan./Feb. 1991), 42; M. F. Bayliss, *The Year Book of Show Horses* (New York: Blackwell Publishing Co., 1936), 13.

20. Newton interview with Riley, Oct. 28, 2004 (quotation); Mildred Hall telephone interview with Fred B. McKinley, June 23, 2004; Mildred Manion Yount telephone interview with Howard Perkins, Nov. 9, 2004. The latter source revealed the attempted abduction by the two men near Dick Dowling Junior High School.

21. *Beaumont Enterprise*, Apr. 13, 1934 (first quotation); June 27, 1938; Newton interview with Riley, Oct. 28, 2004; Amy Spence, Director of Alumnae Relations, Hockaday School, Dallas, Texas, telephone interview with Fred B. McKinley, Dec. 15, 2004; Archie P. McDonald, "Ela Hockaday: More Than A School Omarm," *TexasEscapes.com* [accessed Nov. 20, 2004] (second quotation). According to the latter source, "Ela Hockaday donated the school to the city of Dallas in 1942, but she remained as its president to 1946. Even then, she continued to reside on the campus and interact with her young ladies until her death a decade later." Hockaday School still carries on the tradition of its founder.

22. W. C. "Bill" Grant interview with Greg Riley, Oct. 11, 2004, The Woodlands, Texas (first quotation); Newton interview with Riley, Oct. 28, 2004 (second and third quotations).

23. *Beaumont Enterprise*, Mar. 13, 1936; Mar. 21, 1936 (quotations). Hauptmann's electrocution did not occur until April 3, 1936.

24. Weatherman, "Saga of Spindletop Farm," 26 (first quotation), 28 (second quotation).

25. William Capers Grant, Jr.'s Death Certificate, no. 0114, Hill County Clerk's Office, Hillsboro, Texas; "Caper," *The Random House College Dictionary*, 1968; Monroe, "Famous Saddle Horse Trainers," 247 (first quotation); Bill Grant interview with Riley, Oct. 11, 2004 (second quotation).

26. *Nola Grant v. W. C. Grant*, Jefferson County Divorce Records, file no. 47301, vol. 7, 215, Jefferson County Courthouse, Beaumont, Texas; Anthony McDade "Mickey" Phelan interview with Fred B. McKinley, July 14, 2004, Beaumont, Texas; Nola Ella Grant's Death Certificate, no. 0115, Hill County Clerk's Office, Hillsboro, Texas. The latter source shows that Nola was born on Aug. 11, 1900 at Russett, Oklahoma, and that her parents were Silas and Melinda Jane Miller Sharp.

27. Ransom, *Who's Who and Where in* Horsedom, II, 193 (photo source).

28. "Prominent Horsemen Injured in Automobile Accident," *Saddle & Bridle* (June 1936), 27 (quotations); Weatherman, "Saga of Spindletop Farm," 29; "The Chronology of Spindletop," Internal Reference Section, American Saddlebred Museum, Lexington, Kentucky, 1; Mildred Frank Yount, personal diary entries, Oct. 23, 1935; April 5, 1936. The first diary entry mentions that Carl Pedigo is no longer in Spindletop's employ; and the second indicated that Mildred arrived in Lexington and met Mr. Hailey, the new trainer.

29. "Prominent Horsemen Injured," *Saddle & Bridle*, 27; "Chronology of Spindletop," 1; Richard Hailey, son of Owen Hailey, telephone interview with Kim Skipton, curator, American Saddlebred Museum, Lexington, Kentucky, ca. 1988.

30. Monroe, "Famous Saddle Horse Trainers and Their Methods," 252 (quotation).

31. Ransom, *Who's Who and Where in Horsedom*, I, 102; Bayliss, *The Year Book of Show Horses*, 13 (second quotation); *Saddle & Bridle* (Oct. 1936), 32; Weatherman, "Saga of Spindletop Farm," 29; Pete Monroe, "Chief of Spindletop," *National Horseman* (Oct. 1936), 156, 157 (first quotation). The latter source reflects that Edgar W. Brown, III actually rode Proctor's Red Light during the loss to Beau Peavine. In his position as manager of Pinehurst Stable, Pedigo served as trainer. Some reports reflect that after winning his stake, Beau Peavine became ill; and with the possibility of the Chief not being able to perform due to lameness, Cape Grant faced quite a dilemma. Mr. and Mrs. Charles T. Fisher, owners of Dixiana Farm, donated the trophy in memory of T. Ross Long, popular horse person.

32. "Important Notice! CAPE GRANT," *National Horseman* (Nov. 1936), 179.

33. "Spindletop Hall," 42 (quotation); *Beaumont Enterprise*, Dec. 11, 1938; Weatherman, "Saga of Spindletop Farm," 31; newspaper article, publisher unknown, undated, a copy is in possession of Fred B. McKinley; The Parker Notes, in possession of the American Saddlebred Museum, Lexington, Kentucky. In August 1978, Mrs. Ruth Parker set about to detail Pansy M. Yount's life. She sent out questionnaires to fam-

ily, friends, acquaintances, business associates, members of Pansy's social circle, and various individuals in the horse world. This brief, but informative, package of notes is the culmination of that effort. The actual deeds involved in Pansy Yount's total acreage purchase are in the private collection of Kathryn Manion Haider.

34. Bettye Lee Mastin, "Spindletop Cost Million to Build," *Lexington Herald-Leader*, Apr. 5, 1959; *Beaumont Enterprise*, Dec. 11, 1938 (first quotation); "Spindletop Hall," 42 (second quotation); Richard Stewart, "Beaumont Oil Money Built A Bluegrass Mansion," *Beaumont Enterprise-Journal*, Sept. 3, 1978; "Spindletop Time Line–1937," 1; Kathryn Manion Haider interviews with Greg Riley, Nov. 20–21, Northbrook, Illinois; Elizabeth M. Simpson, *The Enchanted Bluegrass* (Lexington: Transylvania Press, 1938), 280 (third quotation).

35. "A Grand Affair," *American Saddlebred* (Mar./Apr. 1991), 48 (quotation); "Chronology of Spindletop," 1 (additional cite for quotation).

36. *Gazette and Telegraph* (Colorado Springs), July 19, 1936 (first quotation); *Beaumont Journal*, July 25, 1936 (second quotation); Mildred Frank Yount, personal diary entries, July 12, 1935; July 19, 1935; June 26, 1936; Deborah Harrison, Historic Manitou, Inc., telephone interview with Fred B. McKinley, Dec. 13, 2004. Harrison stated that Roland Bautwell, an Englishman, was instrumental in the Colorado Arts and Crafts movement. He used the Craftwood Inn as a studio and showroom, and Onaledge as a communal living space for his sister and other artisans he employed.

37. *Beaumont Journal*, July 25, 1936 (first quotation); *Gazette and Telegraph* (Colorado Springs), July 19, 1936 (second quotation); Bill Grant interview with Riley, Oct. 11, 2004, (third quotation); Haider interviews with Riley, Nov. 20–21, 2004.

Chapter Ten

1. "Spindletop Farm," *American Horseman* (May 1936), n.p.

2. "Spindletop Hall," *American Saddlebred* (Jan./Feb. 1991), 42; Elizabeth M. Simpson, *The Enchanted Bluegrass* (Lexington: Transylvania Press, 1938), 277, 279.

3. "Earl Teater," *Saddle & Bridle* (Aug. 1984), 126–127, 128 (quotation).

4. "The Spindletop Legacy," Internal Reference Section, American Saddlebred Museum, Lexington, Kentucky, 7.

5. Don Edwards, "Without New Plan, White-Elephant Landmarks Vanish," *Lexington Herald-Leader*, undated., copy in possession of Fred B. McKinley (quotations).

6. *Lexington Herald*, Jan. 24, 1938. Senator Barkley later served as Harry Truman's vice president during 1949–1953.

7. Mildred Frank Yount, personal diary entry, Apr. 5, 1938; W. C. "Bill" Grant interview with Greg Riley, Oct. 11, 2004, The Woodlands, Texas; "Garner, John Nance," *Handbook of Texas Online*, http://www.tsha.utexas.edu/handbook/online/articles/view/GG/fga24.html [accessed Dec. 15, 2004] (quotations).

8. "Spindletop Farm Prepares For Inaugural Sale," *Saddle & Bridle* (Apr. 1938), 3, 33; "The Spindletop Sale," *National Horseman* (May 1938), 197; "Spindletop Legacy," 12 (quotation).

9. *Beaumont Enterprise*, June 27, 1938; *Lexington Leader*, June 27, 1938; *Tulsa World*, Apr. 22, 1956; Mildred Frank Yount-Manion, personal diary entries, July 19, 1937; June 27, 1938. The second diary entry puts the wedding at 11:20 A.M.

10. *Lexington Leader*, June 27, 1938; Lynn Weatherman, "The Saga of Spindletop Farm," *Saddle & Bridle* (July 1981), 31 (first quotation); *Beaumont Enterprise*, June 27, 1938 (second quotation); Simpson, *The Enchanted Bluegrass*, 279.

11. *Beaumont Enterprise*, June 27, 1938; newspaper article, publisher unknown, undated, a copy is in the possession of Fred B. McKinley; Mildred Frank Yount-Manion, personal diary entries, June 27, 1938; Oct. 29, 1938; various reports from private detectives to Pansy Yount, in private collection of Kathryn Manion Haider; Kathryn Manion Haider interviews with Greg Riley, Nov. 20–21, 2004, Northbrook, Illinois.

12. Weatherman, "Saga of Spindletop Farm," 31 (first quotation), 32 (second and third quotations).

13. W. J. Harris, "Roxie Highland Enters Land of Immortals," *National Horseman* (Mar. 1939), 97 (quotations), 135; "Spindletop in Mourning," *National Horseman* (May 1939), 232.

14. Weatherman, "Saga of Spindletop Farm," 32; "Spindletop Legacy," 8, 13; "Second Annual Spindletop Yearling Sale Repeats Success of First," *Saddle & Bridle* (June 1939), 20. Tom Murphy later became manager of Reverie Knoll Farm in Danville, Kentucky.

15. Sharon M. Reynolds, "Newborns Brought the Milk of Life," *Lexington Herald*, Dec. 17, 1976 (quo-

tations).

16. *Denver Post*, Jan. 21, 1940 (quotation); Weatherman, "Saga of Spindletop Farm," 32.

17. Lease Agreement no. 630350, between M. F. Yount Estate and A. O. Maltby, et al., El Paso County Courthouse, Colorado Springs, Colorado; *Navajo Gallery & Gifts Online*, http://www.pikes-peak.com/navajo [accessed Dec. 22, 2004]; "Spindletop Legacy," 9; "Chronology of Spindletop," 2; Weatherman, "Saga of Spindletop," 32.

18. Sharon M. Reynolds, "Grandma's House," publisher unknown., ca. July 1977, copy of newspaper article in possession of Fred B. McKinley (first and second quotations); Kathryn Manion Haider telephone interview with Fred B. McKinley, Apr. 1, 2004 (third quotation).

19. "Wartime Economics and Efforts to Support the War," *At Home During WWII Online*, http://www.pomperaug.com/socstud/stumuseum/web/ARHwww3.htm [accessed Dec. 2, 2004]; *The Fabulous Century*, 7 vols. (New York: Time-Life Books, 1969), V, 158 (quotation), 159–173.

20. "Elizabeth Arden Graham," *Hall of Fame-Builder-Elizabeth Arden Graham, 2003,* http://www.canadianhorseracinghalloffame.com/bulders/2003/Elizabeth_Arden_Graham [accessed Dec. 18, 2004]; Bob Wilson, "I Love a Parade," *Classic Automobile Registry* (Feb. 27, 1998), 29 (first, second, and third quotations); unnamed classic car magazine editor, undated communication to Greg Riley (fourth quotation). In his article, Bob Wilson said that his father served as chairman of the Lexington Kentucky scrap iron drive and in that position, he had first-hand knowledge of the destruction of Frank's famous Duesenberg Judkins Berline.

21. "Spindletop Legacy," 10–11.

22. "Beau Peavine Exhibited," *National Horseman* (Aug. 1944), 15; Weatherman, "Saga of Spindletop Farm," 32–33; Kim Skipton (ashmtg@mis.net) emails to Fred B. McKinley, North Myrtle Beach, South Carolina, Nov. 30, Dec. 22, 2004.

23. Quit Claim Deed no. 727422, transfer of property from Mrs. Pansy Yount to Mildred Yount Manion, July 24, 1944; Warranty Deed no. 701205, transfer of property from Mrs. M. F. Yount to Ruth M. Roeser, et. al., June 17, 1944, El Paso County Courthouse, Colorado Springs, Colorado; Deborah Harrison to Fred B. McKinley, Dec. 9, 2004.

24. "Spindletop Legacy," 11; Warranty Deed no. 747181, transfer of property from Pansy Yount to Robert C. Whiteley, Oct. 10, 1946, El Paso County Courthouse, Colorado Springs, Colorado; L. W. "Billy" King and wife, Evelyn, manager and bookkeeper of Magnolia Cemetery, respectively, interview with Fred B. McKinley, July 27, 1987, Beaumont, Texas (both quotations attributed to Billy King); Mary Oxford Englander, "Grave Matters: The History, Lore and Necrogeography of the Magnolia Cemetery," *Texas Gulf Historical and Biographical Record*, vol. 27 (1991), 29 (additional citations for the quotations), 30; Carol Rust, "History Lives in Cemetery," *Beaumont Enterprise*, July 27, 1988; Sara Marsteller, "Body of Miles Frank Yount To Be Placed In Bronze Vault," *Beaumont Journal*, Mar. 28, 1947; Peggy Carter, Frank Yount's great niece, telephone interview with Fred B. McKinley, July 26, 2004; *National Weather Service Forecast Office, Lake Charles, Louisiana*, http://www.srh.noaa.gov/lch/research/txerly20hur4.htm [accessed June 24, 2004]. Accounts of what caused the sand on the mausoleum floor vary. Peggy Carter said that Ida Belle Yount Parrish (Frank's sister) claimed that because the mausoleum's foundation cracked under the extreme weight, the entire structure began to sink. This represents only one explanation for Pansy's action, but most other sources conclude that a hurricane or tropical storm blew through the area, and that prompted her visit and subsequent discovery. According to the National Weather Service web site, the only real possibility of a major storm passing through the area during the timeframe, 1936–Mar. 28, 1947, occurred on July 27–28, 1943. The site states, "Beaumont received 19.48 inches of rain on the 27th and 28th – establishing daily rainfall records that still stand today. Oil Derricks across Chambers and Jefferson Counties met their fate during the [unnamed] hurricane." Another possible explanation according to an article in the *Beaumont Journal*, Mar. 28, 1947, is that "damp atmospheric conditions in this section of the country caused red sandstone acquired from another part of Colorado and employed in the trim of the mausoleum to crumble." This same article, which contains photographs of both the ledger and vault, describes the "ledger" as that being "placed on top of the ground." By the time of the final interment, Frank Yount's body was buried and/or relocated at least four times: the first on Nov. 16, 1933; the second when he was placed inside the mausoleum; the third when he was placed inside a temporary facility while crews tore down the mausoleum; and the fourth when he was buried at the original site of the mausoleum.

25. "Spindletop Legacy," 11–12; J. H. Ransom, "Spindletop Farm and Doss Stanton," *Short Snorts* (Dec. 1951), 54.

26. *Beaumont Enterprise*, Sept. 28, 1949.

27. Bill Grant interview with Riley, Oct. 11, 2004; *W. C. Grant v. Pansy M. Grant*, no. 49117-C, vol. 23, 16, Divorce Records, Jefferson County Courthouse, Beaumont, Texas; David H. Corcoran, "Spindletop Hall," Thirteenth Annual Seminar for Historical Administrators, Photocopy, July 2, 1971, 11–12; Mildred Frank Yount, personal diary entries, July 3, 1934; Aug. 7, 1935.

28. Weatherman, "Saga of Spindletop Farm," 27 (quotation); Mildred Frank Yount, personal diary entries, Sept. 10, 1935 (Mildred mentions that Mr. Van Ronzelen took meals with her while he visited her at Hockaday School in Dallas), and July 3, 1936 (she states that Van Ronzelen came by while she was at Rockledge). From the tone of the entries, Pansy must have asked Van Ronzelen to look in on her daughter at every opportunity, and see how she was doing.

29. Weatherman, "Saga of Spindletop Farm," 33; "Spindletop Legacy," 12.

30. Weatherman, "Saga of Spindletop Farm," 33–34; "Spindletop Legacy," 12; "Spindletop Time Line – 1951," 2; Ransom, "Spindletop Farm and Doss Stanton," 54 (quotation); "Chronology of Spindletop," 2.

Chapter Eleven

1. Pansy M. Yount to Kathryn Manion, Oct. 24, 1960 (quotation).

2. Pansy M. Yount to Mildred Frank Manion, July 8, 1957 (quotations). Pansy's letter also included the statement, "Miss Louise [Ogden] is still with me. I am glad to have her."

3. Joseph E. McKenna to Mr. and Mrs. E. D. Manion, Aug. 29, 1956 (quotations). All of the first-class relics mentioned in this passage are in private collection of Mildred Yount Manion.

4. Lynn Weatherman, "The Saga of Spindletop Farm," *Saddle & Bridle* (July 1981), 34 (quotations); "Spindletop Hall," *American Saddlebred* (Jan./Feb. 1991), 42; *Lexington Herald*, July 4, 1937.

5. "Pleasure Yacht Christened and Blessed," publisher unknown, undated, copy in possession of Fred B. McKinley (first quotation); "Colorado Springs … Polo and Flowers Share Interest of Society," publisher unknown, undated, copy in possession of Fred B. McKinley; Bill Dreggors, Jr. interview with Greg Riley, June 30, 2004, DeLand, Florida (second quotation).

6. Dreggors, Jr. interview with Riley, June 30, 2004. According to Mr. Dreggors, Pansy's home was torn down in 1972 to make way for a large complex of apartments named "The Carriage House."

7. *Beaumont Enterprise*, Apr. 23, 1950 (quotation).

8. "Miss Dixie Rebel Tops Tattersalls For $10,000," *Saddle & Bridle* (Aug. 1952), 25 (quotations); *Lexington Herald*, July 10, 1952.

9. *Beaumont Journal*, Aug. 28, 1957 (first and second quotations); Elizabeth M. Simpson, *The Enchanted Bluegrass* (Lexington: Transylvania Press, 1938), 277; Kim Skipton, American Saddlebred Museum, Lexington, Kentucky to Fred B. McKinley, North Myrtle Beach, South, Carolina, Nov. 10, 2004; *American Saddlebred Online,* http://www.asha.net/progenysearchresults3.asp?Registration1=12027&Gender=S [accessed Oct. 20, 2004]; *Horse Quotations*, http://www.horses.co.uk/horses/quotes.cgi [accessed Nov. 22, 2004] (third quotation), Weatherman, "Saga of Spindletop Farm," 35. According to Kim Skipton, American Saddlebred Museum, Lexington, Kentucky, the location of Beau Peavine's gravesite is lost, and no tombstone now exists.

10. *Courier-Journal* (Louisville), Feb. 21, 1959 (first quotation); Bettye Lee Mastin, "Spindletop Cost Million to Build," *Lexington Herald-Leader*, Feb. 24, 1959; Apr. 5, 1959 (second quotation); J. H. Ransom, "Up an' Atom," *Horse World* (Apr. 1951), 20; David H. Corcoran, "Spindletop Hall," Thirteenth Annual Seminar for Historical Administrators, Photocopy, July 2, 1971, 10, 14. When the University of Kentucky bought nearby Coldstream Farm in Dec. 1956, the price was $1,851,300 or $1,650 an acre. Part of the 1,066 acres included Sunnyview Farm which Pansy purchased from the Ollie D. Randolph estate.

11. Jefferson County Probate Records, Pansy M. Yount, cause no. 21,928, Jefferson County Courthouse, Beaumont, Texas; *Courier-Journal* (Louisville), Feb. 21, 1959; *W. C. Grant v. Pansy M. Grant*, cause no. 49117-C, Divorce Records, Jefferson County Courthouse, Beaumont, Texas. The latter record reflects the exact number of acres involved in the transaction as 1,065.897.

12. *Courier-Journal* (Louisville), Feb. 21, 1959 (quotations).

13. Richard Stewart, "Beaumont Oil Money Built A Bluegrass Mansion," *Beaumont Enterprise-Journal*, Sept. 3, 1978 (quotation).

14. Stewart, "Beaumont Oil Money," (quotation).

15. Helen Locke interview with Howard Perkins, Nov. 15, 2004, Beaumont, Texas; Jeanette Greer interview with Howard Perkins, Nov. 15, 2004, Beaumont, Texas; "A Southeast Texas Broadcast Legend," *KLVI Radio Online*, http://www.klvi.com/history_radio.html [accessed Dec. 5, 2004]; Anthony McDade "Mickey" Phelan interview with Fred B. McKinley, July 14, 2004, Beaumont, Texas; Billy Overton, inter-

view with Howard Perkins, undated, Beaumont, Texas; *Beaumont City Directory, 1953* (Dallas: Morrison & Fourmy, 1953), 194. During this time, KFDM Radio Station located its offices at 1420 Calder.

16. *Beaumont Journal*, May 2, 1958.

17. Ibid (quotations).

18. Jane McBride, "Saving Beaumont Brick-by-Brick," *Southeast Texas Live*, http://nl.newsbank.com/nl-search/we/Archives?p_action=doc&p_docid=0FCDECC4FA5E [accessed Sept. 29, 2004]; William Seale, Ph.D., interview with Greg Riley, Dec. 17, 2004, Jasper, Texas (quotation).

Howard Perkins (hap70119@hotmail.com) email to Fred B. McKinley, Dec. 16, 2004.

19. Perkins email to McKinley, Dec. 16, 2004.

20. Kell Jones' foreman interview with Howard Perkins, undated, Beaumont, Texas (quotation). Perkins email to McKinley, Dec. 16, 2004. Perkins does not know whether Pansy (Mrs. Grant) eventually agreed to an adjustment in the financial arrangements, but at the time of his conversation with the foreman, she was holding the company to its original contract.

21. *W. C. Grant v. Pansy M. Grant*, no. 49117-C, vol. 23, 16, Divorce Records, Jefferson County Courthouse, Beaumont, Texas (quotation); *Beaumont Journal*, Mar. 3, 1959.

22. *Grant v. Grant*, no 49117-C (quotation from Pansy Grant's numerous responses during the trial); Cape Grant's Will and Probate Documents, cause no. 7337, Hill County Courthouse, Hillsboro, Texas; *Pansy M. GRANT v. W. C. GRANT*, Court of Civil Appeals of Texas, Waco, no. 3900, 358 S.W.2d 147; *Pansy M. GRANT v. W. C. GRANT*, Court of Civil Appeals of Texas, Waco, no. 3901, 351 S.W.2d 897. During the divorce proceedings, testimony reflected that Mrs. Lucille Odom, a divorced employee of the Mildred Building in Beaumont whom Carl Kennedy originally hired, carried on a long-standing affair with Cape Grant. Pansy Grant alleged that everyone in Beaumont knew about it except her, until finally, many prominent citizens brought it to her attention.

23. Marriage document, W. C. Grant and Nola E. Grant, May 28, 1962, Hill County Courthouse, Hillsboro, Texas; William Capers Grant, death certificate no. 0114, Bureau of Vital Statistics, Hill County Courthouse, Hillsboro, Texas; "W. Cape Grant," *Horse World* (June 1962), 50; "The Spindletop Legacy," Internal Reference Section, American Saddlebred Museum, Lexington, Kentucky, 13; *Houston Chronicle*, Jan. 13, 1964. Besides the stroke, Grant also suffered from arteriosclerosis. Dr. Silas Grant operated the Grant-Buie Medical Center.

24. Cape Grant's Will and Probate Documents, cause no. 7337 (quotation).

25. *Beaumont Journal*, May 22, 1953; May 9, 1958; Feb. 6, 1959; Feb. 27, 1959; June 1, 1959; *Beaumont Enterprise*, Apr. 7, 1939; May 24, 1953; June 5, 1953; Mildred Frank Yount–Manion, personal diary entry Apr. 6, 1939 announces birth of her daughter, Kathryn Bernadette. Mildred had converted to Catholicism at the time of her marriage to Ed Manion.

26. Mildred Yount Manion telephone interview with Howard Perkins, Oct. 23, 2004; Pansy Merritt Yount's Death Certificate, no. A2592, Jefferson County Courthouse, Beaumont, Texas.

27. *Beaumont Enterprise*, Oct. 15, 1962

28. Simpson, *The Enchanted Bluegrass*, 280 (quotation).

29. Jefferson County Probate Records, Pansy M. Yount' Last Will and Testament, cause no. 21,298, Jefferson County Courthouse, Beaumont, Texas, 4 (quotation).

30. Pansy M. Yount's probate records, cause no. 21,298; Clara Tomlinson, Chief, Austin Service Branch of the Internal Revenue Service, to Peter B. Wells, Beaumont, Texas, Aug. 15, 1969.

31. Mildred Yount Manion telephone interview with Fred B. McKinley, Dec. 19, 2004; *Houston Post*, Jan. 6, 1964; *Beaumont Enterprise*, Jan. 5, 1964 (quotation); Feb. 7, 1964. The Cropper's advertisement reflected that they too had "thousands of items including porcelain, pottery, crystal, brass, copper, vases, pictures, rugs, furniture …"

32. *Beaumont Journal*, Jan. 3, 1964; *Beaumont Enterprise*, Jan. 5, 1964 (first quotation); *Houston Chronicle*, Jan. 12, 1964 (second quotation); Maxine Mesinger, "Big City Beat by Maxine," *Houston Post*, Jan. 13, 1964 (third quotation).

33. *Houston Chronicle*, Jan. 13, 1964 (quotations)

34. Ibid., Jan. 8, 1964; Jan. 27, 1964 (quotations); Catalogue of Auction, Featuring the Legendary Estate of Mrs. Miles Frank Yount, Samuel Hart, Auctioneer, in private collection of Kathryn Manion Haider.

Epilogue

1. "Mildred Yount, Nine, Sells Soft Drinks to Raise Cash to Build Church Addition," unknown publisher, undated, ca. 1929, copy in possession of Fred B. McKinley, North Myrtle Beach, South Carolina

(quotation).

2. Mildred Frank Manion, personal diary entries, May 12, 1937 (quotation). An earlier entry on Aug. 21, 1935 indicated that she was still taking violin lessons.

3. Jeanette Greer interview with Howard Perkins, Nov. 15, 2004, Beaumont, Texas (quotation); Jeanette Greer telephone interview with Fred B. McKinley, Dec. 26, 2004.

4. Billy Overton interview with Howard Perkins, undated, Beaumont, Texas (quotations).

5. Overton interview with Perkins, undated, Beaumont, Texas (quotations).

6. Warranty Deed no. 882235, transfer of property from Mildred Yount Manion to Floyd S. Padgett, Feb. 26, 1952, El Paso County Courthouse, Colorado Springs, Colorado; *Beaumont Enterprise*, Sept. 14, 1955.

7. *Beaumont Enterprise*, Feb. 12, 1958 (first quotation); *Beaumont Journal*, May 16, 1958 (second quotation); Kathryn Manion Haider interviews with Greg Riley, Nov. 20–21, 2004, Northbrook, Illinois; Mildred Yount Manion telephone interview with Fred B. McKinley, Dec. 24, 2004.

8. Mildred Yount Manion telephone interview with Howard Perkins, Oct. 23, 2004; Ed Manion, Jr. (EdDannyBoyJr@aol.com) email to Fred B. McKinley, North Myrtle Beach, South Carolina, Nov. 4, 2004.

9. Sister Mary Richard, administrator of the St. Elizabeth Hospital, to Mr. and Mrs. E. D. Manion and Family, June 27, 1963 (first quotation); *Beaumont Enterprise*, May 17, 1964 (second quotation). St. Elizabeth, in turn, dedicated a wing on the sixth floor expansion in the famous widow's honor. The Manions also donated a cardiac unit to the same hospital.

10. Manion, Jr. email to McKinley, Nov. 24, 2004 (quotation); Haider interviews with Riley, Nov. 20–21, 2004; Mildred Yount Manion telephone interview with McKinley, Dec. 24, 2004; *Beaumont Enterprise*, Jan. 31, 1969; "Mrs. Mildred Manion," *Horse World* (March 1969), 60; Release of Inheritance Tax Lien no. 701900, estate of Mildred Yount Manion, Oct. 24, 1969; El Paso County Courthouse, Colorado Springs, Colorado. Mildred Frank Manion was pronounced dead in Penrose Hospital in Colorado Springs, Colorado. When the State of Colorado released the $152,000 inheritance tax lien that had been placed on Rockledge as a result of Mildred's death, all of the property matters in that area were brought to a close.

11. *Beaumont Enterprise*, Jan. 31, 1969.

12. Jefferson County Probate Records, Mildred Yount Manion, cause no. 29,017, Jefferson County Courthouse, Beaumont, Texas.

13. Reagan Newton interview with Greg Riley, Oct. 28, 2004, Katy, Texas (quotations).

14. Magnolia Cemetery Records, Beaumont, Texas.

15. Kenneth Warren, Kenneth Warren & Son, Ltd., to Trust Department, First Security National Bank, Beaumont, Texas, Feb. 5, 1973; Ed Manion, Jr. to Kathryn Manion Haider and Mildred Yount Manion, Mar. 12, 1973; Manion, Jr. email to McKinley Dec. 13, 2004. In this latter communication, Ed Manion indicates that he does not remember the name of the buyer. First Security National Bank was formed by the merger of the First National Bank and the Security State Bank, both of Beaumont.

16. *Beaumont Enterprise*, Nov. 14, 1974.

17. "McLean, Marrs," *The Handbook of Texas Online*, http://www.tsha.utexas.edu/handbook/online/articles/view/MM/fmcbp.html [accessed Mar. 18, 2004]; "In Memoriam: Verna Hooks McLean (1893–1981)," *The Texas Gulf Historical and Biographical Record* (Nov. 1981), 85–89.

18. James A. Clark and Michel T. Halbouty, *Spindletop* (New York: Random House, 1952): 246–247; "Memorials–Wright F. Morrow," *Texas Bar Journal* (Mar. 1974), 282; *Houston Chronicle*, July 27, 1954; Nov. 2, 1968; Dec. 18, 1973; *Dallas Morning News*, Sept. 24, 1952; June 26, 1955; Dec. 18, 1973; *Daily Texan* (Austin), July 26, 1955; *Austin American-Statesman*, July 28, 1954; June 19, 1955.

19. T. P. Lee's Death Certificate, no. 412, Texas Department of Health, Austin, Texas; Harris County Deed Records, vol. 374, 129–130, Harris County Courthouse, Houston, Texas; Harris County Deed Records, vol. 1510, 22–30; Map Records of Harris County, vol. 4, 3, Harris County Courthouse, Houston, Texas; Madeleine McDermott Hamm, "When Montrose Was Young," *Houston Chronicle*, Aug. 17. 1975; Rev. Sean P. Horrigan, "Links to Houston Pioneers," *UST* (University of St. Thomas) *Magazine* (Winter/Spring 2001), 10–13. According to T. P. Lee's obituary that appeared in the *Houston Chronicle*, Feb. 6, 1939, his active and honorary pallbearers represented a veritable who's who of Texas businessmen, along with other movers and shakers of the time: H. E. L. Toombs, W. W. Kyle, Jr., R. C. Evans, T. F. Rothwell, A. E. Kerr, William K. Taylor, F. L. Bouknight, Wright Morrow, John Henry Kirby, Judge Beeman Strong, Judge Randolph Bryant, Judge W. W. Moore, Captain T. Reiber, John Henry Phelan, R. B. Creager, R. S. Sterling, E. F. Woodward, H. E. Exum, C. K. McDowell, W. W. Kyle, Sr., Orville Bullington, Judge W. C. Morrow, Peter Tighe, Dr. Gavin Hamilton, Col. W. A. Childress, B. S. Horton, Upson Taylor, Preston B. Doty, A. E. Kerr, Sr., J. H. Evans, Frank T. Kincaid, Vice President John Nance Garner, Ben Coyle, E. E. Watts, Dr.

Fred L. Thomson, F. E. Thomas, M. T. Schlicher, John W. Philp, Judge R. D. Armstrong, A. M. Johnson, E. S. Nowery, J. L. Moskowitz, John T. Scott, J. A. Wilkins, D. A. Vann, A. S. Vandervoort, T. J. Donaghue, and Oscar F. Holcombe.

20. Ellis A. Davis and Edwin H. Grobe, eds., *The New Encyclopedia of Texas*, 2 vols. (Dallas: Texas Development Bureau, n.d.), II, 1678; James A. Clark and Michel T. Halbouty, *Spindletop* (New York: Random House, 1952), 221–222; *Houston Chronicle*, Oct. 29, 1936; Bill Lee's Death Certificate, no. 50083, Texas Department of Health, Austin, Texas.

21. "McCarthy, Glenn Herbert," *The Handbook of Texas Online*, http://www.tsha.utexas.edu/handbook/online/articles/view/MM/fmcaw.html [accessed June 24, 2004]; "Glenn McCarthy," *The Celtic Connection: Twentieth Century Texas*, http://users.ev1.net/~gpmoran/20THTX.htm [accessed June 24, 2004]; "Biography of Hedy Lamarr," *Internet Movie Database, Inc.*, http://www.imdb.com/name/nm0001443/bio [accessed Apr. 27, 2004]; "Tierney, Gene," *The Handbook of Texas Online*, http://www.tsha.utexas.edu/handbook/online/articles/view/TT/fticv.html [accessed June 24, 2004].

22. Forest W. McNeir, *Forest McNeir of Texas* (San Antonio: The Naylor Company, 1956), 279; "Woodward, E. F.," *National Trapshooting Hall of Fame*, http://www.traphof.org/inductees/woodward_e_f.htm [accessed Sept. 19, 2004] (quotation); "Woodward, E. F," *Texas Trapshooters Association Hall of Fame*, http://www.texastrap.com/hof.html [accessed Sept. 19, 2004]; "Woodward, E. F.," *Texas Horse Racing Hall of Fame*, http://www.texashorsemen.com/news/news_HallofFame.asp [accessed Sept. 19, 2004].

23. McNeir, *Forest McNeir*, 296 (quotation).

24. Texas Horse Racing Hall of Fame–2001 Brochure, 11 (first quotation); "Woodward," *Texas Horse Racing Hall of Fame* (second quotation); 68th Kentucky Derby, *Kentucky Derby Online*, http://www.kentuckyderby.com/2002/derby_history/derby_charts/years/1942.html [accessed Sept. 19, 2004]; "Forest McNeir Writes of E. F. Woodward," *Sportsmen's Review*, vol. 104, no. 16 (June 5, 1943), 304; Robert R. Woodward telephone interview with Fred B. McKinley, Oct. 4, 2004.

25. "E. F. Woodward as A Horseman," *Sportsmen's Review*, vol. 104, no. 16 (June 5, 1943), 305 (quotation).

26. Emerson F. Woodward's Death Certificate, no. 1615, Medina County Clerk's Office, Hondo, Texas; *Houston Chronicle*, May 25, 1943; "Mr. and Mrs. E. F. Woodward Meet Death," *Sportsmen's Review*, vol. 104, no. 15 (May 29, 1943), 283; Woodward telephone interview with McKinley, Oct. 4, 2004. Ironically, in 1937, the couple's only son, Harley, was killed in a private airplane crash, along with his cousin, when they were flying back to Houston from trapshooting competition. After Emerson Woodward's death, his grandson Robert inherited Valdina Farms. He sold it to former Texas governor, Dolph Briscoe, and his partner "Red" Nunley. Over the years, the property changed hands, and various owners sold off much of the acreage. According to Robert Woodward, Victor Boll of Houston owns what is left of the original parcel–470 acres.

27. Sue Boyt telephone interview with Fred B. McKinley, Nov. 18, 2004; *Beaumont Enterprise*, Dec. 17, 1949; Nov. 15, 1953. According to the latter source, Mable Rothwell was a sponsor of the Beaumont Music Commission, as well as the Beaumont Symphony Society. "She established the Rothwell Bible chair at Lamar Tech [now Lamar University] in memory of her husband."

28. *Beaumont Enterprise*, May 20, 1957; "Phelan, John Henry," *The Handbook of Texas Online*, http://www.tsha.utexas.edu/handbood/online/articles/view/PP/fph1.html [accessed Mar. 18, 2004]; James A. Clark, "New Jefferson County Fields Named for Phelan and McLean," *Houston Post*, Feb. 14, 1954 (quotation).

29. *Beaumont Enterprise*, Feb. 19, 1966; *Beaumont Journal*, Feb. 19, 1966; Kathryn Manion Haider interviews with Fred B. McKinley and Greg Riley, May 14–15, 2004, Northbrook, Illinois.

30. *Beaumont Journal*, Oct. 30, 1961; *Beaumont Enterprise*, Apr. 25, 1988; Apr. 1, 1993.

31. Ellis A. Davis, ed., *The New Encyclopedia of Texas*, 2 vols. (Austin: Texas Historical Society, n.d.), I, 466; *Philadelphia Record*, June 23, 1936; *Beaumont Enterprise*, Mar. 28, 1960; Aug. 16, 1964; Strong Family Records, in private collection of Barbara Moor, Beaumont, Texas.

32. *Beaumont Enterprise*, Jan. 28, 1990 (quotation).

33. Joe Max Guillory telephone interview with Fred B. McKinley, July 26, 2004; Janet McClendon interview with Fred B. McKinley, July 15, 2004, Beaumont, Texas (quotation); *Beaumont Enterprise*, Apr. 1, 1972.

34. *Beaumont City Directory, 1925–1926* (Houston: Morrison & Fourmy, 1925), 579; *Beaumont Enterprise*, ca. Apr. 1961, in possession of Janet McClendon; Marvin W. McClendon interview with Fred B. McKinley, Sept. 9, 1987, Beaumont, Texas (quotation); Janet McClendon interview with McKinley, July 13, 2004;

Janet McClendon (mcclendonjanet@sbcglobal.net) email to Fred B. McKinley, North Myrtle Beach, South Carolina, Aug. 9, 2004; Ryan Smith, Director of the Texas Energy Museum, Beaumont, Texas (rsmithtem@msn.com) email to Fred B. McKinley, North Myrtle Beach, South Carolina, Mar. 23, 2004, indicated that according to a written statement by Janet McClendon, daughter of M. W. McClendon, dated Aug. 7, 1991, the desk suite cost $3,500 in 1927. This is in line with the *Beaumont Enterprise* report, Dec. 17, 1926, that stated, "the desk and table probably will cost about $1700 each; the revolving chair $550; the two side chairs $270 each; the cabinet $950; the phone stand and humidor $350; the coat pole $110; and the waste paper basket $110." Smith then went on to explain that Frank Yount used the furniture until his death, and when Wright Morrow took control of the company, Rothwell bought the furniture and used it until he died in 1949. The furniture was then transferred to the Mable Martha Rothwell Trust, and Marvin W. McClendon used it until his death. Finally in Aug. 1991, the trust administrator, Pamela Parish of First City-Texas of Beaumont, helped arrange the gift of the furniture to the Texas Energy Museum located at 600 Main Street in Beaumont, where it remains on permanent display.

35. *Beaumont Enterprise*, June 27, 1991; Janet McClendon interview with McKinley, July 15, 2004. After July 1935, Stanolind (Standard Oil of Indiana) offered Marvin McClendon a job in its Philadelphia office, but he refused, choosing instead to remain in Texas. Subsequently, he maintained a private accounting practice from 1935 until 1976, and he also served as trustee of the trust funds for Talbot and Mabel Martha Rothwell's six grandchildren from 1953 until 1991. For a period extending from 1935 until 1942, McClendon engaged in an oil and gas business venture with his good friends Frank E. Thomas and Max T. Schlicher. He was a member of the Texas Society of Certified Public Accountants and the American Institute of Certified Public Accountants. He served for about sixteen years on the board of the First National Bank of Beaumont (now Hibernia), which later named him a director emeritus, and he was a member of the First United Methodist Church of Beaumont.

36. "Nelson Eddy – A Brief Biographical Profile," http://www.dandugan.com/maytime/n-biopro.html [accessed Sept. 1, 2004]. American entertainer Nelson Ackerman Eddy starred, danced, and sang in some of the greatest musicals of Hollywood's Golden Age.

37. *Houston Chronicle*, Nov. 7, 2004; Wallace Davis, *Corduroy Road: The Story of Glenn H. McCarthy* (Houston: Anson Jones Press: 1951), 129-130; Jack Donahue, *Wildcatter: The Story of Michel T. Halbouty and the Search for Oil* (McGraw-Hill: New York, 1979), 51 (quotation).

38. *Beaumont Enterprise*, Aug. 4, 1942; "Oakwood Cemetery, Tyler, Smith County, TX," http://www.rootsweb.com/~usgenweb/copyright.htm [accessed Sept. 11, 2004].

39. *Beaumont Enterprise*, Apr. 11, 1926 (first quotation); Glenn H. McCarthy, Speech to Beaumont Optimist Club, Nov. 8, 1948, 1 (second quotation); "Saddle Horse Museum Dedicated," *Horse World* (Aug. 62), 62–63; "Kentucky Opens Saddle Horse Museum," *Indianapolis Star*, July 1, 1962; Kim Skipton (kimasb@aol.com) email to Fred B. McKinley, North Myrtle Beach, South Carolina, Dec. 22, 2004.

Glossary

While the authors do not intend the following to be all inclusive of oil field and Saddlebred terminology and abbreviations, these are some of the most commonly used within this publication. For an in-depth study of oil field terms, we recommend R. D. Langenkamp, *Handbook of Oil Industry Terms and Phrases*, 5th Edition (Tulsa: PennWell), 1994. With full permission of the publisher PennWell Books of Tulsa, Oklahoma, those described herein are quoted directly from the text. Relative to the Saddlebred industry, we wish to thank the American Saddlebred Museum of Lexington, Kentucky for providing such; and for reference purposes, we recommend beginning with the following web sites:

American Saddlebred Museum: www.american-saddlebred.com/museum/asbmusm.htm
American Saddlebred.com:www.american-saddlebred.com/
American Saddlebreds:www.imh.org/imh/bw/ash.html

APPT. Abbreviation for Appointments. Specific equipment and gear required to be carried on, and in the road wagon used in a Roadster to Wagon Appointment Class. Correct saddles, bridles, harnesses, vehicles, and equipment, standardized by custom and used with different types of horses.

ASHB. Abbreviation for American Saddle Horse Breeders.

BHF. Abbreviation for Broodmare Hall of Fame. Status conferred upon mares that have produced a specific number of World's Champion show horses, or dams or sires of World's Champions.

Bit, Spudding. A large-diameter drill bit used to make the initial hole (the top hole) when putting down a well. A spudding bit may be from 15 to 36 inches in diameter, depending upon the depth of the well and the size of the conductor casing. The conductor casing fits into the hole made by the spudding bit. On deep, high-pressure wells, up to 2,000 feet of surface pipe is run inside the conductor casing, which is much shorter; sometimes the conductor is only 50 to 100 feet long.

Blowout. Out-of-control gas and/or oil pressure erupting from a well being drilled; a dangerous, uncontrolled eruption of gas and oil from a well; a wild well.

By. Always refers to the horse's father, the stallion, and never to the mare.

CH. Abbreviation for Champion. Designation earned by a horse that has accumulated a specific number of points at USEF (United States Equestrian Federation) recognized horse shows. The CH becomes part of the horse's name.

Cable-Tool Drilling. A method of drilling in which a heavy metal bit, sharpened to a point, is attached to a line which is fastened to a walking beam that provides an up-and-down motion to the line and tool.

Canter. A three-beat gait; a slow, collected gallop, natural to the American Saddlebred.

Collar. A coupling for two lengths of pipe; a pipe fitting with threads on the inside for joining two pieces of threaded pipe of the same size.

Conformation. The physical characteristics of a horse as compared to an ideal, perfect specimen of a particular breed.

Crown Block. A stationary pulley system located at the top of the derrick used for raising and lowering the string of drilling tools; the sheaves and supporting members to which the lines of the traveling block and hook are attached.

Dam. The horse's mother. The other terms 2nd, 3rd, and 4th dams, refer to the mother's mother, grandmother, and great-grandmother, respectively, listed on the pedigree in descending order from the lower left hand corner of the pedigree.

Derrick. A wooden or steel structure built over a wellsite to provide support for drilling equipment and a tall mast for raising and lowering drillpipe and casing; a drilling rig.

Derrickman. A member of the drilling crew who works up in the derrick on the tubing board racking tubing or drillpipe as it is pulled from the well and unscrewed by other crew members on the derrick floor.

Discovery Well. An exploratory well that encounters a new and previously untapped petroleum deposit; a successful wildcat well. A discovery well may also open a new horizon in an established field.

Drawworks. The collective name for the hoisting drum, cable, shaft, clutches, power take off, brakes, and other machinery used on a drilling rig. Drawworks are located on one side of the derrick floor and serve as a power-control center for the hoisting gear and rotary elements of the drill column.

Drill Bit. The cutting or pulverizing tool or head attached to the drillpipe in boring a hole in underground formations.

Driller. One who operates a drilling rig; the person in charge of drilling operations and who supervises the drilling crew.

Drilling Cable. A heavy cable, 1 to 2 inches in diameter, made of strands of steel wire.

Drilling Mud. A special mixture of clay, water, and chemical additives pumped downhole through the drillpipe and drill bit. The mud cools the rapidly rotating bit; lubricates the drillpipe as it turns in the wellbore; carries rock cuttings to the surface; and serves as a plaster to prevent the wall of the borehole from crumbling or collapsing. Drilling mud also provides the weight or hydrostatic head to prevent extraneous fluids from entering the wellbore and to control downhole pressures that may be encountered.

Drillpipe. Heavy, thick-walled steel pipe used in rotary drilling to turn the drill bit and to provide a conduit for the drilling mud. Joints of drillpipe are about 30 feet long.

Dry Hole. An unsuccessful well; a well drilled to a certain depth without finding oil; a duster.

Duster. A completely dry hole; a well that encounters neither gas nor liquid at total depth.

Fine Harness Division. Fine Harness horses perform two gaits both ways of the ring: the walk and the trot. It is considered bad form to canter or "break"; judges will penalize this. The Fine Harness horse does an animated, springy walk. Speed is not a factor. The good-performing horse should be beautiful, fine, alert, and airy. Like the Five-Gaited horse, the mane and tail are long and flowing, and boots are worn on the front feet. The boots of a Fine Harness horse are not needed for protection, because speed is not a factor, but are traditional and add to the elegant appearance.

Five-Gaited Division. Five-Gaited classes are considered by many as the most spectacular and exciting in the show because of the speed and strength exhibited by these well-trained equine athletes. Five-Gaited horses have long, flowing manes and tails and show both ways of the ring at the walk, trot, canter, slow gait, and rack. Protective boots are worn on the front feet to prevent possible injury from the hind feet when the horse is traveling fast.

Flame Arrester. A safety device installed on a vent line of a storage or stock tank that, in the event of lightning or other ignition of the venting vapor, will prevent the flame from flashing to the vapors inside the tank.

Gait. The manner of locomotion of an animal; the way it moves. Most horses walk, trot, and canter. American Saddlebreds have the natural ability to learn the lateral gaits, the slow gait, and the rack.

Hackney and Harness Ponies. The Hackney is a breed of carriage horse or pony that originated in England and is one of the oldest breeds in the horse kingdom. The high stepper of the show ring, these ponies have extreme action both in front and behind. Judged for brilliance and show ring presence, the Hackney presents a picture of sheer daintiness and perfection being driven to a four-wheeled vehicle called a viceroy. The Hackney is show only at the trot, but in most cases is judged at two speeds: the part-trot and the faster "Show your pony," but never at a sacrifice of form.

Integrated Oil Company. A company engaged in all phases of the oil business, i.e., production, transportation, refining, and marketing; a company that handles its own oil from wellhead to gasoline pump.

KSF. Abbreviation for Kentucky State Fair World's Championship Horse Show.

Kelly Joint. The first and the sturdiest joint of the drill column; the thick-walled, hollow steel forging with two flat sides and two rounded sides that fits into a square hole in the rotary table that rotates the kelly joint and the drill column. Attached to the top of the kelly or grief stem are the swivel and mudhose.

Lease. (1) The legal instrument by which a leasehold is created in minerals. A contract that, for a stipulated sum, conveys to an operator the right to drill for oil or gas. The oil lease is not to be confused with the usual lease of land or a building. The interests created by an oil-country lease are quite different from a reality lease. (2) The location of production activity; oil installations and facilities; location of oil field office, toolhouse, garages.

Lessee. The person or company entitled, under a lease, to drill and operate an oil or gas well.

Log, Driller's. A record kept by the driller showing the following: when the well was spudded in, the size of the hole, the bits used, when and at what depth various tools were used, the feet drilled each day, the point at which each string of casing was set, and any unusual drilling condition encountered.

Low-Gravity Oil. Oil with an API gravity (weight per unit of volume) in the mid to high 20s; heavy oil is designated as oil 20° API or lower.

Open Flow. The production of oil or gas under wide-open conditions; the flow of production from a well without any restrictions (valves or chokes) on the rate of flow. Open flow is permitted only for testing or cleanout. Good production practice nowadays is to produce a well under maximum efficient rate conditions.

Out of. Always refers to the horse's mother, the mare, and never to the stallion.

Paddock. In the Saddlebred industry, this term refers to a small fenced field, where for example, horses are placed to make them easier to catch than in a larger pasture.

Pay. Pay zone; the producing formation in an oil or gas well.

RWC. Abbreviation for Reserve World's Champion. Title earned by being reserve (second) in a class at the Kentucky State Fair Horse Show.

RWGC. Abbreviation for Reserve World's Grand Champion. Title earned by placing reserve (second) in one of the three open championship classes at the Kentucky State Fair.

Rack. The most exciting trait of the five-gaited horse was inherited by the American Saddlebred from its ancestor, the Narragansett Pacer. Each foot hits the ground separately in a four-beat cadence. The rack should be performed at a speed that is comfortable for the rider.

Reserve Champion. In a championship class, the second place winner is designated as "reserve champion."

Ribbon Colors. First place, blue; second, red; third, yellow; fourth, white; fifth, pink; sixth, green; seventh, purple; and eighth, brown.

Rig, Rotary. A derrick equipped with rotary drilling equipment, i.e., drilling engines, drawworks, rotary table, mud pumps, and auxiliary equipment; a modern drilling unit capable of drilling a borehole with a bit attached to a rotating column of steel pipe.

Road Gait. A moderately rapid trot performed by the road horse (roadster) at a speed designed to cover long distance without unduly tiring the horse.

Roadster Division. The Roadster is the speed horse of the show rings, and these driving and riding classes are exciting to watch because of the fast pace set by competitors. Horses must be of the Standardbred breed or of the Standardbred type, of attractive appearance, balanced in conformation, and with manners which make them safe risk in the ring.

Rotary Drilling. Drilling a borehole for an oil or gas well with a drill bit attached to joints of hollow drillpipe that are turned by a rotary table on the derrick floor. The rotary table is turned by power from one or more drilling engines. As the bit is turned, boring, cutting, pulverizing the rock, drilling mud is pumped down the hollow drillpipe, out through "eyes" or ports (holes) in the bit, and back up the borehole carrying the rock cuttings to the surface. The drillstring, to which the drill bit is attached, is made up of the kelly joint, lengths of drillpipe, a stabilizer, several heavy tool joints, and then the bit. When the hole is drilled to the producing formation, the borehole is cased and the casing is cemented to prevent any water above the pay zone from entering the hole. After the casing is cemented, it must be perforated to permit the oil from the pay zone to enter the wellbore.

Rotary Table. A heavy, circular casting mounted on a steel platform just above the derrick floor with an opening in the center through which the drillpipe and casing must pass. The table is rotated by power transmitted from the drawworks and the drilling engines. In drilling, the kelly joint fits into the square opening of the table. As the table rotates, the kelly is turned, rotating the drill column and the drill bit.

Roughnecks. Members of the drilling crew; the driller's assistants who work on the derrick floor and up in the derrick racking pipe, tend the drilling engines and mud pumps, and on "trips" who operated the pipe tongs to break out or unscrew the stands of drillpipe.

Roustabout. A production employee who works on a lease or around a drilling rig doing manual labor.

Royalty, Term. A royalty interest limited by time or productivity of the lease. Most royalty interests are created for a fixed period of time "and so long thereafter as oil and gas are produced." But there are such interests that run only for a specified, fixed length of time with no qualifying "thereafter" clause.

Salt Dome. A subsurface mound or dome of salt. Two types of salt domes are recognized: the piercement and nonpiercement. Piercement domes thrust upward into the formations above them, causing faulting; nonpiercement domes are produced by local thickening of the salt beds and merely lift the overlying formations to form an anticline.

Shale. A very fine-grained sedimentary rock formed by the consolidation and compression of clay, silt, or mud. It has a finely laminated or layered structure. Shale breaks easily into thin parallel layers; a thinly laminated siltstone, mudstone, or claystone. Shale is soft but sufficiently hard packed (indurated) so as not to disintegrate upon becoming wet. However, some shales absorb water and swell considerably, causing problems in well drilling. Most shales are compacted and consequently do not contain commercial quantities of oil and gas.

Sheave. A grooved pulley or wheel; part of a pulley block; a sheave can be on a fixed shaft or axle (as in a well's crown block) or in a free block (as in block and tackle).

Sire. The horse's father.

Skidding the Rig. Moving the derrick from one location to another without dismantling the structure; transporting the rig from a completed well to another location nearby by the use of skids (heavy timbers), rollers, and a truck or tractor.

Slow Gait. One of the gaits of the five-gaited horse, the slow gait is sometimes called a "stepping pace," which means that two legs on the same side of the animal move simultaneously, but the hind foot contacts the ground slightly before the front foot. The slow gait is the precursor to the rack.

Spud [In]. To start the actual drilling of a well.

Stake. A class which is preliminary to a championship class or may be a championship itself.

Strip. Removing the saddle from the horse, to allow the judge to check the conformation.

Tanbark. It is basically large pieces of shavings, much like mulch, used as the footing in many horse show rings. Designed also to prevent slipping, tanbark provides a soft, rather cushiony surface for the horses that is easy on their legs.

Three-Gaited Division. The three-gaited horse performs three gaits both ways of the ring: walk, trot, and canter. The horse should exhibit beauty, brilliance, elegance, refinement, expression, and high action. Gaits are collected, with energy directed toward animation and precision. In contrast to the long, flowing mane, and tail of the Five-Gaited horse, the mane and the dock of the tail are roached (clipped) to accentuate the quality of the horse's appearance.

Tongs (Pipe Tongs). Long-handled wrenches that grip the pipe with a scissors-like action; used in laying a screw pipeline. The head (called the butt) is shaped like a parrot's beak and uses one corner of a square "tong key," held in a slot in the head, to bite into the surface of the pipe in turning it.

Toolpusher. A supervisor of drilling operations in the field. A toolpusher may have one drilling well or several under his direct supervision. Drillers are directed in their work by the toolpusher.

Traveling Block. The large, heavy-duty block hanging in the derrick and to which the hook is attached. The traveling block supports the drill column and "travels" up and down as it hoists the pipe out of the hole and lowers it in. The traveling block may contain from three to six sheaves depending upon the loads to be handled and the mechanical advantage necessary. The wireline from the hoisting drum on the drawworks runs to the derrick's crown block and down to the traveling block's sheaves.

WC. Abbreviation for World's Champion. Title earned by winning a class at the Kentucky State Fair Horse Show, recognized site of the Saddlebred World's Championships.

WGC. Abbreviation for World's Grand Champion. Title earned by winning one of the three open championship classes (five-gaited, three-gaited, and fine harness) at the Kentucky State Fair.

Walk-Trot. Another term for the three-gaited Saddlebred as distinguished from the five-gaited horse; walk-trot horses must perform the canter.

Wellhead. The top of the casing and the attached control and flow valves. The wellhead is where control valves, testing equipment, and take-off piping are located.

Well Naming. The naming of a well follows a longstanding, logical practice. First is the name of the operator or operators drilling the well; then the landowner from whom the lease was obtained; and last the number of the well on the lease or block.

Wildcatter. A person or company that drills a wildcat well; a person held in high esteem by the industry, if he is otherwise worthy; an entrepreneur to whom taking financial risks to find oil is the name of the game.

Wildcat Well. A well drilled in an unproved area, far from a producing well; an exploratory well in the truest sense of the word; a well drilled out where the wildcats prowl and "the hoot owls mate with the chickens."

Bibliography

Books

Arnold, Ralph, and William J. Kemnitzer. *Petroleum in the United States and Possessions*. New York: Harper, 1931.

Bayliss, M. F. *The Year Book of Show Horses*. New York: Blackwell Publishing Co., 1936.

Block, W. T. *Sour Lake, Texas: From Mud Baths to Millionaires, 1835–1909*. Liberty, Texas: Atascosito Historical Association, 1995.

"Caper." *The Random House College Dictionary*, 1968.

Clark, James A. *Marrs McLean, A Biography*. Houston: Clark Book Co., 1969.

Clark, James A., and Michel T. Halbouty. *Spindletop*. New York: Random House, 1952.

Clark, Joseph L. *The Texas Gulf Coast: Its History and Development*. 4 vols. New York: Lewis Historical, 1955.

Crenshaw, Rosa D., and W. W. Ward. *Cornerstones: A History of Beaumont and Methodism, 1840–1968*. Beaumont: First Methodist Church Historical Committee, 1968.

Curcio, Vincent. *Chrysler: The Life and Times of an Automotive Genius*. New York: Oxford University Press, 2000.

Damman, George H. *The Encyclopedia of American Cars, 1919–1929*. Glyn Ellen, IL: Crestline, 1977.

Davis, Ellis A., ed. *The New Encyclopedia of Texas*. 2 vols. Austin: Texas Historical Society, n.d.

Davis, Ellis A., and Edwin H. Grobe, eds. *The New Encyclopedia of Texas*. 3 vols. Dallas: Texas Development Bureau, n.d.

Dedmon, Emmett. *Challenge and Response: A Modern History of Standard Oil Company (Indiana)*. Chicago: Mobium, 1984.

Donahue, Jack. *Wildcatter: The Story of Michel T. Halbouty and the Search for Oil*. New York: McGraw-Hill, 1979.

Duffy, Winifred A. *John Wiley Link*. Houston: D. Armstrong Co., 1974.

English, Alyce Kirby. *Builders of Beaumont*. Beaumont: n.p., 1929.

Federal Writers' Project. *Beaumont: A Guide to the City and Its Environs*. American Guide Series. Houston: Anson Jones, 1939.

_____. *Texas: A Guide to the Lone Star State*. American Guide Series. New York: Hastings House, 1940.

Foster, Marcellus E., and Alfred Jones, eds. *South and Southeast Texas*. N.p.: Texas Biographical Association, 1928.

Giddens, Paul H. *Standard Oil Company (Indiana), Oil Pioneer of the Middle West*. New York: Appleton-Century-Crofts, 1955.

Johnson, Thelma, et al. *The Spindle Top Oil Field: A History of Its Discovery and Development*. Beaumont: Neches Printing, 1927.

Jones, Jesse H. *Fifty Billion Dollars: My Thirteen Years with the RFC (1932–1945)*. New York: Macmillan, 1951.

Kirkland, William A. *Old Bank–New Bank, The First National Bank, Houston, 1866-1956*. Houston: Pacesetter, 1975.

Langenkamp, R. D. *Handbook of Oil Industry Terms and Phrases*, 4th Edition. Tulsa: PennWell, 1984.

Linsley, Judith W., and Ellen W. Rienstra. *Beaumont, A Chronicle of Promise*. Woodland Hills: Windsor, 1982.

Linsley, Judith W., Ellen W. Rienstra, and Jo Ann Stiles. *Giant Under the Hill*. Austin: Texas State Historical Association, 2002.

Marcosson, Isaac F. *The Black Golconda*. New York: Harper, 1924.

McNeir, Forest W. *Forest McNeir of Texas.* San Antonio: The Naylor Company, 1956.
Presley, James. *A Saga of Wealth.* New York: G. P. Putnam's Sons, 1978.
Ransom, J. H., ed. *Who's Who and Where in Horsedom: The Directory for Horseman*. Princeton, IL: Ransom Agency, 1948.
Richardson, Thomas C. *East Texas: Its History and Its Makers*. Ed. by Dabney White. 4 vols. New York: Lewis Historical, 1940.
Rister, Carl C. *Oil: Titan of the Southwest*. Norman: University of Oklahoma, 1949.
Sanders, Christine Moor. *Spindletop: The Untold Story*. Beaumont: Spindletop-Gladys City Boomtown Museum, 2000.
Simpson, Elizabeth M. *The Enchanted Bluegrass*. Lexington: Transylvania Press, 1938.
Stratton, Florence. *The Story of Beaumont*. Houston: Hercules, n.d.
The Fabulous Century. 7 vols. New York: Time-Life Books, 1969.
Tiratsoo, E. N. *Oilfields of the World*. Beaconsfield, England: Scientific Press, 1973.
Vanderholt, Father James F., Carolyn B. Martinez, and Karen A Gilman. *Diocese of Beaumont: The Catholic Story of Southeast Texas*. Beaumont: Diocese of Beaumont, 1991.
Walker, John H., and Gwendolyn Wingate. *Beaumont: A Pictorial History*. Virginia Beach: Donning Publishing Company, 1983.
Warner, C. A. *Texas Oil and Gas since 1543*. Houston: Gulf, 1939.
Webb, Walter P., et al. *The Handbook of Texas*. 2 vols. Austin: The Texas State Historical Association, 1952.
Who Was Who In America, 1897–1942. Vol. 1. Chicago: Marquis, 1950.
Woodhead, Ben. *Beaumonter at Large*. N.p.: n.p., 1968.

Articles

"A Grand Affair." *American Saddlebred* (March/April 1991), 48.
"Beau Peavine Exhibited." *National Horseman* (August 1944), 15.
Brooks, Bradley C. "Owen J. T. Southwell, Architect, and the John Henry Phelan House." *The Texas Gulf Historical and Biographical Record*, vol. 35 (November 1999), 3–18.
"Chicago World's Fair Horse Show." *Saddle & Bridle* (December 1933), 12–13, 15–17, 53.
Cohen, Mat S. "Spindletop's Meteoric Ascent to Prominent Position." *Kentucky Horseman* (August 1934), 23.
Davis, Wallace. "History Repeats Itself–Spindletop is Concrete Example." *Oil Weekly* 40 (August 27, 1926), 34–44.
Doring, Ernest N. "Collecting Violins–The Yount Collection." *Violins & Violinist* (April 1938), 7–13.
"Earl Teater." *Saddle & Bridle* (August 1984), 126–128.
Englander, Mary Oxford. "Grave Matters: The History, Lore, and Necrogeography of the Magnolia Cemetery." *Texas Gulf Historical and Biographical Record*, vol. 27 (1991), 29–30.
Harris, W. J. "Roxie Highland Enters Land of Immortals." *National Horseman* (March 1939), 97, 135.
Horrigan, Rev. Sean P. "Links to Houston Pioneers." *UST (University of St. Thomas) Magazine* (Winter/Spring 2001), 10–13.
"Important Notice! CAPE GRANT." *National Horseman* (November 1936), 179.
"In Memoriam: Verna Hooks McLean (1893–1981)." *Texas Gulf Historical and Biographical Record* (November 1981), 85–89.
Kentucky Horseman (January 1935), 11.
_____ (September 1935), 46.
McKinley, Fred B. "The Yount-Lee Oil Company and the Second Spindletop Oil Field." *Texas Gulf Historical and Biographical Record* (November 1988), 11–29.
"Memorials–Wright F. Morrow." *Texas Bar Journal* (March 1974), 282.
"Miss Dixie Rebel Tops Tattersalls For $10,000." *Saddle & Bridle* (August 1952), 25.
Monroe, Pete. "Chief of Spindletop." *National Horseman* (October 1936), 156–157.
_____. "Famous Saddle Horse Trainers and Their Methods." *National Horseman* (December 1936), 247–254.
"Mrs. Mildred Manion." *Horse World* (March 1969), 60.
"Mrs. Yount of Spindletop Studies Methods at Outstanding Breeding Establishments." *Kentucky Horseman* (May 1935), 17.
"New Oil Fields Are Found Far Beneath Old." *Popular Mechanics* 47 (May 1926), 766.
"New Oil-Fields Under Old." *Literary Digest* 92 (February 12, 1927), 23.
"Prominent Horsemen Injured in Automobile Accident." *Saddle & Bridle* (June 1936), 27.

Ransom, J. H. "Up an' Atom." *Horse World* (April 1951), 20.

_____. "Spindletop Farm and Doss Stanton." *Short Snorts* (December 1951), 54.

Russell, J. H. "Improved Drilling and Production Methods in the Gulf Coast Fields." *The American Institute of Mining and Metallurgical Engineers*, no. 1618-G (November 1926), 1–4.

Saddle & Bridle (October 1936), 32, 55.

"Saddle Horse Museum Dedicated." *Horse World* (August 1962), 62–63.

"Second Annual Spindletop Yearling Sale Repeats Success of First." *Saddle & Bridle* (June 1939), 20.

"Spindletop Farm." *American Horseman* (May 1936), n. p. Copy in possession of Fred B. McKinley.

"Spindletop Hall." *American Saddlebred* (January/February 1991), 41–42.

"Spindletop in Mourning." *National Horseman* (May 1939), 232.

"The Spindletop Sale." *National Horseman* (May 1938), 196–197.

"The Texas Corporation." *Fortune* 1 (April 1930), 49–120.

"The Year in Review: 1934." *Reminisce* (July/Aug. 2004), 19–21.

"W. C. Grant Advertisement." *Saddle & Bridle* (April 1930), 38.

"W. Cape Grant." *Horse World* (June 1962), 50.

Wagner, Paul. "Spindletop's History-Making Comeback Lacks Human Background of Old." *National Petroleum News* 18 (September 22, 1926), 73–78.

Weatherman, Lynn. "The Saga of Spindletop Farm." *Saddle & Bridle* (July 1981), 25–35.

Wilson, Bob. "I Love a Parade." *Classic Automobile Registry* (February 27, 1998), 29.

Newspapers

Arkansas Democrat (Little Rock), March 4, 1935.

Austin American-Statesman, July 28, 1954–June 19, 1955.

Beaumont Daily Journal, September 16, 1915.

Beaumont Enterprise, February 5, 1908–April 1, 1993.

Beaumont Enterprise-Journal, September 3, 1978.

Beaumont Informer, November 18, 1933.

Beaumont Journal, February 15, 1923–January 3, 1964.

Courier-Journal (Louisville), February 21, 1959.

Daily Texan (Austin), November 14, 1933–July 26, 1955.

Dallas Morning News, September 24, 1952–December 18, 1973.

Denver Post, January 21, 1940.

Gazette and Telegraph (Colorado Springs), September 14, 1930–July 19, 1936.

Houston Chronicle, November 27, 1927–November 7, 2004.

Houston Post, November 15, 1933–January 13, 1964.

Indianapolis Star, July 1, 1962.

Lexington Herald, July 4, 1937–December 17, 1976.

Lexington Herald-Leader, Feb. 24, 1959–April 5, 1959

Lexington Leader, September 7, 1935–June 27, 1938.

New York Herald Tribune, November 11, 1934–March 5, 1939.

New York Sun, October 27, 1934.

New York Times, August 1, 1935.

Philadelphia Record, June 23, 1936.

St. Louis Daily Globe-Democrat, September 10, 1935.

Star-Telegram (Ft. Worth), circa 1935.

Tulsa World, April 22, 1956.

Wall Street Journal, August 1, 1935.

Letters

Aaron Jefferson to Mrs. M. F. Yount, November 23, 1933. In private collection of Mildred Yount Manion.

Alford Branch, Rev. Dr. (alford_branch@hotmail.com), email to Fred B. McKinley, North Myrtle Beach, South Carolina, July 29, 2004.

Anne Dunn (trumpetasb1@cox.net), email to the American Saddle Horse Museum (now American Saddlebred Museum), Lexington, Kentucky, November 5, 2003. Original in possession of American Saddlebred Museum.

———. Email to Fred B. McKinley, North Myrtle Beach, South Carolina, November 27, 2004.

Aurelia Norvell to Pansy and Mildred Yount, undated circa November 1933. In private collection of Mildred Yount Manion.

Barbie Scott, Inheritance Tax Section, Revenue Accounting Division, Texas State Comptroller's Office (barbie.scott@cpa.state.tx.us), emails to Fred B. McKinley, North Myrtle Beach, South Carolina, June 1, 24, 2004.

Betty Johnson to Mildred Yount, May 23, 1934. In private collection of Kathryn Manion Haider.

Chilton O'Brien to Allen Grover, *Fortune Magazine*, circa 1934. O'Brien Papers (Box 1). Sam Houston Regional Library and Research Center, Liberty, Texas.

Crystal Ford (cford@academicplanet.com), email to Fred B. McKinley, North Myrtle Beach, South Carolina, August 16, 2004.

David Moerbe, Corporations Section, Office of the Secretary of State, Austin, Texas (dmoerbe@sos.state.tx.us), emails to Fred B. McKinley, North Myrtle Beach, South Carolina, March 19, 22, 2004 and May 10, 2004.

Deborah Harrison to Fred B. McKinley, December 9, 2004.

Ed and Mrs. E. Humphries to Mrs. M. F. Yount, November 23, 1933. In private collection of Mildred Yount Manion.

Ed Manion, Jr. to Kathryn Manion Haider and Mildred Yount Manion, March 12, 1973. In private collection of Kathryn Manion Haider.

———. (EdDannyBoyJr@aol.com), emails to Fred B. McKinley, North Myrtle Beach, South Carolina, November 4, November 24, December 13, 2004.

Emmett A. Fletcher to Mildred Frank Yount, May 2, 1932. In private collection of Kathryn Manion Haider.

George B. Lane, previous owner of Chief of Spindletop, to C. J. Cronan, American Saddle Horse Association, Louisville, Kentucky, September 18, 1933. In possession of American Saddlebred Museum, Lexington, Kentucky.

George H. Sheppard, Comptroller of Public Accounts, Travis County, Texas to Estate of M. F. Yount, February 1, 1939. In private collection of Kathryn Manion Haider.

Hastings Harrison (Dr.) to Mrs. Frank Yount, November 23, 1933. In private collection of Mildred Yount Manion.

Howard Perkins, Director of Student Press, Lamar University (hap70119@hotmail.com), emails to Fred B. McKinley, North Myrtle Beach, South Carolina, July 29, August 2, September 10, October. 11, 2004, December 4, 2004, December 16, 2004.

———. Emails to Fred B. McKinley, North Myrtle Beach, South Carolina, October 20, 2004.

Janet McClendon (mcclendonjanet@sbcglobal.net), emails to Fred B. McKinley, North Myrtle Beach, South Carolina, August 9, December 8, 2004.

Joseph E. McKenna to Mr. and Mrs. E. D. Manion, August 29, 1956. In private collection of Kathryn Manion Haider.

Kenneth Warren, Kenneth Warren & Son, Ltd., to Trust Department, First Security National Bank, Beaumont, Texas, February 5, 1973. In private collection of Mildred Yount Manion.

Kim Skipton, American Saddlebred Museum, Lexington, Kentucky to Fred B. McKinley, North Myrtle Beach, South, Carolina, November 10, December 22, 2004.

____ (ashmtg@mis.net), email to Fred B. McKinley, North Myrtle Beach, South Carolina, November 30, 2004.

Lizzie Edwards to Pansy and Mildred Yount, undated, circa November 1933. In private collection of Mildred Yount Manion.

Nena Wiess Priddie to Pansy and Mildred Yount, November 15, 1933. In private collection of Mildred Yount Manion.

Osler McCarthy, Public Information Staff Attorney, Supreme Court of Texas (osler.mccarthy@courts.state.tx.us), email to Fred B. McKinley, North Myrtle Beach, South Carolina, April 23, 2004.

Pansy M. Grant to Mildred Frank Manion, Europe, July 8, 1957.

Pansy M. Yount to Kathryn Manion [Haider], Lake Forest, Illinois, October 24, 1960. In possession of American Saddlebred Museum, Lexington, Kentucky.

———. To Mildred Frank Manion, Dallas, Texas, February 14, 1935. In private collection of Kathryn Manion Haider.

Paul E. Petosky (ppetosky@chartermi.net), email to Fred B. McKinley, North Myrtle Beach, South Carolina, October 21, 2004.

Philip Margolis (pmargolis@cozio.com), email to Greg Riley, Waycross, Georgia, May 23, 2004.

Reagan Newton (rhnewton@sbcglobal.net), email to Fred B. McKinley, North Myrtle Beach, South Carolina, November 2, 2004.

Ryan Smith, Director of the Texas Energy Museum, Beaumont, Texas (rsmithtem@msn.com), email to Fred B. McKinley, North Myrtle Beach, South Carolina, March 23, August 6, 2004.

Sister Mary Richard, administrator of St. Elizabeth Hospital, to Mr. and Mrs. E. D. Manion and Family, June 27, 1963. In private collection of Kathryn Manion Haider.

Steve D. O'Conor to M. F. Yount, December 22, 1932. In private collection of Mildred Yount Manion.

Treasury Department, Internal Revenue Service, Austin, Texas to R. E. Masterson, July 15, 1936. In private collection of Kathryn Manion Haider.

———. To Peter B. Wells, Beaumont, Texas, August 15, 1969.

W. M. Crook to Mrs. M. F. Yount, November 21, 1933. In private collection of Mildred Yount Manion.

W. M. Schultz to Mrs. M. F. Yount, November 17, 1933. In private collection of Mildred Yount Manion.

Collected Documents

Abstract of the Twelfth Census of the United States, 1900. Washington: GPO, 1902.

Beaumont City Directory, 1904–1905. Houston: Morrison & Fourmy, 1905.

Beaumont City Directory, 1914. Houston: Morrison & Fourmy, 1914.

Beaumont City Directory, 1916. Houston: Morrison & Fourmy, 1916.

Beaumont City Directory, 1921–1922. Houston: Morrison & Fourmy, 1921.

Beaumont City Directory, 1923. Houston: Morrison & Fourmy, 1923.

Beaumont City Directory, 1925–1926. Houston: Morrison & Fourmy, 1925.

Beaumont City Directory, 1927–1928. Houston: Morrison & Fourmy, 1927.

Beaumont City Directory, 1931. Houston: Morrison & Fourmy, 1931.

Beaumont City Directory, 1933. Houston: Morrison & Fourmy, 1933.

Beaumont City Directory, 1937. Houston: Morrison & Fourmy, 1937.

Beaumont City Directory, 1953. Dallas: Morrison & Fourmy, 1953.

Bureau of Vital Statistics. Texas Department of Health. Austin, Texas.

Diocese of Beaumont Records. St. Anthony Cathedral. Beaumont, Texas.

Directory of the City of Beaumont, 1912–1913. Houston: Southern Press, 1912.

El Paso County Deed Records. Colorado Springs Courthouse. Colorado Springs, Colorado.

Fagin v. Quinn, 277 U.S. 606 (1928).

Federal Crude Oil Co. v. Yount-Lee Oil Co. et al., 52 S.W. 2d 56 (1932).

Federal Crude Oil Co. v. Yount-Lee Oil Company, 295 U.S. 741 (1935).

Fifteenth Census of the United States, 1930. Vol. 3, pt. 2. Washington: GPO, 1932.

Fourteenth Census of the United Sates, 1920. Vol. 1. Washington: GPO, 1921.

Hardin County Deed Records. Hardin County Courthouse. Kountze, Texas.

Harris County Deed Records. Harris County Courthouse. Houston, Texas.

Harris County Map Records. Harris County Courthouse. Houston, Texas.

Hill County Bureau of Vital Statistics. Hill County Courthouse. Hillsboro, Texas.

Hill County Divorce Records. Hill County Courthouse. Hillsboro, Texas.

Hill County Marriage Records. Hill County Courthouse. Hillsboro, Texas.

Hill County Probate Records. Hill County Courthouse. Hillsboro, Texas.

Jefferson County Bureau of Vital Statistics. Jefferson County Courthouse. Beaumont, Texas.

Jefferson County Deed Records. Jefferson County Courthouse. Beaumont, Texas.

Jefferson County Divorce Records. Jefferson County Courthouse. Beaumont, Texas.

Jefferson County Marriage Records. Jefferson County Courthouse. Beaumont, Texas.

Jefferson County Probate Records. Jefferson County Courthouse. Beaumont, Texas.

Magnolia Cemetery Records. Beaumont, Texas.

Medina County Bureau of Vital Statistics. Medina County Courthouse. Hondo, Texas.

Minutes of City Commission and City Council. Office of City Clerk. Beaumont, Texas.

Minutes of Ordinances. Office of City Clerk. Beaumont, Texas.

Pansy M. GRANT v. W. C. GRANT, Court of Civil Appeals of Texas, Waco, no. 3900, 358 S.W.2d 147.

Pansy M. GRANT v. W. C. GRANT, Court of Civil Appeals of Texas, Waco, no. 3901, 351 S.W.2d 897.

Register of Baptisms. Westminster Presbyterian Church. Beaumont, Texas.

Standard Oil of Indiana. Board of Directors Minutes. Amoco Corporation. Chicago, Illinois.

Texas Secretary of State. Charter Records. Office of Secretary of State. Austin, Texas.

Thirteenth Census of the United States, 1910. Vol. 3. Washington: GPO, 1913.
Wright C. (Chalfant) Morrow Papers, 1922–1942, Tarlton Law Library, University of Texas at Austin.

Interviews

Behar, Marguerite. Interview with Fred B. McKinley, July 16, 2004, Sour Lake, Texas.
_____. Telephone interview with Fred B. McKinley, July 28, 2004.
Birdwell, Virginia Rothwell. Interview with Fred B. McKinley, August 25, 1987, Beaumont, Texas.
Boyt, Sue. Telephone interview with Fred B. McKinley, November 18, 2004.
Carter, Peggy. Telephone interview with Fred B. McKinley, July 26, 2004.
Dreggors, Jr., Bill. Interview with Greg Riley, June 30, 2004, DeLand, Florida.
Edson, III, Ed. Telephone interview with Fred B. McKinley, November 2, 2004.
Ema, Randy. Telephone interview with Greg Riley, July 20, 2004.
Ford, Crystal. Telephone interview with Fred B. McKinley, June 9, 2004.
Giles, Marjorie Gibson. Telephone interview with Fred B. McKinley, September 24, 1987.
Goolsbee, Ann Moorhouse. Telephone interview with Fred B. McKinley, September 19, 2004.
Grant, Jr., William Capers "Bill." Telephone interview with Greg Riley, June 3, 2004.
_____. Interview with Greg Riley, October 11, 2004, The Woodlands, Texas.
Greer, Jeanette. Interview with Howard Perkins, November 15, 2004, Beaumont, Texas.
_____. Telephone interview with Fred B. McKinley, December 26, 2004.
Guillory, Joe Max. Telephone interview with Fred B. McKinley, July 26, 2004.
Haider, Kathryn Manion. Telephone interview with Fred B. McKinley, April 1, 2004.
_____. Interviews with Fred B. McKinley and Greg Riley, May 14–15, 2004, Northbrook, Illinois.
_____. Interviews with Greg Riley, November 20-21, 2004, Northbrook, Illinois.
Hailey, Richard. Telephone interview with Kim Skipton, curator, American Saddlebred Museum, Lexington, Kentucky, circa 1988.
Hall, Mildred. Telephone interview with Fred B. McKinley, June 23, 2004.
Harrison, Deborah. Historic Manitou, Inc. Telephone interview with Fred B. McKinley, December 13, 2004.
Kelley, Jim. Interview with Fred B. McKinley, July 16, 2004, Sour Lake, Texas.
King, L. W. "Billy," and wife, Evelyn. Interview with Fred B. McKinley, July 27, 1987, Beaumont, Texas.
Lee, III, Thomas Peter. Telephone interview with Fred B. McKinley, September 16, 2004.
Locke, Helen. Interview with Howard Perkins, November 15, 2004, Beaumont, Texas.
_____. Telephone interview with Fred B. McKinley, December 31, 2004.
Look, Mary Clark. Telephone interview with Fred B. McKinley, December 4, 2004.
Manion, Jr., Edward Daniel. Telephone interview with Greg Riley, March 28, 2004.
Manion, Mildred Yount. Interview with Fred B. McKinley, July 12, 2004, Beaumont, Texas.
_____. Telephone interviews with Fred B. McKinley, July 15, December 19, December 24, 2004.
_____. Telephone interviews with Howard Perkins, October 23, November 9, 2004, December 19, 2004.
McClendon, Janet. Interviews with Fred B. McKinley, July 13, 15, 2004, Beaumont, Texas.
McClendon, Marvin W. Interview with Fred B. McKinley, September 9, 1987, Beaumont, Texas.
_____. Interview with Janet McClendon, September 9, 1987, Beaumont, Texas. Tape in private collection of Janet McClendon.
Newton, Reagan. Interview with Greg Riley, October 28, 2004, Katy, Texas.
Overton, Billy. Interview with Howard Perkins, undated, Beaumont, Texas.
Phelan, Anthony "Mickey" McDade. Interview with Fred B. McKinley, July 14, 2004, Beaumont, Texas.
Rollins, Ed. Interview with Howard Perkins, undated, Beaumont, Texas.
Sanders, Christine Moor. Telephone interview with Greg Riley, June 4, 2004.
_____. Telephone interview with Fred B. McKinley, July 24, 2004.
Seale, William, Ph.D. Interview with Greg Riley, December 17, 2004, Jasper, Texas.
Speer, Mary. Telephone interview with Fred B. McKinley, December 16, 2004.
Spence, Amy. Telephone interview with Fred B. McKinley, December 15, 2004.
Teare, Erin Barry. Interview with Fred B. McKinley, July 14, 2004, Beaumont, Texas.
Williams, Mary Reed. Interview with Fred B. McKinley, July 14, 2004, Beaumont, Texas.
Wilson, Rosine McFaddin. Telephone interview with Fred B. McKinley, April 17, 2004.
Woodhead, Ben. Telephone interview with Fred B. McKinley, September 21, 2004.
Yount, Bruce. Telephone interview with Fred B. McKinley, October 18, 2004.

Dissertations, Theses and Unpublished Sources

Corcoran, David H. "Spindletop Hall." Thirteenth Annual Seminar for Historical Administrators. Photocopy, July 2, 1971.

Martin, Everette A. "A History of Spindletop Oil Field." M. A. thesis, University of Texas, Austin, 1934.

Masterson, R. E. *The Low Down on a High Up Man Towit: Miles Frank Yount*. N.p., n.d. Only copy known to exist, in private collection of Kathryn Manion Haider.

McCarthy, Glenn H. Speech to Beaumont Optimist Club, November 8, 1948. Copy in private collection of Kathryn Manion Haider.

McKinley, Fred B. "The Yount-Lee Oil Company." M. A. thesis, Lamar University, 1987.

Web Sources

"A Southeast Texas Broadcast Legend." *KLVI Radio Online*. http://www.klvi.com/history_radio.html [accessed December 5, 2004].

"American Saddlebred." *American Saddle Horse Association*. http://www.imh.org/imh/bw/ash.html#breed [accessed October 12, 2004].

American Saddlebred Online. http://www.asha.net/progenysearchresults3.asp?Registration1=12027&Gender=S [accessed October 20, 2004].

"Bernard Shoninger." *The Jewish Historical Society of Greater New Haven*. http://pages.cthome.net/hirsch/bshon.htm [accessed October 4, 2004].

"Biography of Hedy Lamarr." *Internet Movie Database, Inc*. http://www.imdb.com/name/nm0001443/bio [accessed April 27, 2004].

"Black Monday – 1929." *About.com*. http://mutualfunds.about.com/cs/1929marketcrash/a/black_monday.htm [accessed June 25, 2004].

"Black Tuesday – 1929." *About.com*. http://mutualfunds.about.com/cs/1929marketcrash/a/black_tuesday.htm [accessed June 25, 2004].

"Black Thursday 1929." *About.com*. http://mutualfunds.about.com./cs/history/a/black_thursday.htm [accessed June 25, 2004].

Block, W. T. "Lucas Gusher Fever Affected So Many Folks, Far and Wide." *WTBlock.com*. http://www.wt-block.com/wtblockjr/lucus_gusher.htm [accessed June 25, 2004].

"Charles Lindbergh, An American Aviator." *CharlesLindbergh.com*. http://www.charleslindbergh.com/kidnap/index.asp [accessed September 12, 2004].

Consumer Price Index. U. S. Department of Labor, *Bureau of Labor Statistics*. ftp://bls.gov/pub/special/requests/cpi/cpiai/txt [accessed June 15, 2004].

Conway, John. "Celebrating the Birth of Texas Oil." *Texas Co-Op Power* (January 2001). http://www.texasec.org/tcp/101oil.html [accessed June 24, 2004].

"First City Turns Corner on Final Days." *Houston Business Journal* (November 7, 2003). http://houston.bizjournals.com/houston/stories/2003/11/10/story2.html [accessed October 9, 2004].

Frank Yount's Violins. *Cozio.com*. http://www.cozio.com/Search.aspx [accessed June 24, 2004].

"From Morrow to the Future: A New Home for the Mental Sciences Institute." *University of Texas-Houston*. http://theleader.uth.tmc.edu/archive/2002/july/morrow_house.html [accessed April 1, 2004].

"Garner, John Nance." *Handbook of Texas Online*. http://www.tsha.utexas.edu/handbook/online/articles/view/GG/fga24.html [accessed December 15, 2004].

"Graham, Elizabeth Arden." *Hall of Fame-Builder-Elizabeth Arden Graham, 2003*. http://www.canadianhoreseracinghalloffame.com/bulders/2003/Elizabeth_Arden_Graham [accessed Dec. 18, 2004].

Horse Quotations Online. http://www.horses.co.uk/horses/quotes.cgi [accessed November 22, 2004].

"Jones, Jesse Holman," *The Handbook of Texas Online*. http://www.tsha.utexas.edu/handbook/online/articles/view/JJ/fjo53.html [accessed June 24 9:24:28 US/Central 2004].

"Kochanski, Paul." *Polish Music Journal*, vol. 1, no. 1 (Summer 1998). http://www.usc.edu/dept/polish_music/PMJ/issue/1.1.98/kochanski_part1.html [accessed March 17, 2004].

McBride, Jane. "Saving Beaumont Brick-by-Brick." *Southeast Texas Live*. http://nl.newsbank.com/nl-search/we/Archives?p_action=doc&p_docid=0FCDECC4FA5E [accessed September 29, 2004].

"McCarthy, Glenn." *The Celtic Connection: Twentieth Century Texas*. http://users.ev1.net/~gpmoran/20THTX.htm [accessed June 24, 2004].

"McCarthy, Glenn Herbert." *The Handbook of Texas Online*. http://www.tsha.utexas.edu/handbook/online/articles/view/MM/fmcaw.html [accessed June 24 9:15:15 US/Central 2004];

McDonald, Archie P. "Ela Hockaday: More Than A School Omarm." *TexasEscapes.com* [accessed November 20, 2004].

———. "When Oil Became an Industry." *TexasEscapes.com*. http://www.texasescapes.com/DEPARTMENTS/GuestColumnists/EastTexasallthingshistorical/OilIndustryHistory1200AMD1.htm [accessed June 21, 2004].

"McLean, Marrs." *The Handbook of Texas Online*. http://www.tsha.utexas.edu/handbook/online/articles/view/MM/fmcbp.html [accessed March 18, 2004].

Navajo Gallery & Gifts Online. http://www.pikes-peak.com/navajo [accessed December 22, 2004].

"Nelson Eddy – A Brief Biographical Profile." http://www.dandugan.com/maytime/n-biopro.html [accessed September 1, 2004].

"Northside Belt Railway." *The Handbook of Texas Online*. http://www.tsha.utexas.edu/handbook/online/articles/view/NN/eqn4.html [accessed March 18, 2004].

"Oakwood Cemetery, Tyler, Smith County, TX." http://www.rootsweb.com/~usgenweb/copyright.htm [accessed September 11, 2004].

"Official State Historical Markers of Jefferson County, Texas." *Jefferson County, TX Online*. http://www.co.jefferson.tx.us/landmrks.htm [accessed October 11, 2004].

"Paderewski, Ignacy Jan." *Buckingham Hotel Online*. http://buckinghamhotel.com/Performing_Paderewski.cfm [accessed August 11, 2004].

"Phelan, John Henry." *The Handbook of Texas Online*. http://www.tsha.utexas.edu/handbook/online/articles/view/PP/fph1.html [accessed March 18, 2004].

"Queen Victoria." *Spartacus Educational Online*. http://www.spartacus.schoolnet.co.uk/PRvictoria.htm [accessed June 22, 2004].

Rockledge Country Inn. http://www.rockledgeinn.com/ [accessed May 14, 2004].

"Roscoe, TX." *The Handbook of Texas Online*. http://www.tsha.utexas.edu/handbook/online/articles/view/RR/hjr13.html [accessed August 8, 2004].

68th Kentucky Derby. *Kentucky Derby Online*. http://www.kentuckyderby.com/2002/derby_history/derby_charts/years/1942.html [accessed September 19, 2004].

"Sour Lake, TX." *The Handbook of Texas Online*. http://www.tsha.utexas.edu/handbook/online/articles/view/SS/hjs20.html [accessed September 26, 2004].

"Spindletop Hall Offers Wealth of Amenities for Faculty, Staff, Alumni." *University of Kentucky Online*.
http://www.uky.edu/PR/UK_News/news091503.html#spindletop [accessed June 25, 2004].

"Spindletop Oilfield." *The Handbook of Texas Online*. http://www.tsha.utexas.edu/handbook/online/articles/view/SS/dos3.html [accessed June 24, 2004].

"Sterling, Ross S." *Texas State Library & Archives Commission*. http://www.tsl.state.tx.us/governors/personality/sterling-p01.html [accessed November 9, 2004].

"Sterling, Ross Shaw." *The Handbook of Texas Online*. http://www.tsha.utexas.edu/handbook/online/articles/view/SS/fst42.html [accessed November 9 2004].

"Stock Market Crash." *PBS.org*. http://www.pbs.org/fmc/timeline/estockmktcrash.htm [accessed June 25, 2004].

"Texas Hurricane History: Early 20th Century (July 27–27th, 1943)." *National Weather Service Forecast Office*. http://www.srh.noaa.gov/lch/research/txerly20hur4.htm [accessed June 24, 2004].

"Tierney, Gene." *The Handbook of Texas Online*. http://www.tsha.utexas.edu/handbook/online/articles/view/TT/ftiev.html [accessed June 24, 2004].

"U. S. Crude Prices Hit 21–Year High." *Associated Press Online*. http://dailynews.att.net/cgi-bin/news?e=pri&dt=040728&cat=news&st=newsd843um600&src=ap [accessed July 28, 2004].

U. S. Department of Labor. *Bureau of Labor Statistics. Washington, D. C.* http://data.bls.gov/servlet/SurveyOutputServlet [accessed June 24, 2004].

United States Patent and Trademark Office. http://www.uspto.gov/ [accessed September 8, 2004].

"Wartime Economics and Efforts to Support the War." *At Home During WWII Online*. http://www.pomperaug.com/socstud/stumuseum/web/ARHwww3.htm [accessed December 2, 2004].

"What's Oil Doing on the Spindletop Dome?" *Paleontological Research Institution. Ithaca, New York*. http://www.priweb.org/ed/pgws/backyard/spindletop/spindletop_oil2.html [accessed April 24, 2004].

"Woodward, E. F." *Texas Horse Racing Hall of Fame*. http://www.texashorsemen.com/news/news_HallofFame.asp [accessed September 19, 2004].

"Woodward, E. F." *The National Trapshooting Hall of Fame*. http://www.traphof.org/inductees/woodward_e_f.htm [accessed September 19, 2004].

"Woodward, E. F." *Texas Trapshooters Association Hall of Fame*. http://www.texastrap.com/hof.html [accessed September 19, 2004].
"Yount, Miles Frank." *The Handbook of Texas Online*. http://www.tsha.utexas.edu/handbook/online/articles/view/YY/fyo16.html [accessed June 22, 2004].
"Zaharias, Mildred Ella Didrikson [Babe]." *The Handbook of Texas Online*. http://www.tsha.utexas.edu/handbook/online/articles/view/ZZ/fza1.html [accessed September 15, 2004].

Miscellaneous Sources

American Horseman/Sportologue (July 1952), 7.
Beaumont Real Estate Board. Banquet Program. December 7, 1926.
Board of Directors Minutes. First National Bank of Beaumont, Texas. December 30, 1933.
Catalogue of Auction, Featuring the Legendary Estate of Mrs. Miles Frank Yount, Samuel Hart, Auctioneer. In private collection of Kathryn Manion Haider.
Chief of Spindletop Registration No. 12934 and transfer to M. F. Yount. September 21, 1933. In possession of American Saddlebred Museum, Lexington, Kentucky.
Contract of Sale between Mrs. Laura E. Wiess and M. F. Yount. February 10, 1923. In private collection of Kathryn Manion Haider.
Description of the Improvements: Mildred Apartment Building, Arcade Commercial Building, and Garage Building. Hall & Hall Realtors, 1974 Appraisal. In private collection of Mildred Hall, Beaumont, Texas.
Edwards, J. S. "Tribute to Mr. M. F. Yount." In private collection of Mildred Yount Manion.
Historic Beaumont, Texas, A Driving Tour. Beaumont: City of Beaumont, n.d. Brochure, item no. 18.
Merritt Family Bible. In private collection of Kathryn Manion Haider.
Minutes of Directors' Meeting–Yount-Lee Oil Company, January 3, 1934. In private collection of Mildred Yount Manion.
Minutes of Stockholders' Meeting–Yount-Lee Oil Company, January 3, 1934. Copy in private collection of Mildred Yount Manion.
Original Blueprints of Rockledge, January 1913. In private collection of Kathryn Manion Haider.
Pipkin & Brulin Company. *Registry of Visitors* (Frank Yount's Funeral). Original in private collection of Mildred Yount Manion.
Reports from various private detectives to Pansy Yount. In private collection of Kathryn Manion Haider.
Sales Brochure. *Yount Wire Line Guide or Spooling Attachment—A Dreadnaught Product*. Original in private collection of Mildred Yount Manion.
"Spindletop Time Line." Internal Reference Section. American Saddlebred Museum, Lexington, Kentucky, 1–3.
Stock Purchase Agreement between Yount-Lee Stockholders and Wright Morrow. July 29, 1935. Only copy known to exist, in private collection of Kathryn Manion Haider.
Strong Family Records, in private collection of Barbara Moor, Beaumont, Texas.
Texas Horse Racing Hall of Fame–2001 Brochure. In private collection of Robert and Mary Woodward, Kerrville, Texas.
"The Chronology of Spindletop." Internal Reference Section. American Saddlebred Museum, Lexington, Kentucky, 1–2.
"The Spindletop Legacy." Internal Reference Section. American Saddlebred Museum, Lexington, Kentucky, 1–13.
Yount, Mildred. Baby Book. In private collection of Kathryn Manion Haider.
Yount–Manion, Mildred Frank. Personal diary. In private collection of Kathryn Manion Haider.
_____. Personal scrapbook, in private collection of Kathryn Manion Haider.

Index

T———

The Authors

FRED B. MCKINLEY is a descendant of Revolutionary War, War of 1812, War for Texas Independence and Confederate soldiers, a Texas Ranger, and whose father served in the U.S. Navy during World War II. He embarked on a long and distinguished career in the credit industry and retired with the Louisiana Department of Justice, where he served as a supervisory criminal investigator with the Attorney General's office. A native of Beaumont, Texas, McKinley graduated from Lamar State College of Technology (1964) and Lamar University (1987). He attended Louisiana State University (1995), where he received a law enforcement certification. He is the author of one other book titled *CHINQUA WHERE? The Spirit of Rural America, 1947-1955* and has contributed articles to *The Texas Gulf Historical and Biographical Record*, published in Beaumont, Texas; and to the national magazines of *Country* and *Country Extra*, both published by the Reiman Group in Greendale, Wisconsin. He is the father of three children, grandfather of three, and lives with his wife Dottie in North Myrtle Beach, South Carolina.

GREG RILEY is also a native of Beaumont, Texas. His ancestors emigrated from Ireland to Galveston, Texas, in the 1880s but were forced to relocate when the 1900 storm devastated the island. Afterward, the 1901 Spindletop oil strike attracted the family to the Beaumont area, and they eventually settled in Sour Lake, where they operated a boarding house for oil field workers. Greg's father, Perry Riley, Sr., a career military man, served in World War II and Korea, and later retired with the rank of Lt. Colonel. After attending French High School and Lamar University in Beaumont, Greg Riley has worked for twenty years in sales and marketing. Currently, he is employed as vice president of the General Box Company of Waycross, Georgia. He has written and published one other book, an automotive technical manual titled *The Ultimate Guide to 'Vairs with Air*, and has contributed numerous articles to several different car collector publications. He lives with his wife, Ronnie, and their four children in Cleveland, Texas.